6

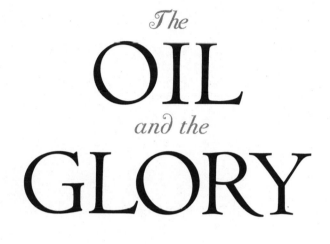

The
OIL
and the
GLORY

The OIL and the GLORY

THE PURSUIT OF EMPIRE AND FORTUNE ON THE CASPIAN SEA

Steve LeVine

Random House   New York

Published in the United States by Random House, an imprint of The Random
House Publishing Group, a division of Random House, Inc., New York.

RANDOM HOUSE and colophon are registered trademarks of
Random House, Inc.

Cartography by Virginia Norey

ISBN 978-0-375-50614-7

Library of Congress Cataloging-in-Publication Data

LeVine, Steve.
The oil and the glory : the pursuit of empire and fortune on the Caspian Sea /
by Steve LeVine.
p.   cm.
ISBN 978-0-375-50614-7
1. Petroleum industry and trade—Caspian Sea Region—History.   2. Caspian
Sea Region—Politics and government—History.   3. Geopolitics—Caspian Sea
Region—History.   I. Title.
HD9576.C372L48 2007
338.2'728209475—dc22   2006101530

Printed in the United States of America on acid-free paper

www.atrandom.com

24689753

Book design by Carol Malcolm Russo

To
Nurilda

CONTENTS

PROLOGUE / *ix*
CHRONOLOGY / *xv*
MAIN CHARACTERS / *xix*
MAPS / *xxi*

CHAPTER 1: The Barons / *3*

CHAPTER 2: A Visitor from Sweden / *14*

CHAPTER 3: Revolution / *28*

CHAPTER 4: Soviet Days / *41*

CHAPTER 5: The Middleman / *54*

CHAPTER 6: Détente / *68*

CHAPTER 7: The Perfect Oil Field / *82*

CHAPTER 8: Crossfire / *102*

CHAPTER 9: The First Deal / *128*

CHAPTER 10: Return to Baku / *144*

CHAPTER 11: The Contract of the Century / *174*

CHAPTER 12: The Near Abroad / *201*

CHAPTER 13: Early Oil / *217*

CHAPTER 14: A Battle of Wills / 236

CHAPTER 15: A Tale of Two Negotiators / 252

CHAPTER 16: An Accidental Pipeline / 273

CHAPTER 17: An Army for Oil / 290

CHAPTER 18: Boom and Bust / 311

CHAPTER 19: Kashagan / 327

CHAPTER 20: A Way to the Sea / 345

CHAPTER 21: The King of Kazakhstan / 360

EPILOGUE / 380

ACKNOWLEDGMENTS / 401

BIBLIOGRAPHY AND NOTE ON SOURCES / 405

NOTES / 409

INDEX / 449

THE FORBIDDING GEOGRAPHY SURROUNDING THE CASPIAN region of Central Asia and the Caucasus has long isolated it from the rest of the world. Situated between the Black Sea to the west and the Tien Shen mountains to the east, this is a vast land of sprawling deserts and jagged, nine-thousand-foot peaks, a bit more than half the size of the continental United States. In the center is the Caspian Sea, five times the size of the next largest inland body of water, Lake Superior.

Over the centuries, Russian novelists and British adventurers romanticized the region, with its camel fights, cacophony of languages, and magisterial kingdoms, known as khanates. But Russian soldiers seeking conquest sometimes became lost and desperate in its daunting wilderness, terrified of the Turkmen, Bukharan, or Chechen raiders whose knives and slave markets might await them. Because the region was so secluded, its exposure to the outside world was limited mostly to the march of conquering armies, starting with those of Alexander the Great more than 2,300 years ago. By the late-middle nineteenth century, its Armenian, Georgian, Persian, and Turkic-speaking Muslim peoples were under the rule of imperial Russia.

Always, there was oil. Marco Polo, the thirteenth-century Venetian trader, reported camel drivers exporting crude from Baku, the capital of Azerbaijan, to points as distant as Baghdad. It was valued both as an illuminant and a balm, he wrote, because "in all the neighborhood no other oil is burnt." Petroleum deposits were so vast that oil and gas issued uncoaxed from the earth.

In 1872, czarist Russia loosened private land ownership rules in

Baku, triggering a feverish oil boom there. At the turn of the century, Baku was providing more than half the world's oil supply, outproducing even Rockefeller's Standard Oil. Great fortunes were accumulated by the city's oil barons, who built imposing mansions and remade Baku into a European-style metropolis, resplendent at night under the glow of electric lights.

The 1917 Bolshevik Revolution claimed thousands of lives in Baku, destroyed its tycoons, and brought its golden age to an end. Oil production plummeted, wiping out Russia's chief source of export dollars. Baku's decline mirrored the industrial paralysis that gripped all of Russia, a nation chronically unable to produce and innovate. Ever since Peter the Great, the Russians had attempted to compensate for this deficiency by importing foreign expertise. Now, his scorn for the West notwithstanding, Vladimir Lenin did the same.

American industrialists like Averell Harriman and Henry Ford answered the call, as did a scrappy New Yorker named Henry Mason Day, who revitalized the Baku oil industry with his state-of-the-art drilling technology. German, British, and other American companies followed Day into Baku, building new pipelines and refineries. The oil fields boomed. By 1928, production had recovered to its turn-of-the-century peak and Stalin was committing more money to spur further growth. So it went for decades, until Baku's oil production and the city itself once again slid into a deep decline. The grand old mansions decayed, and the city became a seedy backwater that stank of oil fumes and garbage.

On December 26, 1991, the Soviet Union collapsed, and the Cold War came to an abrupt end. Fifteen new nations emerged from the wreckage, among them a cluster of states in the Caspian region with names so unfamiliar that few outsiders could spell or pronounce them. (Some foreigners dubbed them the "Stans," since many of their names ended with that syllable.) Although these states were economic failures, together they were said to possess the world's third-largest reserves of oil and natural gas, behind only the Persian Gulf and Siberia.

Thus began a new Caspian oil boom, one that would dwarf its

nineteenth-century predecessor. Oilmen from America, Britain, Italy, France, Japan, China, and elsewhere scrambled to cut billion-dollar deals with the region's emerging strongmen. For a time, the Caspian was at the center of "the greatest sale in the history of the world," as writers Daniel Yergin and Joseph Stanislaw described the period. It echoed the era immediately preceding the First World War, when American and European industrial titans struggled for power and raw economic dominance. The excitement that the Caspian triggered in the global halls of commerce called to mind the openings of the Suez and Panama canals. Western nations relished the prospect of becoming less dependent on Persian Gulf energy suppliers, whom Washington and London increasingly mistrusted. The Central Intelligence Agency fielded Caspian agents, and the U.S. Army trained local soldiers to keep pipelines safe from attack. (Even Hollywood got in on the act. Caspian pipeline intrigue provided the backdrop for the 1999 James Bond film *The World Is Not Enough*, and the CIA, Kazakhstan oil fields, and oil industry corruption drove the 2005 political thriller *Syriana*.)

Oil riches remade the two most important cities of the region—Baku, the Azeri port on the west side of the Caspian, and Almaty, the Kazakh business capital on the east side. New European restaurants and Turkish cafés flourished. Along Baku's faded promenade, Charlie's Bar served American-style hamburgers, and well-dressed couples strolled at night past brightly lit cosmetics and clothing shops. Gamblers risked their oil fortunes in Baku's casinos, and onetime Soviet apparatchiks, flush with bribes, built luxurious homes and imported new Mercedeses. Kazakhstan's president, Nursultan Nazarbayev, built an entirely new capital that resembled an upscale theme park.

But the sudden display of cosmopolitan wealth masked some ugly realities. The larger population remained mired in poverty; in time, the presidents of Azerbaijan and Kazakhstan would be named in U.S. money-laundering and corruption cases.

Fortune hunters and adventurers of all stripes flocked to the Caspian from throughout the West. Some were outright hustlers, like Viktor Kozeny, a smooth-talking Czech American with a Harvard economics degree who lured to his investment scheme former Senate majority leader George Mitchell and some of Wall Street's most seasoned financiers.

Other pitchmen claimed that they could obtain the rights to the region's gold mines; before being unmasked, they managed to float stock issues in Toronto and London totaling $150 million. In both the Kozeny and gold mine deals, all the money was lost.

But the most intriguing players were the middlemen—shrewd American and European dealmakers without whose blessings few foreign companies could gain access to an oil field. Some had flocked to the Soviet Union in the Gorbachev era, eager to participate in the profits they thought could be made from the newly legalized joint ventures between foreign companies and Soviet partners. But before the deals could get off the ground, the Soviet Union began to collapse all around them. Hungry for new opportunities, the boldest of these western entrepreneurs moved on to the former Soviet republics surrounding the Caspian, now independent nations. There they gained the confidence of the region's autocratic rulers, who asked them to protect the interests of the newly independent republics.

John Deuss, a Dutch oil trader with keen and ruthless instincts, was one such operator. He hobnobbed with Arab sheikhs and flew in a Gulfstream jet, often with beauteous models at his side, to visit his offices around the world. Frequently, he dispatched his jet to pick up employees or friends for a weekend at his Bermuda estate. In 1990, he had sent a team to the Soviet Union to look for promising ventures. That led to friendships with the leaders of Russia and Kazakhstan, relationships that he hoped to parlay into billions. In an especially nervy play, Deuss obtained exclusive rights to build a pipeline that would export oil from Kazakhstan's biggest field, leaving its operator, Chevron Corporation, apoplectic and at his mercy.

But no middleman was more influential or had a more spectacular run than James Henry Giffen, a garrulous and worldly-wise New York lawyer who had become a millionaire by the time he was thirty. Giffen had a long history in the region, starting in the Soviet Union in the late 1960s. In the 1980s, Mikhail Gorbachev lent his personal support to a Giffen consortium of blue-chip American companies anxious to do business in the Soviet Union. The Soviet collapse stripped Giffen of his influence in the Kremlin, but he reemerged in Kazakhstan as the president's chief oil adviser. It wasn't long before he helped expel John Deuss. Suddenly, Giffen was the last middleman standing, both envied and feared by other power brokers. For a time, he controlled every major oil deal in the northeastern Caspian. He earned millions from every transaction.

The headlong rush into the region by the world's biggest oil companies was easy to explain. The industry had fallen on tough times—one U.S. oil chairman said that conditions were the worst he had seen in four decades. British Petroleum, Chevron, and the others were hungry to remake themselves after almost two decades of boom, bust, and contraction, and they saw a golden opportunity in the Caspian. They jostled for advantage, led by such outsize personalities as Chevron's energetic Dick Matzke, who made friends and enemies with equivalent ease; Mobil's Lou Noto, who enjoyed the spotlight perhaps even more than the deal; and British Petroleum's prickly John Browne, so powerful that his decisions forged British foreign policy.

But in the Wild West atmosphere of Baku and Almaty, there were few rules and no guarantees. Oil executives spent weeks simply trying to determine who in the government was in charge. One local "agent" after another whispered that he, and he alone, could procure the desired deal. The oilmen spied on one another, and local KGB agents spied on all of them, using bugs that were quickly detected but just as quickly replaced, ever more cleverly.

The Caspian's autocratic rulers, at first dismissed by the oil executives as rubes, turned out to be tough negotiators with few illusions. They had honed their skills in the Soviet era, when the Kremlin shamelessly flattered western businessmen, all the while squeezing them relentlessly for the most advantageous terms. Signed contracts were unilaterally declared open for renegotiation whenever oil companies seemed vulnerable to new demands. Virtually no license or permit—almost every step in a deal demanded one or the other—was awarded without a bribe, politely called a "present." As the competition for oil rights grew more feverish, the cost of graft soared.

Even when these obstacles could be overcome, daunting physical challenges remained. The Caspian's largest fields, in the north, were among the deepest in the world, encased under layers of salt four miles thick or more and suffused with poisonous hydrogen sulfide. Rare mud volcanoes that spewed cold grime dotted the seabed offshore from Baku. Oil company engineers found ingenious ways to cope.

But the biggest obstacle of all was Russia, determined to maintain its hold on the petroleum riches of its former colonies. The Kremlin simply muscled its way into some of the early deals, at one point even threatening that any unauthorized oil platform near Baku would be subject to military attack. But Moscow's most persuasive weapon was its ownership of the Soviet-era pipelines through which all Caspian oil was exported. The oil companies faced the unhappy prospect of forever having to bow to Russia's terms in order to get their oil to market. In a provocative demonstration of the pain it could impose, Moscow intermittently and without warning blocked Kazakhstan crude from entering its pipelines, causing particular anguish at Chevron.

Western oilmen increasingly worried that their crude might literally end up stranded, and stranded it would be worth nothing. By the late 1990s, the U.S. government and the oil multinationals were moving in lockstep to develop an export pipeline route from Baku to the Mediterranean that would touch not an inch of Russian soil. If they succeeded, Caspian oil and natural gas would flow unhindered to the West.

Oil and profit were the irresistible lure, but the struggle in the Caspian was also about geopolitical power and national pride. Now that it had won the Cold War, Washington was determined to establish an American preserve in the region and dismantle the expansionist Russian empire for good. After the breakup of the Soviet Union, Russia was desperate to retain its old imperial influence. The Caspian nations relished the prospect of genuine sovereignty after more than a century of Russian rule. To say the least, these aims were incompatible.

And so "pipeline politics" became a modern-day version of the nineteenth century's Great Game, in which Britain and Russia had employed cunning and bluff to gain supremacy over the lands of the Caucasus and Central Asia. This book is the story of how, at the dawn of the twenty-first century, the game was played once again across the harsh environs of the Caspian Sea.

Pre-Soviet period

1823 Zeynalabdin Tagiyev born

1872 Sale of Baku land legalized; oil rush begins

1873 Robert Nobel arrives in Baku

1878 Ludvig Nobel unveils *Zoroaster,* world's first oil tanker

1883 Edmond and Alphonse de Rothschild arrive in Batumi

1901 Baku supplies 51 percent of world's oil

1905 Worker uprising destroys Baku oil fields

1906 Baku-Batumi oil pipeline completed

1914 World War I breaks out

1917 Bolshevik Revolution

1920 Bolsheviks overthrow Azerbaijan government (April 28)

Early Soviet period

1920 Standard Oil concludes deal with Nobels (July 30)

1921 Lenin's "New Economic Policy" invites foreign businesses

1924 Britain recognizes Soviet Union

Lenin dies

1933 United States recognizes the Soviet Union

Later Soviet period

1968 James Giffen hired by Soviet trader Ara Oztemel

1969 Détente begins; Nixon liberalizes trade with Soviets

1972 Oztemel fires Giffen

1973 John Deuss launches first oil trading venture

U.S.-USSR Trade and Economic Council formed (June 22)

Arab nations start oil embargo (October 17)

Saudi Arabia cuts off oil shipments to United States (October 20)

1979 Iranian Revolution; new Arab oil embargo begins

John Deuss ships oil to South Africa against U.N. embargo

Soviets invade Afghanistan (December 27)

1984 Giffen forms Mercator; becomes president of U.S.-USSR Trade Council

1985 Blowout at Tengiz oil field (June 24)

1987 Gorbachev legalizes joint ventures (January 13)

Giffen forms American Trade Consortium (May)

Heydar Aliyev sacked by Gorbachev from Politburo (May)

Chevron in Moscow to look at Soviet oil properties (September)

1989 Steve Remp arrives in Baku (May)

Nursultan Nazarbayev becomes Communist Party chief of Kazakhstan
(June 22)

1990 Gorbachev signs START II with Bush, and preliminary agreement for
Tengiz with Chevron (June 2)

Baku's new oil rush begins with first oil show (October)

1991 Kazakhstan takes over Tengiz talks with Chevron (July 23)

Attempted anti-Gorbachev putsch (August 19)

Omanis loan Kazakhstan $100 million for grain (November)

Ex-Soviet republics form Commonwealth of Independent States
(December 21)

Gorbachev resigns (December 26)

Soviet Union dissolves (December 31)

Giffen's American Trade Consortium ceases to function (December 31)

Post-Soviet period

1992 Chevron fires Giffen as adviser (January)

Ex-Soviet foreign minister Eduard Shevardnadze returns to Georgia
homeland (March)

Nazarbayev and Chevron chairman Ken Derr sign preliminary Tengiz deal
at Blair House (May 18)

Kazakhs, Omanis form consortium to build export pipeline for Tengiz
(June 11)

Margaret Thatcher helps seal BP's offshore Baku deal (September 7)

Giffen helps Kazakhstan get uranium pact with United States (October)

1993 Preliminary agreement to develop Kazakhstan's Kashagan oil field (January 9)

Clinton, Yeltsin establish Gore-Chernomyrdin commission (April 3–4)

Final Tengiz agreement signed (April 6)

Heydar Aliyev announces assumption of power in Azerbaijan (June 18)

Russia severs Caspian states' natural gas exports (November)

Russia's Yuri Shafranik promised 10 percent of Baku offshore deal
(November 19–20)

1994 Yeltsin declares Russia ex-Soviet regions' "guarantor of stability"
(February 21)

Russia asserts veto rights over Caspian development (April 28)

"Contract of the Century" signed for Baku offshore wells (September 20)

Giffen put in charge of negotiating Kazakhstan's major oil deals (December)

1995 Kazakhstan lets Gazprom into Karachaganak natural gas field (February 12)

Car wreck kills Qais al-Zawawi, Deuss's Omani patron (September 12)

Clinton phones Heydar Aliyev to urge dual pipeline routes (October 2)

Dual Baku pipelines announced (October 9)

Unocal signs for trans-Afghan pipeline (October 21)

1996 Deuss forced out of Tengiz pipeline consortium (January)

Tengiz pipeline consortium restructuring agreed in Moscow (March 11)

Clinton signs Iran-Libya Sanctions Act (August 5)

Taliban captures Kabul (September 27)

1997 Collapse of Thai baht triggers financial turmoil (July 2)

U.S. Army's 82nd flies history's longest airborne operation (September 15)

First new Baku oil pumped (November 12)

Final offshore (Kashagan) contract signed (November 18)

Nazarbayev proclaims new Kazakhstan capital (December 10)

Viktor Kozeny's Aspen, Colorado, party with Baku investors (December 20)

1998 Russia's financial collapse (August)

Unocal "suspends" Afghan pipeline after United States fires missiles
(August 21)

1999 Early Oil pipeline through Georgia opens (April)

Swiss judge freezes Kazakhstan bank accounts (August)

BP says Baku-Ceyhan pipeline ought to be built (October)

Caspian leaders sign Baku-Ceyhan pipeline deal (November 18)

2000 United States asks Swiss aid in corruption probe against Giffen (June 12)

Companies announce oil is struck at Kashagan (July 24)

BP calls Baku-Ceyhan pipeline financially viable and signs deal
(September 21)

2001 Terrorists fly jets into World Trade Center, Pentagon (September 11)

Nazarbayev offers United States use of Kazakh airspace for Afghan
campaign (September 24)

United States says terror attacks won't affect Baku-Ceyhan pipeline
(September 28)

2002 Russia surpasses Saudi Arabia to become world's biggest oil producer

2003 Giffen arrested at JFK International Airport (March 31)

Giffen protégé Bryan Williams sentenced to forty-six months in prison
(September 18)

Heydar Aliyev withdraws as presidential candidate for his son Ilham
(October 2)

Kozeny indicted by New York state prosecutor (October 2)

Ilham Aliyev elected with 76.8 percent of vote (October 15)

Eduard Shevardnadze resigns (November 23)

Heydar Aliyev dies (December 12)

2006 First tanker loaded at Ceyhan (May 27)

Deuss arrested in money-laundering probe (October)

2007 BP's John Browne resigns after allegations by his lover (May 1)

Kazakhstan forfeits $84 million in alleged bribes cited in Giffen case;
money goes to poor children (May 3)

Nazarbayev grants himself the right to be president for life (May 22)

Nazarbayev issues international arrest warrant for son-in-law Rakhat
Aliyev for alleged racketeering (May 28)

Nazarbayev's daughter Dariga divorces Rakhat Aliyev (June 11)

2008 Giffen expected to go on trial

Historic Baku

Zeynalabdin Tagiyev: *Great oil baron of the nineteenth century and the city's leading citizen*

Leyla Tagiyeva: *Tagiyev's favorite daughter, whose flight to Persia crushed his spirits*

Sophia Abdullayeva: *Tagiyev's granddaughter, who witnessed his collapse and suffered in internal exile for decades*

Ludvig and Robert Nobel: *The foreign oilmen whose ingenuity sparked Baku's emergence as a global oil capital*

The Dealmakers

James Giffen: *Bold American who became the Caspian's most successful middleman*

John Deuss: *Dutch oil trader and Giffen's suave challenger*

Jack Grynberg: *Denver oilman in search of one more big deal*

Viktor Kozeny: *Czech-born investment adviser and master schemer*

The Oil Company Bosses

John Browne: *Indefatigable leader of British Petroleum's drive for Caspian primacy*

Ken Derr: *Chairman of Chevron who presided over its pursuit of Kazakhstan's oil*

Dick Matzke: *Geologist who became the tough-minded chief negotiator for Chevron*

Tom Hamilton: *Veteran troubleshooter and executive with BP and then Pennzoil*

The Caspian Autocrats

Nursultan Nazarbayev: *As a Kazakh power broker during the Soviet era, he dared to challenge Gorbachev for control of the region's oil fields; when the Soviet Union collapsed, he emerged as president of independent Kazakhstan.*

Heydar Aliyev: *Banished by Gorbachev during Soviet days, this former KGB general later rose to become president of independent Azerbaijan, a shrewd strategist of multinational oil deals, and the father of the pipeline policy that challenged Russia's dominance over the Caucasus and Central Asia.*

Saparmurat Niyazov: *Turkmenistan's quirky president, whose rule was cultlike and despotic*

The Russians

Viktor Chernomyrdin: *The iron-willed prime minister fought mightily to preserve his nation's influence over the newly independent Caspian states and their oil fields, no longer part of the Soviet empire.*

Yuri Shafranik: *As energy minister, his task was to resist the western incursion into Caspian oil fields, or at least push his way into the most important oil deals on behalf of Mother Russia.*

The Americans

Samuel "Sandy" Berger: *National security advisor to President Bill Clinton, he made sure oil companies adhered to U.S. policy on major Caspian pipeline project.*

Strobe Talbott: *Deputy secretary of state in Clinton administration, and strong voice for a more Russia-friendly policy when it came to Caspian oil fields*

Leon Fuerth: *Foreign policy adviser to Vice President Al Gore, he enabled Caspian issues to get a full hearing at highest policy levels.*

Rosemarie Forsythe: *Director of Russian, Ukrainian and Eurasian affairs, National Security Council (1993–1995)*

Sheila Heslin: *As a government researcher, she was an early proponent of multiple export pipelines for Caspian oil, which would become the centerpiece of U.S. policy in the region. Later named director of Russian, Ukrainian and Eurasian affairs, National Security Council (1995–1996).*

Bill White: *Deputy secretary of energy in Clinton administration, he partnered with Rosemarie Forsythe to promote an assertive U.S. policy in the Caspian.*

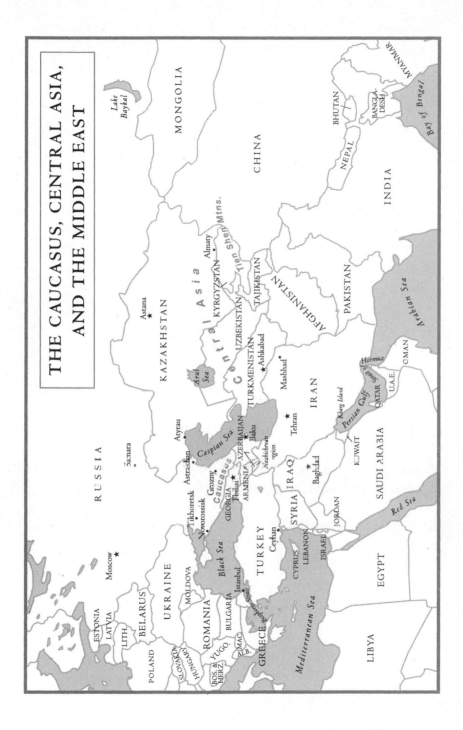

THE CAUCASUS, CENTRAL ASIA, AND THE MIDDLE EAST

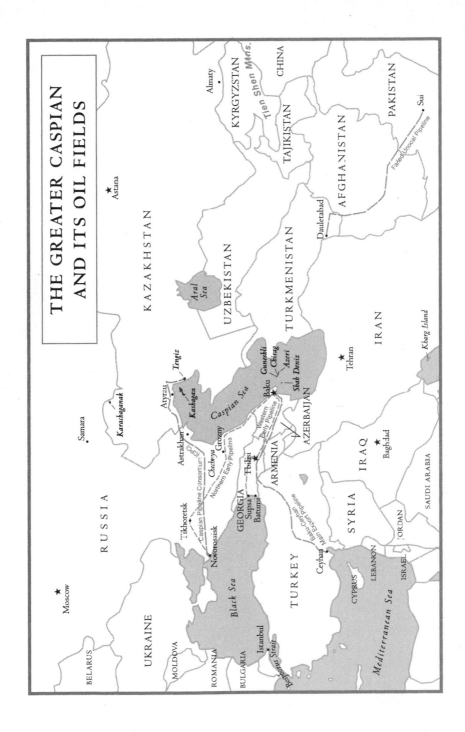

THE GREATER CASPIAN
AND ITS OIL FIELDS

BELARUS

RUSSIA

Moscow ★

UKRAINE

MOLDOVA

ROMANIA

BULGARIA

Istanbul

Bosporus Strait

Black Sea

Novorossisk

Tikhoretsk

Astrakhan

Samara

Karachaganak

KAZAKHSTAN

Astana ★

Atyrau

Tengiz

Kashagan

Caspian Sea

Aral Sea

UZBEKISTAN

KYRGYZSTAN

Almaty

Tien Shen Mtns.

CHINA

TAJIKISTAN

Grozny

Chechnya

Caspian Pipeline Consortium (CPC)

Northern Early Pipeline

GEORGIA

Supsa
Batumi

Tbilisi

Western
Early Pipeline

Baku

Guneshli
Chirag
Azeri
Shah Deniz

AZERBAIJAN

ARMENIA

TURKMENISTAN

Dauletabad

AFGHANISTAN

PAKISTAN

Sui

Failed Unocal Pipeline

IRAN

Tehran ★

Kharg Island

TURKEY

Ceyhan

Baku-Ceyhan
Main Export Pipeline

SYRIA

IRAQ

Baghdad ★

JORDAN

ISRAEL

LEBANON

CYPRUS

Mediterranean Sea

SAUDI ARABIA

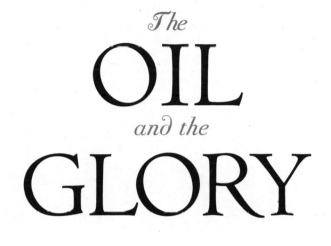

The

OIL

and the

GLORY

The
Barons

IN THE EARLY NINETEENTH CENTURY, Baku was a frontier settlement with the air of a medieval duchy. Within its seven-hundred-year-old walls, narrow cobblestone streets snaked past bustling outdoor markets, small mud-sided homes, and a minaret from which a princess had jumped to her death to escape her incestuous father. Rainbow-colored wooden carts called *arbas*, their wide carriages mounted on irregular seven-foot-tall wheels, transported people and goods across the surrounding desert. The crescent-shaped bay—seven miles from tip to tip and fifteen miles in circumference—teemed with fishing boats from the Russian city of Astrakhan up the coast and black merchantmen from downcoast Persia.

Baku was not regarded as a benign place. Alexandre Dumas *père* witnessed a frightening menagerie in 1858—"Tigers, panthers, jackals that roam through the whole province; the plants; the insects—locusts, scorpions and poisonous spiders." And then there were the relentless dust storms. A British petroleum engineer named A. Beeby Thompson wrote of winds that deposited as much as five feet of sand on roadways, halting all traffic. "There is no complete escape from these sandstorms," Thompson observed. "The fine dust penetrates everywhere; it accumulates in the pockets; it finds an entrance into the watch case, and causes the works to get clogged; it defies double windows and shutters, and the silicious particles accumulate in the house to such an extent that shovelfuls of sand may be removed from a Baku drawing room after a storm." Still, the wonders of Baku astonished those daring enough to visit. At night, when the winds quieted down, it became a magical place. Fire danced from the land and sea; in November and December, it lit the western horizon an eerie blue. A British professor visiting in 1845 described "a fairy castle" in which "multi-colored tongues of fire dance weirdly in the winds." In 1876, a journalist declared the spectacle "as wonderful as the Solfaterra at Naples, or the Geysers of Iceland, and to me infinitely more curious." Other visitors spoke of huge bubbles that suddenly appeared on the surface of the Caspian, capsized ships, and, if a torch were tossed overboard, produced a wall of flame. Visitors also reported a trick of physics in which the fires did not burn hot—Ludvig Nobel emerged unscorched after steering a steamboat straight through the blazing sea.

The source of these phantasmagoric displays was Baku's tremendous store of hydrocarbons. Experts speculated that the region was on top of a seventy-million-year-old residue of dead microorganisms. Another possibility was that detaching from the Black and Mediterranean seas had turned the Caspian into a saline death trap that entombed thousands of fish and other animals every day. Fumes from these ancient petroleum deposits continuously leaked to the surface, where they ignited at the slightest provocation.

Baku's oil earned an early, almost mythic reputation. Marco Polo's was perhaps the first written account. He reported a gusher that in a single hour produced "a quantity of oil sufficient to load up one hundred vessels." Later reports were strikingly similar. Eighteenth-century British trader Jonas Hanway described Russians sipping cordials of Baku's "white oil," a spontaneously occurring mixture of natural gas and petroleum that they thought chic and a certain cure for venereal and heart disease. While nearly all the world cooked by wood fire, a visitor to the district of Surakhani found that fumes escaping from the ground enabled the preparation of heated meals. Villagers simply dug into the soil and, applying a live coal, ignited a blaze. The natural gas that produced this phenomenon could be dangerous. In 1754, a traveler spoke of eight stabled horses being burned alive when the earth beneath them accidentally caught fire.

One peculiarity especially absorbed visitors—the theology attached to Baku. Zoroastrianism, the monotheistic Persian faith that originated the notion of angels, paradise, and the underworld, taught that fire purified the soul. Hearing of Baku and believing that the fires had burned since the Flood, Zoroastrians flocked there. They built temples where flames fed by natural gas jetted through porous limestone—the same jets that created the city's nightly fusing of Lewis Carroll fantasy and Dantean nightmare. The Zoroastrians fled in the middle of the seventh century, after Christian invaders sacked their temples and Arab conquerors insisted that Baku convert to Islam. Some brave followers made pilgrimages to Baku for centuries afterward, but by the 1860s xenophobic Orthodox Russia had all but halted even those short visits.

The first oilmen of Baku simply took out their shovels and dug or used their bare hands—the oil was that close to the surface. Obtaining the rights to do so was simple; you could buy or lease. Written evidence of one such agreement dating back to the Muslim year 1003—about 1595 by the western calendar—was found on a stone unearthed in a Baku oil pit. An Arabic inscription recorded the name of a landowner, Allah Jaz, the son of one Mohammed Nurs. The stone indicated that Mr. Jaz did not himself dig for oil but rather leased his property to an unnamed tenant. The tenant would have collected the oil in a pond lined with stone, then poured the unrefined crude into *boordukes*, goat- or ram-skin bags holding about twelve gallons. If Mr. Jaz's tenant were export-minded, he would have loaded the *boordukes* onto camels, two bags per beast, and shipped them in caravans across the desert. An *arba* could carry ten times as much oil but was not sufficiently sturdy to survive the arduous trek to distant markets.

So it went for the next two centuries. During that time, Mr. Jaz's property, in a district called Balakhani, was absorbed into the Persian Empire, then in 1813 into Russia. On the other side of the world, America had yet to develop a commercially exploitable oil industry. But that was about to change, sending shock waves all the way to Russia and, finally, to Baku. In 1859, a tenacious entrepreneur named Edwin Drake struck a gusher after twenty months of toil in the poor western Pennsylvania town of Titusville. With it, he triggered the world's first oil rush. In the wake of that discovery, a stern and lanky Clevelander named John D. Rockefeller cornered both the U.S. and European markets, earning him history's first great oil fortune.

By the late 1860s, Rockefeller-led advances were revolutionizing the oil business, but production methods at Mr. Jaz's property were substantially unchanged. The latest tenant on this land lacked almost any justification to invest in the new steam-driven wells because unlike his Pennsylvania counterparts, he couldn't be sure he would be the one to profit. Russia, milking the state-owned fields for bribes as Persia had in the past, rotated tenants every four years to obtain fresh payoffs. Hence, Balakhani tenants had every reason to continue to dig and scoop, without bothering to refine, and sell as much oil as they could as fast as they could. The result was that Russia's product was inferior in every way to Rockefeller's, including price.

Three years after Drake's discovery, a few tin containers of kerosene arrived in St. Petersburg. Their appearance might have gone unnoticed except that, improbably, they had traveled all the way from America.

Why would anyone finance an eight-thousand-mile shipment of kerosene when petroleum-rich Baku was so close at hand? The reason was simple. Nights were long for half the year in the Russian capital, and its people had to rely on malodorous tallow to relieve the darkness. The American kerosene was clean-burning by comparison, and tradition-bound Baku was producing only a relative trickle of kerosene. By 1870, gratified Russians were buying 250,000 gallons of U.S.-produced fuel a year, much of it from Rockefeller.

Russian scholars wondered how the United States, which had discovered its oil just a few years earlier, could so brazenly challenge the Empire in its own backyard. The answer, of course, could be found in the self-defeating and corrupt management of the Empire's petroleum riches. Court ministers and the press urged Alexander II to act. The czar was no visionary, nor even very resolute, but after some dithering, he buckled. In December 1872, he ordered the auction of 1,240 desseatines—3,348 acres—of oil land. In that one act, Alexander wiped out much of the state's suffocating hold on the industry and triggered a delirium that would itself spread all the way to upstart America. At first, there was panic in Baku. Somehow the mistaken impression had taken hold that all the region's oil lay within these tracts. Thus, bidders feverish to obtain some of the supposedly limited supply drove up the collective price of the lands at auction by a factor of six.

Not surprisingly, authorities by and large rigged the process. Most of the successful "bidders" were senior officials favored by Alexander, and the remainder were Baku's richest merchants. But there was one unlikely winner. The son of an illiterate shoemaker, he would learn to write his name only later, and even then the resultant signature more closely resembled a chicken scratch.

Zeynalabdin Tagiyev had neither great wealth nor influence. He had made his way in life as a master stonemason after a harsh boyhood in which he was apprenticed as a bricklayer at the age of ten. But by the late 1860s, as he reached middle age, he had achieved a modicum of success. He had a thriving business as a building contractor and owned two retail fabric shops besides.

Baku was not big, but as the main regional trading hub connecting the Persian, Ottoman, and Russian worlds, it did offer considerable opportunity to the observant. Tagiyev noticed some small yet fascinating changes in Baku's rudimentary oil industry. One well-off oil field tenant had built a primitive refinery. Other, smaller operators were erecting more modest kerosene-making plants—each little more than a roof over a couple of stills, but for Baku, real progress. Tagiyev himself soon procured a simple, two-cauldron refinery.

The announcement in 1872 that the state would auction some of

Alexander's oil lands excited Tagiyev, and he and an equally exhilarated Armenian friend named Sarkissov agreed to enter into the bidding. But how could they hope to compete with Baku's wealthiest and most influential figures? In particular, they were vexed by a contractor named I. M. Mirzoyev, who more than anyone had contributed to the auction hysteria. It was not that Mirzoyev was reckless—it was he who had had the foresight to open Baku's first refinery—but he was a bit overenthusiastic. He paid an astounding £254,000 for a 270-acre parcel—85 percent of all monies raised during the auction to buy 8 percent of the land. His tract was among the most highly prized, and no one begrudged Mirzoyev his right to disgorge his fortune this way. But in doing so, he disheartened the few ordinary bidders, such as Tagiyev and his partner, who could not afford to be so profligate.

Their chance finally arrived in the auction's final hours, when the more dubious properties came on the block. The next-to-last parcel was especially suspect. It was a stretch of flatland called Bibi-Heybat, one thought so unlikely to contain hydrocarbons that the state had appraised it at a mere £57. But the participants' zeal after Mirzoyev's example was still intense, and they bid up the price, driving it to fifteen times its assessed value. Sensing that this might be his final opportunity, Tagiyev would not be denied. He bid £906. No one countered. Dubious Bibi-Heybat was theirs.

The oil field was next to a mosque, and "dubious" soon seemed a generous way to describe it. Tortuous months of extracting just a dozen barrels from time to time stretched into years. Finally Sarkissov lost patience and sold out to his partner.

Not until fourteen years after the auction did Tagiyev's payoff come. But when it did, it arrived in a very big way.

On September 27, 1886, there was a rumble at Bibi-Heybat, and a gusher burst 224 feet into the air. It resembled "a colossal pillar of smoke, from the crest of which clouds of oil sand detached themselves and floated away a great distance without touching the ground," the *Baku News* reported. The magnitude of Tagiyev's strike was flabbergasting. Before it was contained, it spewed, and lost, more oil each day than was being extracted at the time by all other major petroleum-producing centers in the world *combined*—including America's twenty-five thousand wells and those in Galicia, Romania, and Burma.

The mosque next door and nearby homes were drenched by the 3,500-barrel-an-hour shower of oil and rock. Even neighbors a mile and a half away were treated to the downpour. On the sixth day, a sudden thrust of crude saturated the square in front of the Baku Town Hall two miles from the well. Two days later, the flow was measured at 81,400 barrels every twenty-four hours. Authorities demanded that the well be capped, and on the fifteenth day Tagiyev's engineers managed some semblance of control—they reduced the daily outflow to 7,000 barrels. "Altogether," the *Baku News* reported, "close on 12 million puds [1.4 million barrels] are estimated to have come to the surface, and most of this was lost for want of storage accommodation. The oil simply poured into the Caspian Sea, and was lost forever to mankind."

Before long, Tagiyev's strike was making him among Baku's wealthiest citizens. His oil, notable for its high quality, fetched twice the price of that extracted in Balakhani, where land cost up to five times as much. Tagiyev proved not only determined but clever and ambitious as well. He built a refinery to process his crude and a dock on the Caspian from which his own private tanker fleet could steam north to the mouth of the Volga River. Waiting there were Tagiyev-owned barges to ship his oil to customers courted by his own Moscow sales office.

Tagiyev became Baku's most influential citizen, a dignified and deceptively quiet man with a bearded, open face and white hair who was astonishingly lean and fit. Peasants, workmen, robbers, and the crustiest oilmen all treated him with deference. When he appeared in public, he extended his hand, and people jostled to kiss it and addressed him as "Haji." He was elected chairman of the city council and was decorated by the Emir of Bukhara and the Shah of Iran. Czar Nicholas II named him an honorary state councilor. Even after he left the city council, few people of consequence would pass through town without dropping by for tea with the oilman who after years of struggle had overtaken all the power brokers and generals to become Baku's elder statesman.

Foreign visitors raved about the oil. Lewis Emery, an oilman from Bradford, Pennsylvania, found that Baku's lamp oil, unlike that at home, produced no smoke when it was burned. British journalist Charles Marvin reported that Baku oil was less dangerous as well, its flash point at 88 degrees, some 20 degrees higher than the American varieties. Other American visitors found the fountains of oil roaring skyward most thrilling. Some recalled that, in the Titusville boom, a few hundred barrels a day was a bonanza. But in Baku, a well called Vermishev spewed oil for four solid months, its stalk forty feet tall and nine feet in diameter.

Even after the introduction of safety measures—storage tanks, caps with specially designed sliding valves—Baku's monsters were not easily controlled. In August 1883, the most famous of all, a well called Friendship, erupted with a gusher that tore its safety cap to shreds, then ripped through twenty-five feet of concrete casing as well as the roof and sides of a seventy-foot-tall derrick. Visible eight miles away and audible at a distance of three miles, the fountain thundered two hundred feet in the air for more than four months.

Outsiders mobbed Baku, causing the city's population to surge from 14,500 to 80,000 in a mere decade (by 1905 it would be 207,000). Most of the newcomers sought work in the fields. But others came with ready cash to invest in the hope of becoming rich, among them Europeans and Americans who paid £35 for the ten-day, 2,500-mile journey from London requiring both rail and sea travel.

The oil fields were transformed; hand digging was abandoned. Seventeen steam-drilled wells quickly materialized, and by 1878 there were 301 of them. The government auctioned off more land, and one new field named Zabrat was so prolific that it was dubbed the "Golden Bazaar." Wild speculation erupted. The oil lands were subdivided, then divided again. Ordinary people began digging in their yards, and some discovered that they, too, were wealthy. Everywhere workers were raising cone-shaped wooden derricks twenty feet square at the base, sixty to eighty feet tall, and three feet square at the top. The greasy structures barely fit onto the slivers of land on which anyone with a bit of means was working.

It seemed that everyone had become a refiner, too. People converted their homes into distilleries, and Baku became a fog of black smoke. Appalled city officials banned refineries, forcing the erection of a new suburb to accommodate them. Aptly, it was called Black Town. By 1880, Black Town was a nightmare picture of gangs of shirtless men toiling in 195 oil-saturated refineries.

The area ultimately under production wasn't large—twelve square miles, but it spawned new millionaires by the day. A fabulously wealthy core of two hundred emerged, and people began calling Tagiyev and his fellow operatives "the barons."

Unabashedly ostentatious, the barons used their money to raise a European-style city outside Baku's old walls. They outdid one another with their construction of inns—the Hotel d'Europe and the Dominique were the most elegant—plus casinos and rows of exclusive shops. Their taste was eclectic, to put it kindly, favoring Moorish, Gothic, Byzantine, and rococo—sometimes all in the same structure. They copied Venetian palaces from postcards. A baron named Isa Bey Hajinski built a three-story mansion that vaguely resembled playing cards. A neighbor saw a photograph of a dragon in a magazine and fashioned his palace into a facsimile; guests entered through the open jaws.

The barons' families lived in old-fashioned Eastern splendor. A middle-ranking baron named Timurbek Ashurbekov employed a cook discharged by the Emir of Bukhara, whose kingdom lay across the Caspian. Some of the barons' homes were served by eunuchs, who escorted their veiled wives on the street and, late at night, read their children bedtime stories. The barons themselves seldom went home. They gathered after hours at a private seaside club called the Oil Producer's Association or in their villas in the northside resort of Mardakhan, developed by Tagiyev.

The reverberation of gunshots was commonplace. Until the government finally outlawed the practice, celebrants at Baku parties fired from their homes at passersby. Even boys of ten carried small revolvers. The violence was not just for fun. Many of the oilmen despised one another, and those tensions, when added to the highway banditry between Baku and the oil fields, made people understandably anxious for their safety. Before long, bands of hired gunmen, called *kotchis*, from the Persian for "daredevil," appeared on the streets. They displayed a kind of fraternal loyalty but used the bullying tactics of racketeers. *Kotchis* went to work when especially quarrelsome oilmen encountered one another on the street. The opposing *kotchi* forces would fire solemnly at one another—not at the actual oilmen, which under *kotchi* rules was normally prohibited.

It was against this rowdy backdrop that Tagiyev's image grew larger than ever. At the age of seventy-three, he married Sona Arablinskaya, the seventeen-year-old daughter of a retired czarist general. An ethnic Circassian, Sona was an exotic beauty. The marriage angered Ismail, Tagiyev's eldest son from his first marriage. For one thing, Ismail himself was twice the girl's age. More irritating still, he was now technically also his own father's brother-in-law, for Tagiyev had married the younger sister of Ismail's own wife. Unmoved by his son's protests, Tagiyev became devoted to Sona—and dangerously possessive.

A few years after the wedding, Tagiyev heard talk of a scandal in his downtown mansion. At the center of the affair was Prince Bebutov, who had once been in Tagiyev's care as a sort of foster child. It was whispered that the prince, now of age, had became a little too friendly with Sona.

Lev Naussimbaum, the son of a Baku oilman, wrote an account of what happened next, embellished somewhat but in general agreement with family oral history. Tagiyev summoned Bebutov to his private chambers and confronted him with his suspicions. Dissatisfied with the prince's response, Tagiyev—whom Naussimbaum called "the general"—clapped three times. Servants entered, and the patriarch commanded: "Deprive him of his sex!"

> The Prince roared, the general cursed, the armed servants proceeded to obey their employer. The general's son hurried to his foster brother's assistance, but was beaten and driven away. By a miracle the prince succeeded in tearing away and running down the steps. There he was attacked again, but was able to attract the attention of his servants, who stood in the street. Now it came to a regular battle between the prince's servants and the general's. Passers-by on the street, who did not want to lose the opportunity to take part in a battle, interfered so that the prince could be

dragged away from the field of manly honor. The fight, which had now lost its objective, was continued for several hours for purely esthetic reasons.

According to Naussimbaum, the prince fled to Paris. As for Tagiyev, he became, in the view of the adoring Russian media, "The Azerbaijani Eunuch-Maker."

CHAPTER 2

A Visitor *from* Sweden

A FEW MONTHS INTO THE BOOM, A visiting Swede stepped off a Caspian Sea steamboat and onto the docks at Baku. At forty-three, Robert Nobel was the eldest of three talented brothers whose family name would ultimately ascend to a nineteenth-century pantheon alongside the entrepreneurial giants Carnegie, Morgan, and Rockefeller. On this day in 1873, his immediate task was to find and purchase a supply of hardwood to be shaped into rifle stocks for imperial Russia's army.

But from the moment he boarded the steamer, on the last leg of a long journey from St. Petersburg, his interest in hardwood had begun to fade. The boat's Dutch captain had regaled the impressionable Robert with colorful stories of Baku. When he disembarked, he was fascinated by what he saw and heard. The oilmen he met were full of swagger and greed and stories about huge gushers sending skyward black columns of crude.

Robert was carrying twenty-five thousand rubles, entrusted to him by his brother Ludvig to buy the hardwood. But all the talk of fortunes to be made in the nearby oil fields was too alluring to resist. Within a matter of days, he had spent the entire twenty-five thousand rubles on the purchase of a Black Town refinery and an oil field property owned by the steamboat captain. The Nobel Brothers Petroleum Company was born.

Robert's impulsive dealmaking went largely unnoticed in frenetic Baku, and he would ultimately become a figure lost to history. Yet his gamble that day would put this backwater city on the path to becoming the world's first great oil capital, and it would set in motion the complete modernization of the global oil industry.

A commanding figure with his bushy eyebrows, beard, and determined gaze, Ludvig would emerge as the architect of this extraordinary transformation. He would revolutionize the way petroleum products were transported around the world by designing and building the first successful version of an oceangoing tanker. He would devise a refining process so advanced that it would still excite American oilmen when they finally embraced it a quarter century later. He would create the first environmentally regulated workmen's village, an advance that over the next century would open the areas with the harshest climates in the world to oil exploration. For decades to come, his name would be synonymous with oil.

For the Nobels, the era had begun in 1838, when their father—the chemist, engineer, and inventor Immanuel Nobel—moved to the Russian capital to try to sell his inventions to the czar's court. The Russians were interested almost immediately in a weapon the Swede had perfected, the underwater exploding mine, and before long, Czar Nicholas I began giving Nobel grants for his work. The insolvent but confident Immanuel uprooted his family to the Russian Empire. For two decades, Immanuel obtained profitable commissions—he created the first central water-heating plant and a customized five-hundred-horsepower engine for Russia's warships. But then Nicholas died, and Immanuel's fortunes died with him.

Wary of outsiders, Alexander II severed his predecessor's contracts. Immanuel returned to Sweden, penniless.

All three sons inherited their father's expertise in the laboratory. Alfred, the youngest, was the first to gain prominence. At age thirty-three, he appropriated Italian chemist Ascacio Sobrero's invention of nitroglycerine and used sand to change it from a dangerously volatile liquid into a stable solid. His patented creation—Alfred called it "dynamite"—was instantly popular with builders and miners. He was soon managing a global dynamite monopoly from an apartment on the chic Avenue de Malakoff in Paris, proving so shrewd a businessman that Europe's premier financiers considered him one of their own.

Ludvig, the middle son, remained in St. Petersburg to settle his family's business affairs after his father's return to Sweden in 1859. He was the logical choice, possessing as he did his brother Alfred's initiative and good judgment but none of Robert's often unappealing personality traits. Over time, Ludvig restored his family's name in the Russian capital and won the favor of the unpredictable Alexander. Operating his own machine shop, Ludvig made himself Russia's largest manufacturer of horse-drawn military supply carriages. When the czar commissioned him to manufacture thirty thousand automatic rifles to replace the Russian military's old muzzleloaders, Ludvig's success seemed assured.

It was in connection with this undertaking that he dispatched his older brother to the Caspian in search of hardwood. Handicapped by a short temper and a persecution complex that together undermined his every venture, Robert had suffered several business failures over the years. He had joined Ludvig in St. Petersburg as perhaps the only dignified opportunity left open to him.

When he returned from Baku with the news that he had spent the twenty-five thousand rubles on an oil field and a refinery, Ludvig had little choice but to make the best of his brother's initiative. He agreed to advance the additional cash needed to cover the initial operating costs. (Brother Alfred would later invest some of his dynamite fortune in the Nobel Brothers Petroleum Company, entitling him to lecture the financially untutored Ludvig about improvident spending. The lectures would fall on deaf ears.)

Robert went back to Baku brimming with ideas. He began with what he knew best—chemistry. The kerosene manufactured in the Nobels' refinery produced copious amounts of smoke and a repellent odor, shortcomings that all Baku refineries shared. Robert quickly identified the source of the problem, an outdated method of purification. He introduced an improved procedure that used caustic soda as the cleaning agent, and then he built an entirely new refinery.

His perfectionism became celebrated. Of all the Black Town refinery owners, only Robert insisted on strict cleanliness—leaks were to be instantly repaired and oil puddles swabbed. Because he didn't trust local specialists, he imported Swedish talent: a production chief, a senior chemist, and a machine shop foreman.

But no one could dismiss the results: Within two years, Nobel Brothers Petroleum's kerosene wasn't just the finest in Baku, but also matched American quality. In October 1876, the first three hundred barrels of Nobel kerosene were shipped to St. Petersburg; their arrival signaled the beginning of the end of Rockefeller's domination of the Russian market. The American oil wizard had conquered Europe, but by 1883 the Nobels would force him to retreat from the czarist empire.

Ludvig finally decided to have a look at the goings-on in Baku for himself. As he stepped off the Caspian steamer with his son Emanuel, the flavor of the city flooded his senses, immediate and pungent. Turbaned stevedores hurried about, and a swarm of Armenian merchants noisily pressed forward to bargain. Baku had seemed to be so much madness when viewed from faraway St. Petersburg. But now, seeing it up close, Ludvig quickly understood his brother's enthusiasm about the city's prospects. He toured the new refinery and saw that the Nobel Brothers Petroleum Company had distinguished itself.

He also saw that his brother's erratic personality was exacting a toll on the company's operations, so he abruptly elbowed Robert aside and put himself in charge. It could not have come as a total surprise to Robert; he knew that his tantrums had demoralized the employees. But he could not hide his disappointment, and in the autumn of 1879, he disappeared, telling no one of his destination.

Robert left behind an important legacy. Baku had practically thirsted for someone with his combination of intellect, ingenuity, and boldness. Without him, its oil industry almost certainly would not have achieved greatness so soon—perhaps never at all. It is nearly as certain that Ludvig would not have scaled the heights he did. Robert's daring brought Ludvig to Baku, and Baku unlocked Ludvig's genius.

When Ludvig settled in Baku in 1876, the city had a vexing problem: how to export its crude oil and other petroleum products to distant markets. Its oil fields and refineries, perched on the shore of the landlocked Caspian Sea, were disconnected from most of the world. Europe was best reached by the Baltic Sea, but that was some two thousand miles away and blocked by mountains.

The Russian Empire was the chief consumer of Baku oil, but even it was difficult to service with ease. Cargo vessels trying to make their way across the Caspian to the Russian shore were blocked by ice floes nearly half the year. The barge system that transported oil up the 2,300-mile Volga River into Russia's interior was underdeveloped. Railroads were in decrepit condition.

Even when the waters were open, the economics of Caspian shipping were such that American kerosene actually retailed in St. Petersburg for less than the Baku product. The same was true for markets closer to home. The regional capital of Tbilisi, 341 miles northwest of Baku, bought its kerosene more cheaply from America—fully eight thousand miles to the west.

How to solve the transportation puzzle became an obsession for everyone whose livelihood depended on breaking Baku out of its landlocked straitjacket. "Grandiose schemes are constantly being discussed for conveying the oil to Europe," British journalist Charles Marvin wrote in 1885. The Briton reported "a great deal of talk of running a pipeline from Baku to the Persian Gulf, with the idea of securing Baku the exclusive control of the markets of Asia." For his part, Ludvig thought the problem was solvable. It simply required a deliberate, step-by-step approach, he decided, starting with the basics: how oil was sent from oil field to refinery within Baku.

A mere eight miles separated the Nobel wells at Balakhani from their refinery in Black Town. Yet there were chronic bottlenecks. The drivers of the two-wheeled carts that hauled the crude in barrels were the cause. There were an estimated ten thousand of them working Baku's fields, and each was supposed to make the trip from wells to refineries twice a day. But they were a cantankerous lot. The *arba* drivers regularly demanded higher pay, often striking till they got it. They took off for Muslim holidays, bad weather, or simply because they felt like it. This was the very problem that Rockefeller had confronted a decade earlier with his teamsters and their horse-drawn wagons, conveying the oil with maddening casualness along the muddy lanes from western Pennsylvania's oil fields to railroad stops. The American had done away with the teamsters. Now Ludvig would send his *arba* drivers packing and replace them with the town's first oil pipeline.

The Crown's representatives had never heard of an oil pipeline. In fact, the idea sounded a tad eccentric. They refused to grant Ludvig the necessary rights of way, relenting only after he brought political pressure to bear and deposited bribes in the right pockets.

America was the world's acknowledged leader in pipeline technology, and Ludvig turned there for inspiration. After examining the size of pipe used in western Pennsylvania and studying American pumps and cisterns, he settled on a design. His pipeline would be manufactured in Glasgow of five-inch-diameter steel; the crude would be pushed through it, from oil field to refinery, by a Nobel-designed, twenty-seven-horsepower steam pump.

In 1877, his workers began putting down the line. The *arba* drivers were livid—along with the coopers who fashioned the barrels—and they organized gangs to disrupt the project. When the police did nothing, Ludvig built eight watchtowers and hired Cossacks to man them. Within a year, the pipeline was complete. The total cost, including pay for the Cossacks, was $50,000. Based on the money saved by firing the *arba* drivers, the pipeline paid for itself within a year.

Ludvig's competitors were astounded. He had offered them partnerships in the pipeline when it was first proposed, but they had rebuffed him, forcing him to finance the entire project himself. Now, those who could swallow their pride began paying him to transport their oil. Those who couldn't tried to duplicate his creation, and the resulting tangle of pipes soon leaked oil everywhere. Ludvig expanded on his success, and by the turn of the century, there would be a network of 326 Nobel pipelines covering nearly seventy miles of territory.

But perhaps his greatest achievement was the development of the oil tanker. Russia's foremost authority at the time declared it "the most important fact in the entire history of the petroleum industry." Nobel biographer Robert Tolf called it "a discovery to rank with brother Alfred's invention of dynamite." The vessels that Nobel designed and built were forerunners of the block-long supertankers that would sate the modern world's enormous appetite for energy. By enabling the uninterrupted movement of oil on a global scale, they would spur one of history's great economic expansions.

Until Ludvig's invention, oil was shipped in wood barrels aboard the steamships that crossed the Caspian to the mouth of the Volga River. This was an improvement over camels hauling *boordukes*, but still primitive. The steamships could carry just a few hundred barrels at a time, and the empties were dead weight on return trips. The barrels themselves were expensive because the wood had to be imported, sometimes from as far away as America. If rising oil production drove down the price of crude, as Ludvig suspected it might, the cost of each barrel could ultimately exceed the value of its contents.

Others had already proposed a ship whose outer skin would serve as one giant container. But the Caspian's turbulence made that impractical. In experiments, ships modified to test the theory were tossed about in the waves as the weight of the oil inside shifted from side to side.

Ludvig rejected the single-container concept that had proved so unstable, instead designing a ship with multiple containers. In his final blueprint, the ship's hold contained a row of twenty-one vertical compartments, or cisterns, linked to one another by pipes. To enhance stability, the engine was placed amidships, and iron tanks capable of holding 242 tons of kerosene were positioned fore and aft. There were several safety modifications. The cisterns were sealed off from the ship's boiler and designed to tolerate the expansion or contraction of their cargo when temperatures changed. The hold was ventilated so that gases could not accumulate.

Russian shipbuilders were unsure how to build the peculiar contraption. Ludvig assigned the task to a master shipbuilder in Sweden, and in late 1878 he accepted delivery of the *Zoroaster*, a 184-foot-long, 27-foot-wide, superlatively buoyant vessel with a gleaming white hull. It was all steel, built according to the most modern specifications.

On its maiden voyage, the ship steamed six hundred miles from Baku to the Russian port of Astrakhan. Word of the successful trip spread quickly, and Americans, Britons, and Germans came to study the design. Eight years later, impressed with the vessel's ability to conquer the tempestuous Caspian but slow to accept that it could manage the Atlantic or Pacific, the Americans and Britons sent their first replica across the ocean, from England to New York. Ludvig had never bothered to patent his creation.

It was perhaps inevitable that a powerful competitor would emerge to challenge the Nobel primacy in Baku and Russia. What Ludvig may not have expected was that the threat would come from another influential European family—the French branch of the House of Rothschild.

Barons Alphonse and Edmond de Rothschild were sons of a great financial dynasty whose interests spanned investment banking, mining, oil, and railways. The brothers themselves owned refineries in Marseilles and the Adriatic port of Fiume. For them, Baku was an opportunity to buy low-cost crude to refine in Fiume—and, not so incidentally, to mount a credible challenge to Rockefeller's dominance in Europe.

From the time of their arrival in Baku in 1883, the Rothschilds always seemed to be a target of mischief. Lev Naussimbaum, the son of an oilman, wrote a probably exaggerated account of how the brothers were victimized for refusing to hire *kotchi* guards. The hired gunmen retaliated by committing a series of burglaries, after which the Rothschilds got the message and put them on the payroll. But even then, the best the brothers could manage was a sort of catastrophic protection plan covering major crimes; the still-disgruntled *kotchis* reserved the right to engage in occasional minor thievery on Rothschild property.

The brothers were blatantly duped, Naussimbaum wrote, by Musa

Jacob, a weapons smuggler-cum-oilman who wanted to dispose of a dry well. The calculating Jacob lined its sides and floor with concrete and poured in enough oil to create the illusion of an active well. He then informed the Rothschilds that the well was for sale and invited an inspection by their agent. Everything seemed in order, so the Frenchmen closed the deal. When they discovered the swindle, they had to contain their outrage. As Naussimbaum wrote, "When the cementing came to light, the Rothschilds' representative demanded restitution of the money, but quickly waived further claims when Jacob explained to him that one usually paid for such ridiculous demands with one's life. The Rothschilds were foreigners and nobody blamed Jacob for this transaction."

It was serious business, however, when a syndicate of Ludvig Nobel's competitors in Baku turned to the Rothschild brothers for help. Ludvig's domination of the Caspian-Volga oil export route had nettled the other oilmen, and they had embarked on a search for an alternative. They came up with a plan to build a 561.5-mile railroad west to the ancient Roman naval base of Batumi, on Georgia's Black Sea coast. From there, access to all of Europe would be theirs. Czar Alexander III, somewhat annoyed by Ludvig's steadily expanding power, approved an outline of the proposal. Then oil prices dropped, expenses exceeded the budget, and the syndicate needed a savior.

Alphonse and Edmond knew something about big rail ventures; the Rothschilds had built Europe's first major railroad, from Vienna to Galicia, as well as the Mediterranean Railway along the French coast. They rescued the syndicate's rail project by providing some $10 million in financing, accepting as collateral mortgages on oil fields and on a refinery. The new railroad began operating in 1883. The Rothschilds put a hundred of their own railroad cars on the tracks and permitted Ludvig to run 450 tankers of his own, a calculated business decision that must have dismayed the other barons.

The railroad project turned Batumi into a boom town. For decades, it had been a tiny Turkish trading port with a bazaar of rickety booths and only one structure taller than one story, belonging to the Russian vice consul. Now thousands of newcomers built houses and shops, and British companies developed yacht clubs and cricket fields. European visitors could billet in the Hotel d'Europe or Hotel de France. Most preferred the latter because it was larger, it was situated next to the train station, and, what with workdays often stretching into the late evening, it kept its dining room open as late as midnight. Perhaps most important, the hotel's location was relatively safe, no small consideration in a town so dangerous that virtually everyone carried a small revolver.

The port of Batumi instantly attained world-class status, busier than frenzied Philadelphia, San Francisco, or Port Arthur, Texas. Crude oil stored in towering dockside tanks was loaded aboard British cargo ships that embarked for European refineries at the rate of more than five thousand a year. Kerosene was shipped in four-gallon Welch tins packed in wooden cases. The Rothschilds ran the biggest such operation, employing 1,400 people who in a day could pack thirty-six thousand tins into eighteen thousand cases. Russia added to the port's congestion by building a naval base. Through it all, Batumi remained a gritty place. Passing through in 1888 on his way to Baku, Calouste Gulbenkian, a twenty-one-year-old Turkish Armenian new to oil trading, found "a filthy mushroom town" where "the water stank of oil and drains and the inhabitants seemed to exist almost entirely by smuggling."

For a time, the railroad's success was tempered by bottlenecks that developed in the Caucasus mountains, where steep grades slowed train traffic from Baku and harsh weather sometimes halted it altogether. The main culprit was the 3,200-foot Suram Pass, so difficult a climb that two engines were required to pull just eight tankers over the crest at a time. Rapidly, crude oil awaiting shipment to Batumi was backing up in Baku.

The logical fix seemed to be a pipeline, one far more ambitious than any built thus far in or around Baku. At first, Czar Alexander's court would have none of it. The opposition there was understandable. The Crown was earning enormous tariffs from the railroad; anticipation of this windfall had been a main reason for St. Petersburg's original keenness in the project. Neither did the czar's avaricious agents in Baku support a pipeline. There were endless ways in which they could meddle with the movement of tanker cars on the railroad in order to generate bribes from oilmen anxious that their shipments of crude be expedited.

Baku's oilmen finally struck a compromise with the Crown, agreeing to a scaled-back pipeline project that kept the trains running at least part of the distance. In 1886, Nobel, the Rothschilds, and Zeynalabdin Tagiyev formed an alliance of convenience, using four hundred tons of Alfred Nobel's dynamite to punch through the Suram Pass and clear a path for their pipeline. The line that they laid from Baku terminated seventy-eight miles short of Batumi, but it did surmount the mountains and speed the shipment of oil. Seventeen years later, in 1906, the line would be extended the remaining distance to the port, at a total cost of $12 million.

When Batumi opened Europe to crude oil and other petroleum products from Baku, Rockefeller responded with a vengeance. He dropped prices across the continent, typical of the predatory "sweating" that he regularly employed to beat back competitors. Rockefeller added rumor, sabotage, and bribery to his campaign and played on widespread suspicions that oil from the Russian Empire was of poor quality. But unlike most of Rockefeller's usual victims, the Nobel Company and the Rothschilds had the financial wherewithal to wait out the American and counterattack with a public defense of their products.

Rockefeller was in unaccustomed circumstances. In America, he had long ago ceded 15 or 20 percent of the market as a sop to competitors—it was too much trouble to attempt to grab everything. Now he had a bitter pill to swallow—Standard Oil's share of global exports would fall from 78 percent in 1888 to 71 percent three years later. Russia would account for the difference; its share, mostly Nobel and Rothschild oil, would rise to 29 percent.

Adding insult to injury, the Rothschilds outwitted Rockefeller with a daring thrust into a new market. It began with a simple problem of supply and demand: The brothers' Batumi facilities were capable of refining and shipping far more oil than Europe could absorb. Casting about for new customers, they settled on the Far East, an extraordinarily large market that had long been ignored. The question was how to move the oil such a great distance without having the profits eaten up by shipping costs.

The Rothschilds turned to a young Briton named Marcus Samuel for help with their Baku problem. The rotund and excitable Samuel, age thirty-seven, was up to the challenge. Over the years, his father had culti-vated strong friendships with a group of Scotsmen who owned Britain's great trading houses in Bangkok, Calcutta, Hong Kong, Manila, and Singapore. Now all seemed willing to cooperate with their old friend's im-pressive son. In 1890, Samuel traveled to Baku on behalf of the Roth-schilds. Fascinated with what he saw, he devised a plan so audacious that the Rothschilds at first backed away. They knew how spiteful the intended victim of Samuel's proposed coup could be—none other than Rockefeller. Eventually, they set aside their apprehension and instructed Samuel to pro-ceed.

Surprise was paramount to the scheme's success—Rockefeller could be expected to retaliate swiftly if any word of the plan leaked—and Samuel operated in complete secrecy. With the support of his father's Asia-based friends and the financial backing of the Rothschilds, Samuel approached the British government. Britain controlled the Suez Canal, and Samuel needed permission to ship Rothschild oil through it if his gambit was to succeed. The reason was simple. By taking this shortcut to Asia, the Rothschilds' ships would make the journey in thirty-five hundred fewer miles than it took Rockefeller's competing fleet to steam from Philadel-phia to Singapore. Conversely, absent the advantage of the Suez, the ven-ture would probably never be profitable.

There was reason to doubt that Samuel would succeed. Already the British, citing safety concerns, had rejected Rockefeller's own, similar pro-posal. But Samuel turned Rockefeller's failure to his own advantage. He commissioned the design of a larger, more technologically advanced tanker than Rockefeller had in mind and convinced the government that the ves-sel would be safe. Most important, Samuel argued that Britain had a stake in his enterprise—unlike Rockefeller, he would be a Briton shipping cargo produced by a company with strong British ties aboard a British tanker through a canal built by Britain. The British government consented.

The last critical step was to arrange for rapid distribution the moment the oil arrived in Asia. Samuel ordered that depots be built in three strate-gic ports—Singapore, Bangkok, and Hong Kong. On July 22, 1892, the first Rothschild tanker, the *Murex*, filled up at Batumi. On August 23, it passed stealthily through the Suez on its way to Samuel's Asian agents.

Within weeks, the success of the Rothschild coup was self-evident, and Rockefeller was flummoxed.

By 1901, Baku was producing a majority of the world's oil supply, and the company that Ludvig Nobel had built was satisfying 9 percent of this global demand. It ranked among the world's largest commercial enterprises, employing more than twelve thousand people with an annual payroll of $2.5 million. By 1916, the company would be transporting its oil on the world's largest private fleet. The Nobel juggernaut was the envy of Baku—sort of. "All the Baku well proprietors hate one another," Charles Marvin wrote, "and the only sentiment they have in common is a general hatred of the Nobel Brothers."

Ludvig would not live to see all of this; he died in 1888 of heart failure, and control of the company passed to his son Emanuel. But it could be argued that in his lifetime, Ludvig had in some ways surpassed Rockefeller. True, the cunning American pioneered vertical integration decades before the term was invented. In the second half of the nineteenth century, his Standard Oil Company grew to control 90 percent of oil sales both in America and Europe. It was a triumph credited to a brilliant, "well-to-wick" transportation network that moved Rockefeller's oil from oil field to retailer faster and more cheaply than any competitor.

What distinguished Ludvig from the more renowned American were the Swede's single-handed accomplishments. While Rockefeller mostly bought, rented, or adapted existing technology to build Standard Oil, Ludvig designed, built, and, through his company, operated every pipeline, ship, and barge in the Nobel empire himself. Rockefeller depended on others; Ludvig Nobel relied on no one—because he had no one on whom to rely. He was not reluctant to borrow ideas from others, but he almost always improved on them. Once, Ludvig dispatched a Russian engineer named Alexander Bary to Pennsylvania for three years to study crude oil processing. Bary's observations led to Ludvig's invention of a system called "continuous refining." The method was unquestionably superior to standard practice, but twenty-five years elapsed before it was adopted in the United States. Similarly, Ludvig examined the design of a U.S. iron boiler car, shrank it, and developed his own unique railroad tank car. By 1883, he had fifteen hundred in operation.

Ludvig was a rarity in another way—a social visionary in an age when fellow industrialists had little regard for their workers, paying just fifty cents a day; housing them in filthy barracks without toilets, baths, or soap; and enforcing few safety rules. Ludvig instead built colonies of stone houses, including separate quarters for married men, and educated his workers' children in free schools. He distributed 8 percent of company profit to laborers and 40 percent of the remainder to salaried personnel. One of his most notable creations was Villa Petrolea, a twenty-five-acre walled employee compound that was the forerunner of fabricated oil camps that would emerge a century later on the tempestuous North Sea, on Alaska's frigid North Slope, and in Indonesia's sweltering tropics. To provide his workers respite in arid Baku, he landscaped Villa Petrolea with soil, trees, and shrubbery hauled in from elsewhere and irrigated the greenery with water fetched from the Volga by his tankers. For recreation, Ludvig installed a billiard room and Baku's first telephone.

Ludwig never engaged in the philanthropy that earned Zeynalabdin Tagiyev widespread respect. Still, this inventive Swede was undeniably a giant of his time. His accomplishments led Marvin to dub him "the Oil King of Baku." Nobel's biographer Robert Tolf called Ludwig "an incomparable, insatiable overachiever. His deeds in Russia at the time were without parallel. On a world scale only a de Lesseps, builder of the Suez Canal, was of equal rank."

Revolution

As the twentieth century dawned, Baku was a truly cosmopolitan city. Its streets pulsed with a dazzling mix of people—turbaned Azeris with red hennaed beards, Dagestanis in long robes, water merchants on donkey carts, Russians in fur-lined caps, and Swedes and Germans in stylish suits. Its electric service was more advanced than almost any city of comparable size anywhere in the world. Other municipal services lagged, according to one gloomy account that called Baku "the worst managed city in the world," its "horse-tram service pitiable, the sanitary arrangements appalling."

Calouste Gulbenkian, the Turkish Armenian oil trader, fretted over the failure of the old-line barons to adopt good conservation practices. While the Nobel Brothers Petroleum Company made sure that its wells were properly capped, its competitors made the Caspian "black with wasted crude oil," Gulbenkian wrote. "Products which are worth their weight in gold today are dumped into the sea." Should that ever be reversed, "the rivalry between Baku petrol and the United States product will be only a memory."

The city enjoyed a vibrant cultural life, thanks mainly to the unlettered Zeynalabdin Tagiyev, whose great oil wealth had allowed him to act on his sense of civic duty. He established a western-style theater, perhaps the first such permanent facility in the Muslim world, and introduced ballet to the city. He spent lavishly on an opera house designed by his favorite architect, a talented Pole named Josef Goslavsky. The building bore a striking resemblance to Monte Carlo's classic Casino et les Jardins.

The old baron also dared to build a secular boarding school for Muslim girls, probably the first in the Islamic world. Baku conservatives and Muslim leaders were outraged by the bold undertaking, but Tagiyev asserted that nothing in the Koran barred the education of girls. He enlisted the support of a leading cleric and persuaded several prominent businessmen to enroll their daughters. Lastly, he won over Czar Nicholas II, who had harbored doubts about such a politically sensitive project, by cleverly appealing to the Crown's vanity—he named the school after Nicholas's wife, Alexandra. Public opinion shifted, and when applications were solicited for the second year, there was a lengthy waiting list. Tagiyev wore a tall lambswool hat for the official class photograph of the first graduates, all without veils.

By that time, he was no longer an oilman, having sold his holdings in 1897 for £600,000 to James Vishnau, a Briton. The divestiture caught almost everyone by surprise, which was compounded when Vishnau struck an enormous gusher within months. In retrospect, however, some people supposed that the shrewd patriarch, now in his eighties, had sensed earlier than most that there were other great windfalls waiting to be had.

Tagiyev became a diversified industry, branching into half a dozen major businesses. He opened a fish-processing factory south of Baku, where the rushing Kura River, teeming with giant, caviar-laden sturgeon on their way to spawn, spilled into the Caspian. He started a shipping line, planted cotton plantations, and helped capitalize Baku's first locally owned bank. And he built the city's first textile factory, importing mechanical looms and bringing instructors from England's expert mills to teach local men the art of fabric design.

Yet underlying Baku's prosperity was an ominous fault line—the hate-filled ethnic divide that roiled the local Azerbaijani Turk and Armenian populations. The Armenians were, to a large degree, members of the wealthy establishment of industrialists, merchants, and managers and, later, the local leadership of Lenin's Bolshevik revolutionaries. The native Azeris, often far less educated, filled many of the jobs in the oil fields, railroad yards, and factories.

Unlike Nobel, other industrialists treated the Azeri-dominated labor force with deplorable disregard. If a man married, he could be automatically sacked, as matrimony was thought to make him unreliable. Those married workers who were tolerated were usually not permitted to live with their families—to provide for a worker's comfort was considered patently absurd. In any case, few oil workers wanted to subject their wives to life in their stinking barracks. The workday lasted twelve to fourteen hours in conditions that were grossly unsafe.

The first stirrings of labor unrest surfaced in 1903, led in part by a young Georgian whom the world would later know as Josef Stalin. The future Soviet dictator trained in Baku and in the oil port of Batumi, and the strikes he helped initiate spread across Russia. Ludvig Nobel unwittingly contributed to the cause—the Bolsheviks surreptitiously used the vast shipping network that he had created to distribute Lenin's revolutionary newspaper *Iskra.*

Baku found itself caught up in violence. A secretive army of toughs called the Black Hundreds carried out assaults and attacked refineries. It was organized by one of the czar's ministers in the hope that the militants demanding better conditions for workers would be blamed for the attacks and thus discredited. Instead, ethnic hatred in Baku only worsened.

Then came Lenin's "Great Rehearsal," the St. Petersburg strikes in 1905 that resulted in the czar's creation of a constitutional monarchy. On the heels of that event, Lenin sent an Armenian lieutenant, Stepan

Shaumian, to lead an uprising in Baku, and the city's czarist authorities panicked. They did not intervene as Muslim Azeris proceeded to massacre their Armenian neighbors and, along with other groups, set the oil fields on fire. Witnesses described entire Armenian families knifed or prevented by lines of gunfire from escaping their burning houses. The aftermath resembled a battlefield from the U.S. Civil War—many of the oil fields were charred ruins, with only the odd derrick still standing. There was no reliable tally of the dead, but they numbered in the hundreds, possibly the thousands. It was a catastrophe from which the city would require decades to recover.

Tagiyev's interests may have helped to inflame the troubles of 1905. The provocation was the newspapers he controlled, particularly *Kaspy*, Baku's first Azerbaijani-owned publication. To run it, Tagiyev had hired a crusading Russian editor who, aspiring to speak for all the Empire's Muslims, promoted pan-Islamism and pan-Turkism. That did not mean that Tagiyev was being disloyal to the Crown. Indeed, when World War I broke out, he and other industrialists and merchants financed a volunteer combat unit to resist the German forces. Manned entirely by Azeris and Dagestanis, it was known popularly as the "Savage Division." Tagiyev had personal links to the division as well: His eldest son, Mehmed—his wife Sona's favorite—was an officer. Stories regarding its practices abounded. It was said that Savage Division soldiers bit through the throats of adversaries they caught and that its officers demonstrated their courage by playing Russian roulette; in 1918, Mehmed Tagiyev died from a head wound inflicted by his own bejeweled Browning.

Lev Naussimbaum, the Baku author, described Mehmed Tagiyev's funeral as the pretext to a second round of bloodlust that followed the 1917 abdication of Nicholas II. The Savage Division had risen against the Bolsheviks, overthrowing them in the southern Azeri town of Lenkoran, and in late March 1918 shifted up the Caspian coast to Baku aboard the *Evelina*. Elements of the Savage Division marched into the city. The attackers were finally disarmed, but not before Russian gunboats in the harbor had shelled Azeri homes in the city. When the fighting was over, several thousand Azeris were dead, and thousands more had fled.

Quite apart from Baku's chronic ethnic hostilities, the Armenian

Bolsheviks had reason to fight. Just a few years after the 1890s massacres of Armenians in Ottoman Turkey, the Crown had confiscated the property of the Armenian Church, and czarist soldiers had fired on a May Day crowd in heavily Armenian-populated Tbilisi. Moreover, there was the logic of revenge—the Armenians had not forgotten the 1905 massacre of their kin in Baku.

The continuing instability in and around Baku in the years before and after the Russian Revolution made western oilmen understandably nervous. The port was under the control of the Bolsheviks, then the British—intervening from their outpost in Persia—then the Turks, then the British again. But through it all, oil field deals went on, and one of the most aggressive players was Henri Deterding, the gambling-minded chief executive of Royal Dutch/Shell. Short but massive and powerful, with lively black eyes and a white mustache, he was called the Napoleon of oil by his detractors.

In 1913, Deterding took over the Rothschild holdings in Baku and Batumi in exchange for 2.9 million pounds' worth of Royal Dutch stock. Thirty years earlier, Alphonse and Edmond de Rothschild, sons of one of Europe's most influential Jewish families, had managed to establish themselves in the Russian Empire despite prohibitions against Jews owning or renting land. Now, however, the brothers were leaving, discouraged by the events in Russia and fearful of rising anti-Semitism. The transaction made the Rothschilds the largest individual shareholders in Royal Dutch.

Deterding next bought prospective oil property in Grozny, the capital of the land of the unruly Chechens, located 280 miles north of Baku. Then, circling northeast around the Caspian shoreline, he laid claim to oil lands in Dosser, in the traditional territory of the Kazakh nomads. By 1916, the combined production from Grozny and Dosser ranked second in the Russian Empire, and Deterding was introducing new refining methods reminiscent of Ludvig Nobel's advances decades earlier. Russia's share of the global oil supply had shrunk from 51 percent to just 9 percent, but an undeterred Deterding foresaw better days ahead. He could not know—and he would never in fact concede—that his time had already passed.

Even as the Bolshevik Revolution in 1917 imperiled the Royal Dutch holdings, Deterding pressed on. He paid Alexander Mantashev, the former Baku tycoon, a £625,000 advance for his dispossessed Baku oil properties. He bought a stake in Baku baron David Lianosov's holdings, plus rights to the Nikopol-Mariupol pipe factory, Russia's largest plant of its kind. Deterding did not regard the Mantashev transaction as unacceptably risky: He was certain of the Bolsheviks' inevitable collapse—and the consequent validation of such transactions—foreseeing "the whole of Baku's wealth falling into his hands, and with it the decisive word in the international oil industry."

But Deterding was not alone in expecting another Baku windfall. Rockefeller's Standard Oil of New Jersey early in 1919 agreed to pay independent Azerbaijan $320,000 in French francs for eleven plots of undeveloped Baku oil land. Sister company Standard Oil of New York negotiated a six-month virtual monopoly on Baku oil shipments. The first deal proceeded unchallenged, but not the second one—Deterding urged Britain's Baku governor general, W. M. Thomson, to derail it. Thomson, who enjoyed veto power over decisions by the "independent" government, exercised his authority.

Great Britain's Anglo-Persian Oil Company chose to negotiate with the Bolsheviks and signed an agreement with a trade commissar to buy Grozny oil lands. To Deterding's chagrin, the deal included Royal Dutch properties that the revolutionaries had confiscated. But the Bolshevik leadership later vetoed the agreement. Standard of Jersey commenced talks with a now-humbled Emanuel Nobel, who figured that his oil empire was lost to the revolution but sensed that a partner able to invoke American diplomatic influence might help him reclaim it.

Emanuel had been a wide-eyed lad clutching his father, Ludvig's, hand when the two had stepped onto the Baku docks for the first time three decades earlier. He had become sole director of the family enterprise upon Ludvig's death, and in many ways he had proved as adroit as his father. With Ludvig's transportation system in place, Emanuel had led Baku to a dominating role in global oil. Under his tutelage, the Nobel empire soon encircled the Caspian Sea. Like Shell's Deterding, Nobel operated in Grozny and Dosser. Photographs of the Kazakh field show oilmen traveling amid caravans of large, hairy camels while Kazakhs rest outside a yurt, their traditional, round tentlike homes. Finally, down the Caspian's eastern coastline, Nobel men pumped oil on the Turkmen island of Cheleken, directly across the sea from Baku, and distributed kerosene from the nearby military port of Krasnovodsk to all of Central Asia and Persia as well. In all, Nobel Brothers Petroleum controlled a full third of Russian oil production. The czar showed the Nobel scion his appreciation in a rare gesture—he awarded him Russian citizenship.

When the Bolsheviks closed in on Baku, Emanuel's heart told him that as heir to one of the world's great enterprises, he could not leave. But now, after the fresh massacres of 1918, common sense told him he should not stay. So it was that eighty-one years after Immanuel Nobel introduced his family's genius to Russia, his grandson found himself in the North Caucasus, where a White Russian rear guard formed a line to defend the Empire's former elite.

It was not certain that Emanuel could escape Russian territory—no one would dare grant exit papers to a Nobel. Only after forged documents arrived from a family friend in the Baku police was Emanuel finally able to flee the Empire disguised as a peasant and escape to safety in Paris.

At stake in his ongoing negotiations with Standard Oil of New Jersey was the sale of half of Nobel's Baku holdings. Standard's president, Walter C. Teagle, dispatched a man for a firsthand inspection. Three weeks later, the aide returned in a buoyant mood, calling Baku "a production engineer's dream" and "a wildcatter's paradise." That was endorsement enough. On May 13, 1919, John D. Rockefeller, Jr., himself sanctioned Standard's payment of $11.5 million to Nobel.

Teagle was so enthralled that even after the White armies crumbled and the Bolsheviks recaptured Baku, he advanced another $500,000 so that Nobel could buy additional oil properties. As Teagle argued to a colleague: "If we do not do it now, I think we will be debarred from ever exercising any considerable influence in the Russian producing situation."

When Baku finally fell to the Bolsheviks in April 1920, the barons were immediately targeted. The city's new revolutionary council invited workers to invade the homes of these "capitalist bloodsuckers and their parasites" and take clothes, money, furniture, utensils—anything the mobs desired. Defiance by any oilman was branded capital treason, punishable by death.

Baku's barons had snickered in disbelief when one of their colleagues, oilman Murtaza Mukhtarov, vowed to kill any Red who entered his home and then commit suicide. But later came the sobering news that he had done exactly that. Two Red Army fighters had forced their way into his mansion—on horseback. Mukhtarov shot them dead. Then he positioned the pistol against his own head and fired.

Zeynalabdin Tagiyev escaped harsh treatment. Many of the leaders of Baku's new order were beholden to him despite their allegiance to Lenin and Stalin. When they were young men without resources, he had put them through college. Now, in an act of deference, they allowed him to choose from among all his properties the home in which he would live out his years. The most exquisite of his holdings was his fifty-room mansion in central Baku. But Tagiyev preferred his smaller, more secluded villa in seaside Mardakhan, north of the city. He retired there and even the hated Cheka officer Baba Aliyev did not disturb him.

Tagiyev himself had founded Mardakhan as an exclusive resort years before, and he had established a landscaping school to make the barren land flower. He had planted his own twenty-acre estate in mulberry, fig, and apricot orchards under the guidance of a landscape artist brought in from Europe. The orchard surrounded the twenty-room, two-story villa, which was virtually self-sufficient—almost a necessity in those turbulent times. Bread was prepared in a bakery, and the estate's own utility systems supplied electricity and water.

Tagiyev and the ever faithful Sona surrounded themselves in exile with seven children and grandchildren. The collapse of the family's outside world was not permitted to sadden life within the estate. The children saw to that, particularly Sophia, scampering with her grandfather's chickens and gazelles, racing the still-robust patriarch up and down the stairs, or playing the rice game. Popular in the family, the game went back to the 1830s, when food in the ancient city was in limited supply. Young Tagiyev and his boyhood friends had played every Friday, creeping under the tables where their fathers were dining. As the debates around the tables grew more heated and the men attacked their food with more abandon, sprinkles of rice fell from the tables' edges to the hungry boys below. Years later, Tagiyev insisted that his grandchildren maintain the tradition.

Sophia was darting between Tagiyev's legs in a spirited lunchtime session of the game when dreadful news intruded on a muggy Friday in August.

Two messengers entered the dining room to tell Tagiyev that his favorite daughter—twenty-six-year-old Leyla—had fled Baku. Some days before, the Persian ambassador had passed along word that Leyla's husband, Ali Assadulayev, was to be arrested. After a bribe was paid in diamonds, a visa was arranged to allow Ali to escape in the guise of a trip to Persia to buy horses. But there had been no talk of Leyla leaving, too. Yet now it was confirmed: Informing no one in advance, Leyla had bundled her three children onto a Turkmen boat and taken flight south to Persia to join Ali. Wordlessly, Tagiyev choked and crumpled.

Two days later, at the age of 101, he was dead.

The funeral was thronged. At its climax, mourners respectfully hoisted the patriarch's shrouded body onto uplifted hands, and he was buried behind his Mardakhan mansion, a magnificent gravestone installed in his memory.

Five days later, Baba Aliyev and his lieutenants appeared at the villa. What followed would forever be etched in little Sophia's memory. Baba Aliyev led her by the hand on a sadistic farewell tour of her grandfather's cherished home. As they paused at each room, Aliyev instructed, "Tell the room goodbye." An innocent Sophia repeated, "Goodbye, room," as the Cheka officer sealed each door.

Baba Aliyev banished the Tagiyev clan to a plain two-room apartment within Baku's limestone fortress.

The barons who managed to escape Baku with their families fled first to Constantinople. Certain the Bolsheviks would soon fall, they "played poker to the last breath" or visited elegant cafés and cabarets like the Black

Rose and the Muscovite, where they drank champagne and sang Russian songs.

The magnificent Turkish port, straddling the Asian and European continents and dotted with remnants of history's greatest empires, was a destination of choice for those fleeing the disorder of former czarist Russia. But getting there from Baku could be a frightening experience, according to accounts by Ummelbanu Assadulayeva, who wrote under the pseudonym Banine. She was the sister-in-law of Leyla, the Tagiyev daughter who had slipped away to Persia.

Banine described how those without passports—almost everyone, since the Bolsheviks had issued so few travel papers—boarded a train south from Baku, followed by a carriage ride, then a fugitive passage by boat to Persia. From there, the refugees went overland west to the Turkish capital.

At the Baku railroad station to bid farewell to departing relatives, Banine watched as Red soldiers burst into the waiting room and began searching the family's bags. When a cousin mumbled a reply to a question, a suspicious soldier forced open the boy's mouth, exposing an enormous diamond ring. The men then searched the whole family. "There were jewels in my aunt's hair, in the mouths of children, in the hems of clothing," Banine wrote. "As my poor relatives lamented this, I pitied them with all my heart; but there was, at the same time, something so comical in this extraction of jewels from the most unbelievable places, normally so badly suited to serve as hiding places, that, at moments, I was taken by the desire to laugh." Luckily the family was released and sent home. Before long, they found an alternative departure route, and this time they were more cautious. When they reached Constantinople, they still had the gold they had dug up from safekeeping in their backyard.

Banine herself reached the Turkish capital by slightly less nervewracking means—her husband, Jamil, bribed a Bolshevik friend to obtain passports. In Constantinople, they found a city inundated with refugees from colonial Russia, rich and poor alike. The influx made for a vibrant nightlife; some of the best dining spots were opened by émigrés, who turned out to be unusually talented restaurateurs.

Once safe in Turkey, Banine and Jamil decided, like many of Russia's most affluent émigrés, to move on to Paris and the European culture that they had always cherished. There, they moved into a grand apartment near the Parc de la Muette, in the prestigious sixteenth arrondissement. Their neighborhood was one of the ethnic ghettos into which the émigrés divided themselves, districts where they were "turbulent, remonstrative, despising of the 'indigenous' population, awaiting with assurance the defeat of the Bolsheviks, but for the time being deprived of fixed incomes," Banine wrote. Calouste Gulbenkian's son, Nubar, described how "the cafes of Paris, rife with rumors from the homeland, were like brokers' branch offices with securities traded on a curb market and icons, paintings, jewelry, and other treasures changing hands like a Baku bazaar." One of these traders, Leon Mantashev, a spendthrift son of Baku's richest oil baron now in need of funds, sold his last remaining painting to Nubar's father for $30,000. It was a much-ridiculed work by a French artist named Paul Chabas, entitled *September Morn*.

Zeynalabdin Tagiyev's daughter Leyla and her husband, Ali, suffered a horrible loss on their confused flight from Constantinople to Paris. At the Berlin train station, they somehow lost sight of their youngest son, Bobik. He was never found.

Once in Paris, the Tagiyev clan was greeted warmly by old friends. Some were members of the Nobel family—minus Emanuel, now back in Sweden—who had great respect for Leyla's and Ali's fathers and gave them a place to stay. Ali knew he had to work, and the Rothschilds produced a job that tapped his equestrian skill—in the family stables.

By the German invasion of France, Leyla and Ali had lost another son, Nadir, who drowned in the Seine River. In 1940, they fled east. Ali was lured into World War II by a Russian military hero, Andrei Vlasov, who had turned against Stalin after being captured by Hitler's troops. The general saw the Nazis as a way to defeat Stalin and then form a new, independent Russian government. Ali fought alongside his eldest son, also named Ali. But in May 1945, Vlasov's forces surrendered to Allied troops, who turned them over to the Soviets: Vlasov and his men were executed. Ali and his son were never seen again, and their surviving relatives assumed that they had met the general's fate. In the Turkish capital, grief-stricken Leyla took her own life, mixing cognac with an overdose of aspirin.

Misfortune seemed to haunt Zeynalabdin Tagiyev's surviving family members. The baron's widow, Sona, never left Baku. She suffered maddeningly from the obloquy following her husband's 1924 death. Before long, neighbors became aware of a wild-haired woman who wandered and begged in the streets. Many readily recognized her. The German manager of a nearby candy shop instructed his employees to serve the woman free coffee if she passed. One morning in 1932, Sona's lifeless body was found in the doorway of the shop. Two years later, soldiers razed the old cemetery in the district of Bibi-Heybat, where, among so many memories, Sona had been buried, erasing the last trace of her life.

Before Sona's death, her son Ilyas had been imprisoned for a year in Moscow by the Soviet secret police. He returned to Baku but, like his mother, had gone insane. He died in 1935 in a psychiatric hospital. His brother-in-law, Zeynalbek Salimkhanov, fearing the attention that the funeral could attract, loaded the body onto a bullock cart and followed on foot from a distance. Salimkhanov's daughter, Sophia, no longer the little girl diving under her grandfather's table for rice, rode in a hired coach with some of the other children.

By then, Salimkhanov technically was no longer a member of the Tagiyev clan—he had divorced Sophia's mother, Sarah, two years earlier. That mattered little, however. Police arrested and, according to family oral history, incarcerated him in a flooded cell, the water up to his knees. After several days, the family found him on their doorstep, badly shaken but still alive. The charges that provoked the arrest were never made clear. Five years later, as Hitler's troops were advancing on Baku's oil fields, the suspicious Soviet secret police searched Salimkhanov's apartment. One officer found Zeynalabdin Tagiyev's passport and tore it up. Another turned up a coin collection containing old czarist-era currency imprinted with the image of Catherine II. Enraged, the officer began punching Salimkhanov in the face. "Were you waiting for the Germans?" he barked before taking him away. The last the family heard was that Salimkhanov had been imprisoned and denied the right to correspond.

Just after her divorce, Sarah moved to St. Petersburg, by this point called Leningrad. In 1934, she was arrested. A gunman had slain Sergei Kirov, Azerbaijan's former Communist Party secretary and now party secretary in Leningrad. Among the millions rounded up on the pretext of conspiring in the killing, she spent two years in prison. Hundreds, including many leading Bolsheviks, were executed for direct responsibility in the murder. Only in the Soviet Union's final years did scholars demonstrate that Kirov was in fact the first major victim of Stalin's murder of almost all of his revolutionary colleagues.

Sophia married at seventeen and took the name of her husband. "I was glad just to be able to change my name," she said. But she was to be treated not much differently from the others. Three months after her father disappeared into a Soviet prison, she was summoned by an Interior Ministry officer and given twenty-four hours to leave the province. Thus, she and her husband, a petroleum engineer, found themselves riding a cattle train to a Siberian oil-producing town in the Ural Mountains called Sterlitamak. It would be the start of decades of wandering from the subzero steppes of Russia to the blistering desert heat of Turkmenistan.

In Baku, it became seditious even to mention a baron's name with anything other than contempt. Tagiyev's magnificent grave, now untended, quickly deteriorated. Along Communist Street, his girls' school was closed. And the three-story mansion of the baron Isa Bey Hajinski, modeled after a house of cards, was turned into a propaganda center.

Soviet Days

IN THE AFTERMATH OF THE REVO-
lution, some aspects of life in Baku improved. The Bolsheviks installed the city's
first electric streetcar, vividly described by
the Baku-born writer Banine: "As red as it
could be—as it should be for a tramway
given birth to by the revolution—it shone at
night with all of its lights, and in the first
days of its appearance the population went
out expressly to admire it." The future
seemed more hopeful for ordinary people
who for years had "lived in unclean shacks,
received laughable salaries and had no legal
means to use against the rich."

But the oil industry was in dire straits;
the boom days were only a faint memory. At
times one could be tempted to doubt that
Baku's zenith had ever occurred. Once the
source of almost a fifth of Russia's hard cur-

rency, the city was now producing just a third of its prewar oil volume, a level last seen in 1890. Much of the decline was the lingering result of the 1905 uprising and burning of the oil fields, after which the barons had sharply curtailed spending on new drilling and even the routine care of existing wells. With no guarantee of security, they simply could not justify the financial risk. Now water seeped into the neglected wells, diluting much of the crude into a runny, brown-green solution.

This crushing turn of events echoed the situation across Russia. Industrial production sank to just 13 percent of pre–World War I levels, by one estimate, and millions starved when famine struck. Lenin feared counterrevolution if the collapse were not rapidly reversed and was painfully aware that his government lacked the requisite money, technology, and expertise. He decided that, enemy or not, he needed the West.

In March 1921, Lenin unveiled his New Economic Policy, or NEP, as it came to be known. The NEP diluted purist Communism by allowing the privatization of small companies and the opportunity to earn profits. And it sought to attract the participation of suspicious western businessmen by offering them a form of ownership rights—called "concessions"—in big industrial concerns, including oil fields.

Standing in the way of such deals was a trade embargo clamped on Russia by western nations after the Bolsheviks repudiated czarist-era debt and murdered the Romanovs. Lenin hoped that his offer would cause business leaders to pressure their governments to lift the embargo. But for American oilmen entertaining Lenin's invitation, it was not as simple as he made it sound. For one, they had to consider the prospect of violent opposition at home. A full-fledged Red hysteria was under way in the United States, led by President Woodrow Wilson's attorney general, A. Mitchell Palmer, and a young assistant named J. Edgar Hoover. The two were in the process of deporting some 250 suspected Communists to Bolshevik Russia and detaining 6,000 others without trial. There was similar hesitation in Europe, where, after Wilson proposed merely inviting the Bolsheviks to the talks that produced the 1919 Treaty of Versailles, French prime minister Georges Clemenceau said that his "middle class would panic. There would be rioting in the streets."

Lenin dispatched Leonid Krassin, an urbane former industrialist, on a charm offensive to soothe the concerns of western businessmen. Krassin plied the powerful foreigners in fluent French and German, along with another language they could understand—capitalism. In 1902, while secretly supporting the Communist underground, Krassin had managed Baku's electric company, and later he had run Siemens-Schuckert's operations in Russia.

Krassin proposed a partnership between Great Britain's Anglo-Persian Oil Company and Standard Oil of New Jersey to revive the Grozny fields. Anglo-Persian had already tried and failed to make a deal with the Bolsheviks, but this time it was Walter Teagle, the mistrustful Standard of New Jersey boss, who scotched the idea. If the Bolsheviks had reneged on Russia's debt, how could they be trusted to adhere to this agreement, he wondered. After a futile attempt at persuading the U.S. government to come to his aid if the deal were to go bad, Teagle opted out. Krassin then offered Grozny to Henri Deterding, the risk-taking boss of Royal Dutch/Shell, under a seven-year contract that would split profits between the Bolsheviks and the oil company. Deterding, who had been Grozny's largest producer before World War I, agreed to the terms with relish. But when bickering broke out among other Bolshevik leaders, the deal unraveled. Krassin's initiatives gave the western oilmen confidence that they held the advantage, yet did not dispel their most worrisome concern: Did the Bolsheviks ever intend to restore the ownership rights of American and other foreign companies whose Russian oil fields were seized in the revolution? If not, how and when would those oilmen be compensated for their losses?

The question spilled onto the world diplomatic arena. Great Britain had backed White Russian efforts to reverse the Bolshevik Revolution militarily, dispatching troops to Baku, Central Asia, and elsewhere, actions that Deterding and the rest watched breathlessly from Paris and elsewhere. But the White Russians collapsed, and the former Baku oilmen took their issue to the Allies' first postwar conference. The venue was Genoa, Italy, an April 1922 gathering meant partly for western reconciliation with the Bolsheviks. The Allies were not ready to extend diplomatic recognition—the British, French, and other Europeans would not do so until two years later, and the United States nine years after that. Rather, they had a more practical purpose in mind. "We have failed to restore Russia to sanity by force," said the conference organizer, British prime minister David Lloyd George. "I believe we can save her by trade."

Krassin arrived at Genoa ready to negotiate new deals for both Baku and Grozny. With the western oilmen backed by diplomats from their respective countries, compromise at first seemed in the air. The conciliatory Lloyd George floated a proposal that the Baku fields be returned to their claimants for ninety-nine years, after which they would revert to state ownership. Then Shell's Deterding crossed a line—he maneuvered to restrict the deal to pre-revolutionary owners, language that would make his almost the only company eligible to reclaim its fields, since Standard of New Jersey had formed its partnership with Nobel after the war; French and Belgian concerns, too, had done their deals after the war. A free-for-all broke out. Now Jersey's Teagle, supported by American, French, and Belgian diplomats, insisted on absolute recognition of private property. U.S. envoy Richard Washburn Child went further—he proposed suspending all treaties with Russia. Genoa collapsed in disarray.

For a time, Deterding and fifteen other former owners of Russian oil property tried to set aside their differences and pledge common cause. They agreed to call themselves "Front Uni" and demand either a collective return of their properties or complete compensation for their losses. Standard of New Jersey, for one, was confident that such an unyielding line of attack would drive a desperate Bolshevik leadership to compromise.

In fact, the Front Uni effort would soon come undone. It didn't help that the Bolsheviks seemed unable to decide what they really wanted. But the more substantive problem was an unrelenting rivalry among the oil companies, one that the Soviets fully exploited. "The hostility toward the Anglo-Dutch group of the Standard interests . . . was so intense, and the strategical and economic value of Baku and Grozny was so great, that each would prefer and did prefer to sabotage the other's progress rather than take merely a share," one writer concluded. Indeed, within months Deterding ignored his Front Uni pledge and bought seventy thousand tons of Soviet kerosene. Standard of New Jersey, too, sent a man to Moscow to try to negotiate its own kerosene deal. Some of the others did the same.

The fracas was perhaps best understood by the Constantinople-born

Calouste Gulbenkian, at the time a key Deterding adviser. The father of twentieth-century oil dealmakers, Gulbenkian earned the sobriquet "Mr. Five Percent" for his share of the original land concession that held Iraq's extraordinary oil riches. "Oilmen are like cats," Gulbenkian's son Nubar quoted his masterly father as saying. "One never knows when listening to them whether they are fighting or making love." As for the son, confidant and secretary to both his father and Deterding, he believed that "in the oil business not even one's best friends are to be trusted."

Although Krassin's mission to Genoa failed, Lenin's campaign to lure the capitalist world into throwing the Bolsheviks a lifeline was yielding results elsewhere. Gulbenkian himself provided £50,000 in much-needed cash for a one-year monopoly on Caspian Sea caviar, doubling his money on fifty tons of sturgeon eggs. Averell Harriman, the Harvard-trained scion of nineteenth-century robber baron Edward Harriman, flirted with an oil venture in Baku before turning to a twenty-year deal for the world's largest deposit of manganese, a mineral necessary in steel-making, located north-west of Baku in Georgia. Armand Hammer, the American son of a Russian émigré, became a money launderer for the Bolsheviks, sneaked cash to secret Bolshevik agents in the United States, and profited hand-somely as the representative in Russia of some thirty American companies. Hammer earned from both sides—his clients paid commissions as high as 30 percent of a transaction's value, and the Soviets paid as well. Such deals were done without the encouragement of the U.S. government, which told any businessman who asked that he was free to risk—and most probably lose—his money if he wished but that he should not expect Washington to bail him out.

The involvement of American business figures like Harriman and Hammer in Soviet deals helped improve the Bolshevik image abroad. But Lenin needed much more than that to turn around his nation's desperate economy. When a white knight did come, he was a little-known New York entrepreneur named Henry Mason Day. Like Robert Nobel five decades earlier, Day walked inconspicuously into Baku—and proceeded to usher in a reversal of the city's oil fortunes.

A profile in *The New York Times* described Day as a swarthy, six-foot-two, 190-pound oilman belonging "to the almost fabulous group of postwar international concession-hunters who trail their game—which involves hundreds of millions of dollars of at least potential wealth—across continents the way a stalker trails a moose over a hill. International-minded, multi-linguistic, their fame is based less upon their practical experience as oil men than upon their super-salesmanship and the glow of mystery and power that surrounds them." The description was breathless, but in his dealings with the Bolsheviks, the nimble Day inarguably outclassed his supposed betters.

The owner of a New York–based oil company called Barnsdall International, Day had arrived in Baku just a month after the formation of Front Uni. His stealth was deliberate, because Day feared litigation for trampling on the claims of the pre-Bolshevik property owners, which he was plainly doing. Under a fifteen-year agreement, he was to repair wells and drill new ones on more than a thousand acres of oil land in Baku's Balakhani district, almost all of it privately owned under the czarist regime. Most important, he was to install state-of-the-art rotary drills—until then, Baku had used percussion, a blunt method by which a heavy object was repeatedly dropped until oil was revealed. In return, he would receive royalties plus 15 percent of the crude from old wells in addition to 20 percent from any successful new wells he drilled. He closed a fifteen-year deal in Georgia as well, giving him exclusive rights on the export of oil, coal, timber, tobacco, and a list of other items.

An impressed diplomat in Constantinople cabled Washington to say that Day had been made "virtually the fiscal agent and minister of foreign trade" not only of Azerbaijan but of Georgia and Armenia as well. The diplomat was correct. Day had won appointment as commercial adviser to the three republics, which, he boasted, had given him $500,000 in gold "to guarantee any outlay American interests may make."

Day's first oil crew, which included six American engineers, arrived in Baku in June 1923. Finding technology that differed little from the time of Ludvig Nobel, they made revolutionary advancements. Their rotary method accelerated drilling by a factor of ten and reduced costs by more than half. Their electric pumps—until Day arrived, oil had been extracted mostly by bailing and natural flow—resulted in similar production improvements.

American, German, and British companies followed Day. They built and repaired two pipelines to replace and augment the 560-mile Baku-Batumi line built by Ludvig Nobel and his contemporaries. American and British companies installed refineries such as Baku had never seen—so-called cracking units that produced not kerosene but the more valuable commodity gasoline by breaking down oil molecules under high temperatures. Soon Baku exports resumed. In nearby Georgia, a group of Britons signed a forty-year deal, as did the Belgians and Italians. A French company acquired oil rights in both Baku and present-day Uzbekistan, and Norwegians signed a forty-year deal in present-day Turkmenistan.

But the best oil deal—on paper, anyway—was concluded by a showboating American who had hired Day as a middleman. He was Harry Sinclair, the head of Sinclair Oil. Appearing "something like a frog, with his popping eyes, his wide mouth and fat cheeks," the Kansan was the most flamboyant figure on the U.S. oil patch and, after Rockefeller, the wealthiest. Now he was setting his sights on greater achievements. In 1922, Sinclair went to London and met Krassin. Accompanying him was Day, Teddy Roosevelt's son Archibald, and an entourage that occupied two decks of an ocean liner called the *Homeric.* For the remaining journey to Moscow, he chartered a train for $193,000. His aim was fittingly hubristic—the Bolsheviks, he said, should give him control of oil in Baku, Grozny, the Kazakh lands, and half the Siberian island of Sakhalin. What was more, he desired a monopoly on Soviet refining, crude transportation, and global oil distribution.

Not visibly put off, the Soviets countered with an offer that, while not wholly compliant, was staggering: a partnership in Baku and Grozny for forty-nine years and a monopoly on Sakhalin. In exchange, Sinclair would invest $115 million and arrange a $250 million loan for the Soviets. The third condition exposed the Soviet ulterior motive: The United States would have to grant the Soviets diplomatic recognition. Japan, which had operated the Sakhalin fields for years, was openly indignant. When Sinclair sent men to examine the properties, the Japanese arrested them. Undaunted, Sinclair grandly announced that he would act as "Russia's salesman to the world."

Sinclair's confidence was grounded in his influence with President Warren G. Harding and some of his cabinet secretaries. But a year later, in 1923, Harding died. Then a scandal surfaced—U.S. interior secretary Albert B. Fall was accused of accepting bribes to lease a government oil property in Wyoming called the Teapot Dome. The alleged paymaster of the operation was Harry Sinclair. Sinclair was acquitted of bribery, but, in a Washington sensation, he and Day were convicted of jury tampering in the trial. Sinclair served almost six months in the District of Columbia jail, and Day just over three months.

The episode marked the end of Day's extraordinary career as an international dealmaker and the turning point in the Soviet attitude toward dealmaking. The revival of Baku's oil fields and other raw materials industries that he had triggered was providing Soviet leaders with cash and confidence, lessening their willingness to compromise with western industrialists, much less with oilmen. Armand Hammer was still useful as a conduit for cash to Soviet intelligence agents, but Stalin, who succeeded Lenin after his 1924 death, began to cancel the preferential oil deals—including Day's—without compensation. He negotiated new contracts under which westerners would be limited to negotiated fees as payment; there would be no opportunity for ownership rights or profit sharing.

By then it had dawned on Baku's dispossessed oilmen that they had been eclipsed. Standard of New Jersey's losses were the $160,000 down payment to independent Azerbaijan and $8.8 million of the promised payoff to the Nobels. Teagle, the Standard chief, was bitter. But his ill will was nothing compared with that of Deterding at Royal Dutch/Shell, whose hostility became ever more acute after his 1924 marriage to Lydia Pavlovna, a White Russian aristocrat. He spent much of the remainder of his life railing against the Soviets and predicting their imminent demise.

In 1928, Stalin launched his five-year plan to revive Soviet industry and unabashedly employed American and European expertise to help carry it out. American engineers and equipment working at his command built the world's largest steel plant, its largest hydroelectric dam, its largest automobile factory, and more. Baku's oil fields, the country's greatest source of foreign exchange, received special attention. Relying on American and German experts, but as hired help rather than as profit-earning co-owners,

Stalin injected money and labor into Baku in "savage determination to get out every barrel with the utmost speed and convert it as quickly as possible into the dollars so desperately needed by the five-year plan." In 1930, production rose to nearly 100 million barrels, just one-tenth of U.S. production but still the third-highest in the world.

An American journalist visiting the city that year was struck by the signs of prosperity. "I drove over twenty miles of perfect asphalt pavement through mile after mile of new settlements, snowy white, the architecture neo-oriental," reported Hubert Knickerbocker, a correspondent for the *New York Evening Post.* "The street car system that replaced horse cars four years ago is the best in Russia. The new electric inter-urban line connecting with the 'Black City' of oil, where wells are thickest, has the most artistic station and almost the only new big city railroad station in the country." Walking through Baku, Knickerbocker heard a shot ring out. He traced it to a shooting gallery with a comic political overtone: "Hit a capitalist and up rises a Social-Democrat; hit a hog and his head changes to that of a fat-jowled banker. . . . Baku, rich, is still red."

As Lenin had hoped a decade earlier, western know-how and equipment was instrumental in making the Bolshevik experiment work. The Great Depression motivated American professionals to seek jobs in the Soviet Union, and Washington not to bar their way. Since the economic plunge also reduced demand for their raw materials, the Soviets tapped national treasures for cash to pay the foreigners. Calouste Gulbenkian improved his already-impressive art collection with exclusive objects from the Hermitage Museum. They included two Rembrandts and *Diana the Huntress,* a popular bronze nude by the eighteenth-century sculptor Jean-Antoine Houdon that had been commissioned by Catherine the Great.

And so it went, until the Second World War.

Stalin's breakneck development of Baku paid dividends in the form of steady export dollars. But its most profound payoff came when Hitler betrayed his 1939 alliance with Stalin and attacked the Soviet Union. In the first year after the 1941 invasion, Baku produced an astonishing 125 million barrels of oil, crucial in mustering the Soviet defense. But then it became clear that a primary German aim was the capture of Baku itself, to fuel Hitler's war machine. So Stalin ordered most of the wells to be plugged with concrete, and Baku's best oilmen—some ten thousand of them—moved on to other petroleum regions like the Volga River basin near the Ural Mountains. Baku still produced oil, but in steadily fading volumes.

When World War II ended, the concrete plugs turned out to have ruined many of the wells. Entire fields were producing less and less because of poor pumping methods, such as a failure to preserve the underground natural gas pressure that propelled the oil out of the ground. Carcasses of old rigs, black with age and use, stood silently on the horizon. Soon, the legendary fields were overtaken by the Volga basin, and Baku reinvented itself as the center of Soviet refining, the nation's main source of lubricating fluids and oil field machines and parts.

Yet Baku was about to prove that it still had the ability to stir up excitement. Local geologists were intrigued by reports from ship captains of oil slicks in the waters around Baku. At one place forty miles off the coast, where the seabed abruptly rose, the Caspian became shallow, and rocks appeared from the depths—rocks covered with a deep black sheen. There was evidently a seepage of oil. But could there be more? A masterful Russian driller, Mikhail Kavyorochkin, was dispatched to find out.

No one—not Nobel, not Day, not Rockefeller, not Deterding—had ever drilled in the middle of a sea. There was no technology to do so. But in 1947, relying on a surfeit of enthusiasm and a fleet of boats that day by day ferried over the parts of an onshore rig, Kavyorochkin and his men built a makeshift platform. They dubbed the oil field that resulted "Oily Rocks."

Oily Rocks was a first—an offshore oil city. A scuttled ship was outfitted with a kitchen to feed workers. Wooden trestles and bridges were built so the oilmen could move from one well to another as they brought in gusher after gusher. Rocks were ferried over to create an island, on which five-story apartment blocks were built to house the workers. Erected to service eighty-four wells, Oily Rocks grew into a wood-and-steel oil town on stilts fifteen miles long and two and a half miles wide. It looked like a demented Venice, divided into five districts, tangled with 174 miles of criss-crossing roads and 29 miles of bridges, and surrounded by an oily glaze on the water. It also was dangerous. A raucous 1957 storm killed Kavyorochkin, along with his entire team of more than a dozen men.

But a twenty-year-old Azeri named Sabir Guseynov boarded a boat in Baku and saw something different—"a place of wonder . . . a legend in the open sea"—and went on to work at Oily Rocks for forty-four years. Others felt similarly. Famous Soviet singers visited. A banquet was held on Platform 408 for Soviet leader Nikita Khrushchev, who according to oral history became drunk and, to reflect the grand stature of Oily Rocks, ordered the construction of a nine-story apartment block. It duly went up, and at once there was sufficient housing for twenty-five hundred workers.

America took note of the activity. A secret CIA report from 1955 concluded that Oily Rocks had become Azerbaijan's largest single producer of crude, turning out some 14 million barrels a year. It also accurately described the deterioration of the onshore oil fields.

But Baku's problem wasn't just the sealed wells or the shift of Soviet interest to oil regions elsewhere. The Allied friendship with Stalin had soured—in 1948, the United States clamped another equipment embargo on the Soviet Union, whose primary import need was oil field machinery and tools. The geopolitical tension was so great that in 1949, *The New York Times* regarded it as front-page news when President Truman permitted the export of $500,000 of electric drilling rigs to the Soviets, calling the relatively modest transaction the "first tangible evidence that the cold war in trade between the United States and Russia is abating."

The report was premature, and the continuing embargo would prove lethal to Baku. And it wasn't long before dismayed Baku geologists learned that they needed more than just spare parts—it turned out that the remainder of their richest oil deposits were east of Oily Rocks, in three fields as much as four miles under water. As the CIA noted, "The future of the Baku area in the production of crude oil depends largely on the offshore operations."

The Soviets lacked the technology to drill in such deep water, and they thought that they had little incentive to try. They were finding some of the world's largest oil fields in the Volga basin, the so-called Second Baku, and in western Siberia. These fields made the Soviets a world petro-power by the end of the 1960s, and they seemed likely to keep producing for decades longer. To make the fields deliver, the Soviets flooded them with water, a practice that forced large volumes of crude to the surface. It was a tricky process, because if not done right it also damaged the fields, and indeed more and more water was now required to produce less and less crude.

In 1960, a bespectacled former CIA oil analyst named Robert Ebel toured Baku along with nine American oil executives. They saw plenty, but they were barred from Oily Rocks. The Soviets had no intention of laying bare their prized operations. Weeks later, in the interest of helping to ease superpower tensions, Ebel led visiting Soviets on a reciprocal tour of U.S. oil fields. Although almost no American oil technology had been available to the Soviets since 1947, they seemed unimpressed by what they saw. Perhaps the tour confirmed what the Soviets suspected. "They felt pretty good about themselves," Ebel thought. "They felt they were as good as us." There was ample reason for the Soviet self-assurance. Quite apart from ideological pride, they had logged an impressive run of success through the 1950s. Their economy racked up annual growth superior to America's, their military sector matched the United States weapon for weapon, and in an especially muscular display of scientific aptitude, Soviet engineers launched the first man into space.

They achieved similar gains in the oil patch. As Ebel witnessed, the Soviets not only were producing at sea, they had also invented the "turbo-drill," a well-digging device that had generated much interest in the West. Improving on a 1923 design by a Baku oil engineer, the Soviets challenged convention by mounting the motor just above the bit rather than stationary at the earth's surface—in a nutshell, they sent the motor down the hole with the drill. The resulting drill dug wells ten times faster than standard technology and at a much lower cost. Most remarkably, it could drill multiple wells in different directions from a single rig—including horizontally inserting what looked like a tree root into a subterranean oil seam.

In 1956, J. B. O'Connor, a Dallas oil executive with a white mustache, saw the drill in operation while on a Soviet visit and was so astonished that he instantly sought manufacturing rights for his company, Dresser

Industries. American engineers had tried and failed to produce such technology, O'Connor noted, while the Soviets "made it so simple that it had to work." As with Ludvig Nobel's invention of continuous refining, however, hubris got in the way of science. Asserting that the deal violated strategic policy, Dwight Eisenhower's commerce secretary, Sinclair Weeks, rejected O'Connor's contract. Three decades later, the West finally borrowed from the Soviet technology. Western oil companies kept their motors on the earth's surface but embraced the multiple-wells technique, renaming it "directional drilling." For their part, the Soviets did not totally shun American oil technology. They regularly attempted to buy stronger well pipes and more durable drill bits. But as the government's veto of O'Connor's contract demonstrated, the United States was not about to relax the post–World War II trade embargo in any meaningful way. And the political climate in America continued to be "violently anti-Russian," further discouraging American companies from trying to do business with the Soviets.

Of the few who did circumvent the barriers, one was a California attorney not long out of law school and eager for a glamorous life. He would become the protégé of a globetrotting metals trader from Boston whose pioneering Soviet ventures had already reaped millions in profits. Together, they would virtually rewrite the rules of U.S.-Soviet trade, and their partnership would prepare the young lawyer for his ultimate role as the unrivaled king of the Caspian oil dealmakers.

CHAPTER 5

The
Middleman

WHEN JAMES HENRY GIFFEN WAS born in 1941, the small, racially segregated town of Stockton, California, had a good-time reputation. Though gambling and prostitution were illegal in the state, officialdom in the Central Valley city—councilmen, police, and judges—was bribed to allow wide open poker rooms and brothels along a half-dozen downtown blocks that locals called "Skid Row." The trade went back to the middle nineteenth century, when Stockton took root as a settlement for men seeking their fortune, first in fur trapping, then in gold prospecting amid the nearby Mother Lode foothills. Men ambled through "crowded bars and card rooms, cafés, pool halls, liquor stores and movies, their paths crossed by lines of urine from darkened doorways," Leonard Gardner wrote in his novel *Fat City*.

By the time Giffen was born, farming was central to its survival; its rich, peaty soil made asparagus seem to grow before one's very eyes, and it whipped up into storms so thick that at plowing time, motorists had to keep their lights on during the day too. Riverboats from San Francisco brought new arrivals who built one of the earliest Jewish communities west of the Mississippi River and thriving Filipino and Chinese neighborhoods south of the railroad tracks. Some of Stockton's own called their town "hick," but there were signs of refinement. When society women strolled downtown, they did so in gloves. And gentlemen shopped in stylish haberdasheries, mainly Bravo & McKeegan and the Threlfall Brothers.

Giffen's father, a handsome raconteur whose stylish appearance prompted some to call him a Beau Brummel, had settled in Stockton in the early 1930s. Lloyd Giffen was an Oklahoma native who told friends that he had gone broke gambling on horses in Louisville, Kentucky. He landed a job at Bravo & McKeegan as a much-valued "display man," meticulously selecting merchandise and dressing mannequins for passersby to view in the shop's windows. After six years, he was store manager.

In 1940, Giffen wed Lucile Threlfall, the widowed eldest daughter of his employer's chief competitor, Richard Threlfall. The marriage catapulted Giffen into a favored position in Threlfall management and admitted him to the upper ranks of local society, a position that a Stockton newcomer might never otherwise attain. Indeed, Lucile brought to the marriage not only her own stature but also that of her deceased husband, George Crane, Jr., the son of a wealthy real estate and insurance man. His death in 1938 was front-page news and left her with an infant boy to raise on her own. Now, just a year after marrying Giffen, she gave birth to a second son, whom they named James.

Lloyd Giffen eventually opened his own haberdashery shop in a smart new downtown strip, called by its promoters the Miracle Mile. Bravo & McKeegan was there, as was John Falls's men's shop. Both sold Ivy League styles like Hickey Freeman. Not Giffen. His Oxford Shop carried the creations of flamboyant Los Angeles designer Louis Roth, chic Countess Mara silk ties, and imported European leather jackets. Competitors envied his window displays—exquisitely placed jackets, shirts, and ties, not a crease anywhere. One clothes presser became so enraged at Giffen's "finicky" demands that he quit and told him to iron his own shirts. So Giffen did.

He could be equally fastidious and even ornery with customers. If he didn't think the man standing before him measured up to the store's standards, he might declare, "I don't have a thing for you. Go up to John Falls' " in a loud, booming voice that could be heard out the door and up the street. Lloyd Giffen's competitors marveled that his shop survived despite such surly outbursts, especially considering its high prices. But he was a masterful salesman when he wanted to be, and he attracted a number of repeat customers who trusted his taste implicitly. Some only had to telephone to say that they were threadbare, after which Giffen would select their entire wardrobe—slacks, shirts, ties, jackets—and notify them when it was ready to be picked up.

His behavior could be downright idiosyncratic; he liked to knit socks at Aptos Beach near Monterey, and late in life his pampered black poodle, J.J., was his constant companion at the shop. But his success finally earned him a place in Stockton society in his own right. He moved his family into a series of successively more comfortable homes in good neighborhoods and bought membership at the exclusive Stockton Country Club, where he was a respected golfer. He socialized with the men of "The Syndicate," an elite group that gathered on Wednesdays at Oakmoore, a private country club, for gin and gambling over dominoes. On weekends, he, Lucile, and another couple were the "Saturday Nighters," sharing cocktails and dancing at the country club or the Stockton Ballroom.

When his son Jim was a teenager, the two were regulars at Fred Eastwood's driving range on the edge of the city, a gathering place for Stockton's upper crust. Jim and his friend Ernie Segale drove balls until the lights were turned off, with the former having the stronger swing. Blond and chubby, Jim wore a flattop and was a natty dresser in his khakis and white buck shoes, which he tidied up with powder he kept in his pocket. He didn't strike friends as a bookworm. Indeed, he dreamed of becoming a professional golfer.

Lloyd Giffen pushed his son to go into medicine, and accordingly in 1958 young Jim enrolled at U.C. Berkeley, an hour's drive away. He joined Delta Upsilon, a down-to-earth fraternity that had a reputation for partying (his pledge class dubbed itself the Rectum Rippers). Giffen seemed always to be talking, often while taking an imaginary golf swing. He dwelled on what the future might hold, which set him apart from the others. Giffen "had an agenda. The rest of us didn't," recalled former roommate Michael Barkett. He "wanted to go places," specifically "where the dough was." Not that Giffen didn't join in the fun, drinking beer and chasing girls. He kept a six-foot boa constrictor, Simon, with which he "would scare the hell out of dates" and thus amuse his fraternity brothers. But his cockiness irritated some, and Giffen knew it. "I've got the kind of face that, when guys meet me, they want to beat me up," he told Barkett.

Years later, he would regale listeners with an inflated account of how he had been Berkeley's number one golfer but quit after the coach scolded him for spending too much time partying and chasing women. In fact, Giffen ranked below the team's best players during the two complete seasons in which he competed, as a sophomore and senior. Dave Newsom, a teammate, remembered him as a stylish figure on the course when few others had the spare cash for fashionable golf wear.

But Newsom also credited Giffen with having a good short game that he used to great effect in match play, in which victory is awarded the player who wins the most holes, regardless of how many strokes are taken overall. Some suppose that golf reveals a great deal about a person. One school of thought is that those gifted at match play are likely to be assertive individuals especially adept at seizing the advantage in one-on-one encounters; those mediocre in such situations perhaps feel less need to control and do best as part of a team. Giffen was a middling stroke-by-stroke player with a reputation for being temperamental. But in match play, he was a force to be reckoned with. Unless he was up against a vastly superior player, he would establish a commanding early position with superior chipping and putting and press home his advantage from there.

In his sophomore year, Giffen noticed a Kappa Delta girl walking down Waring Street, a petite brunette with smooth olive skin, "cuter than a bug's ear." He learned that her name was June Hopkins—and that she was not just any Hopkins. As he breathlessly told his fraternity brothers, she was one of *the* Hopkinses—a granddaughter of President Franklin D. Roosevelt's most trusted aide, Harry Hopkins.

Jim Giffen and June Hopkins were soon a couple. It made him feel important to be dating a socialite, one who had debuted at the 1959 New Year's ball at New York's Waldorf-Astoria hotel and whose personal scrapbook contained a White House invitation. On weekends, the pair would make the seven-hour drive south to her parents' Los Angeles home. June's father, Harry Hopkins's eldest son, David, was a celebrity in love with celebrities—a "stage door Johnny" as a young man who in 1937 had made headlines by eloping with a talented Ziegfeld Follies dancer named Cherry Preisser. He went on to become a motion picture producer, an advertising executive, and a Democratic Party stalwart, all of which made him influential in Los Angeles, not to mention enthralling to June's new boyfriend. Giffen was dazzled by the photographs that lined the walls of his girlfriend's home—Harry Hopkins in various poses with FDR and Soviet officials—and the dinner table talk, of New Deal days and the romance of an international life. So began his lifelong obsession with America's aristocracy, the East and West Coast elites who shaped domestic and foreign policy.

June's father "woke me up" and "started making me think what life was all about," Giffen said, and he returned to Berkeley from these weekends determined to pursue a different path. David Hopkins had earned a political science degree from the University of Chicago, and now Giffen, at the age of twenty, abandoned his own parents' wishes that he become a doctor. He would change his major to political science, like David Hopkins.

In March 1962, June, Giffen, and his friend Dan Wallace were in the stands at U.C. Berkeley's Memorial Stadium when President John F. Kennedy took the stage to deliver a foreign policy speech. The crowd of 88,000 greeted Kennedy with wild enthusiasm and thunderous applause, and Giffen was mesmerized. Here was the most famous living American aristocrat of all, in the flesh. "When he finally walked by, I nearly fell off my chair, though we were standing up," Giffen would later recollect. "His hair was auburn in the sun; he looked ten years old." One intimate would misjudge Jim as a "Kennedy Republican" for his fusion of JFK hero worship and conservative sermonizing. Actually, if Giffen wasn't already a staunch Democrat, he certainly was after that day. He began to style his hair after Kennedy's and would visit the Los Angeles factory of his father's favorite men's designer, Louis Roth, to be fitted out with copies of the president's suits. Soon, he would even develop a passable imitation of JFK's Boston-accented stammer.

In Jim and June's senior year at Berkeley, Giffen abruptly informed his friend Wallace that he and June were eloping and asked him to be his best man. Without informing their parents, they drove four hours to Carson City, Nevada, where they were married in a civil ceremony. Three weeks later, Jim and June took church vows in Los Angeles followed by a reception at the Hopkins home.

Starting then and for years after, it was the rare social occasion or newspaper interview when Giffen would fail to mention whose grandson-in-law he was. It grated on some after the third or fourth mention. But during drinking bouts with colleagues as his career flourished, Giffen would lose any resemblance of subtlety. Openly expressing contempt for his wife, he would bluntly declare that he had married her only for the family's political connections.

After graduating Berkeley, the Giffens moved into a west Los Angeles apartment so that Jim could study law at UCLA. There he formed a special bond with Paul Proehl, a six-foot-five former diplomat who taught international law. He was a generous mentor, old-fashioned but highly respected, a teacher "you didn't bluff." Proehl urged his students to do serious, publishable work. At his first meeting with each new class, he would sternly announce that those who weren't prepared to write a term paper—one that, in his telling, sounded more like a mini-dissertation—why, they could drop out now. And many did. But the diehards remained, including Giffen, who eagerly attacked his assignment to illuminate trade practices in the opaque Soviet Union. Proehl was impressed with the results. It wasn't that he thought either Giffen or his 115-page paper brilliant. But knowing that "brilliance and success aren't the same thing," he decided that this student was going places. Jim's success with the assignment pleased his father, who, when John Falls sauntered by the Oxford Shop, summoned him inside to brag about his son's latest triumph.

Giffen emerged from UCLA with a law degree and a family to support—he and June now had two small children. He turned to David Hopkins for help, and Hopkins called his tax lawyer, a man named Louis Baker, who himself had done some international work. Did Baker happen to have a place for his son-in-law? A job was offered, and Giffen accepted it. Before long the tax lawyer concluded that his new hire wasn't really motivated to be an attorney, and he advised Jim to try something else, perhaps in East-West trade, of which Giffen so often spoke.

About the same time, Giffen had a fortuitous encounter at a TWA ticket office in Paris. At forty, Ara Oztemel was already something of a legend, the genial American metals trader who, it was said, could "open any door" in the Soviet Union and depart with a deal. The twenty-four-year-old Giffen was openly thrilled to meet a walking textbook on Soviet business. He proudly told the older man how he had come across Oztemel's trail while researching the legalities of Soviet trade, the topic of an academic paper he was now expanding into a book. And he introduced June, taking pains to explain her patrician background.

The inexperienced Giffen seemed an unlikely match for Oztemel, a streetwise raconteur with a Northeastern University engineering degree and some fifteen years of international practice behind him. Yet Oztemel sensed something special about this gregarious young man, the promise of talents yet untapped. Himself a superlative salesman, Oztemel recognized one of his own breed. He observed Giffen's polished optimism, an eagerness verging on zeal. With her aristocratic background and bearing, June completed the package nicely. He invited Giffen to come see him in New York.

Oztemel arrived home "very excited," telling his wife, "I've just met this smart young man." A close friend said Oztemel "fell in love" with his new acquaintance. Another thought the attraction more prosaic: "Ara's main interest was not in the monetary rewards, but in the action itself. The more action, the more he enjoyed it. Jim Giffen seemed to promise a lot of action."

Around 1968, three years after they first met, Oztemel met with Giffen in New York and offered him a job at $18,000 a year. Giffen, by this point a deputy public defender in Los Angeles after being politely sacked as a tax lawyer, didn't have to think about it long. Since meeting his wife and her family seven years before, he had dreamed of living the international jetsetting life that was second nature to them. Now a stroke of good fortune might make it possible.

Back in Los Angeles, Giffen telephoned a friend. "I'm moving to New York," he said. "I'm going to work for Ara Oztemel."

Oztemel, a saxophone-playing Turkish Armenian émigré from Boston, had been so poor in the early 1950s that he had to pawn one of his horns to get his wife and their newborn son discharged from a Watertown, Massachusetts, hospital. But in the 1960s, he was navigating the treacherous waters of trade with the Soviet Union probably better than any other American, and he had become a very rich man. A decade before Richard Nixon and Henry Kissinger made the term famous, Oztemel instinctively grasped the essence of détente. Long before the diplomatic thaw that ultimately thrust open the Caspian, this archetypal middleman erected his own trade bridge between the superpowers.

One former employee described the balding Oztemel as a "Middle East potentate," and he certainly lived like one. Leaving his wife, Mary, and five children behind at their forty-room seafront estate in Greenwich, Connecticut, Oztemel and his longtime secretary and mistress, Betty Van Staveren, would fly the supersonic Concorde to London and be picked up by his Rolls-Royce for some high-stakes gambling or perhaps a sumptuous meal at the White Elephant Club. He kept two London apartments in addition to *Sophisticated Lady,* a yacht anchored in Cannes, France.

Dun's Review dubbed Oztemel "The Answer Man in Soviet Trade," a moniker that the CIA appeared to endorse. Upon returning home from Moscow, he was usually met by CIA agents, themselves removed from the direct Soviet contacts he enjoyed and therefore eager to debrief him. The unruffled Oztemel viewed such attention as an unavoidable by-product of the advantageous turf he occupied; after all, the Soviet KGB demanded similar debriefings.

His rise to prominence had begun in 1959, when Oztemel had seemingly come out of nowhere to execute an eyebrow-raising trade: $5.5 million of American-made steel in exchange for military-grade Soviet chromium ore, an essential ingredient in strategic stainless steel. Three years later, he and a Swedish partner named Ralph Feuerring negotiated an unqualified masterstroke—exclusive rights to import Soviet chrome into the United States. A deal that made both men millionaires, it was all the more extraordinary considering that superpower relations at the time were strained to the breaking point over the Cuban Missile Crisis.

Over fifths of Dewar's after business hours, Oztemel regaled his subordinates with his account of landing the deal. The turning point, he would say, was his friendship with a powerful Soviet minister named Anastas Mikoyan, a former trusted aide to Stalin. That no one, including his closest associates and friends, ever actually saw him with Mikoyan didn't seem to matter. As time passed, the story only enhanced Oztemel's reputation as a man with unrivaled influence in the Soviet Union.

Since the nineteenth century, the global metals business had been dominated by German-Jewish traders who regarded themselves as "men who by virtue of their wits are able to operate as powerful and uncontested freelance salesmen of the Earth's resources," men whose "outlaw bravado" could win over almost anyone. And that was doubtless an apt description of their successes almost everywhere. But even they grudgingly acknowledged that U.S.-Soviet metals trading was an exception, an arena that was almost the sole province of Ara Oztemel. Even in the less-constrained 1970s, trading powerhouses such as Philipp Brothers and Marc Rich would form fifty-fifty joint ventures with Oztemel, for it was presumed that there were deals only he could manage.

His modus operandi was bulldog persistence, exaggerated congeniality, and masterful self-promotion. He loved Soviets, and they seemed to genuinely care for him, according to Bernard Majech, an old Moscow hand

from Sweden who escorted him to the city the first time and helped negotiate the chrome import agreement. Oztemel understood how the Soviets
cherished respect. He made them his friends, showered them with gifts,
and—unlike most other American visitors—treated them with deference.
He told his protégés that the best strategy was not to hustle the Soviets, as
some had tried, but to make them feel important and, at the same time,
that they needed you.

It was also crucial that the Soviets have fun, and Oztemel was unsur-
passed in that respect. His parties were notable for "a lot of drinking and
a lot of everything." He financed and organized Moscow's first American
jazz concert, featuring Toots Thielemans on alto harmonica, Bob James on
piano, Milt Hinton on bass—and Oztemel, himself an able jazz musician,
on sax. Soviet trade officials were perennial guests of honor at his lavish
black-tie Christmas parties in London.

He also impressed the Soviets by stepping in when no one else would.
When the Bolshoi Ballet failed to find financing to tour America, Oztemel
shelled out a million dollars to make it happen. When the Soviets wanted
to export their mediocre Lada automobiles and hydrofoils to the West, he
took over the European and American concessions for the vehicles. When
they wanted to export their films, only some of which were accessible to a
broad audience, he did that too.

In the case of the 1962 chrome deal, there was no need to persuade
the Soviets—they fully realized they needed the cash. Nor did Oztemel
have any real competition, at least not from other American traders. Even
Armand Hammer, once Lenin's money launderer, was shut out. The only
initial difficulty was landing a buyer. American steelmakers were so para-
lyzed by the political climate that they shied away from the chance to buy
even a lucrative, difficult-to-acquire metal like chromium. Oztemel and
Feuerring found a customer by dangling a potent incentive—a price cut of
$25 a ton on an initial order of ten thousand tons, for a total discount of
$250,000. It was sufficient to attract an independent Niagara Falls steel-
man named Norris McFarlane, and all three were enriched by the deal.
Oztemel and Feuerring earned nearly $30 a ton, which over the years
added up to tens of millions of dollars.

Giffen began his employment with Oztemel as aide-de-camp. On their business trips abroad, the young man took copious notes during negotiations, presented later to his boss as aide-mémoire. Professional touches like that were rarities at Oztemel's two enterprises—Greg-Gary, the company he formed in 1957 and named after his two eldest sons, and Satra, the holding company he added a decade later, its name an acronym for Soviet-American Trading. These were disorganized, seat-of-the-pants operations almost exclusively serving Oztemel's supreme gift—the deal—and his penchant for the high life. He regarded the deal as the essence of business, often consummated on a mere handshake, as he frequently boasted. Now he had aide-mémoire compiled by a bright young assistant. Both gave him a feeling of pride.

Oztemel was an immigrant, with the predictable insecurities about his place in America. But Giffen—the former U.C. Berkeley golfer with his effortless charm and socialite wife—seemed totally at ease with himself. His manner suggested a maturity beyond his years, and he seemed more polished than many of those around him. In a series of 1970 photos, he is wearing a coal-black pinstripe suit, his closely cropped, neatly gelled hair parted on the side, all of it distinguishing him from the dour middle-aged men with whom he was meeting. Before long, Oztemel, a patron in the old-country style, for whom loyalty was a way of life, was treating him like a son. Greg and Gary, while much loved, were only teenagers, not terribly interested in the business.

For his partner Feuerring and others, Oztemel took too many risks. And it was true that he sometimes plunged ahead without restraint. After receiving a shipment of ten thousand tons of Soviet chromium, Oztemel then wanted to negotiate shipping space for ten times that volume, apparently on a hunch that there must be hidden demand. He thrived on the rollercoaster nature of his chosen profession—the difficult-to-forge friendships, the tense horse-trading until the right price was achieved, and the sumptuous lifestyle it afforded.

Giffen's mind worked differently. When he considered what his boss had accomplished—the creation of a highly successful commodities trading operation—he thought that Oztemel had largely squandered his considerable power and influence. Giffen was thinking bigger. His strong suit was the grand idea and the salesmanship to pull it off, traits that his boss recognized and appreciated. So when Giffen proposed that they launch an international consulting business, Oztemel was ready to agree.

Giffen was put in charge of the new subsidiary, Satra Consulting. His mission: to monetize Oztemel's matchless Rolodex of important Soviet names. He was awarded shares of stock in the company, not enough to make him rich but a definite incentive to do well.

Virginia Proehl detested Jim Giffen, this ambitious young man who had studied law under her husband, Paul, at UCLA. She thought, accurately enough, that Giffen was trying to lure his former professor into joining Satra Consulting, a venture that she regarded as loopy. It wasn't because she was unfamiliar with the ways of flashy, even eccentric individuals. After all, Paul and Virginia were regulars at Southern California society parties where the guests might include film stars such as Zsa Zsa Gabor, celebrity scientists such as oceanographer Jacques Cousteau, and intellectuals like Proehl himself. But Giffen made Virginia recoil. When he telephoned her husband for advice, which he did frequently, Virginia was reminded of *All About Eve*, the Hollywood film in which Anne Baxter ingratiates herself with an aging starlet, played by Bette Davis, milks the woman's acting secrets, then betrays her to take over the stage herself. But Paul felt ready for a change. And Giffen promised precisely that.

At Stanford University, John Huhs, about to be awarded a newly offered super-credential—master's degrees in law and business—noticed a posting on a bulletin board: Was anyone interested in an international business career? A boutique New York startup was recruiting consultants. Huhs and a gangly classmate named Carl Longley liked the sound of it: a chance for adventure, rather than the mundane corporate work to which their classmates were headed. The Stanford pair flew east.

In their interviews, Giffen told them that superpower relations were changing. The chill generated by two decades of hostilities—Moscow's invasion of Hungary, the Bay of Pigs fiasco, the erection of the Berlin Wall, the Cuban Missile Crisis, the Vietnam War, the crushing of the Prague Spring—had passed. Now, as the 1960s neared an end, détente was blossoming, led by the anti-Soviet warhorse Nixon and his brainy German-born adviser Kissinger. Trade barriers between the United States and the Soviets were falling, Giffen told his visitors, and the Park Avenue firm he represented was well positioned to profit from the boom that was sure to come. Satra Consulting would become the nexus between corporate America and the Kremlin. Why, only recently he had escorted American oil-tool company executives to Baku, and they were already earning tidy profits on their sales to the Soviets, who needed western help to rejuvenate an industry in distress. We'll all become millionaires, Giffen promised.

So it was that the three men—Proehl, Huhs, and Longley—became Giffen recruits. The professor would contribute his advice by phone while continuing to teach at UCLA; the other two would join their new boss in New York.

Jim Giffen was well prepared for his new undertaking. He had worked diligently to create a fresh persona for himself—that of an authority on trade between the United States and the Soviet Union. Under Proehl's mentoring, he had fattened his UCLA term paper into a 240-page book manuscript entitled *The Legal and Practical Aspects of Trade with the Soviet Union.*

Frederick A. Praeger, a semi-academic publishing house that had launched a special series on foreign trade, agreed to publish it in 1969, but without any advance payment. His editor at Praeger, Richard Rowson, knew the book would have value nonetheless for Giffen, "establishing him as an expert in this field." As it turned out, Giffen did get an immediate reward for his labors. As he and Rowson stepped outside the Praeger office in New York's Tribeca district on their way to a meal, Giffen pointed out a Rolls-Royce parked at the curb. It was a congratulatory gift for the new author from Oztemel. (Giffen gave Rowson the only gifts the editor ever received from an author—a silver ashtray embedded with a silver dollar and a silver paperweight.)

The book was larded with legal analyses that demonstrated the obvious—that trade with the Soviets was possible. Yet it did provide a useful orientation. One learned, for example, which Moscow building was the usual location for trade talks and that the building had five entrances, each manned by two militiamen, and that choosing the wrong entrance would almost certainly make one late to a meeting. Also included were 130 pages of Soviet trade forms. The book paled in comparison with a genuinely heavyweight account, published a year later, by Samuel Pisar, the Harvard- and Sorbonne-trained lawyer with whom Satra colleague John Huhs would later work. But as Rowson had predicted, the book did provide Giffen with instant cachet as a Soviet expert.

For years Giffen had yearned for such respectability, the kind that whisked one unquestioned through difficult-to-open doors. The reflected glory of being part of the Hopkins family had already nourished his sense of self-importance. But now, in addition to being Harry Hopkins's grandson-in-law and deputy to Ara Oztemel, he was the author of a well-regarded book. "I was flying," Giffen said years later. "I had a job in my area, and had sold a book. That was hot shit."

Some would recall him speculating aloud on further paths to power—perhaps a senator at thirty-five, maybe even president at a younger age than Kennedy, who took office at forty-three. It was his "manifest destiny to be president of the United States," Giffen would declare. Perhaps he was merely trying to impress the secretaries at Satra. But one could never be sure; boundlessly ambitious and, it seemed, able to win over anyone he set his sights on, this young man might end up anywhere.

Détente

THE ATMOSPHERE AT SATRA CON-
sulting was defined by bonhomie. Ara
Oztemel was the convivial ringmaster, always
the center of attention. At lunch, there were
formal sit-down meals prepared for the staff
by his personal cook. After business hours,
all gathered for whiskey in his office, serious
drinking sessions that could last hours. If
Oztemel was so inclined, which he often was,
he and Betty Van Staveren would take those
with stamina out for late dinner and jazz,
occasions in which he himself would frequently climb the stage to jam with the musicians.

Jim Giffen, meanwhile, prided himself
on the aura of credibility he was creating for
the business. His connection to Harry
Hopkins would prove invaluable in dealings
with the Soviets, who remembered the lat-

ter's role in procuring them desperately needed Lend-Lease assistance during World War II. Paul Proehl, not only a law professor but also a former vice chancellor at UCLA, was a man whose gravitas would inspire the instant respect of clients. The firm could additionally boast of its two Stanford law-business graduates, John Huhs and Carl Longley. Giffen made sure that the pair promptly mounted their framed diplomas for prominent display on the office walls.

The team's most immediate task was to devise a sales pitch, one that would emphasize Satra's unequaled access in Moscow. Giffen built it around his boss's own heroic account of his early adventures in the Soviet Union. In this telling, Oztemel's 1959 and 1962 chrome deals were blurred into a single blockbuster exploit starring him and the Bolshevik pioneer Mikoyan and pushed back to 1953—or 1952, depending on whim—a time when Oztemel in fact was living in poverty in Watertown, fending off in-laws nagging him to find a job. There was no logical explanation for Oztemel's inflation of the truth; it was simply the Phineas Barnum in him. He once was interviewed by *Fortune* magazine, which duly reported his boast that Satra had earned about $800 million in revenue the previous year and approvingly took note of supposedly original paintings by Modigliani and Picasso on his office walls. The magazine piece caused mirth among those who knew that the revenue had been magnified at least twofold and that the "originals" were prints.

Armed with their dramatic sales presentation, Giffen and his colleagues wooed an American meat packager, a pharmaceutical firm, chemical and steel companies, automobile parts makers, and oil technology manufacturers. Sure, they said, any company was at liberty to proceed to Moscow on its own—the new world created by détente had made it so. But the Satra consultants already had certain deals in their sights to which only clients would be privy. Instead of fumbling its way around the Soviet capital, an American company could get on the fast track by signing with them. Giffen's closer was that Satra had "leverage in selling to the Soviets," having already guided other American companies to profitable ventures there. He kept his initial fees deliberately low so as not to discourage potential customers. But at ten to twenty-five thousand dollars annually, they were insufficient to cover the cost of a yearlong commercial campaign and would have to be adjusted along the way to assure Satra's profits.

Word of mouth enhanced the fledgling firm's reputation. One early convert, George Helland of Houston's Cameron Iron Works, was greatly impressed by an incident in Moscow. Helland, some twenty other American oilmen, and Giffen were about to board a flight home after touring Siberian oil fields when a Soviet official stopped Giffen. His passport lacked a required stamp, the official told Giffen, who responded that he was the personal guest of a Soviet minister. The official, unmoved, held him back while allowing the others to board. Not long afterward, as the plane sat on the tarmac prepared for takeoff, Helland looked out the window and saw Giffen emerge from one of several limousines that had pulled up. The confident young man boarded the plane and then described how he had gained his release. Giffen said that he had told the airport officials to call a certain telephone number, the private line of a senior KGB official, who "gets angry and says, 'Get him on a plane immediately and give him first-class treatment!' " Helland recalled. "How much he embellished, I don't know. I do know the plane waited for him and he came out with limousines. That gave me a little more faith in his ability to make things happen."

When Proehl visited his Satra colleagues in New York, he was called "the Professor." The title befit him—he was fluent in French and German, a collector of African art, and a voracious reader. But it also bothered him because it seemed to imply that he was of another age, out of his realm when measured against his enterprising colleagues. Once, in London, he tried to loosen up. Ara Oztemel took him in his Rolls to a private club called Annabelle's, handed him a couple of thousand pounds, and told him to have some fun. Proehl proceeded to win—according to his wife, he tripled the sum—and handed Oztemel the winnings. "It's yours," Oztemel said with a wave of his hand.

But while Proehl was a bit stiff, his scholarly demeanor commanded instant respect among people of stature; it was he, not the young hotshots, who originated Satra Consulting's signature deal with a ranking American industrialist. Aboard an airliner, the professor fell into conversation with his seatmate, who introduced himself as Zenon Hansen, chairman of Mack Trucks. Soon, they were discussing the Ford Motor Company's recent rejection of a contract to build a Soviet cargo-truck plant. It was not just any truck plant, but one that would dwarf all those in the United States, with an annual capacity of 150,000 vehicles. Ford's decision not to build, Proehl noted, had been heavily influenced by Nixon's secretary of defense, Melvin Laird, who had fumed that the trucks could end up in the service of the Moscow-backed North Vietnamese. That elicited a rise out of Hansen, who believed that Mack made the best industrial vehicles in the world. "Let me at them," he said.

Hansen went with a Giffen-led team to Moscow and seemed to connect instantly with the Soviets. The Soviets then sent a delegation on a reciprocal visit to the United States, including a stop at Hansen's Allentown, Pennsylvania, home. There, the entire group marveled at his collection of memorabilia devoted to the bulldog, Mack's corporate symbol. When John Huhs's wife remarked favorably on the hats, shirts, and bookends bearing the mark of the bulldog, it stirred evident pride in Hansen: He cupped his hands over the front of his pants and then opened them slowly to expose a bulldog figurine attached to the zipper on his fly.

Less than a year later, Hansen and the Soviet Union signed an agreement allowing Mack Trucks to build and operate a factory there; *Business Week* published a fifteen-page exclusive about it. A black-and-white photo of Giffen and his pleased Soviet partners adorned the cover.

The publicity was a commercial bonanza for Satra. "The phone started ringing off the hook," said Huhs, and Giffen's brainstorm began to pay off. Proehl joined the company full-time as its West Coast executive. Huhs soon found himself squiring America's most powerful blue-chip executives around Moscow, in addition to commercial celebrities such as Col. Harland Sanders, the Kentucky Fried Chicken tycoon, who wanted to open Soviet restaurants. The Satra team symbolically headquartered with proximity to power—near the Kremlin—by taking four rooms at the exquisite Metropol Hotel.

As for Giffen, he had become a millionaire on paper, thanks to the surging price of company stock. Now he increasingly began to be regarded as the boss's heir apparent. He and June bought a home in the Westchester County town of Larchmont, near the ultra-exclusive Winged Foot Golf Club. Giffen was no stranger to country clubs, but the ones he knew were of the Stockton variety. One did not gain admission to Winged Foot by simply applying, and there was no reason to believe that the no-name son of a Stockton haberdasher would qualify. Oztemel intervened, introducing his protégé to friends, who sponsored Giffen's membership.

The only discordant note came when the Mack Trucks deal became embroiled in international politics. In the White House, intense discussion unfolded on whether to approve the venture, reject it, or "use it for linkage to the SALT talks, Vietnam, and so forth," recalled Peter Peterson, Nixon's international trade adviser. In the end, Nixon split the difference—while approving some $500 million in private contracts for the Soviet plant, he turned down Mack, which could play no role in the plant.

The Satra men didn't suffer a complete loss. Even though the value of their stock fell with the collapse of the Mack deal, the fees generated from the Nixon-approved private contracts meant that Giffen and Huhs were still multimillionaires, and new clients continued to pour in. Paul Proehl received no commission, even though it was his encounter with the Mack executive that had led to Satra's sudden rise. Oztemel made amends by telling him to buy a Mercedes-Benz and charge it to the company. So he did—an aqua gray sedan with black leather seats.

Meticulously dressed, with a telemarketing personality, Giffen trolled for new clients wherever high-powered businessmen from America gathered. One of his favorite hunting grounds was the U.S.-USSR Trade and Economic Council (USTEC), a pioneering association formed by Nixon and Soviet leader Leonid Brezhnev to faciliate business activity.

There was already a mystique about Soviet trade. American blue bloods like oil scion David Rockefeller and steel magnate Cyrus Eaton were flocking to Moscow on perceived missions of peace, believing that trade would reduce the chance of superpower military confrontation, and basking in the public adulation of American businessmen seen as able to crack the Kremlin. Nixon and Kissinger encouraged such ventures, rightly seeing trade as Brezhnev's Achilles' heel. They dangled the prospect of a full relaxation of trade barriers in exchange for certain concessions. In this atmosphere, USTEC's membership quickly bulged, ranging from self-made businessmen like Oztemel and Giffen to the aristocratic cream of America's blue-chip corporations. Giffen skillfully took advantage of the opportunity. "He could walk into a room and within an hour know everyone in it," Longley said.

Among those Giffen cultivated was a handsome celebrity executive named Najeeb Halaby, chairman of Pan American World Airways. A Yale and Stanford man, Halaby was a former military pilot who had served in the Truman, Kennedy, and Johnson administrations and had appeared on the cover of *Time* magazine. Later, his daughter Lisa would marry Jordan's King Hussein and become Queen Noor. One thing Halaby was not was wealthy. In late 1971, he candidly revealed to a reporter that he was having severe cash problems. Though he earned $127,000 a year, having to pay for housing, private school for three children, and other such expenses prevented him from amassing any savings. That a perquisite of his airline job was free flying privileges for himself and his family only seemed to mock him. "Jeeb tells me I can go anywhere in the world I want—as long as I don't get off the plane and spend money," quipped Halaby's wife.

In March 1972, Halaby was forced out after eight years at the airline. Now he sought to parlay his social connections, his Washington experience, and his alumni links into serious cash. Jim Giffen's advice was a bold stroke: Halaby should round up enough financing to buy Ara Oztemel's controlling share of Satra Consulting. Halaby and Giffen would then form a new concern, one that would make the former airline executive a very wealthy man. The protégé, it seemed, had outgrown his mentor and was now quite willing to plot against him. An Oztemel intimate said that Giffen "wanted to imitate Ara," but "he didn't know where to stop."

Within days of his dismissal from Pan Am, Halaby was on a plane with Giffen to Chicago, to Los Angeles, to San Francisco, and elsewhere. With prospectus in hand, they worked their way through Satra's stable of clients, promising that the new partnership would deliver bigger and better results. Jerome Komes, a senior vice president at the San Francisco–based engineering giant Bechtel, listened patiently as Giffen and Halaby described how they could help the company procure Soviet deals. Then he asked Giffen, "Are you still with Satra?" Giffen replied that he was. Komes later told Halaby that he would not retain them as consultants; he had little interest in a relationship with someone "who could with equanimity set about putting together a competing company when he was still with his old employer." It did no good when Halaby pledged his intention to buy the Satra subsidiary from Oztemel.

Oztemel found out about Giffen's perfidy while in London. He and Betty Van Staveren grabbed a trans-Atlantic flight, arrived in New York to a spring rain, and drove to the Upper East Side apartment they shared. Oztemel was silent, in a fighting mood. He and a few close associates spent the weekend in long meetings, debating how to respond to the betrayal. On Monday, a shouting match broke out between Oztemel and Giffen. Giffen stormed out, and that was the end of his tenure at Satra.

In three amazing years, thanks to his fateful meeting with the go-to man on Soviet trade, Giffen had realized all of his early dreams. Now he seemed to have thrown it all away. At the age of thirty-one, he was out of a job.

Unemployed, Giffen managed a brave face. He boasted to Proehl that he was fending off a job offer from Borg-Warner, a Satra client. Alert to a bluff, the professor checked with the executive Giffen had named. There had been no offer. The truth was that Giffen was drifting. He tried to assemble a consortium of oil tool companies that would negotiate as a single entity with the Soviets but failed to attract sufficient interest. He attempted, with little success, to line up other trade ventures on his own, while he waited for his next chance at a truly big deal.

Jim Giffen's greatest talent had always been his preternatural ability to win the confidence of powerful older men. Each step of the way in his business career, he would seem compelled to be close to such men, whose approval he would cherish and whose credibility he hoped would transfer to him. An associate who watched him cultivate some of these relationships described the process. Giffen would launch an " 'I want this guy to be my friend' effort," the associate said. "He would sort of pick people like that who he thought could help him. He would work at it. He would call them frequently, keep them updated. He was very charming, definitely intelligent. He could work himself in."

In the summer of 1973, about a year and a half after his banishment from Satra, Giffen's special ability again proved providential, this time intersecting with the sudden need of an old-money Ohio steel tycoon to get into the Soviet Union, and fast.

C. William Verity, Jr., was a white-haired gentleman with a "common touch" and the midwestern values of his birthplace, Middletown, Ohio. But Verity also possessed a sense of entitlement that came with being the grandson of George M. Verity, founder of Armco Steel and the largest employer in the mill town of fifteen thousand people. At eleven, Verity was sent east to Connecticut to board at the prestigious Choate prep school, rooming one year with an athletic Massachusetts boy named John Kennedy. Verity formed a special friendship with the future president, one that continued through college, with Verity at Yale and Kennedy at Harvard "chasing the same girls." It was a good-natured rivalry; once, learning that a "lassy and sexy girl" at Vassar named Dorothy Walker had made dates with both of them on the same night, Verity and JFK decided to stand her up and go out to dinner themselves, stag.

Moving in such privileged circles, playing on the Yale golf team, and touring Asia as a twenty-one-year-old at the outset of World War II, Verity developed a folksy worldliness that later would win him acceptance in drawing rooms and boardrooms alike. In 1940, Verity returned to Middletown to work his way up from Armco's factory floor and eventually run the company; years later, he would become Ronald Reagan's secretary of commerce.

In June 1973, Richard Nixon put the much-traveled Armco chairman on a list of three dozen American businessmen invited by the president to breakfast with Soviet leader Leonid Brezhnev. It was a heady privilege in détente's giddy years, for Verity would be shoulder to shoulder not only with Brezhnev but also with the cream of Soviet trade, including Ara Oztemel, Armand Hammer, and Pepsi chairman Don Kendall. At Blair House, Brezhnev won over the men with his talk of warmer relations and expanded business ties. That led to a statement of intention to form the

U.S.-USSR Trade and Economic Council, with Verity as a founding member of its board of directors. "We're looking forward to building a silicon steel plant for you," the delighted Verity told a Soviet minister.

The trouble was, Verity knew next to nothing about the Soviet Union. How would he get up to speed?

Soon, Verity was introduced to Giffen, who sold himself as an accomplished Soviet trade expert, invoking at one point his authorship of a book on that very subject. Asked about career experiences, Giffen mentioned his employment at Satra, explaining somewhat vaguely that it had ended after a "falling out" with the boss. Verity didn't probe further, thrilled to find someone who seemed so able, and hired Giffen to negotiate steel and oil equipment deals with the Soviets.

A few months later, a two-paragraph item appeared in *The New York Times* headlined "Armco in Soviet Trade Pact." It described a five-year "protocol" involving ferrous metals and offshore oil equipment. Seasoned hands knew that a protocol was what the Soviets signed when there was nothing more concrete to agree on, and indeed the report disclosed that the sides hadn't discussed money. Still, the news item's very appearance demonstrated that, Giffen's ignominious departure from Satra notwithstanding, he was still in the game; four years later, he would take credit for negotiating some $100 million in Soviet contracts for Armco.

One of those was a 1976 deal that provided Baku with its first deep-sea oil rig. Until then, the Soviets could not drill deeper than a paltry three hundred feet underwater, rendering many of their best fields unreachable. Technically, the sale violated U.S. law, which linked trade to a loosening of Soviet restrictions on Jewish emigration. But Giffen's paperwork got around that by showing that the machinery had been sold to Norway. Upon its arrival there, he simply diverted the disassembled rig to the Soviet Union and floated it down the Don River for reassembly.

Giffen operated out of an Armco office in the Seagram Building on Park Avenue. His quarters were large, fitted out with a bathroom, shower, and, in a credenza, a full bar. When the work day ended, his secretary, Terry Nixon, would pour him a Dewar's on the rocks, while he bantered with colleagues who joined him. Anyone who wished to be taken seriously knew that it was a requirement to drink with Giffen, often into the late evening. During these sessions, Giffen would variously indulge in locker-room humor and long monologues. But it was risky to raise business matters; unlike the Satra days, when Giffen never seemed tipsy no matter how much Scotch he consumed, he now would begin to lose focus after the first or second drink.

Giffen luxuriated in his new life. Although still a married man, he dated a series of female employees, most of whom remained on the job after breaking up with the boss. He hosted black-tie dinners for favored clients and political celebrities. He favored corporate boardroom dress shirts—white collars on pastel blues and pinks—and spoke with an assured Brahmin cadence. Depending on what the situation seemed to require, he could be brash or charming, obsequious or threatening. Many of his clients and employees regarded him as "fun," particularly when it came to gifts. At Christmastime, if he had learned of a new electronic gadget, he would order two or three dozen for immediate shipment to clients and friends. He gave each person on his Armco staff a year-end bonus equaling a month's wages along with a cashmere sweater or perhaps something from Brooks Brothers. One day back in Stockton, Lloyd Giffen summoned John Falls to the Oxford Shop: "You know what Jim is doing for me? He's giving me a Cadillac."

All the while, he worked at promoting himself as a Soviet authority. He began to teach an evening course in Soviet trade at Columbia University. On the strength of his book, he declared that he knew more about the subject than any other American, an extravagant claim considering the track record of his former boss, Ara Oztemel, who had been bartering with Moscow for two decades.

He nurtured his ongoing relationship with the CIA, which considered him a valued source. Bud Johnson, a CIA analyst on Soviet oil, recalled how he refused to see Armand Hammer "because the agency thought Hammer was a friend of Lenin's." But, accompanied by one or two trainee analysts, he met frequently with Giffen, whom he described as "really the conduit for the sale of oil field equipment. We wanted to find out about the negotiations." Giffen himself flew to Washington to brief—and be briefed by—CIA political and economic specialists. "He got pretty good treatment because of his good contacts with the Soviet trade people," Johnson said.

Such chumminess traced back to Satra days, when one CIA agent had become an office fixture, even accompanying Giffen and his men to dinner with their wives. Giffen explained that it was "part of the bargain" if one wanted to trade with the enemy, recalled one of his lieutenants. "Your government had questions for you. He'd tell his government what went down." KGB agents would catch up with Giffen in London, introduced to the Satra men as diplomatic attachés, but "you didn't have to be a brain surgeon" to know they were spies, the aide said.

Giffen also continued to widen his circle of blue blood friends. One such person was the Manhattan socialite attorney Michael Forrestal, who ran in the same circles as David Hopkins; his father, James, had been Truman's first secretary of defense. Michael had become, in effect, the adopted son of the renowned diplomat Averell Harriman after the 1949 suicide of his father.

According to Giffen's account of their first meeting, Forrestal, a Soviet authority in his own right, said curtly, "Tell me everything you know about the Soviet Union." The ambushed and startled Giffen quickly retorted, "Well, get out your pad." He talked nonstop while Forrestal listened; Forrestal left with a copy of Giffen's trade book in hand.

With Giffen's fondness for embroidered self-narrative, it wasn't clear where the truth ended and the bravado began. But the two undeniably developed a close relationship. Forrestal later sat on the board of a consulting firm established by Giffen, and at times he publicly promoted the latter's ventures. Giffen was impressed by Forrestal's concern for social issues and seemed to want to emulate it. At one point, the two of them negotiated with the Soviets to relax restrictions on Jewish emigration. Forrestal would die of an aneurism in 1989; a colleague who attempted to console Giffen recalled, "He turned his back to me, and you could see he was choked up. He started staring out the window."

Giffen was so successful at patterning himself after mentors like Forrestal and Verity that he could be easily mistaken for a bona fide member of the Eastern Establishment. Having the Winged Foot membership and Rolls-Royce helped, of course. But it was more the result of having carefully observed the older men in action. "I watched and learned," he said. "I just changed overnight." He seemed loath to discuss his own childhood out west. Once, pushed, he groused about the "rich Giffens" from Fresno, south of Stockton, who were in the cotton business and who supposedly had looked down on his immediate family as the "poor Giffens." Few associates seemed aware that Giffen had in fact had a relatively privileged boyhood. Perhaps his reticence was not so odd, however, when one considered how lofty his definition of success had become.

Four years into the Armco job, Giffen impressed his boss anew. President Jimmy Carter asked David Rockefeller to find a new chairman of USTEC, the Soviet-U.S. trade organization, and he tapped Verity. But the job required frequent summits with senior Kremlin officials, including Brezhnev, and Verity felt out of his league. Again, Giffen came to the rescue.

"I couldn't have taken the job if not for Jimmy," Verity said. "I depended on him for everything. He explained everything to me." When Giffen's role as counselor to the USTEC chairman became known, the still-bitter Ara Oztemel quit the organization. Verity was unmoved by his departure, and the ties between the steel magnate and Giffen only strengthened. Verity and his wife, Peggy, socialized with Jim and June. "I was like an uncle to him," Verity said.

But Verity did not recall those days with total equanimity. Giffen, he conceded, was disliked by many at Armco for flaunting his intimate relationship with the chairman while treating others with barely disguised disdain—"a good way to destroy the organization," Verity said.

Giffen was also thought to be a cheat. It was a grievance shared up the line—even to Verity himself—and it had its origins in the annual employee golf tournament. As is customary in friendly competition, mediocre players with established handicaps were allowed to take extra strokes. The worse the player, the greater the handicap and the more strokes allowed.

Verity, himself a former college golfer with a three handicap, could see that Giffen was a better player. All one had to do was notice Giffen's powerful drives and excellent short game. Which explains why Verity and colleagues were stunned when Giffen announced his handicap—a generous ten. They had guessed him to be a par player or close to it, meaning little or no handicap. "It was terribly unfair," Verity said. "He always won."

Verity and his top deputy, Harry Holiday, tried repeatedly to persuade Giffen to play with an honest handicap, but "he'd make out like we were goody-goodies," Verity recalled. "I told him he didn't have a [moral] compass. He'd say, 'That's all crap.' Once he said, 'Who are you to judge?' That's one of his weaknesses. He wants to win so bad that he's willing to cut corners."

Giffen's Armco colleagues never forgave him. Golf was a gentleman's sport in which honor was assumed. If that trust was violated, one's reputation was forever tarnished. "They stopped letting him play," Verity said. "And if you showed up with him, you were tainted."

At work, Verity and Holiday continued "to tolerate Jim because he knew exactly what we needed, he did it well, he did it on time and within budget," Verity said. But they kept Giffen under close scrutiny. Though they never caught him in any serious deception, they concluded that Giffen was a bit of a schemer. Verity said simply, "I just don't think he cares."

Giffen's marriage collapsed in 1984. June finally tired of her husband's dalliances and announced that she was leaving him for another man. Even after their divorce, though, he continued to invoke his now-frayed Hopkins connection in the presence of prospective clients and others he wanted to impress. He began seeing a beautiful woman of aristocratic Russian blood named Nikita Cheremetoff, and the relationship seemed serious. "Giffen wanted to marry her," said one intimate. He had hired the woman, then in her twenties, as a translator and kept promoting her until she was his assistant. That provoked the ire of her colleagues, who bristled at her growing arrogance, founded, after all, mainly in her sex appeal to the boss. Cheremetoff ultimately resigned and ended the relationship.

That same year, Giffen, with generous support from Verity, struck out on his own. He formed a consulting firm specializing in Soviet-U.S. trade and, at the suggestion of Michael Forrestal, named it Mercator, Latin for "world trader." Many of his Armco staff followed him to the new enterprise. There were handsome rewards for doing so: Giffen raised the salary of executive Michael Sekus, for example, by a whopping 83 percent, to $125,000 from $68,000.

Such largess was due in large part to Verity's financial backing of Mercator. Indeed, though Verity years later would grouse about Giffen and say he could not recall why he had been so munificent, he appeared to have no misgivings at the time. Without the support of his former boss, it is doubtful that Giffen could have survived the startup period. Verity not only awarded the new company an exclusive contract to represent Armco on Soviet matters, he also bankrolled virtually all of Giffen's expenses in the first year and a substantial portion over the next four years. He even turned over Armco's New York office and furnishings to Mercator. Verity described it as bestowing "our blessing" on the new venture. "It was odd," Sekus recalled, everyone sitting at the same desks but suddenly working for a new company.

Trade with the Soviet Union had become difficult, a victim of the invasion of Afghanistan and the Ronald Reagan–inspired chill in superpower relations. But Giffen stayed afloat. Even as he was launching Mercator, he ascended the ranks in USTEC. The council's new chairman, Dwayne Andreas, head of agricultural giant Archer Daniels Midland and a supremely influential figure in Washington, installed Giffen as president of USTEC, second in power only to the soybean king himself.

Andreas, intent on smoothing trade relations between the two superpowers, set out for Moscow with his eager new executive. After a few preliminaries with Kremlin authorities, word came that a meeting had been arranged. Giffen and Andreas would have an audience with a rising star of the Politburo, one Mikhail Gorbachev.

Giffen had already transformed himself from the son of a haberdasher into a merchant banker with important international connections. The meeting with the fresh-faced Kremlin minister, however, would catapult him to even greater heights, putting him on the path toward his first big oil deal, on the shores of the fabled Caspian Sea.

The Perfect Oil Field

MIKHAIL GORBACHEV WAS UNLIKE Soviet rulers of the past. Open-minded and inventive, pragmatic and flexible, "he would look you in the eye, and you were the only person in the room." He was said to be "impossible not to like." Born to a peasant Russian family, he was a young boy when Stalin's purges silently swept up both of his grandfathers along with millions of others. As a college student, he was inspired by Nikita Khrushchev's denunciation of Stalinist bloodshed. Three decades later, energetic and confident at age fifty-four, Gorbachev became Khrushchev's political heir.

His rise to power as supreme leader came at an opportune moment. It was 1985, and "a sort of torpor" had settled over the Soviet Union. Apart from wooden dolls, vodka, and weapons, it manufactured almost no finished products marketable outside the Soviet bloc. It was bleeding from its delusional military adventure in Afghanistan. And the loyalist cadre that had helped to overcome crises in the past wasn't as easily summoned this time.

Like the idealistic generation that produced him, Gorbachev believed that Soviet Communism could be repaired. His interpretation of Marxist orthodoxy made him the inheritor not only of Khrushchev's mantle but of Lenin's too. Studying his nation's past, Gorbachev thought that an entirely different Soviet Union might have evolved had Lenin's market-based economic policy not been abandoned for Stalin's brutal "barracks socialism." Democracy and reform might have prevailed instead of "the omnipotence of violent methods" that had wracked the country and its people.

Now, facing an "alarm about the fate of the revolution" similar to Lenin's, Gorbachev likewise turned to the West for salvation. He welcomed western capital and, as an inducement, legalized 49 percent foreign ownership of profit-making ventures. But the first results disappointed him. Though hundreds of western companies had shown interest in entering the Soviet market, just a dozen or so had actually followed through.

It was in this context that Gorbachev found common cause with Jim Giffen, at that point president of the U.S.-USSR trade council. In a remarkable display of salesmanship, Giffen persuaded the new Soviet leader that he and his friends among America's corporate gentry could help "jump-start" the Soviet economy. Thus was born the American Trade Consortium.

Giffen had long advocated that American businessmen should band together when dealing with the Soviets. A single foreign company had no leverage. The Soviets would "just rip you to pieces," employing bluster and vague threats of competitors waiting in the wings in order to whittle down prices and exhaust even the most determined negotiator. Giffen thought he could draw the cream of corporate America into an alliance able to hold its own with the Soviets—a consortium that would place "so many things on the board that [the Soviets] could not be unreasonable on any one deal."

But there had to be a guarantee that the American companies could convert their ruble profits to dollars and then repatriate the cash home. If earnings were stranded in the Soviet Union, there would be little reason to do business there. Giffen's solution to this dilemma was suitably elaborate. He would recruit an American oil company into the consortium, then persuade Gorbachev to allow the company to drill for an export Soviet crude. The oil company would split its potentially huge earnings with Moscow. It would then set aside a portion of its remaining profits to serve as a kind of currency exchange for consortium members doing business in the Soviet Union. All this would be set up in a way that would leave Moscow functionaries powerless to meddle, and the American companies would be able to repatriate their profits without any trouble.

It was a head-spinning proposal. After all, profit was outlawed, even vilified in the Soviet Union, especially profit denominated in the ideological enemy's currency. Western ownership of enterprises had been illegal since Lenin. Moreover, the Soviets, now the world's largest producer of crude, regarded oil as one of their most strategically important possessions.

But the pragmatic Gorbachev desperately needed to fire up the plodding Soviet economy, so he was more inclined than most to embrace such heresy. Michael Forrestal, Giffen's establishment lawyer friend, liked the idea. Giffen himself allowed that it was "fucking ingenious" and turned to an acquaintance, Nicholas Brady, for tactical advice.

Educated at Harvard and Yale, Brady was chairman of the well-connected Wall Street investment bank Dillon, Read and Company. Giffen knew him as an investment banker for Armco and an occasional golfing partner. Brady was won over, and in a phone call the two debated which oil company might best suit the idea. Exxon? Too big. Mobil? Too maverick. Texaco? Out of the question—it was on the verge of bankruptcy after a vicious courtroom wrangle with Pennzoil. What about Chevron? Brady served as investment banker to the San Francisco–based company. A short time later, Brady phoned back. "Get on a plane," he told Giffen. "You have an appointment with George Keller."

Oil companies were among the most despotic of corporations. When a petroleum geologist had a hunch or an exploration team came across an alluring prospect, it was the chairman of the company—not any committee, not any underling—who decreed what would happen. The chairmen were astonishingly megalomaniacal, indeed almost had to be to succeed. On the road, they behaved—and were often indulged—like heads of state, basking in their collective reputation as men of daring who, without flinching, regularly gambled millions on what their drilling rigs might find.

George Keller, the chairman of Chevron, was no exception, and he almost never deigned to meet with someone like Giffen. Keller was constitutionally hostile to promoters of any stripe but especially the would-be middlemen with, as he put it, "a suede-shoe feeling." They were known to whisper in an oilman's ear that they had a half million barrels of crude for sale at a special discount; if the oilman were naïve enough to fall for the con, only then would the hustlers actually try to find a shipment at that price.

Keller's dislike of middlemen was shared by most western oil executives working abroad. But there was a certain irony to this. Chevron's 1930s evolution from a coastal U.S. oil company to an international player had resulted not from its own acuity but rather from that of middlemen who had actually delivered. It was a New Zealander named Frank Holmes who ushered Chevron, at the time known as Standard Oil of California, or Socal, into Bahrain, and, more important, an American geologist named Karl Twitchell who had midwifed Socal's pioneering oil development in Saudi Arabia. Through the early 1970s, Chevron had so much oil that "we weren't concerned about having to go other places and find it," recalled Ken Derr, who would be Keller's successor.

But abruptly everything changed. Saudi Arabia absorbed Chevron's oil concession, and a mid-1980s oil price collapse, from $31 a barrel to $10 a barrel, cost the company hundreds of millions of dollars in revenue. With no substantial new discoveries expected in the United States, the company turned to the North Sea and found oil there. It acquired Angolan and Nigerian properties in 1984 by buying Gulf Oil. But that still added up to "not a lot of new international joint ventures," in Derr's words. Chevron was still America's fourth-largest oil major, but the future was looking iffy. An oil company's value rested not only on what it produced but also on the reserves it could draw on in the years to come, so-

called booked reserves. The company was desperate to find big new overseas oil deposits to replenish its stocks, but it seemed overly averse to risk.

Yet the worm of adventure was there. Keller and his British deputy,
J. Dennis Bonney, had both worked in Saudi Arabia. Indeed, as a young
man in the late 1950s, the urbane Bonney had cut his teeth as a lawyer for
Calouste Gulbenkian's successors in the Iraq National Oil Company in
Baghdad; he even had a chance encounter with Gulbenkian's captivating
son and heir, Nubar, at the Hotel Ritz in Paris. Now, as the two Chevron
executives considered the possibility of penetrating the forbidding Soviet
Union, their adrenalin started flowing. The company's own studies confirmed that Soviet oil reserves were huge. But how could Chevron get at
them? Keller could not imagine an orthodox Communist government
agreeing to any terms that an American oil company would find attractive.
Yet neither could he disregard the call from Nicholas Brady, whose opinion he greatly respected. If Brady favored Giffen's idea, then Keller had to
put his doubts on hold and listen.

He summoned Giffen to a meeting with senior Chevron executives,
and gave him the floor, declaring: "Brady tells us you have some ideas
about working in the USSR. Tell us about them."

Giffen could be glib, but he was seldom frivolous. He had often-
trenchant ideas and could express them with eloquence, which he did on
this day, speaking for two hours without notes. Wearing a dark suit with a
white handkerchief peeking out from his breast pocket, he began with a
gussied-up version of his own resume, lifted straight from the seventeen-
year-old presentation he had developed at Satra. He talked about his
decade of negotiating for Armco Steel, the rare deals that, even if many
were stillborn because of Cold War politics, he had nevertheless managed
to fashion with the Soviets even in the dark days of Brezhnev. He described the enviable Kremlin contacts he now possessed, especially his relationship with Gorbachev.

Finally, Giffen outlined how Chevron fit into his plan. He would personally introduce Keller and others to the most powerful leaders in the
Soviet Union. Chevron would be in the company of a select group of
blue-chip American corporations, all of which would in all likelihood successfully negotiate ironclad contracts with Moscow. Giffen made it all

sound enticingly real, and he concluded by inviting the Chevron men to Moscow, where he would show them around.

Sizing up his guest, Keller decided that Giffen should be taken seriously. The Chevron boss knew that his own team had no idea how to break into Moscow. Here was someone who already had forged a way through the Soviet bureaucracy, who in fact was already acting as a full-service guide for visiting American businessmen—you landed in Moscow and a Giffen man met you at the airport, a Giffen man arranged the meetings, and a Giffen man did the translating. Keller had also been impressed when Giffen recited his knowledge of Chevron, including its history in Saudi Arabia. That had struck an emotional chord; Giffen might be youthful in appearance and brash in manner, but at least he knew to whom he was speaking.

As the door shut behind their visitor, Keller turned to John Silcox, president of Chevron's overseas operations. "When can you get to Moscow?" he asked. "George, let's talk about it," Silcox replied. He wanted at least to verify Giffen's credentials and claims. "Okay, John—but when can you get to Moscow?" Keller demanded. The resolute chairman had already made up his mind.

With Chevron signing on, Giffen now had the clout to attract others. His corporate dream team came to include Ford, which intended to assemble cars in the Soviet Union; RJR Nabisco, to bake Oreos; Eastman Kodak, to make kidney dialysis machines; Johnson & Johnson, to manufacture tampons; and Archer Daniels Midland, to mix soy-based products. Giffen's own firm, Mercator, would act as investment banker. As their chairman, the group selected Robert Carbonell, an RJR executive who crowed that here, at last, was a winning formula to crack the Soviet market after years in which "it was impossible to make contacts . . . [and one] never got to first base." Carbonell's partners grudgingly agreed that his cheerfulness compensated for the nauseating tobacco-free RJR cigarettes to which he subjected them at consortium gatherings.

In August, just three months after Giffen had recruited Chevron, he obtained the final required blessing—Gorbachev's. The American Trade Consortium was now a reality. Giffen unveiled it at a Moscow news conference and reception attended by influential Soviets, which was followed by a Kremlin dinner with executives from the American companies prominent at the head table.

Amid all the celebrating, there were some who thought the proposal somewhat grandiose. Certain members of the U.S.-USSR trade council grumbled that Giffen had sold out their interests for his personal gain and that of his company, Mercator. Yet, with Gorbachev's unambiguous endorsement, the consortium had become the biggest game in town. Seasoned traders were astounded when the Soviet leader began to enact the very laws Giffen recommended—many for his consortium exclusively, it seemed. American companies not members of the consortium, many of whom had tried unsuccessfully to tap the Soviet consumer market of 290 million people, took notice. Silcox began receiving calls from his counterparts at Mobil, Amoco, and Exxon, themselves desperate for a Soviet oil field, inquiring whether each could partner up with Chevron. "I said it was much too early," Silcox recalled. There wasn't even an oil field yet to explore.

Giffen had accomplished an exceptional feat. Granted, he had started with an advantage—Nicholas Brady's introduction. But in the end it was his idea, and he alone—armed with only a generalist's knowledge of oil and the nerve to engage some of America's most seasoned executives in a scheme of his own making—had closed the deal and won over Gorbachev. A front-page story in *The Wall Street Journal* summed up his achievement: AN AMERICAN IN MOSCOW: JAMES GIFFEN HELPS U.S. FIRMS GET A FOOT IN THE DOOR.

Keller was the undisputed boss at Chevron, but that did not mean that everyone "gripped this opportunity with enthusiasm," as a dubious executive put it. Indeed, his subordinates were worried about the chairman's speedy decision; one or two members of his board of directors were outright antagonistic to the idea. What if Gorbachev's embrace of free enterprise was some kind of ploy? Years of superpower distrust—and Ronald Reagan's denunciation of the Soviets as "the evil empire"—had made many American companies extra cautious. What if there was a repetition of the Soviets' Afghanistan adventurism: If they "started throwing bombs around, it wouldn't be good for the Chevron brand," the same skeptical executive said. The concern about Chevron's image was somewhat assuaged when members of a focus group said that they wouldn't be bothered if Chevron oil came from the Soviet Union.

Keller's overseas deputy, Silcox, still wasn't convinced: What Giffen proposed "was a business concept totally alien to any of us." Chevron seemed to be drifting from its traditional role of hard-driving oil company to one of facilitator for a banking enterprise. Ultimately, however, Chevron executives took comfort from a saying attributed to bank robber Willie Sutton. "They asked him why did he rob banks, and he says, 'That's where the money is.' When you're an oil company, you've gotta go where there is oil," Derr observed.

So it was that Silcox prepared the search for "an oil field that would generate cash in a hurry, something that would be easy to export right away to finance the consortium." First, he needed intelligence on the Soviet oil fields—which were the most promising and what challenges did they pose? A few American geologists, like former CIA analyst Robert Ebel, had examined the fields over the years and written articles and books about them. But the published pickings were slim. One of the best sources turned out to be government agencies such as the U.S. Geological Survey; its brain trust included expert Soviet émigrés who had continued to follow their homeland's oil prospects despite the apparent hopelessness of it ever opening up. They sent Chevron a thick pile of maps, including an eerie CIA satellite photograph in which a blazing fire and two plumes of smoke were visible on the northeastern edge of the Caspian Sea. The Chevron men knew the prevailing wisdom—maintenance at the Soviet fields wasn't a priority. But an inferno like this was a different matter.

In October 1987, Silcox and two deputies arrived in Moscow with a three-ring white briefing book filled with maps and recommendations. They found that, as good as his word, Giffen was "on a first-name basis with every minister." At one function they shook hands with Gorbachev himself. Giffen, immaculately attired and blowing cigarette smoke like a Hollywood star, didn't limit himself to VIPs. At the bar of the National

Hotel, across from the Kremlin, one Chevron man recalled watching their host "flirting with all the prostitutes. They were saying, 'Jimmy, you're back in town. Why don't you give me a call?' "

A Silcox-led team, Giffen, and a Gorbachev emissary whom they dubbed "Mr. Z" embarked on a flurry of meetings with Soviet geologists and oil engineers. Though translators were necessary, it became quickly apparent to the Americans that their counterparts were their scientific equals. Not only were they conversant with western oil journals and English technical terminology, they often could out-talk the Americans about Chevron's own projects, having "read everything that had ever been published" on some of them.

Much of the discussion revolved around the difficult conditions in Soviet oil fields. At Timan-Pechora in the Russian Arctic, some 13 billion barrels of oil were scattered among more than 260 fields in pockets 1,000 to 14,000 feet beneath the permafrost. The crude had a pour point of 80 degrees Fahrenheit, meaning that it would not flow unless heated—but heat would melt the permafrost.

The Soviets wondered if Chevron's proven method of controlling "sour gas" could be applied to the Tengiz oil field near the northeast Caspian Sea. A poisonous brew, sour gas is industry jargon for hydrogen sulfide, or H_2S for short. It is one of the most insidious naturally occurring substances on the planet, destroying one's sense of smell before rapidly paralyzing or killing its victim; it literally eats up any steel with which it comes into contact. (Tengiz, it turned out, was the burning oil field in the CIA satellite photograph. The flames and smoke plumes were the aftermath of an enormous blowout two years earlier, when the Soviets lost control of a well there; to contain it, they were forced to summon American oil field legend Red Adair.)

Silcox began to wonder if every Soviet field came with a shopping list of hazards. But as the talks wore on, he became more optimistic. Tengiz, where oil was first discovered in 1979, could be a prime candidate for modernization if Chevron were a partner, he suggested. The Soviets abruptly turned cool. They had enjoyed the hearty exchange of opinions, but they didn't require any western assistance, thank you very much—why, they had spent their lives drilling hundreds, even thousands, of wells in some of the world's most productive fields. "You sort of felt at all these meetings that the troops hadn't picked up Mr. Gorbachev's view of all this stuff," said a Silcox colleague.

Mr. Z came to the rescue. "You don't have a budget. You need help," he lectured one minister. The reproach had its desired effect. In a Moscow conference room four months later, a half-dozen Soviet geologists began unveiling their inventory.

The sheer number of oil fields astonished the Americans. In dozens of long meetings, the Soviets described hundreds of petroleum reservoirs from the Caucasus and the Volga all the way to Siberia. They impressed their American visitors by producing the bible of oil geologists—seismic maps showing the outlines of the reservoirs, with well logs revealing their precise scientific characteristics. However, it was unclear how many wells had actually struck oil.

The Soviets were enthusiastic about American participation in one field—Timan-Pechora, to which they flew the Chevron team several times for a firsthand look. The early Siberian fields were built up mostly by prisoners confined to a string of Stalin-era concentration camps. The workforce included experts in oil field technology who, like Zeynalabdin Tagiyev's granddaughter Sophia and her petroleum engineer husband, were shipped there in cattle cars. While the experts eventually were permitted to move on, the prisoners were kept behind to work the oil fields even after finishing their long sentences. Khrushchev later burned down the camps, the outlines of which were still visible.

The weather was bitter cold when the Chevron men visited, but they were always greeted warmly. In Arkhangelsk (called Archangel in English), the Americans were seated on a horse-drawn sled, and costumed children danced and sang for them. At Kogalym, a proud roughneck showed off the miles of cattle, greenhouses, and barns that made residents self-sufficient, shielding them from the fallout of a collapsing nation. Alcohol was poured liberally; as the Americans mugged for a home video at their hotel one morning, one quipped, "The guys haven't had any vodka in at least two or three hours. I think they're getting the shakes."

Out in the oil fields, the picture was sobering. One Chevron visitor observed that "if a pipeline leaked, they repaired the leak but didn't clean up the spill," and pools of oil would gather. Unfinished tree logs were fashioned into wellheads. Workers injected excessive amounts of water into the ground to push oil to the surface, causing harmful flooding and ruining otherwise enviable fields. Wells were everywhere, often within a hundred feet of one another, "to suck the oil out as fast as possible," noted one of the Americans. But the practice was shortsighted, he said, like putting "ten straws into a can of Coke."

The Soviet oilmen seemed to harbor no illusions about what they had inherited. Their leaders had become smug during fifteen years of big oil finds in the Volga-Ural region, West Siberia, and Kazakhstan; as former Soviet oil minister Lev Churilov wrote, "exploration and production equipment stood frozen in time, with few technological advances after the 1960s." Although the Soviets exported some 2 million barrels of oil a day, almost all of the profit was absorbed by the insatiable military. "While we were developing one of the richest oil provinces the world has ever known, we were also bankrupting our country," Churilov observed. Indeed, the visiting Americans initially rejected any deal involving these fields, telling the Soviets "not only no, but hell no." Still, they were impressed with the Soviets' ability to make do and their obvious skill at finding oil and producing it in prodigious volumes. Moreover, the Americans felt that these were Russians with whom they could work. "It seemed the Cold War was really over," thought Bill Crain, John Silcox's boss, who led one journey.

As the relationship warmed, Chevron arranged a visit to America for the Soviet oilmen, whose past travels typically had been limited to Eastern Bloc countries, usually as soldiers in Poland or East Germany during the compulsory two-year army service. Chevron's red-carpet hospitality in the United States had left some "literally shaken." Almost none had ever seen a five-star hotel, much less stayed in one, or ordered lunch from a diverse menu that actually corresponded to what was in the kitchen, or rented a car. One Soviet official wanted to sample some American-made martinis, then struggled to follow the bartender's spiel. Would he like vodka or gin? Rocks or neat? Olive or onion? Vermouth, no vermouth? "He was flabbergasted by the choices," a companion said.

The visitors were also bowled over by western-style business practices, what one called the "incredible organization of labor." They were awakened at five A.M., served breakfast at six, and then put in a thirteen-hour workday crammed with meetings and oil field and laboratory tours. After ten days of this, "we simply could no longer stand, we were so tired," one Soviet participant said. As a reward, Chevron whisked them off on mini-vacations to the *Hornblower* dinner ship for a cruise around San Francisco Bay, to Jack London Park, to Disneyland. The famous California amusement park made the group "as happy as children"—particularly "Pirates of the Caribbean"—and "unfathomably grateful to the company that did this for us." Yet that was only how the Soviets spoke among themselves. To their Chevron hosts they rarely betrayed any satisfaction.

The Americans, meanwhile, were growing restive. No one could be sure of Soviet reliability or predict Gorbachev's staying power. To commit enormous sums in such a politically risky climate, Chevron had to be assured of a field that promised huge rewards. That meant a "supergiant," in industry parlance, a field holding a minimum of 1 billion barrels of recoverable reserves. Giffen, arguing on behalf of Chevron, said that it could not be a field that had been fouled by sloppy practices. After some foot-dragging, the Soviets offered Korolev, the "King's Field," a pristine reservoir in the Soviet republic of Kazakhstan, near the wells pioneered almost a century earlier by the Rothschilds, the Nobels, and Henri Deterding.

The Americans were familiar with Korolev—it was part of the same general geologic structure as Tengiz, the field pictured in their satellite photograph. A year earlier, the Soviets had unfurled seismic maps of the area. The Americans distrusted Soviet estimates that Korolev was a supergiant of 1 to 2 billion barrels. But it easily could contain 750 million barrels, which would qualify it as a still-respectable "giant."

As for Tengiz, the Soviets continued to declare it off-limits because, as a senior official told the Americans, "We're just getting ready to turn it on." But its promise tantalized the Americans. Both they and the Soviets believed it contained 10 billion barrels, which would make it one of the world's ten largest fields. Seismic maps revealed Tengiz as Korolev's more beautiful sister, a huge carbonate reef with a column of crude 1,500 feet tall. Chevron geologists, accustomed to oil fields in the Gulf of Mexico,

Nigeria, and West Texas with columns ten to thirty feet in height, were agog. Even Saudi Arabia's Ghawar, the largest oil field on the planet, one that had produced more than 30 billion barrels of oil since its 1951 inauguration, now had an oil column not much taller than 200 feet.

To jog Tengiz's perimeter would require running two marathons—it was about twelve miles wide and fifteen miles long. One senior Chevron geologist compared it with a mountain not far from the San Ramon, California, offices of Chevron—3,850-foot Mount Diablo. He calculated that if one sawed through Mount Diablo at its base, then turned it upside down and buried it far underground, such that its tip reached a depth of 15,000 feet, that mountain would be Tengiz. Geologists called Tengiz a "reef" because that's how it appeared underground, like a tropical Caribbean reef. At first, some 310 million years ago, it was much farther south; if there had been palm trees, they would have grown within this reef. Indeed, some admiring Chevron geologists considered Tengiz a "perfect oil field." Well, not truly perfect—a truly perfect reservoir would be a large cavern that needed merely to be tapped. But that almost never happened—none of the world's supergiants was such a pool. Instead, like most oil fields, Tengiz's subterranean appearance was that of solid rock. Yet its limestone only looked solid—under a microscope, one could see that 6 percent of the stone was pore space. That's where the oil was contained, in the pores, the residue of sea organisms crushed together, the water squeezed out over time until there was a mile-thick section of oil-saturated stone. This oil column was part of what made Tengiz so ideal. But it was only one of its virtues. The enormous volume was combined with high pressure—12,000 pounds per square inch—that served as a natural propellant; unlike Ghawar, which was under so little natural pressure that workers had to inject 7 million barrels of water a day into the reservoir to force the oil to the surface, Tengiz would probably never require such artificial measures.

The final ingredient was the seal—the material that kept the oil from migrating elsewhere. At Tengiz, the oil was contained by a salt crown—a perfect seal. Nothing could escape. The salt—six hundred feet thick at some spots, four thousand feet elsewhere—was the result of the Caspian's evaporation over time; until about ten thousand years ago, the sea had reached far into Russia and across what was now Kazakhstan, accounting for the region's flatness. Subterranean pressure had made the salt perfectly pliable, like toothpaste; when one drilled into it, the salt easily traveled straight up the well bore. Meanwhile, however, it wholly confined the oil.

Other formations in the region also fascinated the American oilmen. The reefs containing Korolev and Tengiz were only part of a larger, oblong-shaped atoll that had yielded major discoveries to the northwest and northeast. Chevron scientists studying the Soviet seismics were especially intrigued by a line that stretched from Tengiz into the sea, to the atoll's western edge. It seemed to indicate the presence of another field offshore containing two subterranean reservoirs, each two to four times the size of Tengiz, or a minimum of 40 billion barrels of oil.

The Soviets were willing to consider some western investment in the area—early in 1988, industrialist Armand Hammer announced plans to build an $8 billion petrochemicals plant there, using Tengiz feedstock. But every indication was that western oil interests would not be welcome in the North Caspian. A classified 1989 CIA report made clear why: The region's petroleum riches were critical to Moscow's strategic future. As had been true since before the Bolshevik Revolution, the country relied on oil income to stay afloat. Soviet production was starting to decline in its existing oil regions—West Siberia and the Volga—and a new Klondike was needed. "Only one new oil region has this potential—the North Caspian Basin," the CIA reported. The agency's own estimate for Tengiz was 18 billion barrels of recoverable oil, and the North Caspian as a whole a stunning 30 to 50 billion barrels, or three to five times the size of Alaska's Prudhoe Bay.

As Chevron executives processed what they had learned about Soviet oil fields, their appetites grew. Soviet strategic sensitivities aside, if the company couldn't have Tengiz, it wanted those huge offshore reservoirs. In the meantime, it would dispatch geologists to see Korolev for themselves. Although the King's Field alone would not be enough to satisfy Chevron, it could always be part of a package.

The inspection of Korolev required a plane flight to the local capital of Guriev, named for the Russian trader who in 1645 established it as a fishing village. The Americans encountered a dry, dusty place built on a white, largely treeless plain and reliant mainly on two industries, oil and caviar. Guriev's clayish soil was so soft that houses slowly sank into the earth. Most streets were unpaved, and many residents had no drinkable water much of the time. By the look of things, the surrounding countryside, inhabited mainly by camels, hadn't changed since the time of the Rothschilds and Deterding.

But the main attraction during the visit turned out to be Tengiz itself. Soviet oilmen, anxious to show off the field, took the Chevron geologists there on a side excursion. When their tour reached Well No. 37, the Americans appreciated why they had been supplied gas masks and briefed on what to do in case of a poisonous gas leak. On June 24, 1985, the well had exploded when oilmen lost control of the reservoir's immense pressure, sending a 623-foot column of oil skyward and spewing a cloud of sour gas. The Soviets did the only thing they could—they set it ablaze, converting the gas instantly into far less dangerous sulfur dioxide and, *Izvestia* reported, avoiding a "continuing flow of unburned toxic gas [that] could poison every living thing within hundreds of kilometers." Still, it was "scary to work there," said a local oilman. The blaze, so hot that water boiled 150 feet from the well, looked as "tall as a fifty-story building" to a visiting French technician and was visible on the steppe some hundred miles away. The ground was littered with the charred remains of ducks that had burst into flames on their way to the marshes abutting the Caspian. The roar from the escaping hydrocarbons overwhelmed the ability of rescue crews to hear one another. All in all, an estimated 34 million barrels were lost before the well was contained some four hundred days later. Amazingly, only one person died, a Ukrainian worker who wandered too close and was sucked into the inferno.

Yet, far from being embarrassed by the disaster, the Soviets appeared proud because, in the words of a Chevron visitor, the blowout had demonstrated that "they were on to a major oil field." As souvenirs, they gave the Americans small pieces broken off from an acre-size pond of hardened oil resembling obsidian—the residue of the accident.

Senior executives of the oil company calculated what it would take to modernize the Tengiz operations. John Silcox, for one, was familiar with squalid field conditions. The son of a Socal chemist, Silcox grew up in a central California oil camp surrounded by decrepit derricks and oil puddles. Though that was four decades earlier, at Tengiz he observed similarities. Safety equipment, for instance, "consisted of a couple of sacks of sand and a shovel." High winds at times blew the shoreline inland thirty miles, submerging part of the oil field and the "very sophisticated equipment [that] can't operate when there is water over it."

The region was peopled by Kazakhs, always mindful of their duty to lay on the hospitality for visitors. Sagat Tugelbayev, an astute and diminutive local leader with years of oil field experience, called a shepherd friend. "Clean up your place and make some *beshbarmak*," Tugelbayev instructed him, referring to the Kazakh dish of flat noodles and lamb. The Chevron delegation arrived in jeeps, and soon a traditional banquet was in full swing, including the presentation of a cooked sheep's head to the guest of honor—Silcox. Tugelbayev instructed the oil company executive how to honor tradition—cut off one of the sheep's ears for a child and remove an eye as a gift "to someone who is supposed to look after everyone." Silcox dutifully handed the eye to Tugelbayev, after which everyone drank *shubat*—camel's milk—and went swimming in the nearby Emba River.

The next day, Silcox flew into the Kazakh capital of Almaty. It was more than a sightseeing trip; he was mindful of the need to build relationships with local leaders rather than relying entirely on his connections with Soviet officialdom.

As he had expected, the Kazakhs told him that the oil fields were theirs; Kazakhstan may be part of the Soviet Union, they said, but Moscow had no right to decide anything unilaterally. The decades of Russian imperiousness over Soviet minorities were deeply resented. The Kazakhs, a Central Asian people unrelated to the Russians by race or language, were particularly sensitive about the environment. They distrusted Moscow-ordered commercial activity on the Caspian, home to the giant sturgeon, from which caviar is produced. And they were livid over nuclear testing in the northern region of Semipalatinsk and the resulting two generations of deformed children.

But there was also a more concealed vein of anger. A traditionally nomadic people who migrated with the seasons with their camels and sheep, hunted with eagles, and lived in round tents called yurts, the Kazakhs were forced by the Soviets in the 1930s to settle down and learn to raise crops. Stalin brought modernization to the Kazakhs—paved roads, universal education, industrial jobs, and equality for women. (When Yuri Gagarin became the first man in space, his craft was launched from the Soviets' sole launching pad—Baikonur Cosmodrome, located in Kazakhstan.) But Stalin also wrought personal ruin. An estimated 1.5 million Kazakhs—a third of the native population—starved to death, were executed, or fled to China, Turkey, and Afghanistan during this period. Stalin used the sprawling land of temperature extremes as a second Siberia: He exiled hundreds of thousands of political and ethnic rejects to the republic, including the entire population of Chechnya, relocated en masse in 1944. In the 1950s, Khrushchev launched his Virgin Lands program, shifting tens of thousands of Russian and Ukrainian settlers to Kazakhstan with the aim of dramatically increasing the Soviet grain harvest. The Kazakhs became a minority in their own land, ruled over by ethnic Russians in every sphere. Kazakhstan became one of the most Russified of the fifteen Soviet republics: In the populous capital, many Kazakhs grew up speaking only Russian and knew next to nothing of their own language or history. Even in 1987, Russians regarded Kazakhstan as "really just oil and fish," and the Kazakhs recognized that only Tengiz had gained them new respect in the national capital.

At this point, the Kazakh claim to sovereignty was wishful thinking more than anything else. But Silcox played along, advising his hosts to insist on a seat at the negotiating table. In fact, the next time Chevron had talks in Moscow, a Kazakh would be there.

Months later, the Kazakhs escorted Silcox's boss, Bill Crain, up the Ural River, which flows into the Caspian from the northeast. Sturgeon used the river to reach a spawning ground. One of the oilman's hosts hooked one of the fish, sliced it open, and removed a "glutenous bag of raw roe," as Crain described the moment. The man slapped the caviar on the table, steam rising from it in the cold; spoons in hand, "everyone dug in." The scene was no mere show: The Kazakhs hoped that the demonstration would persuade Chevron to stay out of the offshore zone rather than risk harming the cherished sturgeon's habitat.

But Chevron believed the area could be drilled safely, so it dispatched a company executive named Dale Wooddy to convince local officials. Wooddy knew his way around oil fields—his father was an Exxon man, and in college he himself had worked in the oil patch every summer and Christmas. So he was at ease escorting a Soviet delegation to Chevron's off-shore platforms in the Gulf of Mexico near Louisiana. The men could see a hundred feet below, to where ling fish fed on shrimp growing on the mostly submerged oil-drilling platform. Issued a fishing pole, one Soviet official caught a thirty-pound ling. Still, one Soviet minister was convinced that the platform was a Hollywood prop erected as a deception, and he demanded to see where Chevron disposed of its refuse. Wooddy showed them the sewage treatment plant, but the minister was still certain that "this was all just an act, that [they] were not producing oil," recalled Wooddy.

In Moscow, Kazakhstan's political leader, Nursultan Nazarbayev, seemed to side with the Americans. In an interview, he noted approvingly that "shrimp is harvested under the Chevron oil derricks." But the company still couldn't seem to transcend the environmental issue. One Soviet official said flatly, "You aren't going to be able to drill there; no one will be able to in our lifetime."

Giffen, trying to help things along, went to the top. In January 1990, he wrote Gorbachev a two-page letter proposing that Chevron lead off-shore development in the North Caspian region. If only Korolev were opened to exploration, Chevron would expect to finance ten to fifteen joint ventures of $100 million each, he wrote. But if the offshore were put into play, the payoff would be many times that, enough to finance 60 to 350 such enterprises, depending on the volume of oil discovered. "Even the Tengiz field might be included" in such a Chevron-led venture, Giffen subtly suggested.

Chevron was not so nuanced. It now stated flatly that it would not de-velop Korolev alone. Unless the company were granted rights to Tengiz or the offshore, it would pull out. The brusque ultimatum reflected a man-agement shift—and a rather stark change of personalities—at the top lev-

els of Chevron. A year earlier, George Keller had retired as company chairman; his successor, Ken Derr, championed delegation of authority. More
important, on January 1 the self-effacing John Silcox retired as well, and he
was succeeded by brash and gregarious Dick Matzke, a geologist with a
shock of white hair and considerable attitude.

Everyone involved at Chevron realized that Tengiz would be a "company maker," meaning it would transform the company overnight by increasing its reserve base by 50 percent. In the words of a colleague, Silcox
had "only wanted to do the right thing" for the company and had largely
stood aside while a Chevron negotiator haggled with the Soviets and
Giffen gave helpful nudges when the need arose. But Matzke, another executive said, was himself an instinctive and shrewd negotiator to whom
"the chance to deal was more [important] than precisely what the deal
was." The new overseas boss looked at the situation and "realized that if he
could land Tengiz, it could get him a shot at the top job," meaning the
Chevron chairmanship. Matzke brushed aside both the negotiator and
Giffen and assumed control of the talks himself. In one of his first en-
counters with the Soviets, he hardened the company's position. "Keep the
offshore. Give us Tengiz," he said. Matzke had decided that, the great potential of the offshore fields notwithstanding, Tengiz's proven reserves
made it the more attractive catch.

Though Tengiz wells were producing, the Soviets knew that they "needed
foreign help" at the field, Lev Churilov would later write. There was no escaping the profound challenges they faced; the frightening blowout at Well
No. 37 "had thrown everything into doubt." They had intended an aggressive increase in output at Tengiz, but now they wondered if their production strategy made sense. Moreover, how would they finance the badly
needed equipment upgrades? No Soviet oil operation had access to the
hard cash needed to replace existing gear, much less buy the ultra-advanced
technology required at Tengiz.

The momentum was swinging in Chevron's direction, and Gorbachev
was about to push it all the way over, even as he was beginning to lose control of his political equilibrium. Startling signs of discontent were arising

throughout the country and the Eastern Bloc. One by one, Moscow's Eastern European satellite nations confronted public demands for independence. The three Baltic republics were in open revolt against Soviet rule. Civil war had erupted in Azerbaijan. In Kazakhstan itself, public demonstrations broke out in four cities after Moscow conducted its sixth nuclear test of 1989; the Kazakh parliament demanded that the explosions be halted. And Gorbachev was in tense nuclear arms reduction talks with the administration of George H. W. Bush; if successful, Gorbachev would be able to divert scarce Soviet budget money to more critical civilian needs.

By May 1990, Gorbachev was making plans to travel to Washington and sign the arms agreements. But, as Ken Derr, Chevron's new chairman, would recall, the Soviet leader "wanted to make a splash" with something more, and Tengiz was "one of the big things they thought they could splash with." So it was that Derr visited Moscow in advance of Gorbachev's Washington trip and found that the Soviet leader "was really excited about this whole thing. He greeted me like a long-lost cousin."

A Soviet delegation was dispatched to California to negotiate a Tengiz protocol with Chevron, the first step toward opening the field to exploration. The oil company's lawyers "tormented us, day in and day out, picking on every comma in every clause" of the proposed protocol, said Churilov, who was a member of the Soviet team. But he was most amazed by the Americans' insider knowledge of Tengiz. One day, Churilov wandered alone down a corridor at Chevron headquarters. "Imagine my surprise when I saw a huge satellite picture of Tengiz on the wall," he said. "You could see every detail, even the cars parked at the side of the road."

On June 2, 1990, in Washington, Gorbachev and Derr signed the protocol, which awarded Chevron exclusive rights to negotiate for Tengiz. Or so it seemed. As it happened, another oil giant, British Petroleum, wanted the same prize and had embarked on a daring strategy to snatch Tengiz from Chevron. The chase was not over.

Crossfire

IN THE LATE 1980S, TOM HAMILTON, British Petroleum's new chief for international exploration, was appalled when he inspected the company's books. Oil reserves once totaling 70 billion barrels had dropped to 4 billion barrels. BP still produced a respectable 1.5 million barrels of oil a day but, with its holdings in Alaska and the North Sea in decline, the trend line was turning negative. In just five years—by 1993—the daily take could fall below 900,000 barrels, an alarming prospect.

Some of the loss could be blamed on a wave of nationalization that had swept away some or all of BP's oil supply from each of six countries. But company managers were also at fault, Hamilton believed. They had become complacent in the fat years, the 1960s and 1970s, when they "stopped exploring" and were satisfied "to harvest what they had." The company had a tradition of boldness; in 1901, company founder William Knox D'Arcy had negotiated the original 480,000-square-mile Persian oil concession that triggered what author Daniel Yergin called "the era of oil in the Middle East." But now, in Hamilton's view, it had become "risk-averse" and "scared to death to drill dry holes."

By the time BP executives realized they had to scramble for new reserves, the company barely possessed the talent to do it. Cutbacks in the workforce had left BP without many of its most expert oil trackers—the crusty old hands who seemed able to divine where to drill on the scantest of evidence. Hamilton regarded their replacements as "Nintendo geologists"— bright but almost wholly reliant on technology that was good, but not always good enough.

BP was not the only one adrift. The industry as a whole was suffering from an identity crisis after fifteen years of shipping embargoes, lost drilling rights, and oil field closures. Such gyrations had driven the companies to diversify. Before withdrawing in the face of ridicule, Gulf Oil agreed to buy the Ringling Brothers/Barnum and Bailey Circus; Mobil purchased the Container Corporation of America and the Montgomery Ward department store chain; Armand Hammer's Occidental Petroleum acquired Iowa Beef Processors; Exxon started making office machines; and BP went into the animal feed and breeding trades. More conventionally, a merger frenzy had erupted. Chevron paid a record $13.2 billion in cash for Gulf, Texaco acquired Getty Oil for $10.2 billion, Mobil bought Superior Oil for $5.7 billion, and BP paid $7.6 billion for the 47 percent of Sohio it didn't already own. But then oil prices went on the skids: In 1985 and 1986, they fell from more than $31.50 a barrel to less than $10.

Now a rueful industry was attempting to regain its footing. At BP, the task fell to John Browne, a German-born Briton who had been trained at Cambridge as a physicist and earned a master's degree in business at Stanford. His rise to senior management was likened to dropping "a Ferrari engine" into the heart of the company. Browne was exceedingly demanding and made it plain that "you didn't bullshit him," said Hamilton. Few in the industry could out-think him. To be sure that no one could beat him on the facts, he installed personal computers in his office before such technology was in vogue, allowing him to plumb the latest in business thinking.

His husky mentor, Bob Horton, and the elfin Browne became known as "Batman and Robin" for their practice of suddenly appearing at a BP division to dismantle and reassemble it, leaving it smaller but in better order as they dashed off to a new challenge. Now, with Horton as chairman and Browne as his overall head of exploration and production, they undertook reconstruction of the entire company. In 1987, British prime minister Margaret Thatcher had sold the state's 51 percent share of BP, making it entirely a private concern. But by then it had grown into an overstuffed hodgepodge of holdings in energy, animal feed, minerals, and finance. Controlled largely by hereditary peers, former military officers, and retired bureaucrats, BP had "the look of a miniature House of Lords," British journalist Anthony Sampson wrote. Some thought it would not survive.

Among Browne's first acts was to order a study of the most important oil field discoveries in the industry's entire 140-year history. If there were any hidden secrets to success, he wanted to know what they were. He appointed Hamilton, a professorial Ohio native with a Ph.D. in geology, to lead the review. The paunchy scientist, slow-talking and deceptively languid, liked to slouch with his stockinged feet propped up. He hardly seemed a Browne man. But then he would bound to his feet and argue a point with unassailable logic while swiftly sketching a geological structure or an economic model on a white board.

With a team of some thirty men, Hamilton figuratively "redrilled every well in the world," scrutinizing more than a thousand fields in all. They concluded that the company was following a doomed strategy. Like its rivals, British Petroleum had fallen into the habit of spending large sums for the rights to ever-smaller shares of proven oil reserves. Such an approach was very low-risk—there was little danger of drilling a dry hole. But it would never produce sufficient volumes to restore the company's health. BP had to undertake more daring explorations, to hunt only the largest elephants, as oilmen called great fields, in places previously uncharted and difficult to reach.

Company after company was reaching a similar conclusion. For example, Rockefeller's Indiana branch, now called Amoco, resolved to penetrate what it labeled "breakthrough countries," those "with high exploration potential but which have previously been, or continue to be, considered inaccessible for political, economic, operating or legal reasons." In general, the oil industry was eyeing Arab nations that in the past had nationalized western holdings; so-called rogue countries, such as Libya and Iran, put off-limits to American companies by U.S. law; and sections of Latin America. Topping almost everyone's list was the Soviet Union, the ultimate inaccessible nation, whose reserves had been closed to foreigners for almost six decades but were prized the world over.

Suddenly, Communist power collapsed in Eastern Europe, and the Soviet Union began a historic transformation. Foreign oilmen ventured into Moscow, certain that the prize was so great that they couldn't afford not to. To their delight, they were led to believe that they might be allowed considerable control over oil fields rather than be consigned to preparing the fields for exploitation by the Soviets.

It was an abrupt turnaround for the Soviets, a telling indication of how desperately they needed the West's expertise to ramp up production. Soviet oilmen accustomed to years of fat proceeds from exports of crude were now "alarmed" by the ground roiling beneath them, Business Week reported. Oil production was falling for the first time in decades—from 12.5 million barrels a day in 1987 to 11 million barrels by late 1990, the CIA would find. Though global prices had recovered, the decline had left the Soviets desperate for hard currency to prop up their teetering economy.

The oil fields presumably open to westerners were deep, troubled, and dangerous, beyond the ability of Soviet technology to exploit. That didn't worry the oil majors, whose mastery of advances in geophysics was fundamentally changing oil field economics. Houston-based oil service companies and high-tech Silicon Valley firms had installed remote devices on satellites that could sense the presence of oil, developed three-dimensional visual tools that peered deep beneath the earth, and expanded on the decades-old Soviet techniques of horizontal and multiple-direction drilling. Oil companies previously might take a peek at a suspected oil basin based on the hunch of a talented geologist but retreat if initial results were disappointing. The new technologies allowed them to do a more exhaustive follow-up and even take a second look at ground already explored. Of all the possibilities, the Caspian Sea was the most inviting "because of the size of the opportunity," Hamilton said. "The southern republics were the largest, most material plays we were looking at any place in the world."

Margaret Thatcher urged BP to move more aggressively in the Soviet Union. The prime minister, who had bet her credibility on Gorbachev by declaring after their 1984 introductory meeting that "we can do business together," urged Browne to get Britain's largest industrial concern to please "start some investment rolling." The BP boss instructed a subordinate to "get to Moscow and make something happen."

How to enter into serious bargaining with the Soviets was something of a puzzle for the foreigners. With whom did one speak? And how did one get to him? For Chevron, though it had not yet concluded the Tengiz protocol with Gorbachev, the way was being paved by Jim Giffen. Now a Denver oilman named Jack Grynberg checked into Le Meridien in London's Piccadilly Circus and sent word to British Petroleum that a special opportunity awaited.

Grynberg had a gravelly voice and a gruff yet effusive manner. He favored tinted glasses and short ties with stripes, and a belt at times dangled loose from his waist. He projected the air of a small-time hustler. Yet he had the reputation of someone not to be trifled with, a man who would quickly retaliate with a lawsuit if sufficiently provoked. It was a combativeness learned early. Born in 1932 in Belarus, Grynberg at twelve began frequenting forests near his boyhood home where members of the anti-German underground gathered. At fifteen he joined Irgun, the Jewish guerrilla group fighting to establish Israel. Grynberg's desk was cluttered with mementoes of those days: his Irgun identification card and a 1983 photo in which he posed with Menachem Begin at a "Terrorist Ball"—a New York reunion of Irgun's North American volunteers. A green bumper sticker was affixed to Grynberg's office door:

"Please God let there be one more oil boom.
I promise not to piss it all away this time."

In fact, Grynberg had not pissed away his earnings. He lived in a $2 million house on two and a half acres in Denver's wealthy Cherry Hills Village district. But he was pining for another killing. A chance encounter in 1989 at San Francisco Airport seemed to present the opportunity he sought. A man speaking Russian was objecting to being bumped from a United Airlines flight to Denver, without much success. Grynberg, who understood Russian from his childhood and was on the same flight, stepped in to help. Before long, the two were sitting together aboard the airliner. Grynberg's seatmate was a natural resources adviser to the Soviet premier, and he wished to know "how he could reciprocate" for the American's kindness. Within two months Grynberg found himself perusing boxes of Soviet geological data inside a six-story marble building on the Moscow River. The data was interesting, but to Grynberg's disappointment none of the officials he met seemed interested in exploring a deal. He returned to Denver empty-handed.

Still, the experience whetted his appetite and prepared him for what came next—a request from the State Department to host the visiting leader of the Soviet republic of Kazakhstan. Nursultan Nazarbayev's state was big in livestock breeding, and he was anxious to see how the business was conducted in America. Grynberg was pleased to oblige. His Fort Morgan spread, sixty miles northeast of Denver, was only a sideline, but it was a serious one, at times feeding forty thousand head of cattle.

The American treated the Kazakh delegation to a catered cocktail party and dinner at his elegant home. Both the guest of honor and his host were engineers by education—Nazarbayev in metals, Grynberg in petroleum. As a bodyguard lingered close by, the relaxed Communist strongman drank vodka and began to describe his little-known corner of the world. If you are truly interested in petroleum, he told Grynberg, Kazakhstan is the place for you. One field alone, called Tengiz, possessed 14 billion barrels of oil. Fourteen billion barrels? "I had never heard of Tengiz. But my eyes lit up," Grynberg recalled. "You don't have to be a genius. I thought to myself, 'This could be another Persian Gulf.' "

Days later, the two met again, this time in New York. Both were attending a dinner honoring former secretary of state George Shultz, who was to receive the Jabotinsky Award for service to Zionism. It was a promoter's dream—the right guests, the right venue (the Plaza Hotel), and Grynberg, a mover in Zionist circles and co-host of the affair, on stage with Shultz himself. The effect on the visiting Kazakh ruler was as Grynberg had hoped—this Denver rancher was evidently an important man with important friends. Nazarbayev invited him to Kazakhstan.

Grynberg made the trip in February. His plane flew along the oil-rich northeast Caspian shore, then on to Almaty for dinner at Nazarbayev's forested home. Waving off the traditional vodka shots, the American got right down to business. If you want serious development, he said in Russian, why not allow me to form an international consortium, a group of foreign companies with the money and expertise to overcome Kazakhstan's technological shortcomings? Nazarbayev expressed the usual concern for the Caspian's sturgeon. Grynberg assured him that this was no problem. If an oil spill was the worry, the consortium could construct an artificial island to guard against just such an eventuality. British Petroleum had done so in Alaska, for example. Nazarbayev had never heard of an artificial island. But he said to proceed.

Back in London, Grynberg approached an aide to BP's Tom Hamilton and described how he had the ear of the Kazakh leader and the glimmerings of a deal for Tengiz. As evidence of his credibility, he brandished photos of himself with Nazarbayev in New York. Briefed afterward, John Browne and Hamilton quickly issued an order: "Check on him." The word came back that Grynberg wasn't making it up. Indeed, the Denver man had produced more photos, this time playing tennis with Nazarbayev in Caracas. The Kazakh leader, Grynberg said, had slipped his arm under the American's and promised, "Jack, you will have Tengiz." Hamilton agreed to fly to Kazakhstan for a firsthand look.

Thus the stage was set for a test of wiles pitting two oil giants against each other. British Petroleum knew that Chevron was making advances on Tengiz with Jim Giffen's help, and Chevron would soon become aware of BP's sortie, guided by Grynberg. (At one point, Browne and Hamilton would probe Chevron's interest in pooling their efforts. While the two BP executives enjoyed "the thrill of the chase," Hamilton explained, there were substantial political risks, and "you clearly didn't want it [all to] yourself." But when Hamilton met Chevron overseas chief Dick Matzke, that gifted dealmaker sat "stone-faced" and "guarded," clearly unenthused about a Tengiz partnership.)

BP's success would depend on Nazarbayev's ability to make a disrespectful end run around Moscow and award the Tengiz oil concession on his own, even though his republic was still under Soviet rule. Chevron's success would rely on Moscow reining in Nazarbayev and standing by Gorbachev's soon-to-be-signed protocol, opening the way for Chevron to negotiate for Tengiz.

Risky as it was, BP's strategy of dealing directly with Nazarbayev was the only shot the company had. "If we were going to steal a march on Chevron, we needed to do something different, because they were in with the Kremlin," said a BP executive.

Complicating matters were unusual divisions within the Soviet bureaucracy. The Oil Ministry was lining up behind Gorbachev's pending deal with Chevron, while the Geology Ministry generally supported the notion of competition for Tengiz, and so welcomed BP's interest. One American oilman reported that the two ministries "hated each other and didn't speak." In Moscow on his way to Kazakhstan, Tom Hamilton was grilled by a suspicious Boris Nikitin, the deputy oil minister. What interest did BP have in Kazakhstan? the minister inquired. Hamilton had no choice but to stall: He could not let slip that BP intended to do what it had done elsewhere in the world—rely on local power brokers to snatch an oil field.

Then came an urgent phone call from Grynberg, who had gone ahead to the Kazakh capital of Almaty. "If you can bring John Browne, you can sign right now for the whole Pre-Caspian Basin," he said, meaning virtually all of Kazakhstan's potential oil reserves straddling the Caspian Sea, offshore and onshore. The BP men and Grynberg, not having seen any oil field data, didn't know precisely what that meant, but they could sense something substantial.

Hamilton received confirmation of the offer from Kazakhstan's envoy to Moscow, and the office of Kazakhstan's prime minister then phoned Browne. The BP chairman was willing to make the hasty trip from London but "absolutely positively would not fly Aeroflot." And he wanted his own interpreter first to accompany Hamilton to Almaty and make doubly certain that the deal was as advertised. Browne got his way. KGB officials not only granted a visa on the spot to his interpreter but also allowed BP's Dassault Falcon to be the first private jet to land in Kazakhstan since that of the Shah of Iran, who had gone there to heli-ski.

In Almaty, Nazarbayev sent his personal car to meet the visitors and transport them to a guesthouse. There, although it was 2 A.M., they were greeted by some thirty Kazakh officials and treated to a feast of jellied camel tendons, fermented camel's milk, and more. Everyone was toasted with vodka shots, including one Kazakh honored for siring five sons and no daughters, which was regarded as a notable achievement. When Hamilton's top negotiator for the Soviet Union, a devout Mormon lawyer named Rondo Fehlberg, boasted of the same accomplishment, the Kazakhs took that as "a sign that we were supposed to be there, and treated us like heroes," Fehlberg recalled.

After grabbing a few hours of sleep, the visitors gathered in front of a snooker table on which their Kazakh hosts unfurled a giant set of two-dimensional seismic charts and well logs, in effect a geological blueprint of the Tengiz field and its surroundings. Inspecting the seismic lines, Hamilton saw that some zigzagged up the coast from Tengiz, and a few drifted offshore, clearly revealing carbonate reefs. Suddenly, said Hamilton, "we saw this enormous feature.... It wasn't continuous coverage—a few lines of 2-D. But you could see the enormous reef," meaning the offshore reservoir, twice the size of Tengiz, that had so tantalized Chevron. As for Tengiz itself, Hamilton could not find the bottom of the oil column, it was so deep.

Hamilton and his companions thanked the Kazakhs and suggested they take a break. "Holy shit," Hamilton blurted out when they were alone. "These were Ray Charles kind of structures—a blind man could see what they were."

There was nothing to do but seize the moment. The BP men negotiated all night. The Kazakhs had no English-language typewriter, so the two copies of the resulting protocol—granting exclusive rights to negotiate for the Pre-Caspian Basin, including Tengiz and the offshore deposits—were typed in Russian and written longhand in English. Nazarbayev repeated that his government would sign—if Browne, who was in Moscow awaiting word on the negotiations, would come to Almaty. The Dassault was dispatched to pick up the BP executive, but when he boarded the plane, the Soviets wouldn't permit it to leave. The plane, which days earlier had taken the group from Moscow to Almaty, had been cleared to fly in and out of the national capital only once. Browne, "an important, busy, impatient man who is not used to wasting his time," stewed in a Moscow hotel built by Armand Hammer. The BP men suspected a stall engineered by Oil Ministry officials who were "smelling a rat, because we have a big shot in," Fehlberg surmised. Browne's aides finally persuaded the KGB to intervene, and the plane was cleared to depart with only an hour to spare before the testy executive was prepared to return to London.

Browne and Nazarbayev's prime minister, Uzakbay Karamanov, signed the protocol that night. Under its terms, a yet-to-be organized consortium of oil majors led by British Petroleum would negotiate with the Kazakhs for Tengiz. For Browne and Hamilton, it was a heady day. They had, it seemed, beaten Chevron to the prize.

The deal was equally pleasing to Grynberg. It gave the Denver middle-man the sole authority to decide who would be allowed to join the consortium, meaning that any oil company wanting a piece of the action would have to negotiate with him. Grynberg would soon sign up British Gas, Venezuela's Mariven, Gulf Resources of Canada, and Marathon Oil; Shell and France's Total would join later. In return for his labors, he would be entitled to a 20 percent cut of all consortium profits—potentially worth tens of millions of dollars. It was a modern-day version of deals made decades earlier in the Middle East by Calouste Gulbenkian, the legendary "Mr. Five Percent."

In their jubilation, BP executives invited Nazarbayev to visit their Alaska operations and see for himself how their company could safeguard a fragile ecology. The Kazakh president pleaded the press of business at home but sent a delegation led by his prime minister, Karamanov. Grynberg escorted the visitors around the United States on a Marathon corporate jet and looked after their every need. Karamanov was suffering from bad dentures, and Grynberg instantly arranged for a new set—at BP's expense, of course. Dentists checked his teeth in New Orleans, took imprints in Houston, and fit them in Anchorage. BP wrote it all off to the cost of retooling the flagging company.

To Karamanov, a diminutive man with sparkling eyes, Americans seemed to have forgotten the Cold War. His delegation received a warm welcome wherever it went, in New York, Colorado, San Francisco, at Disneyland. He found himself pondering why Soviet development had fallen behind that of the United States. Stalin, he decided, should have visited America. "If he had seen it, maybe [things] would have developed slightly differently. It's just that the two ideological enemies, the two systems, feared each other. There was hatred, but of course the main thing was the fear. We couldn't open up."

At the climax of his visit, on June 23, 1990, in Alaska, Karamanov signed a more formal version of the Almaty protocol. Three weeks earlier, Chevron had signed its Tengiz protocol with Gorbachev, putting it on a collison course with British Petroleum. But BP, which quickly learned of the Chevron signing, was not dissuaded. There was a sense that the ground was shifting beneath the feet of the Soviet rulers and that Gorbachev might not be able to maintain absolute control. Republics like Kazakhstan could be on the verge of becoming their own power centers. BP was betting on Nursultan Nazarbayev and his Kazakh government.

The first sign that something might be amiss for BP came three weeks later. Nazarbayev himself suddenly showed up in the United States, flown there at Chevron's expense and escorted by its astute Kremlin-connected adviser, Jim Giffen. *The New York Times*, publishing a photograph of the Kazakh leader provided by Giffen, described Nazarbayev as "a one-man chamber of commerce . . . trying to convince Americans that his mineral-rich region would be a good place to do business." Nervous British Petroleum executives wondered what it all meant.

Then the other shoe fell. In Moscow, geopolitical concerns had begun to drive events solidly in Chevron's favor. The Soviet leadership was coalescing around the idea that a deal with Chevron, and no one else— certainly not a non-American company—was "a precondition for any improvement in relations [with] the United States." Gorbachev also still believed fundamentally in Giffen's consortium of blue-ribbon American companies and its potential for reenergizing the Soviet economy. On meeting Chevron's chairman in September 1990, Gorbachev "paused, grabbed [Ken] Derr's hand, and declared, 'We expect a lot from you.' " The end came swiftly. BP's Hamilton was summoned to Moscow. "We can't stop you from doing this deal with the Kazakhs," Deputy Oil Minister Nikitin said with his usual military bearing. "But if you proceed, you will never get a deal in Russia. And just try to get your oil out." With equivalent drama, Giffen implored Nazarbayev to abandon BP, warning the Kazakh leader that he was risking his republic's future, that "if we scare off Chevron, then not a single western investor will ever come."

Nazarbayev prepared to cancel the deal; before he could act, British Petroleum threw in the towel. But BP emerged with an important consolation prize: The Soviet Oil Ministry agreed to smooth the way for its entry into the legendary Azerbaijan oil region of Baku. Tom Hamilton figured his company had escaped relatively unscathed. Besides Baku, there were other very inviting oil fields in Kazakhstan where BP might later be able to gain a foothold, including the offshore region; the disagreeable Nikitin had said nothing about those. Of course Grynberg retained his contractual rights; if BP ever did a deal in Kazakhstan's resource-rich west, it would owe him a share of the profits.

Nazarbayev did not seem especially distressed by the outcome. He wanted his republic to have a larger say in the exploitation of its resources; he also wished to test Moscow to see how far he could go in that direction. In the end, he could have insisted on a deal for BP. But his government and other foreign oil companies hungry for deals in Kazakhstan seemed likely to suffer mightily at Moscow's wrath, an outcome he was not prepared to risk.

The Kazakh leader was inexperienced, but not unschooled. A convivial former steelworker with a flair for both local politics and global diplomacy, he had gained favor in the Kremlin in recent years by helping to defuse anti-Soviet protests in Kazakhstan. He had exchanged his Communist Party persona for that of a Kazakh nationalist and would soon be recognized as the Soviet Union's third-strongest political leader, below just Boris Yeltsin, his Russian counterpart, and Gorbachev himself. Journalist David Remnick, writing in *The Washington Post*, would describe Nazarbayev as "an essential power broker and soother of egos," sufficiently sophisticated during Soviet political battles to have "pushed Gorbachev toward a more resolute course of change and Yeltsin away from the temptations of impulse." Washington was intensely aware of his talents. Secretary of State James Baker characterized Nazarbayev as an underestimated man to whom more attention was due—"a careful, intelligent figure, one who understands practical politics."

The American government had observed the Tengiz proceedings with interest, notwithstanding the disingenuous claims of some officials that they had kept their distance because of conflict-of-interest concerns. These were men with close ties to the energy industries, such as Baker, a lawyer prominent in Texas oil circles. A decade later, he would assert that while serving in the administration of President George H. W. Bush, he "was recused on energy matters, so was not into any of the deals." Reading the word *Tengiz* aloud from a typewritten question, he pronounced it with studied slowness, as though encountering an unfamiliar name. In fact, Baker had been an avid follower of the Chevron deal. At a Moscow meeting with Giffen and U.S. ambassador Jack Matlock, Baker posed the most fundamental of a seasoned oilman's questions—what oil price would make the deal profitable? Eighteen dollars a barrel, Giffen replied. "At that time, the spot market was $20, so it didn't seem so unreasonable," Matlock recalled. Halyk Abdullayev, Kazakhstan's chief negotiator, said he met Baker in his Washington office three times to seek advice on the deal, and Chevron chairman Ken Derr regarded the secretary as "very, very supportive."

But the deal's biggest fan in the administration may have been the president, himself a former oilman. "Chevron had asked us to say something to Gorbachev," recalled Brent Scowcroft, then Bush's national security adviser. "The President basically said [to Gorbachev], 'Look, you want American investment. Yet you've been negotiating with Chevron a long time. Nothing is happening. There is no better way to attract investment than to sign one big contract. Chevron is one of our biggest companies.

That would be a sign to other companies that you can do business here.'
He mentioned it maybe once, maybe twice, to Gorbachev."

Nor did Bush do so reluctantly. In July 1991, Derr stopped by the
White House for a fifteen-minute photo opportunity and a brief chance
to get Bush "up to date." Bush had a better idea. "I would love to talk to
you about your negotiations with the Soviets. . . . Are you free for lunch?
Today?" the Chevron boss recalled the president saying. Then, said Derr,
"he calls Scowcroft and the three of us went down to the White House
mess, as they call it, and I sat there for an hour and a half and went
through the whole deal, where we were and what we needed."

After vanquishing British Petroleum, an emboldened Chevron pushed
hard to cement its claim on the riches of Tengiz. The company "inundated
us with faxes and telegrams," a Soviet official groused, and some detected
a "commanding intonation" in its corporate voice. When Soviet underlings seemed slow to produce answers, the company invoked Gorbachev's
name. And when Chevron suddenly announced that it wanted both Tengiz
and the offshore territory, and the Soviets balked, arguing that "Tengiz
was quite big enough to keep them busy for 50 years," Chevron threatened
to "abandon Tengiz altogether," former oil minister Lev Churilov would
later write. "Out of their briefcases came document after document, supporting their arguments, all signed by Soviet officials who had no business
to be approving such matters."

It was no secret that Chevron wanted to generate profits as quickly as
possible, but Soviet officials thought the company's behavior was bordering on the impulsive. From the seismic tests, the offshore reservoir looked
enormous, but the presence of oil inside had not yet been proven—a cautionary note in an industry legendary for "mother lodes" that ultimately
produced little more than water. Even Tengiz, alluring as it was, came with
some caveats. The most important was its profitability, no small matter to
Chevron's stockholders. The company's investment would be colossal, an
estimated $10 billion to develop the supergiant, but it had yet to complete
a fundamental examination of the venture's commercial merit.

Among the Chevron specialists now assigned to perform just such a top-to-bottom appraisal was Sandy Cornelius, a Scottish-accented mechanical engineer who made the taming of poisonous gas seem a poetic pursuit. The white-haired Cornelius had spent years managing a showpiece sulfur-removal plant for Chevron in Evanston, Wyoming. For many months, Cornelius had been escorting a parade of Soviets through his operation in an effort to demonstrate that sulfur decontamination could be carried out safely. The next thing he knew, he was on his way to Tengiz itself, part of a twelve-man team that would inspect the field's sulfur equipment, not to mention its drilling rigs, wells, railway lines, power generators, boiler plants, pipelines, and so on.

Cornelius arrived by plane in the west Kazakhstan provincial capital of Guriev (since renamed Atyrau) in July 1990. As his Chevron colleagues had observed a year earlier, the seaside city struck him as "a sorry place" where "there weren't paved roads or anything." Yet the group felt warmly welcomed, particularly when the local Party newspaper splashed three photographs of them on the top half of the front page, a clear endorsement.

A helicopter ferried the Chevron team to Tengiz, and as it prepared to land Cornelius could make out the two sulfur-removal plants that he had come to inspect. The plants were enormous zoos of angled pipe and cylinders, each resembling an oil refinery in the final stages of construction. Two more were planned. Because the Soviets themselves lacked sufficient expertise, they had imported Hungarian specialists, who in turn had employed a Canadian-Italian-French consortium to build the units. Together, the four plants would be capable of cleansing the sulfur associated with four hundred thousand barrels of oil a day, a respectable performance. But work on the plants had nearly ground to a halt because the Soviets were having trouble finding the money to pay for it.

There were additional reasons to be discouraged about the state of affairs at Tengiz. The sole sources of electricity were a dozen ancient turbines bolted to railway cars that "looked like something out of a German concentration camp in the last big war," Cornelius recalled. The more than ten thousand workers at the site endured severe conditions, in sharp contrast with the comforts that Ludvig Nobel had provided his workforce a century earlier. Even the privileged ones like Cornelius who bunked at an exclusive residential camp could count on running water just two hours a day. The camp's boiler was so rusted that the showers flowed brown; Cornelius would emerge from bathing with the appearance of a suntan.

Soviet management practices dismayed the Chevron team. "The administrative processes are broken," Cornelius recalled the team concluding. "Their logistical processes are broken. They have bad values." Cornelius was taken aback by the nonchalance with which some Soviet managers discussed their crews, how on one past project " 'we only killed so many people,' like that was successful." It didn't sit well with the westerners to hear oil field fatalities described so clinically. As far as Cornelius was concerned, "You don't kill anybody. That's just not allowed."

But the promise of the place exhilarated the American oilmen, and they returned to California convinced that "this is something big. This is a company changer." As an understated Cornelius put it: "There is enough natural resource here from what we've seen and what we've read that this is worthy of pursuing as an idea."

In its formal report to Chevron executives, the team praised the technical know-how of the Soviet bosses at Tengiz, whatever their shortcomings as managers. "This is not a third-world intellect. This is a first-world intellect," the report said, echoing the sentiments of John Silcox, the former Chevron overseas executive. It cautioned against "running up the beach and planting the American flag, teaching people to speak English and technology that they don't know and dominating the population."

Chevron's deputy chairman, J. Dennis Bonney, "an oil statesman" with the composure of "a senior professor at a college," listened to the presentation without betraying any emotion. Yet "there seemed to be quite a bit of excitement" from the others, who "just soaked it up," Cornelius recalled.

Chevron was ready to proceed.

While the Tengiz field was drenched with hydrogen sulfide, the poison was almost entirely confined to its natural gas; the reservoir's estimated 10 billion barrels of recoverable oil were virtually untainted. Once the gas was extracted, Tengiz would yield oil of extremely high quality—at the upper end of the world's best crudes. Its oil was much better, for example, than that at Saudi's Ghawar, history's largest oil field. The distinction is crucial, for crude oils bear a unique fingerprint, differing as much as single-malt whiskeys, and are priced accordingly. The most prized are those that produce the most valuable end products—gasoline, benzene, jet fuel.

To make each, refiners and chemists manipulate all manner of technical factors, which in the end can be reduced to a matter so fundamental that it can't be debated: carbon atoms. For example, to produce gasoline typically requires a crude molecule containing five to ten carbon atoms, the much-prized octane molecule being smack in the middle at eight carbon atoms. The slightest variance can produce a much different substance, such as naphtha, a less valuable raw material for chemicals. Manufacturing jet fuel requires eleven to thirteen carbon atoms, or the result might be diesel, a decidedly inferior fuel. A refiner can adjust the chemistry, crack or blend the molecules with those of other crudes, to come up with the desired product. But the most highly prized crude is that which yields the most lucrative fuels without requiring so much handiwork. And that was Tengiz. Its properties were inherently excellent for both gasoline and jet fuel, which was why Chevron expected it to command a 10 percent or greater pricing premium over many other crudes.

It was understandable, then, why Chevron was aghast when it learned how its crude would be transported from Tengiz. Rather than being provided with a dedicated oil pipeline to a seaport tanker terminal, Chevron would have to dump its crude into the Soviet pipeline system. There, it would be commingled with "Urals blend," an inferior export composite of various Soviet grades. Chevron demanded that it be compensated for the insult to its product; Tengiz crude, after all, "was the difference between selling 22-karat gold and 24-karat gold" and presumably would make the Urals blend more valuable. But the Soviets stood fast. In their minds all the component crudes in Urals—light Baku oil, heavier West Siberian grades—were mere parts of a whole and should be treated as such. Why single out Tengiz?

Dick Matzke, negotiating for Chevron, eventually moved on to other issues. He and others on his team knew that the only genuine solution would come some day in the future when, as they saw it, a pipeline would have to be built to link Tengiz directly to a tanker terminal on the open sea.

Much of the talk between Chevron and the Soviets had to do with technical matters: how to split profits, set tax rates, exchange rubles and dollars. But one issue surfaced repeatedly, and that was the environment. Angst over the Caspian sturgeon inspired new and sometimes dubious claims of peril. One Kazakh official said he feared that drilling deep into the earth could allow a tremor from earthquake-prone Iran or Turkey to travel more than six hundred miles to West Kazakhstan and "swallow half the province." (The same official offered an imaginative, if impractical, solution to the poisonous gas—dig a hole thousands of feet into the reservoir's salt dome and install the sulfur-processing equipment there.) Though some environmental complaints sounded peculiar, and some seemed a guise to slow down or halt the western rush into the Soviet patrimony, Chevron had to treat the ecology seriously. For if there were a single major accident, the company risked expulsion; notwithstanding the Soviets' own sorry environmental record, public opinion would not abide a disaster caused by foreigners.

The oil company's negotiators did their best to defuse such worries, voiced most persistently by the same Kazakh official who had imagined half the province in ruins from a quake. Then they got an unexpected opening. Chevron's Dale Wooddy happened upon a microphone behind a picture in his hotel room. Its wiring led to the adjoining quarters of a Soviet team member who had "kind of acted like the typical KGB kind of guy." Rather than confront the Soviets, Wooddy elected to turn the bug to Chevron's advantage. He motioned his team to follow him outside, where he whispered his plan. They would return to the room and stage a fake "strategy session" while the Soviets eavesdropped.

Back inside, Wooddy led what seemed like a routine discussion. Then he singled out the Kazakh official who had been most pesky about the environment and issued a forceful warning. If that official continued to be a problem for Chevron, "we are going to break off talks. We aren't going to do the deal, and we'll go home." The next morning, the offending Kazakh

took a different seat, one in a corner, where he sat silently for the remainder of the talks. Wooddy relished the results of his deception, and "it
wasn't the last time we pulled that trick."

In Almaty, the Kazakh leader Nazarbayev unhappily concluded that "we
had been sidelined" in the Tengiz discussions, as an aide put it.
Nonetheless, he had a "hunch that Tengiz was going to be the instrument"
with which Kazakhstan could leverage some independence from Moscow.

Nazarbayev was not alone in harboring thoughts of independence.
The hinterlands were awakening, and oil regions in Soviet republics distant
from Moscow were wondering whether obedience to the central government was to their benefit. Once, any official in these outposts who failed
to execute orders from the Kremlin could expect to receive a "wolf's
ticket," meaning he would be ostracized. Now, Moscow was "losing its
grip on the republics," just as it "ran out of money" for the republics, a
Chevron executive observed.

In October 1990, the Kazakh parliament declared the republic sovereign, a symbolically important gesture. Almost all the Soviet republics were
doing so, but it was a measure of the times that such gumption had arisen
in Kazakhstan, the largely passive repository for Stalin's exiled peoples.
The western press took note, describing Nazarbayev as "a Marlboro-
smoking metallurgist" who was "decidedly unrebellious" but demanded
that "the locals get their cut." Nazarbayev's newfound stature reached the
attention of Chevron, which invited him to visit the United States. Halyk
Abdullayev, Kazakhstan's voluble chief representative to the Tengiz talks,
recalled it as the time he "had the luck—or bad luck—to meet Mr. Giffen
for the first time."

These were heady times for Jim Giffen. His organization of leading
U.S. companies, the American Trade Consortium, was still in business.
Chevron, his most important client in the group, had withstood the chal-
lenge from British Petroleum and seemed to have Tengiz all to itself. In his
role as middleman par excellence, he moved easily between American and
Soviet officialdom. In fact, listening to him talk, it was understandable that

some mistook him for a kind of superdiplomat operating at the behest of the U.S. government, the Soviets—or both. He nurtured the image by brandishing supportive letters from Bush, then the same from Gorbachev. Kazakhs who needed convincing were told that even their official Soviet counterparts in Moscow "didn't have the kind of access to the Kremlin that Giffen does [in addition to] access to the White House. . . . He told me that repeatedly," Abdullayev said. The Kazakh negotiator came to believe that Giffen's consortium had been "formed by a special order of President Bush." He wasn't alone. Some Chevron men, too, thought that Giffen's consortium enjoyed official Washington sanction. John Peppercorn, Chevron's vice president for chemical production, who went on a 1987 trip to Moscow, considered the American Trade Consortium to be "a U.S. government–sponsored effort. We were part of seven companies asked to go over." In fact, Giffen's organization possessed no U.S. government sponsorship of any type.

Giffen, of course, thrived on such ambiguity and reinforced it at every opportunity. Kazakhs visiting his New York office on the Chevron-sponsored tour gazed at a wall covered with photos of such notables as President Bush, Secretary of State Baker, and Treasury Secretary Nicholas Brady, Abdullayev said. "I even saw his picture with Ms. Condoleezza Rice," at the time a member of Chevron's board of directors. Gesturing toward the display, Giffen promised that, with him as their ally, the Kazakhs would be introduced to such political heavyweights, not to mention the elite of corporate America—"big and significant people" like the heads of RJR Nabisco, Coca-Cola, and more. And he delivered.

In San Francisco, Chevron arranged for Nazarbayev to deliver a speech before local foreign policy specialists; after hours, the president delighted in wandering about on his own, surprising a Chevron couple in the elevator to the penthouse Cornelian Room, where dinner was being served. But most of the Kazakhs felt overwhelmed. Not only were there "all those huge skyscrapers, all that huge, stormy life . . . [meetings] with leaders of companies whose budgets are half of the budget of the Soviet Union," but there was Giffen himself, who "had no problem talking with all those people, hugging, shaking hands, calling them by their first name," recalled

Abdullayev. Though "to a degree he is an actor," the Kazakhs came away believing that if they wished to be taken seriously by important people in America, Giffen could make it so.

In fact, Jim Giffen had become the essential man for all sides. He had ushered Chevron to the Korolev fields and had then urged that "if we are going to risk, it was better to risk big"—meaning change gears and try to snag Tengiz. And it was Giffen who had put the topic on Gorbachev's radar screen, which led to Tengiz being offered to the company. As the talks drifted into 1991, it was Giffen who nudged senior Bush administration officials to apply gentle pressure to Chevron and the Kazakhs, and Gorbachev to have his underlings be more flexible. None of that was acting.

The Tengiz deal began to look like the only silver lining in an immense dark cloud that was forming over the Soviet Union. The previous December, Gorbachev's demonstrative foreign minister and partner-in-arms, Eduard Shevardnadze, had dropped a bombshell in parliament by quitting. With the resignation came a warning from Shevardnadze: "Dictatorship is coming." No one knew precisely what the "Silver Fox" had meant by that, only that it sounded ominous. Gorbachev's power was slipping, and the economy was worsening—in April, Giffen's old mentor Ara Oztemel had to step in and financially rescue the Bolshoi Ballet's first U.S. appearance in sixteen years. Gorbachev and others regarded Tengiz as "the Soviet Union's trump card in the game for the future," Russian economist Yegor Gaidar would later write. Against that backdrop, Chevron and the Soviets signed another document filling in more details of their agreement. Then fresh challenges arose.

A Soviet "committee of experts" was appointed to evaluate the contract. It was directed by Gaidar, a little-known academic who attracted much attention when, in a Moscow meeting chaired by Giffen, he delivered a ringing denunciation of the proposed deal. Later, meeting face-to-face with Chevron in California, Gaidar posed "questions after questions after questions after questions, [and] you just got the feeling it was just never going to happen," said Ken Derr, Chevron's chairman. Under the contract, Gaidar said, "Chevron would end up owning one of the world's richest oil fields without taking on any clear-cut obligations in relation to our country." The newly assertive Soviet press echoed Gaidar's assertions, saying that the country risked being "plundered."

Separately, Nazarbayev made his own dramatic move. Writing Gorbachev, he declared that "Kazakhstan would henceforth take control of the field." Gorbachev, who needed Nazarbayev's help in holding together the Soviet Union and staving off the increasingly powerful Russian leader Boris Yeltsin, had little choice but to consent. In late July, Nazarbayev convened a special meeting at the Kazakhstan mission in Moscow. There, he informed Chevron's Matzke how things were going to be. The Kazakhs were now in charge of Tengiz, and the laboriously negotiated agreement with Chevron was null and void. Nazarbayev "could not accept a deal that had been done by the Soviet Union." While Matzke "didn't understand and wanted the old terms," he at last had to accept that "things are changing," Giffen recalled. The agreement would have to be renegotiated.

It was a frustrating time for Chevron's hard-charging "golden boy." Dick Matzke had joined the company in the early 1960s as a young geologist, and unfailingly impressed his superiors. Bill Crain, his boss in the early years, recalled Matzke undertaking a task that might take weeks, "but he did it in seventy-two hours, and it had the meat of what you were looking for." Matzke "always had a sense of confidence, knowing where he's going and what he's doing." Another Chevron executive recalled that the young Matzke "was a schmoozer and could talk to anybody." A decade later, he had earned an MBA by going to classes at night, after which he let his colleagues know that he no longer wanted "to be considered a geologist. He wanted to be considered a dealmaker."

In 1984, the presidency of Chevron Overseas became open. Matzke felt that he deserved the job and "made a stink" when it went instead to John Silcox. Five years later, Silcox retired and Matzke was tapped to replace him. Crain, also his boss in the Tengiz negotiations, thought that Matzke had "special skills," that he was someone who got things done by building "relationships all over the place, outside the company. . . . We'd get faxes twenty-four hours a day. He kept two secretaries busy all the time. He does not tire. He could work twenty hours a day." Matzke's imperious style irritated some colleagues, but "he had so many talents that I wouldn't even think of replacing him," said Crain.

A week after Nazarbayev had claimed Tengiz for Kazakhstan, President Bush was the honored guest at a Kremlin dinner. At the intervention of the Kazakh president, Giffen was invited to attend. He watched as Soviet prime minister Valentin Pavlov sauntered over to Nazarbayev and asked, "When are you closing [a deal for] Tengiz?" "We are working quickly," the Kazakh leader replied. "Well, do it quickly. I need the money," the prime minister said, bursting with laughter.

In fact, Gaidar's challenge, along with the new assertiveness of the Kazakh leader, had for the moment brought new negotiations with Chevron "to a dead end." The talks adjourned with an understanding that all parties would return to the bargaining table in the fall. Gorbachev embarked on a replenishing Black Sea holiday in the Crimea. Giffen stopped off in Almaty, where Nazarbayev assured him that he had adequate time to go fishing as planned in Montauk, New York. Yeltsin himself appeared in Almaty not long after, and he and Nazarbayev retreated for some fresh air along the banks of a mountain stream. Derr, the Chevron boss, left for his yearly vacation at his Lake Tahoe cabin.

On August 18, 1991, a small group of Communist Party hardliners isolated Gorbachev and his family on their Crimean estate and declared a state of emergency. While the attempted putsch collapsed in just days, it set in motion the events that would lead to the breakup of the Soviet Union four months later and independence for its republics. Nazarbayev, though he sought autonomy for his republic, proceeded with care. At fifty-one years old, he had the acute practicality born of a childhood raising sheep in the mountains and riding a donkey to buy bread in the nearest town. Among his earliest memories was family talk of the fateful year of 1929, when the Soviets forcibly settled Kazakh nomads, and, as he observed, "the animals died without feed and care in the collective farms, and the people died of hunger."

An independent Kazakhstan would never again "consent to be the appendage of another region, and [it] will never be anyone's 'little brother,' " he would later write. Yet he also saw economic advantages if the republics were to band together in a post-Soviet alliance, and he worked to promote that idea while edging slowly toward total autonomy. Finally, he could no longer "hold back. It was necessary to move" along with the crowd, he told his prime minister, Sergei Tereshchenko. On December 16, 1991, Nazarbayev declared Kazakhstan to be an independent state, the last leader of the fifteen constituent republics to abandon the Soviet Union. Still reluctant to part with his accustomed world, on that same day he brought together leaders from eleven of the former republics, who agreed to join him in forming a new, looser grouping called the Commonwealth of Independent States, or CIS. Ten days later—on December 26—the Soviet Union officially perished.

Through the ensuing turmoil, Giffen managed his usual bravado. It was not his consortium but the Soviet "hard-liners" who were sunk, he said, and a new government would have "a chance to replace the dunces with reasonable, experienced people." That belied the unmistakable fact that the conditions under which Chevron had entered the Soviet Union four years earlier no longer existed. Watching the news in Lake Tahoe, Derr turned to his wife, Donna, and said, "Well, I guess we can forget about that Soviet deal."

Still, Giffen did not entirely misread the situation. Nazarbayev knew he needed a deal on Tengiz. A sovereign Kazakhstan was without cash, and it needed to build international alliances that would strengthen its independence. And so the Kazakh leader wrote to Derr, suggesting that they resume negotiations. Derr's reply was positive, and a new round of talks got under way.

But the atmosphere was uneasy, noted Chevron negotiator Dale Wooddy. The Kazakhs had "a real feeling of vulnerability," a by-product of their seven decades of subservience to Moscow. If the talks were to progress, it would be necessary to create "a feeling of comfort." Which is where Giffen again stepped in. First, he persuaded Matzke and his team that they could strike a deal "that would work for us" commercially. Then he went to work on Nazarbayev, establishing himself as "independent verification that we were not going to screw them" and promising that the company would "be there for the long haul," as Wooddy put it. Any time the Kazakhs complained that the talks were stalling, Giffen in New York would ring Nicholas Brady's or James Baker's office and instantly arrange a face-to-face meeting in Washington. Baker, responding to Abdullayev's pleas, would call Derr and say, "It cannot be like that. You need to meet once again." Whatever doubts the participants may have had about Giffen, such interventions "made both parties understand that this was a deal they needed to do," said Wooddy. After that, "it was just numbers."

Giffen's methods sometimes backfired. At dinner in Moscow, he leaned over conspiratorially to the gregarious Morley Dupré, Matzke's new chief lieutenant in the talks. "You ought to become chairman of Chevron," Giffen confided. He seemed to be suggesting that if Dupré would only "follow his path and do the Tengiz deal, that was [the] path to become chairman of Chevron." Dupré was nonplussed. "If I were to become chairman," he thought, "it wouldn't be because of outside influence." A Chevron lawyer said later that others had heard "that line" from Giffen as well. While grateful for his services, the Kazakhs, too, at times felt manipulated, a feeling that "Giffen was never on our side . . . even though he was constantly stressing that he was on our side," said Abdullayev, their chief negotiator.

Giffen's casting as the essential man did not impress Matzke, who rather imagined himself in that role. In fact, the two of them were remarkably similar. In appearance, they could have been cousins, resembling each other in looks and build—shorter than average, athletic and stocky—and the way they routinely swaggered into rooms with body language that insisted they be the center of attention. In character, they were also from the same mold—vain, egotistical, and insecure men who had short fuses but could exhibit infinite patience and even humility when needed; shrewd men who regarded themselves above all as dealmakers and possessed the personal magnetism to carry it off. Ultimately, there wasn't "enough glory in any deal for the two of them to share," summed up one Chevron executive.

Asked about Giffen fourteen years later, Matzke flashed back to the original transfer of corporate power to Derr and himself, when he was informed that "the most important person in my life would be Jim Giffen. Derr and I didn't agree. I instantly hated him. . . . I just sized him up as someone who did business differently from how I was trained. He was ethically a different person. It was just a feeling."

It wasn't hard to persuade Derr, the low-key Chevron chairman, to fire Giffen. He had no affection for middlemen, and he felt that Giffen's value had all but run its course. Now, Derr "demanded from us that Mr. Giffen be removed from the negotiation process on this project," Abdullayev said. The Kazakhs complied, and Matzke made it official in a letter written a month after the Soviet Union's collapse in December 1991.

Giffen could take some satisfaction in knowing that under the terms of his agreement with Chevron, he still had a big financial stake in Tengiz. "This released me from my obligation but left Chevron's intact," Giffen said. Derr's deputy, Dennis Bonney, knew that was true "but couldn't do anything about it." That obligation—a payment to Giffen of 7.5 cents for every barrel of Tengiz oil that Chevron produced—would be worth tens of millions of dollars to the vanquished dealmaker once the deal was consummated, particularly when the company reached its projected exports of 750,000 barrels of oil a day. But there was no mistaking the severe damage that had been done to Giffen's standing as a result of the Soviet Union's demise. His painstakingly built life in the geopolitical fast lane had suddenly come to a grinding halt.

With Giffen out of the picture, Matzke seemed to have rid himself of middlemen. But another was about to appear on the horizon, a Dutch entrepreneur who would become as crucial to Matzke's pursuit of Tengiz as the despised Giffen had been.

CHAPTER 9

The First Deal

JOHANNES CHRISTIAAN MARTINUS Augustinus Maria Deuss was a legend in the oil industry. The Dutchman made his first fortune in the 1970s and was soon recognized as the world's premier oil trader, moving more than a million barrels a day in his own tanker fleet. He smuggled crude to apartheid South Africa in the 1980s in defiance of a worldwide embargo and made a quick profit of more than $300 million in an opportune sale of a big U.S. refinery and gas station chain. Now this granite-willed bargainer was on the hunt for new opportunities.

Deuss was a resolutely private man, guarded in his conversations with outsiders and protective of his close-knit and lucrative relationships with the important and the powerful. Those who met him were impressed by his unfailing courtesy, his European courtliness, and his ramrod self-confidence. He conducted business in the strictest secrecy. When negotiating an agreement, he demanded that he deal only with those empowered to make a decision; he would not bargain with subordinates on the other side of the table, no matter their rank. He was a man in constant motion, frequently off to Paris, Muscat, Oslo, London, or New York in his private jet, often negotiating the takeoffs and landings himself before handing over the controls to his pilot.

His style generated an air of mystery that, combined with his business daring, made him appear a renegade to some. One oil trader claimed that Deuss had an ugly scar crossing one side of his face. Another said he noticed nothing unusual about Deuss's face—but did think the Dutchman wore a toupee. The truth was that Deuss did have a large scar that began at his nape and created a bald spot on the back of his head, the result of a nasty accident with explosives as a teenager. Otherwise he appeared wholly ordinary—fit and boyish, slight of build, with longish, brown hair parted on the side, flapping over his high forehead. But he could create a presence with his usual entourage—two English sheepdogs, British bodyguards, and tall, striking female assistants.

Those around him said he had a tender side. When one of Deuss's dogs was suffering from an ailing tear duct, "in the middle of a meeting, he'd put tear drops in its eyes," said an associate. But more often he displayed intensity and competitiveness, riding championship jumping horses and practicing karate. "I would not get on the tennis court with him without a bulletproof vest," an acquaintance said.

It was Deuss's unfailing intuition in business matters that made him an ally of the ruling dynasties of the Middle East, in particular the royal family of Oman. He had earned the Omanis a premium on their oil by smuggling it to South Africa, leading to a relationship of trust. Later, his highly profitable deal for the U.S. refinery and gas station chain purchased from Atlantic Richfield had whetted the Omani appetite for diversification. But they needed someone to show them the way. So it seemed only natural that the Oman Oil Company be formed in 1991, jointly owned by the country and the company's chairman, John Deuss.

In the autumn of that year, Deuss sent three aides to scout oil-related opportunities in Malaysia, Indonesia, Algeria, and, finally, the Soviet Union. In Kazakhstan, they visited Tengiz and, as one of them recalled, took careful note of Chevron's ongoing negotiations for "this 7- to 8-billion-barrel field and no way to get its oil out." The three Deuss men very quickly sensed that they had struck pay dirt; whoever developed and controlled a pipeline system that would allow Caspian oil to flow unimpeded to the West would make a fortune. It was "the principal industrial opportunity" here, concluded one.

Deuss was sufficiently impressed with their findings to head for Kazakhstan himself and further explore the possibilities. On a stopover in Moscow, a serendipitous introduction to the chief oil negotiator for the Kazakh government gave him an opening he had not expected. It was all the doing of an octogenarian White Russian Frenchman named Alex Moskovich. A year earlier, with the approval of the Gorbachev government, he had brokered Kazakhstan's first exploration deal with a foreign company, awarding Paris-based Elf Aquitaine the rights to look for oil in virgin territory northeast of the Caspian Sea. Like Deuss, he was stopping off in Moscow. So was Halyk Abdullayev, the Kazakh oil negotiator. The Frenchman looked up his Kazakh friend and extended an invitation: Come meet an interesting acquaintance of mine, a European businessman who is also here.

Abdullayev soon found himself seated across from Deuss, who identified himself as a personal representative of the Sultanate of Oman. After some conversation, the two realized they were both headed for Almaty, the capital of Kazakhstan. "We ended up on Mr. Deuss's personal plane," Abdullayev recalled. "As we flew, we started talking." His greatest worry for Kazakhstan spilled out—an oncoming calamity of hunger. It was a nation of traditional livestock herders whose diet was based on meat, a land populated by 10 million cattle, 40 million sheep, 2 million horses, and 3.5 million pigs. But a severe winter and a poor harvest had left the republic critically short of the corn and barley needed to feed the livestock. Moscow, in turmoil after the attempted putsch against Gorbachev, had sent no money to buy grain from abroad. If the herds starved, so might the Kazakhs.

Don't worry, Deuss said, he would arrange financial help. The sultan of Oman is a personal friend, he explained, and "for him a $100 million credit would present no problem." A meeting was quickly arranged in Almaty with the Kazakh prime minister, Sergei Tereshchenko. Deuss took the opportunity to suggest ways that the republic could expand its oil industry and trigger a welcome influx of dollars. The no-nonsense prime minister said that might do for the long term, but first things first—what about our livestock? Deuss repeated his pledge, that the sultanate would be happy to provide a loan. After all, Kazakhstan was already producing enough oil—sixty thousand barrels a day from Tengiz alone—to make it creditworthy.

The Kazakhs were uncertain what to think. They had raised the animal feed issue during the ill-fated negotiations with British Petroleum, only to be rebuffed. Now here was a stranger, a European moreover, portraying himself as the representative of a vaguely familiar Arab nation and freely offering the needed cash. The portly Tereshchenko was dubious. He had already done some homework and had learned of the Dutchman's reputation in some quarters as a shady character. Himself a wily product of the predatory Soviet system, the Kazakh leader also knew that altruism was not what had motivated Deuss. The Dutch dealmaker could end up extracting "tens, hundreds of millions of dollars" from the republic in the way that "all businessmen worked," Tereshchenko thought. Yet Kazakhstan had been "thrown into the sea" by circumstance and simply "didn't have the time to look from side to side at who is who," he concluded. "We had to count on any help."

Deuss flew Abdullayev to Oman, where the Kazakh oil negotiator was ushered in to meet the sultan, the country's oil minister, and Deuss's very good friend, Qais Abdulmonim al-Zawawi, the powerful deputy prime minister for finance. It was apparent that Deuss was close to all three; whatever anyone could say of him, he wasn't an impostor. Three provisional documents were signed. One declared friendship between the two nations. A second effectively made Deuss the Kazakhs' adviser on all oil matters. And the third provided for the loan, to be repaid in Kazakh oil, as

Deuss had suggested. A few months later, the money began flowing. Abdullayev, for one, was astounded by the rapidity of it all.

Deuss grew up in the small town of Berg en Dal, a suburb of the Netherlands's oldest city, Nijmegen, whose preserved Roman walls abut the Waal River and the German border. The grandson of a physicist and son of the manager of an Amsterdam automobile plant, he dropped out of school at seventeen and worked briefly for his father before assembling his own modest empire, a network of filling stations, a taxi service, and a Citroën dealership. When he overreached, trying to launch a competing Japanese assembly plant and dealership network, he lost everything. Through a friend he turned to a new venture: oil trading.

At first the business was only moderately remunerative, what with a barrel of oil selling for less than $2.50. But his enterprise, named JOC for John's Oil Company, found itself perfectly positioned when in 1973, the industry was abruptly transformed: Arab-Israeli hostilities broke out, and Arab producers imposed an oil embargo. In the resulting panic, buyers seemed willing to pay anyone almost anything to satisfy their desperate need for crude. They soon found that the young Deuss had a knack for the split-second decision-making and cutthroat tactics required to outwit rival traders.

Sometimes his considerable nerve got him into trouble. In 1977, he refused to make good on a $101 million Soviet oil cargo he had bought. Deuss argued a technicality, that the Soviets had violated banking rules because only one official had signed the required documents and not two. When international courts disagreed, assessing a $100 million penalty on top of the disputed sum, Deuss claimed he had been "tricked" and vowed to appeal. Carl Longley, the onetime aide to Jim Giffen at Satra and now an overseas representative for Ara Oztemel's oil-trading firm, stumbled across the Deuss escapade and actually ended up playing a bit role in its denouement.

Longley dropped by the Soviet foreign trade office in Moscow one day to bid on a fifty-thousand-ton load of oil aboard a tanker in the Black Sea. To his surprise, he learned that "some mystery buyer" had beaten him to the cargo, someone willing to pay ten cents a ton more. Soon, though, Longley became suspicious. Satra colleagues in New York, without knowing its history, had purchased the very same tanker load at a port in Maine for less than Longley's original bid. If appearances were to be believed, the mystery buyer was swallowing a huge loss, made worse by the cost of transporting the oil 4,500 miles from the Black Sea to Maine. It made no sense.

Satra executives tipped off Soviet investigators, who learned to their embarrassment that the "mystery buyer"—actually John Deuss—had duped them. Deuss had bought the oil using a bank-issued letter of credit, good for ninety days. He then sold the oil and pocketed the proceeds— then, at the end of the ninety days, he defaulted on the letter of credit. Other than the shipping costs, he had paid nothing for the load of crude. That had led to the Soviet lawsuit.

According to Longley, the Soviets were sufficiently angered to "do in" the Dutchman. But Deuss put a story out that he was financed by the CIA, and that reportedly was enough to cause the Soviets to back off. Longley described it as "some sort of 'mad' rule that they didn't kill off one another unless absolutely necessary." A Deuss aide said that a KGB contact finally got the Dutchman "out of his jam" with the Soviets, and an out-of-court settlement was reached.

The 1979 Iranian Revolution indirectly led to a new windfall for Deuss—and even more notoriety. In the aftermath of the revolt against the shah, Iran stopped exporting oil. Its action severely affected South Africa, whose white-supremacist policy of apartheid had made it the target of a global oil embargo under the aegis of the United Nations. The shah's willingness to skirt the blockade had kept the beleaguered country supplied with oil. Now South Africa was scrambling to find a new supplier—and Deuss was willing and able to oblige.

Sometimes operating under false documents and clandestinely transferring oil from one tanker to another on the open sea, he shipped some 115 million barrels of Arab crude to South Africa from 1979 through 1983, according to one investigation. The Shipping Research Bureau, an Amsterdam-based anti-apartheid investigative group, documented his evasive tactics in one 1980 transaction. It began with the Norwegian tanker *Havdrott* filling up in the Gulf, then embarking for a listed destination of

Bahrain, a major refining center. Along the way, it "sailed alongside the partly loaded Danish tanker *Karoline Maersk*," into which "the oil cargo of the *Havdrott* then was pumped into the *Karoline Maersk*" through large hoses. The empty *Havdrott* continued on to Bahrain, where it picked up another crude shipment, while the *Karoline Maersk*, scrapping its stated destination of Singapore, went "directly to South Africa ... to deliver its entire oil cargo." Since the South Africans paid a $2.50- to $4.50-per-barrel premium on top of the oil and shipping price, Deuss earned between $280 million and $500 million during the period.

His willingness to defy the blockade angered anti-apartheid activists, and in 1985 a heretofore unknown group calling itself Pyromaniacs Against Apartheid set his Berg en Dal home ablaze. The ever-composed Deuss continued to dismiss the embargo as "counterproductive to correcting the sociopolitical problems in that country." Nevertheless, two years later he renounced the South Africa market because "the change we had hoped for has not come about. We don't believe in sanctions. They will not work. But that does not mean we have to continue trading with South Africa."

By now he had built an organization that was deep with expertise. He had scouted Harvard University's business school for young talent, hiring three promising graduates, including Michael Fowler, a decorated Vietnam veteran from Houston who would become a key aide. He recruited former senior Arab officials and others who "knew everyone in the Middle East," ensuring that Deuss would be "well connected" there, a Deuss associate recalled. The Dutchman also became an important client of Theodore Shackley, a retired thirty-year veteran of some of the CIA's most legendary—and sordid—missions. Shackley, who now did investigations on his own, was assigned to unearth intelligence that "helped Deuss in his dealmaking" in South Africa, the Middle East, and elsewhere, according to a Washington journalist.

For years, oil-producing countries had been dominated by the "Seven Sisters"—the big U.S. and European energy companies that ruled the world oil business. Now these countries were learning how to earn more— by selling to Deuss, so that "instead of Shell being the price setter, they had an alternative," said a close aide.

More behemoth deals followed, earning and losing Deuss fortunes. In 1985, he paid the fire-sale price of $192 million for Atlantic Richfield's Philadephia refinery, along with its 576 service stations in Pennsylvania and New York and a 986-mile pipeline system. The purchase caused a stir when a friend, the oil minister of the United Arab Emirates, appeared at the opening ceremonies, feeding rumors that Deuss was not buying the system for himself but as an agent for the Persian Gulf country's interests. Yet Deuss dived into the new business, renovating service stations, launching a fresh marketing campaign, and even reconfiguring the chemical formulation of its products. Just three years later, he sold it to the Sun Company for a whopping $513 million, more than doubling his money.

The rapid cash turnaround was masterly, but some of its glow was dimmed by the unfortunate results of a gamble on North Sea Brent crude just months earlier. Betting that supplies would be tight, Deuss had bought all but one of the forty-two cargoes of Brent oil available in a two-week period during January 1988. But rivals detected his move and quickly unloaded their excess oil on the market, causing a glut. The Dutchman would lose some $200 million.

As Deuss consolidated his fortune, he assumed the accouterments of European gentry. He bought an estate in exclusive New Canaan, Connecticut, and a horse farm of rolling meadows in elite West Palm Beach, Florida, calling both Windsome Farms. By one associate's count, Deuss owned 170 champion jumping horses between the two spreads and his main residence in Bermuda. He also bought a ski lodge and half a mountain in fashionable Jackson Hole, Wyoming, and continued to maintain the family's repaired stone-and-brick home in Berg en Dal, where his younger sister Tineke lived.

The Deusses were Berg en Dal's wealthiest residents. In town, a shopkeeper, explaining why Deuss's number was not listed in the phone book, simply smiled and rubbed his thumb and forefinger together. To reach the villa, one turned right from Berg en Dal's tiny downtown (three restaurants, all closed for lunch, an auto parts store, and two hotels) onto Postweg, a long, meandering road with deep forest on either side and occasional sightings of deer or livestock through the trees. The road led to a castle, visible beyond a dark, gated entrance. Although there were no men in balaclavas, it was the very picture of a Mafia don's hideout. Video cameras were posted on either side of the black electric wrought-iron gate. A British-accented voice on the speaker box informed any unexpected visitor that Deuss was not home. "Leave your business card on the gate," it said with finality.

Guests invited to one or another of his residences found John Deuss to be a supremely hospitable host, although not exactly garrulous. He often flew them in, aboard a pair of luxury Gulfstream jets, or ferried them around the Caribbean and along the U.S. East Coast on *Fluertje*, a 150-foot yacht large enough for formal dinners on deck. Even in such settings, he seemed to be "business, business, business," said one visitor.

Some, however, saw a different Deuss, particularly those who met him in the 1970s, when he and his wife, Krystyna, an authority on Guatemalan culture, were a fashionable couple. One who befriended him then was Suzan Mazur, a stunning blonde from New York who in 1974 stepped into modeling when her journalism career temporarily waned. As she told it, Deuss launched a New York line of designer evening dresses called Alexandra Christie, and his manager hired Mazur to model them. One night, she and Deuss dined as part of a foursome at Lutèce, an exclusive French restaurant around the corner from his midtown Manhattan office. Over select Taittinger champagne and Cuban cigars, Deuss and a male business associate impressed her as "a highly entertaining and unique duo." In Bermuda, she remembered, Deuss stood "Bogart-like, at the wheel of his cruise boat attempting to sing the popular Lebanese song 'Susannah.' " He confided the details of the rooftop explosives accident that caused his scar, causing her to think that "it had to be one of the defining episodes of his life. At age fourteen he looked into the face of death and won."

But even as he spent freely on fine estates and thoroughbred horses, life as an oil trader was no longer as satisfying as it had once been. Deuss began looking for a larger role, something akin to that played decades earlier by J. P. Morgan, Sr., who had seen himself as a civilizing force in international finance, ready when needed to stabilize the markets and forestall panic. Deuss's own vision was to stabilize the oil world; he would do it by forging a grand alliance of oil-producing nations, OPEC and non-OPEC alike. United, they could better coordinate production and soak up excess supply in times of surplus, he thought. Though the super-cartel didn't materialize, a front-page story in *The Wall Street Journal* reported that "Mr. Deuss . . . is described as a 'statesman' of world oil by acquaintances." After all the years in the trenches, John Deuss had begun to cherish the idea of being above the fray, grooming his horses while powerful oilmen, financiers, and government officials sought him out.

In Kazakhstan, Deuss's first task as the government's oil adviser was to help move along the Tengiz talks with Chevron. Right away, it seemed apparent that the oil company had had its way when the financial formulas were first calculated. The Kazakhs put the blame on the general ineptness of Soviet officials who had overseen the earlier proceedings, now out of the picture. Kazakh negotiator Abdullayev "discovered to [his] horror that there was not a single lawyer in the Soviet delegation negotiating with Chevron . . . let alone a single qualified translator." Instead, "Chevron's lawyer drew up all the documents" and did "all the financial calculations." Abdullayev concluded that some of the numbers were fundamentally unfair, especially a provision granting Chevron 28 percent of the profit, a share that seemed excessive.

Kazakhstan, it was decided, needed some experienced international advisers to hold its own with Chevron, and two were hired—the venerable J. P. Morgan as investment bankers and Britain's Slaughter & May as lawyers. Deuss himself would act as technical adviser and have the last word on all terms—apart, naturally, from Kazakhstan's supreme leader, Nazarbayev. By February 1992, the team was ready to proceed.

The new round of talks with Chevron got off to a disagreeable start. The company had insisted that all parties sign a standard confidentiality agreement, meaning that anything heard or read during bargaining was to remain a secret. But J. P. Morgan refused. Dick Matzke, the Chevron chief, then obtained a confidential letter that soured him even more on the bank's participation. According to the letter, the bankers "had a side deal with

Kazakhstan" that promised J. P. Morgan $250,000 for every quarter of a percentage point knocked off of Chevron's profit split. Under the agreement, if no oil pact could be settled within six months, the bank "would have the exclusive right to peddle the deal" to other oil companies on the Kazakhs' behalf. To Matzke, the inescapable conclusion was that J. P. Morgan's "incentive was for there to be no deal." He managed to exclude the firm from the talks, at least for the time being.

Distrust ran high. Matzke and Abdullayev at times were acid toward each other. The Chevron team also was wary of Deuss—"There was always the rumor that he was being hunted down by a hit squad," said one of its negotiators—but conceded that the talks tended to make more progress when he was around.

Among the Dutchman's favorite tactics was a luxurious version of shuttle diplomacy, hauling everyone off to Jackson Hole, West Palm Beach, Connecticut, London, or Paris for a time-out to cool tempers. After all, said one oil executive, these were "multibillion-dollar negotiations at the highest level, covered in the press, [in which] the tension is really on." At Jackson Hole, Deuss would ski down a slope with Matzke, then separately with Abdullayev. Indoors, he would place the Chevron team in one room, the Kazakhs in another, and flit between the two.

Another method to "take the edge off" was a traditional one: women. No matter where the talks were, Deuss flew in beauties from the London, Paris, and New York offices of a modeling agency he owned. The women represented a startling range of nationalities and often spoke two or three European languages. When negotiations broke for the evening, the tall, elegant models joined the men. They engaged in relaxed conversation with the Kazakhs and Americans and danced with any who were in the mood. A Chevron man remembered that Abdullayev "always had a sweet thing on his arm." All parties—the Americans, Deuss's subordinates, and the Kazakhs—seemed to tense up when asked years later whether things ever went further. Perhaps—probably—they didn't. If they did, no one was talking.

Even with Deuss in the role of facilitator, an agreement continued to be elusive. The Kazakh team rejected Chevron's demand for 28 percent of the profit, offering 13 percent instead. On March 3, Abdullayev threatened to find a new suitor should no deal be signed by the end of the month. The talks dragged into April with his ultimatum still hanging in the air. Late in the month, Chevron submitted a counteroffer; Abdullayev found the terms so deficient that it put "the realization of this project into serious doubt."

Progress at times seemed so slow that Chevron chairman Ken Derr wearily observed, "I don't know where it's going to go." A deal for Tengiz was assuming even greater importance for his company, where year-to-year profits had fallen for the fourth straight quarter, and analysts were demanding to know why Chevron was spending so much on unrewarding U.S. oil fields. Meanwhile, Nazarbayev, the Kazakh president, was under pressure of a different sort, trying to fend off nationalist complaints that he was about to hand over the country's treasure to a foreign oil company. Lowering his guard with Daniel Sneider, an American reporter, Nazarbayev assailed former Soviet colleagues in Moscow who, he said, had staged "a campaign in the press ... saying this is the plunder of Kazakhstan." He pledged not to approve any deal that was "disadvantageous to Kazakhstan."

Deuss stepped in, and a whirlwind round of negotiations ensued, ending with everyone being flown to Almaty in his Gulfstream (after stopping on the way to the airport to pick up one of his girlfriends). The truth was, nobody wanted the talks to fail. Nazarbayev was about to make his first post-Soviet visit to Washington, including a meeting with President George H. W. Bush. Expectations were high that the Kazakh president would use the occasion to sign the deal with Chevron for Tengiz; without it, Nazarbayev would be entering the White House empty-handed, so to speak. But neither could the oil company expect a bargain.

Deuss advised Nazarbayev that "he needed to give Chevron a take-it-or-leave-it deal. If they did not take it, we would assist the Kazakhs in finding a new partner," an aide recalled. Kazakhstan put its final offer on the table, and Matzke agreed to compromise on the key issue of profit—Chevron would accept 20 percent. The parties had split the stubborn difference separating them almost straight down the middle.

On May 18, 1992, in a formal ceremony at Blair House, President Nazarbayev and Chevron's Derr signed what was called a "foundation agreement"—not a final contract but a statement of terms. The details would have to be ironed out in talks to follow. Yet for Chevron it was cause for celebration—after five exhausting years, there was light at the end of the tunnel. As for Nazarbayev, the following day he had his working lunch with President Bush.

The final round of negotiations took ten months, during which time the Chevron team had an oilman's equivalent of a near-death experience. At the end of one session, Matzke made the rueful discovery that he had inadvertently agreed to let the Kazakhs run Tengiz. His colleagues were mystified and unsure how to repair the damage. One of Chevron's bottom lines was that it wanted to be in charge—in industry parlance, to be the "operator" of Tengiz. After all, the company had solid experience managing big, complex oil fields, and it feared a "friggin' disaster" should the Kazakhs be left in charge. "I thought it was a deal breaker," admitted Morley Dupré.

It was Deuss, counselor to the Kazakhs, who got Chevron out of its self-imposed jam. He proposed a form of joint management in which the most senior jobs would be distributed by nationality: Chevron would appoint the general director, the Kazakhs the deputy general director; Chevron would appoint the manager of operations, the Kazakhs the manager of public relations. The effect was to restore Chevron's upper hand. "Deuss was able to convince [the Kazakhs] that what we eventually ended up with was a reasonable way to operate on a day-to-day basis that wouldn't cause gridlock," said Dupré.

When fresh disputes threatened, the bond that had formed between Nazarbayev and Chevron chairman Ken Derr seemed to have a calming effect. Derr could mix well with dignitaries like the Kazakh president. At Chevron, he was seen as "totally strait-laced," a sentimentalist when it came to the company. Like most big U.S. corporations, it had its codified business principles, called "the Chevron Way," and Derr "felt all Chevron people should live" according to them. He had a subordinate fit the declarations onto a laminated card, which he kept triple-folded in his jacket pocket. Sometimes he would "take it out and weave it into his presentation," one executive said. His comfortable relationship with Nazarbayev perhaps came about because both men were able to distance themselves from the negotiations. So it was that, in quick order, "Derr showed up, they go to Nazarbayev's retreat, spend the afternoon together, then have dinner, and everyone is happy with one another."

On April 6, 1993, the final agreement was signed. Kazakhstan had laid the economic foundation for genuine statehood. Chevron had restored its standing as an oil multinational, in a single stroke raising its worldwide reserves by 50 percent. Both owed much of their success to two remarkable individualists: the brash American Jim Giffen, whose 1987 brainstorm set in motion the events that led Chevron to Tengiz, and the suave Dutchman John Deuss, without whom the negotiations might well have foundered.

After everything they had been through, the Chevron executives decided they respected Deuss. He "was not a benevolent arbiter," yet he had served both sides and had been "able to sway the Kazakhs," so wary of trickery that they might otherwise have refused to sign anything, said a Chevron executive. Indeed, Dale Wooddy, the Chevron negotiator, concluded that "most bad stories about Deuss are a bunch of crap" and continued to admire his capabilities.

Close scrutiny of the final agreement revealed that Matzke had built into it some important financial rewards for his company. One complicated provision had to do with marketing and currency procedures that would benefit Chevron. Another made him especially proud. He had managed to link the payment of a deal-closing bonus for the Kazakhs to resolution of the stickiest remaining issue: the development of a dedicated pipeline from Tengiz to a seaport oil terminal. The bonus amounted to $450 million. But most of it—$420 million—would not be paid until the pipeline was completed and in operation, a huge and costly undertaking that Chevron seemed content to leave in the hands of the Kazakhs. Talking strictly in terms of cash out of pocket, Chevron had obtained the rights to the world's sixth-largest oil field for a paltry $30 million. That was "where Chevron outsmarted the Kazakhs," said Giffen, who thought himself a better negotiator than most.

Perhaps. The pipeline would be critical to Chevron's need to move its oil to the West in large volumes; the existing Soviet lines could accept only sixty thousand barrels a day versus the seven hundred thousand a day that Chevron contemplated for Tengiz. Without the higher volume, Tengiz was hardly worth owning. And only a dedicated pipeline would allow Chevron to keep its high-quality Tengiz crude from being tainted by the Urals blend. Wooddy said that some on the Chevron negotiating team, including himself, thought the pipeline so important that provisions for its development should have been made part of the final agreement. But Chevron's most senior executives did not agree.

For the moment, such concerns seemed academic. Several months before the final agreement was signed, John Deuss had moved to seize control of the pipeline project. The Kazakhs had awarded Oman Oil—the company jointly owned by Deuss and Omani royalty—exclusive rights to develop the Tengiz export pipeline. Operating completely in the open, Deuss then added Azerbaijan and Russia to what he called the Caspian Pipeline Consortium, which one industry newsletter dubbed "the world's hottest pipeline project." Even at that point, Chevron could have tried to negotiate an equity share, but its executives appeared not to be "ready to do the pipeline."

Deuss's team concluded that the company had expected "the Kazakhs would fall on their butt, then Chevron would step in," build the line, and dictate especially favorable terms for the transport of its Tengiz crude, said one associate. But, while appreciating the Dutchman's work on the oil deal, Matzke and other senior Chevron executives had failed to appreciate the full dimensions of Deuss's shrewd thinking and hardball instincts. The Dutchman now was poised to control the movement of Chevron's oil to western markets in the volumes that the company had to have if Tengiz were to pay off. With that kind of leverage, he could effectively control the field itself. For Michael Fowler, his Harvard-educated aide, "It was just perfect."

For those who believed in omens, a scene at the Russian port of Novorossiysk on the Black Sea might have been telling. Soon after its deal with Kazakhstan was sealed, Chevron grandly sent its first tankers to pick up Urals blend oil in exchange for the Tengiz crude the company was sending into the Russian pipeline system. But the seamen had to wait, said an oil company executive. Another tanker was ahead of them, "taking the cargo we thought we were going to get." It was loading crude for a European well-known to the industry—John Deuss. Years later, Wooddy recalled that after the signing of the final agreement, Derr had turned to him and said, "I'll bet you're glad that's all over." "What do you mean?" Wooddy replied. "It's only just begun." The Chevron chairman looked at him "like I had had too much to drink."

Return

to

Baku

ACROSS THE CASPIAN SEA IN AZERBAIJAN, other oil multinationals were struggling for control of offshore Baku fields that together constituted a true colossus. The origins of this campaign dated back three years, to the consolation prize promised to British Petroleum after it failed to steal Tengiz away from Chevron. At the time, the Soviet Union was still ruling the Caspian states. When the Kremlin told the BP executives that they could have first crack at offshore Baku as compensation of sorts for losing out to Chevron, the British company wasted no time getting there.

One of the early arrivals was Tom Hamilton, head of international exploration for BP. As his plane began its final approach to the Baku airport in October 1990, he was in an optimistic mood. A BP negotiator had gone in ahead of him and had been well received. If the Soviets followed through and granted BP the exploration rights, it would make BP the first western oil company in modern times to establish a foothold there.

From the air, the capital of Azerbaijan didn't appear especially promising. What seemed to be many trees pleasantly dotting the landscape were, upon closer inspection, hundreds of old, black-caked oil rigs—the carcasses of once-thriving oil fields now pocked with pools of crude, "like Oklahoma or East Texas in the 1920s." In fact, the Baku oil region was a shadow of its former self. Neglected by Moscow, its fields were in an even sadder state than those of haphazardly maintained Siberia and Volga. Still, crude continued to be produced in sufficient volume to sustain the economy of this city of 1.1 million people.

On the ground, contemporary Baku looked "much like any other Soviet city with its dreary apartment blocks and massive Communist Party buildings," one British visitor observed. But he also sensed its historic Asian flavor, commenting on how "old men pause on the pavement outside coffee houses, discussing the political questions of the day in the shade of overhanging balconies." Another wrote that Baku's waterfront had managed to preserve "a stylish quality rare in Soviet cities" with its "tree-lined promenade" where "pine trees tremble in the breeze." Robert Finn, an American diplomat who would arrive two years later to open the first U.S. embassy there, found more than a breeze—the winds were so fierce that he "had to walk my pug Bobo behind the walls because she'd be blown away." The people he met "loved their city" and "played Baku songs all the time." But he couldn't escape the smell of oil, garbage, and industrial waste. Finn thought the overall scene invoked the image of Marseilles merged with Jersey City—nineteenth-century architecture with an oil refinery in the center. Looking for a place to stay, he finally settled on a $60-a-month apartment in which "the rats had the kitchen, I had the bedroom."

Fleeting traces of Baku's legendary past—the pre–Russian Revolution era of oil barons and their fine palaces—could still be found. The mansion of Murtaza Mukhtarov—the oilman who had fired on Red soldiers from horseback and then killed himself rather than surrender his home—was now the city's wedding hall. Other once-lavish residences of the barons had been divided into apartments and government offices.

There were only a few reminders of Zeynalabdin Tagiyev, the great patriarch who was exiled to his seaside villa at nearby Mardakhan after Baku fell to the Bolsheviks. Two of his ornate, glass-and-wood bookcases had survived in the rare books section of the city library, and a mostly ignored bust of Tagiyev stood on a cornerstone of what was once his downtown mansion, now a museum. As for his proudest accomplishment—the school for Muslim girls that he built in defiance of Islamic conservatives—it now housed an Azerbaijan Academy of Science archive. His villa had become a tuberculosis sanatorium, its water pipes rusted and its wood siding rotting in the ocean air.

Mikhail Gorbachev formally rehabilitated Tagiyev in a 1990 ceremony witnessed by the old baron's granddaughter, Sophia, who at the age of sixty-nine was once again living in Baku. Her white hair parted neatly down the middle, she bore a striking resemblance to her grandfather. She was accompanied by her mother, Sarah, now ninety, and the two of them lingered for a while at Tagiyev's gravesite next to the old villa.

The modern-day equivalents of the barons were the Communist Party functionaries whose control over the oil industry had made them moderately wealthy even by western standards. They enriched themselves by pilfering oil and chemical products and selling their take on the side or pocketing the funds they budgeted for nonexistent work projects. Hamilton thought he had one scam figured out. The Soviets maintained a budget category for "spillage," meaning oil lost to leaky pipes and other routine mishaps. But the size of the estimated loss was absurd—seven hundred thousand barrels a year, 10 percent of total production. That amount of oil would create pools around the city, even be "visible from space," he said. Instead, Hamilton concluded, the Communist bureaucrats "cooked the books" to steal and sell the crude themselves.

Unlike in Moscow, there was no obvious hunger in Baku. Bread shops were well stocked and fruit plentiful. But there were reminders of a harsh environmental toll exacted by the region's heavy industry. In the eerie neighboring city of Sumgait, for example, thirty-two chemical and metals plants had until recently sent some 120,000 tons of waste into the air annually. The foul conditions were believed to have contributed to Sumgait's high infant mortality rate: 36 of every 1,000 babies died before the age of one, triple the U.S. average. Driving into the city for the first time, a United Nations official named Paolo Lembo found that his "eyes started itching. I started smelling something. I thought I was seeing some kind of fantastic scene. It looked like it couldn't be true." A Moscow documentary maker dubbed Sumgait the "dead zone."

Oilmen have a history of hunting for crude in some of the world's most inhospitable places. While Baku was not the worst, BP's Hamilton arrived to difficult conditions that October. Ten months earlier, Soviet troops had invaded the city to put down restive elements among the Azeris, as the Turkic Azerbaijanis are called. The assault came to be known as the Black January Massacre. British journalist Thomas de Waal estimated that 130 died as "tanks rolled over barricades, crushing cars and even ambulances." Now martial law was in effect, and four Soviet armored personnel carriers were stationed in the main square on the waterfront. Baku itself still functioned, but Bill Keller, a *New York Times* correspondent, wondered who was in charge; the city seemed to run "out of habit and clan connections rather than because of any centralized authority."

In contrast with the relative tameness of Kazakhstan on the eastern side of the Caspian Sea, Azerbaijan and the rest of the western territory could only be called disorderly. The region was dominated by the Caucasus mountain range, an undulation of crags and isolated hollows populated by some fifty different ethnic groups speaking more than forty languages. It was a highly belligerent mix that only became more so in the late 1980s, when Mikhail Gorbachev haltingly relaxed the Soviet Union's political grip on its republics. The restive Chechens in the north, for example, chafed for independence after enduring harsh treatment by the czarist empire and its Soviet successors. Large and unruly pro-independence demonstrations erupted in neighboring Georgia, just to the south of Chechnya, protests in which Gorbachev's troops killed twenty people.

And in the southernmost reaches of the Soviet Caucasus, war erupted between Armenia and Azerbaijan. The trigger was a small piece of territory between them that had come to symbolize national honor for both republics. Each invoked a historic claim to the Rhode Island–size spit of land called Nagorno-Karabakh, which aptly translates as "mountainous black garden." In 1988, when the disputed region's Armenian-dominated governing council voted to secede from Azerbaijan, it set off a series of bloody clashes both between and within the republics.

Azeris turned against ethnic Armenians who lived among them; Armenians did the same to the ethnic Azeris in their midst. In Sumgait, an Azeri rampage killed thirty-two Armenians. In Baku, "Armenians were thrown to their deaths from the balconies of upper-story apartments. Crowds set upon and beat Armenians to death," wrote de Waal. Armenians replied with their own attacks. Civilians on both sides fled regions where they were in the minority until, as de Waal observed, "Armenia and Azerbaijan completed their ethnic cleansing of each other's populations." Gorbachev established nighttime curfews and ordered the arrest of the leaders of both camps. But it did no good—nationalists were now dictating events in both republics.

The first western oilman to enter Baku during those volatile times was a tall, amiable American entrepreneur named Steve Remp, curious about opportunities for his oil service company. He arrived in May 1989, almost a year and a half before Hamilton, and was an immediate hit with the Azeris. On the first night at his Baku hotel, he was drawn unceremoniously into a raucous wedding party, amid circular dancing, vodka toasts, and general hilarity. When the celebrants learned that he was an American, Remp became the effective guest of honor.

This open-armed welcome continued over the next few days, as Remp's guide, a Moscow specialist in oil field terminology, organized meetings with the city's oil elite. Remp wore his bloodline proudly: his great-grandfather was a California oilman, his grandfather found oil in his backyard in Oklahoma, and his father invented a well-known oil field tool. For his part, Remp was head of Ramco, a company that cleaned offshore drilling platforms and was headquartered in the Scotland oil town of Aberdeen. The Azeri oilmen were fascinated by their visitor and offered to sell him old platforms that he could salvage as scrap. But Remp was after something more. He had hopes of negotiating "a seat at the table"—a modest stake in the Baku oil fields—and his prospects seemed encouraging.

Soon his sincere manner earned him the trust of the Azeris, who were well aware of their inexperience with western oil companies and were grateful to have such a knowledgeable friend. On this and subsequent trips, he worked to strengthen the relationship, socializing with ease and handing out family photographs as mementoes. Asked years later for recollections of those days, one senior Azeri oilman turned and opened his office safe. Out came his personal copy of the black-and-white Remp family portrait.

Remp formed a particular kinship with an astute oil official named Namik Effendiev, who spoke to the American with unusual candor. Baku's onshore oil industry "was dead," its offshore was "in trouble," and there was "no money from Moscow" to fix any of it, Effendiev said. Azerbaijan oilmen needed western partners who could provide financial resources and advanced technology. Remp agreed, and they sat down with Effendiev's boss to make their case. Kurban Abassov was skeptical at first. He had been a chief developer of Oily Rocks, the pioneering oil field in the sea, four decades earlier. Azeris revered him as "Nefte Kurban"—"Oil Kurban." A muscular giant of a man, he was said to have swum the rough sea between the Oily Rocks platforms on occasion. Azeris and foreigners alike were intimidated by this local legend, who held forth in an enormous office lined with huge oil field maps, shouting into one or another of his dozen phones even while receiving a steady stream of visitors. One oilman complained, "You never felt you were getting the guy's undivided attention." He was also a Soviet man to his bones. Angry at one unfortunate soul, Abassov stood and declared, "We will liquidate him, like in the old days."

Abassov didn't like the idea of foreign involvement in Azerbaijan's oil fields. Yet he could not ignore the terrible deterioration of his beloved Oily Rocks. Miles of platforms, roads, and derricks were in failing condition. If he waited for help from financially strapped Moscow, Oily Rocks would probably never be restored to its former glory. Foreign cash might well be the only answer, he reluctantly agreed. Whereupon a letter was drafted appointing Remp as Azerbaijan's official representative to western oil companies, and Abassov signed it. A similar letter went to the Azeri president, who signed it as well.

It was an astounding triumph for the American oilman, but Effendiev wasn't finished yet. Next he offered Remp access to geological and seismic documents containing the most vital secrets of Baku's "elephants." Until now, the materials had been kept carefully hidden from outside eyes. Remp could see why. They depicted world-class oil fields waiting to be drilled, clearly visible in painstakingly drawn maps and sketches and well logs that revealed what Remp recognized as "super megastructures" offshore.

In August 1990, Remp returned to Scotland, where he drafted a five-page letter to the two big oil companies with U.K. headquarters, British Petroleum and Shell. In it, he noted his appointment as agent for Azerbaijan's oil industry, summarized Effendiev's data, and invited their inquiries. Then he sat back and waited for replies.

A week or so later, British Petroleum's early negotiator in Baku, Rondo Fehlberg, concluded his own visit there and flew back to London. Astonishingly, Fehlberg had also met with Kurban Abassov—and come away with a tentative exploration deal for BP. At first glance, the Azeri oilman would seem to have been double-dealing: engaging Remp to represent its petroleum industry but cutting him out of the process at the first sign of a western oil company ready to do business. But the more likely explanation was simple confusion. BP's Fehlberg, who came to Baku armed with the Kremlin's support, at that point knew nothing of Remp's visit. Nor was Remp, acting on his own, aware of Fehlberg's foray. An expectant Kurban Abassov no doubt regarded the BP man's sudden appearance as the first welcome result of Remp's hard work on the Azeris' behalf. It was a tangle that the Marx Brothers might have appreciated.

Over time, all this would sort itself out. But for now, British Petroleum possessed a letter of intent, signed by Abassov, awarding it exclusive rights to negotiate for a potential supergiant named Azeri. The oil field's original name had been 26 Baku Kommissars, but that designation had troubled Fehlberg. It referred to a group of Bolsheviks who had been executed after the Russian Revolution; in the histories taught to Soviet schoolchildren, the deed was done with British connivance. Fehlberg, worried about potential harm to BP public relations, said the name had to change. "What do you suggest?" Abassov replied. "How about Azeri?" Fehlberg said. "They said 'Okay,' and that's how the Azeri field got its name," he recalled.

Back in London, Fehlberg rushed to prepare a formal agreement to be initialed by both sides at Baku's first post–Bolshevik Revolution oil industry exhibition, a "coming-out party" the Azeris were planning for October. Thumbing through an accumulation of unread faxes on his desk, Fehlberg noticed the letterhead of an unfamiliar company, an outfit named Ramco. It was Steve Remp's five-page invitation to invest in Baku. Fehlberg examined the summarized oil field data. Interesting, he thought—this guy Remp had gotten access to the well logs before he, Fehlberg, had; Fehlberg had thought he was the only western prospector in town.

He showed the fax to his boss, Tom Hamilton. No, Hamilton replied, we're blessed by Moscow. Why do we need another Jack Grynberg?

The disorder that greeted Hamilton when he flew into Baku in October 1990 was impossible to ignore. Gorbachev's bloody attempt months earlier to suppress Azeri nationalists by sending in the troops was proving a colossal failure. The republic's Communist Party leader, Abdulrakhman Vezirov, had fled. In Vezirov's place, Gorbachev named an oil engineer and technocrat named Ayaz Mutalibov, who recognized that he could not hold the republic together without yielding some ground to the Popular Front, an anti-Soviet movement with broad support that would come to dominate Azeri politics. As the Baku oil exhibition began, small gatherings of Popular Front followers could be seen in the streets, and the armored personnel carriers continued their vigil on the main square.

But none of it stopped agents of the western oil multinationals from flocking to the show. They were eager to learn more about the tantalizing offshore Azeri oil fields, three of which alone were said to contain 4 billion or more barrels of crude. The stage was being set for history to repeat itself; another epic brawl for Baku's legendary petroleum wealth was about to begin.

Word quickly circulated that British Petroleum had already sewn up the only deal on the trading block. The reality was a bit different, thanks to the maneuvering of an American citizen of Azeri-Iranian extraction named Michael Hoomani. Impeccable in his tailored suits, Hoomani had established a base of operations in Baku and developed excellent contacts among Azeri officialdom. It helped both that the Virginia man's family hailed from just over the border in northern Iran and that he spoke the Azeri language.

In anticipation of the oil exhibition, Hoomani had telephoned the Houston offices of Amoco, the former Standard Oil of Indiana, and managed to reach a thirty-seven-year-old geologist named Ray Leonard, who oversaw the company's interests in the Soviet Union. Hoomani was no stranger to the company—he had once worked for Amoco in Iran. Though he was now a middleman, his prior affiliation gave him instant credibility. So when he spoke of a big oil deal going down in the Azerbaijan capital, Leonard listened. Indeed, he was impressed by the detail that Hoomani provided. This would-be dealmaker seemed to be among the "one in ten who really was who he said."

Within Amoco, one executive recalled, Leonard was regarded as a "risk-taker" with "a nose for being in the right place at the right time," particularly good at tracking "new frontier stuff" in places like Baku. He ended up at Hoomani's side at the oil show, where his host seemed to know everyone, especially important Azeri officials. Leonard, in turn, made an excellent impression; he was a geologist made welcome by Azeri oil professionals who "liked technical people," as one westerner noted. They also appreciated his willingness to plunge into conversation in Russian, despite his less-than-polished command of the language. As long as he "didn't mind making a fool of himself... they didn't mind and laughed along with him," another colleague said.

After some difficulty, Hoomani negotiated a meeting with Kurban Abassov, the Azeri oil boss. Leonard argued that Amoco should be allowed to compete for the oil field about to be handed over to British Petroleum. Give us a chance, he pressed—Amoco only wants a chance to bid. Surprisingly, the crusty Abassov gave his assent. But he set a demanding deadline: Amoco had to deliver its bid by the next day, before the end of the oil show.

Using a secure telephone line jury-rigged by company technicians through a fax link in Moscow, Leonard told his superiors in Houston of the apparent breakthrough. Then he went to work on the bid. Around midnight, his printer malfunctioned. The Fortune 500 company would have to submit a handwritten offer. In the morning, he handed Abassov a meticulously printed four-page document in English. "This isn't serious," grumbled Abassov, a non-English speaker who couldn't read it even if he were inclined to overlook that it wasn't typed. Without further comment, Abassov ripped it up.

Amoco's gambit, it appeared, had failed. But luck again favored the company. Unbeknown to Leonard, a thirty-year-old American college professor was about to become his inadvertent rescuer. He was Rob Sobhani, an adjunct faculty member at Georgetown University in Baku to deliver a lecture on U.S. politics. Born in Kansas, Sobhani, like Hoomani, was an ethnic Azeri with family roots in northern Iran. And government officials, delighted at having another foreign visitor who spoke their language, arranged a one-on-one meeting for him with the Azerbaijani president, Mutalibov. Naturally, the conversation turned to oil, as the exploration agreement was about to be signed with British Petroleum. As it happened, Sobhani had just read a history of BP, and he wasn't bashful about expressing his opinion. He told the Azeri leader that, considering BP's less-than-praiseworthy history in neighboring Iran, the company might not be the best choice for Azerbaijan. President Mutalibov would do better to consider an American company; unlike Britain, the United States was a superpower and as such was "an insurance policy for a future independent Azerbaijan." After all, Sobhani concluded, "The American flag follows the American dollar."

What company would you suggest? an interested Mutalibov inquired. Again Sobhani drew on the history he had read, recalling one company that had treated the Persians well. It was called Amoco. Sobhani ended by suggesting that they should first put the oil deal out to bid, rather than simply hand it to British Petroleum. Mutalibov grabbed the telephone and dialed Kurban Abassov. "Don't sign that protocol," he said, referring to the agreement with BP. "We're going to have a competition."

At the oil show, a crowd gathered for the closing press conference and official announcement that British Petroleum had won the first exploration contract. Instead, Prime Minister Hassan Hassanov, BP's most stalwart supporter, declared that the Azeri field would be put out to international bid. There was immediate confusion, not only over the surprising turn of events but also over one of Hassanov's concluding remarks. The prime minister's English translator quoted him as saying, rather baldly, that "BP will win." Listening to the announcement in Russian nearby, Amoco's Ray Leonard thought he had heard Hassanov say something different, that his "friends at BP hope they will win." A journalist conversant in Russian nudged Leonard, indicating that he, too, had noticed the mistranslation. Amoco's hopes were still alive. BP's Rondo Fehlberg, meanwhile, was aghast—how could his hard-won deal have unraveled? As the throng at the news conference looked on, he disputed the decision with Hassanov, but to no avail. BP for the moment would get nothing more than a protocol "promising eternal friendship" with Azerbaijan.

But in Azeri oil affairs, things were seldom what they seemed. Later, Hassanov privately assured Fehlberg that the public announcement had been a bit of theater to satisfy his impulsive president. He, Hassanov, would protect British Petroleum's interests; in fact, he would allow BP to draw up the terms under which the bidding would be conducted. When all bids were in, BP would be the winner. "But we have to make it look fair," Hassanov cautioned.

A relieved Fehlberg returned to British Petroleum headquarters in London and, as agreed with Hassanov, set about writing the rules for the competition. But when two weeks passed and he couldn't get a call through to Baku "for love or money," he began to worry. He sought reassurance from Moscow, whose promises of support had sent BP to Baku in the first place. But his contacts there—at the Azeri mission and at the Oil Ministry—had disappeared. His applications for renewed Soviet visas also failed. Something was wrong; Fehlberg had to find a way back to Baku without delay. But how?

He had a brainstorm: An international soccer match was approaching in Glasgow, and he knew that diplomats at the Soviet embassy in London were fans. Fehlberg sent a colleague to buy tickets and shrewdly invited the entire embassy to the match. In that relaxed setting, he began relating his visa troubles. The diplomats, grateful to be at the soccer match, declared: "There should be no trouble. Anyone can get a visa these days. That's what *glasnost* and *perestroika* are all about. We can get you visas."

With that assurance, plans were laid. A team of British Petroleum's top executives would fly to Azerbaijan, but with no advance notice; instead, they would surprise the Azeris with a midnight run into Baku. Fehlberg reached his boss, Tom Hamilton, who was at the Caribbean island of Mustique for some Christmas scuba diving. Okay, Hamilton said, he would head back to London, and they would take the company's Hawker Siddeley jet. A second senior executive also was put on alert, as was a translator.

The flight plan for the British Petroleum jet required it to fly uncomfortably close to a region on the verge of war—some five hundred thousand U.S.-led troops were about to attack Iraqi forces that had invaded Kuwait five months earlier, threatening the world oil supply and thus the balance of world power. The U.S. military air corridor, the zone within which it flew sorties and regarded other planes as enemy combatants, was wide. Some thought it even reached the Caucasus, about eight hundred miles from the front line. BP pilots at one point seemed nervous about proceeding, but Hamilton coolly advised, "Just keep going."

When the Hawker touched down in the darkness of the Baku airport, Azeri security officials, who had heard nothing from Soviet authorities about the flight, were puzzled. "You are invited, right?" one military officer asked uncertainly. Well, said Fehlberg, we know the prime minister, the president, and Kurban Abassov. And they would be happy to see us. The name-dropping failed to impress. Worse yet, the officers noticed that the delegation's Soviet visas didn't mention Baku, as required. The now-anxious oilmen were cordoned off in a corner of the terminal while security officials debated what to do with them. At last Fehlberg recalled that he had the prime minister's home telephone number. Though it was 2 A.M., in desperation he called it. A half hour later, Hassanov showed up and ordered their release. A politician with high aspirations who still smarted from being passed over for the presidency a year earlier, Hassanov "viewed this as a way to further his political ambitions. So he got behind us," Hamilton said.

But the weary BP delegation soon got some bad news—Amoco was now the preferred company, thanks to a startling shift in Azeri politics. While just six months earlier the Azeris had unhesitatingly bowed to Kremlin instructions to welcome BP, President Mutalibov now was following no one's lead. As Fehlberg later reconstructed the events, an increasingly beleaguered Gorbachev "had much bigger fish to fry than worry about Baku," freeing the Azeri president to operate with unaccustomed independence. That meant backing Amoco, mainly because "he wanted to show independence from Hassanov." Seemingly overnight, British Petroleum had become enmeshed in a rivalry between the Azeri president and his prime minister. When Kurban Abassov, the burly protector of Oily Rocks, was suddenly unavailable because of a purported need to undergo kidney dialysis, the British Petroleum executives grew even more suspicious. Trying to preserve BP's rights seemed to have become "very much a cloak-and-dagger kind of affair."

But all was not lost, the relentlessly upbeat Fehlberg told himself. He still possessed the letter of intent favoring BP, signed the previous August by the feared Abassov. The Azeris couldn't very well deny its existence. The company also enjoyed the continued support of Prime Minister Hassanov, who in Azerbaijan's somewhat fluid political atmosphere was delighted to keep signing documents supporting BP; their value seemed questionable, but at least they were something.

In Kurban Abassov's absence, it fell to one of his subordinates to monitor the BP versus Amoco drama. Khoshbakht Yusufzade was the Azeri vice president for geology, a personable man in his sixties who was responsible for many of the republic's oil discoveries. He shared the long-ingrained Soviet distrust of the West, regarding "the foreigners like they were gypsies, fortune-telling us" of how they would help the country, but actually assuming that "they will take away our wealth. They will cheat us." When he examined BP's claim, the suspicious oilman balked. BP was asking too much, he thought, especially in its demand for rights to another offshore field of its choice should Amoco win this round. In fact, Yusufzade was not prepared to grant exploration rights to any field. The Azeris would do the exploring, and the western companies would have to settle for the limited role of developing what was discovered. Now BP's Fehlberg was insulted—his company "was not in the business of developing and producing other people's oil." It could not give up exploration and discovery rights, which had the potential of far greater financial rewards.

Fehlberg provoked a showdown that would end in Kurban Abassov's hospital room, of all places. "Let's draw up two agreements—your version and mine," Fehlberg suggested to Yusufzade. "And let's let Kurban decide." The BP man risked offending his hosts by appearing ill-mannered; Abassov, after all, was supposedly undergoing a serious medical procedure. But Fehlberg instinctively felt that, of all the Azeri oilmen, it was "Kurban [who] had great faith in BP." Moreover, this could be BP's only chance to salvage something of value. Luckily, Yusufzade agreed that his boss should have the last word. Dressed in business suits and carrying briefcases, the Azeri vice president and British Petroleum's negotiator marched together into the hospital and found Kurban Abassov's room. Contrary to BP's suspicions that he had been spirited away, the Azeri lion was in fact draped in a patient's gown and attached to a tangle of tubes. The nurses, however, were horrified at the intrusion and insisted that the unexpected visitors at least don white medical coats. So outfitted, the men watched as an assistant handed Abassov the documents containing the competing ideas. After some brief conversation, Abassov scribbled his assenting signature on one of the papers—Fehlberg's. No matter the outcome of the bidding tender, BP would not be the loser—should Amoco prevail, BP would have rights to the offshore field of its choice.

Yet Fehlberg was still uneasy. BP needed some extra protection for its position. One possibility was to partner up with someone else possessing a preexisting exploration award. The only person meeting that qualification was Steve Remp, the American oilman and erstwhile agent for Azerbaijan whose faxed invitation to BP five months earlier had been summarily discarded. "If anyone's agreement was going to be recognized because he was there first, it was Steve Remp's," Fehlberg now told John Browne. The BP exploration chief agreed, and Remp finally had his seat at the table—"a piece of the action in exchange for getting behind us," said Fehlberg.

As a precaution against any last-minute foul-ups, Fehlberg spent most of the spring of 1991 in Baku, regularly visiting the offices of the state oil company. Telexes were streaming in from oilmen around the world, asking how to get in line for Baku exploration deals. The ministry's workers had little experience answering such inquiries, so they were pleased when Fehlberg volunteered to draft replies. He was amused by the thought that "if these companies knew it was us answering them, they would have hit the roof." His replies, naturally, did not disfavor BP.

In March 1991, BP and Amoco submitted their detailed bids for the oil field known as Azeri. Weeks passed with no decision. But behind the scenes, yet another luck-of-the-draw event favored Amoco. In May, Rob Sobhani, the Georgetown scholar and now unofficial adviser to Azeri president Ayaz Mutalibov, returned to Baku. The morning after his arrival, he headed for the president's office, accompanied by two Houston oil lawyers whom he had befriended on the plane. They had come to Baku in hopes of turning up some legal business. When Sobhani introduced them, the Azeri leader, seeing an opportunity for expert advice, reached for his phone. "We've got some American lawyers," he told Yusufzade. "I want to send them over to help you evaluate those bids."

Two hours later, the two lawyers—Todd Gremillion and his partner, Jack Langlois—were in the geologist's office. Yusufzade grilled them "to see if we were real oil people" and then handed over two twelve-inch binders—the confidential bids from BP and Amoco. Go back to your hotel rooms and look them over, he declared. Gremillion and Langlois were astonished by the trust that was being extended, so much so that for the moment they didn't bring up the subject of fees. "You take a leap of faith," Gremillion recalled.

Joined by Sobhani, they stayed up all night talking over the bids before coming to a conclusion: Each bid had certain advantages, but overall, "Amoco's bid was better on fiscal terms." BP had proposed a fifty-fifty profit split with the Azeri government; Amoco's bid was similar, but its terms seemed more attractive over the long haul. Once production picked up and capital expenses were paid down, Azerbaijan's take eventually would rise to 75 percent. Also weighing on the minds of the Azeris was something that Sobhani had said—that choosing an American company made better sense, geopolitically speaking.

A month later, in June 1991, the winner was announced. Amoco would be granted one-year exclusive rights to negotiate for the big Azeri oil field. The news was "shattering" to a British Petroleum group hearing it in Moscow. Gathered later for a meeting at Heathrow Airport, the BP delegation heard a message relayed from John Browne: "If we don't have a deal in three months, we're out of there"—meaning the entire Soviet Union. The group knew their leader was serious. Well, someone remarked, "we could get something quick in West Siberia." "That's not good enough," replied Eddie Whitehead, the BP negotiator who best knew Browne's thinking. "It has to be on the Caspian." Why wasn't clear, but the bottom line was unmistakable: If the BP men intended to remain in the game, they needed to be creative, and they needed to be fast.

Now began one of the most tumultuous periods in the quest for Baku's petroleum wealth. Over the next eleven months, Amoco tried to lock up its deal, BP made a comeback, and two other oil multinationals—Pennzoil and Unocal—managed to burrow their way into contention. Some key players switched employers, including BP's Tom Hamilton and Rondo Fehlberg, and Amoco put the influential Azeri Americans, Rob Sobhani and Michael Hoomani, on its payroll. As the maneuvering wore on, the oil companies wooed Azeri officials with luxurious junkets, hoping to "make some progress, Middle East style," as one executive phrased it. BP took them to London, Amoco to Houston, and Unocal to both California and Bangkok, where they were given "a couple of days to get their legs out from under them before seeing" Unocal's Thailand fields, said Fehlberg. Such spending, in the tens of thousands of dollars, was small change next to the billions at stake in potential profits.

The first surprise came as Amoco prepared to negotiate its contract for the Azeri field. The government announced that its new chief negotiator would be a "very literate" man "with an analytical mind," and a westerner as well. His name was John Deuss.

At the same time that the cunning Dutchman was courting the Kazakhs, across the Caspian, he had been prowling Baku in search of oil deals. He had won the confidence of Azerbaijan's new oil chief, Sanan Alizade, who had succeeded the ailing Kurban Abassov. Deuss treated Alizade to a trip to Oman for talks with the sultan; the Azeri was so impressed by Deuss that he scoured Italy for a double-breasted steel-gray suit of the type the Dutchman wore, finally managing to locate one. Thus, it was not surprising that he would ask Deuss to run the Amoco talks.

The negotiations were carried out in Deuss's inimitable style. He dispatched his well-appointed Gulfstream to ferry the Amoco negotiators from Houston to Bermuda. Once there, he clamped a tight grip on them. Tom Doss, who led the delegation, recalled what it was like. Deuss dictated "where we had to go eat, where we could go in Bermuda." The Americans were picked up each morning at their hotel without anyone knowing the destination. When their taxi reached a pre-designated landmark, the driver would call for directions on his two-way radio and "from there you'd be told where to go." An Azeri team working with Deuss was also kept under wraps. For most of the time, the two negotiating teams were kept entirely apart, each meeting separately with Deuss in an extreme form of his shuttle diplomacy. "We didn't even know where they were staying," Doss said. "We'd show up [by taxi] and the Azeris would have just left." Amoco's chief negotiator, Bill Young, found Deuss to be "reasonably persuasive." But Doss felt differently, that "we were just marking time." Deuss's style—the women, the stories of his business with South Africa, the secrecy with which he operated—gave Doss and some others at the company pause about dealing with him. "Deuss had a poor reputation to start with. Sleazy. We weren't ever going to make a deal with Deuss, and we knew that," he said. "But the Azeris didn't know."

When the two sides finally did meet, it was on Deuss's yacht, a vessel that Doss found to be "a demonstration of obscene money." With "all kinds of gals around" Deuss, a deck crew in white shorts served a multicourse dinner with fine wine at a banquet table.

British Petroleum negotiators, meanwhile, had followed John Browne's orders and were again pressing the Azeris for a deal of their own. In secret talks over two months, BP won exclusive rights to negotiate for not one but two supergiant fields. The first, called Chirag, abutted Amoco's Azeri field. The second, called Shah Deniz, was a few miles south, offshore. It was a coup for BP, the way smoothed by Kurban Abassov's hospital-room pledge that British Petroleum would not go away empty-handed.

The deal might not have been finalized, however, without a British nod to Azeri national pride. BP had intended to recruit Michael Heseltine, a senior U.K. government minister, as the headliner at a Baku ceremony celebrating the agreement. The Azeri response essentially was, Michael who? So the call went out to former prime minister Margaret Thatcher, who was visiting Hong Kong at the time. Could she alter her itinerary just a bit and make an appearance in Baku? Since it was Thatcher—quite the admirer of Gorbachev—who had originally urged BP to become active in the Soviet Union, she obliged. As Azeri officials beamed, she presented them with a check for $30 million, up-front money that sealed the deal for BP.

(About two years later, even British royalty rallied to BP's side. When further oil field negotiations with the Azeris seemed to stall, the petroleum giant arranged for the president of Azerbaijan to visit Britain for an audience with Queen Elizabeth, hoping that he would feel so honored that he would speed up the talks. The visit was a success, but negotiations remained bogged down.)

Like most multinationals in Baku, BP operated in a constant state of mild paranoia. Anything could undo a deal, and one couldn't build in too many defenses. Accordingly, it formed a strategic partnership with otherwise little-known Statoil, Norway's state-owned petroleum company. The move was a subtle way of discouraging Azerbaijan, Russia, or anyone else from meddling with the deal, for that would invite not only a commercial response from BP but also a diplomatic one from Norway, a small but respected European government.

Amoco followed a similar strategy in its pursuit of the Azeri field. It parceled out small slices of the venture to its Baku rivals—BP, Unocal, and Pennzoil. Outsiders might have thought it odd to share the spoils after such a tough competition, but Amoco was being pragmatic, not generous. Given Azerbaijan's chaotic environment, the company's chief ally, President Mutalibov, could easily end up out of power. Its rivals, meanwhile, had established relationships with politicians who could rise in Mutalibov's place or be influential with whichever faction seized power. Therefore it seemed prudent for Amoco to "get these others with us rather than against us"—to "spread out the percentage exposure," one executive noted.

Pennzoil's arrival on the scene reintroduced Tom Hamilton to Azerbaijan after a six-month absence. This laconic American geologist who had risen to the top ranks at British Petroleum was no longer a BP man. Exhausted by the furious pace he had maintained the previous three years as John Browne's right-hand man and feeling increasingly out of place at BP as an American, Hamilton had left the company in the middle of 1991 and gone home for rest and relaxation. But when two former colleagues approached him with a proposal to form a new oil exploration company, he became intrigued. Hamilton agreed to help refine the idea and shop it around.

He soon got a bite from Pennzoil, the well-connected Houston company known for its ties to auto racing. Its chief executive, Hugh Liedke, started in the oil business with George H. W. Bush, now in his fourth year as U.S. president. The deal that took shape was this: Pennzoil would use the business model to create a new division run by Hamilton, with a $100 million annual budget and responsibility for all overseas exploration and production activities. The division would build up its inventory of oil properties until it was sufficiently valuable to be sold off, along with whatever U.S. oil field and production assets were on Pennzoil's books. The proceeds would be used to pay down Pennzoil's $2 billion debt, with a sizable share set aside to reward Hamilton's team. Pennzoil, in his words run by "financial folks" who "didn't understand" the ways of finding and developing oil, would end up focusing on the marketing of oil products.

Hamilton thought it a splendid idea. He formed a management team and recruited Rondo Fehlberg, BP's top Soviet negotiator, and later Steve Remp, the first American oilman into Baku. Remp, who had been enlisted by BP to strengthen their bargaining position many months earlier, was eager to move on. After the departures of Hamilton and Fehlberg from BP, the British were "treating me like persona non grata," he complained.

Personal touches meant a great deal when conducting business in Baku, Hamilton knew. That explained why he arranged for Pennzoil planes to fly in Kurban Abassov's insulin on occasion. Another deft move was hiring Khoi Tran, Vietnam's former deputy minister of oil and gas. The Soviet Union, which had maintained close relations with the Hanoi government, had sent a number of Azeris to Vietnam over the years to provide training in the oil industry. Tran had met many of them, so it was a comfortable fit for him to be living and working in Azerbaijan. With the Azeri oilmen, he "drank Vietnamese tea and spoke French. They loved him," said Hamilton. When an order of computers arrived at his office, Hamilton funneled some to the Azeris, most of whom had never seen one before. Tran showed them how to run oil economics on Excel spreadsheets.

Hamilton ended up in negotiations for the rights to a prized oil field called Guneshli, on which the rickety remains of Oily Rocks stood. The deal clincher was an unusual agreement under which Pennzoil would help with Azerbaijan's natural gas needs. Valekh Aleskerov, a dapper former wrestler who was now a vice president at the state oil company, explained the problem this way: Oily Rocks was venting into the atmosphere the equivalent of 150 million cubic feet of natural gas per day for lack of equipment to capture it; meanwhile, Azerbaijan was spending scarce dollars to import natural gas. What if Hamilton were to equip Oily Rocks with two big natural gas processors, the machinery needed to solve the problem? That, Aleskerov implied, might clear the way for a Guneshli deal.

Hamilton's top deputy, Dave Henderson, indicated a favorable response. It sounded to him like Aleskerov had "just offered us a 1.8 billion–barrel field for the price of two compressors"—a relative bargain. Over time, installing the compressors would prove more daunting than expected, and the actual costs would balloon to $100 million. But the Pennzoil delegation was untroubled. Practically every oil company had to ante up that kind of money to keep deals moving—usually in the form of favors like disguised payments, scholarships, vacations, and gifts to important Azeri officials and their families. Considered in that light, the $100 million worth of compressor equipment was a kind of bribery insurance—sufficiently valuable to express gratitude to the Azeris while allowing Pennzoil to dodge the necessity of cash payments.

The bribery issue was a thorny one for the oilmen. America's stiff anti-bribery law, known as the Foreign Corrupt Practices Act, prohibited U.S. companies abroad from paying bribes of any type in order to obtain business. But a company that failed to sweeten a deal would likely get nowhere on the Caspian. For Pennzoil, it was a practical matter as well: Hamilton lacked the ready cash to play at the same level as "the big boys." In his mind, the compressor equipment constituted a payment in kind but was strictly legal and delivered "in front of the whole world to see."

Fehlberg, the former BP negotiator now with Hamilton, thought the term *bribery* was an oversimplification when applied to the Azeris. "It is more complex than that," he said.

In their culture, with the old Middle Eastern customs that include friendship and *baksheesh* with a veneer of communism, there is a mix that is difficult to understand. But their culture has a clear morality to it. For me to be befriended by a senior minister and have him work for me and bust his tail to make it happen, in their culture he is entitled to something.

Everyone in the Soviet Union knew that these ministers are paid very little and are entitled to live according to their station. Their morality is that he should be compensated for doing something. The morality is how much he can and can't take. But they view it as immoral if westerners don't compensate them. It's immoral if they expect something just for being a gatekeeper, and they would probably suffer for that. But to expect a reward for working for us, that is moral. But everyone runs around being pious about how everyone is a crook.

It took time for them to trust me. At first when I couldn't pay them, they didn't trust me. It took time for them to get to know me and to know I would help out if I could but that U.S. laws prevented me from doing certain things. That's why Pennzoil did the gas utilization project. We said, "That will be our payment to all of you." We were fought hard by our western colleagues [i.e., competitors], who understood what we were doing.

Meanwhile, as the costs of the compressor equipment grew, so did Pennzoil's ambitions. Henderson and the others began to speculate on what might happen if they could put the finishing touches on their deal and start oil flowing from Guneshli while Amoco and British Petroleum were still tangled up in negotiations for the Azeri and Chirag fields. That might give Pennzoil an opportunity to make its own play for the two oil fields, which Guneshli abutted. "We'd just march down" the peninsula and take all three fields, Henderson thought. It was hard to tell whether such thinking reflected a sudden flight of grandiosity or a realistic game plan. But at this moment on the Caspian, few ideas seemed outlandish.

In the wild scramble to cut exploration deals, there were few secrets. Western oilmen arriving at the airport could figure out who was in Baku by surveying the private jets lined up on the tarmac. Or they could browse the register at the seaside hotel where most visiting oilmen stayed, looking for familiar names or revealing nationalities.

There was a certain grandeur about the hotel, known as the "Old Intourist" to distinguish it from a newer but bland Intourist facility down the road. Western oil companies kept their offices at the Old Intourist, and eventually the U.S. embassy opened there. The Russian embassy was down the hall, and the Turks were downstairs from the Americans. The old building took some getting used to, said American diplomat Robert Finn, who remembered the American embassy "smelling like cabbage soup" most of the time. International telephone calls had to be made at the hotel's reception desk and were routed through Moscow over poor lines. If an oilman threw caution to the wind and shouted his latest business down the receiver, he risked being overheard by everyone in the lobby.

Agents for the Azeris regularly eavesdropped on oil company negotiators, who countered with devices to detect hidden microphones. While he was still with British Petroleum, Fehlberg watched as a sweep of his hotel suite yielded "a dozen or more bugs" in each room. After he joined Pennzoil, he had an even more jolting experience. A colleague offered to demonstrate the workings of a detection device in an office that had been cleared of bugs only the previous evening. When the device was turned on, it surprised everyone by emitting a stream of telltale static. "They had overnight dug out a little plaster in all the walls and put in wall bugs in all the rooms," Fehlberg said.

Once, when BP's Terry Adams had something confidential to discuss with British ambassador Thomas Young, the two went for a rainy walk along the shoreline. Their privacy seemed assured—few cars or people were braving the nasty weather. Just then, a small Soviet-made Lada stopped fifty yards ahead of them, and a sheepdog with a big collar jumped out. The dog trailed after the men, making them suspicious. "When the dog's tail would go up, Tom would say, 'Careful, it must be transmitting,' " Adams recalled. As bizarre as it sounded, the story took on a life of its own, and it helped convince many other oilmen that most if not all conversations were being recorded.

Some oil companies resorted to code names in hopes of confusing those listening in. One member of Azerbaijan's loyal opposition was dubbed "Loyal Avis" by the Pennzoil team. Another who wore alligator shoes became "the Big Bopper," and a third who owned a house near the president's was known as "the Landlord." A fourth who was in the local KGB was "the Lamp."

Oil companies snooped on one another in various ways. When Pennzoil's Fehlberg found himself in need of a translator while in the waiting room at the state oil ministry, he turned to Unocal's Marty Miller for help. "Can I borrow your interpreter?" Fehlberg inquired. Sure, Miller replied. The translator so impressed Fehlberg with his skills that the Pennzoil man employed him on three more occasions—until he caught on to the man's identity. Osman Kaldirim, it turned out, was no ordinary interpreter. He was vice president of Saudi Arabia's Delta Oil, Unocal's partner in Baku, and he expertly briefed an amused Marty Miller on what transpired each time he translated at one of Fehlberg's negotiating sessions.

Kaldirim was an altogether mysterious figure. A Turkish-born American, he was remembered by one Unocal executive as a "deceptive-looking man—shortish and fat, but very clever." His contacts in Azerbaijan were such that he seemed able to set up meetings with virtually any senior Azeri official at a moment's notice. Within Unocal "it was thought that he [was] a CIA operative," the executive said.

Kaldirim held master's and doctorate degrees in electronic engineering from UCLA, but much of his image was shaped by the tales of intrigue that he told. In a quiet voice, he would describe working at UCLA on fiber optics to make military jets impervious to a highly destructive electromagnetic pulse. In one desert test, he said, he had mounted an airplane atop a tower thousands of feet high to determine whether its electronics could withstand a high-tech Soviet weapon that could "fry its electronics."

Naturally, he said, all his university work on electromagnetic pulse theory had been classified.

Other times, Kaldirim would lift a pant leg to reveal a round scar on the inside of his ankle, which he attributed to a bullet wound he suffered in Afghanistan during the 1980s uprising against Soviet occupation. He had fought alongside the Afghan rebels, Kaldirim said, and had transported heat-seeking U.S. Stinger missiles to them.

There was at least some truth to the UCLA story. Before graduation, Kaldirim was recommended by his UCLA dissertation adviser, Professor Cavour W. Yeh, for a job as a research associate for Dikewood Corporation, which was working on the electromagnetic pulse problem. "I don't want to diminish his contribution—he did some good work. But there are hundreds of people working in this area," Yeh said. Kaldirim's master's thesis examined how to make certain receivers for fiber-optic networks; his doctoral dissertation sought a way to attach a magnetic charge to medicine, which once swallowed, would travel instantly to a designated organ. Both papers were available on the Internet.

His account of military adventures in Afghanistan was hotly disputed by Robert Oakley, a former U.S. ambassador to Pakistan during the 1980s who served as a Unocal consultant. Oakley himself was a noted bender of the truth, but his dismissive view of Kaldirim was echoed by leading Afghan rebels and their Arab supporters. Asked about Kaldirim by name, nationality, and physical description, none could recall him. "I discovered I couldn't believe everything he told you," said Unocal's Marty Miller.

While Amoco, British Petroleum, and Pennzoil were deep in negotiations for the three supergiants to which they had laid claim, Unocal was feeling shut out. It had no field it could call its own and little likelihood that the Azeris would offer a consolation prize anytime soon. So Unocal embarked on a clever strategy—one that would rely on a well-kept geological truth about the three fields that were now in play.

Although everyone said otherwise publicly, the big oil multinationals knew that the fields were actually part of one long, curved underwater shelf called the Absheron Sill. It was a formation that started on the Baku shore and stretched east almost all the way to Turkmenistan. Somewhere deep in its geology, there were pathways connecting the three fields—Azeri, Chirag, and Guneshli. In fact, they constituted one large reservoir of crude oil. Amoco, British Petroleum, and Pennzoil, instead of pumping from their own distinct field, could find themselves sucking up one another's crude.

The odd public silence about the true nature of the fields was rooted in the once-rigid demands of Moscow bureaucrats. The Azeris knew full well that it was all one giant reservoir. But to satisfy the Soviet demand that oil field explorations show results, they had always identified the fields as separate entities, thereby allowing them to claim credit for three discoveries instead of one. The practice persisted even after Soviet influence declined.

Unocal set out to persuade the Azeris that it would be to their advantage to face up to the truth. Forget about separate deals with Amoco, BP, and Pennzoil. The three fields should be "unitized"—treated as one huge reservoir and operated by the big multinationals together in a partnership that would, of course, include Unocal. Such an arrangement would speed exploration and development, and riches would flow more swiftly to Azerbaijan, Unocal argued. Its executives reasoned that if this approach were adopted by the Azeris, no one oil company would have an automatic advantage at the outset. Everything would be open to a whole new round of negotiations, and Unocal could "fight like hell for equity," said a Unocal executive.

Amoco, BP, and Pennzoil dug in their heels against the proposal. While it might make geological sense, the atmosphere in the Caspian had come to resemble that of a gold rush; greed or something close to it was the driving force, and no western oil company was about to give up any part of its claim, certainly not to the opportunistic Unocal. But the Azeri oil ministry took the suggestion to unitize seriously, seeing some wisdom in it.

All the while, the region was still wracked by military hostilities, and the Azeri government of President Ayaz Mutalibov was laboring to maintain power. In early 1992, Azerbaijani battlefield defeats drove the populace of Baku to despair. When the Azeri town of Khojali fell to Armenian forces, wrote journalist Suzanne Goldenberg, "a mighty wave of anger built up in Baku. The entire city seemed convulsed by rage. Elderly women approached me on the street, pulling newspapers out of their shopping bags and stabbing fingers at the headlines. They were consumed by grief and anger and desperate to explain the extent of their loss." Robert Finn, the American diplomat in Baku, witnessed the chaos. People "would just disappear," Finn said. A jogger saw an old lady, dead, floating in the water. The city's plentiful food supply began running out, causing more panic. "Someone would come and say, 'There's cheese in the market,' and everyone would run out." Even the oilmen had to make do with less. Amoco's Ray Leonard and Tim Hartnett had brought Fig Newtons, Coke, peanuts, and Saltines in their baggage from abroad; at times, the snacks were their evening meals. Basic household supplies became scarce. When journalist Thomas Goltz managed to purchase three ten-gallon plastic buckets, he was mobbed by passersby "demanding to know where I had found the treasure."

Azeri politics became more frenetic. Only months earlier, the Soviet Union had finally collapsed, and the last vestiges of Moscow's control over Azerbaijan were slipping away. Now the anti-Soviet Popular Front flexed its considerable muscle, demanding the dissolution of the Azeri Communist Party and threatening to field an army of ten thousand volunteers. Goltz found the Popular Front's rise "a breathtaking thing to see in a society thought to be deaf, dumb, and blind."

In a tumultuous sequence of events, the harassed Mutalibov abandoned the presidency and then reclaimed power two months later. Within days of his return, the Popular Front seized parliament and besieged his office. Alarmed, he got on the phone and tracked down Rob Sobhani, the American professor who had talked up Amoco's virtues when the two had first met more than a year earlier. A nervous Mutalibov asked "if there was anything I or the U.S. government could do," Sobhani recalled. "He was being run out of office." There wasn't, and the old Communist Party reliable fled to Moscow.

Mutalibov was succeeded by Popular Front leader Abulfaz Elchibey, a charismatic Middle East scholar with gray hair and beard whose reputation for honesty enhanced his commanding moral authority. Azeris were thrilled when, on the battlefield, their forces rolled back some of the Armenian advances. The multinational oil companies, however, were dismayed when the new government then froze all of their pending oil deals—in effect sending everyone back to square one. The sudden turn of events left the foreign oilmen feeling desperate, and they commiserated with one another about the injustice of it all—how "every time we about reached critical mass on an oil deal, the government would collapse," said one executive. Worse yet, when a new government was ready to resume bargaining, "an old oil deal might be held against you."

But even open warfare, civil unrest, and government ousters didn't kill the bargaining for Baku oil, no matter how nerve-wrackingly disruptive they could become. Too much was at stake for all the players, and not just the multinationals like BP and Amoco. Even the various Azeri factions jostling for power could agree that the fledgling nation's economic future turned on the full development of its oil resources. And so the pursuit of oil deals had a momentum of its own. The state oil company in a sense operated outside of the political system. No matter how many presidents came and went, the technocrats remained, their relationships with foreign oilmen more or less survived intact, and negotiations eventually were revived.

The fledgling government of Abulfaz Elchibey soon got down to business, appointing a new chief negotiator who seemed headed straight for unitization, the scheme promoted by Unocal. This time it would happen, and the Azeris would force the multinationals to form a single partnership. Together, they would explore and develop the vast deposits of crude now acknowledged to be in one supergiant field; the individual deals that had been pending for BP, Amoco, and Pennzoil would be subsumed by the new arrangement. It was not what the three oil powers wanted, but they had no choice. In May 1993, the state oil company made it official.

Now began a fight over which oil company would be awarded the biggest share in the partnership. British Petroleum and Amoco—the most powerful in the group—employed different strategies. BP sought to curry favor with government officials; Amoco tried to charm engineers at the state oil company. Unocal befriended respected Azeri academics and also brought in its biggest gun—John Imle, its self-assured president of international operations—to angle for a decent share. At one meeting to discuss up-front money for the Azeris (more politely, a "signing bonus"), Imle ventured that "a field of this size should be worth way over $100 million." His remark suggested far greater generosity than his fellow oilmen were prepared to display. "We all wanted to shoot him," said Amoco's Tom Doss.

In June, the oil companies and the government finally hammered out a preliminary agreement. Under its terms, the companies would make an initial payment to Azerbaijan of $70 million, one third of an eventual $210 million signing bonus. Imle's estimate of what it would cost to satisfy the Azeris had not been extravagant after all. A ceremony to make the agreement official was scheduled for June 30 in London, attended by Azeri president Elchibey, who would be in Britain on a state visit.

Along the way, John Deuss had been removed from his role as an Azeri negotiator. But the wily Dutchman was still very much a player. In a ceremony at his favorite New York hotel, the swank Pierre on Fifth Avenue, both Azerbaijan and Kazakhstan signed foundation papers for Deuss's pipeline consortium. It was yet another step in his determined campaign to control the export of millions of barrels of Caspian oil.

In the elation of the moment, the oilmen took little account of what seemed to be a minor disruption outside Baku, in a city called Gyanja. A local textile mill owner named Surat Husseinov, once a war hero but discredited after abandoning his post in Nagorno-Karabakh, was proving troublesome to authorities. He and his cohorts had somehow taken possession of a cache of heavy arms abandoned outside Gyanja by hastily departing Russian troops.

Azeri forces were dispatched from Baku to disarm Husseinov, but a firefight erupted and some two dozen men were killed. Now Husseinov vowed to remove Elchibey, the Azeri president, from office. Though there were no actual sightings, Husseinov's troops were said to be marching on Baku. Elchibey's prime minister resigned in panic, as did the chairman of parliament.

Early one morning, Unocal's Marty Miller was awakened by someone pounding on his door at Baku's hilltop Anba Hotel. Outside he found men in "black leather jackets and sunglasses, waving their arms. I could tell they wanted me to leave the hotel." Downstairs, the hotel manager told Miller that "they were afraid there was going to be fighting nearby, in front of the Parliament." Miller gathered his things, walked down the hill, and left the country the next day, along with dozens of other foreign oilmen and western diplomats fleeing to Turkey.

The actual danger posed by Husseinov was never clear. Word spread that his men were on the edge of the city, but the only visible signs of their presence were a few stragglers smoking cigarettes on the road or wandering through town. The threat was sufficient, however, to send the Azeri president fleeing to his home province after only a year in office. Honorable to a fault and a humane leader, Elchibey unfortunately "had no business being president of Azerbaijan," Rob Sobhani reckoned. "He was a good man, but good men don't make good presidents." Especially in the carnivorous atmosphere of Azeri politics.

Now it was the turn of Heydar Aliyev, a blunt statesman and former KGB general infamous in Azerbaijan. Elchibey had summoned Aliyev to try to mediate an accommodation with the rebellious Husseinov. With the Elchibey government now in collapse, Aliyev proclaimed that he was in charge.

Bewildered oil company negotiators, many of them watching all this from the safety of Istanbul, wondered what to do next. Was the signing ceremony in London still on? Aliyev offered vague assurances to the few oilmen still in Baku: "Don't worry, we'll find someone to sign" the contract, he promised at a press conference.

The oilmen's most immediate concern was the signing bonus. The first payment of $70 million was due about a week before the London meeting, on June 22. If the payment was not made, the long-sought deal could be cancelled by the Azeris. The companies, after a collective gulp, made the payment. "Seventy million dollars is a lot to you and me, but it's not that much to the companies," one of the oilmen reasoned.

Then came new cause for consternation. Five days before the scheduled ceremony in London, the chief Azeri negotiator announced without elaboration that there would be no signing. As for the $70 million just handed over by the oil companies, no one knew its whereabouts.

The oilmen issued confident statements for public consumption. One read, "The talks have only been suspended and the delegation has gone back to Baku to report to the new government." Privately, they were less sanguine. "They have an obligation to us," one said. "We hope."

CHAPTER 11

The
Contract
of the
Century

HEYDAR ALIYEV WRAPPED AN ARM around Rob Sobhani, the Georgetown professor, and bid him to "sit down and talk." Foreign oilmen, trying to salvage their suddenly disrupted Azerbaijan exploration deal, were agitating for a new round of negotiations. But the sixty-nine-year-old Azeri leader had something else on his mind: America. How did the United States work? the veteran Soviet strongman inquired. What were its politics, the personalities of its leaders? Two and a half hours of discussion followed. Aliyev seemed surprised to learn that American presidents for the most part lacked the autocratic powers wielded by Soviet rulers. And when Sobhani mentioned the presidential salary of $200,000, the Azeri did a double take. "I thought that was per month," he said. "No," Sobhani repeated, "a year."

Aliyev, pen in hand to take notes as the thirty-four-year-old American academic spoke, impressed Sobhani, by now a seasoned observer of Azeri leadership. Whatever one might say about this man, Sobhani decided, "he was not full of himself." Rather, without swagger, Aliyev spoke with utter confidence of his intention to "bring Azerbaijan to a better place" and projected both "charisma and a human side."

But after six changes of government in Azerbaijan in three years and nearly as many abortive contracts, foreign oilmen were dubious. Some suspected Aliyev to be a Moscow surrogate, not an unreasonable surmise when one considered the mystery and ruthlessness that had marked the man's career.

The son of a railroad conductor, Heydar Aliyev grew up in Nakhichevan, a rural Azerbaijani province bordering Iran, Armenia, and Turkey. According to his official biography, he joined the Soviet security services after gaining espionage experience in a World War II "military counterintelligence group" in Ukraine. But like much of Aliyev's resume—his precise birthday, birthplace, ethnicity, and education—the facts surrounding his early years in government service were sometimes murky.

Gambai Mamedov, a former Azerbaijan prosecutor, for example, served on a Soviet commission that he said established that Aliyev had faked his war record. Aliyev, he said, was hired by the country's Internal Affairs division in 1941, four years earlier than he had claimed. "When the war began, Aliyev, in his desire to avoid being drafted into the Army, went to his native Nakhichevan," Mamedov said. "There he obtained a document stating that he suffered from a serious form of tuberculosis and was relieved of his military obligation."

What was undisputed were the two decades of intelligence work that followed, capped by Aliyev's appointment as head of Azerbaijan's KGB. Two years later, in 1969, Aliyev, now a general, was inducted into political service—as first Communist Party secretary, Azerbaijan's most powerful leadership position.

He moved quickly to purge the ranks of government and academia and surround himself with loyalists. Over a three-year period, he sacked all but two of the ten members of the ruling Party bureau; three of the four Party secretaries; six of the seven members of the Council of Ministers

Presidium; and the heads of eleven of the fourteen Party departments. Allies from his home province and the officer corps of the KGB replaced most of those who had been ousted. The rapid housecleaning did wonders for Aliyev's image, casting him as an "ardent warrior against corruption" and significantly bolstering "Aliyev's political muscle," wrote one scholar. Azeris learned not to challenge this man with the "expressionless eyes and the power to act on what he liked or did not like in a way that made people tremble," observed Audrey Altstadt an American expert on the region.

The punishment accorded Gambai Mamedov was a striking object lesson. In 1976, he was stripped of his job as prosecutor after alleging widespread corruption in agriculture and industry and challenging the authenticity of economic gains claimed by Aliyev. Two years later, as a deputy in parliament, he rose to his feet and repeated his earlier accusations. His remarks set off a storm of protest, according to the Moscow-based *Literaturnaya Gazeta.* One lawmaker declared, "Comrade Aliyev is our pride, the ingenious son of our republic and people, and here comes this Mamedov and libels" him. Mamedov had "simply lost his mind," thundered another. "Who are you speaking against, Gambai? If you believe in God, you might say that before us stands God himself in the person of [Aliyev]. God himself has sent our people this courageous son." Mamedov was expelled from parliament and charged with 124 separate criminal acts. He fled to Leningrad, taking up residence at the "home of his wife's relatives."

Rhetoric aside, Mamedov's offense was simply his refusal to "join the Aliyev gang," observed Arkady Vaksberg, a crusading reporter for the Moscow newspaper. But the disgraced deputy got off easy compared with Ibragim Babaev, an investigator for the Azerbaijan prosecutor's office. Babaev, whose loyalties to Aliyev were suspect, was convicted of corruption, and when "Aliyev personally requested that [he] be shot," the jailed investigator was executed, according to Vaksberg. The Russian journalist decided that such actions by Aliyev were not so much a battle "against the mafia but between one mafia and another." At the Azeri leader's essence, he concluded, was a single-minded pursuit of power—not for the sake of the good life, although Aliyev did not live austerely, but in the deeply held belief that "power itself was heaven."

In 1982, KGB chief Yuri Andropov became the Soviet Union's preeminent leader, succeeding the late Leonid Brezhnev as general secretary. Andropov was a true believer who thought that many Communist ideals had fallen by the wayside in the decades since the revolution. He believed that a Kremlin leadership based on toughness and discipline would restore what had been lost, and he called on someone who had already set an example—Heydar Aliyev.

Brought to Moscow, the Azeri was made Andropov's deputy prime minister and a full member of the elite Politburo. Aliyev was instantly singled out by Kremlin watchers as a possible prime minister, a potential chief of the entire KGB, even a dark horse candidate for general secretary. By 1985, when Gorbachev came to power, Aliyev was the fourth most powerful official in the Soviet Union.

In the national capital, the Politburo's only Muslim was something of an exotic. Moscow diplomats regarded him as "an exceptionally intelligent and self-confident man." Vaksberg, the reporter, saw in Aliyev an "individuality" that put him a cut above his colleagues, most of them nondescript functionaries. The Azeri "stood out because of his energy, ambition, cunning and capacity to see ahead but not to swim with the tide." His personal tastes set him apart from some other senior Party officials who "took pleasure in the company of alcoholics, foul-mouthed swearers and womanizers. . . . Aliyev preferred a different crowd—composers, theater directors, actors and artists."

In the atmosphere of greater openness encouraged by Gorbachev, the Azeri won converts among foreign correspondents by holding a Moscow news conference and actually entertaining their questions. It was a virtually unprecedented performance by a senior Politburo member. American reporter Celestine Bohlen, a longtime Kremlin observer and a daughter of Charles Bohlen, the celebrated former U.S. ambassador to the Soviet Union, was among those impressed. She found that "Aliyev—tall, dark-haired, broad-shouldered and well-dressed—was a good candidate to put before the journalistic pack." He "deftly dodged tricky questions, made a few jokes—one about the small portions of bread offered in western restaurants—and generally handled himself with an ease rarely seen in Soviet press briefings."

Only once did he stumble. Asked about privileges enjoyed by Communist Party leaders, such as access to exclusive stores stocked with imported goods, Aliyev was reported to have initially "denied the shops existed, then said the issue was under discussion, and finally retreated into the defensive," maintaining that Party officials were too busy to submit to the ordeal of shopping in public establishments. His remarks collided with a bold speech to Communist leaders only the previous day by Boris Yeltsin, then a relatively minor figure. Yeltsin called such privileges "the source of the decay of the Party and the lowering of Communist authority" and argued that unless otherwise justified, "they must be canceled."

One year later, Aliyev suffered a stunning fall from grace. It began with Gorbachev forcing the Azeri out of the Politburo. The official explanation, that Aliyev suffered from cardiac problems, had some basis in fact—he had once had a heart attack. But Kremlin disenchantment with him had been building steadily. His years of close association with Azerbaijan's oil, cotton, and caviar barons had tainted Aliyev irreparably; indeed, "for Gorbachev's supporters he exemplified the privilege, nepotism and corruption" of the Brezhnev era, one observer wrote. (In his memoirs, Gorbachev would write that he had been impressed by his "strong opposition to corruption and the black economy" but finally concluded that Aliyev in fact "reigned supreme" over just such a society in Baku.)

Gorbachev unleashed a full-blown, Stalin-style denunciation of Aliyev, including a torrent of derisive Moscow newspaper and television reports. The press especially attacked Aliyev for fawning over Brezhnev years earlier when the Soviet leader, now scorned, had visited Baku, including a speech in which the Azeri strongman had mentioned Brezhnev's name twenty-six times in his presence. Even the Party newspaper in Baku—the city Aliyev had only recently ruled like a Mafia don—threw old loyalties aside and joined in the smear campaign. A long article enumerated the extravagant gifts that the paper said Aliyev had presented to Brezhnev, including a bas-relief portrait "done in white gold," a sword that was "a glittering specimen of the jeweler's art," and a "huge ring embedded with a precious stone."

Aliyev managed for a while to keep his seat in the 301-member Central Committee and its accompanying perquisites. But in 1989, that too was taken away. In a final speech before the ruling body, he insisted that he had "actively struggled against those abusing power and negative phenomena, the result of which is that I earned many enemies and a huge heart attack." Later, he noted to an interviewer that it was de rigueur for regional Communist leaders to butter up powerful visitors from Moscow like Brezhnev. Hadn't his predecessor in Baku treated Nikita Khrushchev "no less triumphantly" on a 1960 visit there? It was all a matter of "status and established tradition." As to Brezhnev's dazzling ring, Aliyev asserted that the general secretary had arrived in Baku already wearing it and that in fact "we didn't give him any kind of special presents." Gorbachev visited a final humiliation on Aliyev by evicting him, along with other former Party leaders, from his plush dacha on Moscow's outskirts.

Unlike many of his similarly disgraced colleagues, Aliyev did not go away meekly. In the days after the Black January massacre by Gorbachev's troops in Baku, he made a surprise appearance at the Azerbaijan mission in Moscow. There, he shook hands with sympathizers of the anti-Soviet Popular Front and talked with reporters. "The absolute majority of the population is behind the Popular Front," he said, an astonishing statement from a still-committed Communist of such recent stature. Aliyev had begun his transition from Soviet loyalist to Azeri nationalist, but not without some hesitation. In an interview just weeks later, he confessed that moves to end the Party's monopoly on power were "a little hard for people like me to accept psychologically. I mean, we're just not used to thinking this way."

Aliyev finally left Moscow in the hope of resettling in Baku. When "they wouldn't give me an apartment—wouldn't let me live [there]," he retreated to the only remaining sanctuary, his boyhood home of Nakhichevan, he would later tell a journalist. There, "everyone embraced me as a native son." Just a few weeks before the 1990 Baku oil exhibition, Aliyev ran uncontested for Nakhichevan's seat in the Azerbaijan parliament and was elected with 95 percent of the vote. Humble as the office was, it marked an exceptional political rebirth for the future architect of resistance to Russia's stubborn post-Soviet embrace.

———

Aliyev's home province kept piling on the honors: In addition to his parliamentary seat, he was soon installed as the territory's leader. Governing with practiced imperiousness and exploiting the language of an arcane 1920s treaty, Aliyev transformed himself into a virtual head of state. He established diplomatic relations with Iran and Turkey and welcomed a steady stream of visitors, though reaching remote Nakhichevan was not easy. Most outsiders had to rely on a single air connection from Baku that operated just twice a day.

One of them was Paolo Lembo, a United Nations representative who flew in humanitarian supplies after border fighting with Armenia severed the province's electricity and fuel. The thirty-three-year-old Italian ended up stranded in a three-day blizzard, spending his daylight hours in "the only heated room in Nakhichevan"—Aliyev's office. "I was impressed how he was dressed, impeccably dressed. His nails were manicured," Lembo recalled. "He talked the whole day, but he was not blathering. He had an incredible analysis of the politics. He talked about his past and the region, about history and the Bolshevik Revolution. I had the perception that I was in the presence of a statesman, unlike the crowd I was used to in Baku. He was a statesman in the middle of nowhere."

Western journalists like Daniel Sneider were also intrigued by this former Communist kingpin holding court in his rural outpost. Aliyev regaled Sneider with stories of "always having been an Azeri nationalist who defied the Russians in the Kremlin," particularly Gorbachev with his "chauvinist sentiments." The journalist experienced firsthand the Azeri's hold on his province. Late getting to the airport for a departing flight, Sneider saw the airliner waiting on the runway, loaded with passengers. The pilots had not dared to take off without him, lest they embarrass Aliyev. Sneider was led to a front-row seat reserved for "a Nakhichevan VIP" and, later, into the cockpit, where he was invited "to fly the plane a bit." Though untrained, Sneider, caught up in the moment, did so.

In Thomas Goltz, a North Dakota native with a shaved head, a booming voice, and an outsize ego, Aliyev met his journalistic match. Before arriving in Baku, Goltz had studied theater in Chicago and had also once been a one-man traveling Shakespeare company in Africa, specializing in the dagger scene from *Macbeth;* he was also a linguist who spoke German, Arabic, and Turkish and was a student of history. Most visibly, though, he was a Hunter Thompson of the Caucasus, a self-absorbed gonzo journalist minus the drugs, practicing what he called "real-life theater" and recording it all in his classic *Azerbaijan Diary.* Visitors to the comfortable Baku apartment he shared with his Turkish wife, Hijran, would often find Goltz slamming down the phone after a shouted exchange with an editor back in the United States who had belittled his latest dispatch. Goltz didn't hold jobs long, but he was responsible for the most knowing, courageous, and vivid accounts of events in Azerbaijan.

Here is how Goltz captured Aliyev in a speech to the Azeri parliament after President Abulfaz Elchibey invited him to mediate with the Gyanja-based rebel Surat Husseinov:

"Yooouuu WORMS!!!" thundered Heydar from his seat. "YOU FAWNING FALSE DOGS AND SELFISH SELLOUTS!"

The capital letters are Goltz's, who wrote that the chamber fell silent as Aliyev continued his diatribe:

> The President of Azerbaijan has asked me to come to Baku in order to determine if there is any possible solution to the well-known problems that beset our country. IT IS A QUAGMIRE CREATED BY YOU, THE POLITICAL DILETTANTES AND DWARFS IN THIS HALL! But here you are again, in this lofty parliament, fawning on me and attempting to play political games! I WILL NOT HAVE IT! I AM NOT HERE TO PLAY! Now it is not time for words. ACTION IS LONG OVER-DUE! . . . To begin with, I will repair to the city of Gyanja within the hour. Alone! I ask the deputy chairman of parliament to provide the necessary transportation for all members of the press who wish to accompany me. Accordingly, I advise you to suspend this session of parliament until my return, at which point I will be able to comment on the Gyanja disaster in an informed and reasonable manner. I have had my say.

With that, Goltz reported, Aliyev decamped, reporters in tow, to Gyanja, where he took Husseinov's measure for the first time.

When Elchibey's national government fell in June 1993 and Aliyev seized control, western oilmen had early cause for optimism. Although Azerbaijan's new leader nullified the offshore Baku contract that was to have been signed in London, he quickly approved a fresh round of talks. In charge for the Azeris were Todd Gremillion and Jack Langlois, the two Houston lawyers who two years earlier had evaluated the original BP and Amoco bids. The pair ran a tight ship as intermediaries between the state oil company, known as Socar, and the foreign oil companies. They did not permit "the Socar folks to talk to us directly or us to talk to the Socar folks directly," one oilman said. But they achieved results in a matter of weeks, producing a draft agreement opening up the offshore fields to the broad partnership of oil multinationals that Unocal had lobbied into existence. Success seemed to be at hand.

In July, Amoco's Tom Doss and BP's Eddie Whitehead presented the document to an assembly of Azeri oil executives. But before they could finish, three men marched from the back of the room, one of them shouting that the contract was a disgrace. He identified himself as President Aliyev's new oil negotiator and instructed his two comrades to open the footlocker they were carrying. Inside were stacks of paper, which the two began handing out to the baffled audience. "This is the model contract," the newcomer declared, making clear that he intended its terms to be the basis for new negotiations.

Doss was incredulous; he thought the uninvited visitors were "a renegade group." But a call to the president's office confirmed it—the negotiations were now in the hands of this dandyish showboater, a thirtyish Azeri businessman named Marat Manafov. He described himself as a former police detective who had earned a fortune dealing in raw materials and owned a soccer club in his current home of Slovakia. A powerful Azeri oilman had persuaded Aliyev to dump the two American lawyers, sideline Socar, and install Manafov in their place.

The model contract that Manafov handed out that day left the foreign oilmen both amused and aghast. Ethiopian in origin, it was a perfect blue-print for desert oil exploration but useless as a guide to framing agree-ments for drilling beneath the ocean. If one didn't know better, one might suspect a perverse example of Azeri humor at play.

Manafov employed an entourage of about a dozen westerners—Britons, Americans, a Canadian, and a German. The oilmen mainly fo-cused on his gorgeous translator, a Slovakian woman named Ivana, "like Ivana Trump." Before her arrival, attendance at the sometimes tedious ne-gotiations had been grudging. But "now we were anxious to go to them," said one Texas oilman who participated in the talks.

At a get-acquainted meeting with Manafov, everyone sat around an enormous table and exchanged business cards. When it was his turn, the blustery fellow reached into a shoulder harness "with a Clint Eastwood type of grin" and slapped a pistol on the table. Negotiations would begin in ten days in London, he said. It was only the first of several times that he would brandish the nine-millimeter weapon.

In London for the start of formal negotiations, Pennzoil's Dave Henderson went to the Hotel Savoy to introduce himself to Manafov. The next thing Henderson knew, he was looking down the barrel of the pistol, which the tough-mannered Azeri was aiming at his head.

"What's your point?" Henderson asked.

Manafov laughed, put down the gun, and asked, "Who are you? What company are you from?"

BP's Eddie Whitehead once emerged "white as a ghost" from a meet-ing with Manafov. "He pointed a gun at me," a dazed Whitehead told his colleagues. "Oh yeah, he did that to me, too," Henderson replied, to which Whitehead's "jaw dropped."

No one witnessed Manafov ever actually firing a shot, and Amoco's Tom Doss concluded that he was simply "trying to scare the hell out of you." Yet, he allowed, "it kind of puts your heart in your throat."

Intrigue seemed to surround the erratic Azeri. He once claimed to Henderson that his bank accounts had been frozen, his cell phone had been switched off, and he was being followed. "I know who it is," the agi-tated Manafov said, adding, "There is a company that has offered us $50 million to throw Pennzoil out and assign it [Pennzoil's] interest. I'm the only one keeping Pennzoil in the deal. Do you believe me?" Manafov demanded. "One company will be thrown out, and it won't be Pennzoil. You go back and tell them that."

Henderson left, unsure what to make of the exchange. Manafov at one point had implied that Amoco was having him tailed. But he had given no hint as to which company was supposedly offering a bribe to scuttle Pennzoil. The American had not pressed the issue, having concluded it was not wise to upset an armed man.

A perplexed Henderson immediately told the other oilmen what had happened. Tom Doss scoffed at the suggestion that his company had someone following Manafov. "Absolutely not," the Amoco executive asserted. But when Doss consulted his superiors, they told him that at least part of Manafov's story was true. "Completely without my knowledge we did have a guy [following Manafov]," a chagrined Doss told his colleagues. "He's been called off." The others were livid, but there was nothing to do but press on.

Still, the question lingered in the minds of some: Had one of them truly offered tens of millions of dollars to steal Pennzoil's share of the deal, or did Manafov manufacture that claim to spice up his story? If it were true, no one was going to confess. The unsettling episode left everyone on guard.

Manafov's next communiqué, relayed to Henderson by the Canadian in the Azeri's entourage, posed a more serious problem. "Dr. Manafov expects a fee if this is successful," the Canadian said bluntly.

"We don't mind doing anything that we wouldn't mind reading on the front page of *The Wall Street Journal*," Henderson replied.

"This can't be in the contract. Dr. Manafov expects $300 million," the Canadian said.

"You're out of your fucking mind," said Henderson.

"But such fees are customary."

"The government will make its money as we make ours."

"Others have paid," said the Canadian intermediary.

"What you have gotten them to do individually you'll never get them to do as a group," Henderson said confidently.

"We expect you to deliver the message."

"Don't expect it to be well received."

Manafov's bold entreaty plunged the oilmen into a whole new state of uncertainty. Was their antagonist acting alone or in a scheme to split the payoff with Aliyev and his family? British Petroleum made discreet inquiries in Baku, and word came back that the president had nothing to do with it.

True or not, the oil companies decided to stand fast and tell Manafov they would pay no such bribe. As Henderson had told the Canadian messenger, even if one company were tempted to accede to the demand privately, there was no chance that it would do so as part of a group. That would make it witness to a criminal plot that could be prosecuted in the United States under the Foreign Corrupt Practices Act.

Manafov feigned ignorance when the oilmen, in a tense meeting, raised the matter and said that they would not pay. "You have impugned my integrity," he exploded, adding that he would never make such a demand. Then came language that the oilmen took as a threat. "I know where each of you live," he said, without elaboration. He ended the meeting with the ominous announcement that he was moving the negotiations from London to Slovakia; they would reconvene ten days hence in the resort town of Piešťany, where he was headquartered.

Back at their hotel, the oilmen went into a panic. Amoco's Tom Doss rang the company's Baku office. "Don't use the phones. Don't say anything. Lay low," he said and hung up. At 2 A.M., he phoned Pennzoil's Henderson with disturbing news: "The lives of our representative here and his family have been threatened, and our employees in Baku have been threatened. We are organizing a charter flight to get them out [of Baku]. We are willing to bring your guys too."

Henderson thought quickly: He had 150 people in Baku, but it would be difficult to assemble them on a moment's notice, and in any event there were too many to squeeze into Amoco's chartered plane. He thanked Doss for the offer, and at 3 A.M. faxed a carefully worded advisory to Pennzoil's

Baku office, urging the staff to heighten security by such actions as traveling in pairs and taking different routes to work. He was deliberately vague as to the cause of his concern.

The Baku office chief, Tom Hickox, was mystified by the message. Four time zones ahead of London, he waited until 7 A.M. to ring Henderson for clarification. "Can you elaborate on this?" he asked. Believing the phone was tapped that very moment, Henderson struggled to think of a suitably oblique reply that nonetheless would mean something to Hickox. "I want you to behave like you're in Bogota," Henderson said, referring to the semi-lawless Colombian oil fields. "Okay, got it," said an understanding Hickox.

As the time to leave for Slovakia drew close, Doss returned to his hotel room to find that someone had rifled through his suitcase and, it seemed, stolen documents. Now the oilmen became "completely paranoid," especially those who were about to find themselves caged up with the unpredictable Manafov on his home turf. But too much was at stake to refuse to go, and the negotiators departed London, some with security details in tow.

To everyone's relief, the Slovakia sessions were remarkably uneventful. Both teams "went back to negotiating as normal," said Henderson, and the unpleasantness in London was not mentioned. Manafov seemed to have been surprised and embarrassed by what had transpired. The westerners could only speculate that he had been testing the possibilities of an under-the-table payoff but had dropped the idea after encountering such determined resistance.

Even so, the talks devolved into a feeding frenzy for the Azeris. The partnership of oil companies more than doubled the signing bonus, to $500 million; it would be an aboveboard payment written into the contract and deposited in a government bank account. Manafov in return signed off on almost every clause precisely as the oil companies had hoped, affording them an even more favorable contract than before. The final draft was completed November 1, 1993, and forwarded to the Azeri government and parliament for ratification.

Henderson, Doss, and the rest of the oilmen were never able to unravel the full extent of the skullduggery. How was it that certain Azeri officials in faraway Baku routinely seemed to know what the oilmen were privately discussing in London? Perhaps the Azeris had access to recordings or transcripts of wiretapped conversations, but "Azerbaijan cannot bug your phones in London," Henderson thought. Was it the KGB? And what about the mysterious searches of hotel rooms occupied by the American oilmen? Could British intelligence have played a role in the snooping? Given the nerve-wracking atmosphere, it was little wonder that the oil companies had secretly rented a room in a second London hotel, the Royal Westminster, so that they could meet with some assurance of privacy.

As for Manafov, his hijinks may have been more bluff than anything else, but the oilmen who lived through them weren't so sure. "He was Mafia, maybe KGB," Henderson reckoned. "He was in their underworld," concluded Doss. The companies had almost no dealings with him after the deal was signed. Years later, the Slovakian police reported that Manafov had vanished after alleging dishonorable relationships between the foreign oil companies and the Aliyev family; authorities were "investigating whether he may have been abducted or killed," according to a British press report.

In Azerbaijan, President Heydar Aliyev was finding himself on the defensive, both militarily and diplomatically. Armenian troops had made broad advances; by October 1993 they had occupied up to a fifth of Azeri territory. The Armenian fighters were a disciplined, determined force. The Azeris, by comparison, were reduced to press-ganging young men in Baku; the quest for the disputed territory of Nagorno-Karabakh had resonance there but less so than in the cities of Armenia, still nursing memories of the decades-old Turkish massacres. The Armenian offensive uprooted at least seven hundred thousand Azeri civilians—some said a million—or a full 10 percent of the population, their towns burnt behind them and their belongings looted. Many of the refugees trudged east, toward Baku. It was as though the entire city of San Francisco were suddenly on the move, looking for a place to stay.

Aliyev turned to the outside for help. The bloodthirsty Afghan warlord Gulbeddin Hekmatyar, in return for an undisclosed payment, sent some one thousand *mujahideen* to spearhead an Azeri push. An ad hoc squad of U.S. veterans of special forces arrived in Baku to train and supply Azeri troops. The Americans called their outfit "Mega Oil," and General Richard Secord, a principal in the 1980s Iran-Contra scandal, played a cameo role. Almost as quickly as they arrived, however, the Americans departed. The Afghans, too, returned home, having caused perhaps more disruption within the Azeri lines than among the Armenians.

Meanwhile, Armenia was outflanking Azerbaijan in the international arena. Hundreds of thousands of dollars' worth of munitions and financial assistance poured into Armenia from diaspora communities in Aleppo, Syria; Beirut, Lebanon; Paris; Boston; Fresno, California; and elsewhere. In Washington, the Armenian lobby had managed to persuade Congress to sharply restrict assistance to Azerbaijan. As a result, aid to Baku through December 1993 totaled about $36 million, compared with some $330 million to Armenia. The limited funding was especially meant to penalize Azerbaijan for its economic blockade against Armenia, denounced in the United States as inhumane. The Azeris, though, were left wondering why in wartime they should be expected to maintain a lifeline to their enemy.

As if Aliyev didn't already have enough to contend with, there was the specter of Russia, unhappy at having lost its empire. Moscow was determined to keep the newly independent Caspian states under its thumb; it was already pressuring Azerbaijan on the battlefield by furnishing military aid and mercenaries to the Armenians. Such Russian meddling was a chilling reminder of its willingness to employ military force in neighboring Georgia; Moscow had dispatched troops the previous October to help a breakaway Black Sea region called Abkhazia secede from Georgia. Azerbaijan and Georgia had both irritated Moscow, in part by resisting membership in the Commonwealth of Independent States, the post-Soviet federation that Kazakhstan's Nazarbayev had midwifed back in 1991; the two republics worried that Moscow would ultimately dominate the federation, enabling it to continue its historical rule over the Caspian. In the end, the Georgians and Azeris reluctantly agreed to join, but relations with Moscow hardly warmed.

Russia especially coveted the huge oil reserves of Kazakhstan and Azerbaijan, arguing that it had a rightful claim to the fields since they were discovered during the Soviet era. On his way to Baku to urge Azeri acceptance of the pending deal with the oil multinationals, U.S. deputy secretary of energy Bill White stopped off in Moscow. There he encountered Russia's energy minister, a brash career oil boss named Yuri Shafranik, who knew White's destination and had a warning for him. "You know, these resources in the Caspian were discovered by Russians, and Russian companies will be the ones developing them," Shafranik said. "But if you want to go to Baku, so be it. We know everything about Baku. That was part of our oil and gas complex. The same with Kazakhstan."

White had agreed to make the trip after the always-nervous American oil companies had lobbied the Clinton administration for help. The offshore Baku exploration agreement negotiated only weeks earlier was still awaiting ratification by the Azeri parliament. There were disquieting rumbles that Aliyev was having second thoughts because, in his view, Washington was penalizing his country while rewarding Armenia.

The American official flew into Baku with Pennzoil's Rondo Fehlberg, who briefed him on the usual: "Assume everything is bugged." The pair was met at the airport by Prime Minister Hassan Hassanov, who shouted demands as the motorcade's lead car swerved in and out of traffic, running other motorists off the road. "America is not doing its job as a superpower," Hassanov insisted, because it was not using its influence to resolve the Nagorno-Karabakh conflict. If the U.S. government continued to stand on the sidelines, "American companies will suffer adverse commercial consequences."

Next came a sit-down with Aliyev himself, during which White did his best both to disarm and reassure the Azeri president. America could not impose a peace on Nagorno-Karabakh, the energy envoy argued, and it made no sense to penalize U.S. oil companies for something Washington could not control. Aliyev should not lose sight of the fact that foreign oil investment by itself could strengthen Azerbaijan. To the Azeris, it seemed clear that Washington felt little impulse to offer them diplomatic or other help.

An unemotional, calculating gambler, Aliyev weighed the odds against him and decided that he still had cards to play. In a world in which giant oil fields were becoming scarce, Azerbaijan had three that were proven and ready to produce. He would use them to move events in his favor. Paolo Lembo, the U.N. diplomat, heard Aliyev predict that he would prevail. "The Armenians are rolling over you," Lembo cautioned him during a visit to Baku. "They have better weapons. You don't have such weapons." Aliyev responded sharply: "You are wrong. My weapon is oil, and with that we will manage to win the war."

The Azeri strongman's first step was to widen the circle of nations whose companies would be awarded offshore oil deals. The heavyweights like America and Great Britain would still receive the biggest chunks, but smaller slices would be distributed to a rainbow of other countries, a veritable United Nations of oil partners. The strategy was simple—each of the newcomers would have a stake in ensuring Azerbaijan's territorial integrity. The more nations he invited in, the more international support Azerbaijan would enjoy against Russia, and Armenia as well.

At the same time, Aliyev attempted to soothe Russia's anxieties. He signaled that he was prepared to grant it a third of Azerbaijan's stake in the pending offshore oil deal with the multinational companies. The share would amount to 10 percent of the total deal. A tentative agreement to that effect was reached with Shafranik, the Russian oil minister, only a day after White, the U.S. energy official, ended his inconclusive meetings in Baku. The Azeris tried to put the best face possible on the pact, insisting that Shafranik had respectfully made "a request, not a demand" that a Russian company—in this case, Lukoil—be permitted "to participate in the consortium on the same terms and conditions as the other companies."

Finally, Aliyev considered the political leverage afforded him by the hunger of oil multinationals to get at his nation's huge reserves of crude. It rankled him that the United States in particular expected its companies to be granted a sizable share of Azerbaijan's national treasure but was unwilling to do much in return, diplomatically speaking. If he was to hand American corporations 40 percent of the deal—the single biggest piece— well, then, political support had to be part and parcel of it. The United States government would have to be willing to stand visibly by his side, in a partnership conspicuous to Russia. He would make sure that American oilmen—and their lobbyists in Washington—understood this condition.

The Azeri parliament never had a chance to ratify the contract negotiated between the oil companies and the pistol-wielding Marat Manafov. The state oil company got to it first and declared the agreement dead on arrival.

Representatives of Pennzoil, BP, and Amoco, summoned to Socar headquarters in December 1993, were the first to learn of the maddening turn of events. "The contract is unacceptable," a senior official told them. "We are going to put together another [negotiating] team, and we will sit down in due course."

"What do you mean, it's not acceptable?" exclaimed a disbelieving Richard Edmonson, Pennzoil's lawyer. "You told us to negotiate with Manafov, we did so in good faith, and now you're telling us it's not acceptable?" The oilmen, in Edmonson's understated words, "were all upset" by the news.

But it was clear what had happened—the foreign companies had been caught in a power struggle between Manafov and the old guard of Azeri oil interests, who still controlled the state oil company. They regarded Manafov as an interloper, and they were particularly bitter at having been forced to stand by while he did all the negotiating. And so the Socar leadership simply picked apart the agreement, especially the sections that reflected its Ethiopian desert origins—one required the companies to provide Azeri villagers with free gravel from their oil drillings, a material not likely to emerge from offshore wells.

Months passed without a resumption of negotiations. The anxious oilmen faulted state oil company functionaries for being either unable or unwilling to focus on what needed to be done. They were additionally dismayed by an Azeri attempt to change the rules of engagement. The unification arrangement successfully promoted by Unocal would no longer be acceptable; instead, each oil company again would have to negotiate separately for its share of the offshore fields. The oil companies balked. Where once they opposed the idea of banding together in a partnership to develop the fields, now they were committed supporters of unification. "We're going to have to take this under advisement," British Petroleum's

Eddie Whitehead told the Azeris. With that, the oilmen departed Baku for a strategy session in London. Tensions were so high that "no one wanted to ride with anyone else," and the rivals flew west on four different company planes.

After some initial bickering in London, the companies drew their own line in the sand. They agreed to form the Azerbaijan International Oil Consortium, a group that "would negotiate jointly, or none of us would go ahead with any of the deal," as one participant described it. The Azeris would not be allowed an opening to divide and conquer. Seven decades earlier, foreign oil companies had similarly formed the partnership called Front Uni to stand together in negotiations with the Bolsheviks in Baku. But Front Uni had soon fallen victim to unrelenting company rivalry and collapsed. This time, the oilmen did not allow their competing interests to undo their coalition, and the Azeris backed off the attempt to jettison unitization.

The Russians, meanwhile, continued to be bothersome in ways that made western oil companies uneasy. Shafranik, the oil minister, pushed to double Lukoil's share in the offshore Baku oil deal, from 10 percent to 20 percent. Aliyev managed to find other sweeteners for Shafranik that allowed the Azeris to hold the line at 10. Separately, Russia's Foreign Ministry wrote Britain that all five states whose land fronted the Caspian Sea must sign off on any undersea development. The boldness of the concept was startling: It would give Russia, one of the five, effective veto power over any offshore oil deal, including the one still in progress between the Azeris and the western oil companies.

Shafranik also began maneuvering for an agreement that would assure the continued export of Baku oil solely through the Russian pipeline system. It was a simple matter of economics, he said. A pipeline already existed between Baku and the Russian Black Sea; for a mere $50 million in upgrades, foreign oil companies could ship their crude through the Russian line directly to oceangoing tankers waiting at Black Sea terminals.

The western oilmen, not wanting to surrender control of their exports to the Russians, reacted with alarm—as did the Azeris. Whoever operated the lines through which the crude was sent to market would have de facto command of the oil fields—and, by extension, of Azerbaijan itself, given the nation's near-total dependence on oil profits. When the land was a Soviet republic, this was a moot point. But now that the Azeris were independent, they shuddered at the prospect of Russia wielding a potential chokehold over their economic lifeline. Dutch dealmaker John Deuss had been truly prescient when he forecast the life-or-death role that export pipelines would play in the Caspian oil rush.

Ominous though these events were, the foreign oilmen were willing to bet that Aliyev could out-think the Russians and "would figure out how to accommodate" them, said one western onlooker. Admittedly, the Stalinist-trained president was a product of the KGB and the ruling Soviet Politburo. But he had proven himself to be no Russian puppet, despite the earlier suspicions of many. He had become a towering figure in his own right, one not to be trifled with. Most Azeris seemed to accept that no one was more capable of standing up for them. Even battlefield losses inflicted by Armenia had little political impact. He somehow managed to deflect fault, scorning one of his failed predecessors ("the traitor Mutalibov") and even the Popular Front ("more a selfish political party than a movement per se"). As Goltz wrote, "There was only one hero of the people, then and forever more: Heydar Aliyev."

So large a shadow did he cast that, with time, the foreign oilmen, as well as the governments in the United States, Europe, Japan, and elsewhere would come to rely on this autocrat's uncanny finesse.

In May 1994, a new round of negotiations for offshore Baku finally opened in Istanbul. Heydar Aliyev sent the person he trusted most—his only son, Ilham—to be his eyes and ears at the talks. Ilham's presence would allow the Azeri president to keep abreast of every turn without having to rely entirely on the reports of his negotiators or resort to something clumsy, like listening devices. Amoco's Tom Doss recognized this when he and the thirty-three-year-old Ilham climbed into a car during a break in talks. After Ilham ended a longish cell phone conversation, Doss inquired, "Who was that?" "Heydar," the son replied simply.

The Azeris were represented by the old oil guard. Key members were Valekh Aleskerov, Azerbaijan's vainglorious and brilliant principal negotiator; Natik Aliyev, the emotional president of Socar (no relation to the country's president); and Khoshbakht Yusufzade, the elderly oil geologist whose well-timed humor often calmed flaring tempers. The bumptious Marat Manafov had been banished, apparently without compensation, in the wake of his failed agreement.

The oil industry team was led by Doss, the plain-talking Amoco petroleum engineer, and BP's Whitehead, who, while having the sharpest mind among the oilmen, nonetheless saw negotiation as "90 percent theater." Whitehead scripted routines for himself and Doss to follow; he would deliver a piece of bad news, and Doss would then step in to explain why it was so. The theory was that, since the Azeris "were all technical people, I'd be more believable," Doss said. Whitehead had even studied acting in order to dramatize such performances; Doss knew when Whitehead was shifting to acting mode "because he'd drop both hands on top of the table, one over the other, look up," and then deliver his punch line.

Aleskerov, an instinctive actor himself, could match Whitehead move for move. (Heydar Aliyev, too, was talented in this respect, having played Hamlet, among other roles, in high school and college.) Aleskerov had a young financial team behind him, trained largely by Pennzoil. Their presence, plus his ability to run many of his economic models independently and his intimate knowledge of past negotiations, made him a formidable opponent. With a beautiful wife, a tastefully furnished Baku apartment, impeccably tailored suits, and a muscular physique, Aleskerov was the very image of elegance. That was before he began negotiating, however, when he would preen, shout, curse, and pound tables to get his way.

The task before everyone was to draft a foundation agreement, a list of principles generally establishing the guidelines for oil field development and the division of profits. Given the number of times these issues had been hashed over in the past, the assignment might have seemed simple. But what followed was a three-week "knock-down, drag-out" fight, as Doss remembered it. The two sides worked out of separate war rooms in the Istanbul Hilton. The oilmen operated so-called white noise generators in their quarters to defeat attempts at surveillance, but the Azeri team at times still seemed to know what they were planning. The only certain way to foil eavesdropping was to go outside for a walk, which Doss and

Whitehead did regularly when plotting bargaining tactics. "You don't want the other side to know the whole damn strategy before the meeting started," said Doss.

The oilmen imported their own team of economists, whose workday commenced when the negotiators finished, toiling through the night to produce a flurry of charts and recommendations. They were backed up by an Amoco technical unit in Houston that stood by to generate whatever supporting data was needed. For example, when the oilmen wanted to know how a proposed bonus would affect the deal, they would drop the question off in the war room and get the answer in the morning.

One day, as Doss was using a flip chart to argue a point, the Socar president called him "a liar" and moved closer to elaborate. The American, a wiry, well-built golfer who usually kept his emotions to himself, poked the Azeri in the chest and indignantly responded, "How long have I known you? This is the truth." Calm was quickly restored; as Doss by now knew, it "was just theater."

Serious differences quickly emerged. The Azeris sought a larger share of profits than the oil companies were offering and a higher pipeline tariff as well. The oilmen balked at both demands and argued that development expenses should be paid down before profits were distributed. There was also the matter of the fields themselves. At first, only two were offered up by the Azeris; the third, Guneshli, had been taken off the table in the abortive Manafov round of negotiations. The oilmen successfully argued for restoration of at least a portion of Guneshli—a pristine deep-water section—by offering a bigger payoff.

When the Istanbul talks ended, the money issues were still not entirely resolved. The negotiators elected to plug in ballpark figures for the time being. But everyone agreed that progress had been made—at last, "both sides understood each other," said Doss. They could proceed to final negotiations.

The two sides moved on to Houston in July, and interpreters labored to present a draft agreement in three languages, Russian, Azeri, and English. As the exhausting talks dragged on, the chain-smoking Socar president,

Natik Aliyev, appeared to be ill. He was perspiring heavily, and his eyes were sunken. Oil company negotiators "were worried he would have a heart attack and die, and we'd be back to square one, and who would that be with?" recalled Doss. So they issued an ultimatum: No more talks until he saw a doctor. Back came the report that Natik had some partially blocked arteries; he would have to restrain his eating habits and his smoking. Two other Azeri negotiators were also chain smokers; to encourage their ailing colleague, they agreed to put away their cigarettes. Their pledge lasted just three days, but by that time Natik's condition seemed to have stabilized. Everyone went back to work.

The intensity of the talks simply reflected the high stakes. "It was a process of life or death," observed Yusufzade, the Azeri geologist. "They do not want to spend more. We do not want to get less." Most evenings all dined together, often at a Greek restaurant where the food was reminiscent of the native fare of Azerbaijan. After the meal, the Azeris would "push the tables away and dance, and make us dance with them," said Doss. Personal friendships developed between the Americans and their guests; to the sentimental Yusufzade, Amoco's Doss "was like my son." But then both sides would retire, to prepare for more hard bargaining the next day.

A stir arose when members of the Amoco delegation demanded that the Azeris guarantee the fields against Russian encroachment. They wanted "a signed release from Russia that the Russians surrender any claim to the reserves," recalled Bill White, the U.S. deputy energy secretary. It was an extraordinary proposal, and Amoco's own partners "looked at them like they had their heads on crooked," said one participant. The Azeris were insulted. President Aliyev himself was "the main guarantee," said Aleskerov, their lead negotiator. That rang true—without a leader of his astuteness, Azerbaijan could not hope to stand up to Moscow.

The Amoco demand so upset the Azeris that Ilham Aliyev immediately flew to Washington, where he urged Bill White to rein in the renegade company. The American official gently informed the surprised Azeri that Washington lacked the absolute power over private companies wielded by his father back in Azerbaijan. But White did follow up with Amoco. He judged the company's demand to be reasonable from a business point of view but politically unrealistic. The demand was withdrawn, and the oil companies took comfort in the age-old belief that possession was nine-tenths of the law along with a contract clause in which the Azeris simply asserted sovereignty over the oil fields.

Two months into the Houston talks, frustration began to mount. Aleskerov now "made it known that he wanted to revisit the economics"—meaning open up the thorny money issues that had been settled with much difficulty in Istanbul. But as the oilmen thought about it, irritation set in. They had compromised enough, said Doss; they were "fed up with the Azeris," and wanted "to end this thing." Oil company lawyers drafted a finished contract that incorporated already settled language plus their desired version of provisions still in dispute. Doss sprung the document on the Azeris.

"This is our final offer," he said. "We want you to show this to President Aliyev and see if he accepts." Doss then slid four airline tickets to Baku across the table and invited Aleskerov and his comrades to use them for a quick trip home and a presidential consultation.

The Azeri negotiator was furious: "That's not the way it is going to be."

Doss stood firm, and declared that if Aliyev didn't agree, "we aren't sure we want to continue negotiating."

The disgruntled Azeris turned to Khoi Tran, the trusted analyst for Pennzoil, and asked him to look at what Doss had presented. Tran spent a day and a half poring over the numbers and pronounced the deal equitable. Still unsatisfied, they appealed to Pennzoil's Dave Henderson, saying that they "felt in a corner, that BP and Amoco were being unreasonable." Henderson rebuffed their feeler for a deal with Pennzoil alone, one that would have left the other companies out in the cold, and told them, "This is as good as it gets." The Azeris still didn't give up. From Istanbul, Socar's top executive telephoned Doss, who said he "wouldn't change anything."

As the negotiations sputtered, the U.S. government prepared to step in and nudge matters to a conclusion. The determined Heydar Aliyev was about to attain what he had wanted all along: an unmistakable signal to Moscow that America was extending its political support to Azerbaijan in exchange "for leaning to the West," as a Washington lobbyist phrased it. The signal sought by the Azeri president was a White House Rose Garden meeting with President Bill Clinton.

Rosemarie Forsythe, the Caspian authority on the National Security Council, swung into action. She had been in constant contact with the oil companies during the roller-coaster negotiations, waiting for the right time to offer what she called "the goody," meaning that Clinton meeting that Aliyev so prized. Washington was just as anxious as the oilmen to wrap up the contract—not just to lend a hand to the oil companies but also to secure a U.S. presence on the Caspian. America was on the verge of a dramatic new initiative in Central Asia; the geopolitical game there was about to get rougher.

Forsythe called Hafiz Pashayev, Azerbaijan's ambassador to Washington: "We are going to go ahead with a meeting if [Aliyev] signs the deal," she said. It would not be in the Rose Garden—privately, the administration knew that such a meeting would inflame Armenian sensibilities—but during the annual meeting of the United Nations General Assembly in New York. That was good enough, came back the reply.

The contract ceremony would be five days hence. Once he made a decision, Aliyev was not a dawdler.

At first, the frazzled oil company negotiators did not believe what they were hearing. Discreet inquiries were made to some of Aliyev's subordinates, asking if the Azeri leadership really was ready to conclude a deal. "They mean to sign the document we sent them, right?" inquired Amoco's Doss. "Yes," the reply came back. The list of signatories to the final agreement would be long. Over the months, the oil consortium had grown substantially, as Aliyev kept taking slices from Azerbaijan's share and distributing them to other countries, in keeping with his strategy of building a diplomatic shield. In all, ten companies representing six countries, including neighboring Turkey, would sign the deal.

But Pennzoil was very nearly not among them. At almost the last moment, the president of Socar notified Tom Hamilton in Baku that his company and that of his partner, Steve Remp of Ramco, had been excluded.

Hamilton was irate, pointing out to the Azeri oil executive "what good friends we had been"—providing free computers and crucial economics training for Socar's team, lending a sympathetic ear during negotiations. But there was also a sharp edge to his response. Was the Azeri aware of Pennzoil's $3 billion courtroom victory over Texaco in 1987, after Texaco decided to tangle with the company? Just such a bludgeoning could await Azerbaijan, he implied. Hamilton then went straight to the president's office, where he told Aliyev: "We have put our careers on the line for this country." If the expulsion stood, Pennzoil's huge natural gas recovery project at Oily Rocks would be abandoned. "There obviously has been some sort of misunderstanding," said Aliyev. Pennzoil and Ramco were back in.

Hamilton was never told why Pennzoil's share had been put in sudden jeopardy. But it was not hard to speculate. Even though the oil companies were now joined in a partnership to develop the fields, each kept trying to fatten its share of the profits at the expense of the others. If the Azeris could be persuaded to lop a percentage point or so off one company's deal and slip it to another, that was just part of the game. Seen in this light, Marat Manafov's earlier tale of being offered $50 million by an unnamed rival to throw Pennzoil overboard didn't seem so fanciful after all.

The final mystery of the Baku negotiations hinted at high-level profiteering of some sort. The consortium of western oil companies was obliged to pay the Azeris a $300 million signing bonus. After receiving credit for the $70 million advance payment feared lost in the turmoil as Aliyev rose to power, the oilmen deposited the remainder in a designated Azerbaijan government bank account abroad. Almost instantly, the money was dispersed to four separate private accounts elsewhere—"offshore accounts in countries with lax banking laws," in the words of Dave Henderson of Pennzoil. The oilmen were never able to identify the beneficiaries of the four accounts. But logic dictated that they were persons in some way connected to the Azeri government.

On September 20, 1994, Heydar Aliyev sat behind a long table inside Baku's Gulistan Palace for the signing of what a banner proclaimed the CONTRACT OF THE CENTURY. Before him were four leather-bound versions of the document—in English, in Russian, and two Azeri renditions in Cyrillic and Latin script. Flanking him were oil company executives and government officials from the United States, Britain, and Russia. They sipped celebratory champagne against a backdrop of flags representing the participating countries, an international front line against anyone who might challenge Azerbaijan's independence.

A Russian deputy energy minister initialed the document as a witness, and the Azeri government interpreted his action as a signal that Moscow "recognized this contract and that this oil field is Azerbaijan's," said Aleskerov, the chief negotiator. Just how wrong he was became clear before the signatories had even left the palace: Declaring that Moscow abhorred "unilateral actions" that "contradict international law," the Russian Foreign Ministry said that the Kremlin did not recognize the deal.

Six days later, Aliyev and Clinton sat in two large armchairs at New York's Waldorf-Astoria. The Azeri president reported on the cease-fire he had reached with Armenia in July and outlined his hopes for an enduring peace between the two countries. Then Aliyev requested a favor—that Clinton persuade Russia's Boris Yeltsin to acquiesce to the oil deal and be flexible on the issue of pipelines. Russia cannot "dictate this question," Aliyev declared. Clinton promised to try.

The Near Abroad

PRESIDENT CLINTON KEPT HIS WORD. Two days after assuring Aliyev that he would take up Azerbaijan's cause with the Russians, Clinton huddled with Boris Yeltsin at a Washington summit meeting. Russian hostility to the oil deal between the Azeris and western oil companies was shortsighted, the American leader gently argued. "Oil development in this region is good for Russia and good for the U.S.," he told the Russian president. "It's in your interest to take another look at this and show a little flexibility."

Vice President Al Gore sat in on the September 28, 1994, discussion. He had developed an interest in the Caspian after visiting there nine months earlier. En route to the Kyrgyzstan capital of Bishkek, he was counseled on the niceties of eating a sheep's ear, a delicacy traditionally offered to important guests: Swallow but don't chew the rubbery appendage, which could be gnawed forever to no effect. Stepping off the plane, Gore resolutely intoned, "Swallow don't chew, swallow don't chew." In Kazakhstan, his hosts treated Gore to a sauna, an especially high honor. Later, President Nazarbayev, his wife, Sarah, and his daughter Dariga sang Kazakh folk songs in three-part harmony, and, it being Christmastime, Gore reciprocated with a hearty rendition of "Jingle Bells."

Now, looking at Yeltsin, the less-restrained Gore charged straight to the point: "You guys will get a 10 percent cut. That's not such a bad deal. And it's a way to get Azerbaijan off the Russian dole." Neither Clinton's moderate approach nor Gore's directness had any visible effect. Yeltsin and his subordinates made it plain that even if Moscow were inclined to permit the Baku deal, it would never do so absent a concession on oil transportation. "Russia is interested that we control the pipeline," one Yeltsin adviser said bluntly.

Aliyev lingered briefly in Washington before heading home. Immediately after his historic meeting with Clinton, the Azeri president was guest of honor at a celebratory dinner hosted by oil company executives. They lauded him with champagne toasts, and he savored his new alliance with America. It was a sweet moment for the old Kremlin campaigner after a year of threats to his rule. But it didn't last long.

In Azerbaijan, with Aliyev out of the country, law and order had rapidly begun to disintegrate. The news that Aliyev received was head-spinning: Four men imprisoned when he consolidated power "miraculously escaped" from a sixth-floor cell in KGB headquarters. Three senior government allies were assassinated. Interior Ministry troops mutinied, irate over the arrest of comrades accused of involvement in the assassinations. The troops assaulted the state prosecutor and barricaded themselves inside barracks. In Gyanja, men loyal to the disputatious Surat Husseinov seized the airport, the train station, and the local Interior Ministry building. Meanwhile, a Baku explosion injured about a dozen people, and someone cut telephone lines out of the country.

Upon his return, Aliyev declared a state of emergency. Described as "weary-looking," he went on television to declare that the nation's survival was at stake and to summon the Azeri people to his side. Though it was past midnight, some five thousand people answered the call, crowding together outside the presidential palace and cheering as their president vowed not to be intimidated. Once again, the Aliyev magic was working.

He quickly ordered the rebels rounded up and undertook finally to rid himself of Surat Husseinov, whose Gyanja-based rebellion fifteen months earlier had driven Aliyev's predecessor from office. In the negotiations that led to Aliyev taking power, Husseinov had demanded and received the title of prime minister, with responsibility for military affairs; the catch was that he enjoyed no real authority. Once Aliyev became confident that the somewhat dim-witted fellow was not a serious threat, Husseinov's days were numbered. The crafty Aliyev administered the fatal blow at a seafront rally following his return from New York; he lambasted traitors "who wish to destroy our land" and then thundered, "one of them is the Prime Minister, Surat Husseinov!" Nobody was more startled than Husseinov, who was standing nearby. He lamely protested that "independent groups" had been responsible for the most recent Gyanja uprising, not his forces. Guilty or not, Husseinov was sacked and arrested. Aliyev then engineered a campaign to make his former prime minister the scapegoat for all sorts of government failings. As Thomas Goltz wrote sardonically, "it was Surat who had lost the war in Karabakh; Surat who had brought the economy to its knees; Surat who had isolated Azerbaijan from the rest of the world." Husseinov managed to escape and flee to the safety of Moscow, a broken man.

Order was soon restored to Azerbaijan, but Aliyev did not rest easy. He suspected that a Moscow-backed plot had contributed to the turmoil, perhaps even instigated it. Western leaders were similarly concerned, and Britain signaled that "relations would suffer if Russia had fomented the trouble."

The suspicions were easy to understand, even though the supporting evidence was largely circumstantial. Ever since the Soviet Union's collapse, Russia had regularly provoked mischief in its former republics, sending in troops without invitation, backing challenges to national borders, and arbitrarily severing supplies of gas, oil, and electricity. Mysterious assassinations, coups, or bomb blasts often seemed to coincide with events that Russia perceived as threats to its interests—for example, the signing of the Baku oil deal. To some observers, it became almost an article of faith that a bullying Russia was behind many such acts and that they were intended as punishment for any former Soviet republic that dared to stray from Moscow's grasp.

The cloak-and-dagger episodes appeared to be mainly the handiwork of disillusioned military officers encouraged by rightist elements within Russia's political hierarchy and espionage agencies. The Caucasus was dotted with former Soviet military bases now in the hands of the Russians, and the senior officers attached to them were among the most imperial-minded in the armed forces. Cash at times was motive enough. So undisciplined was the Russian military that troops could be hired as mercenaries by almost anyone bent on disrupting the former Soviet republics; weapons were also for sale.

No one accused Boris Yeltsin of having a direct hand in the acts of violence. But his increasingly bellicose assertions that Russia had a historical right to maintain its sway over the recently departed republics seemed to leave little doubt about Kremlin intent. In Moscow, the phrase "near abroad" became synonymous with its "sphere of influence"—the fourteen republics outside Russia that once were part of the Soviet Union. Yeltsin's vow to protect ethnic Russians still living in the former Soviet states reminded Nazarbayev, the Kazakhstan leader, "of the times of Hitler, who started off with the question of protecting Sudeten Germans."

The Russian leader had set a very different tone when he succeeded Mikhail Gorbachev a little more than three years earlier. Back then, the masterfully theatrical reformer had indicated that in addition to being "the first democratically elected leader in Russian history," he would also be "the first non-imperialistic one," wrote a senior American diplomat. But Yeltsin soon found himself locked in "a mortal struggle" with hardliners in Russia's parliament who, accusing him of sedition, had curtailed his powers and attempted to impeach him. About two years into his presidency, he had run out of patience and resorted to force: Loyal tank units fired on his opponents holed up in the Russian parliament building, and elite Alpha forces in black masks led them away.

Two months later, new parliamentary elections revived the nationalist forces. Yeltsin and other liberals sought refuge in a rightward lurch, touting the virtues of Russian empire. Soon he was voicing impatience with former colonies that seemed to have forgotten their place, and world powers—such as the United States—that presumed to meddle in the backyard of a great nation like Russia. Though Yeltsin and his pro-western foreign minister, Andrei Kozyrev, were acting out of political expediency, they didn't seem all that uncomfortable in their new roles. By the time of his September 1994 summit with Clinton, the Russian president was spending much time beating his chest in public at America's expense, playing to the fantasies of nationalists back home that Russia still possessed its former clout. Addressing the United Nations, he in effect declared Russian hegemony over the former Soviet republics; *The Economist* called it the "Monroesky Doctrine."

By then, a U.S.-Russia confrontation centered on the oil-rich lands of the Caspian was almost inevitable. History was replete with national clashes over valuable natural resources. It would have been astounding indeed if the heirs to the once-great Russian Empire had not viewed the western oil companies as interlopers feeding on the fruits of Russian ingenuity and investment. But the foreigners would not be turned back easily. Unlike in 1920, when exhausted and circumspect British leaders overruled field officers anxious to finish off reeling Bolshevik forces and seize domination of the Caspian region, this time Washington and London would be eager for the challenge. Russia was in the process of "reinventing itself and, in so doing, reinventing international politics and requiring us to reinvent American foreign policy," a senior U.S. official wrote.

Russian policymakers had watched the negotiations between Azerbaijan and the oil companies with mixed interest, and they initially seemed uncertain how to react. Yeltsin had taken office in mid-1991, on the eve of the Soviet collapse and about the time that Amoco thought it had shoved aside BP and wrapped up rights to the offshore Baku field called Azeri. Preoccupied with the tumult surrounding his presidency, the Russian leader was not "concerned about the Caspian in the first, second, third, or fifty-fifth place," Energy Minister Yuri Shafranik would later say. It fell to Shafranik and Foreign Minister Kozyrev to protect Russia's historical claims to the oil wealth of a region in which its authority was no longer absolute. But relations between the two men were cool, and by late 1993 each was fashioning a very different response to the dilemma.

The forty-three-year-old Kozyrev, a handsome professional diplomat who spoke English with an unblinking, piercing stare, at first had been "unable to really understand what Russia's interests were in totality." But hardliners irked at foreign oil companies scouring Russia's backyard, among other things, increasingly assailed him and his pro-western views. The pressure mounted for Kozyrev to declare "some kind of position" on Baku, and he found it in past dealings between Iran and the Soviet Union. There had been a time in history when they were the only two countries abutting the Caspian Sea, and they had signed treaties dividing the vast body of water between them. Now, the territories of five nations—Iran, Russia, Azerbaijan, Kazakhstan, and Turkmenistan—touched its shores. The old treaty was of dubious value; the Caspian appeared to belong to everyone and no one. Kozyrev proposed what seemed a sensible solution: The five would negotiate a new treaty carving up the Caspian among them.

But some elements of his initiative, revealed to the outside world in April 1994, stirred immediate resistance. First, there was Kozyrev's demand—voiced in the letter his Foreign Ministry sent to Britain—that no undersea development should proceed without the approval of all five states. In practical terms, this would arm Russia with veto power over any offshore Caspian oil deal—a nonstarter for the Azeris and western oilmen alike.

There was also his seemingly esoteric assertion that the Caspian Sea was not a sea at all. It was just a very large lake. The foreign minister's claim, developed with the assistance of Russian government lawyers, drew blank stares. But if he could prevail with this line of attack, it would mean that a multitude of international agreements and maritime laws governing the world's seas would not apply to the Caspian; in effect, it would just be a big puddle, its resources there for all to share. Such a finding would invite an even worse free-for-all than already existed, a climate that could incidentally serve the purposes of those seeking to stultify Caspian oil development. Oddly enough, Kozyrev's argument had some basis in geological history. The world's largest inland body of water, the Caspian was a bit larger than Japan—about 750 miles from north to south and an average of 200 miles wide. Geographically speaking, it was a giant salt lake, many experts said. Yet 5 million years earlier, it had been a great sea, connected to world oceans by the Black Sea. That fact helped to convince other experts that, its eventual isolation notwithstanding, the Caspian remained a sea.

To many outsiders, Kozyrev's road map for the Caspian was a barely concealed scheme to advance imperial designs on Russia's neighbors. It was evident, for example, that some Russians had trouble accepting that their empire had vanished, "that Kazakhstan, say, is a foreign country. To them, its independence is make-believe," said one Yeltsin deputy. Oil company lawyers scrambled to evaluate documents dating back three hundred years, trying to gauge the risks to their clients of Kozyrev's claims. The Russian foreign minister somberly observed that, in the absence of a new offshore treaty, any exploration deal rested on "a volcano." Some of the foreign oilmen were "people who come here as though to El Dorado, and try to take shortcuts," gambling that no one would later determine that "their business dealings are questionable from the point of view of existing law," he said. The western oil company that relied on Heydar Aliyev's word alone to guarantee an agreement could someday face "a change of guards" that "challenged everything." Kozyrev recommended that the foreigners suspend activities on the Caspian.

The murky status of territorial boundaries inspired a flurry of competing claims. Turkmenistan asserted rights to the big formations off Baku known as Azeri and Chirag (dubbing them Khazar and Osman, respectively), and Iran and Azerbaijan registered overlapping claims to three fields. But none of this slowed the oil companies down. As risky as it might seem to sink millions into oil fields the ownership of which was still unsettled, they were willing to take the gamble. The oilmen took some comfort in legal assurances that they would prevail in international courts. Besides, every deal that was signed would make it that much harder to dislodge the westerners later, and one had to be optimistic that boundary disputes would eventually be sorted out to everyone's satisfaction.

Energy Minister Yuri Shafranik scoffed at Kozyrev's Caspian initiative as a legalistic nuisance. Its provisions could take decades to bring to fruition, during which "we will lose" much of Russia's footing there. A more pragmatic strategy was required, something that would yield tangible results without wasting time debating whether the Caspian was a sea or a lake.

A plain-speaking, garrulous man of 42, Shafranik envisioned himself as part of a brotherhood of Russian oilmen "tied together by the same citizenship"—meaning their chosen occupation. He would have felt at home in Texas oil country. He had built his reputation in the contemporary Soviet equivalent, West Siberia, where he had presided over the tough and prolific oil region of Tyumen. After the August 1991 coup attempt against Gorbachev, Shafranik had defied the Energy Ministry's leadership by appearing on Siberian television in support of Yeltsin's appeal for a national strike. Yeltsin made him energy minister less than two years later. The extent of his power was difficult for an outsider to appreciate. It was as though Chevron's Ken Derr were suddenly running not only his own company, but also Exxon, BP, and Shell—all at once. In addition to the state-owned oil companies, Shafranik oversaw Russia's coal production, second-largest in the world behind only the United States. The nation possessed the world's largest natural gas reserves, and the energy minister set the export price. The fate of Russia's economy literally depended on the fortunes of his industries; it could be argued that his domain overshadowed even the military and the KGB in terms of its importance to the nation's future.

That said, Shafranik faced something of a thankless task upon assuming office. As he saw it, Russia was "on the verge of collapse," a situation so grave that "during the war under Stalin, there was more order." The energy industries, though immensely rich in natural resources, were in various stages of decay. He was particularly rankled by the absence of Russian companies from Baku's oil rush, now three years old. After all, it was the birthplace of the imperial Russian oil industry. Baku, he said, was "key to the [Caspian] region. All the roads are there."

And so, while Foreign Minister Kozyrev was proceeding along his path, in late 1993 Shafranik embarked on a bold offensive of his own. He pushed his way into the offshore oil discussions between Azerbaijan and the western companies and made two demands: that a Russian company be cut in for 10 percent of the deal and that the western oil companies export their Caspian crude through Russian pipelines only.

His chosen candidate for the 10 percent share was Lukoil, the Russian energy company. In this pursuit, his interest was not entirely dispassionate. Until 1990, Shafranik had headed a Siberian oil concern called Langepasneftegaz, which the following year became the *L* in Lukoil, a newly formed merger of three Russian oil concerns. Now, as the powerful energy minister, he received shares in Lukoil, compliments of its ethnic Azeri chairman, a friend named Vagit Alekperov.

Azerbaijan willingly made space for Lukoil. In March 1994, it awarded the company a 10 percent share after turning back Shafranik's attempt to push it to 20 percent. Now Russia would have less incentive to interfere with their dealmaking with foreign oil companies, the Azeris thought.

Six months later, Azerbaijan signed the "Contract of the Century," opening offshore Baku fields to the multinationals. But Shafranik's demand for pipeline control was still unresolved, and the prospect of having to rely on the Russian network to export their crude made foreign oilmen jittery. Few trusted Russia's ability to protect the lines from sabotage or other disruptions. In December 1994, Russia attacked Chechnya, exposing the pipelines to the hazards of warfare. More ominous was Moscow's willingness to use pipeline access as a bargaining weapon. Moscow had made Turkmenistan bend to its will by severing its natural gas exports to the West and had signaled displeasure with Chevron by cutting in half the flow from its showcase Tengiz field in Kazakhstan.

Behind the scenes, a few western oilmen began to explore the possibility of outflanking Shafranik. Their evolving strategy was deceptively simple: Preserve a modicum of peace with Moscow by continuing to ship some volume of crude through its network, but at the same time partner

with the Azeris to build a new export line that would skirt Russian territory and therefore be free of Moscow's control. It was a cautious bid for
self-protection, but even so, it seemed a highly dangerous gamble; almost
everyone believed that Moscow would find a way to scuttle it.

Shafranik's stratagems received mixed reviews from his rival in the
Kremlin. Foreign Minister Kozyrev felt that it had been a mistake to accept
the 10 percent deal. Lukoil's financial take in Baku would depend to some
extent on its cooperation with Azerbaijan and the westerners, thereby lessening Russian leverage over the Caspian republics, he thought. Still, he saw
some virtue in what he called Shafranik's "opportunistic" approach and
the energy minister's impatience with legalities that "could not be settled
as quickly as we all wanted."

Despite their tactical differences, Yeltsin's two ministers actually had
the same aim—to bring their nation out of supine post-Soviet bankruptcy
and into parity with the West. Both were intent on protecting Russia's
sphere of influence. At the same time, neither rejected out of hand any
western presence on the Caspian, and they urged colleagues to discard
Cold War thinking and seek a mature relationship between Russia and the
West. Yet it was perhaps inevitable that their pronouncements would be
understood differently by outsiders, particularly in Washington.

President Clinton's top adviser on the former Soviet Union was Nelson
Strobridge Talbott III, the son of a Cleveland investment banker and, according to some admirers, a "lineal descendant of the 'Wise Men,' " the
privileged East Coast–educated thinkers who shaped U.S. policy after
World War II. Strobe, as he called himself, boarded at the Connecticut
prep school Hotchkiss and earned a degree in Russian literature from Yale
and a Rhodes scholarship to Oxford University. There, he roomed with
another American student named Bill Clinton and translated Khrushchev's
memoirs into English. *Time* magazine hired him, and he spent two decades
as a correspondent. When his Oxford friend became president, Talbott was
appointed special envoy to the former Soviet Union and then deputy secretary of state. He had the qualifications—the forty-seven-year-old
Clinton confidant was erudite and supple in his approach to the ideas of

others. His political analyses were often penetrating. Clinton would later write in his memoirs that Talbott "had known and cared more about Russia and the Russian people than anyone else I knew" and that he "trusted both his judgment and his willingness to tell me the unvarnished truth."

Talbott had an ambitious goal: to use his quiet, persistent diplomacy to encourage far more momentous Russian reform and westernization. And he "didn't want anything to distract from that historic process," said one colleague. While he publicly hewed to Clinton's declared policy that Russia was "not the only game in town," in practice Talbott focused on little else. He was able to do so by exploiting his status as an FOB, or Friend of Bill; only Talbott could pass chatty memos directly to the president— which he did frequently—and receive approval of his initiatives from the top. On issues related to Russia, Talbott was more powerful than National Security Advisor Anthony Lake, nominally the president's chief foreign policy adviser. When Clinton met with Yeltsin, it was Talbott, not Lake, who sat prominently with the American president taking notes; Lake was not even in the room during the most sensitive discussions with Yeltsin. Even Talbott's direct superior in Clinton's second term, Secretary of State Madeleine Albright, could be pushed aside. When Albright persuaded Clinton to attack Kosovo and wanted to lead discussions on Russia's role, Talbott called Clinton to say he would handle it. The message was clear: Talbott could trump anyone—and did.

From the outset, Talbott had urged empathy with Russia. The shattered country was transforming itself into a democracy deserving of membership in the community of peaceful nations, he asserted. It was a process that required nurturing by America. But some began to doubt his relatively benign assessment of Russian intentions. The Caspian initiatives mounted by Yeltsin's two ministers were troublesome. So were Georgia's loss of seaside territory to Russian-supported rebels, Azerbaijan's surrender of a chunk of its land to Moscow-backed Armenia, and Moscow's shutdown of Turkmenistan's natural gas exports. When Russia put the squeeze on Chevron's exports from Tengiz, some of Talbott's subordinates thought a line had been crossed. The mounting evidence seemed to discredit the notion that Russia, still in transition, was merely experiencing birth pains.

Rather, Moscow seemed engaged in a deliberate pattern of threatening behavior. The twin motives appeared to be the reassertion of imperial control and the pursuit of profit, with officials like Shafranik standing to gain
financially from some of the dealmaking on the Caspian. "Generally if
someone is holding a knife to your throat they want something," observed
one oilman in Almaty.

But Talbott stood his ground. When Senator Richard Lugar quietly
advised him that America should "contain the problem of Russia redux,"
the bluntness of the remarks bothered Talbott tremendously. He "found it
ominous that an influential and moderate member of the Senate would
reintroduce the concept of containment."

Among those making the case for a harder U.S. line were Bill White,
Clinton's deputy secretary of energy, and Rosemarie Forsythe, who headed
a new National Security Council desk handling the Caspian region.

The thirty-eight-year-old White, who had raised $2 million for
Clinton's successful 1992 presidential campaign, was an up-by-his-
bootstraps Texas lawyer whose "decorous, laid-back speech and courtly,
deliberate movements convey the impression of a much older man," one
journalist wrote. His Houston law practice earned him an early fortune,
and the stogie-smoking White became known as a well-connected political operator with deep pockets for candidates he liked. Only a few months
into his Washington job, he began receiving plaintive phone calls from
Amoco and Pennzoil executives in Azerbaijan: "Please think about coming
to Baku. The companies are in big trouble here." Those calls led to his
November 1993 meeting with Heydar Aliyev, in the hopes of persuading
the Azeri leader to accelerate approval of the then-stalled offshore deal.

When White returned from Baku, he immersed himself in the subject
of Caspian oil. The global petroleum industry had always held a fascination for him; he recalled that during his undergrad years at Harvard, his
classmates "were protesting Vietnam [while] I was volunteering to work
against OPEC." Now he found himself briefing colleagues in the State
Department, the Pentagon, and elsewhere on his belief that the U.S. government had to play a bolder role on the Caspian. The region was never

going to dominate world oil supplies like the Middle East did, but it could help keep prices down by providing the critical difference between shortage and surplus. Say the Caspian produced 2 to 4 million barrels of oil daily, a reasonable expectation. That would be roughly equivalent to the Alaska and North Sea production a couple of decades earlier that "helped break the back of OPEC," he argued.

If the American presence in the region were less than vigorous, the Caspian and its oil resources could easily fall under the sway of its two biggest neighbors: Iran, with "deep antagonism to the U.S.," and Russia, with "nationalism lurking still in their national psyche." The United States spent tens of billions of military dollars to protect its oil supply in the Persian Gulf, so "why not an ounce of prevention by filling Central Asia with independent states?"

One Saturday, White invited Rosemarie Forsythe to brunch at his home near Washington's Glover-Archbold Park. He spoke of how, if he had "to identify where the risk of geopolitical rivalry involving the West could become hot, it was over oil resources in the Caspian." Agreeing instantly, Forsythe added that U.S. policy there could not be driven by fear of disrupting America's relationship with Russia. The pair obviously shared "the same passion"—the Caspian was not a place to ignore, certainly not to pander to Russia.

Forsythe's views had coalesced over several years, influenced by her travels through the old Soviet Union and her frustration after its collapse, when Washington neglected newly independent republics like Azerbaijan. She sympathized with their struggles and with the travails of American oilmen in the region, and she came to believe that the stakes on the Caspian were higher than senior Washington policymakers realized. A thirty-seven-year-old Indiana native, Forsythe wore enormous round glasses and her hair up in an attempt to look older. Like White, her youthful appearance had caused her to be chronically underestimated. She had grown up as a child prodigy, graduating from Indiana University at age sixteen with a triple major—political science, Russian literature, and classical studies. After sticking around for an additional two years "just to get old enough to do something," Forsythe toured the far-flung Soviet republics, acquainting herself with its non-Russian nationalities. "I looked like I was about twelve," she said, "so I was fairly unthreatening to the Russians." In 1987, she entered government service in the State Department.

Her elevation to the National Security Council was rapid, the result of her firsthand knowledge of the republics, where the United States began establishing embassies immediately after the Soviet collapse. She was the one who had given Vice President Gore the advice on how to eat a sheep's ear while traveling with him to Central Asia, and she kept the lines open to American oil companies during the uncertain final months of bargaining for offshore Baku. When Heydar Aliyev demanded a meeting with Clinton before sealing the deal, Forsythe shepherded the Waldorf-Astoria sit-down.

Her interest in the Caspian and its oil intensified after a State Department researcher named Sheila Heslin produced a fiery paper on the subject. Not only was Russia aspiring to renewed empire, it was a "neo-mercantilist" nation that was "slowly undermining the independence" of the Caspian countries through its "iron umbilical cord," meaning the network of Soviet-era pipelines now controlled by Russia. To halt this creeping power play, she argued, "you needed new pipelines." Forsythe agreed, and before long she was immersed in Caspian energy issues.

Her authority on the National Security Council—charged with coordinating the president's foreign policy—was limited. She was its junior-most regional director and so new to the foreign service that she was still a year away from completing her probationary period. Still, her position meant that she could walk point on Caspian matters. That put Forsythe and her opinions, characterized by a Talbott deputy as "very anti-Russian," on a collision course with Clinton's most powerful adviser on post-Soviet policy.

Strobe Talbott was bureaucratically wise enough not to tangle too overtly with doubters like Bill White and Rosemarie Forsythe, whose attitude toward Russia he found hard to fathom. As he usually did, he let his senior advisers take the lead. They argued that the United States had to find ways to reward Moscow for the considerable concessions it was being asked to make, leading some to suspect they were advocating that the United States "throw [Russia] the Caspian as a bone." White got a discouraging reception when he tried to press his case with Talbott and his

staff. As White outlined his reasoning to them, he "could sense an apprehension that I might not appreciate what the 'real stakes' were."

The tension between the two camps was not about absolute right and
wrong, but rather which U.S. policy would most effectively nudge Russia
toward becoming a nonconfrontational partner with the West. Talbott and
his allies put the greatest emphasis on soothing Moscow and not pressing
matters that might irritate it—such as the future of the Caspian. Forsythe
and White thought that no progress would be made until Russia was
forced to halt transgressions such as those on the Caspian and that
America should apply the appropriate pressure.

In Washington, the view that Clinton's Russia policy was soft gained
momentum. Just as Yeltsin had bowed to domestic realities, Talbott finally
was forced to temper his public optimism about Russia's reformist intentions. The changing political climate shifted the advantage to White,
Forsythe, and Heslin, who would soon act to set the course for one of
Clinton's most enduring foreign policies. The unlikely threesome would
make the Caspian an issue of national security. Their case would rest on
the assertion that its oil qualified as a strategic interest for America. This
interest was threatened by Russia's ability to make the region unstable and
harass American oil companies. So it was incumbent upon the American
government to come to the aid of the Caspian republics—in effect, to run
interference for them against Russia.

Some compared the events that would follow with the Great Game between imperial Britain and Russia of the nineteenth century—only with
an expanded cast. Talbott believed that the United States could not be successful in a Great Game strategy; indeed, "we were big on deleting any ref-
erences to the Great Game" from briefing papers and talking points, said a
senior Talbott deputy. Yet there was no mistaking that conditions were
ripening for a twentieth-century struggle for influence and possessions in
traditional Great Game territory. This time, the United States, Britain, and
Turkey would be pitted against Russia and Iran.

The mood was apparent when, on a trip with Talbott, Rosemarie
Forsythe found herself in conversation with a senior Russian diplomat at

the U.S. ambassador's residence in Armenia. Rejecting the notion that western troops might act as peacekeepers in the disputed territory between Armenia and Azerbaijan, the diplomat, Vladimir Kazimirov, pointed his finger at Forsythe, and said, "Over my dead body will you get involved in my backyard."

But this contest would have far greater ramifications than its historic predecessor. The United States would seek to neuter Russia, its great twentieth-century rival, as an expansionist power. If America succeeded, Russia in two or three decades would "feel more comfortable inside its borders" and stop presuming that "it could control every aspect of these countries." Or at least that was the hope.

The U.S. offensive would be two-pronged. On one front, America would engineer the expansion of the NATO military alliance almost to Russia's border, stopping only at Ukraine and Belarus; that would deal a mortal blow to Russian influence in the Eastern European nations that had been swept into the Soviet Union's orbit after World War II. On a second front, the Caspian, Russia would be pushed out as the absolute ruler of lands it had occupied in some cases for almost two centuries. No western military presence was contemplated there, however. Bill White had said to Azeri prime minister Hassanov back in November 1993: "The United States would never commit troops to the region. It was naïve to think we would." Instead, the means of imperial defeat on the Caspian would resemble the mythical Trojan Horse, only less romantic. As Sheila Heslin had envisioned in her policy paper, it would be an oil pipeline.

Finally, in these ancient and volatile territories of Central Asia and the Caucasus, the interests of the U.S. government and the ambitions of American oil companies would converge.

CHAPTER 13

Early Oil

A CENTURY AGO, DURING BAKU'S first oil boom, its crude was sent to market in wooden barrels that were hauled on barges, steamboats, and railcars. The oilmen of the day despaired of the system's inefficiency. Finally, Zeynalabdin Tagiyev, Ludvig Nobel, and the Rothschilds hit upon what was then an extraordinary scheme—they laid a pipeline five hundred miles from Baku to the Black Sea coast, where oceangoing ships took the precious cargo and transported it directly to refineries in Europe. From that moment on, pipelines were the key to exploiting the Caspian's riches.

In early 1995, western oilmen in Baku were learning that lesson all over again. Their companies had spent $800 million to secure the rights to huge deposits of offshore crude, but the question of how to move it to market was still unresolved. The oil would be transported by pipelines, of course. But whose pipelines, and over what route? Whose hand would be on the switch that could keep the oil flowing or shut it down?

The first discussions centered on the proposed development of a single export line with relatively modest capacity, a sort of demonstration project called the Early Oil pipeline. It would be the forerunner of a second, very large line that would become a necessity as production increased. But despite the limited nature of the Early Oil proposal, it would push all the hot buttons associated with pipelines on the Caspian.

Uppermost was Moscow's insistence that it be the custodian of Early Oil. The Russians proposed to fold the new line into their existing pipeline network, a vast system built during the Soviet era and now under firm Kremlin control. Oil had flowed through these lines from Baku to Russia and beyond for decades, and Moscow saw the network as vital to maintaining its stake in the region's petroleum wealth. Moscow's Early Oil pipeline would move Baku crude north through Russia to tankers at its Black Sea port of Novorossiysk.

Despite their misgivings, most western oil companies initially shrugged off the accounts of Moscow's intimidating behavior elsewhere and looked favorably on its Early Oil proposal. While day-to-day operations of the pipeline admittedly would depend on Kremlin goodwill, perhaps going along with Moscow would mollify its displeasure at losing influence in the region.

After all, not that much seemed to be at risk. Industry thinking was that the Early Oil line would merely "show it can be done" and allow the multinationals to begin earning back some of their initial investment, said one company lobbyist.

Economics also favored going with the Russians. Most of the companies wanted to limit spending on Early Oil, since it was in effect an experiment. The Russian option was the cheapest because much of what would be needed was already in place; the companies would only have to build or refurbish a dozen or so miles of pipeline from Baku to the Russian border. That, plus some infrastructure, was estimated to cost a mere $50 million.

British Petroleum's new man in Baku, a brash veteran of Middle East oil fields named Terry Adams, was the most enthusiastic supporter of the

Russian option. He was adamant about holding down costs and argued that "we needed to keep Russia happy," a Pennzoil lobbyist recalled. Some detected a whiff of BP self-interest. The company intended Baku to be a beachhead for its triumphant return to this part of the world after a long absence and envisioned ambitious deals soon in Russia as well as Iran. Adams would later agree that he was there partly "to set the scene—[to do] heavy promotion."

William Courtney, the U.S. ambassador in neighboring Georgia, cautioned Adams and others at British Petroleum that the fighting in Chechnya could disrupt the flow of oil. But the BP officials were not dissuaded. They "had blind faith that the Chechens could be paid off," Courtney said; not only BP but also some of the other companies "thought I was too suspicious and had too low confidence in Russia."

As the debate wore on, a compromise proposal began to emerge: Build not one but two Early Oil pipelines. One would run entirely through Russia, thereby placating Moscow. But a second line would snake across the friendly territory of Georgia to a port on its Black Sea coast, without touching Russian soil.

The concept of a second line under control of the West was already on the radar of the handful of oilmen who had been speculating for months on ways to outflank Russia. But when the Georgia scheme surfaced, it was instantly scorned by most of the oil companies. Its somewhat irregular route, shadowing the path carved by Baku's oil barons a century earlier, would cost the companies about $250 million, five times what they would spend to go through Russia. And the very idea of it would give Moscow fits.

The Georgian option originated in brainstorming sessions presided over by Eduard Shevardnadze, once Gorbachev's celebrated foreign minister and now president of the former Soviet republic. Like Azerbaijan's Heydar Aliyev, Shevardnadze had risen in Stalinist times as a product of the Soviet security services and had been a Communist Party leader. The republic of Georgia occupied a special place in Russian imperial culture. It was the spectacular playland of the czarist and Soviet aristocracies, who cherished its gorgeous Black Sea beaches and sanatoria, its famous Borjomi water, and its vineyards, the source of the world's first cultured grapes. Georgia was a feast, with exceedingly varied and artfully served vegetarian, lamb, and pork dishes; the country's drinking rituals were widely copied, reigned over by a toastmaster called a *tamada*. In the late 1940s, the author John Steinbeck, traveling through the Soviet Union with photographer Robert Capa, heard Georgians described as "great drinkers, great dancers, great musicians, great workers and lovers" and, upon reaching there, found a people who were "better dressed, better looking and more full of spirit than any we saw in Russia."

Shevardnadze was in Moscow, a member of the Soviet parliament in its waning days of 1991, when civil strife wracked Georgia. He decided to return home and help save his native land from ruin. There was almost no electricity; the republic was so poor it couldn't afford fuel for its natural gas–powered turbines. Factories were idle. Only rarely was there heat or running water. Tbilisi—home to a population of 1.2 million notable for its highly literate professional class—was unique among world capitals, living a modern Stone Age existence.

America's James Baker and German chancellor Helmut Kohl rallied to Shevardnadze's side after his return to Georgia in March 1992, according him something resembling hero worship, as did the Clinton administration later. Foreign aid poured in from the United States, Germany, and other countries, though much of it was siphoned off before it could be put to good use. Cash grants seemed to vanish, and goods such as powdered milk, clothes, and medicine were diverted to the black market. Georgia's tradition of corruption would not be easily erased. Nor was Shevardnadze confident that the old Stalinist practices were a thing of the past. Tedo Japaridze, his top foreign policy adviser, recalled how the white-haired leader would put his finger to his lips—"Shhhhhhh!"—and point to the ceiling of his office, indicating that "it was the KGB. They were listening to everything."

Around ten o'clock most nights, the president summoned Japaridze and a cadre of bright young advisers for free-wheeling discussions that often went on until 1 A.M. and later. The men believed that "we were part of history," said one participant. "It was the beginning of the Georgian state." But what, precisely, would define Georgia as a state? Americans were extending support to Georgia mainly because they admired Shevardnadze. But that wasn't sufficient. If Georgia the country could not establish itself as important to the West, "then Georgia will be treated as a province or district of Russia" and lose the fruits of its first independence since 1920, the president thought.

Gogi Tsomaya, a civil servant with long experience in the Ministry of Transportation, thought he might have the answer. Tsomaya had been studying Soviet road maps when he flashed on a thought: Strategically speaking, Georgia was perfectly situated to host a pipeline exporting Azerbaijani oil to the world beyond. As Shevardnadze and the others listened one night, Tsomaya recited the shortcomings of the routes under scrutiny in other countries.

It would be ill-advised, for example, to ship the oil south via Iran to the Persian Gulf and through the Strait of Hormuz. The waterway was already crowded with tanker traffic, and the United States would not countenance an Iranian route, given the still-raw memory of Tehran's imprisonment of fifty-one U.S. hostages a little over a decade earlier.

The same was true for a pipeline west from Baku through Armenia and on to the Turkish coast. The idealistic Abulfaz Elchibey, then the president of Azerbaijan, had suggested that route to Amoco executives. He had dubbed it the "peace pipeline," a shared venture that would give Armenia and Azerbaijan cause to end their hostilities. But the notion that the Azeri government would give the distrusted Armenians leverage over their patrimony seemed far-fetched.

Finally, given recent events, who could entrust the safekeeping of an oil pipeline to Russia? That left Georgia. It could offer the Azeris and the oil multinationals a pipeline route over hospitable terrain the full distance to the Black Sea coast or even beyond, to Turkey and the Mediterranean Sea. Both options presumably would "make Georgia interesting to the West," Tsomaya thought.

Shevardnadze sat in silence for a moment and then shouted, "Get out of here! Do you want the Russians to blow me up?" The men scurried back to Japaridze's office, where the phone was ringing. It was Shevardnadze.

"You know what? You keep exploring this issue," said the Georgian leader. "Whenever I need it, we will have it."

His advisers were not certain whether Shevardnadze had actually lost his temper for a moment or was trying to confuse an eavesdropping KGB. But it didn't matter. Their president had been won over. "Once we left his office he started thinking about it and understood this was real independence," Japaridze said.

Georgia's careful pursuit of an Early Oil pipeline began in 1994, on two fronts. One was Russia, certain to belittle the idea. Shevardnadze wondered if there were sweeteners that might at least dampen the Kremlin opposition. Perhaps some of the hundreds of Russian troops still based in Georgia could be hired to provide security for the pipeline, giving them an "opportunity to make some money legally and not through the illegal sale of arms."

The second front was America. Japaridze flew to Washington and made a timely presentation to Rosemarie Forsythe at the National Security Council and to Sheila Heslin. Both were in the process of firming up their views on a pipeline free of Russian control. He also visited some of his president's "good friends." Over coffee on K Street, he briefed Zbigniew Brzezinski, the former presidential adviser, and the retired general William Odom, onetime director of the National Security Agency, Washington's elite spy organization. Brzezinski was dubious: Rather than move Baku's oil through Georgia, it would be better sent "through Iran" as a way to reopen that country to the United States. Baker was only slightly more encouraging: At his office, he said that a Georgian route would be feasible "if the line could even a little bit be built on Russian territory."

At home, Shevardnadze made better progress with his neighbor, the Azerbaijani president, Heydar Aliyev. Together, they knew "the rules of the game better than anyone," said Japaridze—not only "how to please the Russians, but also how to outmaneuver and outsmart them." Shevardnadze brought to the table his international stature—he seemed to have an inexhaustible supply of chits in Washington. Aliyev was regarded as better able to navigate the bureaucratic hazards of Moscow. This odd couple—one tossed out of the Kremlin by Gorbachev for being too hard-line, the other Gorbachev's helpmate in dismantling the Communist system—began conspiring against the lingering Russian presence in the Caspian. For Aliyev, supporting Shevardnadze's pipeline scheme "wasn't out of love for Georgia, but to survive and survive together."

By the end of 1994, Rosemarie Forsythe's energy task force at the National Security Council had reached a conclusion—the United States government had to protect its interests by moving squarely behind the construction of a pipeline independent of Moscow. However, she still had to contend with Strobe Talbott, Clinton's trusted deputy secretary of state. Aside from his decades-long respect for Russian culture and his belief in the country's ability to transform itself, he had realpolitik problems with the policy that Forsythe was formulating.

Talbott's view was that Russia was the region's single most strategically important country, towering over Azerbaijan, Kazakhstan, and Georgia, and that it made no sense to risk riling it. Quite apart from being nuclear-armed, Russia was bigger, stronger, more populated, and, with its history of absorbing other lands, potentially more dangerous. Moscow surely would be aggravated if the United States championed a non-Russian pipeline, Talbott thought; its nationalists especially might be angered. The fallout could jeopardize other American priorities, such as a Russian troop withdrawal from the Baltics and a halt to the Balkan civil war. And so Talbott's team continued to work in opposition to Forsythe.

Soon after New Year's 1995, the musings of America's newly appointed envoy to Turkey gave Forsythe an opening to strengthen her position. Ambassador Marc Grossman, a forty-three-year-old California native, had heard talk in Washington of a Turkish campaign to share in development of a Caspian pipeline. The Turks were not after Early Oil, which would move just one hundred thousand barrels or so a day. Rather, they wanted a piece of the second line that would eventually be built, a behemoth known as the Main Export Pipeline and capable of shipping seven hundred thousand barrels a day or more. They envisioned a route from Baku through Georgia and then hundreds of miles across Turkey to its Mediterranean port of Ceyhan.

The American ambassador, a political science buff, quickly recognized what was at stake. A project like this could knit Turks and their ethnic kin in the Caucasus and Central Asia closer together, something that both passionately desired. Additionally, Turkey could earn back in pipeline fees and other revenue some of the $250 million lost when Washington had closed an Iraqi export line to Ceyhan, a casualty of the 1991 assault on Saddam Hussein. Since Turkey was America's southernmost ally in NATO, the idea deserved a serious hearing.

Grossman was due in Ankara in three weeks, when he would take up his new post and hold his first press conference. Conferring with his staff, he wondered aloud, "Wouldn't it be great if the headline from this press conference, instead of that there is a new ambassador, was that 'America Supports Baku-Ceyhan'?"

When Forsythe heard what Grossman had said, she saw an opportunity. Soon it would be time for her to rotate into a new diplomatic post. If she could win authorization for Grossman to make such a policy declaration in public, it would establish a bureaucratic bulwark for the future. Talbott's team and others trying to hold the line against a non-Russian pipeline route would lose ground. Forsythe thought of it as a parting "gift" to her designated successor, Sheila Heslin, who a year earlier had written the State Department paper decrying Russia's "iron umbilical cord."

Grossman would need clearance from several deputy secretaries— in the departments of State, Defense, Energy, Commerce, and the Treasury—as well as the CIA. Forsythe had to proceed with care. There could be no overtly anti-Russian tone. On the contrary, she would have to find a way to argue that such a policy statement would complement Talbott's goals, as convoluted as that might sound.

She told the deputy secretaries that she was not suggesting anything adverse to Russia. Rather, the goal was to ensure the "economic viability" of all of the countries in the region. The United States, she said, would advocate the construction of "multiple pipelines" and an "upgrade [of] Russian infrastructure, including pipelines." Precise routes were still being studied by American oil companies and their multinational partners, but one could be certain that the undertaking would "reduce future dependence on the Persian Gulf oil" and "bring economic benefits to the U.S."

Her presentation contained something for everyone, and it left little room for the "Russia First" crowd to object. James Collins, who had succeeded Talbott as ambassador-at-large to the former Soviet Union, provided the final necessary approval, and Grossman delivered his statement on January 31 in Ankara. While the key language was toned down and buried in a tangle of bureaucratese, Turkish reporters perked up their ears when Grossman said that the United States had "notified several governments in the region that we would endorse construction of a pipeline through Turkey." Near pandemonium erupted. "We are overjoyed," said Turkey's foreign minister. America's support would "greatly contribute to the project," predicted the country's oil pipeline director. Grossman was an instant local hero.

The development of a new foreign policy in Washington sometimes proceeds in a circular fashion. Sheila Heslin got a painful reminder of that in March after replacing Rosemarie Forsythe at the National Security Council. She was asked to draft talking points for Vice President Al Gore to use in a meeting with Kazakhstan's prime minister. Heslin blended elements of her "iron umbilical cord" paper with language on the virtues of multiple pipelines; as such, it could be read as a brief against yielding to Russia in the Caspian.

Her work impressed Gore's forceful and articulate foreign policy adviser, Leon Fuerth. But he wondered why the material seemed so unfamiliar and began asking about its history. Had these policy statements gone through the proper approval process? It was decided that Heslin's NSC supervisor, Coit "Chip" Blacker, should pass final judgment. Heslin rushed her notes to Blacker at his home on a Saturday morning, and he okayed them.

Two days later, the vice president used her talking points in his sit-down with the Kazakh prime minister. When Heslin's critics within the administration learned of this, they went on the offensive, especially the

"Russia First" camp. They accused her of bureaucratic sleight of hand—attempting to slip in a new policy position when nobody was looking. Some colleagues "wouldn't talk to me. Whatever I did was considered pretty bad," Heslin said. Collins, the ambassador-at-large, was among the aggravated. "That was no policy. That was a cable," he said of Grossman's pipeline announcement, "a throwaway" intended to mollify Turkey and nothing more.

Heslin was puzzled. Rosemarie Forsythe had collected the presumably necessary signatures and had specifically "made [Collins] sign it to make sure it was policy." But a postmortem of the dustup concluded that the policy statements incorporated into Gore's talking points should have been reviewed at a higher level—at the so-called Deputies Committee, a senior policymaking group. Lacking that, the multiple-pipeline policy so optimistically shaped by Forsythe and enunciated by Grossman in Ankara was not policy at all.

Three months later, Heslin had an opportunity to begin picking up the pieces. Al Gore was about to meet with Russian prime minister Viktor Chernomyrdin, their fifth encounter since opening a back-channel dialogue in 1993 to bridge differences between the two countries. As unlikely as it seemed, the two men—one a policy wonk born into a political dynasty, the other a tongue-tied former Red factory director—warmed to each other, resulting in several important agreements. Now they were to discuss Russia's sale of nuclear technology to Iran. But Gore, at President Clinton's request, also had the issue of oil in the former Soviet republics on his duty list. Heslin thought the time might be ripe to slip in some of her concerns; if he wanted to, Chernomyrdin could defuse some of the tensions over Caspian pipelines.

Once again, she would have to do some groundwork. Heslin walked Leon Fuerth through her central argument that energy was emerging as a major issue in the region—and that the U.S. government lacked a policy to address it. The Gore aide agreed and persuaded Samuel "Sandy" Berger, Clinton's deputy national security adviser, to schedule the issue for discussion in June before the Deputies Committee. Both Talbott and Heslin would be there.

Preparing for the high-level meeting, Heslin knew it would be fruitless to challenge the pro-Russia group head on. Instead, she fashioned an "upside-down Russia policy"—a pro-Caspian strategy in disguise. It would be a package that Talbott and his allies on the committee could accept even as it advanced her policy goals.

Talbott's mantra was that "we had to support the reformers" in Moscow. Well, said Heslin, what better way than to nurture the development of new or modernized oil pipelines in Russian territory? A major project or two would give bragging rights to the Russian "white hats" Talbott wanted to empower. Toward that end, Washington ought to endorse a proposed Russian export line from Chevron's Tengiz fields in Kazakhstan to the Black Sea. And it most certainly should support the Russian Early Oil pipeline from Baku to the Black Sea. But in order to strike an appropriate balance, the United States should also back construction of a second, roughly parallel Early Oil pipeline, the Georgia option so fervently sought by Shevardnadze. And over the long term, it ought to advocate a large capacity line from Baku to Turkey, the so-called Main Export Pipeline for which the Turks were hungering.

Heslin's reference to a new Russian line that would carry more of Chevron's crude from Tengiz to the Black Sea was pure window dressing. No one, including Chevron, had ever suggested anything else. As to supporting the Georgia Early Oil option, who could complain if there would also be a Russian line? And how could the United States not welcome Turkey, its important ally, into the proceedings? Heslin's final, deft touch was to wrap the package in the unassailable language of "independence and sovereignty" for the Caspian states.

"I don't see how anyone could disagree with this memo," Talbott said.

Fuerth turned to Heslin. "Do you have what you need?" he inquired, meaning authority to write her talking points for Gore. Indeed, an elated Heslin finally had the policy that had eluded both her and Forsythe. For tactical reasons, her camp would have to maintain the fiction that it was not a challenge to the Kremlin. But the policy's thrust was most assuredly that.

At the Gore-Chernomyrdin summit in Moscow, Fuerth listened as the vice president questioned Russia's motives for abruptly reducing by half Chevron's Tengiz exports, an action Moscow had blamed on insufficient pipeline capacity. As Gore went on, an irritated Chernomyrdin "knocked his pen on the table with white knuckles" and dug in his heels, Fuerth recalled. "This is not about a shortage of pipeline space," Chernomyrdin protested. "I have plenty of pipeline space. It's about you going around us." It seemed to the vice president's aide that the Russian was saying, "The Caspian is ours. If you're going to take it, you have to show you can take it."

Gore refused to retreat. He made it clear, said Fuerth, that "we are going to move forward with our agenda" anyway; the U.S. companies would have the fields and ship the oil. Heslin felt vindicated. "The gauntlet was down," she said.

In July 1995, the Early Oil debate began heating up. Washington was throwing its weight behind the construction of both pipelines. Most of the oil companies, fretting over the cost to them and not anxious to incur Moscow's wrath, were still supporting the Russian line alone. Sandy Berger laid out the administration's position for the oilmen at a meeting in the White House Situation Room. "We need dual pipelines," Berger said, unless of course the companies wished "to have the Chevron experience." Terry Adams, the British Petroleum executive, stood by the Russian option, arguing that two pipelines would create more export capacity than was needed.

Some of Sheila Heslin's colleagues began to advise a "grand strategy": Give Russia alone the Early Oil pipeline if Moscow would assent to routing the Main Export Pipeline through Turkey later. But Heslin thought that would be risky. An emboldened Moscow might respond with even more aggressive tactics on the Caspian and eventually renege on its acceptance of the Turkish line. This was "a game of chicken, and you needed to go all the way," Heslin thought.

Her determination stiffened in August, when someone tried to kill Eduard Shevardnadze. The Georgian president's motorcade was on the way to a ceremonial event when a hidden bomb exploded. Shards of glass lacerated his face and hands, and a dozen other people were injured as well. To Shevardnadze, Russia was clearly to blame, and Heslin agreed. "What else could they do" to stop the Georgia line? she asked. As if to punctuate her suspicions, Boris Yeltsin made a surprise telephone call to Shevardnadze about three days later. The Russian president meandered through a discussion of regional politics and then issued some cautionary advice. "There are rumors about pipelines," Yeltsin said. "But I understand that you are smart enough to understand that there should be one pipeline." Shevardnadze and his aides were flabbergasted at the attempt by "this idiot, this drunk" to "scare him," said a Georgian official.

Heslin had one important ally among the oil companies, a forty-four-year-old Washington lobbyist for Pennzoil named Frank Verrastro. He was an unusual hybrid, a chemist who had been assistant secretary of energy under President Carter in the 1970s. Verrastro was steeped in Baku's nineteenth-century history and had an incisive grasp of how international oil and geopolitics came together. Neither he nor Heslin were persuaded that its cheaper cost was reason enough to support the Russian line alone. When one considered Russia's unreliable history of transporting oil from other Caspian states, spending $250 million for a Georgia line seemed like a wise investment to Verrastro. He agreed that "Russia should be accommodated in some manner to keep them on the reservation" but argued that both lines should be built "to keep them honest." They made an influential team, Heslin the overseer of America's Caspian policy and Verrastro the seasoned industry hand with Washington know-how.

By the end of August, only the Turkish state oil company had joined Pennzoil in support of dual pipelines. But there were signs that other companies might be having second thoughts. The increasingly anguished stories about Chevron's unhappy pipeline experiences with the Russians in Kazakhstan began to make the Georgia option more palatable. Verrastro, echoing what Sandy Berger had said in Washington, asked his colleagues, "Do we want to end up like Chevron?" Heslin also made inroads when she cautioned the oil companies that Washington's willingness to stand with them was not inexhaustible. If they chose only the Russian option and then Moscow misbehaved, she told them, "don't look for any high-priority bailout. We are not here to protect you from your own decisions."

The oilmen gathered in Houston on September 18 to debate which way to go. Pennzoil's Verrastro and BP's Adams made the familiar opposing arguments, sometimes with barely concealed animosity. At one point, Adams tried a tactical dodge, suggesting that the companies "possibly could consider" the Georgia option at some future time. But right now, "what I'm hearing is that everyone favors" the Russian line.

"If that is what you're hearing, then you are not listening," Verrastro shot back.

In fact, a consensus was forming around the proposition that surplus pipeline capacity would be a good thing, especially in a region where periodic bottlenecks were the norm. The oilmen finally endorsed a preliminary agreement to build dual Early Oil pipelines—with one caveat: As a concession to Moscow, construction of the Russian line would begin a few months before work started on the Georgia line. The clincher was a company lawyer's chance discovery of a forgotten clause in an already existing contract with the Azeris. The clause allowed the oil multinationals to recover the combined $300 million cost of the pipelines from Azerbaijan by charging it to expenses. Later, Verrastro would call it a "save-your-ass sentence" in the contract.

In the aftermath of Houston, feelings continued to run high between the British Petroleum and Pennzoil delegates. In an angry letter, Adams accused the Pennzoil team "of being in league" with the Clinton administration, meaning Sheila Heslin, and "undermining the unity of the group." The claim was partly true—Verrastro and Heslin spoke nearly every day, and Verrastro kept her abreast of the prevailing mood among his fellow oilmen. But Verrastro felt he was simply strategizing on behalf of the oilmen's best course and not crossing the delicate line of violating confidences, while Adams was in effect working against them. Verrastro's boss, Tom Hamilton, responded to Adams that just as BP conferred regularly with the British government, Pennzoil would continue to speak with Washington.

In the end, of course, neither Washington nor the oil multinationals could dictate the outcome of the Early Oil debate. Though the foreign oilmen would build the line (or lines), they could not proceed without the approval of Azerbaijan's headstrong and willful president, Heydar Aliyev. The offshore Baku contract between the Azeris and the oil companies required that all significant decisions be unanimous. Each side had one vote, but Aliyev's was worth at least a fraction more than that of the companies. After all, they needed to keep him content.

Publicly, the Azeri leader vacillated. Though he manifestly favored the Georgian option, he also thought at times that it might be strategically smarter to support only the Russian option. Assuming that Moscow would use its exclusive franchise to play rough, "it would show the Russians for what they were," said Sheila Heslin, who believed that she understood his reasoning. Turkey's glamorous prime minister, Tansu Çiller, telephoned Aliyev to encourage him to tilt in the direction of the West. But Heslin knew it was a difficult decision for the Azeri to make. Despite his career as a KGB tough, "he wouldn't be able to carry all this water by himself." Russia had made it plain that it would not tolerate a loss of influence in the Caspian. All one had to do was look next door to Georgia, and a bit farther to Chechnya, to see what Russia was capable of. (Even within Azerbaijan, Aliyev still faced occasional challenges to his leadership. In the spring, the same Interior Ministry troops that had revolted once before had done it again, this time at a remote police station. Aliyev had reacted with fury, dispatching hundreds of soldiers, who killed the leader of the mutineers and about eighty others by "blitzing the buildings with automatic gunfire and grenades.")

As the end of September approached, the Azeri president was under increasing pressure to choose a side. The oil companies were only days away from a second, critical meeting in London to ratify what they had preliminarily agreed upon in Houston. Even though Heslin believed dual lines now had sufficient support, she also thought that the oilmen "were waiting for a signal from Aliyev" of his wishes. She began pushing for a formal letter from Clinton that would shore up the Azeri leader as he reached a decision. The timing was tight. The letter would have to be in Aliyev's hands no later than October 2, so he would have time to digest it before the London meeting on October 4.

On Saturday, September 30, Heslin got discouraging news. The

White House bureaucracy hadn't kept pace. The presidential letter wasn't finalized, so the right people hadn't signed off on it, and in any case the automatic pen that duplicated Clinton's signature was about to be locked up and put away for the weekend. There ensued a hasty exchange between Heslin and Sandy Berger, who came up with the solution to her dilemma: a presidential telephone call to Aliyev.

On Monday morning, October 2, White House Press Secretary Mike McCurry opened his daily briefing with an item involving a seldom-mentioned country. President Clinton, he told reporters, had made a twenty-five-minute phone call to the president of Azerbaijan and expressed support for "multiple oil pipelines from the Caspian Sea region," specifically "a Transcaucasus route and a route through Russia." It was a green light for the Georgia option, in lockstep with a Russian line.

The phone call had its desired effect. Over the next forty-eight hours, Aliyev signaled his support to the foreign oilmen gathered in London, and they in turn reaffirmed their Houston agreement to build the dual pipelines. Only one hurdle remained, a meeting five days hence in Baku at which the agreement would be submitted to a formal vote by the oilmen.

Would there be any surprises? Sheila Heslin hoped not. But anything could happen. The CIA's position was emblematic of the uncertainty. The morning of Clinton's call, the agency's daily briefing had expressed a sour view of the Georgia option. In the agency's opinion, "there was no way [it] was going to work. The companies were for the [Russian] line. Aliyev was for the [Russian] line. We were going to do this, cause damage with Russia, and get nothing," Heslin recalled. She had to stifle an impulse to ask the CIA whether "you guys really know what you are doing." Among Heslin's most vocal CIA critics was Robert Baer, a cowboyish California native whose posting to Central Asia and the Caucasus began about the time that she joined the National Security Council. In a memoir Baer wrote after resigning two years later, he said that U.S. policy on the Caspian was designed so that "Amoco, Exxon, and Mobil could have some extra reserves for their yearly financial statement." As for Heslin, he wrote, she was "Amoco's ambassador to the NSC," whose "sole job, it seemed, was to carry water for an exclusive club known as the Foreign Oil Companies

Group, a cover for a cartel of major petroleum companies doing business in the Caspian."

The last urgent days of the Early Oil saga played out in Azerbaijan. They began quietly enough, with the arrival in Baku of Zbigniew Brzezinski, who, as President Carter's national security advisor, had famously ridden up Pakistan's Khyber Pass and aimed a rifle at imagined Soviet troops. Brzezinski had since established his credentials as a balanced and serious thinker on Russia's role in its Near Abroad, and President Aliyev saw in him a kindred spirit. Now Brzezinski was on Amoco's payroll, representing its humanitarian efforts in Azerbaijan and Armenia. But he also was carrying a letter from Bill Clinton, reiterating the American president's telephoned support for the dual pipelines.

(The Azeri leader was a reliably genial host to visiting Americans, but especially so with Hazel O'Leary, the U.S. secretary of energy. Aliyev, a widower, developed an apparent crush on the unattached O'Leary when she stopped off in Baku in May 1995. He showered her with flattering remarks and seemed to attempt holding hands with her at dinner. One of Aliyev's diplomats conveyed to the gray-haired Clinton official that "he had the utmost respect for her intellectual capacity and found her attractive," an O'Leary aide recalled. Visiting New York, Aliyev gave her an Azeri carpet that he asked her to take "home and put it in your bedroom and think of me." O'Leary did her best to deflect the attention, responding, "I think we'd both go to jail if we did that.")

Delivery of the Clinton letter was deferred while Brzezinski and Aliyev dined together and then toured the president's "Cave," a hideaway down a circular stairway. In a jovial mood, the Azeri strongman confided that he himself had dictated its decor: dark walls, plastic replicas of stalactites and stalagmites, wild animal heads, and what appeared to be bearskins covering the bar stools. As midnight approached, they repaired to a private office, where the American envoy handed over the letter. "But it is not sealed," Aliyev protested. "It's unsealed as a sign of the American president's respect for me, that I know its contents, but not as a diminution of the importance of the letter," Brzezinski replied. Satisfied, Aliyev read it. Clinton's message was intended to encourage a firm stand against Russian opposition to the Georgia option, and the American visitor stressed that more was at stake than merely a matter of commerce. "This is a relationship with the United States, in effect, and it has implications for the region" as a whole, said Brzezinski. An obviously pleased Aliyev replied: "If the United States sees this as a serious commitment and not just a commercial enterprise, I will do what the president wants, and I will tell the Russians."

Close on the heels of the Brzezinski visit, a Russian delegation led by a deputy of Prime Minister Chernomyrdin arrived for meetings with Aliyev. The ostensible purpose was to execute several protocols between the two countries; Aliyev was showered with comradely messages from Chernomyrdin and Yeltsin, and Aliyev's prime minister pledged friendship between the two countries.

But the pleasantries apparently faded as the hours wore on. Tedo Japaridze, now Georgia's ambassador to Washington, took an urgent call from his counterpart in Baku. The alarmed man said that he had just received a plaintive message from an Aliyev aide, who described crawling to a phone while the visiting Russians stood menacingly over the Azeri president shouting, "One pipeline! There will be one pipeline!"

At this moment, Heslin was in New York dressed in chiffon, serving as maid of honor at her sister's wedding. She had left Washington thinking that, effectively, "the whole thing was put away." But when the ceremony ended, the priest handed Heslin four slips of pink paper, each bearing the same phone message: Call the White House.

A colleague filled her in: Tedo Japaridze believed that Aliyev was "in grave danger." It had to be an exaggeration, Heslin thought. Would the Russians actually rough up the old Kremlin veteran? At the very least, Aliyev seemed in need of another gesture that Washington was firmly behind him. But it was a Saturday, and neither Clinton nor Berger was available. Heslin phoned Japaridze and asked the Georgian ambassador to relay her assurances of American support to his diplomatic contacts in Baku. The Azeris "calmed down," and it was never clear what had actually happened.

On Monday, October 9, 1995, after nearly a year of sometimes bitter argument, the oilmen cast their votes in favor of two Early Oil lines. The former Soviet republics of Azerbaijan and Georgia, in partnership with the oil companies and backed by Washington, had broken through Russia's obstruction of Caspian oil exports. For the first time, Moscow's once-absolute control of the region's pipelines would be breached.

In Georgia, President Shevardnadze asked his secretary to summon Gogi Tsomaya, the transportation expert whose keen reading of some road maps had set the events in motion. "There will be two pipelines," he told Tsomaya with uncharacteristic emotion. "A political decision was taken." The two shook hands. Their newly independent nation had cast its lot with the West.

A Battle *of* Wills

ON THE OPPOSITE SIDE OF THE CASPIAN
Sea, Chevron's grief with Russian interference at Tengiz was rooted in a deliberate
decision by company executives not to build
the pipeline that would move their crude to
world markets. Instead, they left that task to
someone else, preferably the government of
Kazakhstan. This would prove to be a mon-
umental miscalculation.

Their decision had a certain logic at the
time, spring 1992. Three years before other
multinationals would reach agreement on
Early Oil in Baku, Chevron negotiators were
bargaining with the Kazakhs for the rights to
Tengiz. The economics of the deal were
scrupulously balanced. While the oil company would commit to substantial spending
down the line, it would pay relatively little
cash up front. Initial earnings would be rein-

vested in the oil field to renovate worn equipment and add new technology. This pay-as-you-go approach would continue until production reached full throttle. Its success depended on Chevron's ability to increase the volume of exports from Tengiz in a steady manner, thereby generating the cash to finance each new round of investments in the oil field. But if all went well, the venture would be almost risk-free from a monetary standpoint.

The pipeline issue was seen as secondary. The Kazakhs for years had been exporting a relatively modest volume of Tengiz crude through a Soviet-era pipeline network, a relic of limited capacity that ran north into Russia and was owned and operated by Moscow. Nobody disputed the need for a new high-capacity line. That would be a must as Chevron ratcheted up production, and everyone knew it.

But Chevron vice chairman Dennis Bonney was wary about putting at risk the large sums of money—several hundred million dollars at the very least—required to build a big new line. Chairman Ken Derr, meanwhile, thought it most important to concentrate on nailing down the Tengiz contract. If his company simultaneously tried to tackle the question of a pipeline, the bargaining could go on forever, and the oil field—this pearl of Kazakhstan—might never become Chevron's. Better, Bonney and Derr decided, to have the Kazakh government assume responsibility for the pipeline. After all, the former Soviet republic would be Chevron's partner at Tengiz. It was an Adam Smith strategy: Let economic carrots and sticks guide the pipeline into existence. Kazakhstan, lured by the promise of great wealth once the oil field was fully operational, would somehow find a way to finance the project. Even if the line were routed through neighboring Russia, which seemed logical, Chevron could count on Moscow to be cooperative because of the bonanza in tariffs that the Kremlin would reap. Perhaps at that point the oil company itself might become a partner of sorts, as long as someone else was footing most of the bill.

And so Chevron showed no immediate signs of distress when the Kazakhs entered into a pact with a new entity called the Caspian Pipeline Consortium. It was the creation of John Deuss, the Dutch oil trader who had deduced that whoever controlled the flow of crude out of Tengiz could make some real money. The Dutchman had announced the formation of the consortium just a month after Chevron, in May 1992, signed its preliminary agreement with Kazakhstan for rights to the oil field. Now the Kazakhs had granted him and his Omani partners the sole right to build and operate a pipeline large enough to export seven hundred thousand or even one million barrels a day—should Chevron ever fully open the Tengiz tap. The oil company would have opportunities to negotiate for an equity share in the consortium, but it would hang back until the bitter end.

Kazakhstan happily turned project management over to Deuss, who named himself chief executive of the consortium. The still-struggling country was in no position to go it alone and was understandably grateful that someone was stepping up to build the line after Chevron had refused. (Deuss also wanted to sweep some of Baku's exports into the venture, but political turmoil scuttled Azerbaijan's participation.)

Deuss and his partners studied eight possible pipeline routes out of Tengiz terminating at seaports in Iran, Turkey, or Russia. They gathered in Bermuda in October 1992 to reveal their decision, but anyone privy to the guest list could have predicted the outcome. The giveaway was the presence of Russian prime minister Viktor Chernomyrdin, undisputed king of his nation's energy tycoons. This bear of a man had become extremely wealthy thanks to his personal stake in Russia's Gazprom, which controlled 30 percent of the world's natural gas supply. So it was almost anticlimactic when the Dutchman announced the selection of a route stretching 935 miles from Tengiz across Russia to that nation's Black Sea port of Novorossiysk. Not only that, but Russia had now become a member of the Caspian Pipeline Consortium. Rather than simply collect tariffs, Moscow suddenly had a stake in the pipeline itself.

Deuss could rightly argue that Novorossiysk was the shortest, cheapest, and least complicated route to take. But he had also recognized that Russia was a political necessity if his venture were to succeed. Admitting Russia into the consortium enhanced Moscow's influence in the region rather than threatening it. With Russia as a satisfied partner rather than a disgruntled outsider, the path ahead seemed smooth. And for Deuss personally, aligning himself with Chernomyrdin only enhanced his standing in Russian oil circles.

Deuss could be forgiven for thinking that Chevron would welcome his continued presence. Less than a year earlier, the company's veteran negotiator, Dick Matzke, had praised the Dutchman for the "good chemistry that got things moving again" when talks between Chevron and the Kazakhs hit an impasse. Just days after formation of the Dutchman's pipeline consortium, the company had signed a memorandum of understanding that it would join forces in some manner, citing its "desire to obtain priority access" to the line. Matzke and Vice Chairman Bonney even traveled to Bermuda to join Chernomyrdin and others for the unveiling of the route.

In retrospect, it is clear that Chevron misread the significance of what was happening. Morley Dupré, a senior negotiator for the oil company, had thought that Deuss's pipeline accord "and a dime will buy you a cup of coffee." Only after the Dutchman was firmly entrenched did the company's executives recognize their predicament: While they so painstakingly calibrated Tengiz's finances, they had failed to safeguard the key to the oil field's monetization—the pipeline. They had the oil but the means to export it had fallen into not altogether friendly hands.

Deuss made preparations to exact a heavy price for access to the pipeline. The Dutchman "felt he really had Chevron over a barrel," said Ed Smith, a career oilman who had managed the Alaskan pipeline before becoming a Deuss vice president. "It was clear to us that they were losing money [at Tengiz]. . . . Their economics were obvious. We thought they would be obvious to Chevron shareholders. We thought there would be pressure on Chevron to compromise more in Deuss's favor. There was a sense that the cost of [Deuss's] staying was not high in the beginning and [that] being able to hold off for a while was going to yield a fairly good result."

What followed was one of the most prolonged and bitter confrontations of the era. The clash would soon become a contest of wills between two implacable men, dealmaker John Deuss and Chevron boss Ken Derr. Neither man would ever understand the other. Both would amass powerful allies on the Caspian and in foreign capitals. The subsequent war of attrition would pit Washington once more against Moscow, Moscow against Chevron, and, in the worst moments, Kazakhstan against Chevron.

The first sign of trouble came almost immediately after Chevron and Kazakhstan announced that their negotiations to form a Tengiz partnership had succeeded. On April 6, 1993, Derr and Kazakh president Nursultan Nazarbayev met in the republic's capital of Almaty to sign the final agreement. Chevron would pay the Kazakhs approximately $800 million, half to be set aside for field expenses and the rest to be parceled out over several years as the oil field became more productive, in return for a 50 percent share of its riches.

Nearly three years had elapsed since the Chevron chairman's first abortive run at Tengiz had yielded an ultimately worthless agreement signed by Mikhail Gorbachev. Now the long chase seemed to be over. But at eight o'clock the following morning, as the first Chevron engineers arrived at the oil field to take over operations, they were startled by a message from the Kazakhs. Exports from Tengiz would be limited to just thirty thousand barrels of crude a day—less than half the volume required to finance Chevron's carefully structured plan to refit the field.

The Kazakhs said they weren't to blame—it was Moscow, which claimed it was short of pipeline space. At the time, Tengiz crude was being pumped 540 miles to the city of Samara, a hydrocarbon intersection just north of Kazakhstan. From Samara, the Russians shipped the oil through pipelines to the West or to refineries for distribution throughout the former Soviet Union. Moscow was saying that it had no choice—so much crude was flowing into Samara that Chevron's agreed-upon quota of sixty-five thousand barrels a day would unfairly displace somebody else's oil.

Oh, and there was something else—the sulfurous contaminant in Tengiz crude called mercaptans. Even if the Russians could free up enough pipeline space, Chevron would not be allowed to claim its full share unless it lowered the mercaptan concentration. The admittedly awful stench emitted by the mercaptans repulsed anyone unfortunate enough to get a whiff. But to Chevron's Morley Dupré, now the field's general director, everything he was hearing sounded like a pretext. "We had done an examination of the [pipeline] capacity, and it was there," he said. As for the mercaptans, just weeks earlier the Russians had agreed to accept Chevron's full allotment of oil while the company worked on reducing the odor.

One thing would soon become evident: Chevron analysts had miscalculated the willingness of Russian oil barons like Chernomyrdin to accept the loss of Tengiz. The nation's pioneering oilmen for more than a decade had labored to develop the oil field only to see its ownership slip out of their hands as the Soviet Union unexpectedly broke apart. From their point of view, they were owed something, and they intended to collect.

Mercaptans and pipeline space were not the only problems Chevron encountered when it took over Tengiz. The advance guard of a two-hundred-person startup crew found an oil field vulnerable to troubles ranging from the technical to the criminal. It was up to Morley Dupré to come up with solutions.

Even the seemingly routine task of getting out the payroll was laden with difficulties. Chevron had inherited about three thousand workers from their former Soviet overseers, obligating the company to a monthly payroll of about $1.5 million. Since Kazakhstan didn't yet have its own currency and there was no checking system, the money had to be paid in Russian rubles. Sources had to be found for so many ruble notes, and a Dupré deputy had to figure out how to transport them to Tengiz without being robbed. For security reasons, the deputy operated in strict secrecy; even Dupré "never knew and never wanted to know how he got the rubles there," the general director said. Once the currency reached the oil field, it was stored in a vault specially built for that purpose.

On payday, the money was stacked on three tables, counted out, and stuffed into individual envelopes. All went well until workers left the safety of the oil field to take their earnings home. Most were Russians who traveled by train, and they were routinely robbed along the way. The banditry was curbed only when Dupré leased private railcars for his workers and hired guards to ride with them.

The rough-and-tumble villages around Tengiz, which were settled by Hungarians and Russians, were particularly worrisome. Dupré figured that only half the total population of twenty thousand actually belonged there, the rest being "Chechen refugees, dope pushers, [and] whores." He fretted over the trouble that narcotics and prostitution could cause at the oil field and found the solution in an enterprising deal with the KGB, which still maintained a presence in Kazakhstan.

Dupré was no novice when it came to dealing with the Russian security force. During the negotiations for Tengiz, he had gone to great lengths to foil the agency's eavesdropping on the Chevron delegation. Now he approached a KGB general he knew and recited his concerns about conditions in the villages. Could the KGB help Chevron evict the undesirables?

It turned out the general had a problem of his own. With total candor, he explained that his bosses had told him to infiltrate Dupré's project and gather intelligence on Chevron's progress. He had managed to place some agents in the oil field, but they weren't learning much of value. Dupré thought for a moment and then offered the general a deal. Chevron was sending regular reports to the Kazakh government covering all aspects of the field's operations—production levels, spending, and so on. "I will install a fax in your office, and we will fax that information to you, even before we send it to the government," Dupré pledged. That way, the general could boast to his superiors that he had completely penetrated Chevron management. In return, the KGB would clean up the villages. The general agreed. Dupré then hired former agents from Boris Yeltsin's security detail, and they and the KGB "told the whores and pushers to pack up and leave."

On the oil field itself, the first worry was safety. Russian oilmen over the years had accomplished much at Tengiz under difficult conditions. Working with relatively unsophisticated Eastern European equipment, they had successfully drilled some hundred wells but at enormous risk. There were no devices to detect gas leaks. Instead, "they were sending their people to the well and letting them smell around" for gas like so many human canaries, with instructions to report suspicious odors, said Dupré. Thirteen of the twenty-three wells currently in production were not equipped with blowout protectors, valve-bedecked devices that regulated unexpected increases in reservoir pressure. Just eight years earlier, the gargantuan Tengiz eruption detected by Chevron satellite imagery had illustrated the need for such precautions. Now "you had thirteen more potential blowouts staring you in the face," Dupré thought. It took his team six months "to get the bad wells safely bundled up" with new safe-guards.

Deuss moved rapidly on his plan to build the pipeline that would export Tengiz crude. He engaged western engineering firms to design it and estimated that construction would cost between $850 million and $1.2 billion. Others had guessed hundreds of millions more. But the ever-alert Dutchman had spotted four hundred miles of already existing but unused sections of pipeline within Russia and Kazakhstan that could be incorporated into the project, enabling him to shave costs.

Still, he didn't have ready access to that kind of money, nor did he ask his Omani partners to bankroll the entire project. He told them that their share of the cost would be limited to $25 million, which Deuss estimated would cover the consortium's expenses until all planning was completed and pipeline construction was poised to begin. As for the two other consortium members, Kazakhstan and Russia, neither had cash to spare; their only contributions would be in kind—the four hundred miles of unused pipeline. In fact, it would be unwise for Deuss even to suggest that they shoulder some of the financial burden. Much of his credibility with them relied on his assurances that he would take care of everything.

Instead, the Dutchman would have to negotiate a package of bank loans to provide the bulk of the financing, not an easy undertaking since commercial banks regarded the former Soviet Union as exceptionally risky territory. The key would be obtaining support from the European Bank for Reconstruction and Development, a London-based public-sector institution launched by big western governments like the United States, France, and Germany to underwrite promising capital projects in the former Soviet empire. If Deuss's pipeline scheme were seeded with a few million dollars from the EBRD, commercial banks would interpret that as a guarantee by western powers to stand behind the project, thus reducing the risk to financiers.

Lastly, Deuss would need collateral to back up his loans. In the oil pipeline business, the standard collateral was "throughput," industry argot for the oil flow itself. Banks regarded oil throughput as a rock-solid guarantee since crude was instantly salable anywhere in the world. In this case, Deuss would need a throughput pledge from Chevron—a written promise to bankers that it would export its Tengiz crude through the consortium's pipeline. Tariffs paid by Chevron to the consortium for use of the pipeline would satisfy the bankers that the Dutchman and his partners would have sufficient income to pay off the loans. The oil company's cooperation seemed like a mere formality, since no realistic shipping alternative existed and none was proposed.

Deuss submitted a proposal to Ronald Freeman, the deputy chief of the EBRD as well as its oil and gas specialist. Coincidentally, the bookish American had been appointed to the bank by U.S. treasury secretary Nicholas Brady, who himself had initiated the entire Tengiz deal back in 1987 by introducing middleman Jim Giffen to then–Chevron chairman George Keller.

But Freeman had serious doubts about Deuss's business plan. The sticking point was how the Dutchman intended to set the tariff that Chevron would have to pay for each barrel of oil it sent through the pipeline. He outlined bold ground rules. The consortium's board would have "an absolute right to set the tariff" at whatever level it wished, whenever it wished. Even without any board-ordered increases, the tariff would rise 3 percent annually to cover inflation. The terms seemed to assure that the consortium would be awash in cash, meaning that the banks could be rapidly repaid, in as little as a few years. After that, billions of dollars would accrue to the pipeline's owners—Deuss, his Omani partners, Russia, and Kazakhstan. Enhancing the consortium's bottom line was a pledge that the latter two nations would exempt it from taxation, Freeman was told. The consortium "would pay no taxes—forever."

Freeman understood that the Dutchman, a demanding bargainer, was "starting high." Still, he concluded that the concept was "not bankable." Oil pipelines operated according to a fairly standard fee structure. Global oil tariffs were customarily set only high enough to cover loan payments, operating expenses, and amortization plus a reasonable profit for the pipeline owners. Deuss's proposal fundamentally violated the norms, in Freeman's view. The Dutchman and his allies theoretically could set rapacious terms, relegating Chevron and any other oil shipper to second-class, take-it-or-leave-it status. That kind of muscle would alarm any banker worried about the project's financial stability or, for that matter, any oil-man being asked to provide a throughput guarantee.

Neither did Freeman like the "no tax" agreement. The EBRD frowned on such deals because its client states typically were cash-poor. Granting tax-free status to a project like the pipeline starved the states of the revenue they needed to function.

Deuss, on the other hand, thought tariffs should be "context sensitive," as one aide put it. Kazakhstan was landlocked, and his pipeline would be the only way out. So no one should expect the tariffs to be set at the more accommodating level one might find in, say, the United States, where they typically were a little more than a dollar a barrel. (He would eventually settle on triple that amount as the initial tariff to be paid by Chevron.)

In truth, the tariffs were not all that occupied Deuss's thoughts. He was, after all, a trader accustomed to fast money; the possibility that he could "flip" his share of Oman Oil's stake in the consortium had undeni-able appeal. The Dutchman figured its value would balloon by the time construction was ready to begin, even more so once the oil was actually flowing. At that point, he might cash in, walking away with several hun-dred million dollars in profit while retaining a small interest to keep his hand in the deal. It was worth considering. In Deuss's view, such a tidy sum was the reward due the early investors who had dared to plunk down money when the risks were greatest.

His alliance with Oman's rulers bolstered his confidence. They gave him wide latitude in representing their interests; Oman Oil was almost en-tirely a Deuss show, with him at its head. He, in turn, treated Omani roy-alty with deference. His most important ally was the deputy prime minister, Qais al-Zawawi, who respected Deuss and trusted his judgment. While al-Zawawi's critics said he was too easily manipulated by the Dutchman, others said that he was the only Omani—apart from the sultan—who was confident enough to challenge Deuss on occasion.

In Russia and Kazakhstan, Deuss enjoyed sovereign status as a repre-sentative of Oman. It was an imprimatur that carried far more clout than being a mere oilman. Appearing at meetings arranged by the Omani embassy in Moscow, Deuss "didn't go into the same line as all those oil guys with briefcases" but instead was ushered straight in to Prime Minister Chernomyrdin, recalled one aide.

Deuss conducted himself in his usual grand style. When he flew into New York for business talks, a limousine pulled up to his jet; "like an Arnold Schwarzenegger movie," men in suits and dark sunglasses jumped out and encircled the car before the Dutchman climbed in for the ride to his favorite Manhattan hotel, the Pierre on Fifth Avenue. In Florida, meetings were held at horse-jumping competitions near Deuss's West Palm Beach ranch; Deuss would say a few words, then vanish to jockey one of his champion horses before returning for more negotiations.

As the details of Deuss's plan to finance the pipeline became known, Chevron's benign attitude toward the Dutchman and his consortium rapidly faded. Company executives came to believe that they were being victimized. The consortium already had made it clear that it was expecting Chevron to shoulder a share of the construction costs. Now the threat of uncontrolled, open-ended tariffs for use of the pipeline loomed. On top of that, the company in effect was being asked to become party to its own exploitation by signing the throughput guarantee that would secure Deuss his financing.

One company executive fumed that the Dutchman "was basically trying to blackmail Chevron in a deal that would be totally inequitable." Ken Derr, the Chevron chairman, thought that the situation was outrageous. Just months after the company had taken over the Tengiz operations, the first signs of what would become a debilitating standoff between Deuss and Derr were visible.

It was the last thing that Chevron needed. The company had just bought into its biggest oil property since Saudi Arabia in the 1930s, and much was riding on its success. Anything that derailed expectations for a swift ramping-up of production could upset stockholders and attract the attention of the U.S. Securities and Exchange Commission.

The potential for trouble lay partly in Chevron's early accounting of its new assets. On the heels of signing its final agreement with Kazakhstan, the company had "booked" 1.1 billion barrels of Tengiz oil, increasing Chevron's declared reserves around the world by a third. Its stock price, which had already been climbing (partly in anticipation of the Tengiz acquisition), enjoyed an additional lift from the booking, soaring 26.5 percent in one year.

But as the conflict between Deuss and Derr threatened to stall the pipeline project, those 1.1 billion barrels didn't seem a very prudent calculation. While they represented only a third of the most conservative estimate of the field's reserves, of what value were they trapped in the ground? If the dispute became prolonged and Chevron couldn't achieve its production goals for Tengiz, the company would find itself in a real dilemma. Among other things, it might have to take the commercially risky step of restating its reserves in a filing with the SEC. The stock market's reaction to that might well be brutal.

The new pipeline aside, Chevron was already fighting a losing battle to preserve its pay-as-you-go plan to develop the oil field. If the scheme failed, the company could be forced to spend hundreds of millions more out of its own pocket. The problem was Russia's continued refusal to lift its limits on Tengiz exports. Anyone hoping that Moscow would suddenly stop putting the squeeze on Chevron had to be discouraged by Russian behavior elsewhere. Moscow was threatening to attack the rebellious region of Chechnya and confronting the West over its push to expand NATO into Eastern Europe.

And then there were the disturbing events in an area of Kazakhstan abutting the Russian border, where British Gas and Italy's Agip held rights to a world-class oil and natural gas field called Karachaganak. When they came under pressure from Russia's Mafia-style protection racket, the two western companies were able to buy a measure of peace only by granting Gazprom, the Russian energy behemoth, a 15 percent share of the field.

The Kazakh government was also victimized at Karachaganak. There was, for example, the matter of 137,000 barrels of oil condensate shipped daily to Russian refineries. The Kazakhs calculated that they should be netting more than $100 million every six months from the sales. But Russian corruption in the form of phony refining fees and illegal skim-offs of the condensate was so gross that it left them with not a cent.

Kazakhstan acquiesced, fearful that if it did not, "you can expect the tanks to roll in," said an American observer. Nazarbayev, the Kazakh leader, tried complaining to Boris Yeltsin; the Russian president responded that he did not yet exercise authority over all his country's far-flung refiner-ies and couldn't force them to pay up. It was an extraordinary admission that the president couldn't control his own premier, Viktor Chernomyrdin, who was presiding over the squeeze.

The seasoned Chernomyrdin wasn't acting solely out of personal in-terest. He was first and foremost a super-bureaucrat loyal to Russia's state-owned energy industry, one of the few institutions that did not disintegrate when the Soviet Union collapsed in 1991. The fraternal ties that had long united its ranks remained largely intact, beginning in the oil and natural gas fields and extending to refineries, pipeline operators, and finally export offices. The Caspian oil fields had once been part of that great enterprise. Now Moscow not only had lost the fields that had been its property for decades, but the post-Soviet republics were also allowing westerners to crawl over them like so many ants.

Thus the prime minister could reason that his power plays in places like Tengiz were not to obstruct economic progress on the Caspian. Instead, with even the nation's once-mighty military in disarray, he was de-fending perhaps Russia's last citadel of order, an order he himself had helped establish during his long years in the energy industry. His most re-liable lieutenant in this rearguard campaign was Yuri Shafranik, his energy minister. Years later, Shafranik acknowledged that he "always, on all ac-counts . . . coordinated with Chernomyrdin." As to Moscow's negotiating tactics at Tengiz, he observed, "We navigated and pressured and held our ground and made ultimatums with full awareness" of the consequences to Kazakhstan.

As the months slipped by, an increasingly frustrated Ken Derr refused to yield. The Chevron chairman by now had relented on the once-rejected proposition that Chevron should help bankroll construction of the pipeline. But he deliberately held off signing the throughput agreement, his most potent weapon against Deuss. It seemed to Derr that the Dutchman and his Omani partners were trying to pick Chevron's deep pockets and avoid paying their fair share. Put more politely, they were demanding financial rewards far beyond what their investments to date justified.

The Deuss camp thought Derr's reasoning flew in the face of accepted investment practices. It was an article of faith—in any deal anywhere in the world—that the first investors, who obviously take the greatest risk, are entitled to a higher rate of return. Oman Oil had committed millions to get the pipeline project off the ground at a time when no one else— least of all Chevron—had been willing to step forward. The Dutchman and his partners deserved a dividend for the risk they had taken on.

Once the mud began flying, Chevron's image suffered along with Deuss's. Rivals who recently had praised the company as a market champion now called it a "poster child" for the perils of investing in the former Soviet Union. Derr went globetrotting in search of a way out of the predicament. A meeting with Nazarbayev, the Kazakh president caught in the middle, produced little more than hand-wringing. Talks with Chernomyrdin went nowhere, and efforts to enlist the aid of the Russian prime minister's most trusted western adviser elicited only sympathy.

As news of Chevron's pipeline troubles filtered through the oil industry, the company's share price suffered. By June 1994, it had dropped 14 percent from its high for the year and was still declining.

That same month, Chevron received word that "maybe we could have reasonable discussions" directly with Qais al-Zawawi, the influential Omani who was the Dutchman's patron. At sixty, the tall, slender deputy minister of finance had risen to a position of great influence after the government changed hands in a bloodless 1970 coup. Al-Zawawi and the kingdom's fifty-four-year-old sultan kept the secrets of Oman's energy affairs between them, making the deputy prime minister the second most powerful person on such matters.

Two of Derr's most senior executives had already visited the Omani capital of Muscat to try persuading Deuss and al-Zawawi to soften their position. The results had been discouraging. "What's the problem?" al-Zawawi had told the Chevron men. "It's a fair deal. It's proportional. Do you object to the Omanis making money?"

The two Chevron executives offered to match the $25 million that Deuss and the Omanis said they had thus far invested in the pipeline and then evenly split the remaining costs of the project. In return, Chevron would take a 25 percent ownership share, as would Oman Oil, Russia, and Kazakhstan each, a division that seemed acceptable. But the American oil company's proposition would require Deuss and the Omanis to put up more cash than they had intended and would deny the risk-taking dividend they thought they deserved. Deuss refused.

Now Derr would try his hand. The Chevron chairman and his deputy, Dennis Bonney, dropped everything and flew to London to meet with al-Zawawi. The encounter was probably doomed from the start. Neither Derr nor al-Zawawi seemed prepared for genuine compromise, and their personalities were mismatched. The Omani minister was Middle Eastern with an old-fashioned temperament, and he regarded respectful haggling as an indispensable ritual; Derr, a bit priggish and short on small talk, had little patience for the nuanced way of negotiating that made things happen in the Persian Gulf.

Derr went into the meeting seeking one of two outcomes. Oman and Deuss could give up the idea of a risk-taking dividend and pledge to pay what Chevron regarded as a fair share. Or they could allow the oil company to buy out their stake in the pipeline consortium. To al-Zawawi, it sounded like an affront, and he stood his ground. Derr, feeling he had been misled into thinking al-Zawawi would be more accommodating, replied "in so many words that there would be no deal," said Herman Franssen, a longtime adviser to the Oman Oil Ministry. That enraged the Omani, who thought his nation was being treated like a banana republic. The meeting ended in a shambles.

Al-Zawawi may have wrongly expected a Chevron capitulation or at least a bazaar-style bargaining session. But Derr, who along with his own bruised sensibilities was worried that aspects of any settlement with Oman might run afoul of America's Foreign Corrupt Practices Act, had probably crossed the line of Arab civility. "You can't deal that way in the Middle

East," Franssen said. "You have to always be polite. You never publicly offend the person you are talking to."

An infuriated Derr left London vowing that he would never again speak with the Omanis or Deuss. He "ordered all of us not even to speak with the Omanis," either, Chevron's Ed Chow recalled.

And there things rested. One year after Chevron had taken over the Tengiz oil field amid such high hopes, the pipeline that was critical to its success had fallen hostage to a bewildering tangle of events. The fine points as to who deserved the most blame for the stalemate would continue to be debated. But it was fair to say that issues of substance eventually took a backseat to emotions. Ken Derr's contempt of Deuss had become all-consuming. Deuss was aghast at what he viewed as Derr's utter intransigence. Now it seemed more a matter of who would blink first, the Chevron boss or the Dutchman.

$\mathcal{A}$
Tale
of
Two Negotiators

As the standoff between the Dutchman and the Chevron boss became more entrenched, the anguished Kazakhs could do little else than stand on the sidelines and watch. It was their country that held the promise of riches for all, and they were equal partners in Deuss's consortium. But in practice they were the weakest players in the pipeline drama. In board meetings, the Kazakhs, with one third of the votes, lacked the muscle to force any kind of settlement on the Dutchman and the Russians, who held the remaining votes and usually banded together. Likewise, while the Kazakhs were half-owners of Tengiz with Chevron, the company was putting up all the money to develop the oil field and so seemed to wield the power.

The distress of Kazakh leaders was

heightened by mounting indicators that the fledgling nation was descending into economic collapse. Its economy had shrunk by 37 percent since 1990. Its new currency, the tenge, had plunged in value. Defaults by several Kazakh enterprises had led Germany and Israel to restrict lending based on trade.

More bad news was yet to come. Chevron would soon announce a stunning 90 percent cut in annual spending for operational improvements at the oil field, from $500 million to just $50 million. The reduction would roughly correspond with Tengiz's lower-than-projected oil sales and so could be explained from an economic perspective. But it would drastically slow the planned ramp-up of Tengiz production, in turn dampening Kazakh hopes that a big surge in export profits would soon fatten the state treasury.

Nursultan Nazarbayev was frustrated. In a conversation with visiting American diplomats, the Kazakh president complained about John Deuss, who was "tricky" and "afraid to meet with me because I will tell him to his face what he is." Fingering worry beads, Nazarbayev wondered aloud why Deuss and the Omanis refused to put more of their own money into the project.

Chevron's stance also angered him. The Kazakh leader was still aggravated over the oil company's refusal to build the pipeline in the first place. Now it was rejecting any cooperation with Deuss, the man the Kazakhs had found to take over the task. Nazarbayev in fact wasn't much interested in the fine points of the dispute. All he wanted was the Tengiz export line to be built. "The problem is that money has to be invested," he said later. "What difference is it to me if it is Americans, Omanis, Russians? The main thing is that [the] oil comes out."

And so it wasn't altogether surprising when the Kazakhs ended up enlisting the services of Jim Giffen, the consummate American middleman. In the past, Giffen's polish and skill at selling himself and his bold schemes had propelled him from small-town beginnings in Stockton, California, to the innermost circles of corporate America and favored status in Mikhail Gorbachev's Kremlin. He had guided Chevron into its first negotiations for the Tengiz oil field when Kazakhstan was still a Soviet republic and had carefully nurtured an early friendship with Nazarbayev, then a rising political leader. In the waning days of the Soviet Union, Giffen had ushered the Kazakh strongman around the United States.

The enterprising Giffen lived in high style during this period, his reputation for hard drinking and womanizing undiminished. In rapid-fire order, however, the Soviet Union fell apart and Chevron fired him. By early 1992, out of favor in Russia and no longer a player in multinational oil, Giffen seemed to be a has-been.

But then he got to thinking about prospects in Kazakhstan. Its bargaining with Chevron over Tengiz was nearly concluded, but perhaps the Kazakhs could use his assistance in negotiating future deals with western oil companies. It would mean going from being a big fish in a big pond to being a big fish in a little one. Still, it had the look of his best shot at making a comeback. He already had an ally in Nazarbayev, who had easily navigated the new political landscape and settled in as president of the country.

In mid-1992, as John Deuss's Tengiz pipeline consortium was taking shape, Giffen made his move. He came to the defense of Kazakhstan after U.S. officials accused it of dumping uranium on American markets. Giffen assembled legal and academic advisers who helped persuade Washington to drop the complaint and allow the Kazakhs to ship limited amounts of uranium to the United States, a privilege denied to Australia. His ability to marshal forces and get things done impressed Nazarbayev's top energy aide, who promptly sought Giffen's advice on oil-related matters. He was back in the game.

Soon Giffen was attempting to court the Clinton White House, too, promoting himself as the man who could make things happen in Kazakhstan. One object of his attention was Rosemarie Forsythe, then newly arrived at the National Security Council. In June 1993, Giffen telephoned to report that Kazakhstan had still-unexplored petroleum reserves three times the size of Tengiz. In August, he called with inside information on an offshore deal in the making and bad-mouthed John Deuss, who "wanted to control" the pipeline from Tengiz. During a four-week period in autumn, he phoned her twelve times.

In December, Forsythe accompanied Vice President Al Gore to Central Asia. At 3 A.M. in the Kazakh capital of Almaty, the phone rang in her hotel room.

"This is a love call," a voice cooed.

"Who is this?" she replied.

"This is Jim Giffen. Why don't I come up?"

"Don't you ever call me again," Forsythe replied, slamming down the receiver.

A few days later in Washington, Giffen sent Forsythe three dozen red roses. But the damage was done—as long as she remained on the job, "Giffen never got into the White House again."

He was better at building relationships within the Kazakh government. Giffen understood that his friendship with the president was well and good but not enough by itself to assure his success. So the ambitious American undertook to ingratiate himself with the president's ministers— to persuade them that he was on their side and could provide the muscle needed to stand up to foreign oil companies. For openers, he would make sure the Kazakhs got their money up front rather than waiting for it to be doled out in installments, as Chevron had so purposefully negotiated for Tengiz. His campaign for acceptance succeeded. In December 1994, the newly appointed oil minister, Nurlan Balgimbayev, named Giffen his main adviser and Kazakhstan's honest broker with the West.

For Giffen, the incentive was a chance to restore his power and stature in foreign circles and make a good deal of money as well. His contract with the Kazakhs awarded him the equivalent of investment banker's fees on any oil deal he successfully negotiated. The arrangement was a point of pride with him. "We always get paid," he once snapped at the suggestion that his company, Mercator, could be stiffed in a deal. And Giffen would earn his pay. He would prove the tough bargainer that the Kazakhs wanted in the stubborn pipeline dispute between Chevron and John Deuss. He would shape a disciplined strategy to protect Kazakhstan's interests, and his creative thinking and inexhaustible energy would galvanize the powerful forces already stirring against the Dutchman.

Even before his formal appointment as Kazakhstan's chief oil adviser, Giffen had been eyeing Deuss's management of the pipeline consortium with irritation. Some of Giffen's reaction to Deuss was envy, to be sure, but he also thought it was not in the interests of his new clients to allow the impasse with Chevron to continue, and for that he put most of the blame on the Dutchman.

But in the early going, Giffen had to proceed with care. Although the Kazakh leadership was becoming increasingly impatient with Deuss, he still wielded considerable influence there. Espy Price, Chevron's regional vice president, saw that firsthand. He spent an entire afternoon in Almaty with Balgimbayev, the Kazakh oil minister, sorting through the issues separating the oil company and the consortium. They reached agreement on how to resolve some of them. But the next morning, the phone rang in Price's hotel room. It was Giffen. "You know that Deuss came last night, right?" he asked Price, who didn't know of the Dutchman's arrival in the Kazakh capital. Giffen was conveying a guarded warning that Deuss had countermanded whatever it was that the Chevron man thought he had settled with the oil minister. He was "really trying to help us," Price recalled. "On behalf of the Kazakhs, he was trying to make it work." But Giffen was powerless to override Deuss at that point. Sure enough, the oil minister later snubbed Price, who couldn't even get a meeting to ask what had gone wrong.

As Giffen maneuvered to strengthen his position, he employed a tactic that had served him well in the past: He reached out to an old friend with influential connections. J. Bryan Williams was a tall Mobil Oil lawyer who wore tailored suits and slicked back his silvery hair. He and Giffen had known each other since the early 1970s, when Williams was an associate lawyer under Michael Forrestal, Giffen's mentor in New York, and they had remained close; Giffen was godfather to Williams's two sons, and he still invited Williams to his yearly black-tie Christmas parties. The astute Williams was now an oil trader for Mobil, assigned to buy large volumes of crude in Russia and elsewhere for later sale abroad at big markups. It was a risky business, dominated by agents for ruthless mafias. But he was no stranger to hazardous assignments, having plied his trade in West Africa and the Persian Gulf.

Giffen and Williams soon struck up an alliance. The Mobil lawyer had personal contacts that could serve Kazakhstan well. He knew power brokers in Moscow and was friendly with Oman's oil minister, Said al-Shanfari, who had proudly showed the American his private collection of Maseratis and Jeeps. Giffen and the Kazakhs lacked such inside tracks to the Russian oil barony and the shrouded sultanate.

Moreover, Williams had a close relationship with Mobil's Brooklyn-born chairman, Lucio Noto, who was trolling for oil properties in the former Soviet Union. Toward that end, Noto had met in early 1994 with Nursultan Nazarbayev but had come away empty handed. The Kazakh president, anxious to get the Tengiz pipeline project moving, had floated the idea of Mobil financing some of it. Sorry, Noto had said, Mobil would participate only if it had rights to a producing Kazakh oil field that would profit from having access to the pipeline. Otherwise, it would make no sense from a business standpoint. Since no such field seemed available, the talks had broken off.

Giffen, however, saw a possible opening to exploit. He set up a meeting between the Mobil lawyer and Nazarbayev that ended with Williams agreeing to work his personal connections on Kazakhstan's behalf. No oil field rights were offered, but Williams knew that whatever goodwill he engendered could prove extremely valuable for Mobil.

In Russia, he found his way to Peter Castenfelt, a Harvard-educated investment banker who had earned a fortune at hallowed Dillon, Read. Later, as a gentleman investor, he had become remarkably close to the Russian government. News agencies would label Castenfelt the "secret Swede," the "shadowy Swede." In terms of access and influence, he was Moscow's Jim Giffen of the early 1990s, shorn of the latter's overweening impulses for financial gain; though Castenfelt would at times work as a consultant in the private sector, his service to the Russian government was without recompense.

The Swede's ties to Russia predated the Soviet breakup. As a private financier, Castenfelt had helped the struggling Bolshoi Theater obtain independent funding. It was a popular deed that led to his appointment as a financial adviser to the Russian prime minister's office. Astonishing the Russians and many others, he helped arrange the seemingly impossible—a loan from the International Monetary Fund, whose managing director, Michel Camdessus, was an acquaintance. At the time, high-risk Moscow was attracting only a trickle of foreign investment, and the $1.5 billion in IMF money was regarded as a miraculous lifeline. Castenfelt now appeared to enjoy the complete trust of Yeltsin, Prime Minister Chernomyrdin, and other Kremlin influentials, including Russia's traditionally skeptical intelligence agencies.

At the behest of Williams, Castenfelt was soon in Kazakhstan offering his counsel to President Nazarbayev. He almost didn't get in the door. The presidential chief of staff, a loyal Deuss ally, refused admittance and bluntly told the Swede to go back to Moscow. It was an impressive example of the Dutchman's ability to penetrate important offices, but only for so long. The Swede countered with a phone call to the Kremlin, and the chief of staff was forced to stand aside.

Even then, Castenfelt had to overcome Nazarbayev's initial suspicions as to why he was there. The turning point came when the Kazakh leader asked, "Did you really get that IMF loan for Russia?" Assured that accounts of the loan were true, an impressed Nazarbayev opened up. Using derisive terms, he denounced Deuss as an international adventurer. The pipeline morass was crippling Tengiz's prospects, and with it the nation's future. On top of that, the president was catching the blame each time Russia put the squeeze on Chevron's exports from the oil field. Could Castenfelt please tell Washington what was going on, that forces beyond Kazakhstan's control were causing all the problems?

As it happened, Castenfelt had already tried to focus Washington's attention on the pipeline dilemma. But he found officials more interested in what he could tell them about the conservative Chernomyrdin. On a return trip to the U.S. capital at Nazarbayev's behest, Castenfelt again drew blank stares when he broached the subject.

A deputy to Strobe Talbott, President Clinton's trusted adviser, finally pulled him aside. "Peter, you know, you're a good guy. Here in Washington we all have our own horses," said Dan Speckhard. "Don't get hurt by talking too much about what you're talking about." The deputy was dispensing some friendly advice. Washington was still months away from making its abrupt shift on Caspian oil policy; a pipeline in remote Central Asia hardly mattered in comparison with, say, arms control, which was Talbott's top priority.

The discouraging reception in Washington did not shake Castenfelt's support of the campaign being shaped by Giffen and Williams. The Swede was persuaded that Deuss's stance toward Chevron was endangering Russia's largest single foreign investment. From his Kremlin perch, Castenfelt quietly initiated intelligence inquiries on the Dutchman. Back came one especially interesting report: that Deuss, Chernomyrdin, and their Russian and Kazakh allies were willing to break the pipeline stalemate for a payoff of $156 million. Castenfelt valued his close relationship with Prime Minister Chernomyrdin but was offended that Russia's interests might be compromised by a person at his level. He began to slip documents to people who might be able to get the pipeline moving despite Chernomyrdin's opposition—to Yeltsin, to men on Russia's National Security Council, and to the prime minister's cabinet rivals.

The roles in Giffen's loose confederation were now well defined. Castenfelt and Williams would share intelligence duties, the Swede exploiting his sources in Russia and the Mobil lawyer doing the same there and in Oman. Giffen would manage strategy in Kazakhstan and act as the ringmaster. Together, they would do their best to loosen Deuss's grip on the vital pipeline.

A CIA agent witnessed the considerable power that Giffen had by then amassed in Kazakhstan. The agent was an energy specialist planted under diplomatic cover in the U.S. embassy in Almaty, there to gather intelligence on Caspian oil. Giffen occasionally briefed the agent, just as he had others in the CIA years earlier upon returning from trips to the Soviet Union. The practice had its benefits from a business standpoint, in that Giffen could try to trade information with the agents he saw. But he also used his CIA relationships to burnish his public persona. In conversations with others, he would whisper theatrically about an especially revealing map or some other bit of intelligence he suggested was acquired from the agency, creating the aura of a man of mystery. In truth, his relationship with the agency was rather ordinary for that part of the world. But the CIA remained receptive to his overtures because, as the Almaty agent observed, "Giffen ran energy policy" in the Kazakh Oil Ministry. The agent marveled at Giffen's frenetic activity, "xeroxing this, faxing that. He was a real operator."

As Giffen gathered his forces, Chevron chairman Ken Derr was attempting to do so as well. After his disastrous London encounter in June 1994 with al-Zawawi, the Omani deputy prime minister, Derr had reached an important turning point. He had left the meeting in a fury, vowing never again to speak to the Omanis or the now-despised John Deuss. But simply breaking off talks with them would not be a real solution, he came to see. The real solution would be somehow to marginalize or expel the Dutchman and his Omani allies from the Tengiz pipeline project altogether, even though Deuss assembled the deal and was managing it. Chevron would have to push them aside and stake out a power position for itself in the consortium. The company's initial strategy to leave it to someone else to build the pipeline had been an unfortunate misjudgment and would no longer be operative.

Derr spent the following months trying to drum up support for Chevron but with disappointing results. The U.S. government could be counted on to back the oil company's position, he knew. Bill White, the U.S. deputy energy secretary, would soon be telling reporters that Deuss was a carpetbagger who should step aside. But within the consortium, Russia stood firmly with Deuss and the Omanis, and Kazakhstan cared mainly about getting the pipeline built, not who would build it.

Nor could Derr rely on the force of his personality to win allies. He was a highly skilled financial analyst with a strong sense of propriety and keen intuition. At moments of crisis in Chevron's dealings with Kazakhstan, he proved adept at lobbying Nazarbayev. On two occasions, Derr smoothed over disagreements by accompanying the Kazakh president to a mountain retreat, where they sat naked in a sauna drinking vodka. But he generally was not one for conversational niceties while conducting business, and he sometimes seemed oblivious in social situations.

Derr snubbed Nazarbayev outright during a presidential visit to Chevron's California headquarters. During a sightseeing boat ride around San Francisco Bay, the Kazakh leader noted that his country's national capital was being moved to the windswept city of Astana. He asked Derr if Chevron would help build a new soccer stadium there. Derr literally turned his back on Nazarbayev, who was suitably flabbergasted and in-sulted. The Chevron boss perhaps didn't understand that it was quite nor-mal for a Central Asian government to ask a businessman to build a soccer stadium—a bit like an American company sponsoring Little League teams to enhance its public image.

Nazarbayev's displeasure with his Chevron hosts was made apparent one night after dinner. As the meal was wrapping up about 10 P.M., com-pany executives were ready to escort the president to drinks and a pent-house view of San Francisco's magnificent skyline. But the Kazakh strongman declined, saying he was tired and would retire to the apartment that Chevron had rented for him at the luxurious Fairmont Hotel. The next morning, his Secret Service detail reported to Chevron that Nazarbayev and his entourage had not immediately gone to their rooms. Instead, they had moved on to the hotel bar for some partying—with Jim Giffen, who never missed an opportunity to court the Kazakh leader. Nazarbayev "wasn't tired, but tired of spending the time with Chevron people," said Ed Chow, a company executive.

On the next-to-last day of the visit, Derr and Nazarbayev played a few holes at the exclusive San Francisco Golf Club. The Kazakh president, a beginner at the sport, thoroughly enjoyed himself. Perhaps, he said, he should delay his return trip home so the pair could play again. "I think it's going to rain tomorrow," Derr replied coolly. The next day, Nazarbayev's plane departed from Oakland Airport even as another aircraft was being prepared for a short hop—to take Derr for a weekend of golfing at Pebble Beach, where he owned a house. "As a shareholder, I was looking at the corporate jet, all fueled up, to take him and his wife to play golf when he could have been taking the president of Kazakhstan," said a perplexed Ed Chow.

Derr wasn't the only one who had bumpy relations with the Kazakhs. In late 1994, a Kazakh oilman employed by Chevron was given command of the nation's oil ministry. Company executives were elated; it seemed a golden opportunity to have their own man at the very center of Kazakhstan's government. They had no idea that he was nursing a serious grudge against Chevron.

The episode began to unfold when Espy Price, the Chevron vice president, voiced unhappiness over the performance of Kazakhstan's incumbent oil minister. Akezhan Kazhegeldin, then the nation's prime minister, listened closely to the American's complaints. Despite his KGB background, the prime minister was regarded by westerners as a market advocate, and Chevron had welcomed his appointment.

"What do you want me to do?" Kazhegeldin finally asked. "Do you want me to replace him with Nurlan?"

The reference was to Balgimbayev, at the time a local oilman on Chevron's payroll as a trainee. Price couldn't make out if the prime minister was being ironic or serious. After all, Balgimbayev—though he came from a family of oil geologists—was hardly a seasoned manager. But if the prime minister were actually prepared to put the trainee in charge, what a fine opening it was for Chevron to influence Kazakh oil policies. Deciding to take the remark at face value, Price nodded approvingly.

Unbeknown to the Chevron man, President Nazarbayev had already ordered the appointment of Balgimbayev. The cagey prime minister had allowed Espy Price to think he had swayed the decision.

Chevron executives soon regretted their former trainee's elevation to oil minister. Balgimbayev hadn't forgotten the regular slights he had suffered as an employee of the company, when "he was nobody and was treated that way" by corporate officials, and he found small ways to exact his revenge.

He was particularly unforgiving toward the high-handed Dick Matzke. On one occasion, President Nazarbayev was scheduled to meet with the Chevron executive but had to beg off at the last minute because of the press of business. When Balgimbayev made himself available as a substitute, Matzke was suddenly too busy. His office explained that the Chevron man had been "called away urgently to London," but the oil minister didn't buy it. "No, I just wasn't important enough" to warrant Matzke's time, an offended Balgimbayev concluded. Before long, the oil minister's hostility toward Matzke led to the latter's banishment from Kazakh oil circles by Nazarbayev himself. Several months passed before the ban was relaxed.

An Arco vice president named Dan White was startled when the oil minister's dislike for Chevron spilled out during a private dinner. White had always "figured that Balgimbayev was in Chevron's pocket." But the oil minister was openly disdainful of his former employer, remarking in his broken English that "Chevron is son of bitch." (The powerful Russian oil-man Vagit Alekperov, who had arranged the dinner, later made his own, similar feelings known when Arco presented him with a gift—a bronze statue of an Indian shooting an arrow at a buffalo. Pointing at the animal's rear, he remarked, "This is Chevron.")

Russia's lack of respect for Chevron was partly rooted in Moscow's perception that the company had played the game both ways. It had eagerly courted Deuss's help to save floundering Tengiz oil field negotiations with the Kazakhs more than a year earlier. Now Chevron was distancing itself from him as if there were a skunk in the room. Once, the company had given implicit support to the Dutchman's pipeline scheme, but now it was in opposition. As Russia's energy minister, Yuri Shafranik, once asked, "If the deal is so screwy, why was Matzke in Bermuda when it was signed?"

Still, Ken Derr kept trying to enlist Russia's sympathies. The Chevron boss thought its leaders would see that they were backing John Deuss against their own best interests. "Most of the pipeline was going to go through Russia," he said. "They would be an equity owner and receive all this money for nothing," with or without the Dutchman. Derr believed that the Russians would surely jettison Deuss if that were required to move the project ahead.

Moscow greeted Derr's entreaties with studied indifference. It even re-buffed his offer to give up Chevron's tax-free status in Russia, even though the Russian treasury would have been enriched as a result. A decade later, a chilly expression would cross Derr's face as he recalled his brusque en-counters with Chernomyrdin and the energy minister.

An especially low moment came when Chernomyrdin refused to grant the Chevron chairman yet another audience at which he could appeal for Moscow's help. The Russian prime minister relented only after Washing-ton interceded at Derr's request. When the two sat down to talk, Cher-nomyrdin offered no solace. Why should he help an American company profit from a field that was legitimately Russia's? He went "on and on how

Oman had these rights and 'You should give a throughput guarantee' and 'What's the matter, why don't you do this? You're a rich U.S. company,' " Derr recalled.

Derr dispatched a special Chevron team—led by a skilled negotiator named Jeet Bindra, an ethnic Indian—to smooth things over in Moscow. That Bindra, a senior executive, was "not by birth American or a white Caucasian" might earn him a more receptive audience, Derr thought. But when Bindra tried "to sell Shafranik on a win-win solution" that would leave Deuss out in the cold, the Russian energy minister replied that "there is no such thing as win-win in this world. If you win, I lose. And I don't know how to lose."

Meanwhile, the Chevron chairman's edict that his executives were not to speak directly with Deuss or his Omani partners remained in effect. The company was reduced to sending Dick Matzke to a gathering of oilmen in Almaty to deliver a speech arguing that the Dutchman should bow to Chevron's terms. That his remarks were aired not at the negotiating table but at an industry function seemed to demonstrate how desperate Chevron's position had become.

Oil company executives also launched a press campaign to discredit Deuss personally, confiding to reporters that the Dutchman was a dangerous man and that they feared for their physical safety if he ever came to believe that they had crossed him. One only had to look at the bodyguards who always traveled with him to sense the threat, they said. But reporters could find no record of Deuss orchestrating violent acts against his adversaries.

Chevron said the most telling evidence of Deuss's unsavory character was his willingness as an oil trader to violate the United Nations economic embargo against South Africa years earlier. But an examination of the record showed that the oil company itself had remained in business in South Africa throughout the boycott period. It continued to operate a 112,000-barrel-per-day refinery in Cape Town and held a one-third share in a Durban lubricating oil factory. Its Caltex partnership with Texaco ran 950 South African gas stations, accounting at one time for a full one-fourth of all Caltex-branded outlets.

Zeynalabdin Tagiyev, nineteenth-century oil baron and Baku's leading citizen. *Courtesy of Akhundov Library, Baku*

Ludvig Nobel, the Swede whose genius made Baku the oil capital of the world. *Courtesy of Nils Oleinikoff*

Robert Nobel, Ludvig's brother, who used the cash Ludvig gave him for wood to buy oil land and a refinery instead, and launched the brothers in the oil business. *Courtesy of Nils Oleinikoff*

Oil gushers were fairly common during the first Baku oil boom.
Courtesy of Nils Oleinikoff

Oil derricks were built side-by-side in and around Baku.
Courtesy of Nils Oleinikoff

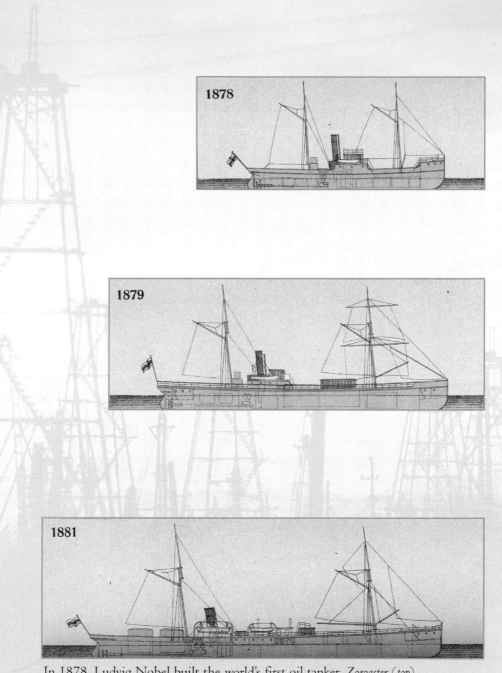

1878

1879

1881

In 1878, Ludvig Nobel built the world's first oil tanker, *Zoroaster* (*top*).
The following year he built *Nordenshild*, and in 1881 *Moisei*.
Courtesy of Nils Oleinikoff

Paul Proehl, Jim Giffen's UCLA law professor and mentor, joined him at Satra, Ara Oztemel's company. The Satra crew jokingly called Proehl "the Professor," but it was he and not the young men who landed Satra's first big deal—the Mack Trucks factory. *Courtesy of Virginia Proehl*

In 1971, Ara Oztemel (*second from right*) and his protégé, thirty-one-year-old Jim Giffen (*right*), were the go-betweens for a deal to build the world's largest truck factory, by Mack Trucks, in the Soviet Union. Zenon Hanson, head of Mack Trucks, is at left. *Courtesy of Virginia Proehl*

George Keller, chairman of Chevron, agreed in 1987 to join the American Trade Consortium, Jim Giffen's vehicle for breaking into Soviet business. *Courtesy of Chevron*

John Silcox, the head of Chevron Overseas. Silcox was charged with taking the company into the Soviet Union. *Courtesy of Chevron*

Dennis Bonney, Chevron's vice chairman, was most responsible for the bungled decision to buy rights to the Tengiz oil field but not take charge of building an export pipeline to ship its crude oil to market. *Courtesy of Chevron*

Ken Derr, Keller's successor as Chevron chairman. Derr finally signed the Tengiz deal and out-lasted John Deuss in a contest of wills over the construction of an export pipeline. *Courtesy of Chevron*

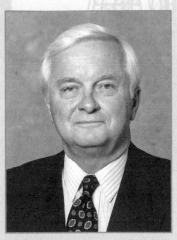

Dick Matzke, Silcox's successor as head of Chevron Overseas, was once shunned by the Kazakhs and couldn't get along with Jim Giffen, but he was an indefatigable and artful nego-tiator. *Courtesy of Chevron*

James Giffen in 1989, near the peak of his influence in Moscow, when he was a regular in Mikhail Gorbachev's Kremlin. *Photograph by Andy Freeberg*

John Deuss, the Dutch oil trader worth hundreds of millions of dollars who finally closed the Tengiz deal for Chevron. A standoff with the company followed when he also exploited its failure to build a pipeline from the field. This photograph, from the 1970s, ran on the editorial page of *Chief Executive*, a magazine he owned. *Courtesy of* Chief Executive

Kurban Abassov (*right*), the father of Baku's Soviet-era resurgence, with Rondo Fehlberg, who was first with BP and then with Pennzoil. Western oilmen courted Abassov in order to get a deal. *Courtesy of Rondo Fehlberg*

For a short time, it looked like British Petroleum's John Browne might steal Tengiz out from under Chevron by getting close to the Kazakhs while Chevron was busy courting Moscow. At this 1990 Kazakh banquet, Browne is respectfully offered the eye of a sheep. He would wrap it in a noodle and chew and swallow it.
Courtesy of Rondo Fehlberg

Chevron's Ken Derr (*seated left*) and Kazakh president Nursultan Nazarbayev (*seated right*) sign the final agreement granting the company half the Tengiz oilfield. Chevron's Dick Matzke stands to Derr's left. *Courtesy of Chevron*

In 1949, the Soviet Union inaugurated the world's first offshore oil platform, a city on stilts in the sea called Oily Rocks. *Photograph by Heidi Bradner*

Steve Remp (*right*), the first Western oilman to visit Baku in the late 1980s, with an Azeri friend. Though he was a small player, his relationships earned him a place alongside the world's biggest oil companies. *Courtesy of Rondo Fehlberg*

Valekh Aleskerov, Azerbaijan's chief oil negotiator. Foreign oilmen often felt they could not get his full attention. *Courtesy of Rondo Fehlberg*

David Henderson (*left*), Rondo Fehlberg (*center*), and Khoi Tran of Pennzoil. Henderson was the number two at Pennzoil's overseas division, and Fehlberg was its key negotiator. Pennzoil hired Tran, a Vietnamese, because of his country's closeness to the Soviet Union. The strategy worked—the Azeris trusted Tran. *Courtesy of Rondo Fehlberg*

Azeri president Heydar Aliyev (*left*) and Tom Hamilton, who headed Pennzoil's overseas division. To avoid having to pay a large bribe to the Azeris, Hamilton built them a giant offshore natural gas refining plant at Oily Rocks. The plant is pictured in the photograph the men are holding. *Courtesy of Rondo Fehlberg*

At the end of 1993, Russia muscled its way into the offshore Baku oil deal as the price for going along with it. Semiprivate Lukoil was Russia's vehicle for entry. From the left in the foreground are Pennzoil's Khoi Tran and Rondo Fehlberg, Lukoil chairman Vagit Alekperov, Pennzoil's David Henderson, and chief Azeri negotiator Valekh Aleskerov. *Courtesy of Rondo Fehlberg*

British Petroleum's internal newspaper featuring the story of BP's "coup" over its rivals, aided by former British prime minister Margaret Thatcher's sudden appearance on behalf of the company. BP's John Browne is at Thatcher's left in the photo. *Courtesy of BP*

The Caspian presidents: Azerbaijan's Heydar Aliyev (*top*), Georgia's Eduard Shevardnadze (*center*), Kazakhstan's Nursultan Nazarbayev (*below left*), and Turkmenistan's Saparmurat Niyazov (*below right*). *Photographs by James Hill*

Kazakh president Nursultan Nazarbayev (*left*) and James Giffen (*seated, center*) on a boat in New York in May 1992. After his Russian relationships collapsed along with the Soviet Union, Giffen moved to Kazakhstan, where he became gatekeeper for the country's biggest oil deals. *Photograph courtesy of Kazakhstan 21st Century Foundation*

Turkmen president Saparmurat Niyazov created a cult of personality. Here, a group of Turkmen women in traditional costume carry a carpet woven with Niyazov's image. *Photograph by James Hill*

A boom economy erupted on both sides of the Caspian. One popular Baku bar-restaurant was Margaritaville, owned by New Orleans couple Charlie and Mary Schroeder. *Photograph by James Hill*

Pushed relentlessly by Washington, British Petroleum finally agreed to build an oil export pipeline from Baku to the Mediterranean Sea, avoiding Russia and Iran. *Photograph by James Hill*

The pipeline was carefully insulated, then buried underground.
Photograph by James Hill

In May 2006, in the Mediterranean port of Ceyhan, the tanker *British Hawthorne* awaited the first load of oil from the pipeline, bound for a customer in Genoa, Italy. Aboard the ship are Michael Townshend (*right*), who led the three-year construction, and David Woodward (*left*), who led British Petroleum's Baku office before and during construction.
Courtesy of Michael Townshend

With the rush of money, President Nazarbayev built Astana, a fabulous new capital on the Kazakh steppe. *Photograph by James Hill*

———

Deuss was greatly frustrated by Chevron's continuing refusal to grant him the throughput agreement, without which he could not finance the pipeline project. He hired Tommy Boggs, among Washington's best-connected political insiders, to enlist support for his scheme. Boggs arranged for Democratic Party supporters to write the White House complaining that Chevron was the villain in the standoff.

Assuming Chevron eventually would relent, Deuss ran calculations on what tariff to impose for its use of the pipeline, settling on $3.25 a barrel. It was a reasonable figure, he thought, and one that might bring the oil company around. At that rate, the pipeline would generate $2.2 million a day in revenue at peak volume, or $830 million a year for the consortium. Once construction costs were paid off, their stake in the project would entitle Deuss and his Omani partners to collect $276 million a year in gross revenue, based on low-end estimates of production. That would add up to more than $6 billion over the pipeline's forty-year life, up to half of which would go to the Dutchman. If Tengiz production reached the high end of Chevron's estimates—9 billion barrels of oil—those figures would rise by 50 percent. They were extraordinary sums.

Word that he would seek a $3.25-per-barrel tariff didn't impress Chevron. But Deuss's next move got everyone's attention. In November 1994, he announced plans to build the final 155 miles of the Tengiz pipeline as a stand-alone project, entirely in Russian territory. The section would stretch from an existing pipeline intersection called Kropotkin to Russia's main Black Sea oil terminal at the port of Novorossiysk. What about the front end of the pipeline, the 780 miles over mostly Kazakh territory, from the oil field to the intersection? That would be put on hold, to be completed sometime in the indefinite future. It would "leave Kazakhstan high and dry," in the words of one Chevron executive.

The message seemed clear: If the oil company didn't like the Dutchman's terms to build the Tengiz line, so be it. He would not force Chevron to have a new pipeline. It was welcome to keep squeezing limited volumes of Tengiz crude through the overburdened Soviet-era pipelines operated by the Russians. His consortium would busy itself elsewhere, away from the Kazakhs and Chevron, at least for the foreseeable future.

Was he bluffing? Startled Chevron executives weren't sure. But if Deuss stuck by his guns and, indeed, pushed completion of the Tengiz line far into the future, it could be a financial catastrophe for the company. Chevron's success at the huge oil field depended on steadily expanding the volume of exported crude; without the big new pipeline, that would almost certainly not happen. With Tengiz oil thus stranded, Chevron would be under that much more pressure to bow to the Dutchman's demands.

There was undeniable genius to Deuss's strategy. The 155-mile section would cost about $350 million to build, about a third of the estimated price for the entire Tengiz pipeline. The Russians would be happy to provide the throughput agreement needed to obtain bank financing. They liked the plan because it would relieve congestion at the Kropotkin pipeline crossroads and would create room for additional crude from the Baku oil fields now under development. Moscow pledged to ship 86,300 barrels a day through the Dutchman's new line, a moderate volume but presumably enough to satisfy the bankers. (Kazakhstan insisted on committing 43,000 barrels a day as well, though it would have no direct access to the line. The worried Kazakhs hoped that this would win them favor with Deuss and Moscow and somehow open up more room for Tengiz exports in the Russian network. It was a vain hope.)

The Dutchman could relish the fact that his plan did not require Chevron's participation. But the important point was how it would change the facts on the ground. He would end up in possession of 155 miles of high-capacity pipeline leading directly to Novorossiysk. In the years ahead, Chevron would need just such a connection to pump its Tengiz crude the final distance to the Black Sea—and Deuss would be waiting there. He still held the exclusive rights to build the oil transportation system from Tengiz and would now have the final stretch of that line already built. The American company would have no choice but to deal with him if its ambitions on the Caspian were to be fulfilled.

On paper, the strategy seemed unbeatable. Deuss promoted it as a two-phase approach to building a full-blown Tengiz pipeline—the 155-mile stretch being phase one and the remaining 780 miles being phase two.

"Some of us were genuinely concerned it might succeed," Chevron executive Ed Chow would later recall. But the ground beneath the Dutchman would soon begin to shift, and his bold gambit would never become a reality.

A month later, Deuss set about collecting the "in kind" payments that Russia and Kazakhstan had pledged more than two years earlier. Short on cash, the two nations had bought their way into his consortium by promising to hand over big sections of existing but unused pipeline in each country. Deuss intended to incorporate the sections into the Tengiz project, significantly lowering its total construction costs. Even though he had no immediate need for Kazakhstan's section—it would be part of phase two—he still wanted it in hand for credibility with bankers.

Russia transferred its share, about two hundred miles of line, without incident in December 1994. But Kazakhstan, which owed about the same amount, unexpectedly balked. It appeared that the beleaguered Kazakhs, with Jim Giffen now directing their strategy, were clinging to one of their few remaining instruments of leverage within the consortium—perhaps their only one.

The foot-dragging by the Kazakhs presented Deuss with a knotty problem. How could he sell his idea to international bankers if he lacked possession of such a significant asset? Tensions within the consortium worsened. At an angry membership meeting in January 1995, Deuss and the Russian oil minister, Yuri Shafranik, took turns demanding that the Kazakhs make the transfer. Shafranik let it be known that if they did not relent, Russia was poised once again to suspend the republic's oil exports. After hours of withering pressure, Kazakh oil minister Nurlan Balgimbayev appeared to give ground. He pledged to transfer the sections of pipeline by March 1.

The meeting was also notable because it marked the first time that Giffen and the Dutchman found themselves sitting across from each other at the negotiating table. For the most part, Giffen stayed in the background. But at one point he offered an opinion, prompting Deuss to ask, "Why is that guy talking?"

"He can talk—he's with me," the Kazakh oil minister replied.

Their encounter seemed oddly anticlimactic, considering the larger-than-life roles that these tough-minded negotiators had assumed in the Caspian oil drama. Each was well aware of the other's activities, and there was no love lost between them. Giffen regarded Deuss as an obstruction-ist; Deuss was simply contemptuous of Giffen. Giffen attempted during casual moments to trade witticisms with Deuss and his lieutenants, behav-ior that the Dutchman found presumptuous. When Giffen once suggested that Deuss "come by my office" if he ever visited New York, the Dutch-man peered at him as if to say, "[Not] in your lifetime."

Even as businessmen, they were in different orbits. The deal seemed to be everything for Giffen, while for Deuss, already possessed of a grand lifestyle, it had become more like serious sport. Giffen could boast of the huge royalties that Chevron was forced to pay him annually, his reward for having brought the company to Tengiz during the Gorbachev years. His royalty was 7.5 cents a barrel; even when Tengiz exports were limited to thirty thousand barrels a day, he was earning roughly $410,000 a year from Chevron's half of the proceeds. Though Chevron had finally dis-missed him, it was stuck with the payments, which galled company execu-tives. Giffen also could express pride in his Westchester County home and Winged Foot Golf Club membership. But impressive as they were, Giffen's royalty deal and badges of East Coast affluence were not comparable to the Dutchman's string of business successes, often measured in the hun-dreds of millions of dollars. And, while Giffen traveled in his Bentleys and Rolls-Royces, Deuss jetsetted around the world in his own Gulfstreams.

The March 1 deadline came and went without the Kazakhs turning over any pipeline assets. Their stalling was deliberate. Secret talks were being conducted with Washington, Kazakhstan, and the European Bank for Reconstruction and Development with the aim of finding alternative ways to finance the stalled pipeline project. At the same time, the U.S. gov-ernment was advising the Kazakhs not to surrender any of their unused pipeline to Deuss. Washington, having thrown its support behind Chevron, was now doing its best to derail the Dutchman.

President Clinton's aides had thought long and hard before falling in line behind Chevron, whose lobbyists had been vigorously pressing for

Washington to intervene. The president's advisers wondered whether doing so could be made an issue by opponents in his 1996 reelection campaign. But they were finally swayed by the oil company's arguments, along with the opinions of junior officers like Sheila Heslin at the National Security Council and analysts at the CIA. The question, all agreed, was clear: Was the United States going to allow a free agent like Deuss—an international dealmaker operating outside Washington's sphere of influence—to exercise control over something as strategically important as the flow of oil from the Caspian? The answer was definitively no, and the administration assigned the Treasury Department to make life difficult for the Dutchman.

Treasury was tapped because of its ties to the global banking community, specifically the EBRD, the linchpin of Deuss's strategy to finance the pipeline. A senior Treasury official named David Lipton phoned EBRD's Ron Freeman to explain why he should resist Deuss's entreaties. Freeman was the senior U.S.-appointed delegate to the bank; he wasn't subordinate to Washington but, practically speaking, he was expected to stay generally in line with American foreign policy. In fact, Freeman's subsequent actions would mirror Lipton's wishes precisely. From that moment forward, Washington and the EBRD would behave like arms of Chevron.

Vice President Gore tried to do his part for the oil company on a trip to Oman to discuss U.S. naval rights there. Over dinner, Gore questioned Qais al-Zawawi, Deuss's staunch supporter in the sultanate. What expertise did Oman bring to the pipeline consortium? Gore inquired.

"We bring our management experience," his host replied.

Gore burst into hearty, exaggerated laughter at al-Zawawi's dubious assertion. The vice president was signaling to the Dutchman's partners that the United States was ready to do battle on Chevron's behalf; when she heard about it, a buoyed Sheila Heslin called it "the laugh heard around the world."

Gore also sent aides to Russia to argue that Chernomyrdin should stop backing Deuss and his Omani allies and instead allow Chevron to lead the Tengiz pipeline project. The Russians didn't budge. Kazakhstan, meanwhile, had isolated itself from its consortium partners by siding with the U.S. government and the European development bank against Deuss.

The Kazakhs told themselves that, uncomfortable as their position might be, they were simply bowing to reality. Since the United States was solidly on Chevron's side and former Soviet republics like theirs needed the Americans as a counterweight to Russia, it was the best choice to make.

The tensions exploded at an April meeting of the pipeline consortium. Deuss had come into possession of a diplomatic note from the U.S. embassy to the Kazakhs that revealed the secret plotting against him. He brandished the note before the assemblage and, in a rare flash of anger, accused the Kazakh delegates of treachery. They had violated consortium rules; he was the only one contractually authorized to pursue financing for the Tengiz pipeline. They had gone behind his back, and he wanted an explanation.

Startled by the appearance of the note, Balgimbayev, the Kazakh oil minister, lamely proclaimed his innocence. Even Giffen was thrown off balance. Doing his best to sound indignant, he braced a Deuss lieutenant and demanded, "Where did you get that letter? That's funny, how that ended up in your hands. Because, you know, that is theft." In fact, it was probably nothing of the kind. One of Deuss's many allies behind the scenes in Kazakhstan or elsewhere had likely slipped the note to him.

Even before the meeting began, it was evident that feelings among some consortium members were being rubbed raw. As delegates gathered, Said al-Shanfari, the gentlemanly Omani oil minister, approached Balgimbayev to present him with a coffee table book on Oman. The Kazakh oil minister reacted with undisguised indifference, a notable insult in the Arab culture.

The tumultuous April meeting was a turning point for Deuss. The diplomatic note unmasking the behind-the-scenes maneuvering by Washington was troublesome enough. But what followed as the session wore on was perhaps more unsettling.

It began with the Kazakhs questioning how Deuss intended to finance his plan to build the Tengiz pipeline in two phases. The Dutchman and his Omani partners had already guaranteed financing for phase one, the 155-mile segment. They would arrange bank loans, or the sultanate itself would foot the bill. Al-Shanfari reiterated that pledge but left unresolved the financing of phase two, the 780-mile stretch.

Coached by Giffen, the Kazakhs put a further question to the oil minister: Would he mind if they looked for ways to raise money for phase two? Al-Shanfari, ignoring Deuss's consternation at the direction the discussion was taking, replied that he didn't mind at all.

By the time the meeting ended, a protocol had been drafted that authorized Kazakhstan to explore financing for phase two outside the consortium's confines. The Kazakhs effectively had been granted a license to bypass Deuss. On the face of it, they could recruit their own bankers. The Dutchman's single greatest advantage—his exclusive right to call all the shots when it came to financing the pipeline—had been seriously compromised. The consortium's utter dependence on him to raise the necessary $1 billion had been the source of much of his power. Now that was slipping away.

What had gone wrong? Al-Shanfari, in all likelihood, had acted out of innocence. The Omani oil minister apparently failed to appreciate how important an opening he was giving the Kazakhs, and how much he was weakening his own position. He seemed to have lost sight of Deuss's strategy: Either the Dutchman and Oman won the game big, or it wasn't worth the effort to build the pipeline. Quickly recognizing the opportunity, Giffen seized it. Deuss had to swallow his dismay. He could not risk offending his Omani allies by seeming to contradict or insult their oil minister in public. And despite his influence with them, the sultanate's leaders reserved the right to be the decision-makers when they felt so inclined.

Yuri Shafranik, the Russian energy minister, was livid over Kazakhstan's sudden empowerment. At one point, he retreated with a flourish to a far corner of the room and placed a call on a mobile phone. He returned to the meeting without explaining the interruption. But the Kazakhs deduced the purpose of his call when a fax arrived later that day. The message said that a freak storm had erupted on the Black Sea, and Russian pipelines could accept no more Kazakh oil exports until further notice.

Shafranik didn't regard the flexing of Russian muscle as a particularly hostile act. It was simply a reminder to the Kazakhs of who was in charge, and after all, it could have been much worse. Moscow had been "ready to cut off Kazakhstan in its entirety. . . . We were so fed up with persuading" the republic, he recalled. "At that moment, we were ready to say, 'That's it, enough. Tengiz is done for. . . . To hell with you. Live your own life.' " The Kazakhs ought to be grateful that he had resisted the angrier impulses of others in the Kremlin, he thought.

John Deuss was left to ponder ways he might blunt Kazakhstan's intrusion into what had been his exclusive domain. Russia's continued allegiance would be critical. But he was confident that Moscow would stand by him as long as he had the support of Qais al-Zawawi, the Omani deputy prime minister. Al-Zawawi was not only his protector but also the guarantor of Oman's willingness to continue bankrolling the pipeline consortium's startup costs.

Then, on September 11, 1995, everything turned upside down. Al-Zawawi and his brother, Omar, a corpulent foreign affairs adviser in the government, were riding in a Mercedes sedan driven by the sultan on a deserted road. A Toyota Land Cruiser smashed into them from behind. Qais al-Zawawi was killed.

The minister's death shook the kingdom, and it also cast into doubt Deuss's privileged status there. Suddenly, the Dutchman's dealmaking days on the Caspian hung by a thread.

CHAPTER 16

An
Accidental Pipeline

EVEN BEFORE THE HIGHWAY CRASH that killed his powerful Omani patron, John Deuss's support within the sultanate had shown serious signs of slippage. Now, with Deputy Prime Minister Qais al-Zawawi dead, the government officials who had become increasingly disenchanted with the Dutchman's stewardship of Oman Oil felt emboldened to act.

Some of their unhappiness was over the millions being spent by the company to support the Tengiz pipeline consortium. There were suspicions that the Dutchman was inflating expenses at Oman Oil, a joint venture of Deuss and the government. His critics were further inflamed when the consortium's startup costs had spiraled upward, requiring Oman to pump in more cash.

The Dutchman's camp thought the criticism was unfair. The surge in spending was mostly the result of Russia deeding its two hundred miles of unused pipeline to the consortium four months earlier at Deuss's behest. The problem was that the pipeline, though idle, came with a bloated workforce—typical of the post-Soviet era—ostensibly required to keep it in working condition. Oman Oil was instantly saddled with the salaries of hundreds of workers it didn't want but was obligated to retain. Right away the Dutchman's "burn rate of money increased dramatically.... What started out as $10 million in risk money was headed to $100 million," said an associate.

On top of the grumbling over costs, some of the sultanate's officials wondered why a foreigner like Deuss was running Oman Oil. The company was now a global player, and national pride demanded that Omanis manage it. This argument required that one overlook the country's ineptitude in exporting crude and its inability to run overseas oil ventures before Deuss took over. Al-Zawawi, though a supporter of eventual "Omanization" of the oil company, had appreciated the Dutchman's visionary strategies and had managed to hold back the tide of criticism.

With al-Zawawi's death, a new lineup of ministers assumed management of Oman's economy and decided that they "didn't see eye to eye with Deuss." The sultan, who himself had steadfastly supported the Dutchman's work for years, now "had to choose between his new ministers or an outsider—Deuss," said Herman Franssen, the Omani Oil Ministry adviser. The sultan sided with his ministers.

Of the anti-Deuss forces, Bryan Williams was first to grasp the importance of the events. He hastened to alert his cohorts, Jim Giffen and Peter Castenfelt, that Deuss might be in trouble in Oman. Before long, the Mobil lawyer's suspicions were validated by a diplomatic note from the Omani government to Kazakhstan's leadership. It requested copies of all recent correspondence sent by the Kazakhs to Oman. Indications were that al-Zawawi's successors suspected tampering at the Omani end intended to benefit the deputy prime minister and Deuss.

Meanwhile, rumors swept the Middle East and elsewhere that the deputy prime minister had been brutally murdered. Some wondered if tensions between members of the pipeline consortium had had something to do with his death. As the mistrustful Sheila Heslin told Chevron's Ed

Chow, "Maybe the Russians solved your problem for you." The notion that parties in Moscow might have plotted the Omani's death seemed conspiratorial, but it reflected the paranoid atmosphere in Russia and the Middle East, since that was the way that relationships were sometimes severed—in both places.

Deuss found himself under mounting pressure outside the sultanate as well. The Kazakhs declared that he had missed a key deadline to produce financing for the Tengiz pipeline project, conveniently forgetting that they had crippled his ability to do so by refusing to surrender their two hundred miles of unused pipeline. They appeared even more intent on proceeding independently of the Dutchman and in fact were already striking a new alliance that would greatly strengthen their hand.

Mobil Oil and Kazakhstan had been circling each other ever since the sit-down a year earlier between Lucio Noto, Mobil's chairman, and Nursultan Nazarbayev, the Kazakh president. Noto had been seeking a foothold on the Caspian, and Nazarbayev had been looking for someone to help him finance the Tengiz pipeline. The meeting had ended on an inconclusive note, but it had planted the seeds of opportunity in the mind of Jim Giffen, Kazakhstan's increasingly self-assured hired gun.

In March 1995, Giffen tried to move the halting courtship along by arranging a meeting between Noto and a Kazakh delegation visiting Washington to confer with Vice President Gore. Akezhan Kazhegeldin, at the time prime minister of Kazakhstan, would later describe the encounter as "not very friendly."

He and Noto went over familiar ground. The Mobil chairman probed for a deal that would reward him with a large, producing oil field. Mobil had spent some $1 billion trying to find oil over the last decade or so, with decidedly unimpressive results; the company badly needed a triumph somewhere. But the Kazakh prime minister, like his president before him, was chiefly interested in Mobil investing in the pipeline project. The meeting ended with the two sides far apart. A Noto lieutenant especially soured the day by making plain his personal opinion that the Kazakhs were hayseeds.

That night, Mobil lawyer Bryan Williams tried his hand at peacemaking. At dinner with Giffen and Nurlan Balgimbayev, the Kazakh oil minister, he posed a question: Putting aside pipeline financing for the moment, what might open the door to a deal for Mobil?

Direct financial relief for Kazakhstan, the oil minister replied. Though a nascent petro-power, the republic continued to be in desperate straits. It seemed to owe everyone—its debts added up to some $5 billion in all. And its one large investor thus far, the resolutely businesslike Chevron, still refused to offer the Kazakhs anything against future earnings from their Tengiz partnership or to accelerate payment of the $420 million in future bonuses pledged by the oil company. Balgimbayev told the Mobil lawyer that an oil field might be the reward for anyone who engineered a cash infusion for his nation. He pointedly noted how Deuss himself had originally cultivated Kazakhstan by arranging a $100 million loan from Oman.

Williams said his boss would be a tough sell unless the Kazakhs had something genuinely tempting to offer—such as a slice of Tengiz itself. Though Balgimbayev barely reacted to mention of the treasured oil field, he didn't say no. Williams took it as an encouraging sign, but he knew that his oil company would have to demonstrate its serious intent by starting with something less than Tengiz. Soon the two sides had signed an agreement for Mobil to explore a territory north of the Caspian Sea called Tulpar. The transaction was not especially noteworthy—Tulpar was thought to hold only modest deposits of crude—but it laid the groundwork for further talks between Mobil and the Kazakhs. Lucio Noto, a raconteur with street smarts, was on his way to parlaying Kazakhstan's desperation into one of the era's most enviable oil deals.

Events unfolded rapidly. Kazakhstan signaled that it was ready to open Tengiz negotiations with Mobil, and the oil company invited President Nazarbayev for talks in Nassau. It made sure his surroundings were luxurious; in one photograph, he is seen swimming next to a company-rented yacht in the Caribbean. To demonstrate its goodwill, the company offered Noto's personal jet as a gift to the Kazakh president and promised to build an Almaty tennis court—enclosed in an all-weather bubble—for use by him and select Mobil executives. Neither of the gifts materialized, but the suggestion served the purpose of flattering Nazarbayev.

By July 1995, Jim Giffen had drafted a tentative agreement. Mobil would be awarded exclusive rights to negotiate for a large, unspecified chunk of Kazakhstan's half of Tengiz in exchange for a $145 million advance payment. Both sides would get what they wanted. The Kazakhs would have the cash needed to tide them over, and Mobil would possess rights to a part of one of the world's great oil fields without having to compete with another company. The final agreement was signed in October 1995—just weeks after the auto crash that killed al-Zawawi— and it added to the formidable forces arrayed against Deuss. A second American oil company now had a stake in Tengiz, and, like Chevron, it would demand a resolution of the pipeline mess.

Giffen emerged triumphant from the episode, dazzling the Kazakh leadership with his performance. President Nazarbayev became his unabashed admirer, and it seemed to all in Almaty that their American adviser could do no wrong. That he dared to demand so much cash from Mobil simply to talk about a deal seemed to awe Nazarbayev. As Giffen later told it with typical panache, he and the president had spent an hour and a half discussing what Mobil might be willing to give for the advance payment. The opening figure suggested by Giffen was $100 million.

"[Nazarbayev] said, 'Do you really think we can get $100 million just for negotiating rights?'

"I said, 'You bet. In fact, I'm gonna ask for $150 million. How do you like that? I also think I can get $5 million to you by Friday—a couple of days to arrange the meeting, then a couple of more days for the money to get here.'

"He said, 'Go ahead.'

"We finally settled on about $145 million."

The deal also demonstrated the wisdom of Giffen's early alliance with Bryan Williams. The two worked hand in hand to engineer the Tengiz agreement, behaving at times as if they were on a great adventure even though they were ostensibly on opposite sides of the fence. In the heat of negotiations, they would withdraw to a corner to confer in whispers. It was an intimacy that Giffen didn't extend to the others from Mobil, or for that matter to his actual client, Balgimbayev, the Kazakh oil minister. In conversations with the latter, Giffen's tone often seemed to suggest that he really wanted to blurt out, "You stupid ass, let me explain the world to you."

From Moscow, Prime Minister Chernomyrdin monitored the Tengiz developments and began to wonder about the wisdom of his reliance on Deuss. The standoff between the Dutchman and Chevron persisted, with the oil company's chairman, Ken Derr, still refusing to talk with his adversary and the Dutchman refusing to soften his terms for Chevron's use of the pipeline. That continued to put a drag on the Dutchman's original grand plan for pipeline financing. Washington was openly working against Deuss; in Chernomyrdin's contemptuous view, the United States was abusing its powers of diplomacy and had become a shill for Chevron. That aside, the inescapable fact was that the Dutchman didn't seem to be making progress on any front.

Relations among the members of the pipeline consortium—Russia, Kazakhstan, and Deuss and his Omani allies—were increasingly strained. Jim Giffen and his Kazakh clients were talking up a new scheme to rescue the entire project by admitting Chevron and Mobil to the consortium, as well as British Gas and Italy's Agip. The price of admission would be cash to pay for construction of the pipeline. In exchange, the energy companies would become part owners of the line. The Dutchman's camp reacted by angrily branding the oil companies the "Gang of Four."

In November 1995, Kazakh president Nazarbayev showed up in Moscow with a report prepared by Giffen and bound with a red cover. The "Red Book," as Giffen dubbed it, posed the ominous question, "If [the consortium] were to collapse, what alternative pipeline arrangement might be appropriate?" Nazarbayev's visit ended with President Boris Yeltsin supporting a search for other ways to build the Tengiz line.

Still on the table was Deuss's notion to outflank Chevron by building the Tengiz pipeline in two stages. Months earlier Oman had promised to arrange financing for the first 155-mile leg and perhaps the rest. But when Chernomyrdin later inquired whether the Omanis were still prepared to put up their own money if necessary, their reply was equivocal. That disquieted the Russian, as did events in Baku that undercut some of the rationale for the proposal. Deuss's two-stage plan had been specifically tailored to ease congestion at Kropotkin, the key Russian pipeline intersection. Chernomyrdin presumed that this would position Russia's proposed Early Oil pipeline to be the exclusive mode of transportation for Baku's increased exports of crude. Then, in October, Azerbaijan and the foreign oil companies in Baku announced that there would be two Early Oil pipelines—the one running through Russia that Chernomyrdin stubbornly thought would be unchallenged and a second one through Georgia. The decision to create the Georgia leg put the Russian prime minister on notice that his nation's primacy in the region was definitively at stake. If Moscow could no longer maintain absolute control over Azerbaijan's economic lifeline to the world, what was next? Might Russia also lose its leverage over Kazakhstan, Azerbaijan's neighbor across the Caspian Sea? Chernomyrdin would do whatever was required to reduce that risk.

Chernomyrdin had not only political concerns over the turn of events but economic ones as well. Deuss's original proposal for the 935-mile line running from Tengiz through Russia to Novorossiysk on the Black Sea coast had promised great wealth for Moscow. State-run Russian industry would likely make hundreds of millions of dollars by building the project, and the port authority at Novorossiysk would collect big fees for use of its facilities. But the greatest profits would come from the steep (unregulated) tariffs that the Russians had envisioned themselves imposing on each barrel of crude shipped through the line. The prospect of this huge financial payoff had made the prime minister a staunch supporter of Deuss.

Now the outcome was less predictable. While it was true that no pipeline could be built across Russia without his approval, Chernomyrdin feared that Kazakhstan and the Americans might, like the foreign oilmen in Baku, find another route for some significant volume of Tengiz oil.

The consortium that Deuss had so adroitly created seemed in danger of imploding. Ever the realist, Chernomyrdin would no longer tie his country's fortunes—and his own—to the Dutchman's survival. It was time to redefine the game. Simply being a partner in the Tengiz pipeline was not enough for Russia; Chernomyrdin would now demand a share of the oil field itself. A stake in Tengiz would more than compensate for any dent in Moscow's earnings from the pipeline. It would also preserve for Russia at least a remnant of the empire's once-vast petroleum holdings in this region of the Caspian.

In return, Chernomyrdin would agree to proceed without Deuss—to break the standoff with Chevron and see to it that a new pipeline came into being.

Not surprisingly, Chernomyrdin decided that Russia's share of Tengiz should be carved out of Chevron's holdings there, rather than be taken from Kazakhstan's percentage. He was motivated both by tradition and his animosity toward the oil company. A profit-driven commercial enterprise like Chevron did not merit the same respect the prime minister would accord a sovereign government. Add to that his lingering hostility toward the energy giant for taking over an oil field his own men had developed during the Soviet era. Why should he have any sympathy for the Americans?

Chevron, half-owner of Tengiz, seemed ill-equipped to resist. As if to remind the company of what it was up against, the Russians operating the Kazakhstan pipeline network had shut down Chevron's exports of crude for the entire month of November. It happened even as Yeltsin in Moscow was lending a sympathetic ear to the Kazakh president and his Red Book, still another indicator that all power in Russia did not rest with its blustery president. Ken Derr and his lieutenants had always understood that someone had to keep Russia on board. But they had thought that Chevron's allies in Washington and elsewhere would accomplish that, and they had never fully appreciated the power that Moscow could wield on the Caspian. As an article in one trade publication said at the time, the eventual success of a Tengiz pipeline deal was not up to Washington, not the banks, "not the international oil companies, and [not] even the Kazakh government. The key lies in Moscow." It was a hard truth that the perceptive Deuss had grasped from the outset.

Chernomyrdin now declared his price for standing aside: an ownership stake in Tengiz for Lukoil, the Russian energy company and Moscow's usual stalking horse. He assigned Lukoil boss Vagit Alekperov to lead the negotiations. The steely, gray-haired executive was regarded as Russia's most professional oilman. From the early days, when Chevron and British Petroleum were first prospecting on the Caspian, they and other westerners had felt comfortable with Alekperov. He seemed to understand the customary give-and-take of dealmaking, as opposed to the fist-clenched demands of negotiators schooled in the ways of the former Soviet Union. That didn't mean, however, that he was a pushover when it came to Tengiz.

Alekperov's initial instinct was to demand terms as good as—or better than—the deal that Moscow had cut in Azerbaijan nearly two years earlier. There, the Russians had muscled Lukoil into talks between the Azeris and western companies for rights to a 4-billion-barrel oil reserve off the coast of Baku. When the dust had settled, Lukoil had made off with a 10 percent share, for which it paid Azerbaijan a mere $15 million.

Peter Castenfelt, the Russian government's adviser and ally of Giffen in his anti-Deuss campaign, warned that a stake in Tengiz could not be acquired at a bargain-basement price like Baku accepted. In Azerbaijan, it had been the government that supplied Lukoil's share; in this case, it would be Chevron. Even if the oil company were inclined to accommodate Russia, it could not be seen as compromising shareholder value—or violating U.S. anti-bribery law. That, Castenfelt told the Lukoil boss, ruled out any sweetheart deal.

Alekperov flew to Kazakhstan and braced Prime Minister Akezhan Kazhegeldin. "We want to be a partner and want some part of Tengiz," he said, according to the prime minister. The Kazakhs should "force Chevron to sell 5 percent to Lukoil." About that time, Nazarbayev conveyed a similar message to Ken Derr. The Kazakh president had already unsettled the Chevron chairman by declaring that he would entrust Mobil Oil to resolve the pipeline imbroglio. But Derr had little room in which to maneuver.

Still, the oil company had to set terms that it could defend to Wall Street and the American government. Chevron negotiators told Alekperov that they would consider nothing less than an all-cash sale at a fair market price. That drew a wry response from the crusty Lukoil boss. "Price is not a problem because I have no cash," he said.

Alekperov then turned to the chief Kazakhstan negotiator and said, "I guess I have to get my 10 percent from your side of the deal." One way or another, Lukoil was going to own part of Tengiz, and if it had to come from the Kazakhs, then they would have to be as generous to Moscow as the Azeris had been in Baku.

Just as an ugly new stalemate seemed to be in the making, another American oil company rode to the rescue. Arco, based in Los Angeles, had been on the hunt for new reserves to compensate for the depletion of its big Alaska holdings. A partnership in Russia with Lukoil seemed like a sure vehicle to rich deposits of crude in that part of the world. And so Arco agreed to provide the cash that Lukoil needed to pay Chevron's price. Kazakhstan was off the hook, and a third U.S. oil major was about to become a player at Tengiz, joining Chevron and Mobil.

The deal was struck silently, out of public view and absent an auction of any type. The Arco-Lukoil partnership paid $200 million to Chevron in exchange for 5 percent of its Tengiz holdings. The price was eye-popping; it represented more than a doubling of the oil field's market value in just two years. (If Chevron's original buy-in at Tengiz had been priced accordingly, the oil company would have paid Kazakhstan $2 billion instead of $800 million for its 50 percent share. If nothing else, the price disparity indicated the bargain that Chevron had obtained on its purchase of Tengiz.)

During the negotiations, Alekperov readily acknowledged the centrality of the pipeline issue. Chevron's Ed Chow recalled asking the Lukoil executive, " 'If you were in Tengiz, would you help [with the consortium]? Would you help on the pipeline?' We wanted to get full value of letting them in. He said, 'Yes. That's why you should sell me [a share]. That's also why you aren't getting anywhere—because there is insufficient Russian involvement.' "

In December 1995, John Deuss's luck ran out. Oman's new ministers informed him that it was time to go. "Omanization" of the sultanate's oil enterprises would proceed immediately; he would no longer be in charge. The joint venture between Deuss and the kingdom that had been the engine of his ambitious pipeline scheme would be dissolved. For all his brilliance and negotiating skills, there was nothing the Dutchman could do.

He was finished on the Caspian. He had expected one of his biggest pay-days ever in Kazakhstan, but he ended up having to settle for much less. In negotiations with the Omanis at London's Connaught Hotel, he reluctantly accepted a settlement "in the tens of millions of dollars, [and not the] hundreds of millions" that Deuss thought he richly deserved, one of his men said.

Ken Derr, the Chevron chairman who never wavered in his refusal to reopen pipeline negotiations with the Dutchman, was able to claim victory in their baffling war of wills. In fact, it could be argued that Derr's stubborn resistance was the underlying cause of Deuss's failure. The Chevron boss had managed to gather sufficient firepower—mainly the U.S. government and the EBRD—to make a strong stand at the outset. He was then able to drag out the pipeline dispute until an act of God—al-Zawawi's death—triggered the final chain of events that undid the Dutchman.

But whether Deuss's demise benefited Chevron seemed debatable. It was not clear, for example, that the company saved money by pushing him out. Financial issues central to the feud were later resolved in ways that seemed to have always been within reach. In the critical matter of pipeline tariffs, the rate eventually imposed by Russia would steadily rise far higher than what Deuss had proposed. One could also speculate that, compared with the players who survived him on the Caspian, the Dutchman might have better managed Moscow's predatory instincts in the years that followed.

The Tengiz pipeline consortium that was Deuss's legacy would live on after him. But it would be drastically restructured in several rounds of frantic bargaining over the next four months. At times, oil companies would find themselves at one another's throats, and alliances that seemed to emerge suddenly would just as quickly be remade. Nothing seemed nailed down for long. When the way was finally cleared actually to build the big Tengiz line, nobody could say with total confidence how it had happened. It was as if the warring parties had fathered an accidental pipeline.

The pivotal event took place at a Moscow meeting of the consortium board in March 1996. On the table was a proposal from Oman, Arco, and Lukoil: With Arco putting up the necessary funds, the three would combine forces to build the first phase of the pipeline as proposed months earlier by Deuss, the 155-mile leg ending at the Black Sea. It appeared to be a breakthrough moment. Russia's budding Rockefeller, the Lukoil boss Alekperov, even made a rare appearance to witness the proceedings.

An aide to Russia's energy minister displayed a pie chart showing how ownership of the pipeline would be divided between oil companies and the consortium nations. But as the aide prepared to call for a vote of approval, Energy Minister Yuri Shafranik suddenly took the floor. "We have some friends outside," he told the startled audience. "I think we should invite them in." Into the meeting strode Jim Giffen, flanked by Kazakhstan's oil minister and senior executives from Chevron and Mobil.

Ed Smith, the former Deuss executive now on the Omani management team, remembered that his "jaw dropped" as the newcomers filed in. What was going on? On the face of it, Mobil, Chevron, and Kazakhstan had secretly formed an alliance, with Giffen playing a pivotal role. Not only that, the intruders were prepared to trump the pending offer from Oman, Arco, and Lukoil. They declared their readiness to finance and build the entire 935-mile Tengiz pipeline. The coalition of energy companies that Deuss had derisively called the Gang of Four—Chevron, Mobil, British Gas, and Agip of Italy—would put up all the money in exchange for 50 percent ownership. The three consortium countries—Russia, Kazakhstan, and Oman—would divide the other 50 percent among themselves. It soon became apparent that Chernomyrdin, the Russian prime minister, had switched allegiances. He had pulled the rug out from under Oman and thrown in with Giffen's forces and the Gang of Four, who easily carried the day. When the dust settled, Arco and Lukoil would also be participants.

Some time later, oil ministers from the three countries gathered to settle accounts. Their 50 percent share of the pipeline was divided according to the dollar value of contributions already made. Russia and Kazakhstan were credited with $520 million for their combined four hundred miles of existing pipeline and collected ownership shares of 23 percent and 20 percent, respectively. Oman, after having already dropped its claim to 10 percent, had to settle for 7 percent, despite the pleadings of its beleaguered spokesmen. It had invested $110 million in pipeline startup costs and deserved better treatment, they argued. But the sultanate drew no sympathy, an indication of its waning influence without Deuss at its side. As Chevron executive Jeet Bindra remarked coldly, "Oman already gets too much."

Nobody could quite explain why events in Moscow had played out in such theatrical fashion. Perhaps Shafranik, the Russian minister presiding over the meeting, didn't actually know the ground had shifted until the last minute. Perhaps it was an inevitable result of the fluid and even chaotic nature of the negotiations, many aspects of which were shrouded in secrecy. Bryan Williams, the Mobil lawyer, later confessed amazement that a deal was ever reached. Control over events constantly changed hands, and each player in the complicated cast of characters had his own agenda to pursue, leading to frequent conflict with the others.

But for the first time, the puzzle of how Chevron and the other western energy companies would move their anticipated petroleum riches from Tengiz and other parts of Kazakhstan to world markets seemed to have been solved. Wall Street quickly indicated its satisfaction; the price of Chevron stock, which had been steadily rising as its opposition to Deuss had become evident, climbed more than 5 percent above its two-year high.

Hostilities kept erupting in the wake of the Moscow meeting. Jim Giffen was angered upon learning that Dan White, an Arco vice president, had dined with the Kazakh oil minister, Nurlan Balgimbayev. Balgimbayev was Giffen's guy, and the Arco man needed to be reminded of that.

The three came together at check-out time at the Metropol Hotel. "Dan, nice to see you. I enjoyed the dinner," the Kazakh remarked, and then strolled off. Giffen looked at White. "Balgimbayev is the smartest man I've ever met in my life, and no one gets to Balgimbayev without going through me," he said. After a short pause, he continued: "This is a strange place over here. People carry guns here. People get killed. And anyone who wants to get to Balgimbayev has to go through me." White walked away wordlessly.

It was Giffen's classic junkyard-dog side, nasty at any sign of trespass on his hard-won turf. Arco had been a nonplayer in the region until it joined hands with Lukoil. That threatened Giffen, who had worked hard to cultivate his image as the impassable keeper of the gate to Kazakhstan, particularly for American companies. An Arco executive dining in private with a Kazakh minister was not something to be ignored. (Power brokers on the Caspian often appeared to be operating from the same playbook. In the early days of the pipeline consortium, Chernomyrdin had delivered an almost identical warning to Ron Freeman, the executive at the EBRD. Commenting disapprovingly on Freeman's rebuff of Deuss, the Russian prime minister had told the banker, "Things happen to people.")

On a trip to Vienna, Dan White caught heat from two Chevron executives who were "madder than hell" at him for wedging Arco into a deal that they insisted was rightfully theirs. White thought they ought to be grateful. "That project was going nowhere" before his company showed up, he believed. "We put the Russian and Omani pieces in a package and in essence delivered the deal." White had a valid point. Arco's willingness to bankroll Lukoil and accept Oman as a partner—entities that Chevron had treated as odious—had propelled events forward.

Elbows continued to be thrown at a meeting the following week at London's Hyde Park Hotel. The Gang of Four had agreed in principle to allow others to invest in the Tengiz pipeline consortium. The idea was to spread some of the costs around. Now, oil company representatives gathered to hash out their participation.

Almost immediately, Chevron's Jeet Bindra and Mobil's Art Golden tried to take over the affair. The companies were an odd fit. Chevron, in a typical display of the company's outsize ego, had been scornful when Mobil first appeared on the scene. But Mobil, personified by chairman Lucio Noto and lawyer Bryan Williams, was everything that Chevron was not. Mobil was fleet-footed, willing to mix it up in business dealings, and not prissy about the company it kept. Where Chevron's agents seemed tentative, Williams was resourceful; where Chevron's Ken Derr and top aide Dick Matzke were too often offended, Noto got along with people who mattered.

But as the hotel meeting room filled with industry executives, Chevron and Mobil seemed joined at the hip. The two executives tried to impose ground rules, the purpose of which seemed to be to intimidate rival companies. "Our boards have approved this—have yours?" Golden told the others. "If you don't have a firm commitment, you will be required to leave the meeting."

The price they set for a company to get in the game was stiff: $3 million to $4 million almost immediately, then a collective $70 million to $100 million within four months, and another $800 million after that. Right away, that discouraged some participants. For good measure, Bindra and Golden trotted out one more demand: Unless a company had a producing oil field that could feed into the line, "you're out."·

Onlookers, irritated at the men's attitude of entitlement, accused them of trying to "bully everybody" so that Chevron and Mobil could end up with the biggest shares of the pipeline.

"Who appointed you God?" shouted Lukoil's representative. Arco's Dan White marched up to the Chevron and Mobil men, poked a finger in their faces, and asked, "Who is going to keep Arco and Lukoil out?" Bindra and Golden conceded his point.

More turmoil followed when someone shouted that Mobil itself had no producing oil field. Jim Giffen declared, "I'm authorized by the Kazakhstan government to state that Mobil is an imminent producer." Mobil's purchase of rights to a stake in Tengiz was not widely known, and everyone present could only guess what field Giffen was talking about— everyone except Russia adviser Peter Castenfelt, who had been sitting quietly in a chair, largely unnoticed. At once the Swede sprang to his feet "like a doll" and declared: "I represent the Russian government" before launching into a defense of Mobil's right to sit at the table.

Lukoil's representative lost his temper. "He can't be the Russian representative. I represent Russian interests," the man insisted and then rebuked Castenfelt.

The reality, of course, was that Chevron and Mobil lacked the power to decide by themselves who would participate in the deal. Cooler heads would finally prevail, and participation in the pipeline project would be opened up to a number of companies.

A month later, on April 27, 1996, Boris Yeltsin met in Moscow with the leaders of Oman, Kazakhstan, and the oil companies. There they signed a joint agreement ratifying the restructuring of the Tengiz pipeline consortium and admitting western energy companies as members for the first time. The oilmen eventually would ante up $2.6 billion to build the line, more than twice what Deuss had estimated would be required.

Chevron, which early on had wanted nothing to do with the pipeline, ended up paying some $400 million to own 15 percent of it, the largest oil company share. But its relationship with the Russians did not improve. Moscow played a powerful role in the management of the consortium, and it used its position at every opportunity to benefit financially. The Kremlin required Chevron to send its agents to every principal Russian locality along the 935-mile route and negotiate individual rights-of-way agreements, a process made more tedious by the bluff and threatening Russian style of negotiating. Much time was spent reaching a settlement at Novorossiysk, the Black Sea tanker port, where official corruption was rampant. Although the pipeline's actual terminal would be built offshore and a bit north of Novorossiysk, the Russian port authorities demanded—and got—a piece of the action.

Soon after the agreement to restructure the pipeline consortium was reached, Kazakhstan announced that ownership of the Tengiz oil field itself had been reshuffled once again. Mobil Oil, it was disclosed, had bought a 25 percent share from the Kazakhs for $1.05 billion. That left Kazakhstan with a 25 percent share, Chevron with 45 percent, and the Arco-Lukoil partnership with 5 percent. Nearly three-fourths of Tengiz, one of history's greatest oil finds, had ended up in the hands of American energy companies.

Jim Giffen collected a $51 million fee for shepherding the Mobil deal on behalf of Kazakhstan. He spread the wealth around, servicing the cash requirements of not only the republic but also its senior leaders. Giffen parceled out payments to numbered bank accounts in Switzerland and elsewhere—$22 million to President Nursultan Nazarbayev, about $2.5 million to Oil Minister Nurlan Balgimbayev, and $2 million to his trusted ally at Mobil, Bryan Williams. It was not altruism on Giffen's part. He was operating on Kazakh turf, and doing so required blurring the lines between what was due the country and what was due its leaders. As for Williams, there never would have been a deal without his dexterous turns of state-craft and bargaining.

Mobil, meanwhile, went the extra mile to ease the republic's cash worries. Custom called for Giffen's $51 million fee to be paid by the Kazakhs, but Mobil chairman Lucio Noto agreed to cover it. Similarly, at Williams's instigation, Mobil came to the republic's rescue in its dispute with Russian refineries over oil condensate shipped from fields in Karachaganak. The refineries still were not compensating Kazakhstan for the shipments. Williams signed an agreement to make the Kazakhs financially whole at Karachaganak at the same time they were signing off on Mobil's deal to buy into Tengiz. The bailout was an added effort to induce Kazakhstan to close the Tengiz deal.

But the details of the arrangement were complicated and highly unorthodox. Mobil's cash did not go straight to the Kazakhs. Instead, it was funneled to a mysterious figure named Friedhelm Eronat, a longtime partner to Williams in Nigerian oil trading. Eronat's role was to use the money to buy the oil condensate from the Kazakhs, after which he would sell it to the Russians and use the proceeds to compensate Mobil. Over time, Eronat received $78 million from Mobil, of which he paid back just $48 million. The remainder appeared to end up in Russian hands—their price, perhaps, for allowing the Kazakh oil industry to function. (Eronat's Russian buyers were gangsters; Mobil wrote off the loss after hearing of their violent reputation.)

As the bargaining was wrapping up in Kazakhstan, the vanquished John Deuss summoned the key members of his team to his secluded family estate in the Netherlands. There to say their farewells were the Harvard man Mack Fowler, Deuss's scrappy lawyer Tim Alrich, and Ed Smith. The Dutchman was still bitter over being expelled from his own deal. But after a while it was time for the men to catch their flights home, and Deuss called an end to the brief reunion. "We worked hard, [but] we didn't make it," the Dutchman said with his usual aplomb. "Good luck—and goodbye."

An Army for Oil

BY THE MID-1990S, THE OIL MULTI-nationals could claim substantial victories on both sides of the Caspian Sea. They had at turns bullied, cajoled, bluffed, and bargained their way to enormous shares of some of the world's richest remaining caches of oil and natural gas. In Azerbaijan, British Petroleum, Amoco, Pennzoil, and others had begun developing Baku's offshore fields. In Kazakhstan, Chevron was well along in its expansion plans.

Agreements to build new export pipelines, the last pieces of the puzzle, were falling into place. But a nagging worry remained for the foreign oil companies: Even with the anticipated new lines, Russia would still be well positioned to play havoc with crude exports if it chose to. Most of the oil would still move through pipeline networks under the direct control of Moscow or pass over Russian terrain.

Western oilmen began talking among themselves about long-term pipeline ventures that might finally render Moscow powerless to disrupt their shipments. By one reckoning, eighty-two different schemes that would entirely avoid Russian territory were proposed, some of them verging on the absurd. Exxon suggested the most eccentric: a $12 billion, 4,400-mile line traversing almost one fifth the circumference of the globe to China's Yellow Sea. It was greeted with more than a few snickers.

Many of those anxious to try their hand were motivated less by concern over the Russian threat and more by the opportunity to profit from everyone's preoccupation with Moscow. One such player was John Imle, president of California-based Unocal. With his gray hair and wire-rimmed spectacles, Imle hardly seemed the adventurous type. In fact, the Texas A&M alumnus was one of oil's biggest gamblers. It was a trait he had inherited from his father, John Imle, Sr., an electrical engineer who, with an amateur's interest in geophysics, had helped to pioneer Venezuela's oil fields in the 1920s and 1930s.

The younger Imle spent three quarters of his time on a Unocal jet overseeing wildcat ventures in Burma, Indonesia, the Gulf of Thailand, and elsewhere. Each of these now-profitable operations had been highly speculative at the outset. But none had been as risky as the undertaking that Imle had in mind for the Caspian.

His plan was to lay 1,040 miles of oil and natural gas pipelines from Turkmenistan on the eastern edge of the Caspian Sea across hundreds of miles of neighboring Afghanistan to export terminals in Pakistan. He would channel the Caspian's energy wealth into potentially the world's most profitable market—the Far East, opposite the direction in which everyone else was going. The estimated cost: $8 billion. In the end, his grand vision would prove somewhat less grand. But it was probably the best example of how far some oilmen pushed the limits in the superheated atmosphere of the Caspian.

There were many reasons to fault Imle's scheme. Perhaps the most sobering was the necessity for Unocal to cozy up to the Taliban, the radical Islamic insurgents about to impose harsh rule over most of Afghan-istan. It would be a rare instance of an American company incorporating a full-blown civil war into its corporate strategy.

Questioned early on about the obstacles he faced, the broad-chested Imle would not be dissuaded. Instead, he recalled the naysayers his father had confronted in Venezuela. "If skepticism were a problem, this industry wouldn't exist," the Unocal executive grumbled in his air-conditioned hotel suite in dusty Turkmenistan.

Imle ordered up a flashy video that took viewers on a computer-simulated flyover of his imagined pipelines; whenever he sought to promote his idea, he would shove it into a tape player. Anyone who knew the territory could see that the lines would cross vast sections of Afghan desert wracked by fighting, making security a dicey question. Some remembered that in the 1980s, the CIA and its Pakistani counterparts had taught Afghan forces how to sabotage the very sort of infrastructure depicted in the video.

Imle's doubters didn't dispute the logic behind his thinking. The shortest and most profitable non-Russian route was in fact straight south to the Persian and Arabian gulfs and on to the surging markets of East Asia. All the oil companies had studied the same maps. All had examined the same forecasts for the twenty-first century: The West's energy demand would taper off as its population and economic growth slowed, while Asia's appetite for energy would rise sharply, driven by economies expand-ing at an annual rate in the high single digits or, in places like China, higher.

Yet routing energy pipelines south from the Caspian seemed a dreamy notion. There were only two possible paths in that direction: one led through Iran and the other through Imle's Afghanistan. The former was politically impossible. America's ongoing economic embargo against Iran was not about to be lifted, not soon anyway. After the humiliating 1979 hostage crisis, Washington viewed Tehran as an unforgivable outcast. That meant that no American multinational and none of the U.S.-dominated international lending institutions, such as the World Bank or the European Bank for Reconstruction and Development, could invest in Iran. As for

Afghanistan, setting aside the practical difficulties of conducting operations there, no bank would finance the construction of a pipeline through an active war zone.

But the Unocal president assessed the Caspian puzzle differently. Where others saw nothing but troubles, he saw possibilities. His company was already a partner in Azerbaijan's Early Oil pipelines out of Baku, which would serve the western Caspian fields; here was a chance to control a substantial piece of the energy flow from the eastern Caspian as well. Russia might even use his line for exports from petroleum-rich western Siberia, he thought.

Imle's opportunistic scheme fit perfectly with his strategy to remake Unocal. Just a decade earlier, the company had barely won a debilitating battle against corporate raider T. Boone Pickens. It was still recovering from the costly buy-up of shares necessary to beat back Pickens's attempted takeover; its shareholder dividends were among the lowest in the industry.

The new Unocal did not aspire to be a fully integrated producer like the world's biggest oil companies. Instead, Imle sold off its California oil fields, its refineries, and its U.S. pipelines and went in search of high-octane profits wherever and however they could be had. Already the formula had produced double-digit profits for Unocal's overseas division, an industry-leading performance that he held up as an example to the company's domestic side.

In carrying out this strategy, Imle's trademark was his willingness to do deals in countries that most others would shun, such as outcast Burma, from which he was building a natural gas pipeline across the Andaman Sea to Thailand. The Unocal chief viewed civil conflict and despotic governments as far less speculative—and thus more attractive—than the sand dunes, mile-thick ice, and snow drifts that other oilmen were more willing to hazard.

By that measuring stick, the economics of his trans-Afghanistan pipeline project looked exceptional. As far as Imle could tell, Pakistan, India, and the rest of the subcontinent had perhaps the greatest growth potential in all Asia. His pipelines would be capable of exporting 1 million barrels of oil and 2 billion cubic feet of gas each day. That translated into $2 billion in annual revenue, sufficient to pay off the entire project in an astounding three to five years and propel Unocal into the top tier of global oil companies.

"It was a huge mother lode," an Arab oil analyst said at the time. "Imagine you are between Bill Gates and IBM, and you get a cent on every PC sold in the world."

Yet not everyone at Unocal was convinced. "We were like a team sent on a suicide mission," said Marty Miller, an Imle family friend and his deputy on the Afghan project. "If it worked out, we would be heroes. But there was a good chance we would be slaughtered." Indeed, in-house critics thought that this time Imle had gone too far. They "constantly badgered us as to why we were doing it," Miller said. He was "half nuts," one executive put it simply.

Unocal's involvement in the tangled and often bewildering politics of Afghanistan began innocently enough. In July 1995, Imle—on the hunt for new oil fields—traveled to Central Asia to meet one of the world's most frustrated rulers. He was the president of largely desert Turkmenistan, Saparmurat Niyazov.

Turkmenistan sat atop the world's fourth-largest proven supply of natural gas. After gaining independence in 1991 following the Soviet collapse, the republic had been earning $2 billion a year exporting its gas through Russian-controlled pipelines. Suddenly, at the end of 1993, the Kremlin cut off Turkmenistan's access to the network. Moscow wanted the entire market for itself. Only the continued export of commodities like oil and cotton kept the young nation from slipping into bankruptcy.

Like many of the region's other rulers, Niyazov was a dictatorial strongman who had never aspired to democratic government. He had been a Communist Party functionary in Soviet times and then won election as a post-independence nationalist. Later, he would declare himself to be "Turkmenbashi"—Ruler of the Turkmen. He commissioned palaces and monuments in his own honor, including a sculpture modeled on the Eiffel Tower with a revolving penthouse restaurant. The cult of personality was visible everywhere. A visiting western oilman counted fifteen portraits of the president in one minister's office—on a lapel button the official wore, on a desk souvenir, on a book, and more.

Local obeisance, however, was not enough for the pudgy Niyazov. He was desperate for western validation. Once, the official state newspaper published a front-page photograph of a smiling Niyazov standing next to Bill and Hillary Clinton, a U.S. flag draped behind them. No such meeting had taken place; the images had been spliced together.

In the hopes of attracting foreign visitors, Niyazov built a dozen five-star hotels, fronted by fountains that kept gushing water while most of the rest of the country suffered through shortages. The establishments extended an especially warm welcome to VIPs. As Unocal's Marty Miller recalled, a knock would sound at the door to his room and there would stand a young woman in a fur coat.

"Are you lonely?" she would ask, simultaneously revealing that she was "completely naked underneath."

Even if he had been inclined to invite her in, Miller realized that "if I'd done that, there were probably cameras in the room" taking photographs that could be used as leverage with Unocal.

Other foreign oil companies also came calling on Niyazov. But they rapidly learned that the rules of the oil game were so different in Turkmenistan, the policies so lopsided against investors—and the possible returns for that reason so modest—that it wasn't worth staying. The only ones that did put down stakes were the very brave, the very dubious, or the very naïve.

Among the latter was a storefront operation called U.S.-CIS Ventures. It was managed by Alexander Haig, chief of staff to Richard Nixon and secretary of state under Ronald Reagan. The retired general, a man with a megalomaniacal streak, boasted of his Washington connections and tried without success to promote the idea of a natural gas line through Iran. Haig simply couldn't navigate the geopolitics, and finally left empty-handed.

But the Turkmenistan president was delighted by Imle's presence. The Unocal boss was not some political has-been but a bona fide executive of a major western oil company—and a tall, distinguished former Texan at that. An enthusiastic Niyazov was soon proposing ventures for Unocal to undertake.

First, he suggested that Imle examine an offshore Turkmenistan oil field called Chelikan I. It had been producing for years and, if modernized, probably could continue for years more. There was one small problem. Niyazov had a lamentable tendency to award "exclusive rights" to energy properties several times over, and Chelikan was already under contract to a small New York–based outfit called Oil Capital Limited. But that was a mere nuisance, Niyazov hastened to add, because Oil Capital was in breach of contract. Imle said he would consider the proposal.

The conversation drifted to Turkmenistan's captive gas fields. It was well-known that the nation hadn't exported a single cubic foot of gas since Russia had shut off its access to Europe. Niyazov inquired of Imle if he, the president of a powerful American oil company, would consider building a pipeline so that Turkmenistan could market its natural wealth.

Again, there was a small problem. Imle knew that Niyazov had already awarded gas pipeline rights to a competitor, an Argentine company called Bridas. But the Unocal president was confident that he could prevail in a showdown. Within a matter of months, he reached an agreement with the Turkmen dictator to build export pipelines for both oil and natural gas.

Imle knew that Niyazov adored pomp, so he arranged for a glitzy contract signing affair in New York at the Park Avenue offices of the scholarly Asia Society. The highlight of the event would be a $25,000, twenty-minute geopolitical chat by the don of global diplomats, Henry Kissinger. When word of the plans reached Niyazov, he seemed suitably thrilled. But then the signing was almost derailed.

Boris Shikhmuradov, Turkmenistan's foreign minister, an ally of the Argentine company, Bridas, moved to sabotage the deal. He commissioned a review by a team of American lawyers, who produced a long list of questions about the structuring of the agreement. The list went straight to Niyazov. Meanwhile, Shikhmuradov, confident that he had outfoxed Unocal, telephoned the oil company's man in Turkmenistan and declared, "You should call John Imle and say that the deal probably will not be signed in New York and that all the ceremonial stuff should be called off. None of it is going to happen."

Unocal executives were frantic. Imle and aides immediately flew to Turkmenistan in the company jet but got nowhere with Khyakim Ishanov, the oil minister. When the Unocal boss asked if he could see President Niyazov, the minister replied, "No, you can't. I can't do anything for you." Ishanov then crumpled up a scrap of paper on which he had seemed to be doodling, and tossed it on the floor. Tsalik Nayberg, the Unocal representative in Turkmenistan, was seated nearby. He bent over as if to tie his shoe and picked up the scrap, which turned out to be a note.

"Tsalik, I can't do anything," it read. "Don't say anything."

Only later did Imle learn the reason for the cloak-and-dagger routine. A second government official sitting quietly in the room was there to monitor the meeting and report back to the foreign minister, who was plotting against Unocal. The man's presence had intimidated Ishanov.

All seemed lost, so a discouraged Imle headed out the door. Suddenly, he was called back. The president himself was on the phone, asking to say hello to the Unocal president. After a halting but genial conversation—Imle only knew enough Russian to say "How are you?" and "I'm fine"—the receiver ended up in Nayberg's hand. Summoning his nerve, the Russian-born naturalized American persuaded Niyazov to grant his boss an audience the next morning.

It was unclear whether the president had paid any attention to the questions raised by the American lawyers. But Imle and his entourage took no chances. They worked all night, amending the contract to remove any doubts about its provisions, and walked Niyazov through the changes the next day. When they were done, the Park Avenue ceremony was still on. In retrospect, it was less anything that Imle had done with the contract and more his statesmanlike attentiveness that carried the day. The dramatic appearance of a powerful American oilman in need of Niyazov's blessings fed the strongman's vanity and preserved the deal.

Documents finally signed in New York in October 1995 and afterward revealed the complexity of Unocal's undertaking. Rather than a straightforward partnership, the plan consisted of a web of interlocking agreements. One tied Unocal to Turkmenistan. Another linked Unocal with Pakistan. A third committed Turkmenistan, Pakistan, Afghanistan, and Uzbekistan to support the project and, more importantly, named Turkmenistan as the arbiter of who would build the lines. Only later did Turkmenistan complete the circle by formally selecting Unocal.

The documents were silent on the matter of financing. Though Unocal planned to open offices in the region, it had committed not a penny to build the pipelines, nor had it yet sought loans from international bankers. This was no oversight. Imle intended first to clear a safe path for his project by courting tribal leaders along the route. He would build roads, schools, and hospitals and provide jobs and free natural gas. In exchange, the tribes would protect the lines. Unocal could then assure lenders that their investments would be secure. Experts at agencies like the World Bank were skeptical. They noted that outsiders including the British, the Soviets, and the Americans had been trying to negotiate their way through the labyrinth of mutually hostile Afghan clans for a century and a half without success.

Also missing was an endorsement from the Taliban, the religious army whose fighters were deployed across the very territory that the pipeline would cross. Unocal had tried without success to obtain approval from the mullahs who commanded the movement. But Imle remained confident that the right combination of incentives would eventually bring the Taliban, like the tribal leaders, to Unocal's side.

In the beginning, the Taliban represented a modest revolt against chaos. It was September 1994, a chaotic time in Afghanistan. Five years after the end of a decade-long Soviet occupation, banditry and rape were unchecked in parts of the country. At a mosque in the southern province of Kandahar, an angry group of men decided that they could no longer tolerate the outrages. If the government would not act, they would.

Led by a thirty-seven-year-old mullah named Mohammed Omar, conspicuous for his missing right eye, they ambushed the outlaws in their neighborhood one by one. When it caught one, the Taliban was merciless— its members would summarily hang him and leave his corpse as a message to others.

The men called themselves the Taliban in acknowledgment of their years of study in the religious schools known as *madrasahs;* the word *taliban* means "students" in Afghanistan's Persian language. The group was quickly lionized by the general population, and converts rushed to join their ranks.

One was Bashar Noorzai, whose finely tailored, flowing cotton garments and silk turbans were fitting for the son of a successful businessman. Bashar was also an old friend of Mullah Omar and funneled cash and weapons to the Taliban. It was a mutually advantageous relationship, for Bashar and his family were longtime opium traffickers, regularly harassed by thugs demanding protection money. The mullah's forces put the extortionists out of business, and Bashar became the biggest drug lord in Kandahar, one of the richest opium-producing regions in the world. Others in the province who also relied on the drug trade for their livelihood would likewise be grateful to the Taliban, especially truckers no longer victimized by bandits.

As popular as they were locally, Mullah Omar's fighters attracted little notice outside Kandahar. But that was about to change. A pragmatic alliance with the security forces of neighboring Pakistan would soon enable this isolated band of religious vigilantes to mount a bloody offensive for all Afghanistan.

Pakistan at the time was all but broke. Its economy produced nowhere near enough export dollars to pay for the nation's daily needs, and the United States—its main foreign patron—had cut off most aid to protest Pakistan's nuclear arms program.

Benazir Bhutto, the country's Harvard- and Oxford-educated prime minister, seized on a possible solution. She would use Central Asia's need for new export pipelines to make her nation the center of revived trade along the path of the historic Silk Road. Pakistan would funnel foreign products to Central Asia via Afghanistan as Caspian oil and gas arrived by pipeline from Afghanistan for shipment to world markets. Bhutto calculated that the tariffs and other profits to be earned from this two-way traffic could surpass the lost American assistance.

Lawlessness on the key road across Afghanistan was a major sticking point. Truck drivers confronted thieves nearly every half mile along just the fifty-mile stretch from the Pakistan border to Kandahar. To demonstrate that the route was manageable, Bhutto resorted to some theater.

Pakistan would send a convoy of food and medicine across Afghanistan all the way to Turkmenistan, a display of bravado that surely would convince any doubters.

Early on October 29, 1994, a column of thirty trucks crossed into Afghanistan protected by two Pakistani intelligence officers and a contingent of Taliban fighters recruited for the mission by Bhutto's security officials. All went well until they encountered a notorious Afghan militia commander named Niyaz Wayand, who objected to the presence of the Taliban.

As the commander had understood the arrangements, he was to safeguard the trucks until they reached the Turkmenistan frontier. In exchange, he was to receive part of the cargo as booty. When the Pakistanis protested, his militia seized the convoy and everyone in it, including the Taliban fighters. There matters stood for a few days until a band of armed men, moving with military precision, suddenly materialized from the direction of Kandahar, the Taliban stronghold. The Afghan militia commander and his followers panicked and fled.

Eyewitness accounts of the episode suggested that the rescuers had been Pakistani troops. The stories became early cause for suspicion that Pakistani security forces had entered into more than a casual relationship with the Taliban. Each side had something to gain from such an alliance. Pakistan would benefit if the Taliban army were deployed against unruly former *mujahideen* who were running amok along Bhutto's hoped-for trade route into Central Asia, and generally flouted Pakistan's opinion on the conduct of Afghan matters. The Taliban stood to profit if Pakistan's generals were to provide badly needed supplies, such as fuel and communications equipment. Tribal allegiances that spilled across both sides of the Pakistan-Afghan border also encouraged cooperation.

The alliance became more evident in the weeks that followed. On one day alone, some three thousand bearded young men were seen pouring into Afghanistan aboard trucks and on foot, carrying new Kalashnikov rifles and military radios. Most appeared to be teenagers, smiling and talkative. Most tellingly, the majority spoke Urdu, Pakistan's official language, rather than either of the Afghan tongues, Pashto and Dari. Their origin was clear—though ethnically Afghan, they had been educated in Pakistani *madrasahs.* They were on their way to join the ranks of the Taliban.

Within a year, Mullah Omar's forces controlled most of Afghanistan's southern and western lands. Afghan men deposed in earlier power struggles returned from exile in Pakistan to join the Taliban fighters. They even set up a phone system in Kandahar with the same area code as the Pakistani border city of Quetta, making it a local call to ring Taliban offices.

In each territory they seized, the Taliban imposed one of the world's most bizarre versions of fundamentalist Islam. Women were forbidden to click their heels in a way that purportedly could arouse men. Music, posters with images of people, and trimmed beards were banned. Despite such eccentricities, many Afghans—particularly those who were tribal Pashtuns like the Taliban—supported the movement, grateful for the law and order it established.

Unocal watched approvingly as the Taliban widened their hold on the country. While the company insisted publicly that it was taking no sides in the civil war, in fact its executives were staking the future of Imle's project on the Taliban's rise to power. The Unocal men were now looking to the insurgents to make the pipelines safe from sabotage or other disruptions once they ruled Afghanistan. Then Unocal could land the huge loans it would need to proceed.

Not surprisingly, there arose a widely held presumption that the oilmen were conspiring with the insurgents. Colluding was a more appropriate term. Imle and his subordinates didn't actually sit in a war room devising strategy with Taliban commanders; that role was handled by the Pakistanis. But Unocal cultivated the Taliban in the belief that the success of its pipeline scheme hung in the balance. Communications with the insurgents were made easier by the installation of a fax machine in a Taliban office in Kandahar, arranged and paid for by the oil company.

Three years earlier, when Unocal was in Azerbaijan angling for a share of offshore Baku, the company had enlisted the help of its Saudi Arabian partner, Delta Oil, to bridge the cultural gap. Now Unocal's president was doing the same to help his cause in Afghanistan.

Imle's lieutenants were oddly reticent about Delta's role. Oilmen working the Caspian generally were a tight-lipped bunch. But the wall of silence at Unocal when inquiries were made about Delta was something entirely different. The faces of the company executives sometimes contorted into expressions of discomfort bordering on fear. That something pained them was obvious. Precisely what was not.

Delta Oil itself seemed to exist only in Unocal literature; searches of public records turned up no trace of the company. Its chairman was a resourceful University of Southern California economics graduate named Badr al-Aiban. He had no background in the oil business. But his diamond-studded watch and matching cufflinks demonstrated that the thirty-six-year-old Arab had access to money. He also had access to power, an asset inherited from his late father, Mohammed al-Aiban, a former officer in the Saudi National Guard.

Al-Aiban kept his distance from Afghanistan. His affairs there were managed by a garrulous New Yorker named Charlie Santos, a former United Nations political analyst on Afghanistan. One did not phone Santos directly. A message was left at a Manhattan number, and then, from Rome, Istanbul, London, or somewhere in Afghanistan, Santos might return the call from the $3,000 laptop satellite telephone with which he always traveled. Adding to this elusiveness was an awkward, whispery manner that seemed to shout, "I am a spy."

It made the Afghans—and many of his professional contacts—exceedingly distrustful. Their suspicions were heightened by the clouded reputation of Osman Kaldirim, the Delta executive who had been prominent in Baku negotiations; his claim of having been wounded in the 1980s Afghan war had been greeted with considerable skepticism. The presence of characters like Santos and Kaldirim in Delta management provoked talk in industry and diplomatic circles that the company was an intelligence front for the Saudis, the CIA, or both. While there was no supporting evidence, the hint that Delta was involved in espionage made potential sources of pipeline financing even more nervous about Unocal's project.

In seeking the favor of the Afghans, Charlie Santos had many tools at his disposal. First was a program of "non-cash bonus payments." This was purported to be humanitarian aid, but it looked more like payoffs, many of them hardly disguised. Santos rented a home from a powerful leader in the northern city of Mazar-i-Sharif for a whopping $1,500 a month, about ten times its market price. He put on his payroll an influential intermediary with Mazar's top warlord, a hulking Uzbek named Abdul Rashid Dostum.

What was more, Santos could count on American political backing. State Department officials in Washington, aware of their government's desire to control Caspian export pipelines, put themselves and U.S. embassies squarely behind Unocal and its chosen partner.

Even so, Santos was making little actual progress on his ostensible mission to advance the oil company's pipeline scheme. The Afghans wondered about his motives. They took umbrage when he suggested—as he constantly did—that they strike truces with their enemies. The Afghans preferred to let the field of combat determine who would rule the country. Who was this American to interfere in their politics?

From his satellite telephone, Santos assured increasingly edgy Unocal executives that such setbacks were to be expected in Afghanistan. Everyone simply had to keep at it. The Unocal president himself was a persistent sort, but even he was starting to lose confidence in his Delta partners, especially as Imle's rival for Afghan pipeline rights seemed to be gaining ground.

The rival was Carlos Bulgheroni, dapper chairman of Argentina's family-owned oil company, Bridas. He cut a magnificent figure with his tailored Italian suits and swept-back silver hair, and his smile, style, and confidence seemed to charm everyone he met. Still determined to win the race to export Turkmenistan's natural gas, he often seemed a step ahead of the Americans. While Imle simultaneously juggled a fistful of major global projects and could only hope that Santos was doing some effective lobbying, Bulgheroni made frequent sweeps through Afghanistan, studying potential pipeline routes and befriending all the main factions. It was as though he had nothing else to do. At that point, the Argentine was hoping to capitalize on the Taliban's latest offensive, one that in September 1995 had carried the Islamic warriors all the way north to the Afghan-Turkmenistan border.

Until he became obsessed with Central Asia, Bulgheroni had done barely any business outside his native Argentina. He was inexperienced in geopolitics, unlike the worldly Imle. Yet in the quest for an Afghan pipeline to the sea, Bulgheroni had some advantages. He was a masterful operative, politically incisive and culturally skillful. Unlike Unocal and its partner Delta, for example, he realized early that the Taliban was different from its opponents—it could not be bought but rather had to be persuaded. And he treated it accordingly. Moreover, he avoided the appearance of doing anything sinister, like spying. He was there only to transact a little business—something that the Taliban could understand, being Afghans, among the world's legendary traders.

Bulgheroni had difficulty getting a fix on the Taliban's ultimate intentions. Mullah Omar, unschooled in commerce, appeared likely to cut a deal with Unocal if the company could arrange U.S. diplomatic recognition of his insurgency. Yet the Taliban leader also took a liking to Bulgheroni's company and even seemed to favor it at times.

To complicate matters, the Argentine oilman also courted the enemy of the Taliban—the government in Kabul—with good results. President Burhannudin Rabbani awarded Bulgheroni thirty-year exclusive rights to develop any Afghan energy reserves or pipelines he wished. It was an essentially symbolic act since the beleaguered president controlled less and less of Afghanistan with each passing season. Yet it was a reminder that Bulgheroni was not to be underestimated.

Benazir Bhutto's husband, the convivial Asif Zardari, was particularly fond of the confident Argentine. Both enjoyed flirting with women and fancied themselves as men's men; when he saw Zardari, Bulgheroni would throw an arm around the Pakistani's shoulders. Soon, Bhutto endorsed the Argentine's bid to build a pipeline, infuriating both Unocal and the American government.

In a meeting with the Pakistani prime minister, U.S. ambassador Thomas Simons argued that Bulgheroni had inadequate experience to undertake such a project. The Argentine oilman, Simons insisted, intended to tie up exclusive agreements and then force Unocal to buy him out. It was, he said, tantamount to "greenmail," or corporate blackmail, and could badly damage Pakistan's global reputation.

The ambassador then apologized in advance for the unpleasant nature of what he had to say next—that several hundred thousand dollars had been paid to someone "very, very close" to Bhutto to sway her decision. The implication was clear—Simons was accusing her husband of taking bribes from Bulgheroni.

While that notion should have shocked no one, since Zardari was famously corrupt, Bhutto was extremely sensitive when it came to her husband and would not tolerate criticism of him. She demanded that Simons withdraw the accusation. When he stood his ground, she ended the meeting.

Bulgheroni seemed undaunted by the U.S. attempt to undo the Bhutto endorsement. Nor did he seem troubled by the refusal of western bankers to finance a pipeline while Afghanistan remained so chaotic. Bulgheroni simply smiled and said that independent financing was in the works. Publicly, he wouldn't say from whom. To his subordinates, Bulgheroni confided that it was Saudi Arabian money, without specifying whose precisely.

The Argentine's mysterious Saudi partner was a company called Ningharco, whose role was as murky as Delta's. Not only did Ningharco lack industry experience, it didn't appear to have existed prior to Bulgheroni's Afghan project. The head of Ningharco wasn't even a businessman but rather the obscure director of a Paris-based strategic institute. Yet Bulgheroni led people to believe that Ningharco provided entrée to a very important person—Saudi prince Turki al-Faisal, the kingdom's refined, Georgetown-educated intelligence chief.

Prince Turki, distinctive with his squarely trimmed beard, was deeply involved in Saudi foreign policy, particularly when it came to Afghanistan. In the early 1980s, he oversaw the kingdom's billion-dollar-a-year covert aid program to the Afghans resisting the Soviet invasion. He dropped out of sight soon after the Red Army withdrawal in 1989, then resurfaced in September 1995, when the Taliban captured its biggest prize to that point—the exotic western capital of Herat. Intrigued by the benefits that might accrue to Saudi Arabia should the Taliban conquer all of Afghanistan, Prince Turki became the insurgency's chief paymaster.

His interest was especially whetted by the seeming opportunity to make inroads against Iran, a religious and political rival of the kingdom. Supporting a pipeline project like Unocal's was appealing because it would keep Turkmenistan's natural gas from being exported through Iran. In addition, the prince for years had spent large amounts of Saudi money in Afghanistan without seriously denting Iranian influence there. Iran shared the language and culture with many Afghans, and Afghan political alliances were not reliable. But an infrastructure project—such as a pipeline—would not just come and go like politicians. Saudi Arabia would finally have a concrete role in Afghanistan.

Sitting down with Bulgheroni, Turki declined an offer to be his business partner in the pipeline, but he gave the Argentine important referrals to Saudi businessmen and the Pakistan government. Bulgheroni would later tell senior aides that he had been promised $500 million in private Saudi financing once the Taliban victory was complete.

In Kabul, Afghan president Rabbani clung to power. Though his government controlled an ever-shrinking share of territory outside the capital, the world at large still treated him as Afghanistan's rightful ruler. As successful as the Taliban offensives had been, it seemed doubtful that the insurgents could dislodge Rabbani from Kabul itself.

And then the Taliban acquired a new friend. Like its other principal patron, he was a Saudi national. But he was of a different sort. Osama Bin Ladin was wealthy; he had inherited millions from his father's construction fortune. In the 1980s, he had led an Arab regiment against Soviet troops in Afghanistan. But now he was a globally hunted terrorist, seeking shelter in Afghanistan for his al-Qaeda organization. Soon he would declare holy war against the United States.

Bin Ladin came on the scene at a propitious time for the insurgency. Prince Turki, for his own reasons, had temporarily stopped the Taliban's cash flow. Now, Bin Ladin stepped in with a gift of $3 million. That was just the kind of sum the movement needed. For while the Taliban itself could not be bought, there was no stricture against it buying the allegiance of other Afghan leaders. With Bin Laden's cash, the Taliban and its Pakistani allies initiated a round of visits to militia leaders still loyal to the Rabbani government. Pocketing the largess, these Afghan commanders laid down their arms or, if welcomed by the Taliban, switched sides. Less than a month later—on September 27, 1996—Kabul fell to the insurgents, who now controlled two thirds of the nation.

Unocal, its pipeline gamble seemingly about to pay off, was jubilant. "We regard it as very positive," a company official named Chris Taggart said in a comment on the Taliban conquest that would be widely quoted. Taggart went on, "I understand Pakistan has already recognized the government. If the [United States] follows, it will lead the way to international lending agencies coming in. If the Taliban leads to stability and international recognition, then it's positive." And it seemed that Washington was prepared to do just that. In a news conference, a State Department spokesman expressed official approval, and a delegation was hastily organized to fly to Kabul and greet Afghanistan's new rulers.

Then news reporters began broadcasting troubling images from the capital—the Taliban had executed Afghanistan's former ruler, Mohammad Najibullah, and dragged his corpse through the city; photographs showed the bodies of Najibullah and his brother hanging from a post with rolled-up dollar bills stuffed into their noses. Taliban followers were seen with sticks beating burka-clad women, who were forbidden to walk through marketplaces unless accompanied by a male family member.

Unocal and the Clinton administration suffered an immediate public relations crisis. Their hastily framed statements of support for the takeover now sounded glib, as if they had been reacting to the results of an election, not an insurgent grab for power. Their eager endorsements of the Taliban reinforced the long-held suspicions of some that the oil company, the CIA, or both had backed the group's long march. Mavis Leno, the wife of American talk show host Jay Leno, and her Los Angeles–based Feminist Majority Foundation were furious. The State Department backpedaled; a spokesman said that the United States was dismayed about Taliban social attitudes. Unocal weakly claimed that its official spokesman had been misquoted.

Imle scoffed at assertions that Unocal had supported the Taliban. "It's a ridiculous thought," he said. "I guess some people are always looking for a big oil company conspiracy." His protestations were Shakespearean. After so many flirtations with repellent foreign leaders, this time he had gone too far; anyone could see that the Taliban's successes were synonymous with Unocal's.

As for the U.S. government, the rumors also had a basis in fact. American officials had helped to prepare the ground for the Taliban. They had openly championed the movement almost from the time it surfaced, enhancing its worldwide image. In early 1995, even after word began circulating that the Taliban was staging grisly public executions, U.S. diplomats in Pakistan had portrayed the group as "the will of the people." At dinners, the Americans had taunted envoys from nations such as France that favored the Rabbani government. In Washington, senior advisers to Assistant Secretary of State Robin Raphel, who was responsible for Afghanistan, had hotly accused Rabbani's government of harboring terrorist training camps. One American diplomat incredibly asserted that the president had rocketed his own capital in order to win public sympathy.

Sher Mohammed Abbas Stanikzai, then a Taliban Foreign Ministry official, attended a series of meetings with officials in Washington just months before the capture of Kabul. He recalled Raphel, the State Department officer, expressing support for the insurgency "because we had been positive for security." He said her remarks echoed what other American officials told his delegation, that the Taliban was bringing peace wherever it went, while the Rabbani government supported terrorists.

Through it all, the United States vigorously disputed reports of Pakistani and Saudi aid to the Taliban. But American diplomats in the Pakistan capital of Islamabad were aware that there was truth to the talk. Charlie Santos, Delta Oil's operative there, regularly briefed one of the U.S. embassy's military attachés. Staffers in the embassy submitted to their managers eyewitness accounts of Pakistan's activism and the renewal of Prince Turki's patronage, accounts that the managers refused to pass on to Washington, claiming that the evidence wasn't strong enough. Neither they nor their superiors in Washington wanted to interrupt what was broadly viewed as a positive development in a long-troubled nation.

The two pipeline adversaries, John Imle and Carlos Bulgheroni, tried to weather the storm, even as the Taliban's harsh rule took a pounding in international news coverage. No nation recognized the new government. Russia and the Central Asian states put their forces on alert to prevent any

Taliban intrusion. Now no banker would take seriously the idea of building a pipeline across Afghanistan, whether it be Imle's or the Argentine's, at least not any time soon.

Bulgheroni was ostracized by Afghanistan's neighbors and the United States but kept the lines to the Taliban open. He promised to begin building as soon as Mullah Omar's government signed a formal contract. Where Bulgheroni would obtain the money was still not publicly spelled out. But a Taliban delegation that visited him in Buenos Aires to work out some details made one stopover before returning home to Afghanistan. It was in Riyadh, where their host was Prince Turki.

Stanikzai, the Taliban Foreign Ministry official, said that the Argentine's oil company and the Taliban spoke face to face for almost two months. The Taliban was ready to sign, he said; all it needed was a written agreement from Turkmenistan assuring cooperation on that end. But Bulgheroni was never able to produce one, Stanikzai said.

Imle, meanwhile, said that Unocal would start work only when there was some semblance of peace in Afghanistan. Regardless, in February 1997 his company paid for four Taliban representatives to visit Houston and Washington. The Unocal oilmen were ultra-careful not to offend their Afghan visitors. In discussions at company headquarters, the Taliban officials were provided with a private bathroom installed with a bucket of water, since many Afghans wash rather than use toilet paper. Taliban sensibilities also were honored when the delegation dined at the home of Unocal executive Marty Miller. Nude Indonesian sculptures near the swimming pool were covered with plastic trash bags so as not to offend a Taliban dictum against depictions of human beings. When it was time to shoot souvenir pictures, the oilmen readily agreed to remove a statue of Buddha so it wouldn't appear in the photo. By all appearances pleased with their visit, the Taliban then embarked on a religious pilgrimage to Mecca, with Unocal's partners at Delta Oil footing the bill.

In May, Imle's determination appeared to be paying off. A major northern warlord defected and handed over to the Taliban the bustling city of Mazar-i-Sharif—one of the last remaining opposition strongholds. Pakistan and Saudi Arabia swiftly granted the movement its first formal diplomatic recognition, which for form's sake had been withheld until then. The two Islamic nations argued that the international community now had no choice but to do the same.

Four days later, Unocal executives were again on edge. Mazar-i-Sharif residents abruptly arose and expelled the Taliban occupiers, slaughtering some two thousand of them in the process. Malik Palawan, the warlord who had surrendered the city, was forced to flee. The portly thirty-three-year-old had to abandon ownership of an especially lucrative piece of property—the house that Unocal operative Charlie Santos had been renting from him for $1,500 a month.

A year later, the Taliban recaptured Mazar, this time marching into the Iranian consulate and slaying nine diplomats. They followed that with a grisly murder spree against native Shiites, acts that helped cement Taliban rule there.

Imle pressed on. He got a lift when Bhutto fell from power, after which her successor, Nawaz Sharif, endorsed Unocal's pipeline plan. In October, Imle announced that a broad international consortium—Unocal and Delta, along with partners from South Korea, Japan, and Indonesia— would begin building the trans-Afghan line by the end of 1998.

Two additional public relations blows finally spelled defeat for Unocal and its dogged president. First, the Feminist Majority Foundation organized a ferocious campaign against the oil company. Mavis Leno disrupted a shareholder's meeting with a speech opposed to any deal with the Taliban. Then, in August 1998, truck bombs blew up at U.S. embassies in Kenya and Tanzania, attacks attributed to cohorts of Osama Bin Ladin. Days later, the United States fired dozens of Tomahawk missiles into an al-Qaeda camp in Afghanistan in a failed attempt to assassinate Bin Ladin.

The missiles were the last straw. Marty Miller called Imle. "John, it's time to quit. It's crazy." Imle agreed.

The next day, Unocal announced it had "suspended" the pipeline project. Just before the end of the year, it withdrew entirely. Stanikzai, the former Taliban diplomat, recalled Unocal saying that it had to drop the deal because "all its partners had walked away, and they were alone."

Years later, over lunch at an Austin, Texas, golf course, Miller still seemed in disbelief over Unocal's Afghan adventure. "It's the black hole of my life," he said. "I don't know whether to laugh or cry."

Boom

and

Bust

AS THE CASPIAN SEA BOOM GAINED momentum in the 1990s, it unleashed a display of wealth not seen since the time of the first oil barons a century earlier. Baku, the capital of Azerbaijan, was transformed into a showplace of cosmopolitan cuisine and fine European jewelry, where men gambled oil field fortunes in glittering casinos.

Visitors making the thirty-minute drive from the new international airport into the city could gas up at a sparkling red, western-style service station staffed by attendants in red jumpsuits. They could buy coffee and Coke at the station's convenience store. If they were having mechanical problems with their automobile, they could buy a new one at the Chrysler showroom next door.

Just down the road, they could visit Ramstore, the best-stocked grocery and department store anywhere on the Caspian. The Turkish-owned establishment offered washing machines, watches, and French-made cooking utensils in addition to shelves of fresh vegetables, fruit, baked goods, and meat. The lunch menu at its café featured a $1.75 baked potato smothered in corn kernels, ketchup, hot dog slices, and sour cream.

"Next, we are opening a flower section," the store's general manager, Ibrahim Kesemer, said proudly.

Local shoppers, accustomed to decades of Soviet-era deprivation, were positively giddy at the variety. But the store's most important customers were foreigners. Thousands of expatriates—Germans, Belgians, Britons, Americans, and others—now lived in Baku, with tens of millions of dollars to spend. Most were oilmen, shipped in by their companies to start producing crude from newly acquired offshore fields. There were also diplomats dispatched to decipher the realignment in the region, relief workers to aid the hundreds of thousands of people made homeless by post-Soviet strife, and businessmen hoping to strike it rich.

Among the latter were New Orleans natives Charlie and Mary Schroeder, who moved to Baku from Dubai, where for years he had worked in the oil industry. In 1994 they opened the city's first western-style bar, Charlie's, a place where oilmen could plop down for a beer and a burger. It was an immediate success, prompting them to open two more eateries: The Ragin' Cajun served the couple's native Louisiana fare, and Margaritaville dished out Mexican food and drew raucous crowds that cheered rugby matches on satellite TV and afterward sang karaoke.

Other saloon keepers followed rapidly. Thomas Goltz, writing in *Fortune* magazine, described a watering hole called the Sherwood as "the bar of choice for the lonely oilie," adding: "If the girls are not at the tables, it means that the police have just effected another bust, but that the talent will soon return." Faced with the prospect of going "on the dole" at home in the English city of Swindon, a Briton named Charlie Christmas instead launched a pub called Lord Nelson. Someone else opened a waterfront Chinese discothèque called the Dragon.

But foreigners weren't the only ones throwing around cash. In the top-floor gambling room of the renovated Apsheron Hotel, Azeri men casually peeled hundred-dollar bills from thick wads, tossed them onto roulette tables, then placed chips on every number. Next door at the new Hyatt Regency, a forty-year-old man named Fedos said he had already lost seven hundred dollars. Now he was playing the slots while he waited for a friend who was trying his luck in one of the high-stakes card rooms. The friend "wants me to join him, but I refused," said the glum Fedos. "There, you can't stop gambling. At least here you can get up if you want."

The gambling habits of Ilham Aliyev, son of Azerbaijan's president, attracted special attention. He frequented Turkish casinos and became heavily indebted to a gambling kingpin there, according to a government report. Turkish newspapers gave differing estimates of what Ilham owed—one said $500,000, another $6 million. But all reported that President Heydar Aliyev paid off his son's debt by granting the Turkish gambler ownership of a luxury Baku hotel and casino, the Europa.

Many of Azerbaijan's elite were corrupt government officials, their wallets fattened by skim-offs and bribes. Others were connected to influential families profiting from illicit dealings in Baku's oil and chemical industries ranging from kickbacks to outright thievery. These men of wealth numbered perhaps two thousand, not even one percent of the city's population. But their prolific spending literally remade the face of Baku.

The seaside district of Patandert, for example, was a virtual wilderness in 1996. A year later, the scenic land atop its cliffs was dotted with luxury homes under construction, most of them being built by powerful businessmen and political insiders with easy money to spend. New cafés and shops selling French and Italian fashions and perfumes opened along a promenade. The Improtex store offered a gold lighter with diamond stud by S. T. Dupont for just $4,600, with a matching pen priced at $3,650. For those unable to stop pacing while watching television, there was a Bang & Olufsen set that automatically rotated when the viewer changed his or her location in a room. The price: a mere $10,500.

"We serve a certain market," said sales manager Oktai Akhverdiev, twenty-two, "and day by day we think this market will increase."

Baku's nouveaux riches showed less interest in the turn-of-the-century mansions that stood in various stages of elegant disrepair, survivors of the age of the first oil barons. Few appreciated the remarkable history that they represented, and fewer still were willing to spend the millions of dollars it would cost to restore one of these hundred-room behemoths.

Still, some were put to use in small ways. Berenice Webb, a well-spoken Briton, arrived in Baku in 1995, pursuing a romance. When the romance collapsed, the twenty-seven-year-old founded a language school in one corner of a seventy-room palace. Her timing was perfect; English was all the rage in Baku, and demand for lessons was high.

Webb, though, was realistic about her success. "Everyone is here because of the oil. It all depends what happens with that, with the politics, with Russia and Iran," she said, sipping a cappuccino at the hilltop Hyatt Regency. "It's all living day to day. We're all exploiting the situation. We don't know what will happen next."

Perhaps the biggest fan of the old mansions was an Interpol lieutenant named Fuad Akhundov, an amateur historian with a Clark Gable mustache and infectious enthusiasm. He spent hours scouring government archives for old maps and photographs to document the era of the barons who were driven into exile (or worse) by the Soviet Revolution.

"When I was in school, no one could write anything about these houses except negative," said the twenty-seven-year-old Akhundov. "People have been deprived of their past."

He tracked down the remaining descendants of the barons, including the three mischievous granddaughters of Timurbek Ashurbekov, whose palace now housed the Webb Academy. Sarah, ninety, Miriam, eighty-eight, and Adela, eighty-two, shared a cramped apartment in Baku with six warring cats. Over tea, the sisters talked about their privileged upbringing, before the arrest and execution of their father by the Soviets.

They fondly remembered their French teacher, Mademoiselle Grilot, a resourceful woman who once shielded them from a Baku mob by unfurling a French flag and claiming the mansion was a diplomatic mission.

Did the sisters have wet nurses? "No, none of us did," Sarah said. "Our mother herself fed us."

"You had a wet nurse," asserted Adela.

"No, I didn't."

"Yes, you did. You had a wet nurse," confirmed Miriam.

Sarah sat with a frozen, silent smile. Her sisters stared.

Akhundov smiled. "They do this all the time," he said, then turned to coax more stories out of them.

Sophia Abdullayeva, the eighty-year-old granddaughter of the legendary baron Zeynalabdin Tagiyev, was discovered living in a rundown apartment in Baku. Her grandmother had been driven insane by the family's ruin, her uncle and her father had been persecuted by the Soviet authorities, and she herself had been exiled to Siberia.

She was hard-pressed to see similarities between the gentry of her time and the newly affluent in Baku. "We saw cold and we saw starvation," Tagieva said. "Those who are rich now are full and don't give a single kopeck to help anyone. They don't understand."

Fortune hunters in the West heard stories of opportunity in the offing and flocked to the Caspian. None was more daring or more flamboyant than Viktor Kozeny, a smooth-talking Czech American with a Harvard economics degree who arrived in Baku in 1997.

Two years earlier, he had fled Prague with an estimated $200 million in profits from a huge privatization scheme. The government accused him of victimizing some eight hundred thousand Czechs, and *Fortune* magazine branded him "the Pirate of Prague." The thirty-six-year-old Kozeny insisted he had done nothing illegal.

He turned up in London, where he bought playwright Andrew Lloyd Webber's Eaton Square mansion for $9.7 million; he took a seaside estate in the exclusive Bahamas retreat of Lyford Cay; and, finally, he went shopping for a villa in Aspen, Colorado, winter playground of America's wealthy.

There he met Frederick Bourke, chairman of a designer handbag maker called Dooney & Bourke; his mansion overlooked the mountain resort. The two became fast friends and ended up touring the Caspian together. In Baku, Kozeny sensed an opportunity much like that which had so enriched him in Prague.

State-owned enterprises were being transferred to the private sector through the distribution of ownership certificates to the populace. Each of

Azerbaijan's 7.5 million citizens was to receive four "vouchers" redeemable at auctions where the enterprises were up for sale. But foreigners could participate, too, and Kozeny began buying up vouchers at cut-rate prices from ordinary Azeris anxious for quick cash. Over time, he would accumulate $15 million worth. Kozeny's primary target was Socar, the state oil company. It was a gem, if a tarnished one. The company was in need of modernization, and its financial condition was uncertain. But its oil fields and refineries were undoubtedly worth billions of dollars, and it owned percentages in every foreign oil deal negotiated since the Soviet breakup. Government officials gave assurances that Socar would be put up for sale.

Back in Aspen, Kozeny paid $19.7 million for a property called Peak House, twenty-three thousand square feet of luxury on three mountaintop acres—at the time, the resort's most expensive piece of real estate. The *Rocky Mountain News* chronicled its "nine bathrooms, a 15-car garage, two swimming pools and a mural-walled wine cave for candlelight dining," and Kozeny outfitted it extravagantly. There was a couch hand-sewn with thirty-three alligator skins, a Tiffany grandfather clock, a tapestry made in 1650, and a French armoire made in 1750. The wine cellar contained five hundred bottles of rare merlots, and twenty-three cases of vintage port. His wife, Ludka, had her own gymnasium. In the event someone invaded the house in pursuit of Kozeny, a secret passageway led from a bedroom closet to a space in which he could conceal himself, known as a "panic room." A second hiding place was located beneath the enormous house.

Kozeny's big spending ways quickly established him as "the darling of the social scene," and on December 20, 1997, he threw himself a million-dollar coming-out party with 150 of the resort's biggest celebrities on the guest list. Ivana Trump showed up, as did Natalie Cole, who sang a Christmas song. Waiters served buckets of beluga caviar and thousand-dollar bottles of Château Pétrus before a lavish sit-down dinner. The hors d'oeuvre menu included black and white truffles, the first course shark fin and bird's nest soup. "The small, rare, delicate nests were retrieved from a cave in Vietnam and, like most of the dinner fare, carefully crated and jetted overnight to Aspen's airport," a Denver newspaper reported.

As Kozeny circulated among his guests, he tantalized them with vivid accounts of his coming windfall. Using the vouchers that his agents were buying on the streets of Baku, Kozeny said, he would take control of Azerbaijan's most valuable assets. Socar alone would return a hundred times his investment, he estimated.

Kozeny was a charmer, tall and red headed, and he excited people with the possibility that they might participate in one of his exploits. It no doubt helped that he sent party guests home with souvenirs from the London jewelry store Asprey & Garrard. In the weeks that followed, Kozeny's neighbors lined up to join his Baku adventure.

Bourke invested $8 million. Real estate mogul Richard Friedman threw in another $1 million. Florida investment adviser Aaron Fleck staked $4 million. While Fleck dismissed the talk of a hundredfold profit as "just hype by Viktor," he did think he might earn twenty times his investment, perceiving the opportunity "almost like an Internet boom."

Fleck was so impressed that he introduced Kozeny to investment banker friends at Smith Barney and Goldman Sachs, suggesting they put up $25 million each. But it was Leon Cooperman, chairman of Omega Partners and a highly respected hedge fund manager, who contributed the biggest chunk of Kozeny's outside financing. Cooperman invested $180 million, including cash scooped up from a Columbia University trust fund and the giant American International Group insurance company. Finally, former Senate majority leader George J. Mitchell was persuaded not only to invest but also to head a Washington lobbying effort that Kozeny suggested would help cement the investment.

All signs seemed encouraging. Three investor representatives met in Baku with President Aliyev and privatization authorities and came away convinced that Kozeny had the inside track to Socar. On a subsequent visit, they were told that privatization would proceed after the elections in October 1998, when Aliyev would be better positioned to enact the controversial reform.

Kozeny's flashy presence in Baku impressed his visitors. He cruised the city in an armored jeep with bodyguards and spent freely in pricey restaurants. He rented two floors in an expensive office building, where he established an investment house called Minaret, complete with a computerized "trading floor," even though Baku as yet had no stock market. His 180-person staff was well paid and treated royally at his luxury seaside dacha.

In April 1998, Kozeny celebrated Minaret's formal opening with a pool-side soirée at Baku's premier hotel, the Hyatt. George Mitchell was the marquee guest. But something seemed amiss. Not a single senior Azeri leader appeared, nor did any of Baku's most prominent foreign residents, such as the U.S. ambassador.

By autumn, the elections had come and gone without any movement on Socar, and the investors began to fret. Kozeny assured them there was no cause for worry. At least one of them, Aaron Fleck, recalled Kozeny saying that President Aliyev himself, "the big boy," now had a financial stake in the deal. But when Fleck and Bourke flew to Baku, they found that Kozeny had fired most of Minaret's trading staff and abandoned nearly all of its office space. Cooperman, with the most money at stake, sought a meeting, but Kozeny failed to return his calls or answer his letters.

The anxious investors began to fear that they were being snookered. Soon their lawyers concluded that Kozeny had used a complicated options requirement imposed by the Azeri government to enrich himself wrongly. He had amassed millions of these options, sets of matching certificates that validated foreign-owned privatization vouchers. He bought the options for an average of 40 cents apiece and then sold them to his investors for $25 each. Kozeny, the lawyers said, had pocketed an instant profit of $73.9 million. The investors were aghast: They had thought they were paying no more for the options and vouchers than it had cost Kozeny to acquire them.

The venture went downhill from there, amid a flurry of lawsuits. It soon became clear that President Aliyev had no intention of privatizing Socar. That should not have been surprising. Anyone with a passing knowledge of Azerbaijan would have scoffed at the notion that its notoriously corrupt state officials would surrender their biggest cash cow to a maverick financier and his naïve American investors.

Suspicions arose that the Azeri leader himself had deliberately inflated the voucher price paid by the Americans so as to collect a handsome payoff from Kozeny. In legal filings, Kozeny asserted that $83.3 million of investor money had been funneled to the president after Aliyev had elbowed his way into the scheme in late 1997, demanding a two-thirds share.

Kozeny claimed that everyone, including himself, had been deceived by the Azeris. In reply to an investor suit, he called Cooperman and the others "men possessed with rabid greed" who were unwilling to admit their own "embarrassing, reckless and expensive misjudgment."

He scoffed at those who claimed to be surprised at the extent of Aliyev's involvement. In a legal paper, he described a meeting in which Cooperman "asked Mr. Kozeny if 'the big man,' meaning President Aliyev, was 'in on the deal.' Mr. Kozeny said yes, along with his son and others of his associates. Mr. Cooperman's response was to smile and to say that if [Aliyev] makes this into a 'ten-bagger' . . . meaning a $10 billion return, then [Aliyev] would be a hero, that a 'five-bagger' would be okay, but only a 'one-bagger' would suck."

If what Kozeny said was true, the Americans could be liable for prosecution on foreign bribery charges. But Cooperman and the others denied his account, which they said was invented.

His investors lost everything—more than $200 million, according to a conservative estimate.

A sometime CIA asset named Roger Tamraz had an adventure of a different sort. He arrived in the early 1990s, on the cusp of the Caspian boom, and ended up in the middle of an American political scandal.

Tamraz, the businessman son of Lebanese parents, was a naturalized U.S. citizen who once ran a Beirut bank and had founded a chain of European gas stations. Along the way, he aided the CIA with a variety of matters in Lebanon, including providing cover for two agents.

His big idea was to build an oil export pipeline from Baku in Azerbaijan straight across Armenia and Turkey and on to the Mediterranean. Half the line would be financed by China and the rest by the companies building it, among them Bethlehem Steel.

Tamraz was not inexperienced in Caspian oil matters. In Turkmenistan, one of his companies, Oil Capital Limited, won control of the offshore oil field called Chelikan, the one that Saparmurat Niyazov, the country's autocratic president, would later offer to Unocal as an inducement to build a pipeline through Afghanistan. But his pipeline scheme was an astounding reach even in a region long accustomed to outlandish ideas when it came to transporting oil.

Azerbaijan and Armenia were sworn enemies; they only recently had called a cease-fire to a bloody war. The Armenians and the Turks were foes as well. The idea that all three countries would join together in such a project seemed laughable, despite Tamraz's blithe description of his plan as the "peace pipeline." (The former Azeri president, Abulfaz Elchibey, had used identical language for such a pipeline route in 1992 before he was unceremoniously ousted after just a year in office. His successor, Aliyev, refused even to see Tamraz to discuss his idea.)

So Tamraz went looking for help in Washington, which had recently embraced Baku as a policy priority. If he could pitch his plan to President Clinton in a face-to-face meeting, maybe even win the president's support, the Azeris and the others would take him seriously, he figured.

Tamraz managed to get an audience with Sheila Heslin, then the National Security Council's point person on Caspian Sea oil. He was frank. He had no interest in building the pipeline—somebody else could do that. Instead, he intended to secure the rights to its proposed route and then "force everybody to come to [him] to put a deal together." In the tradition of oil trader Calouste Gulbenkian, "Mr. Five Percent" of the Middle East a century earlier, Tamraz's fee would be 5 percent of the pipeline's projected $3 billion cost—$125 million.

But Heslin had run a background check on her visitor, which turned up allegations in Lebanon that he had looted $200 million from his bank before it failed. She concluded that he was "shady and untrustworthy," so she brushed off the idea of a meeting with the president.

Tamraz's campaign to get to Clinton was unrelenting. He contributed $300,000 to the Democratic Party on behalf of the president's 1996 bid for reelection. And he enlisted the help of Washington friends, including Robert Baer, a mid-level supervisor at the CIA, and Don Fowler, co-chairman of the Democratic National Committee.

Baer sent Heslin a more favorable report on Tamraz. He saw this as support for an asset who had been highly useful to the agency, and could be again.

Fowler, however, was feverishly in pursuit of more contributions to Clinton's campaign. Soon, Heslin received a call from Jack Carter, a senior official in the Department of Energy. Normally a gentlemanly sort, Carter was adamant: She should endorse Tamraz's request to meet with Clinton because "if he got a meeting with the president, he would give the [Democratic National Committee] another $400,000."

Heslin refused, promising "to block this if such a meeting was scheduled." Carter got tough: Don't "be such a Girl Scout," he said. She didn't budge.

In the end, Tamraz managed to get around Heslin and land invitations to six White House social functions attended by Clinton. But he was never allowed to make a full-blown pitch for his pipeline scheme, and he had to settle for a photograph of himself and the president over coffee. It wasn't a total loss for Tamraz; he could at least use the photo to enhance his image back in the Caspian.

In the fall of 1997, the testimony of Heslin and Tamraz enlivened the otherwise humdrum U.S. Senate hearings into possible illegal campaign contributions to Clinton. Heslin was praised as "a real hero" by Senator Susan Collins, a Maine Republican, and the usually acidic *New York Times* columnist Maureen Dowd called her "a good guy."

Tamraz disarmed the senators with his openness. When Senator Carl Levin, a Michigan Democrat, asked gingerly, "Was one of the reasons you made these contributions because you believed it might get you access?" Tamraz coolly replied, "Senator, I'm going even further: It's the only reason—to get access."

However, getting into the White House and talking to Clinton were two different matters, he said. "The same handlers that get you into the White House are sure, once you get in, [to see to it] that you don't get the chance to get what you want," Tamraz lamented. "They act like a basketball team . . . around the President, and anyone getting too close to the President is waltzed away."

On the other side of the Caspian Sea, the boom was having a similar impact in Almaty, the capital of Kazakhstan. Expatriates piled into the Texas-style Stetson Bar for hamburgers and beer and partied at the Tequila Sunrise discothèque. The athletically inclined could ski the spectacular mountains that towered over the city, so tall that they were covered with snow all year round.

But the most startling example of unbridled spending was the government's sudden decision to move the capital about 750 miles to the north, to an inhospitable city of 300,000 called Akmola. In the winter, temperatures dropped to 40 below; just the previous year, more than a hundred people had died of the cold. In the 90-degree summer heat, enormous mosquitoes swarmed over the marshy region. Water, heat, electricity, and telephone services were scarce, as was housing.

Official reasoning for the move sounded strained, having to do with earthquake safety and blunting any designs Russia might have on the territory. A more likely explanation came from Oraz Kurpishev, spokesman for Akmola's mayor: "The president decided we will move here." Kazakhstan president Nursultan Nazarbayev had something of a Peter the Great complex, and some thought that the leader might be trying to replicate the iconic czar's creation of St. Petersburg.

The vision for Akmola was certainly grand: a fine new city center of marble and granite, complete with presidential palace, parliament building, various ministerial offices, railroad station, a twenty-four-story hotel and casino, and a supermarket. The cost for this first stage of Akmola's development was estimated at $400 million, paid in part by "contributions" solicited from oil companies. Chevron, Texaco, and Agip all committed to build gas stations.

Construction began in 1997, and six months later Nazarbayev came to visit. His motorcade made its triumphant way down Respublikansky Prospekt to the main square, where the huge complex was taking shape. "The new capital will be the face of the Kazakh state," the president told a select audience of several hundred in a chilly wind that at one point blew off his fur cap.

Yet something was awry. Close by, in the city's premier hotel, the Soviet-style Intourist, a twenty-five-year-old government bureaucrat named Aybek Nurtaev was anxiously searching for a bathroom.

"Welcome to Akmola," he glumly remarked to some drinking pals.

"In the main hotel on the main square of the new capital, there are no working toilets."

"It's all a show," declared a builder named Andrei Kadrubinsky. He went on: "The buildings have three sides and no back."

That was an exaggeration, but there was some truth to it. Crews from a workforce of fourteen thousand had been frantic to dress up the blocks of drab Soviet-era shops and apartments that the president's motorcade would pass as it moved along Respublikansky Prospekt. And so they had slapped thousands of yards of white and brown vinyl onto the front and sides of more than a hundred buildings, giving them a halfway cheerful look. Nobody bothered disguising the back walls, since they would be out of sight. The overall effect was that of a Potemkin village.

There was one other problem—the city's name. The word *akmola* means "white grave," which prompted much mocking from Kazakhs and foreigners scornful of their president's grandiose venture. Nazarbayev, stung by the jibes, promptly ordered that the city be renamed Astana, which simply means "capital." (One joke that made the rounds had a man meeting a friend on the street. "Hello," he says, "I'd like you to meet my wife. Her name is 'Wife.' And here is my dog. His name is 'Dog.' ")

Meanwhile, in the shadows of the capital's imposing new buildings, ordinary people struggled to survive. Kulban Aidarova lived in a neat yellow wooden home guarded by a yellow-eyed half-breed wolf. Her feet were resting on a hot water bottle in anticipation of "how we suffer in the winter. It's cold, so cold." She and her seventy-year-old husband, Jumabek, described a spartan lifestyle, with little heat and electricity in the winter and little food at any time of the year. "If you pay for your apartment, you can't pay for your food," she said. "If you pay for your food, you can't pay for your apartment."

In Baku, some expressed dismay at the way the new wealth was being thrown around. Leyla Yunusova, a former deputy defense minister–turned–government critic, noting the rush to build luxury homes at Patandert, commented wryly: "At the same time, we are demanding humanitarian aid."

Azerbaijan still relied on the United Nations and other foreign agencies to care for some eight hundred thousand of its citizens, a full 10 percent of the population. They were refugees from the republic's long war with Armenia, now reduced to living in underground pits, mud houses, and other makeshift shelters.

Roughly two thousand of them lived in 250 railroad freight cars in the rural town of Berda. The cheerful occupant of one offered cabbage soup boiled on a makeshift wood stove to a couple of foreign visitors. He pulled aside a curtain to reveal his family, seven people in all. "No one from the government has come to see how we live," said the man, Shakhir Shakhirov, forty. In a two-room apartment in Baku, schoolteacher Taisya Istayena served tea and pastries to her friends Lyuda and Azrat Razaev. Taisya earned fifteen dollars a month teaching high school physics and astronomy but made her real living raising and selling exotic plants from home, including fifteen types of begonia and six kinds of fuchsia. "It's a bit of a shame for a schoolteacher to be selling plants," she said, "so no one around me knows I do this. It's sort of hidden."

The question of the country's coming oil windfall was raised. "We hope the eventual profits will reach everyone," said Azrat, a policeman. "But I am doubtful."

All three said that they were cutting corners to get by and expressed disappointment at what Azerbaijan had become after the Soviet collapse. "The good was destroyed, and the bad is still here," Taisya observed.

The bust came without warning. Oil companies like Chevron and Shell, eager to follow in the promising tracks of British Petroleum and the Amoco-led consortium, had scrambled to sign a dozen deals to explore offshore Baku properties. Then, one by one, the discouraging results had trickled in—nothing but dry holes. It was an alarming development that cast an immediate pall over the region.

A second, devastating blow soon followed, generated by a little-noticed currency crisis in Thailand. Pummeled by foreign speculators trying to get rich on its shaky currency, the Southeast Asian nation in the summer of 1997 stopped spending scarce dollars to prop up the baht and instead allowed it to fluctuate against the dollar. The value of the baht plummeted, triggering a financial seismic wave across Southeast Asia, where big investors from around the world had parked tens of billions of dollars in hopes of huge profits.

One by one, other currencies and stock markets among the "Asian Tigers" collapsed—in Indonesia, Malaysia, the Philippines, South Korea. The result was a plunge in economic activity that triggered an abrupt drop in demand for oil—the Tigers were enormous energy consumers, and the sudden global oil surplus sent prices plunging.

By November 1998 market-setting Brent crude had dropped to $10.90 a barrel, far below the break-even point in most parts of the world for delivered oil—the combined cost of production and transportation.

Western oilmen around the Caspian reacted by drastically scaling back operations. Only a year earlier, ABC, CNN, and CBS had telecast President Aliyev, U.S. energy secretary Federico Peña, and oil company executives on an offshore Baku platform daubing their cheeks with crude. It was a traditional oil field ceremony, celebrating the first flow of crude into a new export pipeline. Now the exuberance of that moment had faded. The line they had celebrated would continue to be fed by existing wells, but plans to swell its volume by greatly expanding offshore production were suspended. British Petroleum cut its projected annual spending by 40 percent, from $6.3 billion to $3.6 billion.

"It is getting very sticky," a European ambassador said of the outlook for Baku.

As the oil companies retreated in the face of falling prices, the boom economy rapidly deflated. Baku's expatriate community of eight thousand oil workers and others shrank to fewer than a thousand in a matter of months. Upscale boutiques and restaurants went under, and one visitor pronounced the city "dead." Charlie Schroeder noticed the change almost immediately. The Ragin' Cajun and Margaritaville were empty. "All the good money you made, you lost again," Schroeder recalled years later, putting his own losses at about a million dollars.

The malaise that engulfed Baku spread throughout the Caspian. The Red Cross opened soup kitchens in several Kazakh cities. In the former capital of Almaty, families without electricity or gas were reduced to cooking dinner over open fires in their courtyards, some using furniture as fuel.

Almaty apartment dweller Bulat Atabayev, a rotund theater director with a wicked sense of humor, said that he had electricity on alternating days only. Over dessert and tea at his niece's sixth birthday party, Atabayev joked: "We wanted freedom, but we weren't ready. Now we are free from gas, free from electricity—free from everything."

Kazakhstan's revenue slumped by a third, and it was forced to begin auctioning state assets, including its 7.5 percent slice of the big Kashagan oil field for $500 million. President Nazarbayev's pet project, the new capital city of Astana, stumbled. Citing hard times, foreign businessmen backed away from investments there; of the two dozen countries invited to do so, only Uzbekistan committed to building an embassy.

In the West, there was an outpouring of recriminations. Academics at Princeton University, Rice University, London's Institute for International Studies, and others declared the Caspian to be a petroleum white elephant. They accused Washington of grossly inflating the region's estimated oil reserves for political purposes.

A front-page headline in *The New York Times* speculated that America's entire Caspian Sea policy was on the "brink of failure." In the story that followed, various critics heaped doubt on the future of the big Baku pipeline project that had become the centerpiece of the Clinton administration's policy.

Suddenly, the widely embraced assumption that the Caspian would prove to be another Kuwait seemed to be collapsing. It had all been a myth, the critics said. Nobody had a ready answer.

Kashagan

A YEAR AFTER IT BOTTOMED OUT, the global price of oil slowly began to recover. By the end of 1999, it had roughly doubled, to more than $20 a barrel. But the rise in price was not enough to relieve the sense of gloom that had settled over the Caspian oil fields.

Western oilmen were unnerved by what they had just gone through, a plunge in prices so severe that it had for a time utterly deflated the Caspian's fortunes. Nor could they take encouragement from the alarming string of dry holes recorded by the new exploratory wells drilled in offshore Baku, a region assumed to be brimming with untapped oil reserves.

The Caspian seemed to need an event that would excite it all over again, in the tradition of the great oil booms of the past.

The best hope seemed to lie in Kazakhstan, across the sea from Baku. There, a drilling crew was working feverishly to penetrate the secrets of an alluring offshore formation called Kashagan. In an industry in which a field of 100 million barrels of crude was highly admired, and 1 billion barrels was regarded as a giant, there was talk that 15 billion barrels of recoverable reserves might be awaiting discovery there—or more.

Six years earlier, an international consortium of six companies— France's Total, Italy's Agip, Great Britain's British Gas and British Oil, the Dutch-British company Royal Dutch/Shell, and America's Mobil Oil— had agreed to put up tens of millions of dollars for the rights to explore Kashagan. The competition to be a player had been intense; Ray Leonard of Amoco was tearful as he walked out of the negotiating room, no longer authorized by his company to stay in the high-stakes bidding.

Much was riding on the consortium's hopes for success. A strike at Kashagan could lift the oil industry out of its depressed state. The Caspian would be confirmed as one of the world's great oil regions, and Kazakhstan's future as a petro-state would be assured. The muscular geopolitical policies pursued by Washington and the region as a whole since the collapse of the Soviet Union would be validated. Failure would mean that the doubters had judged correctly, and cause oilmen to dismiss the Caspian as a place that never lived up to its promise.

Most of the foreign oil companies had, at one time or another, gazed covetously at a particular section of the Caspian Sea—the northeastern quadrant, the shallow waters of which lapped over a salt dome four miles below. Such domes, when situated in carboniferous zones, often were indicators of great stores of oil and natural gas beneath.

In 1990, executives from British Petroleum were the first outsiders allowed to view raw Soviet data that hinted at something remarkable there. In a Kazakh government guesthouse, they were shown the findings of a primitive seismic study based on decades-old technology. Though the study was unsophisticated by western standards, it plainly revealed the presence of a giant geological structure beneath the salt-covered structure.

But what was inside this reservoir? In the best of all worlds, it would contain high-quality crude oil, like its sister field, Tengiz. But in the oil game it was likelier that there was nothing. Even if there were natural gas, that wouldn't be much better than finding water, in the view of most oil-men; at the time, shipping natural gas from the region was even harder than shipping oil because of Russia's outright refusal to export non-Russian natural gas.

Still, the foreign oilmen were intrigued. Previous Soviet exploration had revealed a giant ring of deep, ancient reservoirs that traversed southern Russia and Kazakhstan for hundreds of miles. The likelihood was that these reservoirs had contained oil and natural gas at some point in the long arc of geological time. The Soviets had already found huge deposits of oil and natural gas in three of these basins—Astrakhan, Karachaganak, and, of course, Tengiz, situated just to the east of this new, hidden reservoir. Tengiz itself was a supergiant—the sixth-largest oil field in the world—but this heretofore unexplored basin was almost three times the size of Tengiz.

In May 1994, a British Petroleum man named Paul Jeffery arrived in the western Kazakhstan capital of Atyrau—the new name for Guriev, the city where Chevron's first teams had decamped in 1989—with three colleagues and $80,000 in cash. A salt-of-the-earth Englishman who seemed able to get along with anyone, Jeffery was a specialist in organizing important projects in difficult places. His job was to put down stakes for the off-shore work to come. Atyrau, a dusty, backward oil town that had been largely forgotten since the Bolshevik Revolution, would be the staging point for the assault on Kashagan.

Jeffery might as well have arrived in the wilderness. Nothing seemed to have been painted in years. Since few streets were paved, mud blanketed the city when it rained. Abandoned and rusted vehicles were everywhere. Running water was scarce and so brackish as to be almost undrinkable. In their quarters at the run-down Kaspi Hotel, the bathtub faucet dribbled water so slowly that the BP crew had to let it run all day to fill the tub—then everyone would bathe in the same water.

Most of the Kazakhs in Atyrau had never encountered foreigners. Steve Green, a Briton deplaning at the airport, had to work his way through hundreds of curious onlookers who had braved freezing winter weather merely to witness the arrival of an airplane with foreigners aboard. Green attracted special attention. Many in the crowd reached out to touch his skin and his hair; apparently, they had never seen a black man.

Jeffery's immediate task was to organize the largest and most expensive seismic shoot ever done. The goal: to produce subterranean images that would help determine whether large deposits of oil indeed lay under the North Caspian. The project would cost more than $300 million, cover sixteen thousand square miles of seabed, and be accurate to within five or so yards.

Though foreign oilmen had snickered at the crude seismic methodology employed by the Soviets, the consortium itself was relying on outdated technology. After shooting sound waves into the seabed, the oilmen stored the resulting seismic images on tape cassettes that were converted into two-dimensional representations of the reservoir. While this produced maps with more clarity than the Soviet method, the industry standard was three-dimensional technology, a far more costly technique. Three-dimensional seismic shoots produced a continuous view of the reservoir that, when projected onto giant screens, allowed geologists wearing special glasses to "walk through" the structure and determine with remarkable accuracy where would be optimal to drill.

But the companies in the consortium—already paying out more than ever before simply to examine a prospective field—were intent on holding down expenses. They would settle for the 2-D, single-slice images of the reservoir. Perhaps down the road—if evidence accumulated that Kashagan was as promising as it seemed—they could reshoot using the superior technology. Aboard twin-engine air boats, Jeffery's seismic teams navigated marshes sometimes just a yard deep and lined the seabed with cables linked to listening devices called geophones. Air guns were then discharged to generate the necessary sound waves, sending startled marshland ducks into the air with each blast.

The seismic mapping, completed in 1997, produced a nearly seamless representation of the entire Kazakhstan section of the North Caspian. The results confirmed the earlier Soviet findings, that a vast reservoir with the potential to contain significant oil and gas deposits did exist. Now the oilmen would attempt to determine what in fact was there.

The consortium, meanwhile, had expanded. There were now nine foreign partners—another American company, Phillips Petroleum, plus a Japanese partner, Inpex, had bought shares. In addition, Exxon had become a partner after having bought Mobil, as was the case with a big new French conglomerate, TotalFinaElf, a combination of original partner Total with Elf and Fina. Together, the oilmen decided to place their bet on a section of seabed where seismic mapping indicated the presence of four reservoirs. The biggest was the giant called Kashagan, forty-seven miles southeast of Atyrau.

Kazakhstan's president, Nursultan Nazarbayev, had signed the go-ahead contract amid the usual ceremonial flourishes in Washington. Now it was time to drill.

The exploration of Kashagan would begin with the drilling of two test wells, each requiring five months to complete. It would take that long to drill through the salt dome that covered the huge underwater basin, which rested 2.3 miles below the seabed.

The venture invited fears of another Mukluk. Mukluk was an Alaskan reservoir, the memory of which chilled oil field veterans. In 1983, word of its existence had electrified the industry, just as Kashagan would years later. Mukluk was believed to be the greatest find in years, comparable to the richest fields of the Middle East. An oil consortium led by one of the future Kashagan partners—British Petroleum—spent $2 billion on a test well. The results were shocking: Mukluk was dry. It was the most expensive such failure in history and all but undid industry interest in exploring risky oil regions in the United States.

Mukluk also was a reminder of the first lesson of oilmen: Regardless of technological advances, there was no way of truly knowing what was underground until wells were drilled. In the case of Kashagan, it didn't much matter what the seismics seemed to show. Only test wells—at $50 million each—could tell with certainty what was there.

But where to drill? The oilmen needed not only to find crude, but needed to find it in sufficient volumes to justify tens of billions of dollars in probable development spending. In short, they had to select the precise location, in a thousand-square-mile field, where there was the greatest likelihood of an extremely rich find. If the consortium did not quickly strike paydirt, its members might walk away from Kashagan rather than pony up millions more for additional test wells.

Enter Harry Cook, a geologist with the U.S. Geological Survey office in Menlo Park, California. A local newspaper characterized the dressed-down, bearded Cook as the "Indiana Jones" of rocks, and the sixty-year-old Santa Barbara native did in fact bear some resemblance, both physically and professionally, to the film character. Cook combined adventurousness, geological skill, and a flair for relating his exploits to audiences.

Cook's specialty was "outcrops," or rock oddities. Like a mirror, some outcrops could tell a geologist what might be hidden deep underground, even hundreds of miles away; standing on the surface, one could look across the land and see a horizontal representation—an analog, in industry parlance—of what lay vertically below.

Though it might seem counterintuitive, there was logic to the concept. Hundreds of millions of years ago, the Earth's land masses were all scrunched up together. Then plate tectonics moved the masses apart and manipulated them into their current contorted positions. A horizontal stretch of land might seem unremarkable, but it might have the same DNA, so to speak, as a vertical section in which oil was trapped.

Oilmen respected the role that analogs could play. In the best of circumstances, a geologist studying the layering of rocks could make a fairly precise estimate of where oil was most likely to be found.

In 1991, Cook had told an industry conference in London that he had found an analog to Tengiz, the supergiant Caspian oil field that was then the talk of the industry. In the mountains of Kazakhstan about 750 miles southeast of the Caspian Sea, he had found a sister structure of Tengiz, hundreds of millions of years old, lying horizontally on the Earth's surface.

His remarks had caused a stir, and they later attracted the attention of geologists who were assembling to study Kashagan for the consortium of oil companies. Perhaps his discovery could help them decide on the most promising locations for Kashagan test wells; after all, Kashagan was a sister of Tengiz. Soon they asked Cook to take them to see the analog.

The geologists walked its entire length, examining every layer of rock. They searched in particular for clues to underground rock formations with the greatest "porosity," suggesting the greatest concentration of trapped oil. Out of that exhaustive process came the decision to sink the wells roughly in the center of Kashagan.

Drilling conditions in the North Caspian Sea were unusual. Unlike the moderately deep waters off Baku, the North Caspian was extremely shallow—about ten feet deep in spots above Kashagan. Highly mobile ice formations were a threat during winter months.

Such conditions dictated that the test wells would have to be drilled from a barge rig, and the only one available was known as a "swamp queen," a flat-bottomed boat deployed until recently by Shell in the muddy waters of Nigeria. Just retrieving the rig and making it ready for use at Kashagan proved to be a daunting task.

Parker Drilling, an Oklahoma specialty company hired to drill the test wells, took the barge under tow to refitting yards in New Iberia, Louisiana, and the work began.

Craftsmen rebuilt the sides of the barge to protect it from ice damage, retooled the drilling rig, and added a helipad. New cabins were built to double the space for live-aboard housing, allowing for a crew of 110 men. After nine months, the job was done. What began as a 1,500-ton, 60-by-25-yard tropical barge had been converted into a 9,500-ton, 95-by-45-yard vessel fit for arctic conditions. It was roughly the size of a football field, the largest of its type in the world.

A vessel this size was too unwieldy to be transported to Kazakhstan by conventional means. So Parker's workers cut it into three sections and shipped them on transport barges roughly six thousand miles around the world to Russia's Don and Volga rivers and then to Astrakhan, on the northern Caspian Sea. There, some four hundred men—including

Europeans, Americans, Russians, and Azeris—were put to work welding the sections back together and installing electronics and ice deflectors.

Strict environmental rules were imposed on the operation of the drilling rig. The ecology of the sea had become a concern in post-Soviet Kazakhstan, particularly the protection of caviar-producing sturgeon and Caspian seals. The oil company consortium agreed to a zero-tolerance policy—essentially, it could destroy nothing, emit nothing into the natural surroundings, and leave nothing behind. Garbage and other waste—even the earth and rock cuttings brought up during drilling—would be sent ashore by barge for safe disposal.

To help supply the operation, the oilmen built an $11 million port south of the ice line in a place called Bautino. And to anchor the barge, twenty-four steel piles, each weighing sixty-three tons, were driven twenty-two yards into the sea bottom.

But in Astrakhan progress was slow. The work site attracted a parade of lowlifes. Prostitutes, gamblers, and drunkards regularly gathered outside the security fence, intent on lining their pockets at the expense of the workers, who soon became willing participants. Parties went on all night; Ross Murphy, Parker Drilling's manager in Kazakhstan, had trouble sleeping in his hotel room because of the loud music. Men reported for work in the morning still drunk. Expensive tools kept disappearing. One shipment of bacteria used to dissolve the waste in portable toilets went missing. But within a few days, presumably after the thieves had examined their loot, the bacteria reappeared. A fire broke out, burning up mechanical instruments and some of the housing units.

By summer 1998, the project was running well behind schedule, causing consternation among the consortium's partners. It was bad enough that world oil prices were on the skids, casting doubt on what Kashagan crude would be worth, assuming it was ever found. But the more immediate problem was the tight timetable that the Kazakh government had imposed on the consortium.

The timetable was the work of Jim Giffen. The shrewd American wheeler-dealer was now managing all major contract negotiations on behalf of the Kazakh government and had driven a tough bargain with the consortium.

The timetable established a series of drilling and production benchmarks that the oil companies were obliged to meet. Failure could mean that they would have to give up the project and forfeit all that they had invested, leaving the Kazakhs free to invite other oilmen to bid for rights to Kashagan. At the least, the consortium could be forced to pay steep penalties for its tardiness.

The oil companies had wanted to begin drilling the first exploratory well by September, which would enable them to meet a deadline two years hence to declare their commitment to develop Kashagan to the hilt. But before anyone knew it, the year was gone and the rig was not ready. Meanwhile, there was much explaining to do in boardrooms back home—project costs were outracing budget estimates by a considerable margin.

More months passed with preparations for drilling still incomplete. Among other problems, the level of the Caspian dropped by a yard, and the barge had to be modified accordingly, on-site, at a cost of additional millions. Finally, in July 1999, the decision was made to move the barge into position, finished or not.

In a contest, Kazakh schoolchildren named the drilling platform Sunkar, which means "falcon." On September 4, Kazakh prime minister Nurlan Balgimbayev, the geologist who had suffered humiliation years earlier as an intern for Chevron, arrived for dedication ceremonies. The Kazakhs slaughtered a ceremonial sheep for good luck, sprinkling its blood on the rig floor. Balgimbayev insisted on initiating the drilling; lowering the apparatus, he drilled about four feet into the seabed before handing over controls to the anxious platform crew.

The drilling plan called for sinking a 30-inch-diameter "pilot hole" for the first 3,300 feet to test for natural gas in the reservoir. The crew would then switch to a 26-inch drill through a depth of 9,900 feet, followed by a 12¼-inch drill for the next 2,600 feet—which would bring them all but through the salt dome. At that point, they would turn to the final bit—8⅜ inches in diameter—that would actually perforate the reservoir. Once inside, they would drill as much as 1,650 additional feet.

Along the way, the oilmen would line the well with a protective steel casing and continually inject an oil-based "mud"—a concoction that would reduce wear on expensive drill bits and bring up rock fragments to be tested for the presence of crude.

But the most important role for the mud was to regulate the enormous pressure between the underwater reservoir and the outside atmosphere. In the absence of mud, a reservoir like Kashagan could erupt into a destructive gusher, sending out poisonous fumes of sulfur dioxide and quite possibly causing an ecological catastrophe. To guard against such an occurrence, Kashagan's "mud engineers" designed a heavy muck that would allow the pressure to dissipate before reaching the surface.

When it actually came time to perforate the reservoir, they would switch to a lighter, water-based mud. This would reduce the chances of contamination, should the presence of crude suddenly be detected in the well. Above all, the oilmen didn't want anything to skew the results of tests performed on such traces. They needed to know precisely what was inside Kashagan. If they struck oil, the well—even though it was only one hole—could allow them to make a ballpark estimate of the minimum volume of crude contained in the reservoir. And if there were no crude? The likelihood was that the consortium would go ahead with the second well, twenty-five miles east of the first, but with greatly lowered expectations. At that point, thoughts of how to make a smooth exit might begin to creep in; the mounting cost of the project might be deemed too alarming, and the mood in the oil industry too discouraging, to proceed.

Paul Jeffery and his team were alert to the threat posed by winter ice on the Caspian Sea. He had observed the remains of Soviet fishing boats trapped in ice in the North Caspian and had seen how the ice sometimes piled forty-five feet atop itself like crazed snow cones. But in view of the timetable imposed by their contract with the Kazakhs, the consortium's partners had no choice but to drill through the winter.

That explained the hiring of Michel Metge, a Frenchman who loved to climb mountains. He was a rare breed—an engineer whose specialty was ice. Only a few dozen such men could be found around the world, most of them in Arctic oil fields. Metge observed the drilling preparations with the meticulous care of a watchmaker. He knew that, for oil rigs, ice was among the most lethal of natural phenomena. It moved like an organism and, since it was solid, could take an offshore platform with it; indeed, moving ice had been known to bring down lighthouses in its path.

Or it could pile up on top of itself and engulf a rig and the trapped crew. In previous decades, such a threat was hardly given a thought; oil field fatalities were considered part of the cost of exploration. But safety was now a top priority in the oil industry. Accordingly, the consortium paid $1 million apiece for a Swedish company to build two tanklike tracked vehicles to carry every man out should an ice emergency arise.

To test the ability of Sunkar to withstand ice floes, the oil companies built a scale model of the platform and studied its behavior in an "ice tank" in Hamburg, Germany. The facility duplicated the conditions an offshore oil rig might confront in nature, with particular attention paid to the expected thickness, density, and strength of the ice.

Caspian Sea ice, it turned out, was a particularly hard variety, posing a special hazard. The reason was the sea's low salinity. Freshwater flowing into the sea from the Ural River lowered salinity to 4 to 5 parts per 1,000 parts of water, compared with a normal ocean level of 30 to 35 parts per 1,000 parts of water. As a result of the ice tank study, engineers designed concave sides for platform Sunkar, the purpose being to force accumulated ice to shatter or fall away rather than fracture the platform itself.

Once drilling began, Metge would be empowered to order the rig evacuated if ice became too threatening. His day would begin at 4:30 every winter morning; in the hours that followed, he would continually survey the hundreds of yards of frozen sea surrounding the platform, looking for telltale signs of dangerous ice movement. One such clue would be "rafting"—stacks of ice three to four meters tall formed by shifting sheets of frozen sea. Seals congregated on these ridges, which provided a place for their pups to rest.

Metge's field of vision would be limited to five hundred yards in any direction. Beyond that, a radar dish set at a 16-degree angle would monitor the ice, picking up echoes even from slight edges on the floes and building an image that he could examine.

On the winter day when the first ice appeared, the sight startled a crewman on the platform. In fact, the ice didn't so much appear as rush toward the rig. "It's not going to stop. Holy smokes!" Michael Schlegel, an Alaskan, thought as the ice crashed against Sunkar, rose up one side of the platform, and began depositing shavings on deck. Then, just as suddenly, the ice lost its momentum and halted its advance. It was a frightening introduction to this new oil frontier.

The life of an oilman on Sunkar was measured in segments of twenty-eight days. Crews worked twenty-eight days on call around-the-clock, then took twenty-eight days off. Charter flights ferried them to Budapest and beyond for rest and relaxation.

Paul Jeffery and his British Petroleum colleagues, who had been forced to share bathwater when they had arrived in Atyrau five years earlier to set up base camp, now lived in relatively comfortable surroundings—a makeshift western-style hotel with 110 rooms. The building had to be hauled into the town in pieces, aboard eighty or so trucks.

Their quarters hardly compared, however, to the "American Village" that Chevron had established to attract executives to its Tengiz project. The 50 million-dollar, self-enclosed enclave of twenty-one acres boasted eighty-six four-bedroom, California-style townhouses, two swimming pools, tennis courts, a clubhouse, and a school, all of it surrounded by a tall fence.

The presence of western oilmen made a mark on towns all along the north Caspian area. The wildest place was Aksai, near the North Kazakhstan natural gas field called Karachaganak. There, Jeffery saw buses ferrying prostitutes into the work camp and retrieving the women the next day.

In Atyrau, some independent contractors took apartments in town and found Kazakh or Russian girlfriends. Oilmen from Sunkar sometimes managed to strike up romantic relationships, too. Jeffery and others were amused by two paramedics on alternating twenty-eight-day work schedules who unknowingly had the same girlfriend. Because one was on duty while the other was on break, neither realized they were courting the same woman. "She pulled it off for quite some time," Jeffery said. "No one talked about it. But everyone knew it."

The strong-minded mayor of Atyrau managed to wheedle millions of dollars out of the oil companies for his pet projects. Twenty-one miles of roads were paved, and sixty railcars were filled with accumulated garbage from all around the city. City crews freshened blocks of apartments with new coats of pastel and brown paint and built new parks and sidewalks. Drainage troughs were installed to capture rainwater, although streets still filled with mud after a good downpour.

Walt Marshall, a New York–born helicopter pilot who took a job flying for Chevron, recalled when "five cars at a traffic light was a traffic jam" and outhouses dotted the town because the water pressure wasn't strong enough to activate indoor plumbing. Now the streets were filled with cars, and water was available most of the day, even hot water.

Townspeople catering to the needs of foreigners found themselves flush with cash, and that set off a construction boom. Inevitably, corrupt local officials figured out how to skim dollars from some of the projects; they built some enormous brick houses along the riverfront.

While the lucky ones were suddenly earning several hundred dollars a month, most Atyrau townspeople remained among the poorest in Kazakhstan, earning an average of less than thirty dollars a month. Yevgeny Karamashin, a twenty-seven-year-old ethnic Ukrainian, longed to find a new home with indoor plumbing for himself, his wife, and a dozen relatives. He survived by poaching catfish, which his wife sold at a nearby bazaar.

Samarbek Bukebayev, Atyrau's forty-eight-year-old chief architect, was the city's number-one dreamer. He talked about razing 1,777 decrepit buildings and erecting offices and apartment buildings in their place, plus a one-thousand-room luxury hotel, a supermarket, and a modern city hall. New bridges would span the Ural, with Asian architecture on one side of the river and European on the opposite side to acknowledge the presence of the two different cultures.

"In Saudi Arabia there aren't oil fields as rich as ours, and we've only just begun," Bukebayev said with some hyperbole. His grand redevelopment plan was not entirely far-fetched—some of the construction he described was already under way. But it was yet another reminder of how the hopes of so many were riding on an oil strike at Kashagan.

———

On platform Sunkar, drilling had to be suspended after the first 3,300 feet so the rig could be retooled to withstand the rigors of the greater depths ahead. The project's hasty start had saddled crews with a "poor boy" rig, oil field argot for equipment built on the fly. One vital piece of machinery that failed repeatedly was the air compressor; it appeared to be at least twenty-five years old and to have been assembled with parts from several different sources. Without a working compressor, the drill could not operate. Work was also halted for days to fetch a wrench accidentally dropped down the hole.

In April 2000, an important milestone was recorded. The first test well reached the top of the reservoir, some 2.3 miles below the seabed. Drilling was halted, and nonessential workers were evacuated from the platform to minimize the number of people at risk should the well begin emitting hydrogen sulfide.

The oilmen declared the well to be a "tight hole," meaning it was now protected by the strict code of secrecy traditionally imposed when drilling reached a critical stage. If anyone leaked word of the well's progress or lack thereof, the company's stock price could be affected or a rival could be tipped off to a competitor's sudden vulnerability. It was a matter of honor among oilmen not to violate the code.

But the industry was already abuzz with speculation as to what the well might reveal. Oilmen, diplomats, political leaders, and journalists who followed energy matters were intently focused on Kashagan. Kazakh president Nazarbayev stirred the pot by suddenly declaring that his country would exceed Saudi Arabia's oil production by 2015. Did he mean that oil had been found at Kashagan? His assertion seemed an obvious exaggeration. Yet, in the charged atmosphere of the moment, couldn't be dismissed outright.

Tension mounted on Sunkar. The scaled-down work team switched to water-based mud, and operations resumed. Finally, the drill perforated the reservoir and was inside. Oil company engineers peered closely at the rock shavings that the drill bit brought up amid the mud, looking for evidence of hydrocarbons within the reservoir. Other crewmen, unable to get a close look, called out, "What do you see? What do you see?" But tight hole rules prevailed, and they got no response.

On the third day, Parker's Ross Murphy, in charge of the drilling crew, heard something revealing from his men. "These guys are excited out here. They won't let us near the cuttings," they told him.

It was too much for Murphy to endure. He marched over to the consortium's general manager and asked point-blank what had been found. "It's everything we hoped for," the man said.

Paul Jeffery, on a rest break in England, answered his phone. The caller was a Kashagan colleague in Atyrau. Their conversation was guarded, but Jeffery quickly realized the importance of his call and the information that was being conveyed.

"So, things are going well out there?" Jeffery asked.

Yes, just fine, his colleague replied.

Jeffery knew—Kashagan had oil. A lot of oil.

Oilmen generally are a taciturn breed, as reflected years later when Murphy and Jeffery talked about the moment when they knew Kashagan would be a success.

His reaction was "a celebration of relief . . . that the seismic was correct and that the field was potentially bigger than anyone really expected," said Murphy. "There were no parties, no overt celebrations, just a solid realization that something special happened."

Jeffery said he was too preoccupied with the work that remained to think about celebrating. Not until two months later did he and his BP men have "a bloody good party," able to savor the thought that "we were all experiencing something that most of us will only ever do in our careers once, discovering a giant oil field."

Original plans called for capping the hole at that point and moving on to drill the second exploratory well. But now that the oil companies knew that there were hydrocarbons in Kashagan, curiosity took over. They decided to keep drilling the first well until they found what was known as the "oil-water contact line," a critical indicator of the volume of oil in a reservoir. Since oil floated on water, drill crews could determine the height of what they called the "oil column" by measuring how deeply into the reservoir they had to go before hitting water.

But results were proving elusive in the case of Kashagan. Day after day, the oilmen kept drilling with no sign of water. "We gotta hit the water contact line" sometime, Ross Murphy recalled one of the crew saying.

At 4,500 feet and still no water, the implications of what they were finding were stunning. In a Texas oil field, an oil column of 10 or 20 feet was regarded as impressive. A 4,500-foot column was otherworldly.

At one point, the crew removed a 90-foot long core for examination, and it was "all oil-saturated. We are all looking at it and thinking, 'This is going to be a hell of a well,' " Murphy recalled. "These guys had never seen anything like it."

He did a back-of-the-envelope calculation that took into account the dimensions of the oil column and the reservoir and the 16 percent porosity of the rock—meaning the percentage of space in the rock likely harboring oil. His rough conclusion: Kashagan contained 40 billion barrels of crude, 15 billion barrels of which could be recovered by conventional drilling. That would make it at least twice the volume of Tengiz.

The oil companies delayed announcement of their find, in part because of timetable considerations. Once they confirmed success with the test well, the clock would begin ticking on their contractual obligation to develop the field and begin exporting crude. The unavoidable bottom line, however, was that Kashagan oil would have to start flowing by 2005, a deadline that most consortium partners thought almost impossible to meet. But news of the discovery could not be contained. Too many Kazakhs and foreigners with inside knowledge were too elated to keep it quiet, and reports that Kashagan was a success finally broke in American newspapers in May 2000.

The story of Kashagan would be incomplete without a tribute to the ingenuity of the oilmen at Sunkar when confronting the power politics of Kazakhstan. It was a moment of pure theater and, when it was over, a source of lasting amusement.

Drilling crews were making preparations to assure the smooth flow of oil out of the well and into a pipeline system. This would require lining the well with a steel casing, then using a powerful gun to perforate the casing.

Oil would then seep through the resulting holes and safely travel up the well. As the oil flowed, workers would ignite any accompanying natural gas, a safety measure called flaring intended to prevent the explosive fumes from escaping into the open.

Without such protective measures, the well could erupt into an uncontrolled gusher, spewing poisonous hydrogen sulfide for miles around. Just such a gusher once raged for a year at Tengiz.

After weeks of installing equipment and making practice runs, the drilling crews were ready to proceed. Then politics intervened.

Kazakhstan president Nazarbayev announced that he wished to see the process firsthand. The oilmen were dismayed. No one wanted to undertake the delicate and risky perforation operation while the president of the country stood by. As some of them joked darkly, it wouldn't be helpful to kill the president.

On the other hand, they couldn't tell him not to come. And so they devised a clever ruse. The crew acquired six thousand gallons of diesel fuel and jury-rigged a tank with an on-off valve. For two days, workmen practiced turning the valve and lighting it—imitating the appearance of gas being flared from Kashagan. Making Nazarbayev think that the burning diesel fuel was natural gas from the reservoir would allow them to stall the actual work until he left. There was one other problem—what to do about the traditional smearing of faces? Nazarbayev would certainly insist on a bucket of Kashagan oil to daub on his and everyone else's face as a sign of good luck. But so far the oilmen had recovered only scant amounts of hydrocarbons from Kashagan, nowhere near enough to wipe anyone's face with.

So they did the equivalent of borrowing a quart of milk from a neighbor, sending for a five-gallon container of crude from Tengiz. They then devised a way for the crude to flow from a valve on the oil rig.

All was in readiness when the president arrived on July 4. Ross Murphy greeted him with a flourish, declaring: "We present to you Kashagan." Nazarbayev was so pleased by what he thought was natural gas being flared that he stood and watched the burning diesel fuel for more than twenty minutes.

Murphy began to fear that their six-hundred-gallon supply of diesel would be exhausted, and "the gig would be up. And that wouldn't have been good at all."

Finally, a contented Nazarbayev moved to the oil valve that emitted Tengiz crude so authentically that Murphy himself thought, "It looked real." The president then smeared the oil on everyone.

Speaking later to reporters at Atyrau's airport, he was ebullient. "I can tell you today that there is oil, big oil, and it is good quality oil," he said. He added, "This is a great aid to our independence, to our future and our future prosperity. The hopes of the Kazakh people have been realized."

A Way
to the
Sea

THE DISCOVERY OF VAST DEPOSITS
of crude at Kashagan was a fitting moment
of triumph for the Caspian. It verified the
region's ascendancy as a global oil giant for
decades to come. But an old question had yet
to be answered: how to move the ever-
increasing volumes of Caspian oil to world
markets?

The existing network of pipelines
strained to keep up with the flow of crude,
and was subject to disruptions that heightened the anxieties of western oilmen. It was
ill-prepared for the huge surge in production
that everyone knew was coming. A bold new
approach was required, or the oil companies
could find themselves with millions of barrels of additional crude to sell each day but
without the means to export it. It would be
an oilman's worst nightmare.

The warning signs could be seen on both sides of the landlocked Caspian Sea.

In Azerbaijan, the Early Oil project—two new pipelines from Baku to Black Sea tanker terminals—finally was up and running. One line, terminating at the Georgia port of Supsa, was controlled by western oil companies and entirely avoided Russian territory. The other, a concession to a restive Moscow, crossed Russia on the way to its port of Novorossiysk. But each had limitations. The Baku-to-Supsa line was rated at a relatively modest 115,000 barrels a day. The Russian line was regularly disrupted by the conflict in Chechnya.

In Kazakhstan, the prospect of Kashagan coming online created new pressure. Russia, meanwhile, kept finding ways to hamper construction of the Tengiz pipeline, even though the consortium trying to build it had been realigned to be more Russian-friendly. Determined that Moscow not be allowed to cripple the company's operations at the big oil field, Chevron responded with an elaborate end-around scheme. It shipped most of its Tengiz production—about two hundred thousand barrels a day—by rail through Russia and Finland, and some smaller volumes by barge to Baku and then overland to the Georgian port of Poti on the Black Sea. Though these routes were long and costly to maintain, Chevron was able to continue exporting its crude—it even turned a small profit, though nowhere close to the sums it could earn if Russia halted its interference with the dedicated Tengiz pipeline.

Conditions seemed ripe for the grand solution that had been talked about for years: a big new Caspian export pipeline able to move eight hundred thousand or more barrels of oil daily, free of harassment by the Russians or anyone else.

Washington liked the idea for several reasons. The nascent Caspian states could reap lasting economic benefits and political allegiances from such a project, making them better able to resist Russia should it attempt to march back into Central Asia and the Caucasus one day. The pipeline could be routed so as to skirt not only Russia but also Iran, whose policies the American government abhorred. America and its allies could collect a huge energy dividend, assuming that most or all of the pipeline's oil were funneled to the West.

Finally, the Clinton administration thought that the pipeline could be the catalyst to reorder historic north-south trade routes in the region—an outcome that would favor the West and disfavor Russia. Central Asia and the Caucasus traditionally shipped raw material like oil, natural gas, and cotton north to Russia, which sent back finished products in return. Washington imagined that the pipeline and its related network of barges, highways, and railroads could redirect trade along east-west routes, with Turkey playing the role that had once belonged to Russia. Critics called the scheme grandiose, but the United States took every opportunity to tout what it called its "East-West Corridor."

Two states in the region—Azerbaijan and Georgia—early on embraced the idea of being strung together like pearls along a great oil pipeline tied to Washington, affording them protection from their enemies. Now that the United States was behind it, they liked it even more. Turkey did, too, believing that participation in such a project could renew its historical influence over the region. Though less fervent, Kazakhstan and Turkmenistan also showed interest.

So it was that the American government breathed new life into the long-incubating proposal for a 1,081-mile-long pipeline from Baku to export terminals at the Turkish Mediterranean port of Ceyhan. It would be the longest such line in the world, and it would be built entirely on territory friendly to America. Azerbaijan would become the energy transportation hub for the entire Caspian basin, exporting some eight hundred thousand barrels a day by 2007—and more in later years. That, at least, was the vision.

While the region itself stood to gain the most, the United States became the idea's loudest promoter. Washington cloaked its strategy with a slogan on bumper stickers that promised a veritable blossoming of pipelines across the Caspian: HAPPINESS IS MULTIPLE PIPELINES. But its real aim was clear—finally to put an end to Moscow's bullying of the region and create a pro-western swath of self-sufficient nations.

Always fiercely jealous of its independence, the oil industry balked. Yes, more pipeline capacity was urgently needed. But spending billions of dollars of their money to build a pipeline on the scale of Baku-Ceyhan seemed an extravagance to the multinationals. Some, resenting the drumbeating by the Clinton administration, derided it as a "political pipeline."

The reaction might have been less vehement had world oil prices not been so low. After all, it was the industry that had originated the idea of Baku-Ceyhan back in the early 1990s, when engineers from British Petroleum and Amoco, with photographs of the region on hand, drew rough sketches of its path on scraps of paper.

But cost was a major concern now, and some in the industry rallied around an alternative route that they argued would be much shorter and far cheaper: south through Iran to the Persian Gulf. Iran had another attraction as well. The nation was inviting foreign investment in oil and gas projects worth billions of dollars, and American oil companies like Exxon, Chevron, Mobil, and Conoco wanted to join in the bidding.

Now it was Washington's turn to resist. Since the 1979 hostage crisis, relations between the U.S. government and Iran had been virtually nonexistent. Legislation signed into law by President Clinton barred American companies from doing business with Iran and provided for sanctions against foreign enterprises that did so.

Washington's tough stance was largely in reaction to Iran's support for Hezbollah, the anti-Israel militia based in Lebanon. Powerful pro-Israel groups such as the American Israel Public Affairs Committee, or AIPAC, heavily lobbied the Clinton administration, and some of AIPAC's closest contacts were senior Clinton foreign policy advisers who were strong opponents of Iran's regime—among them Stuart Eizenstat, an undersecretary in the State Department, and Leon Fuerth, Vice President Al Gore's chief foreign policy adviser.

Despite the oil industry's entreaties, Washington wouldn't budge. "It has to be admitted there is a problem with American companies," Eizenstat said. "But this is a situation where the strategic interests of the United States are so great that they outweigh the temporary advantages of American companies."

For a brief time, the jockeying over Iran turned the Caspian alliance between Washington and the oil companies on its head. Some oilmen fought harder for the right to do business with Iran than they had ever disputed the rationale behind Washington's anti-Russia policy. And Washington, after years of resisting Russian control of Caspian pipelines, seemed even more hostile to a line crossing Iranian territory.

Relations between the oil companies and the U.S. government grew more prickly. British Petroleum especially regarded American officials as meddlesome nannies sticking their noses into commercial matters that were far beyond their ken, too willing to let politics trump wise economic policy. Washington viewed BP and many of the other oil companies as an obstreperous and narrow-minded lot that failed to understand that the Caspian was unlike other places—commerce couldn't be divorced from politics.

In autumn 1998, the oilmen shelved their Iranian option, at least for the time being. They began drafting yet another alternative to Baku-Ceyhan: a $700 million enlargement of the Early Oil pipeline that ran from Baku to the Georgian port of Supsa. The expansion would double the daily flow of exports to three hundred thousand barrels or more, enough to absorb the predicted increase in crude oil production at least through 2003. It was not even half of what Baku-Ceyhan would accommodate, but it would provide at least some short-term relief, and it would cost the oil companies much less.

When word of the proposal leaked to outsiders, it appeared that Baku-Ceyhan was in trouble, perhaps even doomed. The drive to get the pipeline built, "a campaign that has become a centerpiece of American foreign policy, appears to be on the brink of failure," *The New York Times* said. The influential paper took note of Clinton's political problems, specifically the mounting evidence that he had had sex with twenty-one-year-old intern Monica Lewinsky in the Oval Office. "A stronger or more focused President might have made a persuasive case" for Baku-Ceyhan, the paper said. It was a stretch, but it was too tantalizing to ignore. Picking up the theme, Turkey's daily *Hürriyet* ran the headline A MONICA SETBACK FOR BAKU-CEYHAN.

The pipeline's supporters pushed back. Azerbaijan's president, Heydar Aliyev, said *The New York Times* didn't decide American policy. Even Strobe Talbott, the pro-Russia deputy secretary of state, was driven to say, "An obit for the Baku-Ceyhan pipeline is premature at the least and, we believe, wrong and inaccurate."

In fact, the oil industry's counterproposal had a serious flaw. It overlooked crowded conditions at the Bosporus Strait, the majestic waterway passing through Turkey and connecting the Black Sea with the Mediterranean Sea. Tankers exporting crude from the Caspian and Russia loaded their cargo at Black Sea terminals, then proceeded through the strait to the Mediterranean and world markets beyond.

The Bosporus wound for more than nineteen miles, turning twelve times like a river. At its narrowest point, a tree-covered rise called Kandilli, it was a mere 739 yards wide, requiring tankers to navigate a 45-degree turn. At another point, an area of waterside mansions called Yenikov, the turn was a harrowing 80 degrees, or almost a right angle. An average of twelve oil tankers made the journey each day.

A 1936 treaty required Turkey to keep the shipping lanes open. But it already had agreed that Chevron could add more tankers to carry crude from Tengiz. Now the oil industry was proposing to double the volume of exports coming from Georgia, meaning yet another big increase in tanker traffic through the Bosporus. This was more than the Turks were willing to accept. Should any of the huge ships rupture or crash, it could be an environmental disaster for Istanbul, the city of 10 million through which the strait flowed. Skeptics noted that the environmental objections neatly dovetailed with the political and economic preference of the Turks—that Baku oil be transported via an overland Turkey pipeline. But the risk seemed real. There had been nine major tanker accidents on the strait since 1951.

By contrast, the Baku-Ceyhan pipeline would send Caspian crude directly to Turkey's Mediterranean coast, entirely bypassing the Black Sea and the Bosporus Strait.

At a White House meeting with oil executives in October 1998, Clinton administration officials were blunt. Richard Morningstar, the coordinator of Caspian Sea policy, agreed that the Supsa alternative was cheaper, but "that is irrelevant, because you can't have it." Turkey's opposition to increased tanker traffic made it "as politically practicable as putting a nuclear power plant on Manhattan Island," he said.

Tempers flared. The oilmen repeated that Baku-Ceyhan was too ambitious an undertaking, and they questioned the willingness of international bankers to finance such a scheme. But in a statement afterward, a designated spokesman played down the differences. Dick Matzke, Chevron's temperamental overseas president, told reporters, "There was a great degree of agreement as to the logical pattern of pipeline development . . . and that Baku-Ceyhan should be the next logical development. The question was on timing and on financing."

In fact, large gaps of understanding remained. The companies left the meeting thinking they had made it clear that the Baku-Ceyhan pipeline could be built only if by some remote chance it suddenly became as cheap, for example, as the Iran route. Exxon, "convinced that the wave of the future would be pipelines through Iran," continued to lobby quietly for that route, all the while complaining that administration officials were "nuts and not paying attention to commercial realities."

Morningstar, meanwhile, had the impression that the companies had grasped his point, and he rallied the Turks, the Azeris, and the Georgians to stand with Washington and "foreclose all alternatives besides Baku-Ceyhan." Turkey, with so much riding on the success of the latter, vowed that the Bosporus would not be "transformed into a pipeline for Caspian crude."

When Mobil Oil chairman Lou Noto asked for government permission just to swap relatively small volumes of Turkmen and Kazakh oil with Tehran in exchange for Iranian oil delivered on the Persian Gulf, the Clinton aide told him no. "It makes no sense to agree to swaps because that will make Baku-Ceyhan untenable. That's our policy," Morningstar said.

Washington, in short, had adopted a variant of Henry Ford's dictum that any customer could have a car painted any color that he wanted, so long as it was black. The oilmen could build any pipeline they desired, so long as it ran from Baku to Ceyhan without touching either Iran or Russia. In a way, the oil companies were right—this had evolved from U.S. policy into an obsession.

In Moscow, America's determination to build a major pipeline that bypassed Russian territory continued to rankle. Foreign Minister Igor Ivanov told Morningstar, "We know what you are doing and we don't like it." Months earlier, some Washington officials had unsuccessfully attempted to dissuade Morningstar from attending the ceremonial opening of the Early Oil pipeline in Georgia. They thought it too dangerous for him to be standing next to President Eduard Shevardnadze, the repeated target of assassination attempts linked to Russia's displeasure over Baku-Ceyhan.

No single event broke the back of resistance to the Baku-Ceyhan pipeline project. But the tide began to turn in the spring of 1999, when British Petroleum announced that it was paying $29 billion for Arco, the Los Angeles–based oil company. Just eight months earlier, BP had bought Chicago-based Amoco for $55 billion.

The two transactions brought into sharp relief the increasingly common interests of Washington and the British multinational. If the United States approved the Arco purchase, some 30 percent of BP's total oil production would come from Alaska. Meanwhile, the Amoco purchase swelled British Petroleum's share of offshore Baku oil rights to 34 percent, making it the biggest player there; as such, it led oil industry negotiations with Washington over Baku-Ceyhan.

Although BP had thus far opposed the American-backed pipeline, the last thing it needed—with the Arco purchase pending—was a hostile relationship with the U.S. government. As Dick Olver, its chief of international exploration and production, diplomatically put it: "We thought of ourselves as a large American company because of the Alaska interests. We said, 'Because of that we need to behave like a good global and a good American citizen.'"

Right away, BP found itself scrambling to keep the peace. Its move to buy Arco ran into a buzz saw of objections from federal regulators and politicians in Alaska and California. The British company would eventually prevail, but only after agreeing to settle antitrust complaints by selling off some Alaskan holdings and, in California, bowing to demands for environmental and fuel price agreements and pledging to increase charitable giving.

Meanwhile, Washington and the Turks kept the pressure on British

Petroleum to accept Baku-Ceyhan. At one point, Turkey invoked a boycott of BP gasoline and other products—all but shutting down the company's retail operations there. In a hotel lobby confrontation, a senior Turkish energy official berated a BP executive. "We're going to do everything in our power to keep you from sending your oil through Supsa," the Turk shouted.

John Wolf, an acerbic and pushy career diplomat, took over as point man for the United States and immediately went on the offensive. He began showing audiences an animated video—produced by his staff—of the horrors that could result if oil tankers crashed on the Bosporus. One scene showed a tanker bayoneted against a bridge. British ambassador Roger Thomas found Wolf to be "an absolute terrier. He didn't suit very well the British form of diplomacy. He went for the throat every time."

The clash of cultures was evident at a working lunch in autumn 1999 between John Browne, BP's wily chairman, and Leon Fuerth, the vice president's adviser. The Americans in the meeting unwrapped deli sandwiches from the commissary below Fuerth's office. Across the room, a Browne adviser set up china and silverware for his courtly boss, carefully laying out smoked salmon bought at Sutton Place Gourmet, an upscale Washington shop.

Despite the culinary differences, glimmers of agreement began to appear. Browne conceded that shipping more crude through the Bosporus Strait was "not an option" and told Fuerth that his company would now "apply itself to the business of determining whether Baku-Ceyhan could work." The cautious statement meant that BP was ready to take a hard look at whether banks would finance construction of the pipeline, estimated to cost from $2.4 billion to $3 billion.

The staggering price tag had always been the central reason for oil industry opposition to Baku-Ceyhan. It would be up to BP and its consortium partners to raise the money and find a way to operate the pipeline without it becoming a drain on their earnings. While the U.S. government and its allies were driven by geopolitical considerations, the oilmen saw the pipeline as strictly a commercial venture, and a risky one at that.

On October 19, the company went public with its change of heart.

"We recognize the strategic importance of the Baku-Ceyhan line. We said we will do everything we can to bring it about," BP announced in a statement issued simultaneously in Washington and London.

After so many years of British Petroleum and other companies deriding the pipeline as an ill-conceived gambit by an intrusive American government, few knew what to think. Would the company and its partners really build the pipeline? That the October statement was at least in part an attempt to gain Washington's support for the Arco merger seemed transparent. Viktor Kaluzhny, Russia's fuel and energy minister, summed up the doubts: "Ceyhan is, above all, a political issue, I think. I do not believe that the pipeline will ever be constructed."

But while it was hard for outsiders to believe that BP was serious, Browne in fact did order his people to try to make the pipeline work. Time was growing short for his company. The Arco merger had to go forward, some version of a new Baku pipeline was undeniably needed, and Iran—the route pressed so long by the companies—didn't seem willing after all to strike the kind of bargain the oilmen had hoped for.

Wref Digings, a 50-year-old negotiator for BP and trusted aide to Browne, played a crucial role. He had been assigned by the CEO almost two years earlier to "find a way to get major oil out of the Caspian." Digings entered into intense talks with Turkey, on whose land two thirds of the pipeline would be built, and emerged with important assurances. The Turks would guarantee a cap on construction costs for their portion of the line as well as a low tariff for the oil companies shipping crude through it. The sweeteners "tilted the balance on the commercial side," BP executives now believed.

Still, each side continued to jockey for favorable bargaining positions. British Petroleum fretted that the projected flow of crude would be hundreds of thousands of barrels a day below what was needed to secure bank loans. Some in Washington groused that BP was trotting out a worst-case scenario to stall negotiations. Indeed, the company later revised its estimate and said that the flow would be sufficient. The episode seemed to illustrate that BP and Washington were equally skilled at the art of spin: Washington by exaggerating the volume of oil underlying the Caspian to drum up support for its campaign, and BP by low-balling its offshore reserves to make the pipeline venture seem overly daunting, if not outright impossible.

Assembling all the pieces of a Baku-Ceyhan deal was a laborious process. BP had to persuade others in the oil company consortium to accept the terms of the agreement; Exxon was the notable footdragger, still nursing its hopes for an Iranian pipeline. Azerbaijan and Georgia, the starting point and the midpoint of the pipeline route, respectively, had to sign off on the tariff rates, among other issues.

Washington was still pursuing its vision of an East-West Corridor. With that in mind, American diplomats were hopeful that BP could bring Kazakhstan and Turkmenistan into the negotiations. The Kazakhs could ship some amount of their crude across the Caspian Sea and export it through the Baku-Ceyhan pipeline. Turkmenistan could participate by exporting natural gas through a 1,250-mile pipeline to the Turkish city of Erzurum. Talks began with Kazakhstan, but Turkmenistan would prove to be a nonstarter. Construction of the gas line stalled when the republic's eccentric president, Saparmurat Niyazov, kept demanding a $500 million bribe from the western companies that were prepared to build it.

British Petroleum emerged from final negotiations with most of what it and its partners had wanted, especially the participation of quasi-government financial agencies—in effect lowering the oil industry's risk. Nations along the route of the pipeline agreed to share responsibility for protection against sabotage and the cleanup of leaks or spills—usually the obligations of oil companies alone. Another provision elevated the deal to the status of an international treaty, unheard of in the oil industry but giving the companies an extra layer of legal protection. British Petroleum's message to the U.S. government and its allies at times seemed to be, *If you want a pipeline so badly, here are the terms.*

Bargaining sessions were mind-numbing and sometimes tense. Lawyers plodded through draft agreements paragraph by paragraph in rooms "so filled with smoke that you couldn't see the other end of the table." At one point, John Wolf, the Caspian czar for the United States, became upset when Digings, the BP negotiator, expressed disapproval of a proposal from

Georgia. As Digings turned to speak to someone else, Wolf grabbed him by the shoulders and spun him around to continue their conversation. "Get your hands off of me," Digings said. The men eventually calmed down.

To some, the BP-led consortium had walked away with a sweetheart deal, thanks to Washington being intimidated by the more experienced oil company negotiators. New York lawyer Jenik Radon, hired to protect Georgia's national interests, thought that the agreement was terribly one-sided, a "monstrosity . . . from the environment, to liability, to police powers." He managed to win some tariff and liability concessions on behalf of his client.

But from BP's standpoint, the guarantees it demanded were fully justified, given the unknowns of building a multibillion-dollar, long-term capital project through three countries, all of which struggled with ethnic-based hostilities.

On November 18, 1999, President Clinton and the presidents of Georgia, Azerbaijan, Turkey, and Kazakhstan gathered in Istanbul to sign documents signaling their support of the Baku-Ceyhan pipeline. Clinton had wanted to add a romantic touch by staging the event on a yacht cruising the Bosporus, but the waters were too rough and the ceremony was switched to the Ciragan Palace Hotel, an elegant former Ottoman palace on the water's edge.

Russia expressed its displeasure in a statement from Deputy Foreign Minister Ivan Ivanov who complained that "the U.S. administration brought political pressure to bear on the companies involved in the construction." Azerbaijan, he said, should leave the transport of oil to his nation because "Russia's infrastructure is already in place," while the Baku-Ceyhan pipeline existed only on paper.

But Carlos Pascual, Clinton's deputy national security advisor, felt that a critical stage had been passed and that the future looked "pretty positive." The united front presented by the United States and the three Caspian states assured financing for the project. Washington's was the most influential voice in the banks that counted—with its own Export-Import Bank and Overseas Private Investment Corporation as well as with the World Bank and the EBRD. All could be relied on to put up money and make it safe for commercial banks to participate. Several months later, BP would commit to building Baku-Ceyhan.

Clinton called the four-nation agreement "truly historic" and declared: "I'll bet if you polled the citizens of the United States and Turkey, over 90 percent of them would never have heard of the Baku-Ceyhan pipeline or the trans-Caspian gas pipeline. But if we do this right, twenty years from now, 90 percent of them will look back and say, 'Thank you for making a good decision at a critical time.'"

Some tired of waiting for construction to begin. Among them was the flamboyant American author Thomas Goltz, who led three whimsical motorcycle expeditions the length of the pipeline's 1,081-mile route from Azerbaijan to the Turkish coast. He carried with him containers of Azeri crude and natural gas, to be presented to the Turks as the first installments of Baku's promised exports.

The entourage rolled through Azerbaijan's dusty desert, then across the Georgia border to the capital of Tbilisi and into the hills beyond. Always, people were curious about the pipeline. "Is it all decided?" asked a bearded man standing outside a fifth-century Georgian Orthodox monastery on one of the journeys. "We haven't been sure." Outside one village, Turkic shepherds living in the open invited the visitors to stay overnight and slaughtered a sheep that, by 2 A.M., had been turned into a fatty stew. They seemed unworried that the pipeline might disrupt their nomadic lives. "There is lots of land," one said.

Upon entering Turkey, the Goltz group was treated to a royal reception. Young dancers in red-and-black velvet costumes greeted them, and a police escort guided them on the long journey to the coast. At the town of Erzurum, local officials cheerfully accepted the keg of natural gas and presented their visitors with a cake shaped like a pipeline. The icing read, BAKU-CEYHAN.

After ten days on the road, the bikers descended into Ceyhan itself, population 92,000. In the distance, one could see the waiting oil terminal, built to handle some 600 million barrels of crude a year from Iraq but inoperative during much of the 1990s because of hostilities with Saddam Hussein's army. Dancers tied bouquets of roses to each motorcycle and policemen burst into applause. Triumphal music blared, and flags of the

Caspian states flapped in the air. Some two hundred dignitaries in grand-stands looked on as Gökhan Bildaci, the chairman of BOTAS, the Turkish pipeline company, embraced Goltz. Baku oil had arrived—or a symbol of it, anyway.

Nearly two years later, on a wind-whipped section of the northern Azerbaijan marshes, a work crew wrestled with chest-high lengths of steel pipe on ground as slippery as "custard on a sheet of glass." Their assignment: to lay the first section of Baku-Ceyhan, from Azerbaijan to Georgia.

Neil Clough, a balding fifty-one-year-old British pipeline specialist, was in charge. His men had advanced sixty-five miles since embarking from Baku five months earlier, after the groundbreaking ceremonies on June 30, 2003. They had another 210 miles and months to go before they would reach the Georgian border to the north. Meanwhile, in Georgia and beyond in Turkey, other workers were assembling more sections of the massive pipe.

Clough's crew carefully positioned the ten-ton sections of pipe end to end, exactly two centimeters from one another, then stood back. An automatic welding arc, dangling from a crane in an odd, pantry-size contraption called a "habitat," made five passes over each joint, the final sweep lasting a full four minutes. Inspectors x-rayed the welds for flaws and electronically swept the huge tubes of steel for "holidays," the curious term for miniscule holes that might appear in polyethylene coating. Other workers sent violent blasts of water through the line, a test of its resistance to pressure.

Only after all that could the crew bury its creation under three feet of earth. When the hot oil finally flowed, Clough knew, the compacted sand would act "like a thousand hands," holding the pipeline to its original size and assuring that the steel would not expand lengthwise and bust the joints.

A satellite tracking system would keep watch once the pipeline went operational. In anticipation of this, each weld was assigned a code number, handwritten in white paint on the pipe, and its GPS coordinates were entered into a computer. Similarly, each 38.5-foot-long section of pipeline bore a unique bar code, allowing it to be traced from the moment it left the Sumitomo factory in Japan.

Clough, in his trademark orange jumpsuit with silver stripes, gestured toward the ground: "If a pipe is bad, we can know what other pipes were made that day, and where they are. Then we can go down and inspect them. If it's a weld, we can check who welded it and what other welds he did that day, and check those. We know we have to dig right here, because the welds are in the system." Finally, a black fiber-optic line the diameter of a garden hose was buried along the path of the pipeline to allow instant monitoring of, for example, the vital pumping stations.

When Clough's men reached the Georgia border, they would turn and start back toward Baku. This time, they would lay a companion natural gas line and then restore the ground to its original state. "I want to lay down the two pipelines and drive by and not see a thing," Clough vowed. "I don't want to see a scar on the earth."

Six years after U.S. policymakers first identified the Caspian as a strategic interest and almost a decade after pioneering foreign oilmen had first sketched the pipeline's most likely route, all the pieces were finally falling into place.

CHAPTER 21

The
King
of
Kazakhstan

IT HAD BECOME AN AGREEABLE ROUTINE: Once a month or so, Jim Giffen slid into his Bentley and drove from his eleven-acre Westchester County estate to JFK International Airport, where he boarded the first-class section of an overnight flight to Europe and then on to Kazakhstan. Upon his arrival in Almaty, the Kazakh business capital, a waiting limousine whisked him to the four-story hilltop villa that was his home away from home. Giffen called the retreat his "San Francisco House," a tribute to its stunning views. From one side, guests could gaze at the snow-topped Tien Shen mountains and, below, a panorama of tree-covered slopes. From the other, they could view the entirety of the city and the glow of its lights at night.

The villa was a perquisite provided by Nurlan Balgimbayev, a former prime minister of Kazakhstan with lucrative connections in the oil industry. He was a longtime protégé of Giffen's and lived next door; a gate connecting the two properties made the whole arrangement quite neighborly.

An upstairs bedroom closet was stocked with identical blue (and blue pinstriped) suits and white dress shirts with colored collars, the American visitor's preferred business wardrobe. Should he require casual wear, he could select from a supply of identical tan slacks and white polo shirts, some of them embossed with the name of his beloved Winged Foot Golf Club in Westchester County. Always immaculately turned out, Giffen wasn't one for sartorial variety.

He shared the bedroom with a girlfriend, Lana, a local pop violinist he met one night as she played for diners at an Italian restaurant. She had bangs and a coquettish smile and, at 29, was three decades younger than Giffen. He bought her a Cartier diamond ring and financed a recording session and video shoot that made her a star in Almaty.

As the 1990s drew to a close, James Henry Giffen was as influential in Kazakhstan as any foreigner could ever dream to be in any country.

He had landed in the former Soviet republic seven years earlier—just after it had gained independence—with the intention of reviving his fading career as a deal-making middleman. He succeeded by outsmarting the best that the big oil multinationals could throw at him. A grateful Kazakh government, on whose behalf he negotiated, showered him with millions of dollars in commissions and admitted him to its innermost circles of power.

Now he was the close confidant of Nursultan Nazarbayev, the autocratic president of Kazakhstan, whom he had first met when the state was still under Soviet rule. The office walls at Giffen's merchant bank in New York were lined with photographs from trips they took together; in one, the Kazakh president is huddling with former secretary of state James Baker and National Security Adviser Brent Scowcroft from the old George H. W. Bush crowd. When Nazarbayev appeared as guest of honor at his black-tie Christmas party in New York one year, Giffen was so moved that he became tearful while delivering a tribute to Kazakh democracy.

His relationship with the strongman ruler fit a familiar pattern: Jim Giffen had made himself the envied intimate of a powerful man, something he had done so often over the years. With that came the requirement that he be on constant alert for a summons from "the boss," as he called Nazarbayev. One Kazakh diplomat, pondering the American's role, told the story of a circus worker cleaning up the droppings of elephants as they moved through the big top. Asked why he didn't find a more dignified job, the worker was said to have replied, "What, and leave show business?"

Similarly, Giffen accepted whatever indignities arose as a small price to pay for the glory and status of being close to power. He and Nazarbayev sometimes retreated together into the countryside for days at a time, accompanied by young Kazakh women and well supplied with whiskey. He vacationed with the president in the south of France, golfing and partying.

The thought that all this could end, that his storied survival as the Caspian's last reigning middleman might be threatened, must have seemed impossible even to consider.

Some four decades earlier, while a university student in Berkeley, California, Jim Giffen had become fascinated by the globetrotting life of Harry Hopkins, a diplomat of the New Deal era. Hopkins had been President Franklin D. Roosevelt's trusted aide, sent on secret World War II diplomatic missions to see Stalin and Churchill. His granddaughter June was Giffen's girlfriend at the time, and the two would listen as her father told stories about the family's famous relative.

The stories fueled Giffen's attraction to power and to those who wielded it, and by the 1980s he was a global operative himself. Mikhail Gorbachev blessed his business deals in the Soviet Union, and corporate America paid handsomely for his advice. As he gained confidence, his ventures became more daring. Often eloquent and persuasive, he could also play the tough guy, his language rough and frequently vulgar.

The collapse of the Soviet Union left him adrift until his extraordinary comeback in Kazakhstan. He negotiated most of the nation's major deals with foreign oilmen, including development of the giant offshore field Kashagan, employing a swaggering but skillful style that did not endear him to oil companies.

By 1995, he was calling himself "Counselor to the President." Giffen's vision of why he was in Kazakhstan seemed to have expanded accordingly. It would perhaps be too much to say that the brash American had decided that he was going to civilize the natives, but there was a hint of that. He preferred to say that he was a loyal friend of Kazakhstan, there not to enrich himself in oil deals but to help build a self-sufficient democracy.

Toward that end, he commissioned a blue-ribbon team of American and Canadian academics to write step-by-step proposals for new social security, monetary, and judicial systems, and even how to eradicate tuberculosis. He also arranged for the brightest stars in the Kazakhstan leadership to be tutored in politics and economics by professors from Harvard University's Kennedy School and Graduate School of Business.

Giffen called the sessions his own "private technical assistance program to Kazakhstan," though the Kazakh government paid the bills. During a weeklong gathering at Harvard, he showed up with a young Kazakh woman whom he introduced as a friend's daughter. He explained that she was thinking of applying to the university, but she made the distinct impression that she was more interested in shopping than investigating what Harvard had to offer. Meanwhile, she stayed with Giffen in his room.

For months, expert groups filtered into Kazakhstan. Among them was Michael McFaul, a leading academic authority on Russia. Over dinner one night, Giffen told the visitors that it was his mission to make Kazakhstan a better place. To McFaul, his passion seemed real. But when he began gulping shots of single-malt whiskey, Jim Giffen's manner deteriorated. He began boasting of his various triumphs in life, leaving the impression that he had held a full professorship at Columbia when in reality he had taught one-night-a-week business classes.

Then he whipped out his pass to Nazarbayev's presidential palace. "Ever seen an American with one like this?" he demanded to know. His guests seemed nonplussed, whereupon Giffen said they didn't "understand the world" because they were academics, unlike people such as him who "run the world." "He was doing things that had world implications. We were an ivory tower group," McFaul said.

The Americans treated his remarks with cheerful tolerance, but the Kazakhs present stiffened each time he bragged of his influence with their president.

Stories portraying Giffen as a mean drunk circulated widely in Almaty. At a restaurant one night, an American at a nearby table asserted that the Soviets had relied on the blood of people like the Kazakhs to defeat Nazi Germany. Overhearing the remarks, Giffen abruptly stood and demanded to know why the American was talking such rubbish. "Haven't you ever heard of Lend-Lease?" Giffen shouted.

"Haven't you ever heard of keeping your mouth shut?" replied the American, an excitable accountant named Bill Minarovich.

No one made a move then. But later, as Minarovich was on his way out, Giffen extended his foot and tripped the man. As he went down, the accountant tried taking a swing at his tormentor. Instead, he found himself flat on his back, with a Giffen bodyguard pointing a pistol at him. Militia men arrived within minutes. While the bodyguard loaded Giffen into a limousine, three soldiers kept the accountant on the ground, guns at the ready.

Former prime minister Balgimbayev, probably his closest Kazakh ally, advised Giffen to curtail the drinking. "That's not relevant. Next subject," Giffen responded. When the president himself suggested that Giffen regulate his intake of whiskey, Giffen retreated into silence. He didn't believe he had a problem, and it was true that each morning he showed up eager to tackle the day's problems, seemingly fresher than those who the night before hadn't touched a drop.

In advance of the 1999 national elections, Giffen added Kazakh presidential politics to his portfolio. He imported political operatives from Washington to advise him. At least once he traveled to a regional capital to speak on behalf of Nazarbayev before local political bosses, who "saw him as the pseudo-president, because that's what he wanted them to think," recalled Janet McElligot, an American consultant who went along on the trip.

Giffen's main assignment was to persuade the outside world that Kazakhstan was a democracy in the making. It was essentially a public relations problem: President Nazarbayev, already in office for a decade, needed to retain his grip on power without stirring unease in the West about his one-man rule.

That meant overcoming a persistent troublemaker named Akezhan Kazhegeldin, a former KGB officer whose intelligence contacts helped to make him a prosperous dealer in chemical fertilizer and black-market scrap metal. In the mid-1990s, the president had plucked him from obscurity and named him prime minister of Kazakhstan.

Soon, the new prime minister was busy heading a privatization program that sold decrepit but still valuable pieces of the nation's industrial base—oil fields, refineries, and the like. Giffen claimed that the sales made no business sense, and that the prime minister was motivated mainly by the opportunity to skim cash for himself. The assertion sounded more than a little self-serving on Giffen's part, since Kazhegeldin had barred him from some of the biggest deals.

Relations between the Kazakh president and his prime minister finally soured. Accurately believing that he was about to be fired, the forty-five-year-old Kazhegeldin went off to Switzerland, claiming to need treatment for a blood clot in his lung. But when the call for the 1999 elections was issued, he resurfaced to announce that he would be a candidate for president. In a country where Nazarbayev's reelection was regarded as preordained, it was a startling, even a dangerous gambit.

Shots were fired at Kazhegeldin outside a restaurant. An opposition newspaper funded by him was firebombed, people were beaten by thugs, and other similar incidents were reported. Asked later about the intimidation, Nazarbayev said Kazhegeldin had "organized it himself."

Kazhegeldin had succeeded in the public relations contest—western diplomats and journalists portrayed him as a more democratic candidate than Nazarbayev. But Nazarbayev held all the cards where it counted—in the rigged voting system. So Kazhegeldin offered to make peace if he could run for vice president. But Giffen advised Nazarbayev to say no because "that vice president could then go to a certain northern neighbor and say, 'I've got a little problem, and if you can help me solve it we'll split the pot.'" Giffen was suggesting that Kazhegeldin might ally himself with Russia to oust and then succeed the president.

Kazhegeldin had other cards to play. He had formed strong friend-ships with a number of westerners, who saw him as an advocate of eco-nomic reform. (One of them was with Bruce Kososki, a local Chevron representative. When the oilman's son was badly injured after coming into contact with a fallen electric wire, Kazhegeldin showed up with a stack of hundred-dollar bills, $20,000 in all, and told the oil executive to make sure his boy was well cared for.)

Vice President Al Gore was enlisted to telephone Nazarbayev and argue that Kazhegeldin should be allowed to run for the sake of the pres-ident's prestige in the United States and elsewhere.

But in the end the Kazakh strongman couldn't bring himself to agree. His onetime prime minister was fundamentally poisonous, he seemed to conclude, someone aspiring not for a place in Kazakhstan politics but for the president's destruction.

The day after Gore's call, the Kazakh Supreme Court disqualified Kazhegeldin. When a reporter asked why, Nazarbayev snapped: "Fifteen hundred companies are working here and no one wants a different presi-dent. Do you understand this? Write about it."

Nazarbayev won the election with an official 81 percent of the vote. Yet Kazhegeldin wouldn't give up. Calculating somewhat optimistically that he could leverage U.S. political support into a powerful position in his home-land, he launched an anti-Nazarbayev campaign in Washington. Russian and Kazakh tycoons looking to hedge their bets agreed to bankroll him.

He hired a lobbyist, an English-speaking former Soviet Army counter-intelligence officer named Rinat Akhmetshin. The stylish Akhmetshin looked harmless enough, with his designer spectacles and fresh, youthful face. But armed with a seemingly bottomless expense account and a sheaf of inside documents, the skilled Akhmetshin burrowed in with Washing-ton reporters, think tank experts, administration bureaucrats, and key po-litical figures. In a matter of months, he had managed to persuade many of them that Nazarbayev—arguably the most progressive leader in Central Asia—was the vilest of dictators.

All the while, Kazhegeldin was able to portray himself as a persecuted underdog—largely because he was. It was an image enhanced by the Kazakh government's repeated—and clumsy—attempts to put him behind bars.

First, he was arrested in Moscow on an international warrant requested by Kazakhstan; he won release by feigning a heart attack. Ten months later, he was taken into custody at Rome's Fiumicino Airport on the same charges. After that, European governments tired of the game and simply ignored the Kazakh warrants, which were seen as inherently political.

Then there was the plot by some Nazarbayev ministers to sell forty MiG jets to North Korea, apparently unaware that it was on a list of rogue nations barred by the United States from receiving arms. The 1960s-era planes were no match for modern fighters, but Washington objected nonetheless—they could make a difference on the Korean peninsula. Suddenly, about $75 million in much-needed U.S. aid to Kazakhstan was in jeopardy. Giffen helped persuade Nazarbayev to sideline the offending ministers and scotch the transaction, but not before the Kazakh president's reputation in the West had suffered additional damage.

Despite its rich petroleum reserves, Kazakhstan's government seemed continually short of cash. As Giffen put it, the country was bound to become "filthy rich" between 2005 and 2015, when crude oil exports would surge in a dramatic way. But the Kazakh fields were still some distance away from this bounty, and the nation was looking at a $1 billion budget deficit in 2000.

His solution was to sell off another piece of the government's share of Tengiz, the giant offshore field under development by Chevron. The idea troubled some ministers, especially those who already resented Giffen's influence with their president; it seemed to them that the American was about to fritter away Kazakhstan's patrimony for short-term gain. But Giffen had used the same strategy to raise about $1 billion in previous years to tide over the national treasury without doing notable damage to the long-term value of Kazakhstan's oil holdings. The government's immediate need for economic stability trumped all else, he argued. Besides, he had in mind a scheme that he asserted could enrich Kazakhstan several times over. In addition to demanding that the buyer pay double what Giffen had collected only a year earlier for an unproven slice of the Kashagan field, he had his eye on a long list of extras.

The most extraordinary of these was a profit-sharing formula that would generate additional cash for the Kazakh government if the market price of crude oil surged in the future. The buyer would have to relinquish excess profits when oil prices climbed above, say, $35 or $40 a barrel—at the time, thought by oilmen to be an unlikely prospect, but that actually did occur in 2005, when prices soared above $70 a barrel. In addition, the buyer would have to provide Kazakhstan with a low-interest loan of several hundred million dollars.

Giffen would use the resulting pool of money to balance the state budget and open two investment funds. One would be a carbon copy of the Alaska Natural Resources Fund, the often thousand-dollar-plus annual dividend that each Alaskan received as his or her share of the state's oil revenue. The second fund would be a lure for western pension funds and government-backed institutions like the World Bank to invest in Kazakhstan. Giffen envisioned attracting perhaps nine dollars of outside money for every one dollar put up by Kazakhstan. He figured he could generate $4 billion for the investment funds this way.

It was a typically bold Giffen venture. He was confident that a Tengiz sale would attract great interest even though the oil industry was still in shock after the plunge in crude prices a year earlier. In fact, he figured, that scare would play into his hands, since the suddenly risk-shy oil multinationals had largely stopped exploring for new fields and were trying to build up their inventories by buying already-found oil. Tengiz, the world's sixth-largest oil field, posed no exploratory risk.

Moreover, he had access to sophisticated financial models similar to those used by oil companies to assess prospective deals, thanks to his Swiss banker, a youthful executive from Crédit Agricole Indosuez named Jean-Jacques Bovay. With Bovay's expert bank colleagues and reams of computer calculations, Giffen always seemed to know "exactly how much blood was in the turnip." The trick, Giffen said, was to leak out just a bit of well-timed information and create a "feeding frenzy."

So it was that he sent off letters to twenty-eight private and national oil companies in nineteen countries announcing the sale. Eleven replies of interest came back almost immediately, five of which Giffen took seriously.

In January 2000, he settled on Italy's ENI, a state-owned company that only recently had emerged as a global competitor in energy. For ENI, capturing a piece of Tengiz would be equivalent to its winning the trifecta, making the Milan-based company the only one with shares in all three Kazakh oil giants—Tengiz, Kashagan, and Karachaganak, all among the world's ten largest fields.

ENI's negotiating team agreed to every one of his demands and offered $1.05 billion for 10 percent of Kazakhstan's holdings in Tengiz— a dazzling price that seemed to indicate that Giffen had not lost his touch.

But the company's executive committee, troubled by some of the details in Giffen's list of "extras," rejected the deal at the last minute.

It was an embarrassing setback for the American, who had relied on his personal influence with President Nazarbayev to steer the elaborate proposal past its opponents in the Kazakh government.

In some quarters, Giffen's stumble was cause for satisfaction. At Chevron, for example, the letter inviting bids on Tengiz had been treated with seeming indifference. In fact, Dick Matzke, the California company's wheeler-dealer executive, had been intensely interested. And no wonder.

It was the white-haired Matzke who had negotiated his company's original Tengiz contract; later, he had been forced to yield 5 percent of the prized field to Russia's Lukoil to mollify Moscow's objections to an export pipeline project. But Chevron's current 45 percent ownership of Tengiz was still by far the most valuable of the firm's global oil holdings. When Giffen suddenly put more of Tengiz up for sale, it seemed a golden opportunity for the company to push its share over 50 percent.

Even so, Matzke, now the company's vice chairman, had taken a pass. He so mistrusted Giffen that he had been unwilling to make a bid; he thought the boisterous middleman had forced other companies into outrageous financial concessions. In fact, the Chevron executive had detested Giffen from the time they first met a decade earlier, and the years of occasional contact since then hadn't softened his feelings. Giffen felt the same way. Though the men were alike in temperament, self-regard, and love of the deal, neither could see past their mutual hatred.

Now Matzke, who would do almost anything to move his nemesis out of the way, wondered if the ENI rejection had given him an opening. What if he could finesse the Tengiz acquisition without having to deal with Giffen? Perhaps he could form an alliance with someone powerful in Kazakhstan who disliked this guy as much as he did.

The Chevron executive was about to set in motion a chain of events that would leave Giffen a significantly weakened player.

Matzke's chosen ally was Nurlan Kapparov, an accomplished business-man who owned Almaty's best French restaurant and a chain of luxury re-tail shops. Until recently, Kapparov had also been the head of Kazakhoil, the state oil company; then he made the mistake of leading the opposition to Giffen's scheme to sell off part of Tengiz and was expelled from his ex-ecutive position as punishment. Now a mere vice minister of energy, he was delighted by any opportunity to exact revenge on Giffen.

Kapparov had argued against the sale on the grounds that its terms would have left Kazakhstan owning slightly less than one fifth of the en-tire oil field. At that level of ownership, the nation would lose its "block-ing rights," its ability to halt anything that its foreign partners wanted to undertake at Tengiz.

Matzke, aware of Kapparov's fear of losing all control of the field, shrewdly tailored his proposal accordingly. Instead of buying 10 percent of Kazakhstan's Tengiz holdings—what Giffen had put out to bid— Chevron would settle for 5 percent. The difference would be just enough to allow the Kazakhs to retain blocking rights.

Moreover, the company would accelerate payment of a $420 million bonus due Kazakhstan the following year. Chevron chairman Ken Derr only months earlier had refused a Kazakh plea for early payment. But now that Matzke wanted more of Tengiz, he would do whatever he could to make his offer appear more generous.

Kapparov liked what Matzke was proposing. Both realized that if to-gether they could engineer a Chevron victory on Tengiz, it would demon-strate that a major deal could be done without Giffen. The oil world would see that the King of Kazakhstan wore no clothes, so to speak.

And so the Chevron man and the wealthy Kazakh bureaucrat struck up a clandestine partnership, each separately lobbying the president of Kazakhstan for support. Kapparov argued that it was time for the Kazakhs to run their own negotiations. In years past they may have lacked the skills, but now they were able to hold their own with the oil companies. No outside help was needed. His pitch appealed to Nazarbayev's nationalist instincts. "Okay, just for this deal," the president replied. "Let's see what you can do."

When it was Matzke's turn, he and Derr went on a hunting trip with Nazarbayev to make their pitch. The president seemed receptive; on a piece of paper he scrawled the three conditions that were most important to him: The oil company would pay $400 million in cash for 5 percent of the Kazakh share of Tengiz, it would donate $20 million to a fund to build the new capital of Astana, and it would make the $420 million accelerated bonus payment offered by Matzke.

Nazarbayev handed the paper to his new prime minister, Kasymzhomart Tokayev, and then issued a surprising instruction. The two Chevron men should negotiate with the prime minister only. "Don't deal with anyone else," he said. Matzke took that to mean that he could freeze Giffen out of the process and that Nazarbayev would not object.

It was odd, seemingly a sudden act of presidential disloyalty to Giffen. A charitable explanation might be that Nazarbayev simply rushed to embrace the Chevron deal now that the Giffen-brokered sale to ENI was dead. But in Matzke's view, "it was clear that if it happened without a middleman, there would never be another middleman in another deal again. It was the impression I had, and the impression that the president gave me."

In other words, deliberately or not, Nazarbayev was empowering Matzke and Kapparov to proceed without consulting Giffen. And that is what they did. In May 2000, with Giffen out of the country on a business trip, the prime minister of Kazakhstan signed a preliminary agreement granting Chevron the 5 percent share of Tengiz. In a stroke, the Kazakhs had signaled that a big oil deal could be negotiated without their American gatekeeper.

It was a stunning loss of prestige and influence for Giffen. His boastful warning to foreign oilmen anxious to do business in Kazakhstan—deal with me or you'll never get through the front door—had lost all credibility.

Hearing the news when a reporter reached him in Rome, Giffen was asked for comment on the transaction.

"That's news to me," he responded, wholly surprised.

Back in Kazakhstan, Giffen insisted that he could negotiate a better deal with Chevron and was allowed to take part in the final round of contract talks. But he was reduced to the role of adviser to Kapparov, Matzke's secret partner in the scheme to undo him.

From the sidelines, Giffen did his best to exact concessions from the oil company. When the talks stalled on the issue of profit sharing, he produced calculations that argued for terms more favorable to Kazakhstan.

Chevron dismissed his numbers as a negotiating ploy, and Kapparov in a memo to his Kazakh colleagues said that Giffen had likely fabricated them. In fact, Kapparov was wrong—the calculations were solid. But his memo further undermined Giffen's standing with the Kazakhs.

Giffen persisted, declaring that the deal would fall apart if Chevron did not give ground. There were two other suitors waiting in the wings, he said, seeming to imply that France's Total and, once again, ENI were ready to make offers.

Matzke called both companies that night and was told they had no bids in the works. When the Chevron executive reported his findings the next day, Giffen remained silent. His bluff had been called. The Chevron contract would be concluded by the Kazakh negotiators.

Later, at the Intercontinental Hotel, Chevron financial analyst Irwin Lichtblau, an old hand in Tengiz negotiations, watched a subdued Giffen enter the bar. "Congratulations. You won this one," said Giffen, extending his hand with apparent sincerity to the Chevron man.

Giffen never was certain why, after all he had done to make Kazakhstan a world class player in the oil industry, Nazarbayev had not come to his rescue. Perhaps the Kazakh president had decided to cut down to size someone who had become too influential. He did that from time to time, and Giffen may have been only the latest to be reminded who was really in charge.

Years later, a still-gloating Matzke observed that perhaps Nazarbayev simply "wanted to clean up the system, and this was a way to do it." But he also acknowledged that Chevron's brazen challenge to Giffen had been a risky play. At times, he said, "I felt I could die" chasing the 5 percent. That seemed an exaggeration—opposing Giffen was not known to have ever resulted in a fatality. Yet it was no more exaggerated than Giffen's occasional hints that physical harm could come to those who crossed the wrong people.

Giffen embarked on a determined effort to restore his standing in Kazakh ruling circles. But he was about to be overtaken by something far more serious than being an outcast middleman. Investigators for the American government had him in their sights. Giffen's fresh troubles were among the fallouts of a chain of events unwittingly set in motion many months earlier by Rakhat Aliyev, President Nazarbayev's eldest son-in-law. Aliyev, deputy secret police chief of Almaty, had been searching for a way to punish his father-in-law's old political foe, the former prime minister and erstwhile presidential candidate Akezhan Kazhegeldin. He hit on a scheme to unmask the former prime minister as a financial criminal.

The son-in-law claimed to have intelligence that Kazhegeldin was planning to buy a house outside of Brussels for his daughter. He told the Belgians that the former prime minister intended to pay with cash that he had skimmed from his privatization deals and squirreled away in Belgium. Out went a request via Interpol that Belgian authorities look into Kazhegeldin's financial dealings there. Back came the answer Aliyev was seeking—Belgium would be happy to oblige. What the Belgians didn't tell him was that they had, as a matter of routine, copied his request to the neighboring country of Switzerland, where shady individuals might be more likely to attempt money laundering.

Daniel Devaud, a prosecuting magistrate in Geneva, responded with an equally routine request to Swiss banks, asking them to search records for any account held by Kazhegeldin. Because it was an unusual name that could be easily misspelled, he asked that the search include accounts containing the word *Kazakhstan*. While Swiss banks were well-known for the discretion they offered the world's wealthiest people, the government could be brutal if it detected violations of banking rules.

As the responses came in, there was nothing implicating Kazhegeldin. Instead, two other transactions stood out. In the first, $85 million in a Kazakh government account at Crédit Agricole Indosuez had been transferred into a personal account after the magistrate had issued his request for information. In the second, the money had been transferred to yet another Kazakhstan state account at a second bank, Pictet & Cie.

It appeared that whoever controlled the personal account had been warned of the magistrate's inquiry and was trying to camouflage the money—but couldn't decide precisely how. His curiosity piqued, Devaud looked up the name of the account's beneficial owner. It was Nursultan Nazarbayev, the president of Kazakhstan.

The magistrate, suspecting that something irregular was going on, ordered all the suspect accounts frozen. His action was not publicly announced, but news of it broke in *The New York Times* four months later, in October 1999. The report went largely unnoticed. Nazarbayev banned the story from his own media, and when a Russian television station aired a version, he blocked the station's transmissions into Kazakhstan for three days.

Nazarbayev put his lawyers to work trying to unfreeze the accounts while the Swiss magistrate pondered what to do next. It was a frustrating situation. Only recently, the Swiss had been unable to prosecute a case of alleged money laundering involving the eldest daughter of Russian president Boris Yeltsin. Swiss law effectively required the participation of a foreign suspect's government in the prosecution of such cases, something Russia would not do when it came to the president's relatives.

The Kazakh case appeared to be going the same way. There was no likelihood that his own government was going to supply evidence against President Nazarbayev. But then, poring over the bank records, the magistrate came across an American connection.

A U.S. businessman named James H. Giffen had been wiring money into the Swiss accounts of well-connected Kazakhs. As Devaud dug more deeply, he established that U.S. oil companies operating in Kazakhstan had been sending "bonus payments" to a New York bank account officially belonging to the Kazakh government but secretly controlled by Giffen. The American, in turn, had channeled the payments to the accounts of Kazakh insiders, including the president. Such payments to foreign governments for rights to oil fields were standard in the industry. But they were illegal under U.S. law if the money went to a foreign official with the intent of influencing his actions. Then they became bribery.

Devaud saw a possible opening. Swiss law allowed him in effect to piggyback on the prosecution of a foreign national in another country if the alleged misdeeds had a connection to Switzerland as well. Indeed, virtually anyone entangled in such situations could be prosecuted by the magistrate. This meant that if Giffen were indicted in the United States, Devaud could charge any of the Kazakhs linked to the transactions, from Nazarbayev on down.

In April 2000, the magistrate brought his findings to the U.S. Department of Justice, and the two governments began cooperating in a money-laundering investigation aimed squarely at Jim Giffen.

The particulars were spelled out in a confidential eighteen-page letter from American prosecutors to Devaud, sent in June. The letter asked for assistance in a probe of "the alleged use of U.S. banks to funnel funds belonging to certain oil companies through Swiss bank accounts and shell companies in Switzerland and the British Virgin Islands for ultimate transfer to present and former high-ranking officials of Kazakhstan."

The letter asserted that Nazarbayev and other senior Kazakhs had received under-the-table payments from at least six major oil deals going back to 1995—almost every big transaction that Giffen had negotiated. The payments from U.S. oil companies alone were said to have totaled $85 million. Additional bonuses had been paid by European oil companies, but they were not under scrutiny because bribery was legal at the time under the laws of their countries.

Documents in the case were obtained almost immediately by Akezhan Kazhegeldin, the politician whom Nazarbayev's police chief son-in-law had set out to incriminate. Through his well-connected Washington lieutenant, Rinat Akhmetshin, he was delighted to pass them on to human rights lawyers and journalists, and soon the tribulations of Giffen and the Kazakh leadership were being reported around the world.

Former prime minister Nurlan Balgimbayev, Giffen's close ally and next-door neighbor in Almaty, was one of those implicated in the transactions. Dispatched to defend the Kazakh elite, he told a news conference: "I can directly say and even guarantee that I am clean." Balgimbayev then suggested that oil envy was behind a foreign conspiracy to harm his nation.

"Why did similar articles appear simultaneously in three respected Western publications?" he asked. "Why, if anyone intends to conduct an investigation, did they allow such publications before the end of the case?" He concluded: "Somebody cannot sleep because we found first oil at the first exploratory well" at Kashagan.

Giffen called the allegations "bullshit," arguing that he had only been "doing what we were told." He said he had wondered if he should list the Kazakh accounts on his income tax returns, but a lawyer said it was unnecessary since he was only a trustee and not a beneficiary of the Kazakh accounts. He began showing the lawyer's letter around as proof that he had nothing to worry about.

He also thought he held a trump card—his decades of close contact with U.S. intelligence services. Since his days with Ara Oztemel starting in 1968, Giffen had made a point of always reporting his activities to contacts at the National Security Council and the CIA and regularly socializing with CIA agents.

According to former agent Robert Baer, Giffen was instrumental in halting Kazakh sales of advanced surface-to-air Russian missiles to Iran and North Korea. A senior State Department official "made the problem quietly disappear with a couple of phone calls to Giffen," Baer wrote.

Of course, Giffen had his own reasons for cooperating with the CIA and other U.S. agencies. It was a way to enhance his prestige, not only in Washington but in foreign capitals as well. In Kazakhstan, for instance, by helping to smooth the MiG controversy, he had strengthened his own hand with Nazarbayev. And at almost any opportunity he fed his reputation for having powerful friends by dropping suggestive hints of intelligence he possessed, implying that the CIA was the source.

Now he viewed himself as Washington's best source of information on the inner workings of Kazakhstan, and he was confident that that would protect him from prosecution. He told Nazarbayev the same— everything was under control.

In fact, everything was out of control. By spring 2003, a federal grand jury in New York had assembled a fifty-five-page sealed indictment of Giffen, accusing him of violating American law by bribing foreign officials, racketeering, laundering money, and engaging in fraud.

The document, later unsealed, described a complicated web of transactions through which millions of dollars from American oil companies had been secretly funneled to Nazarbayev and other Kazakh insiders and their families. Giffen was accused of directing the entire scheme and of passing along some $77 million to Nazarbayev and Balgimbayev, his protégé. The indictment alleged some of the ways that the two officials spent the money, including Balgimbayev's purchase of about $180,000 in jewelry and a stay at a Swiss spa and Nazarbayev's payment of $45,000 in tuition at an exclusive Swiss school for his youngest daughter, Aliya. Giffen personally bought millions of dollars in gifts for the two officials and their wives, including jewelry, fur coats, and an $80,000 Donzi speedboat, according to the indictment.

The convoluted string of financial dealings, resembling the way organized crime rings moved money around, seemed hard to defend. Giffen's claim, when the scandal first broke, that he was simply following instructions was unpersuasive. While the Kazakhs certainly made clear their appetite for a share of the proceeds, it was difficult to believe that they had specified that the money be divided into small parcels, moved from account to account, then reassembled.

It wasn't clear how much Giffen himself had profited financially. When one added up all the transfers, some $39 million was left over for him. But out of that, he covered the fees of the various private consultants he had hired on behalf of Kazakhstan to stand up to the teams of oil company negotiators.

On March 31, 2003, Giffen arrived at JFK International Airport, intending to meet up with his lawyers for an evening flight to Europe. The trip would be an opportunity for them to review material for his defense; they would disembark in Paris to take depositions while Giffen flew on to Kazakhstan alone.

Making his separate way into the terminal, Giffen lawyer Steven Cohen bumped into an old colleague from his days at the U.S. Attorney's Office.

"We're arresting a guy. We're doing a takedown," he told Cohen, without mentioning a name.

Moments later, Cohen heard a commotion behind him. Turning, he saw a cluster of FBI agents and a familiar face—Giffen, smirking and rolling his eyes, under arrest. Federal authorities had made a last-minute decision to seize him at the airport after learning that he had purchased a one-way Air France ticket to Kazakhstan via Paris. They concluded that he must be fleeing the country. In fact, Giffen had simply divided his trip between two different airlines; his return ticket, on Lufthansa through Frankfurt, was in his pocket.

The chief FBI agent present spotted Cohen. "How did you get here so fast?" he asked.

After the mix-up was sorted out, federal prosecutors were apologetic. They had not known that Cohen and Giffen's chief lawyer, William Schwartz, would be accompanying their client. Obviously, if Giffen were on the run, his attorneys were not going to be part of it. Both were former federal prosecutors and not likely to make themselves parties to a felony.

But there was no way to repair the awkward situation. The warrant and other paperwork were too far advanced to allow Giffen to go free and surrender voluntarily later. He was handcuffed, then photographed and fingerprinted in Manhattan before being placed in a holding cell at the New York Correctional Center, the prison facility attached to the federal courthouse. The next day, bail was set at $10 million; he put up his two Westchester houses as collateral and was released.

A few months later, Bryan Williams, the Mobil Oil lawyer to whom Giffen had wired $2 million for his crucial role as valiant ally in the pipeline wars, pleaded guilty to tax evasion for not reporting the payment as income. Federal prosecutors tried to get him to testify against Giffen, but Williams insisted he knew nothing about the Swiss accounts. He was sentenced to forty-six months in prison.

Giffen's predicament left at least one of his former mentors unmoved. In Beaufort, South Carolina, Bill Verity, his former boss at Armco, saw it as convincing evidence of Giffen's willingness to cut corners to get ahead. "Now he's getting his comeuppance," Verity said.

Jim Giffen vowed to wage a tenacious legal fight. He said that he would not bargain with the federal attorneys; either the government would absolve him or he would go to trial. After all, he insisted, he effectively had been operating as a U.S. agent in Kazakhstan—Washington's man on the inside in one of the most strategic regions of the world. If that had required him to act as the Kazakh president's private banker—not that he was admitting to it—well, then, he was delighted to have served his country.

But his reign as the Caspian's most powerful dealmaker was over. The King of Kazakhstan had finally been dethroned.

MICHAEL TOWNSHEND STOOD ON A TURKISH BEACH ON
the Mediterranean and peered at the *British Hawthorn,* an oil tanker moored
offshore. It was an emotional moment for the British Petroleum executive.
The Italy-bound ship was about to take on six hundred thousand barrels
of crude, the first cargo of oil to be released from the Baku-Ceyhan
pipeline. In May 2006, more than fifteen years after the great pipeline had
first been envisioned, it was finally operational, a thousand-mile cylinder
of steel entirely filled with crude.

Townshend had been a Washington lobbyist for BP in the mid-1990s,
when the pipeline was only the vague idea of a few oilmen and Clinton administration officials. The tall, lanky Briton ended up managing the global
consortium of oil companies that built the $3.8 billion project. Now, their
task done, he and some colleagues donned swim trunks and dived into the
warm sea—a "cleansing moment" he had long dreamed about.

"It's a strange pipeline in that the more you do, the less you see,"
Townshend said. "You actually know when it's all done when you see that
physical tanker at the other end, and it's not until that moment you can say
that it's all done."

When Baku-Ceyhan officially came on line a few months later, in the
summer of 2006, it symbolized the fulfillment of America's Caspian initiative, a campaign to draw the region away from Russia and Iran and into
the embrace of the West. As such, the pipeline represented a rare
post–Cold War foreign policy triumph for the United States, chiefly an
achievement of the Clinton administration with the later support of the
George W. Bush White House. It anchored America's physical presence on

the Caspian, already conspicuous in the wake of the September 11, 2001, terrorist attacks on New York and Washington. For a few years after those signal events, Central Asia and the Caucasus became effective U.S. protectorates, with the establishment of military bases and the deployment of military advisers throughout.

The judgment of those in the U.S. government who had promoted the pipeline was harshly criticized at times by academics, European leaders, and even oilmen. But the policy seemed prescient indeed when the first tankers loaded at Ceyhan. Hundreds of thousands of barrels a day of new crude were entering the market just as global oil supplies were becoming extremely tight.

The timing of the pipeline project seemed especially fortuitous in geopolitical terms. It had its beginnings when Russia's economy was in tatters and Moscow's ability to resist western incursions in territory it once ruled was at low ebb. A delay of a few years might well have changed the outcome. For Russia roared back onto the world stage more rapidly than anyone could have expected, powered by a startling surge in oil revenue. Around the time that Townshend and his BP crew were bathing in the Mediterranean, Russia was overtaking Saudi Arabia as the world's largest oil producer. New technology introduced after the breakup of the Soviet Union had reinvigorated Russian oil fields, and the price of crude soared—at one point reaching almost $78 a barrel, more than seven times its low just eight years earlier.

Flush with oil export dollars, Russian president Vladimir Putin gathered state power to himself by bringing much of the country's energy sector under his direct control. Extremely favorable exploration deals that foreign oilmen had extracted from Boris Yeltsin and a weakened Russia in the early and mid-1990s suddenly were subject to renegotiation. Exxon, BP, Royal Dutch/Shell, and Total of France were particular targets. To make his resolve unambiguous, Putin temporarily shut down a Shell project on Sakhalin Island, in Russia's Far East, forcing the Anglo-Dutch company and its Japanese partners, Mitsui and Mitsubishi, to sell half their holding to the mostly state-owned Russian giant Gazprom. There was grumbling that in Russia a deal was a deal—until Moscow decided it wasn't. The Russians and many oil experts countered that the newly confident nation was simply recovering the ground it had lost to foreigners, who had exploited its previously perilous condition.

Western anxiety over Moscow's intentions heightened especially in early and late 2006, when Russia briefly suspended natural gas and oil exports to Europe. The Kremlin's history of using energy as a blunt instrument to conduct business in the Caspian and elsewhere seemed to be repeating itself. This time, a pricing dispute had prompted Moscow to shut down its gas pipeline to Ukraine, through which Russia's natural gas flowed to Europe, in January 2006. Although the Europeans were not the intended target, the event alarmed a continent that relied on Russia for about 30 percent of its natural gas and oil. Those apprehensions were exacerbated in December 2006, when a dispute with Belarus severed part of the oil flow to Europe.

Russia was also frustrating the Europeans by keeping its grip on gas exports from Turkmenistan and Kazakhstan. The two Caspian nations were forced to sell their gas at cut-rate prices to Russia, which profited handsomely by marking up the fuel and selling it at export. Moscow used its accustomed leverage: It denied the two states the use of Russian export pipelines, effectively marooning their large gas reserves. The strategy for cowing the states continued to work despite U.S. offers of leverage—in May 2007, Moscow persuaded Turkmenistan and Kazakhstan to decline a renewed U.S. plan to build an independent natural gas pipeline from Central Asia to Baku, bypassing Russia. Instead, the two countries agreed to erect yet another pipeline connecting their fields to Russia, locking in their dependence.

Once again, Turkmenistan and Kazakhstan had failed to replicate the will and vision through which Azerbaijan and Georgia had realized the Baku-Ceyhan pipeline. Consequently, they appeared likely for the forseeable future to remain politically marooned amid larger and stronger states.

Europe's most outspoken states, like Poland, tried to step in and persuade Moscow to allow them to import the Turkmen and Kazakh gas without Russian intervention. "We feel very unsafe" relying on Russian gas, said Piotr Woźniak, the economy minister in charge of Poland's energy policy. But Moscow wouldn't relent, and appeared to be marching west with its economic power, a different kind of challenge to Europe from the military one it had posed decades earlier.

Russia continued to needle Georgia, apparently unwilling to yield what remained of its leverage over the former Soviet republic. The Kremlin backed separatists who controlled swaths of Georgian territory, and it frequently squeezed the country's supply of natural gas, ostensibly to enforce price increases. But by 2007, British Petroleum was sending natural gas through a pipeline that it had built across Georgia as a companion to the Baku-Ceyhan oil pipeline. By tapping the line, Georgia said it could reduce its reliance on Russian natural gas from 100 percent to just 30 percent or so of its needs.

Along with its pipeline policy, the United States promoted western-style democratic practices in the former Soviet republics not only to usher in reform but also to prevent a resumption of Russian domination. Elections were held and judged to be fair in some cases. The results almost always favored existing rulers, with Georgia being the notable exception.

While the existence of the Baku-Ceyhan pipeline created the opportunity for change, the autocrats now in control around the Caspian were unlikely to weaken their hold on power, nor to alter political course dramatically. The foundation for reform existed, made possible by the pipeline's guarantee of economic security and independent statehood, but it would be up to future generations to act.

Nursultan Nazarbayev

The president of Kazakhstan continued to build his new capital of Astana. One addition was a 203-foot-tall glass pyramid, designed by British architect Norman Foster. Nazarbayev also commissioned a steel observation tower, at the top of which was a gold-and-silver triangle impressed with his palm print.

Grandiosity aside, by 2007 he had led Kazakhstan to the brink of vast wealth. Everywhere was a building boom. A fairly large and affluent middle class was expanding. The economy had grown by nearly 10 percent a year since 2000, per capita income had more than tripled to about $5,000 a year, and the percentage of the population in extreme poverty had fallen to 10 percent. Some $17.5 billion of the country's revenue was deposited in a national rainy day fund, and any future acceleration in crude oil production would build it further.

Nazarbayev had failed to build geopolitical leverage by linking up

Kazakhstan's pipeline infrastructure to the West. Yet he had otherwise shrewdly balanced the demands of the great powers—Russia and China, right on Kazakhstan's borders, versus the United States—and made his country relatively secure for the first time in a century and a half. There was a measure of personal freedom and qualitative distance from its Central Asian neighbors—Uzbekistan's systematic torture, Tajikistan's civil war, Turkmenistan's descent as a failed state, Kyrgyzstan's perpetual disorder.

Yet in summer 2007, Nazarbayev assumed some of the more dictatorial aspects of those regimes, granting himself the constitutional right to be president for life if he so decided, rather than being forced to step down in 2012. At the same time, he lifted the sole remaining grounds on which he could be impeached, allowing himself to retain power even if he committed treason. Scandal always seemed to be in the air. His appetite for personal fortune and the evidence of Swiss bank accounts fattened by oil company payoffs gave him the appearance of a sultan who thought it his due to feed off the country's wealth.

Nazarbayev was still an unindicted co-conspirator in his former oil adviser Jim Giffen's legal entanglement in New York. But in May 2007, the Kazakh president tried finally to cut the political damage inflicted by the continuing Swiss bank scandal, agreeing to a deal with U.S. prosecutors to forfeit the $84 million in alleged bribes underlying the case against Giffen. Under the arrangement, the World Bank would supervise distribution of the money to programs benefiting poor children in Kazakhstan.

Then the Nazarbayev name became more tarnished: That same month, Nazarbayev ordered the arrest of his eldest son-in-law, Rakhat Aliyev, on racketeering charges involving the roughing up of a pair of executives at a bank Aliyev controlled. Aliyev long had a reputation for using intimidation to his advantage in business, but the irony was rich. Eight years after he had hunted down former Kazakhstan prime minister Akezhan Kazhegeldin across Europe, Aliyev himself was on the run when his father-in-law issued an international arrest warrant for him. Austrian authorities finally arrested Aliyev, but he was fighting any return home, and it looked like he might prevail since there was no extradition treaty between the two countries. "In Kazakhstan I am now enemy No. 1 and if I returned, I would be a walking corpse," Aliyev said.

There was reason for Aliyev's apprehension. For if Kazhegeldin, the former prime minister, were to return to Kazakhstan from exile, for instance, he certainly would face immediate imprisonment, regardless of any assurances to the contrary, or even murder.

It was now in some cases deadly to be a Nazarbayev opponent. Two of them—one named Zamanbek Nurkadilov and the other Altynbek Sarsenbayev—were murdered execution-style in separate incidents. Police ruled the former a suicide, although the man was found with two bullet holes in his chest and one in his head.

The following month more bad news for the now-exposed Aliyev arrived in the form of a fax: Dariga Nazarbayeva, his wife, had divorced him; he said someone forged his signature on the legal document. Whatever the case, by falling afoul of Nazarbayev, Aliyev was stripped of his titles, his connection to Central Asian royalty, and perhaps his fortune.

Meanwhile, Nazarbayev's younger son-in-law, Timur Kulibayev, accumulated more and more power. He controlled the state oil sector on Nazarbayev's behalf, and was the country's biggest private oilman at the same time that he was deciding who could drill in Kazakhstan. Energy companies often had to make the fellow a partner in order to do business there.

In 2007, Sacha Baron Cohen won a Golden Globe award for his work in *Borat: Cultural Learnings of America for Make Benefit Glorious Nation of Kazakhstan*, in which he played a Kazakh television reporter whose cultural and ethnic bumblings revealed America's own biases. After Kazakh officials initially expressed outrage over the misportrayal of their country, for example as anti-Semitic, it was Aliyev, before his downfall, who recognized the film as a potential publicity bonanza. He invited Cohen to visit his country and discover that "women drive cars, wine is made of grapes, and Jews are free to go to synagogues."

In May 2006, Vice President Dick Cheney flew into Astana to shore up relations with the leader of a country that within a decade was expected to be exporting more than 2 million barrels of oil a day. Asked by reporters about Nazarbayev's human rights record, Cheney said he felt "admiration for all that's been accomplished here in Kazakhstan."

Heydar Aliyev

Azerbaijan's ruler died in the Cleveland Clinic in Ohio in December 2003, and he left behind a mixed legacy. He had governed as an autocrat and failed to lay a foundation for eventual power sharing and honest elections. But he ingeniously conceived the multinational oil consortium that underpinned Azerbaijan's independence, and he led the way for the Baku-Ceyhan pipeline that cemented the autonomy of his country and of the region as a whole. The contribution of those who partnered with him—Georgia, Turkey, the United States, and, of course, the oil companies—could not be discounted, but he influenced events more than any single person.

In October 2003, Heydar was succeeded by his son Ilham, whose rise to power had been carefully engineered by his father. President George W. Bush telephoned congratulations, and Ilham, while a less dominant personality than the senior Aliyev, soon proved up to the task of wielding power in chaotic Azerbaijan. By 2007, he had fired and begun prosecuting some of his father's closest business associates, men who had held powerful positions in the government and in state-owned enterprises.

From the start, Azerbaijan had been a prime candidate for the so-called resource curse—the phenomenon of oil-rich countries becoming lazy once petrodollars started rolling in and then misallocating the profits and ending up economically worse off. The Azeri economy was growing in double digits for the fifth straight year in 2007, thanks to oil revenue. But Ilham, like his father, failed to take advantage of a brief window of opportunity to build a balanced economy so that when the oil dollars began to wane, other industries could pick up the slack. Nor had he built up sizable reserves for the eventuality of hard times; Azerbaijan had just $1.4 billion in its national oil fund, about 10 percent of Kazakhstan's savings.

The Kazakhs, with oil fields that would produce through the middle of the twenty-first century and beyond, could afford such mistaken judgment. Azerbaijan could not; the peak of its oil dollars was on the visible horizon—between 2015 and 2020. After that, it seemed likely to struggle.

Eduard Shevardnadze

A popular revolt in 2003 drove the famous former Soviet statesman out of office. Georgia's first post-Soviet president had held power too long, lost his feel for the people, and squandered his reputation in election fraud and corruption scandals. He had allowed the region's most dynamic democracy to take hold in Georgia, and in the end it brought him down.

His successor, a 36-year-old U.S.-trained lawyer named Mikheil Saakashvili, belittled Shevardnadze for so single-mindedly focusing on the Baku-Ceyhan pipeline while failing to resolve the republic's systemic difficulties. There was some truth to Saakashvili's criticism of his predecessor's rule, but no one could deny the pipeline's inestimable value to the young nation.

Its fundamental importance was that it firmly aligned Georgia with the West. While Russian harassment on various fronts would persist, the Kremlin's sway over the Georgian economy was irrevocably weakened, as evidenced by the natural gas turnabout in 2007; Russia's ability to use its natural gas monopoly to squeeze Georgia was lessened. And the stronger Georgia's bonds with the West and neighboring Turkey became, the less vulnerable it would be. Credit for all of that belonged to Shevardnadze.

The deposed ruler symbolized the improbable alliance of Kremlin-trained autocrats and young American diplomats who equated an oil pipeline with national independence, and willed it into existence. In 2007, he was living in his former presidential home in the capital of Tbilisi.

Saparmurat Niyazov

The eccentric ruler of Turkmenistan, who created a cult of personality at his people's expense, died in December 2006 of cardiac arrest. Another autocrat, a deputy prime minister named Kurbanguly Berdymukhamedov, succeeded him. None of the monuments raised to Niyazov's glory was immediately removed, but large portraits of Berdymukhamedov started to go up in public places.

John Deuss

After his defeat by the combined forces of the U.S. government and Chevron, the Dutch oil trader left Kazakhstan far behind and retreated to his estate on the island of Bermuda. He kept his hand in oil, exploring for crude in places like Nigeria and Indonesia and running a refinery in Louisiana. But his days as an important force in the energy sector were over.

He went into finance, focusing especially on two small banks that he controlled, both of which catered to global investors. He continued to ride jumping horses in competition, regularly winning events in the seniors category. Divorced from his first wife, Deuss married a younger rider named Francis Jardine. Their marriage ended in divorce in 2005.

The next year, investigators in the United Kingdom and the Netherlands began examining what became known as the "carousel" scandal, in which hundreds of cellular telephone traders allegedly earned tens of millions of dollars in fraudulently collected import and export tax refunds. A common link soon became apparent—virtually all of the traders were clients of First Curaçao International Bank, one of the Dutchman's two banks.

In September 2006, authorities raided the Deuss family home in the Netherlands, where his sister, Tineke, a director of the banking enterprises, lived. She and Deuss were separately detained—she in the United Kingdom, he in the Caribbean—for investigation of alleged money laundering.

A press report described the sixty-four-year-old Deuss as "painfully thin" and "a strangely lonely and still figure" in a Bermuda courtroom after three nights in jail. "He kept his head mostly bowed and his eyes down. His right hand held one leg of his spectacles, betraying the slightest tremble." The Dutchman was voluntarily extradited to the Netherlands, where he was released on bond just before New Year's of 2007. As the year wore on, he was forced to stay in the Netherlands, his passport having been confiscated as the investigation proceeded.

Deuss's bank accounts were frozen, and he began selling off assets— land in Florida, his banking properties—to pay his bills. He even put *Fleurtje,* his 150-foot yacht, up for sale. It was a staggering fall. Deuss had crossed many boundaries of acceptable behavior in his lifetime, but was he a mere money launderer, a seeming step down from the player he had always been? Friends said that if the Dutchman indeed was involved, his take would not be inconsiderable. "One thing about old John—big numbers, that's what counts," said one. In any event, the small-time image bore almost no resemblance to the man who had brought Chevron and the Kazakhs together to strike the Tengiz deal, and very nearly forced the oil company to course all its crude through his pipeline.

Jim Giffen

In the months after his arrest, Giffen didn't so much deny the accusations against him as bitterly complain that he had been arrested in the first place. The years of acting as a sometimes self-appointed, sometimes genuinely sought-after expert on Soviet and Kazakhstan affairs; the fine nights of black-tie dinners and whiskey with the cream of American industry; the access to the upper reaches and inner sanctums of foreign governments; the Bentleys, first-class cabins, private golf courses, and country clubs—all of it seemed to have persuaded Giffen of the inviolability and even right-eousness of his cause. Often, he seemed actually to believe that his role in Kazakhstan had been to bring democracy to the Kazakhs and to serve American interests. He could not seem to see that, in terms of its impact, the democracy he championed was all about entrenching his patron, Nazarbayev, and cementing and exercising his own power and influence. As for his undertakings on behalf of U.S. interests, they were useful, but seemed to be more an amusement to him than an objective.

The once-unrivaled middleman of the Caspian continued to declare that he would be vindicated. Indeed, there were hints that political influ-ence might give him a fighting chance. Casting himself as a super-spy pa-triot whose activities had been either known or encouraged by federal intelligence agencies seemed a promising defense. At worst, his trial could be delayed for a long time, maybe enough to wear out the prosecutors. At best, the ultrasecretive Bush Justice Department might drop most or all of the charges rather than expose U.S. intelligence agencies to scrutiny by re-sponding to Giffen's claims.

Bryan Williams, the Mobil oil trader who had been indicted along with Giffen, was released from prison after serving half of his forty-six-month sentence for tax evasion. But he and Giffen avoided contact to avert the possibility that associating would be seen by Giffen's prosecutors as ev-idence of a conspiracy. Giffen also pressured old friends, family, and asso-ciates to stay silent if approached by anyone asking questions.

By summer 2007, his strategy didn't seem half bad. A New York ap-peals court had effectively upheld Giffen's right to use his CIA defense. While the judges sharply questioned the relevancy of the defense, their ruling fed suspicions that the government's case wasn't as open-and-shut as it had once seemed. The lead prosecutor, Peter Neiman, an energetic lawyer who had become deeply immersed in the complex case, left to work in the private sector. That seemed to make Giffen's hopes of weakening the prosecution's zeal not so fanciful.

He still had a presence in Kazakhstan, though his offices were moved from an expensive downtown building to a small, out-of-the-way location. The Kazakhs continued to honor his consulting contract. Although the once-indispensable American was no longer an intimate, President Nazarbayev needed some measure of loyalty from Giffen, who had been at the very center of the scandalous financial transactions that had made the Kazakh leader a wealthy man. It would be out of character for Giffen to reveal secrets, but allowing him to be part of a charade in which he played the part of a Kazakh mover and shaker would ensure his steadfastness.

The Oil Companies

The oil industry virtually remade itself during the Caspian era. Competition among the multinationals fighting for advantage in Azerbaijan, Kazakhstan, and elsewhere was so fierce that several did not survive. The fatalities included Amoco, Unocal, Arco, Texaco, Phillips, Elf, Mobil, and Fina.

The winners were companies that took risks in the beginning and stayed in the struggle. The rewards were greatest in Kazakhstan, which met all expectations. Just between its three largest fields—Karachaganak, Kashagan, and Tengiz—Kazakhstan possessed more than 30 billion barrels of recoverable oil reserves. Kashagan, the biggest Kazakh "elephant," expected to deliver its first crude by 2011 or 2012. Though Azerbaijan did not deliver on its promise of a Klondike of rich new oil fields, the previously discovered 5-billion-barrel offshore reservoirs were nonetheless world-class.

Predator companies stuffed their portfolios with some envied assets. Chevron swallowed Texaco and Unocal, thereby acquiring an interest in Kazakhstan's Karachaganak natural gas field, part ownership of the Baku-Ceyhan pipeline, and rights to offshore Baku oil. Exxon, chronically slow in the race for exploration rights, bought its way into the Tengiz and Kashagan oil fields by purchasing entrepreneurial-minded Mobil. Conoco got a piece of Kashagan, too, by buying Phillips. British Petroleum bought

Amoco, its toughest competitor in Azerbaijan, and Arco as well. France's Total snapped up both Elf Aquitaine and Fina.

ENI, the Italian oil company, had spectacular success on its own. When the Soviet Union broke up, ENI was a relatively minor player in global oil. Sixteen years later, it was an operator of both Karachaganak and Kashagan, had built a natural gas pipeline from Russia to Turkey, and was a full-fledged partner of Russia's in big natural gas deals. Moscow seemed truly to trust the Italians.

Relations between Moscow and Chevron, on the other hand, continued to be problematic. In 2005, the company was prepared to expand the capacity of the trans-Russian pipeline out of Tengiz, a move that would allow Chevron to double its exports from the rich Kazakh field to roughly six hundred thousand barrels daily, an immense flow. But in 2007, the expansion was in grave doubt. Moscow was the hangup. Russia said it would approve only if the company paid higher tariffs for use of the Tengiz line (already more than three dollars a barrel) and promised to ship some of the crude through a yet-to-be-built pipeline crossing Bulgaria and Greece.

The demands were typical Moscow hardball. Russia had all the cash it needed to pay for the line, and it intended to open another route for the country to carry oil from the Black Sea to the Mediterranean. But the Kremlin preferred to shop around for financing instead, using Chevron crude as the so-called throughput guarantee needed to satisfy bankers. What else was on Moscow's mind was not clear. The situation felt like a replay of the company's war with the Dutchman John Deuss, whose insistence on a $3.25-per-barrel tariff plus a throughput guarantee for his version of the Tengiz pipeline had been thought outrageous at the time. Chevron again refused and reverted to its default position—the costly barging of crude across the Caspian to Baku. But this time there was a silver lining: Thanks to the company's purchase of Unocal, part owner of the Baku-Ceyhan pipeline, Chevron could pump its oil directly from Baku to the Turkish tanker terminal instead of having to ship it over a circuitous route by rail.

British Petroleum continued to prosper. It paid $6 billion for a half share of old Russian oil fields controlled by a company called TNK; the deal turned out to be mostly cream, paying for itself quickly and giving BP another 750,000 barrels of oil a day to sell. Oilmen were reminded of the company's experience at an offshore Baku field called Shah Deniz, where BP had struck natural gas and condensate, a high-quality oil. It was the same reservoir that a company executive had snagged in 1994 by dressing up in hospital whites and persuading the ailing Azeri oil boss Kurban Abassov to sign it over. At first, BP was disappointed that Shah Deniz was not a pure oil field. But the condensate made the economics of the Baku-Ceyhan pipeline more attractive, and the gas deposits inspired the construction of the parallel pipeline to export that fuel. Together the oil and natural gas lines were expected to be big cash earners for decades to come.

A cloud on British Petroleum's horizon was lingering resentment, especially among Georgians, that they had been intimidated and bullied by BP while negotiating the pipeline agreement. In their view, BP and other companies in the Baku-Ceyhan consortium had made sure that their investment would quickly pay off while the countries were saddled with most of the risks. Now that the oil and natural gas were flowing smoothly, Georgia was sure to demand better terms; Azerbaijan and Turkey might too. And BP might well have to grant them.

After the years of attempting to placate Russia, BP faced trouble there, too, along with the other multinationals. Moscow forced the company out of one natural gas field, and its longevity in other Russian fields could also come under threat.

At almost the same time that Baku-Ceyhan came on line, Kazakhstan began to export oil east through a pipeline into China's Xinjiang region. The initial flow was forty-five thousand barrels a day; later, it could ramp up to a not-insignificant two hundred thousand barrels. At first glance, the shipments seemed to flout America's policy of sending Caspian oil to the West. But in a larger sense, the exports to China were entirely compatible with America's aims. After all, the U.S. policy also was meant to put large volumes of crude beyond the reach of Russia and Iran; to the extent that it helped do that, the Chinese line complemented Baku-Ceyhan in particular and western interests in general.

The Oilmen

John Browne, the boss of British Petroleum, saw his invincible image scuffed up in the years after 2000. Fifteen employees were killed at a BP refinery explosion in Texas City, Texas. A year later, the BP-managed Alaska oil pipeline leaked and was found to be so corroded that whole sections had to be shut down for repairs, momentarily alarming U.S. consumers. Examinations of the refinery explosion concluded that part of the problem was that Browne had reduced company maintenance costs to the bone, and he announced that he would step down ahead of his scheduled 2008 retirement. In May 2007, however, Browne abruptly advanced his retirement even further after a bitter former lover, a twenty-seven-year-old former professional escort named Jeff Chevalier, went public with claims that Browne had misused company funds to help him. Browne said he was resigning for reasons of honor, and the company rejected Chevalier's allegations of misspending. It was a wrenching end for Browne's BP career after years of keeping his personal life private. Yet BP certainly would not have become a global powerhouse without Browne, and, like many of the oil companies that vanished during his reign, it might not even have survived.

The risk-taking John Imle retired as chairman of Unocal in 2004 and sailed around the world on his yacht. But the man who thought he could do business with the Taliban continued to prospect for oil ventures in countries that were not models of stability. He helped America's Vanco Energy, for whom he served as president, obtain an offshore drilling contract with Ukraine, in addition to deals in Ghana and the Ivory Coast.

Ken Derr, whose epic standoff with middleman John Deuss stalled the Tengiz pipeline project, retired as chairman of Chevron in 1999. He briefly served as chairman of Calpine, a large power generator, and was earning $125,000 a year as a company director. He regularly took time out for golf.

Dick Matzke, the hard-driving Chevron negotiator and Jim Giffen's nemesis, retired as vice chairman of the company and was named vice chairman of Lukoil's board of directors. In addition to his duties at the Russian oil company, he was exploring private oil deals in West Africa.

Morley Dupré, the talented Chevron negotiator who successfully launched his company's operations at the rough-and-tumble Tengiz oil field, died of a heart attack in 2006.

Viktor Chernomyrdin, tough-minded guardian of Russia's historical oil interests on the Caspian and occasional thorn in the side of Chevron, stepped down as prime minister in 1998. In 2001, he was appointed ambassador to Ukraine, a host country of Russia's natural gas pipeline to Europe. Chernomyrdin was rightly regarded as ambassador of both President Putin and Gazprom, the largely state-owned natural gas behemoth that he once led. His appointment was intended to deepen Moscow's influence in Ukraine, a former Soviet republic crucial to Russian economic and political aspirations in Europe.

Russian energy minister Yuri Shafranik, who shoved his nation into some of the biggest oil deals on the Caspian, left government in 1997. He ran his own energy company, called Soyuzneftegas, which drilled for oil and gas in Kazakhstan and Uzbekistan and as far away as Syria, Algeria, and Colombia. He also chaired Russian business interests in Saudi Arabia and Libya. As Saddam Hussein's regime neared its end, Shafranik's name turned up on a list of those who had received huge allotments of crude oil from the Iraqi dictator as part of the U.N.-administered oil-for-food program. Shafranik said that he had merely been seeking access to Iraq's oil fields. In 2005, a Russian magazine estimated his personal fortune to be $100 million, a portion of which was attributed to the shares in Lukoil awarded to Shafranik when he was energy minister.

Jack Grynberg, who showed a rising Kazakh strongman named Nursultan Nazarbayev around his Denver ranch and ended up as a Caspian middleman, cashed in handsomely. The combative oilman settled a lawsuit against British Petroleum in which he demanded a share of the Kashagan oil field for his role in making the deal happen in 1990. The terms were confidential, but one report said he had collected $90 million, or a 15 percent cut. He was said to have pocketed perhaps double that sum by settling a similar claim with British Gas, another partner in the field. But a federal judge threw out his suit against France's Total for a piece of its share of Kashagan. Grynberg continued to pursue oil projects in the Central African Republic, the Caribbean, and Cameroon.

Ara Oztemel

The powerful New York metals trader, who felt betrayed when Jim Giffen tried to orchestrate a takeover of Satra Consulting, triumphed on several fronts after ousting his onetime protégé from the firm.

In 1976, Oztemel outmaneuvered America's big three television networks to win U.S. television rights for the 1980 Moscow Olympics. The networks were livid, and NBC teamed up with the U.S. Olympic Committee to reverse the decision and claim the games for itself. None of that mattered after President Jimmy Carter ordered an Olympic boycott in retaliation for the 1979 Soviet invasion of Afghanistan. In addition to the satisfaction of seeing NBC lose millions in anticipated advertising, Oztemel won a civil suit and restitution, paid partly in Soviet chrome.

A Soviet film distributed by Oztemel—*Moscow Doesn't Believe in Tears*—won an Oscar in 1980 for best foreign film. Six years later, once again demonstrating his prowess at trade with the Russians, he closed a $30 million contract to bring Coca-Cola to Soviet consumers. It was his last big deal.

The 1989 death of Betty Van Staveren, his longtime secretary and mistress, devastated him. For the first time that anyone could recall, Oztemel appeared at work drunk. At one meal he was so inebriated that he "couldn't keep food in his mouth." He developed peripheral neuropathy (a condition that can afflict alcoholics), lost all feeling in his feet, and walked with the help of a cane. He began an affair with another secretary, but his depression did not lift. Satra effectively failed, overtaken by the rush of a new breed of western businessmen to post-Soviet Moscow and by shifts in the metals trade. Sad and angry over his fortunes, he refused to talk about the old days. He died in 1998 at the age of seventy-one.

John Huhs

The adventurous Stanford graduate, who had flown east with such optimism to work for Jim Giffen at Satra Consulting, lasted only a year after his mentor was fired. He fell out of favor because of his close relationship with Giffen and left to work in the Ford administration's Office of Management and Budget. Later, he joined the global trade practice of a wheeler-dealer named Samuel Pisar, a much-celebrated Polish escapee from Dachau. He ended up practicing international corporate law. In late 2006, Huhs retired as head of international operations for LeBoeuf Lamb, the Manhattan law firm, and in 2007 he began teaching international law full-time at Stanford University.

Carl Longley

Recruited from Stanford along with John Huhs to be part of the Satra startup, he survived mainly because Jim Giffen did not. Longley had gotten into trouble by dating the secretary to Betty Van Staveren, whom Giffen disliked. Longley recalled Giffen telling him that the secretary "was a dangerous woman and if I valued my job I better stop dating her." When he refused, Giffen transferred him to a lower-profile job and, Longley presumed, eventual termination. But Giffen's own expulsion intervened. Longley became Ara Oztemel's deputy and married the secretary, Beth Kaplan, with the boss paying for the wedding and giving away the bride. Longley later opened a law practice in La Jolla, California.

Paul Proehl

The third member of Giffen's brain trust at Satra, Proehl also weathered the management shake-up and continued to run the company's affairs on the West Coast. The former professor was especially fascinated by Occidental Petroleum chairman Armand Hammer, an early figure in Soviet trade. He orchestrated a meeting with Hammer at which Satra chief Ara Oztemel enthusiastically described his latest idea—to export Soviet nickel. Hammer suggested a joint venture but then negotiated a nickel deal for himself. Oztemel was furious, as was the normally reserved Proehl. When Hammer launched a personal campaign for the Nobel Peace Prize, Proehl wrote to one influential friend that Hammer's "success hangs by his acquaintance/friendship with Lenin and some other imponderables too deep to fathom at this point, including how much business you can buy with the gift of million-dollar Goya paintings to the Hermitage."

Proehl, who had taught law to a young Jim Giffen at UCLA, later returned to academia, becoming president of Southern California International College. He had little contact with his former student and later boss, dying in 1998. He was "probably fooled by [Giffen] for a while," said Proehl's widow, Virginia. "But when he realized that everything he was doing at Satra was for [Giffen's] own self-aggrandizement, he realized they didn't have much in common."

Bill Verity

The Armco Steel chairman who employed Giffen after he was fired by Ara Oztemel died in January 2007. He was eighty-nine.

Bill White, Rosemarie Forsythe, and Sheila Heslin

They were the Clinton administration's pioneers of Caspian policymaking. White, a deputy secretary of energy, and Forsythe, a newcomer at the National Security Council, together put Caspian oil on Washington's agenda. Heslin, a strategic thinker and skilled bureaucratic infighter, deserved the lion's share of credit for formulating eventual U.S. policy and pushing it to fruition. She went on to raise three children full-time in Maryland, writing occasional analyses of oil, geopolitics, and the former Soviet Union. White was elected mayor of Houston. Forsythe became an Exxon Mobil executive at company headquarters in Irving, Texas.

Viktor Kozeny

Late in 1997, Kozeny had dazzled his wealthy neighbors in Aspen, Colorado, with tales of how he was cornering the market in Azerbaijani privatization vouchers, which he would use to buy the state-owned oil company on the cheap. Eager to cash in, some big-name American financiers and a former U.S. senator signed up with him. Eight years later, the scheme came crashing down. Kozeny and two others were indicted in October 2005 by a federal grand jury in New York, accused of bribing high officials of the Azeri government to grease the transaction, which never took place.

The indictment said that a "senior Azeri official" and two others in the government had received the payments. It did not cite the names of the then-president, Heydar Aliyev, or his son, Ilham, who succeeded him. But it noted that the oil company could not have been privatized without "a special decree from the president of Azerbaijan." In other words, the father and son were unindicted co-conspirators.

Kozeny was said to have arranged for jewelry valued at more than $600,000 to be sent to Baku on the occasion of the "senior Azeri official's birthday on May 10, 1998." That was the date of Heydar Aliyev's seventy-fifth birthday. Other alleged bribes included millions in cash, a large share of the privatization vouchers, and a photo frame with clock valued at more than $100,000.

Federal prosecutors surmised that the Americans had thought they would outsmart the Azeris but ended up being outsmarted themselves. Indicted along with Kozeny were Frederick Bourke, the chairman of a designer handbag maker, and David Pinkerton, managing director of AIG Global Investment. All were charged with violating the Foreign Corrupt Practices Act.

Kozeny was arrested by Bahamas authorities the day before the indictment was announced. As of summer 2007, he was still in a Bahamaian jail, fighting extradition to the United States.

The Nobels

Some twenty cousins of Baku oil pioneers Ludvig, Robert, and Emanuel Nobel visited the Azeri capital in 2004 at the government's invitation. Among them was Nils Oleinikoff, a sixty-four-year-old Swedish pollution control expert whose grandmother was Emanuel Nobel's youngest sister and whose great-great-grandfather was Ludvig Nobel. Oleinikoff said that the Azeris apparently hoped that the Nobel clan could provide financial aid to Baku, perhaps to help restore historical sites.

"They expected the whole family to be as wealthy as the Rockefellers, but we told them everything was taken from us [after the Russian Revolution]. There was nothing left," Oleinikoff said. "They sighed and said that, 'if we can use the Nobel name without offending . . . that would be good enough for us.' "

After touring the city and the old family estate, now an amusement park, he was impressed by Baku's new oil age. "But it's also what I would call a banana republic. They are serious to do something serious. But I'm afraid some of the leading characters in the regime have personal goals rather than goals for the general public."

The Rothschilds

On an estate two hours north of Paris that was modest considering the heritage of its occupant, ninety-four-year-old Guy de Rothschild regaled two luncheon guests with memories of the storied European family, including grandfather Alphonse and his gambles in the oil fields of Baku.

The Rothschilds had stopped doing business with Russia after the pogroms against the Jews and the sale of the Baku properties to Royal Dutch/Shell's Henri Deterding in 1911. But Guy had recently accepted an invitation to visit Moscow, and he found his hosts remorseful over what they called a lost century. Russia, they lamented, had caused itself to become estranged from the rest of the world, very nearly forgotten.

"I tried to reassure them that Pushkin was still known," he ventured.

Guy de Rothschild died June 12, 2007, about four years after the remarks over lunch. He was ninety-eight.

The patriarch's sixty-one-year-old son, David, was now chairman of the family bank. While the Russians wanted the Rothschilds to return and help revive the country's finances, the family was doing so only in a limited way. "We are opening a correspondent bank in Moscow," said David, with Alphonse's portrait hanging nearby.

Sophia

The granddaughter of Zeynalabdin Tagiyev, Baku's powerful oil baron of the early 1900s, lived out her remaining years in the city of her childhood. Memories of the past came alive one day when a visitor appeared at her Baku apartment. "God sent me Leyla again," Sophia blurted out.

She remembered herself as a little girl many decades ago, frightened to see her grandfather collapse upon hearing that his favorite daughter—twenty-six-year-old Leyla—had fled to join her husband in Persia.

The woman standing before her was also a Leyla—the granddaughter of the young woman whose flight had undone the old baron, and the great-granddaughter of Tagiyev himself. Sophia had never seen her, but the forty-seven-year-old woman standing before her—tall, slender, and elegant—bore a remarkable resemblance to her aunt. Leyla had traveled from her Virginia home to see the birthplace of her mother and their famous forebear, Tagiyev.

In 2003, Azerbaijan president Aliyev gave Sophia permission to return to the place where her grandfather had spent his last days in exile, the seaside villa at Mardakhan. She lived there until her death two years later, at the age of eighty-four.

ACKNOWLEDGMENTS

THIS BOOK BEGAN AS AN IDEA IN 1993, ONE YEAR INTO WHAT I DID NOT know would become an eleven-year residence as a correspondent in the Caucasus and Central Asia. It is not possible to list every person to whom I owe a debt of gratitude. However, the book was made possible mainly because of the belief of two men—Noel Greenwood and Thomas Wallace. When I was stumped on how to weave together the strands of the events under way following the Soviet collapse, a friend recommended Noel, the former associate editor of the *Los Angeles Times*, as a crackerjack book editor who might help. Over beers in Santa Monica in 1994, I told him the nub of the story of Russia and its former colonies, along with the new Great Game that was playing out, and he instantly agreed to work as private editor on the project. So began a great collaboration in which Noel was adviser, teacher, and friend. Then Bill Keller, my foreign editor at *The New York Times*, arranged an introduction to Tom Wallace, an agent with a long history as a book editor in his own right. Tom also intuitively grasped what I aimed to do, and in a display of faith rare in the business, he led me around personally to editors at New York's premier publishing houses, and Random House bought the rights. To Noel and Tom, thanks for your faith. This book is as much yours as mine.

I am grateful for the generous financial assistance of the Smith-Richardson Foundation and its expert on the former Soviet Union, Nadia Schadlow, who, when I did not know how I would support the full-time research-and-writing period, made the project happen. David Holloway and Chip Blacker, successive directors of the Stanford Institute of International Studies, made my family and me welcome for two years and provided generous financial assistance. The Kennan Institute provided an early research grant. Stu Auerbach, Fiona Hill, and Jim Steinberg led me to the right doors to find the grants.

Paul Steiger, managing editor of *The Wall Street Journal*, granted me a year off when I had been at the paper for just eighteen months, then extended the leave for another year when it was obvious that the book otherwise would not get done. John Bussey, deputy managing editor at the *Journal*, recommended the dual leaves, and was a good friend and crucial adviser throughout. Thanks, Paul and John.

Will Murphy is a superlatively gifted editor, one of the best in the publishing world, and a rare writer's editor besides. Joy DeMenil commissioned the book when no one else would, and Robert Loomis provided encouragement all the way along. Lea Beresford is a terrific professional. Carol Malcolm Russo and Rick Pracher produced an elegant design for the book and dust jacket, Virginia Norey managed to create order from chaos in clear maps, and Martin Schneider made sharp improvements in the book with his careful copyediting. Evan Camfield brought everything together.

In 1992, the BBC's Chris Bowers and I met in Kabul, both of us having decided to shift bases to Tashkent, the Uzbekistan capital, and cover Central Asia. We agreed to pool our resources in a single office. Chris said I could choose the house/office and hire the staff as long as he could select the dishes. So was born the *Newsweek*-BBC office, the first western-style news bureau in Central Asia. At about the same time, I opened a similar residence/office in Tbilisi, the capital of Georgia, to cover the Caucasus as well. It is not possible to describe briefly the difficulty of outfitting such offices and providing western-quality coverage in regions unaccustomed to such exposure. I want to salute those who, more than anyone, made both operations the wonder of most of the journalists who came in contact with them: in Tashkent, Aziza Nuritova, Malek Nuritov, and Bahora Tajibayeva, and in Tbilisi, Nana Kiknadze, Yuri Bekauri, and Manana Endeladze.

For most of the period, I was a freelance correspondent working for *Newsweek, The New York Times, The Washington Post,* and the *Financial Times.* Freelancers rely on the loyalty of editors in New York and London and bureau chiefs in Moscow. I was blessed with the most supportive in the business. The list is long. First, Andy Hernandez arranged for me first to be hired as *Newsweek's* Peshawar-based correspondent during the Soviet withdrawal from Afghanistan and the three years following, then got me a Russian visa so I could make the shift to the former Soviet Union. Najam Sethi also was crucial to obtaining the visa. Also at *Newsweek,* Fred Coleman, Carroll Bogert, Dorinda Elliott, Bill Powell, Michael Glennon, Peter McGrath, and Melinda Liu were all tremendous bosses. Andrew Nagorski was bureau chief during some of the most difficult times, including my expulsions from Russia and Uzbekistan and my injury by the backfire of a rocket-propelled grenade in Chechnya. Andy fought to get my visas restored and made sure that I was paid by *Newsweek* through nine months of recovery, even though I was technically on assignment for *The New York Times* when I was wounded. At the *Times,* Steve Erlanger, Michael Gordon, Len Apcar, Jeff Sommer, Tim Weiner, Ray Bonner, Jane Perlez, and James Hill were fabulous colleagues. Special thanks to Michael Specter and Alessandra Stanley, who acted quickly to get me out of Chechnya and to California when I was injured. At the *FT,* John Lloyd, Leyla Boulton, Chrystia Freeland, and John Thornhill made sure my copy got in the paper and provided good company in Moscow. At the *Post,* Michael Dobbs taught me how to write a nut graf, and Margaret Shapiro, Fred Hiatt, and Lee Hockstader were friendly voices on the other end of the line from isolated places.

In 2000, *The Wall Street Journal* decided to open a bureau in Almaty—the only western newspaper to have an actual staff bureau in the region, rather than using freelancers—and hired me to run it. In addition to those mentioned earlier at the *Journal*, I want to thank Marcus Brauchli, Guy Chazan, Alan Cullison, Jonathan Dahl, Andrew Higgins, Cathy Panagoulias, Jim Pensiero, Hugh Pope, Imran Raja, Jerry Seib, Bill Spindle, and Lora Western.

My closest colleagues were at the BBC, whose foray into Central Asia was led by Behruz Afagh, Lis Robson, and Baquer Moin. The successive correspondents were Chris Bowers, Alan Johnston, Monica Whitlock, Louise Hidalgo, and Catherine Davis. Reuters opened next, starting with Elif Kaban and James Kynge, who were followed by Douglas Busvine, Chris Bird, Mike Colette-White, Sebastian Alison, and Dmitri Solovyov. Jim Rupert showed all of us the way. In the Caucasus, the pioneers were Alexis Rowell, Natalie Nougayrede, Thomas Goltz, Lawrence Sheets, Andrew Harding, David Stern, Hicran Oge, Liam McDowell, and Rosalind Russell.

Thanks to Denise Albrighton, Birgit Brauer, Yan Cienski, Charles Clover, Nick Moore, and Chris Pala. Thanks also to Nasiba Abieva, Robert Adams, Haroon Akbar, Danabek Bimenov, Heidi Bradner, Tom de Waal, Carlotta Gall, Kathy Gannon, Nicola Harford, Zahid Hussain, Nino Ivanishvili, Yuri Kushko, Alek Nuritov, Aziz Nuritov, Vera Nuritov, Oleg Panfilov, Daud Qarizadah, Andrew Rearick, Nana Talakhvadze, and Nata Talakhvadze.

All of the correspondents who served in the region stood on the shoulders of two men: Peter Hopkirk, who chronicled the Great Game, and Daniel Yergin, the scholar of the intersection of modern history, geopolitics, and oil. This book could not have been written without the existing scholarship of Fitzroy Maclean, the British diplomat; Charles Marvin, the nineteenth-century British reporter who witnessed the Great Game firsthand; Antony C. Sutton, the investigator of America's construction of the Soviet Union's industrial might; and George F. Kennan, America's Cold War–era diplomat and writer.

Karl Garcia and Michelle Teofan are wonderful friends. Thanks to Dilda Baimukhamedova, Paul Bergne, Jim Falk, Ed Guzman, Seymour Hersh, Richard Hoagland, Scott Horton, Riffat Hussain, David Katz, Rick Kellett, Gulzhar Khan, Ismail Khan, Kodyr Kholmatov, Matt Kissinger, Stuart Korn, Scott LaFee, Paolo Lembo, Donald LeVine, Marina Liakhovitser, Maleeha Lodhi, Walt and Marzhan Marshall, Don Mayhew, Doug Mazzapica, Michael Ochs, Martha Olcott, Patrick O'Mara, Sam Patten, Pat Patterson, Bill Perkins, Andy Plowman, Debbie Puente, Chris Reynolds, Christoph Rosenberg, Michael Rosenthal, Dan Russell, Melissa Russell, John Schoberlein, Merrie Spaeth, Richard Spooner, Adam Sterling, Charlie Stewart, Bill Swartz, Linda Swartz, Hiroshi Takahashi, and Rauf Yusufzai.

This book was written at Stanford, where my close colleagues and advisers were Mary Dakin, Terry Karl, Gail Lapidus, Amichai Magen, Gene Mazo, Michael McFaul,

John McMillan, Paul Milgrom, Eva Myersson-Milgrom, and Dan Sneider. Thanks to Maria Sidorkina for her translation of books and research, and to Dave Sare for his always cheerful technical genius.

Médecins Sans Frontières and the International Committee for the Red Cross treated me and got me out of Chechyna, and the Paris-based Committee for the Protection of Journalists worked to get my visas restored.

Several experts in the areas of oil and Soviet, Russian, and international affairs graciously agreed to read the entire book in manuscript form. I am solely responsible for any mistakes, but all of them prevented basic errors. The readers were Robert Ebel, David Holloway, Robert Crews, James Tanner, John Bussey, David Victor, Jon Auerbach, Gregg Jones, Aleli Nucum-Jones, and Tom Wallace.

Respects to fallen comrades: Mark Brunereau, Sharon Herbaugh, Mirwais Jalil, Mohammad Massoum, Daniel Pearl, Rory Peck, Kurt Schork, Natasha Singh, and Sander Thoenes.

Thanks to my parents, Avery LeVine and Dolores LeVine, and my brothers, Edward LeVine and David LeVine.

Without the support of my wife, Nurilda Nurlybayeva, the book would not have been possible. Thanks also to my daughters, Alisha and Ilana.

BIBLIOGRAPHY AND
NOTE ON SOURCES

THIS BOOK IS LARGELY THE PRODUCT OF SEVERAL HUNDRED INTERVIEWS conducted from 1992 through 2007. The sources of the material used in the book can be found in the endnotes.

Most of the history recounted in chapters 1 through 4 is from primary published sources, including books and newspaper articles. The episodes described in the remainder of the book are almost wholly from interviews with participants in or firsthand witnesses of the events described. I have often buttressed these interviews with newspaper accounts in order to include how events were seen at the moment; I also relied on memoirs and journalistic books for these chapters. Chapters 14 through 16, on the Caspian Pipeline Consortium and the oil trader John Deuss, are unique in that they rely on a number of unidentified sources. Many of the people involved in the CPC deal, accustomed to staying behind the scenes, insisted on anonymity.

Modern history is becoming harder to write. Important figures devote less and less time to writing letters, a traditional source of information for researchers. And because of legal considerations, they often do not record their thoughts at length in e-mails, or they delete these e-mails as soon as practicable. In addition, for a variety of reasons, people involved in events seem ambivalent toward describing their experiences to a writer. Given these circumstances, I am extraordinarily grateful to the people—and there are many—who realized they were part of a historic era and agreed to often long and repeated discussions with me. I want to mention some of them.

I spoke with Jim Giffen for the first time in 1995, an approximately four-hour discussion in his Almaty office. Dozens of meetings followed over the years, ending in September 2002, when his legal problems had become such that he preferred to sever contact.

Former Kazakhstan prime minister Akezhan Kazhegeldin sat for numerous interviews over the years, as did Rinat Akhmetshin, his Washington representative.

Ed Smith and Mack Fowler helped me to understand John Deuss in many interviews.

Tom Hamilton, Dave Henderson, Frank Verrastro and Rondo Fehlberg of Pennzoil submitted to many face-to-face, telephone, and e-mail interviews, and replied patiently to numerous follow-up questions. They were always candid and provided valuable detail and context while describing their dealings in Kazakhstan and Azerbaijan. George Keller, Ken Derr, and John Silcox sat for lengthy interviews to explain Chevron's entry into the oil rush. So did Chevron's Edward Chow, and Amoco's Tim Hartnett.

Valekh Aleskerov granted three long interviews to describe Azerbaijan's approach to the negotiations. Tedo Japaridze, Peter Mamradze, Alex Rondeli, Gia Chanturia, and Levan Mikeladze each made themselves available for many hours, as did Rakhat Aliyev, President Nazarbayev's son-in-law.

Virginia Proehl, Mary Öztemel, and their families patiently shared their experiences so that I could understand the days of trade with the Soviet Union before and after détente.

Sheila Heslin and Bill White sat for numerous detailed interviews, explaining the origin of U.S. policy on the Caspian. Bill Courtney also devoted many hours to discussing American policy. So did Caryn McClelland.

Dulat Kuanishev helped me to understand Kazakhstan.

The names of scores of others who were exceedingly generous with their time over the years do not appear by name in these pages. They know who they are, however, and I am grateful.

Primary Published Works

Abramson, Rudy. *Spanning the Century: The Life of W. Averell Harriman* (New York, 1992).

Altstadt, Audrey. *The Azerbaijani Turks* (Stanford, Calif., 1992).

Baer, Robert. *See No Evil* (New York, 2002).

Banine. *Jours Caucasiens* (Paris, 1985).

Bey, Essad. *Blood and Oil in the Orient* (repr. Baku, 1997).

Brzezinski, Zbigniew. *The Grand Chessboard* (New York, 1997).

Churilov, Lev. *Lifeblood of Empire: A Personal History of the Rise and Fall of the Soviet Oil Industry* (New York, 1996).

Clinton, Bill. *My Life* (New York, 2004).

Coll, Steve. *Ghost Wars* (New York, 2004).

Conquest, Robert. *The Great Terror* (London, 1990).

Copetas, A. Craig. *Metal Men* (New York, 1985).

Corn, David. *Blond Ghost* (New York, 1994).

Davies, R. W., Mark Harrison, and Stephen Wheatcroft, eds. *The Economic Transformation of the Soviet Union, 1913–1945* (Cambridge, Eng., 1994).

de Waal, Thomas. *Black Garden* (New York, 2003).

Ebel, Robert E. *The Petroleum Industry of the Soviet Union* (New York, 1961).

Epstein, Edward Jay. *Dossier: The Secret History of Armand Hammer* (New York, 1996).

Fairbanks, Charles, C. Richard Nelson, S. Frederick Starr, and Kenneth Weisbrode. *Strategic Assessment of Central Eurasia* (Washington, 2001). Policy paper.

Ferguson, Niall. *The House of Rothschild.* Volume 2, *The World's Banker: 1849–1999* (New York, 1999).

Finder, Joseph. *Red Carpet* (New York, 1983).

Forsythe, Rosemarie. "The Politics of Oil in the Caucasus and Central Asia" (London, 1996). Booklet.

Fromkin, David. *A Peace to End All Peace* (New York, 1989).

Gaidar, Yegor. *Days of Defeat and Victory* (Seattle, 2000).

Gardner, Leonard. *Fat City* (New York, 1969).

Gibb, George Sweet, and Evelyn H. Knowlton. *History of Standard Oil Co.*, volume 2 (New York, 1956).

Giffen, James Henry. *The Legal and Practical Aspects of Trade with the Soviet Union* (New York, 1969).

Goldenberg, Suzanne. *Pride of Small Nations* (London, 1994).

Goldman, Marshall. *The Soviet Economy: Myth and Reality* (Upper Saddle River, N.J., 1968).

Goltz, Thomas. *Azerbaijan Diary* (Armonk, N.Y., 1998).

Gonta, T. *The Heroes of Grozny* (Moscow, 1932).

Gorbachev, Mikhail. *Memoirs* (New York, 1995).

Gulbenkian, Nubar. *Portrait in Oil* (New York, 1965).

Gustafson, Thane. *Crisis Amid Plenty* (Princeton, 1989).

Hagelin, Karl K. *Moi Trudovoi Put* (New York, 1945). Grenich Printing Corporation.

Hanighen, Frank C. *The Secret War* (New York, 1934).

Hendrix, Paul. *Henri Deterding and Royal Dutch Shell* (Bristol, Eng., 2002).

Henry, James Dodds. *Baku: An Eventful History* (repr. London, 1977).

Hersh, Seymour M. "The Price of Oil" (New York, 2001). Article.

Heslin, Sheila N. *Key Constraints to Caspian Pipeline Development* (Houston, 1997).

Hewins, Ralph. *Mr. Five Percent* (Oxford, Eng., 1958).

Hobsbawm, Eric. *The Age of Empire* (London, 1987).

Hopkirk, Peter. *On Secret Service East of Constantinople* (London, 1994).

————. *The Great Game* (Oxford, Eng., 1990).

Jaffe, Amy Myers, and Robert A. Manning. "The Myth of the Caspian 'Great Game': The Real Geopolitics of Energy" (Houston, 1997). Rice University paper.

Joseph, Jofi. *Pipeline Diplomacy: The Clinton Administration's Fight for Baku-Ceyhan* (Princeton, 1999). Woodrow Wilson Case Study.

Karaulov, Andrei. *Vokrug Kremlya* (Moscow, 1990).

Karl, Terry Lynn. *The Paradox of Plenty* (Berkeley, 1997).

Kennan, George F. *Russia and the West Under Lenin and Stalin* (New York, 1960–1961).

Kissinger, Henry. *White House Years* (Boston, 1979).

Klebnikov, Paul. *Godfather of the Kremlin* (New York, 2001).

Knickerbocker, H. R. *The Red Trade Menace* (New York, 1931).

Levinson, Robert E. *The Jews in the California Gold Rush* (Jersey City, N.J., 1978).

Lloyd, John. *Rebirth of a Nation* (London, 1998).

MacMillan, Margaret. *Paris 1919* (New York, 2001).

Marvin, Charles. *The Region of the Eternal Fire* (London, 1884).

Matlock, Jack F., Jr. *Autopsy on an Empire* (New York, 1995).

McCain, William D., Jr. *The Properties of Petroleum Fluids* (Tulsa, Okla., 1990).

Nanay, Julia. "The U.S. in the Caspian: The Divergence of Political and Commercial Interests" (Washington, D.C., 1998). Article.

Nash, George H. *The Life of Herbert Hoover,* volume I (New York, 1983).

Nazarbayev, Nursultan. *Without Right and Left* (London, 1992).

Nixon, Richard M. *RN: The Memoirs of Richard Nixon* (New York, 1978).

O'Connor, Richard. *The Oil Barons* (New York, 1971).

Olcott, Martha Brill. *The Kazakhs* (Stanford, Calif., 1987).

Palazchenko, Pavel. *My Years with Gorbachev and Shevardnadze* (University Park, Penn., 1997).

Petroleum Encyclopedia of Kazakhstan (London, 1999).

Pipes, Richard. *The Formation of the Soviet Union* (Cambridge, Mass., 1954/1964).

Pisar, Samuel. *Coexistence and Commerce: Guidelines for Transactions Between East and West* (New York, 1970).

Pratt, Joseph A. *Prelude to Merger: A History of Amoco Corporation, 1973–1998* (Houston, 2000).

Polo, Marco. *The Travels* (London, 1958).

Rashid, Ahmed. *Taliban* (New York, 2000).

Remnick, David. *Lenin's Tomb* (New York, 1993).

Roberts, Glyn. *The Most Powerful Man in the World* (New York, 1976).

Ruge, Gerd. *Gorbachev* (London, 1991).

Sampson, Anthony. *The Seven Sisters* (New York, 1975).

Smith, Hedrick. *The New Russians* (New York, 1991).

Siegel, Katherine A. S. *Loans and Legitimacy* (Lexington, Ken., 1996).

Steinbeck, John. *A Russian Journal* (New York, 1948).

Strik-Strikfeldt, Wilfried. *Against Stalin and Hitler* (New York, 1973).

Sutton, Antony C. *Western Technology and Soviet Economic Development, 1917 to 1930* (Stanford, Calif., 1968).

Swietochowski, Tadeusz. *Russian Azerbaijan, 1905–1920* (Cambridge, Eng., 1985).

Talbott, Strobe. *The Russia Hand* (New York, 2002).

Thompson, A. Beeby. *The Oil Fields of Russia and The Russian Petroleum Industry* (London, 1908).

Tolf, Robert W. *The Russian Rockefellers* (Stanford, Calif., 1976).

Vaksberg, Arkady. *The Soviet Mafia* (New York, 1991).

Villari, Luigi. *Fire and Sword in the Caucasus* (London, 1906).

Willerton, John P. *Patronage and Politics in the USSR* (Cambridge, Eng., 1992).

Yeltsin, Boris. *Against the Grain* (New York, 1990).

Yergin, Daniel. *The Prize* (New York, 1991).

Yergin, Daniel, and Joseph Stanislaw. *The Commanding Heights* (New York, 1998).

Prologue

ix "in all the neighborhood": Marco Polo, *The Travels* (London: Penguin, 1958).

xi "the greatest sale": Daniel Yergin and Joseph Stanislaw, *The Commanding Heights* (New York: Random House, 1998), 13.

Chapter I: The Barons

3 In the early nineteenth century: Principal sources for this description of nineteenth-century Baku are Charles Marvin, *The Region of the Eternal Fire* (London: W. H. Allen and Co., 1884) and James Dodds Henry, *Baku, An Eventful History* (London: A. Constable, 1905; reprinted by Arno Press, 1977).

4 "Tigers, panthers, jackals": Alexandre Dumas, *Adventures in Caucasia* (Philadelphia: Chilton, 1961), 141, 150; quoted in Robert W. Tolf, *The Russian Rockefellers* (Stanford, Calif.: Hoover Institution Press, 1976), 40.

4 "There is no": A. Beeby Thompson, *The Oil Fields of Russia and the Russian Petroleum Industry* (London: Crosby Lockwood and Son, 1908), 66.

4 "a fairy castle": Prof. Beresin quoted in Henry, *Baku, An Eventful History*, 27.

4 "as wonderful as the Solfaterra": *The New York Times*, January 24, 1876, p. 2.

4 Other visitors spoke of huge bubbles: Marvin, *The Region of the Eternal Fire*, 189.

4 The source of these phantasmagoric: Thompson, *The Oil Fields of Russia*, 85.

4 "a quantity of oil": Henry, *Baku: An Eventful History*, 27.

4 Eighteenth-century British trader: Marvin, *The Region of the Eternal Fire*, 173.

5 While nearly all the world: Marvin, *The Region of the Eternal Fire*, 170–71.

5 An Arabic inscription: Henry, *Baku, An Eventful History*, 20–21.

6 Russia, milking the state-owned: Henry, *Baku, An Eventful History*, 29–34; Tolf, *The Russian Rockefellers*, 43.

6 Three years after Drake's: Marvin, *The Region of the Eternal Fire*, 208–11; Henry, *Baku: An Eventful History*, 37; Daniel Yergin, *The Prize* (New York: Simon and Schuster, 1991), 57.

7 **In December 1872:** Henry, *Baku: An Eventful History*, 35.

7 **Most of the successful:** Marvin, *The Region of the Eternal Fire*, 211.

7 **Zeynalabdin Tagiyev:** Tolf, *The Russian Rockefellers*, 101; author interview with Baku historian Fuad Akhundov.

8 **Their chance finally arrived:** Henry, *Baku: An Eventful History*, 51–53.

8 **Finally Sarkissov lost patience:** Henry, *Baku: An Eventful History*, caption in photo plate facing 118.

8 **"a colossal pillar":** Henry, *Baku: An Eventful History*, 104–5.

9 **Before long, Tagiyev's strike:** Henry, *Baku: An Eventful History*, 68–69.

9 **Tagiyev became Baku's:** Author interview with Akhundov.

10 **Lewis Emery, an oilman:** *The New York Times*, February 20, 1880, p. 3.

10 **British journalist Charles Marvin:** Marvin, *The Region of the Eternal Fire*, 248.

10 **Some recalled that:** *The New York Times*, January 24, 1876, p. 2.

10 **In August 1883, the most:** Marvin, *The Region of the Eternal Fire*, 216.

10 **The oil fields were transformed:** Henry, *Baku: An Eventful History*, 60–61, 70.

11 **It seemed that everyone:** Marvin, *The Region of the Eternal Fire*, 240–42.

11 **A fabulously wealthy core:** Author interview with Akhundov; Tolf, *The Russian Rockefellers*, 102.

11 **The barons' families lived:** Author interview with Ashurbekov's four surviving daughters, Sarah, Miriam, Nazima, and Adela, February 27, 1997.

11 **Before long, bands of hired:** Ibid.; Essad Bey, *Blood and Oil in the Orient* (1929; repr. Baku: Aran Press, 1997), 60–64.

12 **It was against this rowdy:** Author interview with Akhundov.

12 **A few years after the wedding:** Bey, *Blood and Oil in the Orient*, 85.

12 **Lev Naussimbaum, the son:** Author interview with Zuleha Weber, the seventy-seven-year-old sister-in-law of Tagiyev's daughter Leyla, January 9, 2000. Weber was the granddaughter of oil baron Shamsi Assadulayev.

12 **"Deprive him of":** Bey, *Blood and Oil in the Orient*, 86.

13 **"The Azerbaijani Eunuch-Maker":** Bey, *Blood and Oil in the Orient*, 86.

Chapter 2: A Visitor from Sweden

15 **For the Nobels:** Principal sources for Nobel family history are Tolf, *The Russian Rockefellers*, 4–22, 38–39; Marvin, *The Region of the Eternal Fire*, 284–88; Henry, *Baku: An Eventful History*, 83–91.

16 **Ludvig, the middle son:** Tolf, *The Russian Rockefellers*, 26, 28–31, 39, 45.

17 **The kerosene manufactured:** Tolf, *The Russian Rockefellers*, 46–47, 69.

17 **Ludvig finally decided to have:** Tolf, *The Russian Rockefellers*, 49, 74.

18 **"Grandiose schemes are":** Marvin, *The Region of the Eternal Fire*, 205.

19 **Now Ludvig would send:** Tolf, *The Russian Rockefellers*, 50–53; Marvin, *The Region of the Eternal Fire*, 288–89.

20 "the most important fact": Stephen Goulishambarov quoted in Tolf, *The Russian Rockefellers*, 52.

20 "a discovery to": Ibid.

20 Ludvig rejected the single-container: Tolf, *The Russian Rockefellers*, 53–59; Yergin, *The Prize*, 59; Marvin, *The Region of the Eternal Fire*, 290–93.

22 "When the cementing": Quote and account of Musa Jacob: Bey, *Blood and Oil in the Orient*, 40, 63.

22 The railroad project turned Batumi: Marvin, *The Region of the Eternal Fire*, 95–97; Tolf, *The Russian Rockefellers*, 87.

23 "a filthy mushroom town": Ralph Hewins, *Mr. Five Percent* (Oxford: Rinehart and Co., 1958), 21.

23 The logical fix: Tolf, *The Russian Rockefellers*, 97.

24 The Rothschilds turned: Yergin, *The Prize*, 62–68; Tolf, *The Russian Rockefellers*, 105–7; Henry, *Baku: An Eventful History*, 232–35.

26 "All the Baku": Marvin, *The Region of the Eternal Fire*, 224.

26 What distinguished Ludvig from: Tolf, *The Russian Rockefellers*, 61–67, 72–73; Marvin, *The Region of the Eternal Fire*, 302–7; Yergin, *The Prize*, 58–59.

27 "an incomparable, insatiable": Tolf, *The Russian Rockefellers*, 61.

Chapter 3: Revolution

28 "the worst managed city": Luigi Villari, *Fire and Sword in the Caucasus* (London: James Pott and Co., 1906), 182.

29 "black with wasted crude": Hewins, *Mr. Five Percent*, 24–25.

29 The old baron also dared: Author interview with Akhundov.

29 Tagiyev became a diversified: Tadeusz Swietochowski, *Russian Azerbaijan, 1905–1920* (Cambridge, Eng.: Cambridge University Press, 1985), 23, 27, 35, 76; author interview with Akhundov.

30 Yet underlying Baku's prosperity: Principal sources on 1903–05 violence are Swietochowski, *Russian Azerbaijan*, 37–46; Tolf, *The Russian Rockefellers*, 151–60; Yergin, *The Prize*, 129–31.

31 Indeed, when World War I: Swietochowski, *Russian Azerbaijan*, 76.

31 Lev Naussimbaum, the Baku author: Bey, *Blood and Oil in the Orient*, 89–90.

31 The Savage Division had risen: Swietochowski, *Russian Azerbaijan*, 113, 115.

31 Elements of the Savage Division: Peter Hopkirk, *On Secret Service East of Constantinople* (London: John Murray, 1994), 283–87; author interview with Sophia Abdullayeva, July 15, 1998; Bey, *Blood and Oil in the Orient*, 89.

32 But through it all: Glyn Roberts, *The Most Powerful Man in the World: The Life of Sir Henri Deterding* (New York: repr. Hyperion, 1976), 389.

33 He bought a stake: *The Wall Street Journal*, May 11, 1922, p. 3; Roberts, *The Most Powerful Man in the World*, 228.

33 "the whole of Baku's wealth": Roberts, *The Most Powerful Man in the World*, 183.

33 Rockefeller's Standard Oil: Tolf, *The Russian Rockefellers*, 214–17.

33 The first deal proceeded: George Sweet Gibb and Evelyn H. Knowlton, *History of Standard Oil Co.*, vol. 2 (New York: Harper and Row, 1956), 330.

33 Great Britain's Anglo-Persian: Paul Hendrix, *Henri Deterding and Royal Dutch Shell* (Bristol, Eng.: Bristol Academic Press, 2002), 176.

33 Emanuel had been a wide-eyed: Tolf, *The Russian Rockefellers*, 109–11, 144.

33 Photographs of the Kazakh: *Petroleum Encyclopedia of Kazakhstan* (London: Anglo-Caspian Services Ltd., 1999), 48–56.

34 When the Bolsheviks closed: Tolf, *The Russian Rockefellers*, 210–11.

34 "a production engineer's dream": Memo by Everit J. Sadler quoted in *History of Standard Oil Co.*, vol. 2, pp. 331–32.

34 On May 13, 1919: *History of Standard Oil Co.*, vol. 2, p. 334.

34 Teagle was so enthralled: *History of Standard Oil Co.*, vol. 2, pp. 332–33.

34 "If we do not": Teagle memo to A. C. Bedford quoted in *History of Standard Oil Co.*, vol. 2, p. 333.

35 "capitalist bloodsuckers": Tolf, *The Russian Rockefellers*, 210.

35 Baku's barons had snickered: Author interview with Akhundov.

35 Tagiyev himself had founded: Author interviews with Akhundov and Abdullayeva.

35 Tagiyev and the ever faithful: Author interview with Abdullayeva.

36 Some days before: Author interview with Zuleha Weber.

36 Wordlessly, Tagiyev choked and: Author interview with Abdullayeva.

36 Five days later: Author interview with Abdullayeva.

36–38 "played poker to," "There were jewels," "turbulent, remonstrative, despising": Details of Banine's escape and life in Istanbul and Paris are from Banine, *Jours Caucasiens* (Paris: repr. Gris Banal, 1985), 198–99.

38 "the cafes of Paris": Nubar Gulbenkian, *Portrait in Oil* (New York: Simon and Schuster, 1965), 217.

38 One of these traders: Tolf, *The Russian Rockefellers*, 217.

38 Zeynalabdin Tagiyev's daughter Leyla: Author interviews with Abdullayeva's granddaughter, Gulnar Safyurtlu; her great-granddaughter, Leyla Aru; and Assadulayeva, January 9, 2000, in Vienna, Virginia.

38 Ali knew he had to work: Author interview with Abdullayeva.

38 By the German invasion: Author interview with Weber.

39 Misfortune seemed to haunt: Author interviews with Abdullayeva and Akhundov.

39 "Were you waiting": Author interview with Abdullayeva.

39 Just after her divorce: Author interview with Abdullayeva.

40 A gunman had slain: Robert Conquest, *The Great Terror* (London: Hutchinson, 1994), 37.

40 "I was glad": Author interview with Abdullayeva.

40 And the three-story mansion: Tolf, *The Russian Rockefellers*, 232.

Chapter 4: Soviet Days

41 "As red as": Banine, *Jours Caucasiens*, 180.

42 Much of the decline: Robert E. Ebel, *The Petroleum Industry of the Soviet Union* (New York: American Petroleum Institute, 1961), 74.

42 Industrial production sank: R. W. Davies, "Industry" in *The Economic Transformation of the Soviet Union, 1913–1945*, ed. R. W. Davies, Mark Harrison, Stephen Wheatcroft (Cambridge, Eng.: Cambridge University Press, 1994), 135.

42 "middle classes would panic": Margaret MacMillan, *Paris 1919: Six Months That Changed the World* (New York: Random House, 2001), 69.

43 In 1902, while secretly: Hendrix, *Henri Deterding and Royal Dutch Shell*, 174–75.

43 Krassin proposed a partnership: Hendrix, *Henri Deterding and Royal Dutch Shell*, 196–98.

44 "We have failed": Quoted in George F. Kennan, *Russia and the West Under Lenin and Stalin* (Boston: Little, Brown, 1960–61), 172.

44 They agreed to call themselves: Roberts, *The Most Powerful Man in the World*, 229–43; Hendrix, *Henri Deterding and Royal Dutch Shell*, 230–35.

44 "The hostility toward": Hendrix, *Henri Deterding and Royal Dutch Shell*, 232.

44 Indeed, within months: Hendrix, *Henri Deterding and Royal Dutch Shell*, 244–45.

45 "Oilmen are like cats": Gulbenkian, *Portrait in Oil*, 96.

45 Gulbenkian himself provided: Gulbenkian, *Portrait in Oil*, 127, 131.

45 became a money launderer: Gulbenkian, *Portrait in Oil*, 127, 131.

45 Hammer earned from both sides: Gulbenkian, *Portrait in Oil*, 73–76, 95.

46 "to the almost fabulous": *The New York Times*, November 5, 1927, p. 4.

46 The owner of a New York–based: Antony C. Sutton, *Western Technology and Soviet Economic Development, 1917 to 1930* (Stanford, Calif.: Hoover Institution Press, 1968), 17, 20, 22.

46 "virtually the fiscal agent": Katherine A. S. Siegel, *Loans and Legitimacy* (Lexington, Ken.: University Press of Kentucky, 1996), 120–22.

46 "to guarantee any outlay": *The New York Times*, November 16, 1921, p. 19.

46 Day's first oil crew: Sutton, *Western Technology, 1917 to 1930*, 1, 25.

46 Their electric pumps: Sutton, *Western Technology, 1917 to 1930*, 25–26.

47 American, German, and British companies: Sutton, *Western Technology, 1917 to 1930*, 33–35.

47 American and British companies: Sutton, *Western Technology, 1917 to 1930*, 35–37.

47 In nearby Georgia: Sutton, *Western Technology, 1917 to 1930*, 19, 28–29.

47 But the best oil deal: O'Connor, *The Oil Barons*, 256–58.

47 **"something like a frog"**: Richard O'Connor, *The Oil Barons* (Boston: Little, Brown, 1971), 242.

47 **Japan, which had operated:** Frank C. Hanighen, *The Secret War* (New York: John Day Co., 1934), 225–26.

47 **"Russia's salesman":** Hanighen, *The Secret War,* 254.

48 **The revival of Baku's oil fields:** Hanighen, *The Secret War,* 109–10, 115, 118–19.

49 **"savage determination":** H. R. Knickerbocker, *The Red Trade Menace* (New York: Dodd, Mead, 1931), 132–34.

49 **"I drove over":** Knickerbocker, *The Red Trade Menace,* 135.

51 **"a place of wonder":** Author interview with Sabir Guseynov, October 7, 1995.

51 **A secret CIA report:** CIA report SC/RR 100 of June 1, 1955, p. 36.

51 **"first tangible evidence":** *The New York Times,* September 23, 1949, p. 1.

51 **"The future of the Baku":** CIA report SC/RR 100 of June 1, 1955, p. 6.

52 **"They felt pretty good":** Author interview with Ebel, August 24, 2004; Ebel, *The Petroleum Industry,* 53–55.

52 **they had also invented:** *The New York Times,* March 3, 1956, p. 4; *The Wall Street Journal,* May 12, 1956, p. 1; and *The Wall Street Journal,* June 8, 1956, p. 1.

53 **"made it so simple":** *The New York Times,* March 1, 1956, p. 47.

53 **"violently anti-Russian":** Author interview with Ralph Feuerring, July 4, 2004. A Swede, Feuerring was one of the few westerners who did business with the Soviets in the 1950s.

Chapter 5: The Middleman

54 **"crowded bars and card rooms":** Leonard Gardner, *Fat City* (New York: Farrar, Straus and Giroux, 1969), 85.

55 **Riverboats from San Francisco:** Robert E. Levinson, *The Jews in the California Gold Rush* (Jersey City, N.J.: Ktav Publishing House, 1978), 94, 174.

55 **"hick":** Author interview with Briggs.

55 **a Beau Brummel:** Author interview with Melvin Corren, a prominent eighty-year-old Stockton merchant who knew Lloyd Giffen, January 15, 2004.

55 **Lloyd Giffen was an Oklahoma:** *Stockton Record,* August 14, 1995.

55 **He landed a job:** 1939 Stockton telephone directory.

55 **His death in 1938:** *Stockton Record,* January 6, 1938, p. 1.

55 **His Oxford shop:** From author interviews with his competitors, John Falls and Dick Briggs, January 20, 2004.

56 **"finicky":** Author interview with Falls.

56 **"I don't have a thing":** Author interview with Falls.

56 **he attracted a number:** Author interview with Falls.

56 **he liked to knit:** Author interview with Briggs, who witnessed the episodes.

56 **He socialized with the men:** Author interview with Falls.

56 **On weekends, he, Lucile:** Author interview with Ernie Segale (February 23, 2004), who, along with his father, was friends with Lloyd and James Giffen during the latter's boyhood. Segale's parents were part of the Saturday Nighters.

56 **Blond and chubby:** Author interview with Segale.

56 **Indeed, he dreamed:** Author interview with Giffen.

57 **"had an agenda":** Author interview with Michael Barkett (July 29, 2004), Giffen's roommate at that time. In a separate interview, DU member John Montgomery used the same "had an agenda" language to describe Giffen.

57 **"wanted to go places":** Author interview with fraternity brother John Montgomery, July 27, 2004.

57 **"where the dough was":** Author interview with fraternity brother Larry Costa, September 2, 2004.

57 **"would scare the":** Author interview with Costa.

57 **"I've got the kind":** Author interview with Barkett.

57 **But Newsom also credited:** Author interview with Dave Newsom, February 27, 2004.

58 **"cuter than a bug's ear":** Author interview with Barkett.

58 **It made him feel important:** Author interview with Costa.

58 **whose personal scrapbook:** E-mail correspondence with Marijean Huesman, a former roommate of June Hopkins, August 16, 2004.

58 **"stage door Johnny":** June Hopkins quoted in *New Orleans Magazine*, August 2003.

58 **Giffen was dazzled:** Author interview with Costa.

58 **"woke me up":** Author interview with Giffen.

58 **"When he finally":** Author interview with Giffen.

59 **He began to style:** Author interview with Dan Wallace, October 11, 2004.

59 **Giffen abruptly informed:** Author interview with Wallace.

59 **Without informing their parents:** Author interview with Wallace; *Stockton Record*, November 7, 1961; author interview with fraternity brother Lee Greiner, August 30, 2004.

59 **"you didn't bluff":** Author interview with Virginia Proehl.

60 **"brilliance and success":** Author interview with Virginia Proehl, January 8, 2004.

60 **Jim's success with the assignment:** Author interview with Falls.

60 **He turned to David Hopkins:** Author interview with Louis Baker, September 29, 2003; author interview with his law partner, Mark Ancel, September 29, 2003.

60 **Before long the tax lawyer:** Author interview with Baker.

60 **About the same time:** Author interview with Giffen.

60 **"open any door":** Author interview with Agop Chalekian, an Oztemel partner, August 10, 2004.

60 **"very excited":** Author interview with Mary Oztemel, July 19, 2004.

60 **"fell in love":** Author interview with Stanley Weiss, an Oztemel partner, August 17, 2004.

60 **"Ara's main interest"**: Author interview with Feuerring, July 4, 2004.

61 **Giffen, by this point a deputy public**: L.A. Public Defender's Office personnel records show that Giffen's employment was February 3, 1967 to July 26, 1968.

61 **"I'm moving to New York"**: Author interview with Virginia Proehl.

61 **Oztemel, a saxophone-playing**: Author interview with Mary Oztemel.

61 **"Middle East potentate"**: Author interview with John Huhs, one of Giffen's first hires after going to work for Oztemel. Huhs sat for numerous interviews from 1999 to 2006.

61 **"The Answer Man"**: *Dun's Review*, October 1975, p. 58.

61 **Upon returning home**: Author interviews with Oztemel's colleagues, wife, and sons, 2003 and 2004.

62 **"men who by virtue"**: A. Craig Copetas, *Metal Men* (New York: G. P. Putnam's Sons, 1985), 11.

62 **"outlaw bravado"**: Copetas, *Metal Men*, 21.

62 **He loved Soviets**: Author interview with Bernard Majech (July 11, 2004), who as Ralph Feuerring's agent in Europe negotiated the deal with Oztemel.

63 **"a lot of drinking"**: Author interview with Bernt Rathaus, former Satra executive, May 2, 2004.

63 **When the Soviets wanted to export**: *War and Peace* won the Oscar for Best Foreign Film in 1965, and for *Moscow Doesn't Believe in Tears* in 1980.

63 **In the case of the 1962**: Author interview with Majech.

63 **The only initial difficulty**: Author interview with Feuerring.

64 **the predictable insecurities**: Author interviews with Chalekian and with Oztemel's longtime secretary, Beth Longley.

64 **For his partner Feuerring**: Author interviews with Feuerring, longtime Oztemel lawyer Hanno Mott, April 22, 2004, and Mary Oztemel.

65 **He was awarded shares**: Author interview with Huhs.

65 **Virginia Proehl detested Jim**: Author interview with Virginia Proehl.

65 **At Stanford University**: Author interviews with Huhs and Carl Longley, 1999 to 2005.

65 **In their interviews**: Author interviews with Huhs and Longley.

66 **without any advance payment**: Giffen claimed that he received a $20,000 advance payment. Rowson, however, said Praeger did not provide such payments.

66 **"establishing him as"**: Author interview with Richard Rowson, March 16, 2004.

66 **As he and Rowson**: Author interview with Rowson.

66 **One learned, for example**: James Henry Giffen, *The Legal and Practical Aspects of Trade with the Soviet Union* (New York: Frederick A. Praeger, 1969), 161.

67 **"I was flying"**: Author interview with Giffen.

67 **"manifest destiny to be"**: Author interviews with Longley, in 2003 and 2004. On

Giffen's presidential aspirations, author interviews with Huhs, Mott, and Robert DeMaria, a Giffen colleague at Satra.

Chapter 6: Détente

69 **In this telling:** Author interviews with Chalekian and Mary Oztemel.

69 **"leverage in selling":** December 22, 1972, letter from Paul Proehl to Duane O. Wood, vice president of Lockheed Aircraft.

70 **"gets angry and says":** Author interview with Helland, March 23, 2004.

70 **"It's yours":** Author interview with Virginia Proehl.

71 **Aboard an airliner:** Author interviews with Longley, Huhs, and DeMaria.

71 **When John Huhs's wife:** Author interview with Huhs.

71 **"The phone started ringing":** Author interview with Huhs.

72 **Oztemel intervened:** Author interview with Mary Oztemel.

72 **"use it for linkage":** Author interview with Peter Peterson, October 14, 2003.

72 **Even though the value:** Author interview with Huhs.

72 **Meticulously dressed:** Author interview with Longley.

73 **"He could walk":** Author interview with Longley.

73 **"Jeeb tells me":** Halaby and his wife quoted in *The Wall Street Journal,* October 5, 1971, p. 37.

73 **"wanted to imitate Ara":** Author interview with Oztemel intimate who requested not to be identified.

73 **Jerome Komes, a senior vice president:** April 28, 1972, letter from Paul Proehl to Oztemel describing Proehl's face-to-face conversation that day with Komes about the Halaby-Giffen meeting.

74 **Oztemel found out:** Author interviews with Huhs, Carl and Beth Longley, Chalekian, Mott, and Gilbert Mathieu, another Satra principal.

74 **He boasted to Proehl:** Proehl letter of May 10, 1972, to Oztemel regarding Giffen's claims to a job offer from James Ingersoll, Borg-Warner's president.

74 **"I want this guy":** Author interview with Michael Sekus (March 11, 2004), who worked for Giffen at Armco and then Mercator.

75 **"common touch":** *The New York Times,* August 12, 1987, p. D1.

75 **"chasing the same girls," "lassy and sexy":** Author interview with C. William Verity, September 16, 2004.

75 **Moving in such privileged:** Verity, *Fifty-Nine Years with the Right Woman* (self-published, 2003), 44; *The New York Times,* August 12, 1987, p. D1.

75 **In June 1973:** *The New York Times,* June 23, 1973, pp. 1, 9; author interview with Verity; Joseph Finder, *Red Carpet* (New York: Holt, Rinehart and Winston, 1983), 254–55.

76 **"We're looking forward":** *The Wall Street Journal,* June 25, 1973, p. 7.

76 **"a falling out":** Quotes and account of the origin of Verity's relationship with Giffen are from author interviews with Verity, September 16 and 28, 2004.

76 **A few months later:** *The New York Times*, December 8, 1973, p. 49.

76 **four years later:** *Journal of Commerce*, March 15, 1977, p. 1.

77 **Although still a married:** Among Giffen's office romances was Terry Nixon, who dated him in the 1970s and remained his executive secretary after their romance stopped. Another, Adrian Hoenig, dated Giffen in the early 1980s and remained on Giffen's staff in Kazakhstan until her death in 1998. From author interview with a longtime former executive.

77 **Many of his clients:** Author interviews with Sekus and other friends and former executives.

77 **"You know what Jim":** Author interview with Falls.

77 **"because the agency":** Author interview with Bud Johnson, September 28, 2003.

78 **"part of the bargain":** Author interview with DeMaria, July 27, 2004.

78 **"Tell me everything":** Author interview with Giffen.

78 **"He turned his back":** Author interview with Sekus.

79 **"I watched and learned," the "rich Giffens," "poor Giffens":** Author interview with Giffen.

79–80 **"I couldn't have taken," "I was like," "a good way," "It was terribly," "he'd make out," "They stopped letting," "to tolerate Jim," "I just don't":** Author interview with Verity.

80 **"Giffen wanted to marry":** Author interview with a former executive to Giffen.

81 **"It was odd":** Author interview with Sekus.

Chapter 7: The Perfect Oil Field

82 **"he would look":** Author interview with J. Dennis Bonney, former vice chairman of Chevron, November 16, 2004.

82 **"impossible not to like":** Pavel Palazchenko, *My Years with Gorbachev and Shevardnadze* (University Park: Penn State University Press, 1997), 26.

82 **"a sort of torpor":** Lev Churilov, *Lifeblood of Empire: A Personal History of the Rise and Fall of the Soviet Oil Industry* (New York: PIW Publications, 1996), 19–20. After a career in the Soviet oil industry, Churilov was oil minister near the end of Gorbachev's rule.

83 **"barracks socialism," "the omnipotence of," "alarm about the":** Mikhail Gorbachev, *Memoirs* (New York: Doubleday, 1995), 239.

83 **"jump-start":** Author interview with Giffen.

83 **"just rip you," "so many things":** Author interview with Giffen.

83 **"Giffen had long advocated":** Account of ATC's origin from author interview with Giffen.

84 **"fucking ingenious":** Author interview with Giffen.

84 **Brady served as:** Keller conversation with Brady from author interview with George Keller, June 17, 1999.

84 **"Get on a plane":** Author interview with Giffen.

85 **"a suede-shoe feeling":** Author interview with Keller.

85 **"we weren't concerned":** Author interview with Ken Derr, March 25, 2004.

85 **"not a lot":** Author interview with Derr.

86 **Yet the worm of adventure:** Author interview with Bonney.

86 **"Brady tells us":** Author interview with Keller.

87 **"When can you get," "George, let's talk," "Okay, John—but":** Author interview with John Silcox, former head of Chevron Overseas, June 17, 1999. In interviews, accounts of the meeting by Keller, Silcox, Derr, and Giffen generally coincided.

87 **"it was impossible":** *The New York Times,* July 31, 1988, p. F4.

88 **"I said it":** Author interview with Silcox.

88 **"An American in Moscow":** *The Wall Street Journal,* May 3, 1988, p. 1.

88 **"gripped this opportunity," "started throwing bombs":** Author interview with Bill Crain, Chevron's former executive for overseas exploration and production, October 8, 2004. Details on survey from Crain and Derr.

89 **"was a business concept":** Author interview with Silcox.

89 **"They asked him":** Author interview with Derr.

89 **"an oil field that":** Author interview with Chevron geologist Norman Jokerst, October 18, 2004.

89 **"on a first-name basis":** *The New York Times,* July 31, 1988, p. F4.

90 **"flirting with all":** Author interview with Jokerst.

90 **"read everything that":** Author interview with Allan Martini, Chevron's former vice president for exploration and production, one of the three-man team with Silcox, October 7, 2004.

91 **"You sort of felt":** Author interview with Martini.

91 **"You don't have a budget":** Recalled by Martini in author interview.

91 **The early Siberian fields:** Churilov, *Lifeblood of Empire,* 138.

91 **"The guys haven't":** Crain in a personal video he showed to author.

91–92 **"if a pipeline leaked," "to suck the," "ten straws into":** Author interview with Chevron's Malcolm Boyce, December 29, 2004.

92 **"exploration and production":** Churilov, *Lifeblood of Empire,* 19–20.

92 **"While we were developing":** Churilov, *Lifeblood of Empire,* 138.

92 **"not only no":** Author interview with Boyce.

92 **"It seemed the Cold War":** Author interview with Crain.

92 **"literally shaken," "He was flabbergasted," "incredible organization of":** Author interview with Jokerst, who led most of the Moscow trips.

93 **"we simply could no longer," "as happy as," "unfathomably grateful to":** Author interview with Sagat Tugelbayev, May 26, 2004.

93 **"We're just getting ready"**: Author interview with Boyce, quoting a senior Soviet official.

95 **"Only one new"**: CIA report, "The North Caspian Basin: Salvation for Soviet Oil Production?" April 1989, p. 1. Report released as part of the Princeton Project, a collection of Soviet-era CIA documents declassified and presented at a public conference at Princeton University in March 2001.

96 **When their tour reached:** Author interview with Nahum Schneidermann, the first Chevron employee on Tengiz soil, November 4, 2004.

96 **"continuing flow of unburned"**: *Oil and Gas Journal*, February 3, 1986, p. 29.

96 **"scary to work there"**: Author interview with Tugelbayev.

96 **"tall as a"**: French technician quoted in *Platt's Oilgram News*, February 21, 1986, p. 2.

96 **The ground was littered:** Author interview with Tugelbayev.

96 **"they were on to"**: Author interview with Jokerst.

97 **"consisted of a couple"**: Author interview with Silcox.

97 **"very sophisticated equipment"**: Author interview with Boyce.

97 **"Clean up your place," "to someone who"**: Author interview with Tugelbayev.

98 **"really just oil"**: Churilov, *Lifeblood of Empire*, 206–12.

98 **"glutenous bag"**: Author interview with Crain.

99 **"this was all"**: Author interview with Dale Wooddy, January 4, 2004.

99 **"shrimp is harvested"**: *Rabochaya Tribune*, July 6, 1991.

99 **"You aren't going"**: Author interview with Wooddy.

99 **"Even the Tengiz"**: Giffen's January 9, 1990, letter to Gorbachev, obtained from Giffen.

100 **"only wanted to do"**: Author interview with Wooddy.

100 **"the chance to deal"**: Author interview with Sandy Cornelius, at the time general director of TengizChevroil in Atyrau, on May 26, 2004.

100 **"realized that if"**: Author interview with Wooddy.

100 **"Keep the offshore"**: Author interview with Dick Matzke, March 2, 2004.

100 **"needed foreign help"**: Churilov, *Lifeblood of Empire*, 206.

100 **"had thrown everything"**: Churilov, *Lifeblood of Empire*, 205.

101 **"wanted to make a splash"**: Author interview with Derr.

101 **"tormented us"**: Churilov, *Lifeblood of Empire*, 207.

Chapter 8: Crossfire

102–3 **"stopped exploring," "to harvest what"**: Author interview with BP's Tom Hamilton, September 18, 2004.

103 **"the era of oil"**: Yergin, *The Prize*, 134.

103 **"risk-averse"**: Author interview with Hamilton.

103 **"Nintendo geologists"**: Ibid.

103 **"a Ferrari engine"**: Ibid.

104 **"the look of a miniature"**: Anthony Sampson, *The Seven Sisters* (New York: Viking, 1975), 200.

104 **"redrilled every well"**: Author interview with Hamilton.

105 **"breakthrough countries," "with high exploration"**: Joseph A. Pratt, *Prelude to Merger: A History of Amoco Corporation, 1973–1998* (Houston: Hart Publications, 2000), 160.

105 **In general, the oil industry:** Chevron, Amoco, BP, and others had produced nearly simultaneous internal studies targeting the same countries for exploration.

105 **"alarmed"**: *Business Week*, June 11, 1990, p. 36.

105 **Oil production was falling:** Declassified CIA report, "Falling Soviet Oil Production: No Quick Fixes," August 1, 1991.

106 **"because of the size"**: Author interview with Hamilton.

106 **"we can do"**: *The New York Times*, December 18, 1984, p. A3.

106 **"start some investment," "get to Moscow"**: Author interview with Rondo Fehlberg, Hamilton's top deputy in the Soviet Union, February 1, 2005.

107 **A chance encounter:** Author interview with Grynberg, April 16, 1998.

107 **"I had never heard"**: Author interview with Grynberg.

108 **"Check on him"**: Author interview with Fehlberg, April 1, 1996.

108 **"Jack, you will"**: Author interview with Grynberg.

108 **"the thrill of the chase"**: Author interview with Hamilton.

109 **"If we were"**: Author interview with Fehlberg.

109 **"hated each other"**: Author interview with Boyce.

109–10 **"If you can bring," "absolutely positively would"**: Author interview with Fehlberg.

110 **In Almaty, Nazarbayev:** Author interview with Hamilton.

110 **"a sign that"**: Author interview with Fehlberg.

110 **"we saw this enormous," "Holy shit"**: Author interview with Hamilton.

111 **"an important, busy, impatient," "smelling a rat"**: Author interview with Fehlberg.

111 **Karamanov was suffering:** Ibid.

112 **"If he had seen"**: Author interview with Uzakbay Karamanov, December 29, 2002.

112 **"a one-man chamber"**: *The New York Times*, July 30, 1990, p. D1.

112 **"a precondition for any"**: Churilov, *Lifeblood of Empire*, 206–12.

113 **"paused, grabbed"**: *Fortune*, October 22, 1990.

113 **"We can't stop you"**: Encounter recalled by Hamilton and Fehlberg in author interviews.

113 **"if we scare off"**: Author interview with Halyk Abdullayev, Kazakhstan's deputy prime minister who led Kazakh negotiations with Chevron through about April 1992, on September 10, 2002. In a separate author interview, Giffen also described the admonition.

113–14 "an essential power broker," "a careful, intelligent": *The Washington Post*, July 30, 1991, p. A10.

114 "was recused on energy": Author interview with James Baker, May 14, 1999.

114 "At that time": Author interview with Jack Matlock, May 5, 1999.

114 "very, very supportive": Author interview with Derr.

114 "Chevron had asked": Author interview with Brent Scowcroft, June 1, 1999.

115 "up to date," "I would love," "he calls Scowcroft": Author interview with Derr.

115 "inundated us with faxes": Churilov, *Lifeblood of Empire*, 206–12.

115 "commanding intonation": *Moskovskie Novosti*, June 23, 1991, p. 10.

115 "Tengiz was quite big": Churilov, *Lifeblood of Empire*, 206–12.

116 "a sorry place": Author interview with Sandy Cornelius, May 26, 2004.

116 Yet the group felt: Photographs appeared in *Kazakhstanskaya Pravda*, July 20, 1990, p. 1.

116 "looked like something": Author interview with Cornelius.

117 "The administrative processes": Ibid.

117 "this is something big," "There is enough": Ibid.

117 "This is not a third-world": Ibid.

117 "an oil statesman": Ibid.

118 To make each, refiners: William D. McCain, Jr., *The Properties of Petroleum Fluids*, 2d ed. (Tulsa, Okla.: PennWell Books, 1990), 2.

118 "was the difference": Author interview with Wooddy.

119–20 "swallow half the province," "kind of acted," "strategy session," "we are going," "it wasn't the": Ibid.

120 "we had been sidelined," "hunch that Tengiz": Author interview with Halyk Abdullayev.

120 "wolf's ticket": Ibid.

120 "losing its grip," "ran out of": Author interview with Boyce, who noticed the change from Moscow and Kazakhstan.

120 "decidedly unrebellious": *Washington Post*, November 1, 1990, p. A33.

120 "a Marlboro-smoking metallurgist," "had the luck": Author interview with Abdullayev.

120 "the locals get": *Business Week*, August 13, 1990, p. 48.

121 "didn't have the kind," "formed by a special": Ibid.

121 "a U.S. government–sponsored": Author interview with John Peppercorn, November 1, 2004.

121 "I even saw," "big and significant": Author interview with Abdullayev.

121 after hours, the president: Author interview with Boyce, December 29, 2004. In the elevator with his wife, Boyce encountered the Kazakh leader.

121–22 "all those huge," "to a degree": Author interview with Abdullayev.

122 **"if we are going"**: Author interview with Chevron source who asked not to be identified.

122 **in April, Giffen's**: *The New York Times*, April 3, 1991, p. C15.

122 **"the Soviet Union's trump"**: Yegor Gaidar, *Days of Defeat and Victory* (Seattle: University of Washington Press, 2000), 39.

122 **"questions after questions"**: Author interview with Derr.

122 **"Chevron would end up"**: Gaidar, *Days of Defeat and Victory*, 40.

123 **"plundered"**: *Moskovskie Novosti*, June 2, 1991, p. 10.

123 **"Kazakhstan would henceforth"**: Churilov, *Lifeblood of Empire*, 206–12. Churilov gave the date of Gorbachev's assent as May and said word filtered down to him in June.

123 **"could not accept"**: Author interview with Derr.

123 **"didn't understand and wanted"**: Author interview with Giffen.

123 **"golden boy"**: Author interview with Boyce.

123 **"but he did it," "always had a"**: Author interview with Crain.

123 **"was a schmoozer"**: Author interview with Espy Price, September 21, 2004.

123 **"to be considered," "made a stink"**: Author interview with Boyce.

123 **"special skills"**: Author interview with Crain.

124 **"When are you"**: Author interview with Giffen.

124 **"to a dead end"**: Author interview with Abdullayev.

124 **Yeltsin himself appeared**: Nursultan Nazarbayev, *Without Right and Left* (London: Class Publishing, 1992), 148.

124 **"the animals died"**: Nazarbayev, *Without Right and Left*, 4.

124 **"consent to be"**: Nazarbayev, *Without Right and Left*, 160.

125 **"hold back"**: Author interview with Sergei Tereshchenko, June 13, 2003.

125 **"hard-liners"**: *The New York Times*, August 25, 1991, p. F12.

125 **"Well, I guess"**: Author interview with Derr.

125 **"a real feeling," "that would work"**: Author interview with Wooddy.

126 **"It cannot be"**: Author interview with Abdullayev.

126 **"made both parties"**: Author interview with Wooddy.

126 **"You ought to become," "that line"**: Author interview with Morley Dupré, March 26, 2004. Dupré was Matzke's deputy in the negotiations beginning in September 1991.

126 **"Giffen was never"**: Author interview with Abdullayev.

126 **"enough glory in"**: Author interview with Chevron official who asked not to be identified.

126 **"the most important"**: Author interview with Matzke.

127 **"demanded from us"**: Author interview with Abdullayev.

127 **"This released me," "but couldn't do"**: Author interview with Giffen, confirmed in author interview with Bonney.

Chapter 9: The First Deal

128 Johannes Christiaan Martinus: Dutch websites estimated Deuss's wealth in the hundreds of millions by the 1990s, and at $1 billion by 2003, when he was judged the eighteenth-richest man in the country by a new site: www.allesopeenrij.nl.

129 "in the middle": Author interview with Ed Smith, a vice president of Deuss's Caspian Pipeline Consortium, September 30, 1996.

129 "I would not": *Business Week,* June 30, 1986, quoting J. P. Donlon, editor of *Chief Executive,* a Deuss-founded magazine.

130 "this 7- to," "was the principal": Author interview with Mack Fowler, Deuss's principal subordinate on the pipeline deal, November 20, 1996.

130 "We ended up," "for him a": Author interview with Abdullayev.

131 A meeting was quickly: Author interview with Tereshchenko.

131 The portly Tereshchenko: Author interview with Tereshchenko.

131 "tens, hundreds": Author interview with Tereshchenko.

131 "thrown into the sea": Author interview with Tereshchenko.

132 "tricked": Quotation and description of Deuss's boyhood from *Business Week,* June 30, 1986, which reflected a series of Deuss's written replies to the magazine's questions.

132 "mystery buyer": Longley's account from a September 18, 2003, e-mail exchange with author.

133 "out of his jam": Author interview with Smith.

133 Sometimes operating under: The investigation was by South Africa's advocate general and was released in a confidential June 1984 report to the country's parliament.

134 "sailed alongside the partly": Ibid., p. 4B.

134 Since the South Africans: "John Deuss / Transworld Oil," January 1985 report by the Shipping Research Bureau, Amsterdam. The Shipping Bureau's report included a cargo-by-cargo list of Deuss's shipments to South Africa it traced. Deuss permitted his executives to speak with the author during the 1990s, but declined to respond to queries himself. As noted, in some cases people close to him requested anonymity, usually because they thought it could rupture their relationship with him.

134 "counterproductive to correcting": *Business Week,* June 30, 1986.

134 "the change we": United Press International dispatch, October 14, 1987.

134 "knew everyone": Author interview with a former Deuss associate who asked to remain anonymous.

134 "helped Deuss": David Corn, *Blond Ghost* (New York: Simon and Schuster, 1994), 372.

134 "instead of Shell": Author interview with Fowler.

135 The purchase caused a stir: *The Wall Street Journal,* April 4, 1986, p. 1.

136 **"Leave your business card"**: Author visit to Deuss's home, September 7, 1998.

136 **"business, business, business"**: Author interview with Dupré.

136 **"a highly entertaining"**: Mazur's September 15, 2004, article in the *Royal Gazette* (Bermuda). Mazur confirmed some of the details in a January 27, 2005, interview with the author.

137 **"Mr. Deuss . . . is"**: James Tanner, *The Wall Street Journal,* June 14, 1988, p. 1.

137 **"discovered to [his] horror"**: Author interview with Abdullayev.

137 **The new round of talks**: Author interview with Matzke.

138 **"There was always"**: Author interview with Dupré.

138 **"multibillion-dollar negotiations"**: Author interview with Wooddy.

138 **"take the edge off"**: Author interview with Smith.

138 **"always had a sweet"**: Author interview with Dupré.

139 **"the realization of this project"**: *Christian Science Monitor,* World Section, April 24, 1992, p. 1.

139 **"I don't know"**: *The Washington Post,* April 9, 1992, p. D10.

139 **"a campaign in the press"**: *Christian Science Monitor,* April 24, 1992.

139 **"he needed to give"**: Author interview with Fowler.

140 **"friggin' disaster"**: Author interview with Dupré.

140 **"Deuss was able"**: Ibid.

140–41 **"totally strait-laced," "felt all Chevron," "take it out," "Derr showed up"**: Author interview with Dupré.

141 **"was not a benevolent"**: Author interview with Dupré.

141 **"most bad stories"**: Author interview with Wooddy.

141 **"where Chevron outsmarted"**: Author interview with Giffen.

142 **"the world's hottest"**: *Platt's Oilgram News,* July 27, 1992.

142 **"ready to do," "the Kazakhs would," "It was just"**: Author interview with Fowler.

143 **"taking the cargo"**: Author interview with Wooddy.

143 **"I'll bet you're glad"**: Author interview with Wooddy.

Chapter 10: Return to Baku

145 **"like Oklahoma or"**: Author interview with Scott Barber (October 28, 1998), who first served with Amoco and then Unocal in Baku.

145 **"much like any"**: Michael Dobbs, *The Washington Post,* February 16, 1990, p. A1.

145 **"a stylish quality"**: [London] *Guardian,* October 15, 1990.

145 **"had to walk my pug"**: Author interview with Robert Finn, August 9, 1999.

146 **"spillage"**: Author interview with Hamilton.

147 **"eyes started itching"**: Author interview with Paolo Lembo, February 1997.

147 **"tanks rolled over"**: Thomas de Waal, *Black Garden* (New York: NYU Press, 2003), 93.

147 **"out of habit"**: Keller, *The New York Times,* February 18, 1990.

148 "Armenians were thrown": De Waal, *Black Garden*, 90.

148 "a seat at the table": Author interview with Steve Remp, September 6, 1996.

149 Out came his personal: Khoshbakht Yusufzade took the photograph from his office safe, November 28, 1996.

149 "was dead": Author interview with Remp.

149 "You never felt": Author interview with Tim Hartnett, August 29, 1996.

149 "We will liquidate": Author interview with Tom Doss (September 15, 2004), who headed Amoco's Baku negotiations starting in 1991.

150 "super megastructures": Author interview with Remp.

150 "What do you suggest?": Author interview with Fehlberg, April 1, 1996.

151 "coming-out party": Ibid.

151–52 an American citizen, "one in ten": Author interview with Ray Leonard, Amoco's vice president for frontier exploration, February 7, 2005.

152 "risk-taker," "liked technical people": Author interview with Doss.

152 "didn't mind making": Author interview with Sammy San Miguel (December 12, 2003), who represented McDermott, a British-based oil service company that was Amoco's partner in the competition.

153 "This isn't serious": Author interview with Leonard.

153 "an insurance policy," "Don't sign that": Author interview with Rob Sobhani, who spoke in numerous interviews in January 2005.

153 At the oil show: Author interview with Leonard; Pratt, *Prelude to Merger*, 182–83.

154 BP's Rondo Fehlberg: February 12, 2005, e-mail exchange with Hugh Pope, who covered it for the *Independent* of London.

154 "promising eternal friendship": Author interview with Leonard.

154 "But we have": Author interview with Fehlberg.

154 "for love or money," "There should be": Ibid.

155 "Just keep going": Author interview with Hamilton.

155 "viewed this as": Author interview with Hamilton.

156 "had much bigger fish," "very much a": Author interview with Fehlberg.

156 "the foreigners like": Author interview with Yusufzade, November 28, 1996.

156 "was not in the business": Author interview with Fehlberg.

157 "Let's draw up": Ibid.

157 "If anyone's agreement,": Ibid.

158 "if these companies": Ibid.

158 "We've got some," "to see if": Author interviews with L. Todd Gremillion, a partner in the Houston office of Akin Gump Strauss Hauer and Feld, February 12, 2004, February 10, 2005.

158 "Amoco's bid was": Author interview with Jack Langlois, Gremillion's colleague at Akin Gump, February 10, 2005.

158 BP had proposed: Pratt, *Prelude to Merger*, 183.

159 "shattering," "If we don't," "we could get," "That's not good": Author interview with a BP executive who spoke on condition he not be identified.

159 "make some progress": Author interview with Hartnett.

159 "a couple of days": Author interview with Fehlberg.

159 "very literate": Author interview with Sanan Alizade, November 28, 1996.

159 He had won: Author interview with Alizade.

160 "where we had," "from there you'd": Author interview with Doss.

160 "reasonably persuasive": Author interview with Amoco's Bill Young, September 3, 1996.

160 "we were just": Author interview with Doss.

160 "a demonstration of obscene": Author interview with Doss.

161 "get these others": Author interview with Hartnett.

162 "financial folks": Author interview with Hamilton.

162 "treating me like": Author interview with Remp.

163 "drank Vietnamese tea": Author interview with Hamilton.

163 "just offered us": Author interview with Dave Henderson, September 29, 2004.

163 "the big boys": Author interview with Fehlberg.

163 "in front of": Author interview with Fehlberg.

164 "It is more complex": Author interview with Fehlberg.

164 "We'd just march down": Author interview with Henderson.

165 "smelling like cabbage soup": Author interview with Finn.

165 "a dozen or more," "They had overnight": Author interview with Fehlberg.

165 Just then, a small: Author interview with Terry Adams.

166 "Loyal Avis": Author interview with Henderson.

166 When Pennzoil's Fehlberg: Author interview with Marty Miller, February 25, 2005.

166 "deceptive-looking man": Author interview with Tsalik Nayberg, a Unocal executive in the former Soviet Union, April 9, 1998.

166 "it was thought": Author interview with Nayberg.

166 "fry its electronics": Author interview with Miller.

167 "I don't want to diminish": Author interview with Cavour Yeh, February 22, 2005.

167 His account of military: Author interview with Miller.

167 Asked about Kaldirim: Author interviews in Peshawar, Pakistan, 1999.

167 "I discovered I": Author interview with Miller.

168 "fight like hell": Ibid.

169 "a mighty wave": Suzanne Goldenberg, *Pride of Small Nations* (London: Zed Books, 1994), 119.

169 "would just disappear," "Someone would come": Author interview with Finn.

169 "demanding to know": Thomas Goltz, *Azerbaijan Diary* (Armonk, N.Y.: M. E. Sharpe, 1998), 92.

169 "a breathtaking thing": Goltz, *Azerbaijan Diary*, 46.

169 "if there was anything": Author interview with Sobhani.

170 "every time we," "an old oil deal": Author interview with Hartnett.

171 "a field of this size," "We all wanted": Author interview with Doss.

172 "black leather jackets": Author interview with Miller.

172 "had no business": Author interview with Sobhani.

172 "Don't worry, we'll find": Aliyev news conference, June 30, 1993.

172 "Seventy million dollars": Author interview with oilman who described the decision on condition of anonymity, June 22, 1993.

173 "The talks have": BP company statement quoted in *The Independent* [London] June 29, 1993, p. 22.

173 "They have an obligation": Author interview with oilman who requested anonymity, June 27, 1993.

Chapter 11: The Contract of the Century

174 "sit down and talk," "I thought that": Author interview with Sobhani.

175 "he was not full": Ibid.

175 "military counterintelligence group": Audrey Altstadt, *The Azerbaijani Turks* (Stanford, Calif., Hoover Institution Press, 1992), 177.

175 "When the war began": *Literaturnaya Gazeta*, September 21, 1988, p. 13.

175 He moved quickly: John P. Willerton, *Patronage and Politics in the USSR* (Cambridge, Eng.: Cambridge University Press, 1992), 198.

176 "ardent warrior": Willerton, *Patronage and Politics*, 179, 203.

176 "expressionless eyes": Author interview with Audrey Altstadt, March 4, 2005.

176 "Comrade Aliyev is our pride," "simply lost his," "home of his": *Literaturnaya Gazeta*, September 21, 1988, p. 13.

176 "join the Aliyev gang": Arkady Vaksberg, *The Soviet Mafia* (New York: St. Martin's Press, 1991), 183. Full account of the Babaev case, 183–85.

176 "against the mafia": Vaksberg, *The Soviet Mafia*, 178, 182.

177 "an exceptionally intelligent": Dusko Doder, *The Washington Post*, November 24, 1982, p. A1.

177 "individuality": Vaksberg, *The Soviet Mafia*, 199, 203.

177 "Aliyev—tall, dark-haired": *The New York Times*, February 28, 1986, p. A30.

178 "denied the shops," "the source of": Gary Lee, *The Washington Post*, March 2, 1986, p. A13.

178 "for Gorbachev's supporters": Gerd Ruge, *Gorbachev* (London: Chatto & Windus, 1991), 168.

178 "strong opposition": Gorbachev, *Memoirs*, 144. In his book *Against the Grain* (New York: Summit, 1990), Boris Yeltsin wrote that in the leadup to Aliyev's fall, he had

approached Gorbachev, waving a folder of incriminating documents, and pleaded that the Soviet leader get rid of "this deeply corrupt man" (151–52).

178 **"done in white gold"**: *Bakinskii Rabochii*, August 14, 1988, p. 3.

179 **"actively struggled against"**: From Aliyev's remarks to the Soviet Central Committee, *Pravda*, April 27, 1989, p. 4.

179 **"no less triumphantly," "status and established"**: Author interview with Aliyev; Andrei Karaulov, *Vokrug Kremlya* (Moscow: Novosti, 1990), 256.

179 **"The absolute majority"**: Keller, *The New York Times*, January 25, 1990, p. A10.

179 **"a little hard"**: Remnick, *The Washington Post*, February 7, 1990, p. A18.

179 **"they wouldn't give"**: Interview with Betty Blair, of *Azerbaijan International*, Summer 1994.

180 **"the only heated room"**: Author interview with Lembo, March 2, 2005.

180 **"always having been"**: E-mail exchange, March 1, 2005, with Dan Sneider.

180 **"chauvinist sentiments"**: *The Christian Science Monitor*, April 21, 1992, p. 4.

180 **"a Nakhichevan VIP"**: E-mail exchange, with Sneider.

181 **"real-life theater"**: Goltz interviewed by Harry Kreisler, November 17, 2003.

181 **"Yooouuu WORMS"**: Goltz, *Azerbaijan Diary*.

182 **"the Socar folks," "This is the"**: Author interview with Henderson.

182 **"a renegade group"**: Author interview with Doss.

183 **"like Ivana Trump," "now we were"**: Author interview with Hartnett.

183 **"with a Clint Eastwood"**: Author interview with Miller.

183 **"What's your point?"**: Author interview with Henderson.

183 **"white as a," "He pointed a"**: Author interview with Henderson.

183 **"trying to scare"**: Author interview with Doss.

183 **"I know who it is"**: Author interview with Henderson.

184 **"Absolutely not," "Completely without my"**: Author interview with Doss.

184 **"Dr. Manafov expects"**: Author interview with Henderson.

185 **"Don't use the"**: Author interview with Hartnett.

185 **"The lives of our representative"**: Author interview with Henderson.

186 **"completely paranoid"**: Author interview with Doss.

186 **"went back to"**: Author interview with Henderson.

187 **"Azerbaijan cannot bug," "He was mafia"**: Ibid.

187 **"He was in their underworld"**: Author interview with Doss.

187 **"investigating whether"**: *The Sunday Times*, March 26, 2000.

187 **The bloodthirsty Afghan warlord:** Details in author's August 11, 1993, report in *The Washington Post*.

188 **An ad hoc squad:** Goltz, *Azerbaijan Diary*, 270–79.

189 **"You know, these resources"**: Author interview with Bill White, August 30, 1996.

189 "Assume everything is," "America is not": Author interview with Bill White.

190 "The Armenians are rolling": Author interview with Lembo.

190 "a request, not": Author interview with Valekh Aleskerov, May 31, 2003.

191 "The contract is unacceptable" "What do you," "were all upset": Author interview with Richard Edmonson, Pennzoil's chief lawyer, March 24, 2005.

191 one required the companies: Author interview with Henderson.

191 "We're going to have": Ibid.

192 "would negotiate jointly": Ibid.

193 "would figure out": Ibid.

193 "the traitor Mutalibov," "more a selfish," "There was only": Goltz, *Azerbaijan Diary*, 411–12.

193 "Who was that?": Author interview with Doss.

194 "90 percent theater": Ibid.

194 Heydar Aliyev, too, was talented: From his interview with Blair, *Azerbaijan International*, Winter 1999.

194 "knock-down, drag-out": Author interview with Doss.

195 "a liar": Ibid.

195 "both sides understood": Ibid.

196 "were worried he": Author interview with Doss.

196 "It was a process": Author interview with Yusufzade.

196 "push the tables": Author interview with Doss.

196 "was like my son": Author interview with Yusufzade.

196 "a signed release": Author interview with White.

196 "looked at them": Author interview with Henderson.

196 "the main guarantee": Author interview with Aleskerov.

197 "made it known," "fed up with," "to end this": Author interview with Doss.

197 "felt in a corner": Author interview with Henderson.

197 "wouldn't change anything": Author interview with Doss.

198 "for leaning": Author interview with Frank Verrastro, senior vice president and Washington lobbyist for Pennzoil, March 18, 2005.

198 "the goody," "We are going": Author interview with Rosemarie Forsythe, September 14, 1999.

198 "They mean to sign": Author interview with Doss.

199 "what good friends," "We have put": Author's e-mail exchanges on February 10, 2005, with Hamilton.

199 "offshore accounts": Author interview with Henderson. That the bonus was $300 million, e-mail exchange with Hamilton.

200 "recognized this contract": Author interview with Aleskerov.

200 "unilateral actions": September 20, 2004, statement by Grigory Karasin, spokesman for the Russian Foreign Ministry.

200 "dictate this question": Author interview with Aliyev, New York, September 27, 1994.

Chapter 12: The Near Abroad

201 "Oil development in this region": *Platt's Oilgram News*, September 29, 1994, p. 1.

202 "Swallow, don't chew": Author interview with Forsythe.

202 "You guys will get": *Newsweek*, October 31, 1994, p. 30.

202 Yeltsin and his subordinates: *East European Markets*, October 14, 1994.

202 "Russia is interested": Jim Hoagland quoting Sergei Karaganov, *The Washington Post*, September 27, 1994, A21.

202 "miraculously escaped": Hugh Pope, *The Independent* (London), September 24, 1994, p. 9.

203 "weary-looking": Anatol Lieven, *The Times* (London), October 5, 1994.

203 "who wish to destroy": Goltz, *Azerbaijan Diary*, 448.

203 "it was Surat": Ibid.

203 "relations would suffer": Anatol Lieven, *The Times* (London), October 5, 1994.

204 "of the times of Hitler": Zbigniew Brzezinski, "The Premature Partnership," *Foreign Affairs*, March/April 1994.

204 "the first democratically elected": Strobe Talbott, *The Russia Hand* (New York: Random House, 2002), 26, 27.

205 "Monroesky Doctrine": *The Economist*, August 28, 1993.

205 "reinventing itself": Talbott, *The Russia Hand*, 5.

205 "concerned about the Caspian": Author interview with Yuri Shafranik, November 27, 2003.

206 "unable to really understand," "some kind of": Author interview with Andrei Kozyrev, November 27, 2003.

207 "that Kazakhstan, say": Boris Fedorov, Yeltsin's finance minister, quoted in *The Economist*, September 28, 1993.

207 "a volcano": Author interview with Kozyrev.

208 "we will lose": Author interview with Shafranik.

208 "tied together by," "on the verge of collapse": Ibid.

209 Now, as the powerful energy minister: Paul Klebnikov, *Godfather of the Kremlin* (New York: Harcourt, 2001), 193. Klebnikov, a *Forbes* reporter who was murdered in Moscow in 2004, quoted Alekperov as disclosing his bestowing of the shares on Shafranik.

210 "opportunistic": Author interview with Kozyrev.

210 "lineal descendant": Charles Lane, *The New Republic*, March 7, 1994.

211 "had known and cared": Bill Clinton, *My Life* (New York: Alfred A. Knopf, 2004), 504.

211 "didn't want anything": Author interview with Sheila Heslin, May 26, 1999.

211 "not the only": Talbott, *The Russia Hand*, 78.

212 "Generally if someone": Author quoting anonymous official, published in *The Washington Post*, March 18, 1994.

212 "contain the problem," "found it ominous": Talbott, *The Russia Hand*, 110.

212 "decorous, laid-back speech": Alan Bernstein, *Houston Chronicle*, March 7, 1993, p. CI.

212 "Please think about coming": Author interview with White.

213 "just to get old": Author interview with Forsythe.

214 "neo-mercantilist": Author interview with Heslin.

214 "very anti-Russian": Author interview with a top Talbott deputy who asked not to be identified, May 27, 1999.

214 They argued that the United States: Author interview with Forsythe.

215 "could sense an apprehension": Author interview with White.

215 "we were big": Author interview with senior Talbott aide who asked not to be identified.

216 "Over my dead body": Author interview with Forsythe.

216 "feel more comfortable": Author interview with Heslin.

216 "The United States would": Author interview with White.

Chapter 13: Early Oil

218–19 "show it can be done," "we needed to": Author interview with Verrastro.

219 "to set the scene": Author interview with Terry Adams, October 27, 1998.

219 "had blind faith": Author interview with William Courtney, May 22, 1999.

220 "great drinkers, great dancers": John Steinbeck, *A Russian Journal* (New York: The Viking Press, 1948), 150, 154.

220 "Shhhhhhh!": Author interview with Tedo Japaridze, May 12, 2004.

220 "we were part of history": Author interview with Giga Makharadze, one of the participants, May 14, 2004.

221 "then Georgia will": Author interview with Gia Chanturia (May 13, 2004), who became Shevardnadze's ambassador to Baku and the main conduit to Aliyev during the development and execution of the pipeline strategy.

221 "peace pipeline": Author interview with Doss.

221 "make Georgia interesting": Author interview with Gogi Tsomaya, May 13, 2004.

221–22 "Get out of here," "You know what," "Once we left": Author interview with Japaridze.

222 "opportunity to make": E-mail exchange with Japaridze, April 10, 2005.

222 "good friends," "through Iran," "if the line": Author interview with Tsomaya, who accompanied Japaridze.

222–23 "the rules of the game," "wasn't out of": E-mail exchange with Japaridze.

224 Additionally, Turkey could earn: *FT Energy Economist*, February 1, 1995, p. 8.

224 **"Wouldn't it be great"**: Author interview with Marc Grossman, March 21, 2005.

224 **When Forsythe heard**: Forsythe had been reassigned as U.S. delegate to the European Union in Brussels, a relatively unimportant "promotion" that appeared to reflect the Talbott team's middling appreciation for her NSC work.

224 **"gift"**: Author interview with Heslin.

224 **"economic viability"**: "The Politics of Oil in the Caucasus and Central Asia," Adelphi paper by Rosemarie Forsythe, 1996, which was adapted directly from Forsythe's policy memo.

225 **"notified several governments"**: From State Department's formalized press guidance dated February 4, 1995, signed by Secretary of State Warren Christopher.

225 **"We are overjoyed"**: Turkish Foreign Minister Murat Karayalcin quoted in *Platt's Oilgram News*, February 2, 1995, p. 4.

225 **"greatly contribute"**: Turkish pipeline company director Hayrettin Uzun, ibid.

226 **"wouldn't talk to me," "That was no"**: Author interview with Heslin.

226 **"made [Collins] sign"**: Ibid.

227 **"upside-down Russia," "we had to," "white hats," "independence and sovereignty," "I don't see," "Do you have"**: Ibid.

228 **"knocked his pen," "This is not," "The Caspian is," "we are going," "The gauntlet was"**: Author interview with Heslin, who was briefed on the meeting.

228 **"We need dual pipelines"**: Ibid.

228 **"a game of chicken," "what else could they"**: Ibid.

229 **"There are rumors," "this idiot, this"**: Author interview with Japaridze.

229 **"Russia should be"**: Author interview with Verrastro.

229 **"Do we want"**: Ibid.

229 **"don't look for any"**: Author interview with Verrastro, to whom Heslin made the comment.

230 **"possibly could consider"**: Author interview with Verrastro.

230 **"save-your-ass"**: Ibid.

230 **"of being in"**: Ibid.

230 **But Verrastro felt**: At least one of the oilmen—Pennzoil executive Dave Henderson—thought that Adams was "posturing" the entire time and that he secretly favored dual lines. The BP man was simply trying to improve the terms, Henderson speculated. If indeed the BP man had been playacting, he did such a superb job that he fooled almost everyone.

231 **"it would show"**: Author interview with Heslin.

231 **"blitzing the buildings"**: Andrew Harding, *The Guardian*, March 18, 1995, p. 12.

231 **"were waiting for a signal"**: Author interview with Heslin.

232 **"multiple oil pipelines"**: White House Briefing, October 2, 1995, issued by Federal News Service.

232 **"there was no way"**: Author interview with Heslin.

232 **"Amoco, Exxon, and Mobil"**: Robert Baer, *See No Evil* (New York: Three Rivers Press, 2002), 243, 251.

233 **"he had the utmost," "home and put," "I think we'd"**: According to a Department of Energy aide of O'Leary's who asked to remain anonymous.

233 **"But it is not sealed"**: Author interview with Zbigniew Brzezinski, March 9, 2005.

234 **"One pipeline!"**: Author interview with Japaridze.

234 **"the whole thing," "in grave danger," "calmed down"**: Author interview with Heslin.

235 **"There will be two"**: Author interview with Tsomaya.

Chapter 14: A Battle of Wills

238 **This bear of a man**: Republican congressman Henry Hyde used the occasion of an April 30, 1996, House hearing to ask CIA Director John Deutch about a report that the Russian prime minister was worth $5 billion. Deutch did not dispute the figure but replied that he wished to discuss it outside the public hearing. "I'd be happy to talk about this particular point elsewhere," he said. The hearing, before the House International Relations Committee, was entitled, "Threat from Russian Organized Crime."

239 **"good chemistry"**: *East European Energy Report*, July 8, 1992, p. 4.

239 **"desire to obtain"**: *Platt's Oilgram News*, June 23, 1992, p. 1.

239 **"and a dime"**: Author interview with Dupré.

239 **"felt he really"**: Author interview with Smith. Ed Smith was interviewed more than a dozen times, in person, by e-mail, and by telephone, from 1996 through 2006. This particular interview was on September 30, 1996.

240 **"We had done an examination"**: Author interview with Dupré.

241 **"never knew and never wanted," "Chechen refugees"**: Ibid.

242 **"I will install," "told the whores"**: Ibid.

242 **"they were sending"**: Ibid.

244 **"an absolute right," "would pay no"**: Author interview with Ronald Freeman, April 25, 2005.

245 **"context sensitive"**: Author interview with Fowler.

246 **"didn't go into"**: Ibid.

246 **"like an Arnold Schwarzenegger"**: Author interview with Smith.

246 **"was basically trying"**: Author interview with Ed Chow, April 25, 2005.

248 **"you can expect"**: Author interview with Giffen.

248 **It was an extraordinary admission**: Chernomyrdin had his cousin, Vitaly Chernomyrdin, a thuggish man whose guards often brandished their weapons in business meetings, appointed as deputy director of the region's premier natural gas refining complex in Orenberg, Russia. The complex processed Karachaganak's natural gas.

248 **"always, on all accounts"**: Author interview with Shafranik.

249 **"poster child"**: Author interview with Verrastro.

249 **"maybe we could"**: Author interview with Chow.

250 **"What's the problem?"**: Author interview with Forsythe, who was briefed on the meeting by Chevron.

250 **"in so many words," "You can't deal"**: Author interview with Herman Franssen, September 9, 2004. The general tenor of the meeting, based on interviews with Derr, Chow, and Franssen, was that Zawawi asked for a payment from a source who was briefed by Chevron, and asked not to be identified.

251 **"ordered all of us"**: Author interview with Chow.

Chapter 15: A Tale of Two Negotiators

253 **"tricky"**: Author interview with Forsythe.

253 **"The problem is that money"**: *East European Energy Report*, January 27, 1995, p. 4.

254–55 **"wanted to control," "This is a"**: Author interview with Forsythe.

255 **"We always get paid"**: Author interview with Giffen.

256 **"You know that Deuss"**: Author interview with Price.

257 **"secret Swede"**: BBC News, March 9, 2000.

257 **"shadowy Swede"**: *The Guardian*, March 9, 2000.

257 **In terms of access:** Castenfelt received no fees or other compensation from Russia; in 1996, after the CPC pipeline deal was settled, Mobil hired him as a paid consultant.

258 **"Did you really"**: Author interview with source present at the time who asked not to be identified.

258 **"Peter, you know"**: Author interview with source present.

259 **"Giffen ran energy"**: Author interview with the agent, who spoke on condition of anonymity, November 26, 2003.

261 **The Chevron boss perhaps:** For several years, Chevron in fact was a major sponsor of a Little League organization in Almaty, run by Giffen's Kazahkstan-based vice president, Richard Spooner. A patron of former Soviet artists and a longtime promoter of Little League during the Soviet period, Spooner ran and coached in Almaty on his own time with no backing from Giffen himself.

261 **"wasn't tired"**: Author interview with Chow.

261 **"I think it's," "As a shareholder"**: Ibid.

262 **"What do you want"**: Author interview with Price. In an interview with the author, Kazhegeldin did not deny Price's account but said that in fact he—Kazhegeldin—had been ordered by Nazarbayev to promote Balgimbayev.

262 **"he was nobody"**: Author interview with Chow.

262 **"called away urgently"**: Author interview with Giffen.

263 **"figured that Balgimbayev," "This is Chevron"**: Author interview with White.

263 **"If the deal is so"**: Author interview with Chow.

263 "Most of the pipeline": Author interview with Derr.

263 A decade later: Author interview with Derr.

263 "on and on": Author interview with Derr. No member of the Deuss alliance ever directly requested a payoff in talks with Chevron representatives. The alliance's willingness to stand aside for $156 million was passed along to others in the negotiations, and was learned, for example, by Russian intelligence operatives.

264 "not by birth": Author interview with Derr.

264 "to sell Shafranik": Author interview with Chow.

265 "leave Kazakhstan high": Ibid.

267 "Some of us": Ibid.

267 "Why is that guy": Author interview with Giffen.

268 "come by my office": Author interview with Fowler.

268 The March I deadline: A letter on U.S. Embassy stationery dated December 27, 1994, referred to a December 15–16 meeting between Chernomyrdin and Gore in which the two sides agreed that the EBRD would conduct "an independent and objective study of the proposals put forward by the Chevron Company and Oman Oil Company." The letter made Washington's own position plain: While the study was going on, "The United States of America is kindly asking [Kazakhstan] not to transfer the pipeline assets to other consortiums or companies."

269 A senior Treasury official: Lipton's and Freeman's roles, from author interviews with Forsythe, Heslin, and Chow.

269 "We bring our": Author interview with Heslin.

270 The tensions exploded: Deuss had a copy of the December 27, 1994, letter on U.S. Embassy stationery detailing the agreement between Gore and Chernomyrdin. Account of tension from author's separate interviews with Smith and Giffen.

270 "Where did you get": Author interview with Giffen.

270 Even before the meeting: Author interview with Smith, who was present.

270 The tumultuous April meeting: Author interview with Giffen.

271 At one point: Author interview with Giffen, confirmed by Shafranik.

271 "ready to cut off": Author interview with Shafranik.

Chapter 16: An Accidental Pipeline

274 "burn rate": Author interview with Smith.

274 "didn't see eye to eye": Author interview with Franssen.

274 Before long, the Mobil: Author interview with Giffen.

275 "Maybe the Russians": Author interview with Chow.

275 "not very friendly": Author interview with Kazhegeldin, May 3, 2005.

276 Kazakhstan signaled that: Author interview with Chow, who was shown the photograph by a Mobil executive. The remainder of the account of Mobil's entry into

Kazakhstan is from an official involved in the acquisition who spoke on condition of anonymity.

277 **"[Nazarbayev] said, 'Do' "**: Author interview with Giffen.

278 **"You stupid ass"**: Author interview with Chow.

278 **"If [the consortium] were"**: *Platt's Oilgram News*, November 2, 1995, p. 1.

278 **Nazarbayev's visit ended:** The Red Book included maps prepared by the CIA, causing consternation among Yeltsin's aides. They thought the maps were evidence that the Kazakh president was conspiring with American intelligence. Peter Castenfelt, the worldly Swedish adviser to the Russians, tried to explain that such maps were sold commercially and easy to obtain. The Yeltsin men remained unconvinced; whether the Russian president himself noticed, or cared, is not known.

280 **As if to remind:** *Platt's Oilgram News*, October 27, 1995, p. 1.

280 **"not the international":** *Platt's Oilgram News*, November 2, 1995, p. 1.

281 **"We want to be":** Author interview with Kazhegeldin.

281 **"Price is not a problem":** Author interview with Chow.

282 **"If you were in Tengiz":** Ibid.

283 **"in the tens of millions":** Author interview with Fowler.

284 **"We have some":** Author interview with Smith.

285 **"Oman already gets":** Author interview with Dan White. White spoke with the author in several interviews in 2005.

285 **"Dan, nice to see you":** Ibid. Giffen has denied making the remark.

286 **"Things happen to people":** Author interview with Heslin.

286 **"madder than hell":** Author interview with White.

286 **"Our boards have approved":** Ibid. Oman's Ed Smith confirmed the general events of the meeting, and a source who asked not to be identified confirmed some of the remarks.

287 **"I'm authorized," "like a doll," "He can't be":** Author interview with White.

288 **Soon after the agreement:** Federal indictment of Giffen, April 2, 2003, p. 10; Seymour M. Hersh, "The Price of Oil," *The New Yorker*, July 9, 2001. The details were confirmed with a principal in the transaction who spoke on condition of anonymity.

289 **"We worked hard":** Author interview with Smith.

Chapter 17: An Army for Oil

291 **In fact, the Texas:** Author interview with John Imle, May 13, 1997.

292 **"If skepticism were":** Ibid.

293 **In carrying out:** Ibid.

294 **"It was a huge":** Author interview with Farid Mohammedi, head of the Washington-based Petroleum Finance Company, May 8, 1997.

294 **"We were like a team":** Author interview with Miller.

294 **He commissioned palaces:** Author interview with Miller.

295 **Once, the official:** Published December 13, 1995, in *Neutral Turkmenistan.*

295 **"Are you lonely?":** Author interview with Miller.

295 **But the Turkmenistan president:** Author interview with Joseph Huling, former U.S. ambassador to Turkmenistan, November 4, 1996. Imle confirmed the conclusions of the account in an interview with the author.

296 **Imle knew that Niyazov:** Author interview with Imle.

296 **But then the signing:** The last-minute setback described in general terms by Miller. Author interviews with Nayberg, April 9, 1998, and November 9, 1998.

298 **Experts at agencies:** Author interview with Scott Barber, who was Unocal's Turkmenistan representative at the time, October 28, 1998.

298 **In the beginning, the Taliban:** Author interviews with Kandahar tribal leader (and future Afghan president) Hamid Karzai, Islamabad, April 17 and 24, 1997; with former Kandahar governor Gul Agha, Quetta, Pakistan, April 27, 1997; with Kandahar political leader Mohammed Yusuf Pashtun, Quetta, Pakistan, April 22, 1997; and with former Kandahar *mujahideen* leader Abdul Razzik, Quetta, Pakistan, April 22, 1997. All switched allegiances to the Taliban in 1994 before severing relations for various reasons. Also, interviews with two Kandahar-based Afghans in 1997, who asked for anonymity. The most commonly conveyed story of the group's beginning was that, in reaction to the rape of young local boys by former *mujahideen* fighters, Omar and others hanged the perpetrators from a tank turret and went on to repeat such summary executions against other abusive thugs. However, the interviews then and since produced no firsthand corroboration of the story, which has taken on the suspicious character of legend. While the incidents possibly did take place as the Taliban and its champions said, it isn't clear why well-armed and seasoned fighters would allow themselves to be repeatedly ambushed and hanged in such a manner; more likely was that the Taliban simply helped to galvanize and lead the popular 1994 uprising against the criminality in Kandahar province.

299 **One was Bashar:** Author interviews with a former senior Kandahar-based *mujahideen* leader who requested anonymity, 1997; basic biographical details confirmed in 1997 by United Nations and U.S. drug enforcement officers who knew of Bashar.

299 **Others in the province:** Author interview with a United Nations official who worked in Kandahar during the Taliban's rise and spoke on condition of anonymity, 1996.

300 **Early on October 29:** Author interviews with Agha, Pashtun, and Zia Mojadeddi, a former Kandahari journalist who served as an interpreter for U.S. diplomats and intelligence officers traveling to Pakistan and Afghanistan.

301 **Unocal watched approvingly:** In interviews at the time and a decade later with the author, Unocal officials insisted they were even-handed and never favored one side in Afghanistan over the other. The assertion defies both the realities on the ground and common sense. The Taliban were the dominant force in the country, controlling most of it while its enemies were steadily falling back to isolated pockets; the pipeline would cross the Taliban's tribal stronghold. There was no foreseeable situation in which President Burhannudin Rabbani, clinging to power in the capital of Kabul, would reassert his power over the Taliban or its terrain. The only way to plan for the success of the pipeline project was either through an outright Taliban military triumph or the highly unlikely scenario of the movement finding a modus vivendi with its enemies.

301 **Communications with the insurgents:** Author interview with ISI officer who spoke on condition of anonymity.

302 **The faces of the company executives:** The author witnessed such reactions by Unocal executives during interviews in the mid-1990s.

302 **Its chairman was a resourceful:** Author interview with Delta Afghanistan representative Charlie Santos, October 27–28, 1998, other senior Delta officials who requested anonymity, Abdelrahim Rashid, editor of *Al-Majalla* magazine, June 16, 1997, and two former American employees of Aramco.

302 **It made the Afghans:** Author interviews with Karzai, Mojadeddi, and a U.N. official in Afghanistan.

302 **Their suspicions were heightened:** The view within Unocal that Delta was an intelligence front from author interview with Tsalik Nayberg, Unocal's former representative in Turkmenistan. This opinion of Delta was a standard feature of interviews at the time with U.S. and European diplomats and executives of other oil companies.

303 **Santos rented a home:** The home belonged to Balkh governor Malik Palawan. Author interview with one of Palawan's aides-de-camp, who spoke on condition of anonymity, 1997.

303 **State Department officials:** Author's 1996 and 1997 interviews with U.S., French, and British embassy diplomats, and westerners who attended Islamabad dinner parties, where American diplomats expressed their support for the Taliban.

303 **From his satellite telephone:** Author interview with Santos; Imle's loss of confidence in Delta from Nayberg and September 20, 2004, interview with Robert Todor, who was Marty Miller's deputy.

303 **He cut a magnificent figure:** From author's 1997 conversation with and observations of Carlos Bulgheroni in Islamabad.

304 **Until he became obsessed:** Bulgheroni decided in 1991 to diversify from Latin America and toured the Soviet Union, leading him to Turkmenistan, according to author interview in 1997 with Malcolm Hurlston, his publicist.

304 Yet in the quest: Author interview with Nayberg, who had to contend with Bridas's competition in Turkmenistan.

304 Benazir Bhutto's husband: Author interview with Huling.

304 In a meeting with the Pakistani: Author's 1997 interviews with U.S. diplomats who spoke on condition of anonymity.

305 Intrigued by the benefits: Author's 1997 interviews with Afghans familiar with Taliban trips to Saudi Arabia to pick up Turki's cash payments.

306 Sitting down with Bulgheroni: Steve Coll, *Ghost Wars* (New York: Penguin, 2004), 306.

306 Bulgheroni would later tell: Author's 1997 interview with a former employee of his who spoke on condition of anonymity.

306 Now, Bin Ladin: Author's 1997 interview with an intelligence officer with a long-established record of accuracy with the author.

306 With Bin Ladin's cash: That the Taliban used the Bin Ladin money to buy off commanders, from author's 1997 interviews with Afghans familiar with the payoffs.

307 "We regard it": Reuters, October 1, 1996.

307 And it seemed that Washington: State Department deputy spokesman Glyn Davies said in remarks within hours of the Taliban takeover that the United States interpreted Taliban "statements as an indication that the Taliban intends to respect the rights of all Afghans." Davies did not rule out diplomatic recognition. "I just think it's really too early to pronounce ourselves on questions like diplomatic relations yet," he said. Reuters, September 27, 1996. In interviews with the author, diplomats in the U.S. Embassy in Islamabad said that the Embassy had prepared a plane to take U.S. diplomats to Kabul to speak to Afghanistan's new rulers. The flight was canceled at the last moment, they said, once the Taliban's behavior in Kabul began getting a negative reception in the United States, where President Clinton was five weeks away from an election.

307 "It's a ridiculous": Author interview with Imle.

308 "the will of the people": Quotation from a European diplomat who was at an Islamabad reception where an American diplomat made the remark; accusations of Rabbani's forces rocketing themselves were made by a State Department official in an interview with John Jennings, an AP reporter, Jennings told the author.

308 "because we had been positive": Author interview with Sher Mohammed Abbas Stanikzai, a Taliban Foreign Ministry official, May 15, 2308.

308 Through it all: Washington regularly rejected assertions of Pakistani or Saudi support to the Taliban; Santos's briefings in the U.S. Embassy from author interviews with Santos and the attaché; that U.S. diplomats issued eyewitness reports, from author's interviews with these diplomats.

309 The Taliban was ready: Taliban agreement to allow Bulgheroni's pipeline if he obtained Turkmen permission, from author interview with Stanikzai.

309 **Regardless, in February 1997**: Author interview with Todor.

310 **"John, it's time"**: Author interview with Miller.

310 **"suspended"**: Unocal news release of August 21, 1998.

310 **"all its partners"**: Author interview with Stanikzai.

310 **"It's the black hole"**: Author interview with Miller.

Chapter 18: Boom and Bust

312 **"Next, we are opening"**: Author interview with Ibrahim Kesemer, March 1, 1997.

312 **Among the latter**: Author interview with Charlie Schroeder, February 3, 2006; author's visits to the establishments during the 1990s.

312 **"the bar of choice"**: Goltz, *Fortune*, March 7, 1998.

312 **"on the dole"**: Author interview with Charlie Christmas at Lord Nelson, February 28, 1997.

313 **"wants me to join"**: From March 1, 1997, interview with Fedos by Nana Kiknadze, author's research assistant.

313 **But all reported**: Agence France-Presse, January 26, 1998, February 13, 1998.

313 **"We serve a certain market"**: Author interview with Oktai Akhverdiev on February 27, 1997.

314 **"Everyone is here"**: Author interview with Berenice Webb, March 2, 1997.

314 **"When I was in school"**: Author interview with Akhundov.

314 **"No, none of us"**: During author's February 27, 1997, visit to their apartment.

315 **"We saw cold"**: Author interview with Abdullayeva.

315 **"The Pirate of Prague"**: *Fortune*, December 23, 1996

316 **"nine bathrooms"**: *Rocky Mountain News*, April 9, 2000.

316 **There was a couch**: *The Denver Post*, May 13, 2000.

316 **In the event someone**: Plaintiff documents filed in 2000 in U.S. District Court in Denver.

316 **"the darling of the social"**: Aspen attorney Michael Herron quoted in *Rocky Mountain News*, April 9, 2000.

316 **threw himself**: Peter Elkind, "The Incredible Half-Billion-Dollar Azerbaijani Oil Swindle," *Fortune*, March 2000.

316 **"The small, rare"**: *Rocky Mountain News*, April 9, 2000.

317 **"just hype"**: *Rocky Mountain News*, April 9, 2000.

317 **Fleck was so impressed**: Author interview with Aaron Fleck, September 5, 2000.

318 **In April 1998**: Author interview with Wayne Walz on July 30, 1999.

318 **"the big boy"**: Author interview with Fleck.

318 **Cooperman, with the most**: Author interview with Leon Cooperman, August 31, 2000.

318 **In legal filings**: Kozeny first filed his allegations in July 2000 in a sealed, thirty-eight-page defense to the civil suit in London High Court. Kozeny asserted that

about $83.3 million of the investors' money eventually went to the Aliyevs and unidentified others in an attempt to ensure their support for the investment.

319 **"men possessed with rabid"**: Brief filed by Kozeny in U.S. District Court in Denver in June 2000.

319 **"asked Mr. Kozeny"**: Ibid.

319 **Along the way**: Tamraz's relationship with the CIA went back to the 1970s, including the cover provided to two CIA agents, according to former CIA agent Robert Baer, *See No Evil*, 221.

320 **"peace pipeline"**: Author's 1992 interview with Abulfaz Elchibey.

320 **"force everybody"**: Heslin's quoting of Tamraz's remarks in her Senate testimony, September 17, 1997, as reported in *Platt's Oilgram News*, September 18, 1997.

320 **"shady and untrustworthy"**: *Platt's Oilgram News*, September 19, 1997.

320 **He saw this**: *The Washington Post*, October 10, 1997.

321 **"if he got a meeting"**: Heslin quoted her conversation with Carter in the September 17, 1997, Senate hearings, as reported in *The New York Times*, September 18, 1997.

321 **"a real hero"**: *The Washington Post*, September 18, 1997, p. 1.

321 **"a good guy"**: *The New York Times*, September 23, 1997.

321 **"Was one of the reasons"**: Associated Press account, *Peoria Journal Star*, September 19, 1997.

321 **"The same handlers"**: *Los Angeles Times*, September 19, 1997.

322–23 **"The president decided," "The new capital," "Welcome to Akmola," "It's all a"**: From interviews with the author, November 8, 1997, in Akmola.

323 **"how we suffer"**: Author interviews with Kulban Aidarova and Jumabek Aidarov, November 8, 1997, in Akmola.

323 **"At the same time"**: Author interview with Leyla Yunusova, November 28, 1997.

324 **"No one from the government"**: Author interviews with Shakir Shakhirov, November 29, 1997.

324 **In a two-room apartment**: Author interview with Taisya Istayena and Lyuda and Azrat Razaev, March 4, 1997.

325 **"It is getting very sticky"**: Author interview with the ambassador, December 1, 1997.

325 **"All the good money"**: Author interview with Schroeder.

326 **"We wanted freedom"**: Author interview with Bulat Atabayev, February 6, 1997.

326 **"brink of failure"**: *The New York Times*, October 11, 1998.

Chapter 19: Kashagan

329 **In May 1994, a British**: Author interview with Paul Jeffery, who sat for numerous interviews from March 2001 through July 2001.

329 **Steve Green, a Briton**: Author interview with Steve Green, March 19, 2001.

331 **The consortium, meanwhile:** Later the consortium would change again when Phillips merged with Conoco, and BP and BG sold their interests to the other partners.

331 **Kazakhstan's president, Nursultan:** The contract was signed November 18, 1997, at the State Department.

332 **"Indiana Jones":** *The San Francisco Chronicle,* December 22, 2000, p. A25.

333 **Craftsmen rebuilt the sides:** Author interview with Ross Murphy, May 2, 2006.

334 **A fire broke out:** Author interview with Michael Schlegel, an engineer hired to help design the barge, April 26, 2006.

335 **On September 4:** Author interview with Murphy.

336 **And if there were no:** Author interview with John Foulkes, drilling manager for the Kashagan project, July 22, 2001.

336 **Paul Jeffery and his team:** Author interview with Jeffery.

336 **That explained the hiring:** Author interview with Michel Metge, March 20, 2001.

337 **Beyond that:** Author interview with Metge.

338 **"It's not going to stop":** Author interview with Schlegel.

338 **The building had to be:** Author interview with Jeffery.

338 **"She pulled it off":** Author interview with Jeffery.

339 **"five cars":** Author interview with Walt Marshall, May 13, 2001.

339 **Yevgeny Karamashin:** Author interview with Karamashin, May 17, 2001.

339 **"In Saudi Arabia":** Author interview with Samarbek Bukebayev, May 18, 2001.

340 **On platform Sunkar:** Author interview with Foulkes.

340 **Yet, in the charged:** Author interviews there at the time.

341 **"What do you see":** Author interview with Murphy.

341 **"So, things are going":** Author interview with Jeffery.

341 **"a celebration of relief":** From author's May 20, 2006, e-mail exchange with Jeffery.

342 **"We gotta hit":** Author interview with Murphy.

342 **reports that Kashagan:** *The Wall Street Journal* and *The New York Times* both declared that oil had been found.

343 **"We present to you":** Author interview with Murphy.

345 **"I can tell":** Reuters, quoted in *The Toronto Star,* July 5, 2000.

345 **"This is a great aid":** Agence France-Presse, quoted in *Houston Chronicle,* July 5, 2000.

Chapter 20: A Way to the Sea

348 **Since the 1979 hostage crisis:** In the 1980s, the Reagan administration held secret, unofficial talks with Iran in an attempt to buy the freedom of American hostages in Lebanon.

348 **"It has to be admitted":** Quoted by Jane Perlez and Steve LeVine, *The New York Times,* August 9, 1998, p. 8.

349 **"a campaign that has become"**: *The New York Times,* October 11, 1998, p. 1.

349 **"A stronger or more focused"**: *The New York Times,* October 12, 1998, p. 1.

349 A MONICA SETBACK: Published October 12, 1998.

349 **"An obit"**: Quoted in October 14, 1998, Reuters report, "U.S.-backed Caspian Pipeline Project Said Not Dead."

350 **"that is irrelevant"**: Author interview with Richard Morningstar, June 1, 1999.

351 **"There was a great"**: Quoted in *Alexander's Gas and Oil Connections,* Vol. 3, Issue 27, October 12, 1998.

351 **"convinced that the wave"**: Author interview with Elizabeth Jones, May 22, 2006. She served in various senior diplomatic capacities in the region from 1995 to 2005.

351 **"nuts and not"**: Interview with a U.S. diplomat who was present at several meetings with the oil companies. The diplomat agreed to speak only without attribution.

351 **"foreclose all alternatives"**: Author interview with Morningstar.

351 **"transformed into a pipeline"**: Quoted in "Turkey Moves to Limit Bosporus Traffic," *Platt's Oilgram News,* October 27, 1998.

351 **"It makes no sense"**: Author interview with Morningstar.

351 **"We know what you"**: Author interview with Morningstar.

352 **"We thought of ourselves"**: Author interview with Dick Olver, April 6, 2006.

353 **"We're going to do everything"**: Author interview with Wref Digings, who was quoting Turkey's Yurdakul Yigitguden, undersecretary for energy, May 15, 2006.

353 **"an absolute terrier"**: Author interview with Roger Thomas, March 16, 2006.

353 **"not an option"**: Author interview, March 17, 2006, with meeting participant who asked not to be identified. Details on the meeting come from author interviews with four meeting participants.

354 **"We recognize the strategic"**: Quoted in "BP Backs Baku-Ceyhan Route for Caspian Oil," *The Oil Daily,* October 20, 1999.

354 **"Ceyhan is, above all"**: Quoted in BBC Monitoring Service, translating Interfax of October 21, 1999.

354 **"find a way"**: Author interviews with Digings.

354 **"tilted the balance"**: Author interview with Townshend.

354 **The episode seemed:** Throughout the early days, BP asserted that the pipeline required a minimum of 6 billion barrels of oil to be economically feasible, that the oil had to flow at a rate of 1 million barrels of oil a day for seventeen years, and that it could pay no more than $2.50 a barrel as a pipeline tariff. The problem, BP said, was that the offshore possessed just 4 billion barrels of oil—a maximum 4.5 billion barrels of oil—not sufficient to create a commercially sustainable daily oil flow.

But in February 2001, David Woodward, the offshore consortium president, said that in fact 6 billion barrels weren't required to make the pipeline feasible; 5 billion barrels would be sufficient. Moreover, the three offshore fields contained that volume—5 billion barrels—and not the 4 billion to 4.5 billion barrels that the companies had been claiming; indeed, according to Dick Olver, then company CEO for exploration and production, BP figured that it had somewhere between 5 billion and 6 billion barrels, right around the original volume of oil that it had demanded to proceed with the line. Finally, it turned out that the pipeline didn't require a flow of 1 million barrels of oil a day for seventeen years to be commercially stable; 800,000 barrels were sufficient.

355 **"so filled with smoke"**: Author interview with John Wolf, June 2, 2006.

356 **"Get your hands"**: Author interview with Digings.

356 **"monstrosity...from the environment"**: Author interview with Jenik Radon, June 4, 2006

356 **"the U.S. administration"**: Interfax as quoted in *Houston Chronicle*, November 19, 1999.

356 **"pretty positive"**: Author interview with Carlos Pascual, June 5, 2006.

357 **"truly historic"**: Quoted in Knight-Ridder, "Clinton Cheers Proposed Caspian Sea Oil, Gas Pipelines," November 17, 1999.

357 **who led three whimsical**: Author's August 24–September 3, 2001, journey with the Goltz-led group.

358 **"custard on a sheet"**: Author interview with Neil Clough, November 20, 2003.

Chapter 21: The King of Kazakhstan

361 **When Nazarbayev appeared**: Party as reported in David Glovin, "Mobil, CIA Secrets May Come Out in Bribery Trial of Oil Adviser," Bloomberg, August 28, 2005.

363 **"private technical assistance"**: Author interview with Michael McFaul, Stanford University professor, April 29, 2004. McFaul was part of one of the scholarly teams brought to Almaty.

363 **"Ever seen an American"**: Author interview with McFaul.

364 **"Haven't you ever heard"**: Author interview with Bill Minarovich, May 2, 2001. General details of incident confirmed by a person close to Giffen who spoke on condition of anonymity.

364 **"That's not relevant"**: Author interview with a source who asked not to be identified.

364 **"saw him as"**: Author interview with Janet McElligot, September 28, 2003.

365 **"organized it himself"**: Nazarbayev's interview with a small number of journalists including the author, November 17, 1998.

365 **"that vice president"**: Author interview with Giffen.

365 **When the oilman's son**: Author 1999 interview with Bruce Kososki.

366 **"Fifteen hundred companies"**: Nazarbayev's November 17, 1998, interview with journalists including author.

367 **"filthy rich"**: Author interview with Giffen.

368 **"exactly how much blood"**: Author interview with Fred Tresca, former head of Price Waterhouse's Central Asia operations, September 19, 2004. He sat in on some of Giffen's negotiations with oilmen.

368 **"feeding frenzy"**: Author interview with Giffen.

371 **"Okay, just for this deal"**: Author interview with a witness to the exchange who spoke on condition he not be identified.

371 **"Don't deal with anyone"**: Author's March 2, 2004, interview with Matzke.

371 **"That's news to me"**: Author interview with Giffen.

372 **Matzke called both:** Author interview with Matzke.

372 **"Congratulations. You won"**: Author interview with a witness who spoke on condition of anonymity.

372 **"wanted to clean"**: Author interview with Matzke.

374 **His action was not:** Details from Steve LeVine, "Swiss Freeze Bank Account That May Be Linked to Kazakhstan President," *The New York Times*, October 16, 1999.

374 **But they were illegal:** The law is the 1977 Foreign Corrupt Practices Act.

375 **Devaud saw a possible:** Author interview with Devaud by the author and *Newsweek* reporter Bill Powell, July 10, 2000.

375 **"the alleged use"**: June 12, 2000, Justice Department letter to Swiss authorities.

375 **Additional bonuses had been:** Europe adopted a law similar to the U.S. Foreign Corrupt Practices Act in 1999, about a year after the last transaction documented in the Giffen case.

375 **"I can directly say"**: Balgimbayev quoted in July 4, 2000, Kazakhstan Newswire.

376 **"bullshit"**: Author's confidential interviews with individuals who did not want to be identified.

376 **"made the problem quietly disappear"**: Baer, *See No Evil*, 242.

377 **The document, later unsealed:** One example in the indictment involved a $51 million payment from Mobil Oil to Giffen, his fee for brokering the company's purchase of a share of the Tengiz oil field. Sharing the windfall with his benefactors, Giffen didn't simply transfer it to their accounts. Instead, he spread it among an array of shell companies and foundations with names like Hovelon Holdings, Orchard, and Nichem. The beneficiaries were the Kazakh leaders and others, but Giffen himself was trustee of the accounts, which gave him control. To assemble President Nazarbayev's cut from the Mobil deal, Giffen wired four payments of $5 million each from his New York merchant bank to the Swiss bank account of an intermediary. The money was then moved in like amounts to Giffen's own Swiss account. He then added another $500,000 and wired the total—$20.5 million—to Nazarbayev's account. After all other payoffs were made, Giffen ended up with $17.5 million to divide between himself and colleagues in the deal, including $2 million that he wired to Mobil Oil executive J. Bryan Williams.

378 **"We're arresting a guy"**: Author interview with witness.

379 **"Now he's getting"**: Author interview with Verity.

Epilogue

380 **"cleansing moment"**: Author interview with Michael Townshend, June 1, 2006.

381 **For a few years:** Uzbekistan forced the United States to close its military base there in 2005 in a confrontation over President Islam Karimov's massacre of hundreds of civilians in the city of Andijan.

381 **Hundreds of thousands:** The oil companies pumped an initial volume of about four hundred thousand barrels a day of crude through the pipeline, which had a capacity of 1.8 million barrels a day.

382 **"We feel very unsafe"**: *The Wall Street Journal,* November 13, 2006.

383 **The economy had grown:** Economic data from the International Monetary Fund.

384 **"In Kazakhstan I am"**: **"women drive cars"**: Quoted June 13, 2007, RIA Novosti. *The New York Times,* October 20, 2006, p. E5.

385 **"admiration for all"**: *The Washington Post,* May 6, 2006, p. A13.

387 **"painfully thin"**: description from issue of *The* (Bermuda) *Royal Gazette,* October 17, 2006.

388 **"One thing about old John"**: Author interview with a Deuss friend who asked not to be identified, November 22, 2006.

393 **In 2005, a Russian:** "The Fullest List of Russian Billionaires," *Finance* (Moscow), February 7–13, 2005.

394 **"couldn't keep food"**: Author interview with Jeffrey Barrie, an Oztemel aide, February 20, 2004.

395 **"was a dangerous woman"**: Author interview with Longley.

395 **He orchestrated a meeting:** From Proehl letters to Neil Jacoby, a Hammer intermediary, dated March 30, 1972, November 14, 1972, and November 29, 1972, to Occidental Petroleum vice president Marvin Watson; Proehl telex July 19, 1972, to Oztemel.

395 **"success hangs by his"**: December 26, 1972, Proehl letter to Jack A. Sulser, deputy principal officer, U.S. consulate, Frankfurt, Germany.

395 **"probably fooled by"**: Author interview with Virginia Proehl.

396 **Kozeny and two others:** The federal indictment, announced October 6, 2005, charged Kozeny, Frederick Bourke, and David Pinkerton.

397 **"They expected the," "But it's also"**: Author interview with Nils Oleinikoff, September 7, 2006.

398 **"I tried to reassure"**: Author interview with Guy de Rothschild, July 2, 2003.

398 **"We are opening"**: Author interview with David de Rothschild, July 1, 2003.

398 **"God sent me Leyla"**: Author interview with Leyla Aru, January 9, 2000.

Abassov, Kurban
   ailing and in hospital, 156, 157, 159,
      160, 162, 391
   and Amoco desire to bid on Azeri oil
      field, 152–53
   and British Petroleum, 150, 155, 156,
      157, 160
   signs letter agreeing to Remp as
      Azerbaijan's official representative
      to western oil companies, 149
Abdullayev, Halyk
   meets John Deuss, 130–31
   role in Chevron Kazakh talks, 114,
      122, 126, 137–38
   view of Giffen's role, 120–22
Abdullayeva, Sophia, 35, 36, 39, 40, 91,
      146, 315, 399
Absheron Sill, 168
Adair, Red, 90
Adams, Terry, 165–66, 218–19, 228,
      229–30
   See also British Petroleum
Aeroflot, 109
Afghanistan, and Unocal pipeline plans,
      291, 292–93, 294, 298–99, 300,
      302, 306, 307, 308
Agip. See ENI
Aiban, Badr al-, 302
   See also Delta Oil
Aiban, Mohammed al-, 302

Aidarova, Kulban, 323
Akhundov, Fuad, 314
Akhmetshin, Rinat, 366
Akhverdiev, Oktai, 313
Akmola, Kazakhstan, 322–23
al-Qaeda, 306, 310
Alekperov, Vagit, 280–82
Aleskerov, Valekh
   at Baku signing of oil field contract,
      200
   negotiations with Pennzoil, 163
   at offshore Baku talks in Houston,
      196, 197
   at offshore Baku talks in Istanbul,
      193, 194
Alexander II, Russian czar, 7, 16
Alexander III, Russian czar, 22
Alexandria, Russian czarina, 29
Aliyev, Baba, 36
Aliyev, Heydar
   and Armenia, 187–88
   as Azeri leader, 172, 174–75
   background, 175–76
   denounced by Gorbachev, 178, 179,
      180
   and Early Oil pipeline debate, 231
   epilogue, 386
   fall from grace, 178–79
   and foreign oil investment issues,
      189–90

Aliyev, Heydar (*cont'd*)
  and Hazel O'Leary, 233
  and Kozeny, 318–19
  meets with Bill White, 189–90, 212
  meets with President Clinton, 198,
    200, 214
  named Soviet deputy prime minister
    under Andropov, 177–79
  negotiations for Azeri oil fields, 167,
    168, 170–71, 191, 193, 197–98,
    199
  relationship with Russia, 188–89,
    190, 234
  relationship with Zbigniew Brzezinski,
    233–34
  retreats to boyhood home,
    Nakhichevan, 179–80
  seizes control of Azerbaijan after fall
    of Abulfaz Elchibey, 182
  signs oil field agreement documents,
    199–200
  and Socar, 317, 318
  and son Ilham, 193, 196, 313
  and Thomas Goltz, 180–82
  visit to U.S., 198, 200, 202
Aliyev, Ilham, 193, 196, 313, 385–86
Aliyev, Natik, 194, 196
Aliyev, Rakhat, 384–85
Alizade, Sanan, 159
All About Eve, 65
Alrich, Tim, 289
American Trade Consortium
  Chevron's support, 87, 89
  Giffen creates, 83–84
  Giffen's decline, 125–26
  Giffen's ongoing role, 87–88, 89,
    120–21
  Gorbachev's blessing, 87–88, 112, 121
Amoco
  vs. British Petroleum, 154, 155–56,
    157, 158
  Brzezinski connection, 233
  and draft multinational oil
    partnership, 182
  formerly Standard Oil of Indiana,
    104–5
  granted one-year exclusive rights to
    negotiate for Azerbaijan oil field,
    158–59
  negotiations for Azerbaijan oil fields,
    167, 168, 170–71, 191
  See also Doss, Tom; Leonard, Ray
Andreas, Dwayne, 81
Andropov, Yuri, names Heydar Aliyev as
  his deputy prime minister, 177
Anglo-Persian Oil Company, 33, 43
Arablinskaya, Sona, 31, 35, 39
Aramco
  pursues Azeri oil field, 161
  seeks talks for Azeri deals, 159–60
Archer Daniel Midlands, 81, 87
Arco
  acquired by British Petroleum, 352,
    354, 391
  agrees to partnership with Lukoil,
    282, 283–88
  observes Balgimbayev's dislike for
    Chevron, 262–63
  as oil industry fatality during Caspian
    era, 389
  role of Dan White, 262–63, 285,
    286, 287
Armco Steel
  blesses Giffen's Mercator venture, 81
  founder, 75
  Giffen has New York office there,
    76–77
  trade talks with Soviet Union, 76
  view of Giffen at, 79–80
Armenia
  vs. Azerbaijan, 147–48, 170, 187,
    188, 200, 320
  vs. Turks, 320
Armenians, 30, 32

Aru, Leyla, 412, 449
Ashurbekov, Timurbek, 11, 314–15
Assadalayev, Ali, 36, 38
Assadalayev, Bobik, 38
Assadalayeva, Leyla (Tagiyeva), 36–39,
    398
Assadalayev, Nadir, 38
Assadulayeva, Jamil, 37–38
Assadulayeva, Ummelbanu (Banine),
    37–38, 41
Assadulayeva, Zuleha (Weber), 412, 414
Astana, Kazakhstan, 260, 323, 326, 371,
    383, 385
Astrakhan basin, 329
Atabayev, Bulat, 326
Azerbaijan
    after collapse of Soviet Union,
        169–70
    Aliyev takes control, 182
    announces two Early Oil pipelines, 279
    vs. Armenia, 147–48, 170, 187, 188,
        200, 320
    Caspian oil field claims, 207
    controlling offshore Baku fields, 144
    involvement in military hostilities,
        168–69
    vs. Kazakhstan, 147
    law and order disintegrates in Aliyev's
        absence, 202–3
    politics in, 169–70
    relationship with Russia regarding oil
        reserves, 188–89
    surrenders land to Armenia, 211
    viewed as energy transportation hub
        for Caspian basin, 347
    See also Aliyev, Heydar, British
        Petroleum; Amoco; Baku-Ceyhan
        pipeline; Early Oil pipelines
Azerbaijan International Oil
    Consortium, formed, 192
Azeri oil fields, 150, 164, 168, 190,
    195–99, 205, 207

Babaev, Ibragim, 176
Baer, Robert, 232, 320
Baker, James
    aftermath of Soviet Union breakup,
        126
    interest in Chevron oil deal, 114
    in photo with Nazarbayev, 361
    and Shevardnadze, 220
    view of Nazarbayev, 114
Baker, Louis, 60
Baku
    in 1800s, 3–4
    and 1948 U.S. equipment embargo, 51
    aftermath of Russian Revolution,
        41–42
    Balakhani district, 6, 9, 19, 46
    Bibi-Heybat oil field, 8–9
    BP gains entry to oil region, 113
    description, 145–46
    as early regional trading hub, 7–8
    early secular boarding school in, 29
    eavesdropping in, 165–66
    enterprises of Viktor Kozeny, 315,
        316–19
    ethnic divide in, 30–32
    falls to Bolsheviks, 32, 34–35
    first deep-sea oil rig, 76
    first oil boom, 5–40, 217
    Friendship oil well, 10
    historic buildings, 313–14
    instability surrounding time of
        Russian Revolution, 32
    modernization, 311–12
    Nobel brothers in, 15, 16, 17–18
    offshore operations, 50–52
    oil barons build European city outside
        walls, 11
    and Oily Rocks, 50–51, 149, 156
    part of Stalin plan to revive Soviet
        industry, 48–49
    personal gestures important when
        conducting business, 162–63

Baku (*cont'd*)
pipeline to Black Sea coast, 217
revival of oil fields, 46–48
role in supplying world's oil in late
nineteenth and early twentieth
centuries, 26
Savage Division in, 31
at start of twentieth century, 28
store of hydrocarbons, 4–5
Tagiyev diversifies in, 29–30
Vermishev oil well, 10
during World War II, 49–50
Zabrat oil field, 10
Baku-Ceyhan pipeline
becomes reality, 358–59, 380, 382,
383
effect of condensate, 390
first envisioned, 223–25
negotiations over, 349–58
part ownership by Chevron, 390
relationship to Chinese pipeline,
391–92
revival of proposal, 346–48
role of Aliyev, 386
Balakhani district, 6, 9, 19, 46
Balgimbayev, Nurlan
and Chevron, 262–63
and Deuss, 267, 270
and Giffen, 255, 285, 360–61
and Mobil, 276
at Sunkar drilling platform dedication,
335
Barine. *See* Assadulayeva, Ummelbanu
Barkett, Michael, 57
Barnsdall International, 46
Bary, Alexander, 26
Batumi naval base, 22–23, 24
Bebutov, Prince, 12–13
Bechtel, 73
Belarus, 216
Berger, Samuel "Sandy," 226, 228, 229,
232

Bhutto, Benazir, 299–300, 304, 305, 310
Bibi-Heybat oil field, 8–9
Bildaci, Gökhan, 358
Bin Ladin, Osama, 306, 310
Bindra, Jeet, 264, 285, 286
Black January Massacre, 147, 179
Blacker, Coit "Chip," 225
Boggs, Tommy, 265
Bohlen, Celestine, 177
Bohlen, Charles "Chip", 177
Bolsheviks, 32, 33, 34–35, 41–45
Bonney, J. Dennis, 86, 117, 127, 237,
239, 250
*Borat: Cultural Learning of America for Make
Benefit Glorious Nation of Kazakhstan*
(movie), 385
Bourke, Frederick, 315, 317
BP. *See* British Petroleum
Brady, Nicholas, 84, 86, 88, 126
Brent crude oil, 135, 325
Brezhnev, Leonid
and Aliyev, 178–79
and Giffen, 86
trade relations with Nixon
administration, 72–73, 75–76, 79
bribery issue, 163
British Gas, 111, 278, 284, 328
British Oil, 328
British Petroleum (BP)
acquires Amoco, 352, 390–91
acquires Arco, 352
aftermath of Chevron-Gorbachev
signing of Tengiz protocol,
112–14
vs. Amoco, 155–56, 157, 158
change of heart regarding Baku-
Cehyan pipeline, 353–55
competes with Chevron for Tengiz oil
field, 101, 108–11, 113
epilogue, 391–92
first to examine offshore Kazakhstan
raw seismic data, 110, 328–29

gains consolation prize of offshore
Baku opportunity, 113, 144
Hassanov agrees to protect, 154
and Jack Grynberg, 106
living conditions for Tengiz, 338
negotiates for Azeri oil field, 151,
158–59, 160, 161, 167, 168,
170–71, 191
oil reserves, 102–3
views American officials as nannies,
349
See also Adams, Terry; Browne, John;
Fehlberg, Rondo; Hamilton, Tom;
Jeffery, Paul; Whitehead, Eddie
Brothers, Philipp, 62
Browne, John
and Baku region negotiations, 157,
159, 160
description, 103–4
and Hamilton, 162
as head of BP, 103–4, 106, 108,
109–11, 157, 159, 160, 162, 392
meets with Fuerth, 353
since 2000, 392–93
support for Baku-Ceyhan pipeline,
354
and Tengiz negotiations, 108, 109–11
Brzezinski, Zbigniew, 233
Bukebayev, Samarbek, 339
Bulgheroni, Carlos, 303–4, 305, 306,
308–9
Burma, 293
Bush, George H. W.
and Giffen, 121, 122
meets with Kazakh president, 139–40
roles for old friends, 114–15, 162,
361
and Soviet relations, 101, 124
Bush, George W.
congratulates Ilham Aliyev, 385
and Giffen case, 388
support for Baku-Ceyhan pipeline, 380

Camdessus, Michel, 257
Carbonell, Robert, 87
Carter, Jack, 321
Carter, Jimmy, 79, 229, 233
Caspian Pipeline Consortium
Deuss creates, 142, 237
Deuss vs. Chevron, 239–40, 250,
252–53, 255, 256, 260, 265–67,
269–270, 278
end of, 282–84
financing issues, 243–46, 270–71
Kazakhstan joins, 237–38
role of Giffen, 254–56, 267
role of Oman, 245, 272, 273–74,
282
Russia joins, 238–39
U.S. policy intervention, 268–70
See also Deuss, John
Caspian Sea
ice in, 337–38
oil-rich lands bordering, 205, 206–7,
216
oil shipping economics, 18
pipeline issues, 345–59
Castenfelt, Peter, 257–59, 281, 287
Central Intelligence Agency. See CIA
Chabas, Paul, 38
Chechnya, 147, 209, 219, 346
Chelikan oil field, 296, 319
Cheney, Dick, 385
Cheremetoff, Nikita, 80
Chernomyrdin, Viktor
aligns with Giffen, 284
and Derr, 264–65
and Deuss, 238–39, 246, 278–80
epilogue, 393–94
as loyal Russian bureaucrat, 248, 249
meets with Al Gore, 226
and pipeline proposals, 279
and Tengiz, 241, 248, 249, 269,
279–80
and wealth, 436

Chevron, 85–87, 88, 89, 90, 95, 97, 100
  alliance with Mobil and Kazakhstan,
    284
  and American Trade Consortium,
    83–87, 88, 89–91
  arranges American visit for Soviet
    oilmen, 92–93
  buys Gulf Oil, 103
  buys Texaco and Unocal, 390
  Clinton administration support for,
    268–69
  competes with BP for Tengiz oil field,
    108–11
  deal with Gorbachev, 113
  Derr persuaded to fire Giffen, 127
  Deuss role in Tengiz talks, 137–39
  epilogue, 390–91, 392
  George H. W. Bush administration
    support for 114–15, 139
  impact of Soviet Union breakup, 125
  implements claims on Tengiz, 115–20
  interest in Iran, 348
  internal politics, 123
  issue of paying Russia's share of
    Tengiz, 280–82
  James Baker's interest in Soviet deal,
    114
  and Mobil Oil, 286–87
  signs Tengiz agreement (1990), 112
  signs Tengiz agreement (1992),
    139–40
  signs Tengiz agreement (1996),
    287–88
  talk of admitting to Tengiz pipeline
    consortium, 278
  Tengiz issues, 99–101, 108, 209,
    211, 236–51, 346, 350
  view of Deuss, 239, 246, 247,
    248–51, 263, 264
  as viewed by Russia, 263
  visits Soviet oil field, 91–92, 95–98
Chevron Overseas, 123

Child, Richard Washburn, 44
China's Xinjiang region, 391–92
Chirag oil field, 160, 164, 168, 207
Chow, Ed, 251, 261, 267, 274–75, 282
Christmas, Charlie, 312
CIA (Central Intelligence Agency)
  in Afghanistan, 292, 307
  agents and former agents, 134, 166,
    232, 319, 320
  Deuss claims connection to, 133
  information on Baku, 51, 52
  information on Soviet oil, 89, 95, 105
  question of Delta Oil connection,
    302
  relationship with Giffen, 77–78, 90,
    259, 376, 389
  relationship with Oztemel, 61
  relationship with Tamraz, 319
  and U.S. policy, 269
Çiller, Tansu, 231
Clemenceau, Georges, 42
Clinton, Bill
  and American oil companies, 189
  bars American companies from doing
    business with Iran, 348
  and Caspian initiative, 380–81
  initial support for Taliban takeover of
    Afghanistan, 307, 308
  meets with Boris Yeltsin, 201, 202,
    205, 211
  meets with Heydar Aliyev, 198, 200,
    214
  view of Caspian pipeline issue, 200,
    215, 216, 347
Clough, Neil, 358–59
Cohen, Sacha Baron, 385
Cole, Natalie, 316
Collins, James, 225, 226
Collins, Susan, 321
Commonwealth of Independent States
  (CIS), 125, 188
Communist power, collapse, 105

Cook, Harry, 332, 333
Cooperman, Leon, 317, 318, 319
Cornelius, Sandy, 116–17
Courtney, William, 219
Crain, Bill, 92, 98, 123, 124
Crane, George, Jr., 55

D'Arcy, William Knox, 103
Day, Henry Mason, 45–47, 48
de Waal, Thomas, 147, 148
Delta Oil, Saudi Arabia, 166, 302
Derr, Ken
    and Chernomyrdin, 263–64
    description, 127, 260
    and end of Soviet Union, 125
    epilogue, 393
    focus on Tengiz contract, 139–40,
        237, 240
    and Gorbachev, 101, 113
    and James Baker, 114, 126
    as Keller's successor at Chevron, 85,
        100
    meets with al-Zawawi, 250, 260
    persuaded to fire Giffen, 127
    relationship with George H. W. Bush
        administration, 115
    relationship with John Deuss,
        239–40, 246, 247–51, 252, 255,
        260, 264, 278, 283
    relationship with Nursultan
        Nazarbayev, 140–41, 260–61, 281
    resumes negotiations with Kazakhs,
        125–27, 142
    role in Chevron-Kazakh talks, 139
    view of Soviet oil, 89, 101, 122–23
Deterding, Henri, 32, 33, 43, 44, 45, 48,
    399
Deuss, John
    and Alex Moskovich, 130
    as Azerbaijan governments oil adviser,
        159–60
    and Azerbaijan oil agreement, 171

and Qais al-Zawawi, 131, 245, 272
    and Said al-Shanfari, 271
    background, 128–29, 132
    and Carl Longley, 132–33
    creates Caspian Pipeline Consortium,
        237–38
    description, 128–29
    end of Caspian joint venture with
        Oman, 282–83, 289
    epilogue, 387–88
    full name, 128
    Giffen's view, 255–56, 268
    investigates Caspian oil opportunities,
        130, 193
    and Iranian Revolution, 133
    as Kazakhstan government's oil
        advisor, 137, 267
    lacks U.S. support, 268–70
    lifestyle, 135–36, 138
    meets Halyk Abdullayev, 130–31
    meets with Viktor Chernomyrdin,
        238–39
    and pipeline project, 142, 265–67
    relationship with al-Shanfari, 270, 271
    relationship with al-Zawawi, 131,
        245, 274
    relationship with Ken Derr, 239–40,
        246, 247–51, 252, 255, 260, 264,
        278, 283
    relationship with Oman sultanate,
        129, 142, 159–60, 245–46,
        273–74, 282
    role in Chevron-Kazakh agreement,
        137–39, 141
    Russia makes "in kind" payments, 267
    seeks financing for Tengiz pipeline,
        243–46, 270–71
    stance toward Chevron, 239, 246,
        247, 248–51, 259, 265
    and Tengiz pipeline proposal, 265–67,
        278–79
    view of Giffen, 267–68

Deuss, Krystyna, 136
Digings, Wref, 354–56
Doss, Tom, 160, 171, 182, 184, 185, 187, 193, 194–95, 196, 197, 198
Dostum, Abdul Rashid, 303
Drake, Edwin, 6
Dresser Industries, 52–53
Dupré, Morley, 126, 140, 239, 240–43, 393
dynamite, 16, 24

Early Oil pipelines
    background, 218
    opening, 352
    outcome, 230, 233–35
    proposal to build two, 219, 227, 235, 279
    proposal to enlarge, 349
    pursuit by Georgia, 219–23, 230, 233, 235, 352
    and Unocal, 293
    U.S. policy role, 227–30, 233
Eastman Kodak, 87
Eastwood, Fred, 56
Eaton, Cyrus, 72
eavesdropping, 165–66, 194–95
Ebel, Robert, 52, 89
Edmonson, Richard, 191
Effendiev, Namik, 149, 150
Eisenhower, Dwight, 53
Eizenstat, Stuart, 348
Elchibey, Abulfaz, 169, 171, 172, 182, 221, 320
Elf Aquitaine (French oil company), 130, 331, 389, 391
Emery, Lewis, 10
ENI (Italian oil company)
    Agip, 247, 278, 284, 322, 328
    rejects Giffen's deal for Tengiz, 368–69, 371, 372
    success after breakup of Soviet Union, 391

environment
    and drilling rig apparatus, 333–34
    Tengiz issues, 119
Eronat, Friedhelm, 289
European Bank for Reconstruction and Development (EBRD)
    and Baku-Ceyhan pipeline, 356
    defined, 243
    and Deuss's pipeline scheme, 244–45, 268, 269, 283, 286
    and Iran, 292
Exxon
    buys Mobil Oil, 331, 390
    diversifies, 103
    hires Rosemarie Forsythe, 396
    interest in Caspian oil, 88, 232, 291, 331, 355, 381, 390
    and Iran, 348, 351, 355
    and U.S. foreign policy regarding Caspian region, 232
    Wooddy's connection, 99

Faisal, Turki al-, 305–6, 308
Fall, Albert B., 48
Falls, John, 56, 60, 77
Fehlberg, Rondo
    as BP's negotiator, 110, 150, 151, 154, 155, 156–58
    Hamilton recruits to Pennzoil, 159, 162, 164, 166, 189
Feminist Majority Foundation, 307, 310
Feuerring, Ralph, 62, 63
Fina, 331, 389, 391
Finn, Robert, 145, 165, 169
Fleck, Aaron, 317, 318
Ford, Henry, 351
Ford Motor Company, 71, 87, 351
Foreign Corrupt Practices Act, 163, 185, 250
Forrestal, Michael, 78, 80, 84, 256
Forsythe, Rosemarie
    in Armenia, 216

background, 213–14
as Caspian authority, 198
and Early Oil pipeline options, 222,
    223, 224–25, 226
epilogue, 397
and Jim Giffen, 254–55
viewed as anti-Russian, 214–15
Fowler, Don, 320–21
Fowler, Michael (Mack), 134, 142, 289
Franssen, Herman, 250, 251, 274
Freeman, Ronald, 244–45, 269, 286
Friedman, Richard, 317
Friendship oil well, 10
Front Uni, 44, 46, 192
Fuerth, Leon, 225, 226, 227–28, 348,
    353

Gagarin, Yuri, 98
Gaidar, Yegor, 122–23
Gang of Four, 278, 284, 286
Gardner, Leonard, 54
Georgia
    Baku-Ceyhan pipeline becomes reality,
        358, 359, 383, 391
    and Early Oil pipeline debate,
        219–23, 230, 233, 235, 346, 352
    loss of seaside territory to Russian-
        supported rebels, 211
    new pipeline up and running from
        Baku to Supsa, 349, 350, 353
    as option for proposed Baku-Ceyhan
        pipeline, 223, 227, 229–32,
        234–35, 351, 355–57
    pro-independence demonstrations in,
        147
Giffen, James Henry
    ability to win over powerful men,
        74–75
    in aftermath of Chevron deal for
        Tengiz, 120–22
    and American Trade Consortium,
        83–84, 86–88, 89, 120–22

at Armco Steel, 79–80
background, 253–54
and Balgimbayev, 278, 285
birth, 54–55
and breakup of Soviet Union, 125, 126
changes college major from medicine
    to political science, 58
and Chevron oil deal, 114
chumminess with CIA, 77–78
collects money for Mobil deal on
    behalf of Kazakhs, 288–89
college degrees, 59–60
creates American Trade Consortium,
    83–84
creates timetable for Kazakh
    government, 334–35
cultivates ambitious new persona,
    66, 67
and deputy public defender, 61
description, 72, 364–65
Deuss' view of, 267–68
embroidering of self-narrative,
    78–79
end of marriage to Hopkins, 80
epilogue, 389–90
escorts American executives
    to Baku, 66
escorts Nazarbayev on U.S. visit,
    112–13
ethics, 79–80
financial stake in Tengiz deal, 127
fired by Derr and Matzke, 127
fired by Oztemel, 74
forms Mercator, 80–81
friendship with Nazarbayev, 253–54,
    261
goes to work for Oztemel, 64–65, 66
and Gorbachev, 83, 99, 362
hired by Verity for Soviet deals, 76
and J. Bryan Williams, 288–89
junkyard-dog nasty side, 285
Kazakh standing diminished, 369–73

Giffen, James Henry (*cont'd*)
  as Kazakhstan's bargainer in pipeline
    dispute between Chevron and John
    Deuss, 255
  as Kazakhstan's chief oil adviser,
    255–56, 360–70
  lifestyle, 77, 360–61
  meets and marries June Hopkins,
    58, 59
  meets Ata Oztemel, 60–61
  meets with head of Chevron, 86–87
  at Moscow Tengiz pipeline
    consortium meeting, 284
  moves with June from LA to New
    York, 61
  negotiates deep-sea oil rig sale to
    Baku, 76
  operates from Armco Steel's New
    York office, 76–77
  plots against Oztemel's interest at
    Satra, 73–74
  and private lawyer for Louis Baker and
    Mark Ancel, 60–61
  promotes himself as Soviet authority,
    77–79
  publishes *The Legal and Practical Aspects of
    Trade with the Soviet Union,* 66–67
  put in charge of Satra Consulting, 66
  recruits John Huhs and Carl Longley
    for Satra Consulting, 65–66
  relationship with J. Bryan Williams,
    256–57, 274, 276, 277, 288–89,
    389, 446
  relationship with Najeeb Halaby,
    73–74
  relationship with Nazarbayev,
    361–62, 363, 369, 372, 384
  relationship with Verity, 79
  relationships with Soviets, 121–22,
    123, 124
  removed from Chevron negotiations
    process, 127
  role in Chevron-Kazakh agreement,
    141
  and Rosemarie Forsythe, 254–55
  at Satra Consulting, 68–69, 71–72
  sells himself as accomplished Soviet
    trade expert, 76
  serious legal problems, 373–79
  as student, protégé, then boss of Paul
    Proehl, 59, 65–66, 69–72, 74, 396
  supports trade alliance of U.S.
    businesses, 83–84
  transformation, 81
  at UC Berkeley, 57–59
  and USTEC, 72–73
  view of Deuss, 255–56, 259, 268
  woos prospective Satra clients, 69–70
Giffen, June Hopkins, 58, 60, 72
Giffen, Lloyd, 55–56, 57, 77
Giffen, Lucile Threlfall, 55, 56
Goldenberg, Suzanne, 169
Golden, Art, 286
Goltz, Thomas, 169, 180–82, 193, 203,
    312, 357
Gorbachev, Mikhail
  1990 U.S. trip, 101
  and American Trade Consortium,
    87–88, 89, 121
  attempt to suppress Azeri nationalists,
    151
  attempted putsch against, 124, 130
  audience with Giffen and Andreas, 81
  background, 82–83
  denounces Aliyev, 178, 179
  description, 82
  encourages atmosphere of openness,
    177
  and Jim Giffen, 83, 99, 122, 362
  Kazakhstan asserts control over Tengiz
    oil field, 123
  and Nazarbayev, 114
  question of staying power, 93
  rehabilitates Tagiyev, 146

relaxes Soviet political grip on
 republics, 147
and Soviet Communism, 83
Soviet deal with Chevron, 100–101,
 109, 112, 113, 240
succeeded by Yeltsin, 204
Gore, Al
 accompanied by Rosemarie Forsythe,
  254
 Heslin's initial work for, 225
 interest in Caspian, 201–2, 214, 275
 meets with al-Zawawi, 269
 meets with Viktor Chernomyrdin, 226
 support for Chevron, 269
Goslavsky, Josef, 29
Great Game, 215
Green, Steve, 329
Gremillion, Todd, 158, 182
Grynberg, Jack
 background, 106–8
 competes with Jim Giffen for Tengiz,
  108–9
 contractual rights, 113
 epilogue, 394
 trip to Kazakhstan, 108–11
Gulbenkian, Calouste
 as adviser to Deterding, 45
 as art collector, 38, 49
 as Mr. Five Percent, 45, 111, 320
 in Paris, 38
 view of Baku and oil trade, 23,
  28–29
Gulbenkian, Nubar, 38, 45, 86
Gulf Oil, diversifies, 103
Gulf Resources of Canada, 111
Guneshli oil field, 163, 164, 168,
 195
Guseynov, Sabit, 51

Haig, Alexander, 295
Hajinski, Isa Bey, 11, 40
Halaby, Lisa, 73

Halaby, Najeeb, 73–74
Hamilton, Tom
 and BP's Baku deal, 108, 113,
  144–45, 146, 147, 151
 at British Petroleum, 102, 103,
  109–10, 111
 defends Pennzoil's relationship with
  government, 230
 job change, 159, 162
 joins Pennzoil, 162
 leads review of oil field discoveries,
  104, 106
 leaves British Petroleum, 162
 at Pennzoil, 162–63, 198–99
Hammer, Armand
 announces plans for petrochemical
  plant in Tengiz, 95
 and Brezhnev, 75
 Bud Johnson's recollection, 77
 and Lenin, 45, 77, 396
 as Moscow hotel-builder, 111
 and Occidental Petroleum
  diversification, 103
 and Oztemel, 63, 396
 Proehl's fascination with, 396
 and Stalin, 48
Hansen, Zenon, 71
Hanway, Jonas, 4–5
Harding, Warren G., 48
Harriman, Averell, 45, 78
Harriman, Edward, 45
Hartnett, Tim, 169
Hassanov, Hassan, 153–54, 155, 156,
 189, 216
Havdrott (Norwegian tanker), 133
Hekmatyar, Gulbeddin, 187–88
Helland, George, 70
Henderson, Dave, 163, 164–65,
 199
 and Marat Manafov, 183–87
Hermitage Museum, 49
Heseltine, Michael, 161

Heslin, Sheila
  and Caspian issue, 215, 269, 275
  and Early Oil pipeline options, 222,
    224–29, 230, 231–33, 234
  epilogue, 397
  initial work for Al Gore, 225
  and "iron umbilical cord" remark, 214
  and Tamraz, 320–21
Hickox, Tom, 186
Hinton, Milt, 63
Holiday, Harry, 80
Holmes, Frank, 85
Hoomani, Michael, 151–52, 159
Hoover, J. Edgar, 42
Hopkins, David, 58, 60, 78
Hopkins, Harry, 58, 67, 68, 362
Hopkins, June, see Giffen, June Hopkins
Horton, Bob, 104
House of Rothschild, 21–24
Houston, Texas
  Azeri oil field negotiations in, 195–98
  meeting of oilmen to debate Caspian
    pipeline options, 229–30, 232,
    235
Huhs, John, 65–66, 67, 69, 71, 72, 395
Hussein, King of Jordan, 73
Hussein, Sadam, 357
Husseinov, Surat, 171, 172, 202, 203
hydrogen sulfide, 117–18

Imle, John
  background, 291
  dealings with Turkmenistan, 294–98
  later oil dealings, 393
  proposes scheme for Turkmenistan to
    Pakistan pipelines, 291–94
  relationship with Taliban, 291–92,
    301, 302, 303, 307, 308–10
  as Unocal negotiator for Azeri oil
    fields, 171
Impex, 331
India, 293

International Monetary Fund, 257
Intourist, Baku, 165
Iran
  Caspian oil field claims, 207
  and possible pipeline routes, 348–49,
    351
  as Saudi rival, 305, 306
  U.S. economic embargo, 292
  U.S. hostage crisis, 221
Iranian Revolution, 133
Iraq National Oil Company, 86
Irgun, 106
Ishanov, Khyakim, 296–97
Istayena, Taisya, 324
Ivanov, Igor, 351
Ivanov, Ivan, 356

Jacob, Musa, 22
James, Bob, 63
Japan, Sakhalin oil fields, 47
Japaridze, Tedo, 220, 221, 222, 234
Jaz, Allah, 5
Jeffery, Paul, 329, 330, 336–38, 341
  See also British Petroleum
Johnson, Bud, 77–78
Johnson & Johnson, 87

Kadrubinsky, Andrei, 323
Kaldirim, Osman, 166–67, 302
Kaluzhny, Viktor, 354
Kaplan, Beth, 395
Kapparov, Nurlan, 370–72
Karachaganak natural gas field, 329,
  389
Karamanov, Uzakbay, 111–12
Karamashin, Yevgeny, 339
Karoline Maersk (Danish tanker), 134
Kashagan
  background, 328–29
  drilling results, 344, 345
  export issues, 345–47
  Kazakh share, 326, 367

oil company consortium, 328,
    330–31, 339, 390
oil company exploration, 331–44
as one of world's ten largest oil fields,
    369
platform oilmen vs. Kazakh power
    politics, 342–44
role of British Petroleum, 328–30,
    336, 338, 341
role of Giffen, 362, 367
size of field, 389–90
as trigger for Caspian pipeline issues,
    346–52
Kavyorochkin, Mikhail, 50, 51
Kazakhstan
    alliance with Mobil and Chevron,
        275–78, 284
    asserts control over Tengiz oil field, 123
    vs. Azerbaijan, 147
    believes itself to control Tengiz oil
        fields, 97–98
    desire for independence, 120, 124–25
    enters into pact with Caspian Pipeline
        Consortium, 237–38
    fails to make "in kind" payments to
        Deuss, 267
    Kashagan offshore formation, 328–36
    relationship with Russia regarding oil
        reserves, 188–89
    Russia flexes muscle over, 271–72
    signs joint agreement ratifying
        restructuring of Tengiz pipeline
        consortium, 287–88
    Tengiz pipeline issues, 209, 237,
        252–53, 284, 346
    See also Nazarbayev, Nursultan
Kazhegeldin, Akezhan, 262, 275, 281,
    365–67, 373, 384–85
Kazmirov, Vladimir, 216
Keller, Bill, 147, 399, 401
Keller, George, 84, 85–87, 88, 100
Kendall, Donald, 75

Kennedy, John F., 58–59, 75
kerosene, Nobel Brothers Petroleum
    Company, 17
Kesemer, Ibrahim, 312
Khrushchev, Nikita
    burns down Siberian prison field
        camps, 91
    inspires young Gorbachev, 82, 83
    memoirs translated into English by
        Strobe Talbott, 210
    at Oily Rocks, 51
    Virgin Lands program, 98
    visit to Baku, 179
Kirov, Sergei, 40
Kissinger, Henry, 61, 65, 72–73, 296
Knickerbocker, Hubert, 49
Kohl, Helmut, 220
Komes, Jerome, 73–74
Korolev oil field, 93, 95–96, 99
Kozeny, Viktor, 315, 316–19, 397–98
Kozyrev, Andrei, 205, 206–7, 210
Krassin, Leonid, 42–43, 44
Kulibayev, Timur, 385
Kurpishev, Oraz, 322
Kuwait, 155

labor unrest, 30–31
Laird, Melvin, 71
Lake, Anthony, 211
lamp oil, 10
Langlois, Jack, 158, 182
The Legal and Practical Aspects of Trade with the
    Soviet Union (Giffen), 66–67
Lembo, Paolo, 180, 190
Lenin, Vladimir, 30–31, 42, 45, 48, 49
Leno, Mavis, 307, 310
Leonard, Ray, 152–53, 154, 169,
    328
    See also Amoco
Lianosov, David, 33
Lipton, David, 269
Lloyd George, David, 44

Longley, Carl
  epilogue, 396
  and John Deuss, 132–33
  recruited to work for Satra
    Consulting, 65–66, 69
Lugar, Richard, 212
Lukoil
  gains ownership stake in Tengiz,
    280–282, 283, 284, 287
  Matzke named vice president, 392
  partnership with Arco, 282, 283–288
  and Shafranik, 192, 209, 210, 393

Mack Trucks, 71, 72
Majech, Bernard, 62
Mamedov, Gambai, 175, 176
Manafov, Marat, 182–85, 186, 187,
  191, 193, 199
Mantashev, Alexander, 33
Mantashev, Leon, 38
Marathon Oil, 111
Mardakhan resort, 35
Mariven, 111
Marshall, Walt, 339
Marvin, Charles, 18, 26
Matlock, Jack, 114
Matzke, Dick
  and Baku-Ceyhan development, 351
  and Deuss, 264
  epilogue, 393
  meets with Chernomyrdin, 100, 108,
    118, 123–24, 125, 239
  relationship with Balgimbayev, 262
  role in Chevron Kazakh talks,
    137–38, 140
  view of Giffen, 126–27
Mazar-i-Sharif, Afghanistan, 303,
  309–10
Mazur, Suzan, 136, 427
McCurry, Mike, 232
McElligot, Janet, 364
McFarlane, Norris, 63

McFaul, Michael, 363
mercaptans, 240–41
Mercator
  formation of, 80–81
  as investment banker for American
    Trade Consortium, 87–88
  See also Chevron; Deuss, John; Giffen,
    James
Metge, Michel, 336, 337
Mikoyan, Anastas, 62, 69
Miller, Marty
  assessment of Unocal's Afghan
    adventure, 310
  hosts Taliban officials, 309
  storytelling, 166, 167, 172, 294, 295
Minarovich, Bill, 364
Mirzoyev, I.M., 8
Mitchell, George J., 317, 318
Mobil Oil, 256, 275–78, 281, 286, 328
  alliance with Chevron and
    Kazakhstan, 284
  and Baku-Ceyhan, 348, 351
  bought by Exxon, 331, 390
  buys Superior Oil, 103
  comparison with Chevron, 286–87
  diversifies, 103
  early interest in Caspian oil, 88, 232
  interest in Iran, 348
  and Kashagan, 328
  negotiations for Kazakh oil, 275–78,
    281, 282, 284, 285, 286–89
  signs joint agreement ratifying
    restructuring of Tengiz pipeline
    consortium, 287–88
  talk of admitting to Tengiz pipeline
    consortium, 278
  See also Williams, J. Bryan
Monroesky Doctrine, 205
Morgan, J.P., Sr., 136
Morningstar, Richard, 350, 351
Moskovich, Alex, 130
Mount Diablo, 94

Mukhtarov, Murtaza, 35, 145
Mukluk reservoir, 331
Murphy, Ross, 334, 341, 342, 343–44
Mutalibov, Ayaz, 151, 153, 156, 158,
    161, 168–69, 169

Nagorno-Karabakh, 148, 171, 187, 189
Najibullah, Mohammad, 307
NATO, 216
natural gas
    and Baku, 4–5
    shipping, 291–92, 329
Naussimbaum, Lev (Essad Bey), 12–13,
    21, 31
Nayberg, Tsalik, 297
Nazarbayev, Nursultan
    asserts control over Tengiz oil field for
        Kazakhstan, 123
    background, 113–14
    and British Petroleum, 109–11, 112
    cautiously seeks autonomy for
        Kazakhstan, 124–25
    description, 113–14
    desire for Kazakhstan independence,
        120
    entertains Vice President Al Gore, 202
    epilogue, 383–85
    and Grynberg, 107–8, 109, 111
    issues challenge to Saudi Arabian oil
        production, 340
    as Kazakhstan's leader, 99, 137, 322,
        383–85
    and Matzke, 262
    meets Chevron head Ken Derr to sign
        Tengiz agreements, 139–40, 240
    meets J. Bryan Williams, 257
    meets Peter Castenfelt, 258
    meets with Yeltsin, 278
    and Mobil Oil, 275–77
    relationship with Jim Giffen, 253–54,
        261, 361–62, 363, 369, 372
    relationship with Kazhegeldin, 365–67

    relationship with Ken Derr, 140–41,
        240, 260–61, 281
    relationship with Moscow, 113
    role in Chevron-Kazakh talks, 137,
        139
    San Francisco speech, 121
    signs go-ahead contract, 331
    view of Chevron, 253
    view of John Deuss, 253, 258
    visits Kashagan, 343–44
Nazarbayeva, Dariga, 385
New Economic Policy (NEP), 42
Newsom, Dave, 57
Nicholas I, Russian czar, 15
Nicholas II, Russian czar, 9, 29, 31
Nikitin, Boris, 109, 113
Ningharco, 305
Nixon, Richard M.
    and Brezhnev and USTEC, 72–73, 75
    and détente, 61, 66
    and Mack Trucks, 71, 72
Nixon, Terry, 76
Niyazov, Saparmurat, 294–96, 319, 355,
    386
    See also Turkmenistan
Nobel, Alfred, 16, 24
Nobel, Emanuel (son of Ludvig)
    achievements, 33–34
    arrives in Baku as child, 17, 33
    as Baku oil pioneer, 397
    returns to Sweden, 38
    takes control of company after
        Ludvig's death, 26
    See also Nobel Brothers Petroleum
        Company
Nobel, Immanuel (father of Ludvig),
    15–16, 81
Nobel, Ludvig
    accomplishments and legacy, 15,
        26–27, 32, 33, 46, 47, 53, 116,
        217, 398
    as Baku oil pioneer, 397

Nobel, Ludvig (cont'd)
  background, 15–16
  death of, 26
  develops oil tanker, 20–21
  as middle of three brothers, 16
  and petroleum transportation issues,
    18–21, 30
  physics trick, 4
  vs. Rothschild brothers, 22–24
  takes charge of Nobel Brothers
    Petroleum, 17–18
  travels to Baku, 17
  See also Nobel Brothers Petroleum
    Company
Nobel, Robert
  as Baku oil pioneer, 397
  as eldest of three brothers, 14
  disappearance, 17–18
  starts Nobel Brothers Petroleum, 15,
    16–17
  travels between Sweden and Baku,
    14–15, 16, 17, 45
Nobel Brothers Petroleum Company
  Alfred Nobel as investor, 16
  birth of enterprise, 15, 16–17
  conservation practices, 28
  control shifts from Ludvig to
    Emanuel, 28
  Emanuel's achievements, 33–34
  impact of Bolshevik revolution, 30, 34
  Robert loses leadership to Ludvig,
    17–18
  sells half of Baku holdings to
    Standard Oil of New Jersey, 33, 34
  statistics on company's oil production,
    26, 34
  See also Nobel, Ludvig
Noor, Queen, 73
Noorzai, Bashar, 299
Noto, Lucio, 257, 275, 276, 286, 289,
    351
  See also Mobil Oil

Nurkadilov, Zamanbek, 385
Nurs, Mohammed, 5
Nurtaev, Aybek, 322

Oakley, Robert, 167
Occidental Petroleum, 103
  See also Hammer, Armand
O'Connor, J. B., 52
oil, shipping, 20
  See also pipelines
Oil Capital Limited, 319
oil industry
  aftermath of Russian Revolution,
    41–42
  Baku's first pipeline, 19–20
  company retreat, 325
  epilogue, 389–92
  identity crisis, 103
  industry reviews its failures in late
    1980s, 102–3
  multinational successes in Caspian Sea
    ventures, 290–91
  nine-company Kashagan consortium,
    331
  offshore formation, 328–44
  oil price collapse of 1980s, 85, 103
  oil price collapse of 1998, 334, 348
  regarding Caspian as an El Dorado,
    207
  six-company Kashagan consortium,
    328
  snooping among companies,
    165–66
  See also British Petroleum; Chevron;
    Mobil Oil; Royal Dutch/Shell;
    Unocal
Oil Producers Association, 11
oil tankers
  development of, 20–21
  first successful, 15
oilmen, epilogue, 392–93
Oily Rocks, 50–51, 149, 156

O'Leary, Hazel, 233
Oleinikoff, Nils, 398
Oliver, Dick, 352
Oman
    Deuss's relationship with sultanate,
        129, 142, 159–60, 245–46,
        273–74, 282
    as Tengiz consortium country, 283,
        284–85
Omar, Mullah, 298, 299, 300, 304, 309
Oztemel, Ara
    background, 69
    breakfast with Brezhnev and American
        businessmen, 75–76
    description, 61
    epilogue, 394–95
    as expert in trade with Soviet Union,
        61–64, 77
    and Giffen, 60–61, 64–65, 66, 79
    grand gestures, 66, 70, 72
    mistress, Betty Van Staveren, 61
    at Satra Consulting, 68
    wife, Mary, 61
Oztemel, Mary, 61, 406

Pakistan, 291, 293, 299, 300–301, 308
Palawan, Malik, 310
Palmer, A. Mitchell, 42
Pan American World Airways, 73
Parker Drilling, 333
Pascual, Carlos, 356
Pashayev, Hafiz, 198
Pavlov, Valentin, 124
Pavlovna, Lydia, 48
Pennzoil
    and dual pipeline concept, 229–30
    negotiations for Azeri oil fields, 167,
        168, 170–71, 191, 197, 198–99
    pursues Azeri oil field deal, 159,
        161–64
    See also Fehlberg, Rondo; Hamilton,
        Tom; Henderson, Dave

Persia, 5, 6
Peterson, Peter, 72
Phillips Petroleum, 331
Pickens, T. Boone, 293
pipelines
    from Baku to Black Sea, 217
    Caspian Sea issues, 345–59
    Chevron learns that Tengiz oil field
        exports would be limited by
        competing demands, 240
    concerns of western oilmen, 217–18
    Deuss proposes two-stage solution to
        Tengiz, 265–67, 278–79
    dual, as issue, 228, 234, 235
    Early Oil pipeline, 218, 219, 222–23,
        228, 230, 233–35, 279
    failure to safeguard options, 239
    Georgian option, 219–23, 279
    and Gore-Chernomyrdin meeting,
        227–28
    Imle's plans for oil and natural gas
        pipelines from Turkmenistan to
        Pakistan, 291–92
    needed by Chevron at Tengiz, 119,
        130
    proposed through Armenia, 221
    purposes trans-Afganistan project,
        291–94
    role in success of Tengiz deal, 142,
        237
    Russian interest in controlling, 200,
        202, 209, 279
    significance of control, 192–93
    Tengiz consortium, 283–84, 286,
        287–88
    U.S. government support for dual
        option, 232
    See also Baku-Ceyhan pipeline; Caspian
        Pipeline Consortium; Early Oil
        pipeline
Pisar, Samuel, 67, 394
Polo, Marco, 4

Popular Front (Azerbaijan political movement), 151, 169, 179, 193
Praeger, Frederick A., 66
Preisser, Cherry, 58
Price, Espy, 256, 261
Proehl, Paul
  epilogue, 396
  at Satra Consulting, 69, 70–71, 72
  at UC Berkeley law school, 59–60, 65
Proehl, Virginia, 65, 395, 406
Putin, Vladimir, 381, 394
Pyromaniacs Against Apartheid, 134

Rabbani, Burhannudin, 304, 306
Radon, Jenik, 356
railroads, Rothschild ventures, 22–23
Ramco, 148
  See also Remp, Steve
Raphel, Robin, 308
Razaev, Lynda and Azrat, 324
Reagan, Ronald, 88
Red Cross, 325
Remnick, David, 113
Remp, Steve, 148–50, 151, 157, 162, 198
Rich, Marc, 62
RJR Nabisco, 87
Rockefeller, David, 72, 79
Rockfeller, John D.
  competition with Nobel Brothers, 17, 24
  revolutionizes oil business, 6
  Rothschild challenge in Europe, 21, 24, 25–26
  and teamsters, 19
  as wealthiest oilman, 47
  See also Standard Oil of New Jersey
Rolls-Royce, as congratulatory gift from Oztemel to Giffen, 66
Roosevelt, Archibald, 47
Roosevelt, Franklin D., 58, 362
Roth, Louis, 55, 59

Rothschild, Baron Alphonse de, 21–24, 32
Rothschild, Baron Edmond de, 21–24, 32
Rothschild, David, 399
Rothschild, Guy de, 398–99
Rowson, Richard, 66
Royal Dutch/Shell
  as aggressive participant in Caspian oil field deals, 32, 33, 44, 45, 48
  and Baku oil properties, 44, 45, 399
  and Front Uni, 44, 45
  subject to Putin's desire to renegotiate Russian oil deals, 381
Russia
  after loss of its empire, 188–89
  and Azerbaijan oil deal, 200
  and Baku-Ceyhan pipeline, 224, 348, 349–58, 380
  epilogue, 380–83
  and global oil supply, 7, 18, 32
  interest in oil-rich lands bordering Caspian Sea, 205–8
  introduced to American kerosene, 6–7
  known to provoke trouble in its former republics, 203–4, 382–83
  as member of Caspian Pipeline Consortium, 238
  new pipeline, 346, 380–83
  relationship with Kazakhstan and Azerbaijan regarding oil reserves, 188–89
  relationship with United States, 200, 216
  as Tengiz consortium country, 284

Saakashvili Mikheil, 387
Safyurtlu, Gulnar (Tagiyeva Assadulayeva), 414
Sakhalin oil fields, 47
Salimkhanova, Sarah (Tagiyeva), 39–40
Salimkhanova, Sophia (Tagiyeva), 39, 40

Salimkhanov, Zeynalbek, 39
Samuel, Marcus, 24–25
Sanders, Col. Harland, 71
Santos, Charlie, 302–3, 310
Sarkissov (friend of Tagiyev), 8
Sarsenbayev, Altynbek, 385
Satra Consulting
    adds new clients, 72
    description, 68
    formation, 66
    Giffen put in charge, 66
    and John Deuss, 133
    plot against Oztemel, 73
    Proehl's role, 70–71, 72
    recruits John Huhs and Carl Longley,
        65–66
    sales presentation, 69–70
    woos prospective clients, 69–70
Saudi Arabia
    and Chevron oil concession, 85–86, 87
    Delta Oil, 166
    Ghawar oil field, 94, 118
    interest in Taliban, 305
Schlegel, Michael, 338
Schroeder, Charlie and Mary, 312, 325
Scowcroft, Brent, 114, 115, 361
Secord, Richard, 188
Segale, Ernie, 56
Sekus, Michael, 81
Shackley, Theodore, 134
Shafranik, Yuri
    after 1997, 394
    and Aliyev, 190
    and Caspian oil, 206, 208–10, 212,
        248, 263, 264, 267, 271, 284, 285
    and Lukoil, 192, 209, 210, 393
    warns Bill White, 189
Shah Deniz oil field, 160, 392
Shakhirov, Shakhir, 324
Shanfari, Said al-, 256–57, 270, 271
Sharif, Nawaz, 310
Shaumian, Stepan, 30–31

Shevardnadze, Eduard
    attempted assassination, 228–29, 352
    background, 219–20
    as Georgian leader, 220–21
    and Georgian pipeline option,
        219–23, 235
    and James Baker, 220
    quits Parliament, 122
    since 2003, 386–87
Shikhmuradov, Boris, 296
Shipping Research Bureau, 133
Shultz, George, 107
Siemens-Schuckert, 43
Silcox, John
    background, 96–97
    doubts about Giffen's proposal,
        88–89
    hears from other oil companies
        interested in Soviet oil fields, 88
    initial meeting with Giffen, 87
    and Kazakhs, 97–98
    retires from Chevron, 100, 123
    visit to Tengiz, 96–97
Simons, Thomas, 304–5
Sinclair, Harry, 47–48
Smith, Ed, 284, 289
Sneider, Daniel, 139, 180
snooping, 165–66
Sobhani, Rob, 153, 158, 159, 169, 172,
    174–75
Socar
    declares Manafov agreement
        unacceptable, 191
    defined, 182
    and foreign oil company
        intermediaries, 182
    at Houston negotiations for offshore
        Baku, 195–96, 198, 199
    at Istanbul negotiations for offshore
        Baku, 194, 195
    Kozeny bid for control, 316–18
South Africa, 133–34, 264

Soviet Union
  difficult oil field conditions, 90
  and Giffen, 66–67, 76–81, 121–22,
    123, 124, 125, 126
  as global oil force, 52–53
  impact on economy of fall of
    Communism, 105
  and Mack Trucks deal, 71, 72
  oilmen visit America, 92–93
  and Oztemel, 61–64, 77
  putsch leading to breakup, 124–25,
    130
  replaced by Commonwealth of
    Independent States, 125
  and Tengiz oil field deal, 96, 109,
    122–23
  See also Gorbachev, Mikhail; Russia
Speckhard, Dan, 258
St. Petersburg, Russia, 6, 17, 18
Stalin, Josef, 30, 48–49, 50, 51, 120,
  208
Standard Oil of California, 85
Standard Oil of Indiana, 152
  See also Amoco
Standard Oil of New Jersey, 33, 34, 43,
  44, 48
Standard Oil of New York, 33
Stanikzai, Sher Mohammed Abbas, 308,
  309, 310
Statoil (Norway's state-owned petroleum
  company), 161
Stockton, California, as home of James
  Henry Giffen, 54–55, 56
Suez Canal, 25, 27
Sumgait, Azerbaijan, 146–47
Sun Company, 134
Sunkar (drilling platform), 335–36,
  337, 338, 340–44

Taggart, Chris, 307
Tagiyev, Ilyas, 39
Tagiyev, Mehmed, 31

Tagiyev, Sona (Arablinskaya), 12, 31,
  35, 39
Tagiyev, Ismail, 12
Tagiyev, Sophia, 146, 399
Tagiyev, Zeynalabdin
  alliance with Ludvig Nobel and
    Rothschilds, 24, 217
  background, 7
  death and burial, 36, 40
  description, 9
  diversifies business interests, 29, 31
  in exile, 35–36
  family scandal, 12–13
  granddaughter, 315, 399
  as philanthropist, 27, 29
  as pipeline pioneer, 24, 217
  reminders in 1990 Baku, 146
  successful oil field bid, 8–9
  tagged as oil baron, 11
  as target of revolutionaries, 35
Talbott, Strobe, 210–12, 214–15, 226,
  227, 258
Taliban
  background, 298–99
  and Bulgheroni, 303, 304, 306,
    308–9
  conquers Herat, Afghanistan, 305
  and Osama bin Laden, 306
  Pakistani alliance, 300
  and Prince Turki, 305–6, 308
  Unocal's relationship with, 291–92,
    307, 309–10
  U.S. government and, 308
Tamraz, Roger, 319–21
tariffs, 244–45, 246
Teagle, Walter C., 34, 43, 44, 48
Teapot Dome scandal, 48
Tengiz oil field
  Chevron implements claims, 101,
    115–20
  Chevron learns that exports would be
    limited, 240

competition between BP and Chevron
for, 108–11
condition Chevron found it in, 116–18
description, 90, 93–94, 95, 96, 100,
101, 107, 110
Deuss pipeline proposal, 265–67
Deuss role in Chevron-Kazakh talks,
137–39
drenched with hydrogen sulfide, 117–18
environmental issues, 119
high quality of product, 118
impact of Soviet Union breakup, 125
joint agreement ratifying restructuring
of Tengiz pipeline consortium,
287–88
Morley Dupré as general director,
240–43
pipeline consortium, 283–84, 286,
287–88
proposal for transporting crude oil
from, 118–19
protocol signed between Chevron and
Gorbachev, 112
reservoir, 329
Russian interference with Chevron
interests, 236, 390
Tereshchenko, Sergei, 125, 131
Texaco
bought by Chevron, 390
buys Getty Oil, 103
Thailand, 324
Thatcher, Margaret, 104, 106, 161
Thielmans, Toots, 63
Thompson, A. Beeby, 4
Threlfall, Lucile. See Giffen, Lucile
Threlfall
Timan-Pechora oil field, 90, 91
Titusville, Pennsylvania, 6
Tolf, Robert, 20, 27
Total (French oil company)
and Grynberg, 111, 394
Kashagan consortium, 111, 328

merger with Elf and Fina, 331, 391
and Putin, 381
Townshend, Michael, 380
Tran, Khoi, 162, 197
Treaty of Versailles, 42
Truman, Harry, 51, 78
Trump, Ivana, 316
Tsomaya, Gogi, 221, 235
Tugelbayev, Sagat, 97
Turkmenistan
and Argentinian bid to export natural
gas, 303–6, 309
asserts rights to Azeri and Chirag oil
fields, 207
background, 294–96
and Chelikan oil field, 296, 319
interest in Baku-Ceyhan pipeline, 347,
355
Niyazov's cult of personality, 294–95,
296, 319–20, 355, 383, 386
relationship with Moscow, 209, 211,
294, 382
and Unocal's plans for Central Asian
pipelines, 291, 294, 295–97
Twitchell, Karl, 85

Ukraine, 216, 394
United Arab Emirates, 134
United Nations, 323
Unocal
advocates partnership of oil
multinationals, 182, 191
bought by Chevron, 390
negotiates for Azeri oil fields, 159,
161, 166, 167–68, 170–71
plan to lay pipelines across Afghanistan,
291–94, 295, 296–98, 301, 302,
303, 307, 308–10
U.S. embassy bombings, 310
US-USSR Trade and Economic Council
(USTEC), 72–73, 76, 79, 81,
83, 88

Vaksberg, Arkady, 176, 177
Van Staveren, Betty, 61, 68, 74, 395
  See also Oztemel, Ara
Vanco Energy, 392
Verity, C. William, 75, 76, 79–80, 397
Vermishev oil well, 10
Verrastro, Frank, 229–30, 406, 435
Vezirov, Abdulrakhman, 151
Villa Petrolea, 27
Vishnau, James, 29
Vlasov, General Andrei, 38

Walker, Dorothy, 75
Wallace, Dan, 58
Wayand, Niyaz, 300
Webb, Berenice, 314
Webber, Andrew Lloyd, 315
Weber, Zuleha (Assadulayeva), 412, 414
Weeks, Sinclair, 53
White, Bill
  and Amoco, 196–97
  and Chevron, 260
  since 2000, 397
  and Strobe Talbott, 214–15
  trip to Baku, 189, 190
  and U.S. strategic interest in Caspian
    oil, 212–13, 215, 216
White, Dan, 262–63, 285, 286, 287
  See also Arco
white oil, 4–5
White Russians, 43
Whitehead, Eddie, 159, 182, 183, 192,
    194–95
  See also British Petroleum (BP)
Williams, J. Bryan
  as anti-Deuss, 259, 274, 285
  and Giffen, 256–57, 277, 288–89,
    389
  imprisoned for tax evasion, 378, 389
  and Mobil-Chevron alliance, 286
  See also Mobil Oil

  See also Caspian Pipeline Consortium;
    Giffen, James; Mobil Oil
Wilson, Woodrow, 42
Winged Foot Golf Club, 72, 78, 268,
    361
wiretapping, 194–95
Wolf, John, 353, 355
Wooddy, Dale, 99, 119–20, 125–26,
    141, 143
  See also Chevron
World Bank, 292, 298, 356, 368, 384
Wozniak, Piotr, 382

Yeh, Cavour W., 167
Yeltsin, Boris
  addresses United Nations, 205
  and Bill Clinton, 200, 201
  and Caspian initiatives, 210, 211
  as leader under Gorbachev, 113, 123
  pipeline conversation with
    Shevardnadze, 229
  as Russian leader, 200, 201, 202,
    204–5
  and Tengiz pipeline, 278, 287–88
Yergin, Daniel, xi, 103, 402
Young, Bill, 160
Young, Thomas, 165–66
Yunusova, Leyla, 323
Yusufzade, Khoshbakht, 156, 157, 158,
    194, 196

Zabrat oil field, 10
Zardari, Asif, 304
Zawawi, Qais Abdulmonim al-
  and Chevron, 249, 250
  death of, 272–73
  meets with Vice President Gore,
    269
  relationship with Deuss, 131, 245,
    272
Zoroastrianism, 5

STEVE LEVINE was a foreign correspondent covering the Caucasus and Central Asia from 1992 to 2003. From offices in Almaty, Baku, Tashkent, and Tbilisi, he covered the region for *Newsweek, Financial Times, The Washington Post, The New York Times,* and finally *The Wall Street Journal.* Before that, he was *Newsweek's* correspondent for Pakistan and Afghanistan from 1988 to 1991, and from 1985 to 1988 he wrote for *Newsday* from the Philippines. He has a master's degree in journalism from Columbia University.

This book was set in Centaur, a typeface designed by the American typographer Bruce Rogers in 1929. Rogers adapted Centaur from the fifteenth-century type of Nicholas Jenson and modified it in 1948 for a cutting by the Monotype Corporation.